Strategic Management

Strategic Management

a fresh approach to developing skills, knowledge and creativity

Paul Joyce & Adrian Woods

KOGAN
PAGE

First published in 2001

Kogan Page Limited
120 Pentonville Road
London
N1 9JN
UK

Kogan Page US
22 Broad Street
Milford
CT 06460
USA

British Library Cataloguing in Publication Data

A CIP record for this book is available from the British Library.

ISBN 0 7494 3583 6

Typeset by Saxon Graphics Ltd, Derby
Printed and bound in Great Britain by Bell & Bain Ltd, Glasgow

Contents

About the book   viii

Part 1 Strategic Management: Processes and Contexts   1
1 What is strategic management?   3
2 Does strategic management work?   16
3 The strategic manager   26
   Reading 3.1 How persuasion works by Peter Thompson   42
   Reading 3.2 From Shakespeare to Tom Peters *and* Listening to fools and
   knaves, both by Paul Corrigan   49
4 Formulating missions and goals   64
   Reading 4.1 Lead from voice and vision by Warren Bennis   78
5 Evaluating performance   82
   Reading 5.1 What you measure is what you get by Mick Broadbent   93
   Reading 5.2 12 ladders to world class performance by David Drennan and
   Steuart Pennington   106
6 Analysing markets and customers   115
   Reading 6.1 Analysis: turning information into intelligence by Michelle Cook
   and Curtis Cook   128
   Reading 6.2 Knowledge management by Nigel Ghent   150
7 Identifying and addressing issues   153
   Reading 7.1 Social and ethical issues for sustainable development by Richard
   Welford   164

 8 Formulating scenarios   181
   Reading 8.1 Strategic planning in the greenhouse by Joseph J Romm   195
   Reading 8.2 The next industrial revolution by Paul Hawker,
   Amory B Lovins and L Hunter Lovins   205
 9 Suggesting new business opportunities   221
10 Evaluating strategic options   231
11 Key factors for success (KFS) and core competencies   243
12 Identifying creative strategic options   256
   Reading 12.1 Creating more options by Simon Wootton and Terry Horne   269
13 Planning implementation   277
   Reading 13.1 Plan to implement by Stephen G Haines   291
   Reading 13.2 Working through the change process by David Hussey   302
14 Multi-businesses   314
   Reading 14.1 Strategy and tactics by Jorge Vasconcellos e Sá   329
   Reading 14.2 Trends by Clifford Matthews   347
15 Small businesses   359
16 The public sector   373
   Reading 16.1 The new manager and learning to manage strategically by
   Paul Corrigan, Mike Hayes and Paul Joyce   393
17 E-business   403
   Reading 17.1 The information economy and competitive advantage by
   Colin Turner   415
   Reading 17.2 Does your product or service suit the Internet? by
   Martin Lindstrom and Tim Frank Andersen   437

Part 2 Case Studies   455
 1 The Body Shop by Graham Beaver   457
 2 Ford   460
 3 Fujitsu and ICL   469
 4 Glaxo-Wellcome   472
 5 Idealab by Graham Beaver   476
 6 J D Wetherspoon   480
 7 Maison Novelli by Graham Beaver   485
 8 Manchester United   488
 9 Matcon Engineering by Graham Beaver   500
10 Nissan and Renault   504
11 Powderject Ltd by Graham Beaver   509
12 Procter & Gamble   514
13 Raytheon by Graham Beaver   520

14 Shell   526
15 Starbucks Coffee   535
16 Toyota   544
17 Vodafone   549

Notes and references for the readings   554

Index   564

About the book

This textbook is designed for use on strategic management courses in universities. It has been written to suit final-level undergraduate courses and postgraduate management courses. We hope that it will prove its worth, particularly on MBA programmes.

The book is supported in two ways. First, the authors have designed and maintain a Web site that provides updates to the case studies featured in the book. This is provided free. The address of the Web site is www.pragmaticstrategy.org.uk. Second, there is an accompanying lecture presentation package, which contains the case studies and mind maps from the book, and should be of considerable use to lecturers. This package is available on CD ROM from the publishers.

This book has been written for the changing world of management education in the universities. Nowadays, management students are being asked not only to learn the basic knowledge of management disciplines, but also to handle complex issues both competently and creatively. They are challenged to show not only that they understand the issues, but also that they can systematically arrive at judgements and propose suitable solutions. They are required not only to critically evaluate current research into management, but also to develop the capacity for learning independently so that they can manage their own continuing professional development. The emphasis is on academic discipline; but it is also on professional management practice. In summary, management education in universities is increasingly addressing two very different but related worlds: the world of theory, research and scholarship, and the world of professional practice. The individual student is being invited to move between the two worlds and to learn how to be a superior student and student manager by enriching his or her experiences in both worlds by taking them both seriously.

We have, without exaggeration, written this book with a continuing concern for this transition in management education. We have written it to engage rather than merely inform the reader, and have sought to do this through our approach to the writing of each chapter. We have tried to ensure that the main issues and ideas stand out clearly and boldly. Then, through careful selection of readings, we have paid attention to the techniques managers use in the professional practice of strategic management (e.g. how to measure performance, how to develop competitive intelligence, and how to manage change). We have, however, recognized the rapidity of developments in the practice of strategic management and have therefore also selected readings that are looming larger and larger, though which are still often not well covered in existing textbooks. Environmental issues and e-commerce are good examples of what we have in mind here. Finally, since higher education places increasing stress on personal qualities and transferable skills, we have also selected readings that illuminate aspects of strategic management that are often neglected in texts *about* strategic management rather than *for* strategic management. You will find, for example, some readings that explore how managers can be persuasive, while others probe the responsibilities and challenges of leadership. The case studies included in this book also show our determination to address the modern global business developments that fill the business sections of newspapers.

We would like to thank all the contributors of readings. We would like to express a special thanks to Professor Graham Beaver at Nottingham Trent University for his contribution of six case studies. We would also like to thank Paul Corrigan for a couple of his jokes that we have borrowed and adapted.

We have appreciated the encouragement and practical assistance of various people at Kogan Page, especially Pauline Goodwin and Emily Steel.

Finally, we would like to thank Theresa, Thomas, Caitlin and Patrick Joyce and Mary, William and Anthony Woods for the usual but true reasons.

Part 1

Strategic Management: Processes and Contexts

1

What is strategic management?

INTRODUCTION

Strategic management is difficult in part because it requires contradictory qualities and skills in dealing with the paradoxical demands of situations. We can understand this by first seeing the different types of managers there are and then realizing how the qualities and skills of the different types may be present in single individuals, who have to bring them together in complementary ways to deal with the strategic tensions they confront.

Charles Handy, an influential management writer, wrote a famous book about different management types (1991). He argued that there are in fact only four types of managers. The first type is Zeus – an all-powerful autocrat named after the Greek god Zeus. The second is Athene – a daughter of Zeus who, while less powerful than Zeus, occasionally hurls the odd thunderbolt to punish humans that have upset her. She had a temper and her big weakness was that she often exacted revenge! She was also the goddess of the arts. Apollo is a managerial type who likes routine and order. He is also a bit of an athlete. And lastly there is Dionysus, who traditionally invented wine and is often portrayed with drunken humans. To put a positive light on Dionysus, he is associated with having a good time as opposed to Apollo who can be boring and stuck in bureaucratic routine.

Interpreting Greek myths and gods requires us to use our imagination fully in order that the stories (myths) still speak to us today. One possible interpretation of the polar opposites, Apollo and Dionysus, is that there are two contradictory requirements.

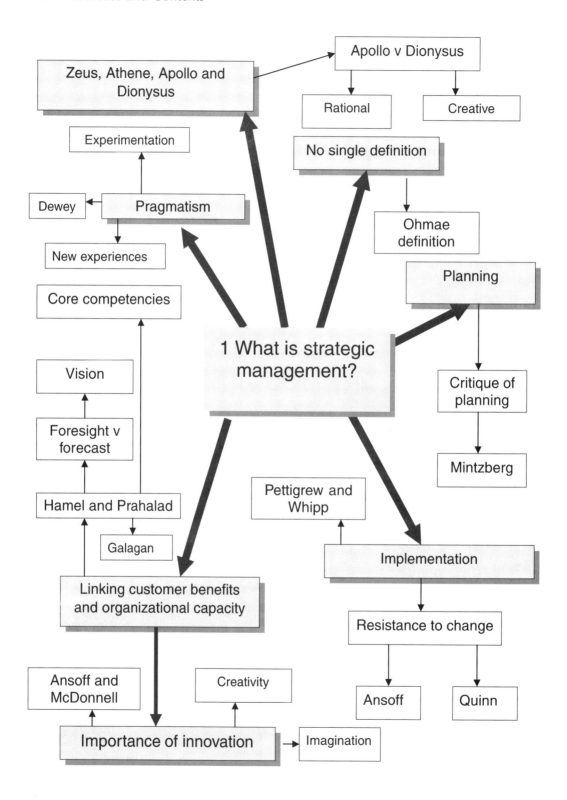

Basically, to do well in strategy, you need both some of the typical Apollo skills and some of the Dionysusian ones. Apollo's skills are required to make sure things happen to plan, in an orderly and predictable fashion. Dionysus' skills (on a generous interpretation) are about not only having fun but also being creative and imaginative. While not wanting you to go out and get drunk to fire your imagination, we would say that there is something in Dionysus that suggests a freeing of thought and hence a flowing of creativity and imagination.

Strategy formulation takes place in the tension between what is and what could be. If you have too many of Apollo's skills you can become trapped in an over-attachment to what is, without giving your creative and imaginative side a chance. With too many of Dionysus's skills you could be forever building castles in the air without turning them into reality. Strategic management takes place within the overlapping boundaries of thinking and action associated with Apollo and Dionysus.

The study of strategic management in business schools and elsewhere has increased for one good reason. Strategic management works. We will look at the evidence for this in the next chapter. In this chapter we want to provide a simple working definition of strategic management, although we recognize that there is no single universally agreed definition. In fact, there are hundreds if not thousands of definitions of strategic management and probably the main variants of them can be justified on numerous grounds. However, we can give a specific definition that probably reflects the kind of themes and strategic thinking capabilities we wish to address in this book. Subsequent chapters will obviously add more and more nuances to this initial statement of strategic management.

We will be assuming throughout this book that the study of strategic management provides current or future managers with frameworks and approaches that can enrich their strategic thinking and reinforce their abilities and readiness to take strategic initiatives (Thurley and Wirdenius, 1989).

PLANNING

Strategic management has become widely established in all sectors of modern economies, although mainly in larger organizations. The rise of strategic planning in the 1960s and its use in the private sector in the 1970s was noted, advocated, and analysed in many influential studies (Quinn, 1980; Ohmae, 1982; and Ansoff, 1987). Its development and application in the public sector in the United States has also been studied (Heymann, 1987; Moore, 1995). The earliest and most prescriptive studies tended to advocate the development of strategic planning systems and the use of analytical patterns of strategic thinking.

This prescriptive view of strategic planning emphasized the importance of the organizational environment as a source of threats and opportunities and the need for effective responses by the organization if survival was to be assured and success achieved. The response was expressed in a plan. Typically this plan formulated major decisions about entry to new industries or the development of new products or services and was guided by sets of objectives and goals. In the 1980s, under the influence of Porter's (1980) writings, the emphasis was less on the plan then on the selection of an appropriate generic strategy to position the business unit in its competitive environment. Porter appeared less concerned with trends and events that might pose threats and opportunities than with an environment. He suggested that the competitive environment could be analysed using what is now often referred to as a Five Forces Analysis. This entailed mapping the environment primarily as a pattern of competitive pressures from rivals, suppliers, buyers, entrants, and substitutes. Then he broadly distinguished two strategic options. The business could either position itself as offering a low cost product at a standard price, or it could offer a product that was different from that offered by rivals. These are referred to as generic strategies. However, Porter still placed emphasis on the analytical strategic thinking needed to formulate an appropriate response to an organization's environment. This analytical thinking extended to the planning of implementation of cost reductions or additions to value through differentiation. This planning of the implementation of a generic strategy could be done using Porter's concept of the value chain. This involved essentially characterizing different types of activity within an organization and analysing them in sufficient detail to identify opportunities for cutting unproductive costs or adding value as perceived by customers. We will look again at Porter's ideas in Chapter 6.

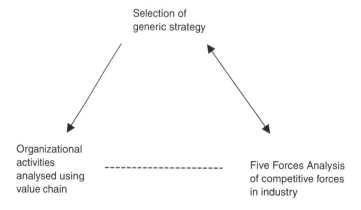

Figure 1.1 Porter's analytical contributions to strategic management

Alongside such approaches there were other studies that advocated widening the narrow view of strategic management offered by strategic planning theorists.

IMPLEMENTATION

Quinn (1980), whose study had a more descriptive intent than some earlier studies of strategic management, emphasized the emergent but rational quality of strategy formulation. This meant that strategic thinking was logical but issues of organizational politics and managerial ignorance affected the way in which strategy might be implemented. This and other studies alerted managers to the issues of strategic implementation. Ansoff (1987), for example, took on board the importance of resistance to change and modified his earlier normative conceptions of strategic planning. In consequence, he defined strategic management as being where strategic planning is coupled with strategy implementation.

LINKING CUSTOMER BENEFITS AND ORGANIZATIONAL CAPACITY

Mintzberg (1994) claimed in the 1990s that strategic planning had fallen from its pedestal. He also claimed to understand why so many middle managers welcomed its 'overthrow'. In fact, in the late 1990s strategic planning continued to be widely used. According to Galagan (1997) strategic planning was back in favour after some years of unpopularity. She credits Hamel and Prahalad with being very influential in the return of strategic planning to popularity (Hamel and Prahalad, 1994). She also quotes the results of a survey showing that strategic planning was a top management issue. More recent survey evidence among nearly 500 global firms showed that while ideas of knowledge management and core competence were becoming unpopular among business managers, strategic planning and mission and vision statements were still popular (Rigby and Gillies, 2000).

Current strategic planning might almost merit a new name if it is the kind of strategizing that Hamel and Prahalad favour. In our view what is most important about their ideas is that they are concerned with strategy as making the future rather than with the types of strategy that are based on predicting it. This point needs underlining because there is a common tendency to pay most attention to their views on core competencies, and consequently to subsume their views within a resource-based view of strategy. This is a perfectly reasonable thing to do. They certainly endorsed the view of seeing a business as a portfolio of competencies, and defined

core competencies as skills and technologies that companies used to provide particular benefits to customers. They said core competences were needed to meet the challenge of future opportunities and that companies were in competition to develop
competences so there is a justification for reading their contribution as mainly one of
advocating a resource-based theory. However, we see their proposal that managers
should develop a foresight about the future and then make it come true as the bigger
idea. For us the interesting point in their views is the harnessing of a resource-based
approach to a foresight perspective. To quote them (1994: 198): 'Preemptive investment in core competence is not a leap into the dark nor a megabet on the unknown…
It is the simple desire to build world leadership in the provision of a key customer
benefit, and the imagination to envision the many ways in which that benefit can be
delivered to customers, that drives the competence building process.'

Our reading of Hamel and Prahalad's work is that they emphasize the creative and
imaginative work that strategists need to engage in to develop a vision of a desired
future. Clearly, visioning the future has to be carried out within some boundaries but
the strategist needs consistently to push boundaries back in terms of what is possible
using intellectual foresight. The very top strategists somehow manage to persuade
others of their vision for the future, even when most people believe it to be unreach-
able at first sight. They force us to stretch ourselves to achieve new possibilities outside of what was previously thought possible. This probably requires considerable
courage. It may involve thinking the unthinkable. Strategists, in a sense, have to be
unreasonable. They have to believe that they can inspire others to join with them in
creating something new that many will see as being unreasonable.

WORKING DEFINITION OF STRATEGIC MANAGEMENT

Ohmae's (1982) ideas of strategic management offer a simple but robust initial definition. He draws attention to three key groups – the corporation, the customer, and the
competitors. Strategic management might be defined, therefore, as the pursuit of superior performance by using a strategy that 'ensures a better or stronger matching of corporate strengths to customer needs than is provided by competitors' (Ohmae, 1982: 91).

Ohmae also emphasizes the importance of moving from abstract ideas of strategy
to concrete planning of implementation. This means that he favours properly
worked-out action plans for line managers. Pettigrew and Whipp (1993) also make
the point about the importance of properly linking strategic and operational changes.
This is based on their in-depth case studies of specific organizations. Strategic intentions should be broken down to what they call actionable pieces, made the responsibility of change managers. They identify target setting, communication mechanisms,

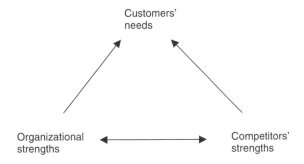

Figure 1.2 Ohmae's strategic triangle

and reward systems as important in carrying strategic intentions through into operational activities. This suggests, as does Ohmae, that strategic management is based on an interdependent relationship between strategic ideas or intentions and operational level changes.

We have emphasized the creative and imaginative part of strategy formulation up to now. What Ohmae and others rightly stress is the need to move from the realm of the abstract to the realm of the concrete. In terms of what we said in the introduction we need to become a bit more like Apollo and a little less like Dionysus.

STRATEGIC MANAGEMENT AND CAPABILITY PROFILE

We suggest that the durability of strategic planning (both old and new variants) reflects a long-run trend for management capability profiles to change in large organizations in all sectors of the economy. Innovation and creativity have always been important in market economies, but the emphasis on both seems to have grown in significance in recent decades. They are seen as the key to growth. Consequently, organizations want managers to seek opportunities for innovation and growth. They want managers that are prepared to take managed risks, and use planning to cope with the dynamism and volatility of their environments (Ansoff and McDonnell, 1990). It is certainly the case that many private sector companies have been using growth strategies. A recent survey found evidence that 65 per cent of US companies and 44 per cent of European companies have used growth strategies (Rigby and Gillies, 2000).

In so far as there is a simple key to becoming a successful strategist, it lies in the capacity to use creative and imaginative thinking to produce innovation, while at the same time using up-to-date planning techniques to reduce the level of uncertainty and disorganization in the modern world. As you move up the managerial hierarchy you will face more and more problems that refuse to be solved easily. They become more fuzzy and difficult to get a purchase on. The information required to aid you in resolving them also becomes harder to find and interpret. The truth is, of course, top managers are expected to solve the problems that more junior managers are not able to solve using standard analysis and techniques. The special skills of a top manager would not be at a premium if the problems were easy to solve. Top strategists inhabit a world where it is hard to see clearly what to do but by using their hard-won skills they somehow manage to envisage what is required and then begin the process of making it happen. They move from fuzziness and disorganization to clarity and organization.

THE INTENTIONS OF THIS BOOK

The main intention of this book is to help students on educational courses in strategic management to learn about the subject and to develop skills and expertise in using strategic tools. It is also our intention that this is done in a way that gives due importance to the role of creativity and innovation in strategic management. Obviously, then, this book is mainly intended for students and teachers in an academic setting – but we would also hope it is of interest to practitioners who want to develop their personal capacity for thinking and acting strategically.

There are many books on strategic management. What makes this one different from most of the rest? Our aim is to provide a textbook that enables students of strategic management to acquire new knowledge and learn new techniques for thinking and acting. We also want this book to help individuals become more self-conscious in their experiences of strategic management, and to encourage them to pursue a greater capacity for lifelong learning as strategic thinkers in their management careers. These aspirations come in part from our experiences – successes and failures – as teachers in university business schools and management departments. They also fit into a decade-old movement to modernize education by centring it on the experience of the student and the importance of personal growth through education.

Usually the philosophical foundations of management books are buried out of sight and often to such a depth that the authors themselves are unaware of them. We think it is important that we indicate the philosophical underpinnings of our views so that you are aware of them and how they mould what we have to say about strategic management. We have attempted quite consciously to use an approach based on pragmatism. According to *The New Shorter Oxford English Dictionary*, pragmatism is 'the view that the truth of any assertion is to be evaluated from its practical consequences and its bearing on human interests'. We have been influenced by such pragmatists as Dewey and James, who wrote key works on pragmatism in the early part of the 20th century, and by Rorty, a pragmatist philosopher of the late 20th century. While drawing ideas from pragmatism we should admit that we have used these as we think fit and in what scholars of pragmatism will probably see as a cavalier manner. We would say we have a pragmatic approach to pragmatism!

One result of our interest in pragmatism is that throughout this book we have sought to present a style of strategic management in which practitioners are reflective. This is a style in which practitioners place great value on the importance of acting on the basis of thought and on evaluating the results of their experimental action. Such practitioners believe in putting themselves into new and novel environments within which they can learn new skills and abilities. Doing and reflecting upon the outcome of action is central to their type of strategic management. So is listening to others in order to try to understand their viewpoints. Having listened, they enter into discussion in the hope that they might change others a little by influencing their position. They accept that others might influence them in turn.

How can strategic managers be developed? How can strategic thinking be encouraged? Knowledge is important but not sufficient. Pragmatism stresses that knowledge is valuable and thus worth mastering if it can be used for practical consequences. Strategic managers and strategic thinking cannot be developed merely by the provision of knowledge to receptive minds. There may be knowledge gaps that need to be filled, but strategic management and strategic thinking are about using as well as having knowledge. And the challenge of lifelong learning suggests that strategic management should be learnt in such a way that individuals can learn what they need to learn from their life as a manager – now or in the future – as well as from books. Often strategic management education is more characterized by pouring knowledge into the student than by the student learning to apply that knowledge in the organizational environment.

Experimentation plays an important part in the development of strategic managers. They try out various ideas and note what happens. We believe that strategic managers should strive to become reflective practitioners by continually testing ideas out and asking questions: Why am I doing this? What reasons have I for doing this? What evidence is there that if I do this the desired end will be achieved? Ideas are 'true' if they achieve what we want them to achieve. It is through experimentation with, and application of knowledge in the managerial environment that strategic managers consolidate their learning.

John Dewey, who we referred to above, continually stressed the importance of the environment and changes in it for experience and learning. This approach can be summarized as an evolutionary approach to learning. Just as in evolution changes in the environment favour some species and adaptations over others, changes in our environment have the potential to change us. It is our interaction with the environment that changes us by challenging us to do things differently. And just as in evolution generally, where changes in one animal or species have knock-on effects, so the changes we make in response to our environment may have repercussions. So it is the changing nature of the environment we experience that provides the framework within which learning can take place. Changes give us the chance to experiment, to try out new ideas, and to note their consequences. Learning is achieved by doing and the value of knowledge or skills achieved through learning is judged by their practical consequences.

One issue that arises from centring the education of strategic managers on the interplay between the individual and his or her managerial environment is the extent to which the environment is rich and varied enough to give the range of experiences required. It might prove impossible for you to experience sufficiently varied situations in a reasonably short period of time to be exposed to enough strategic management techniques or tools to be able to become more skilled. One way of increasing the number and richness of experiences encountered is to use substitutes for first-hand experience. In this book we have provided numerous readings and case studies that should help you in experiencing, albeit at a distance, strategic management, but it is your use of this in practical situations that will foster depth and richness in learning. The task you have to set yourself to get the maximum benefit from the book is hard. You have to move from reading about and perhaps, if you are on a course, writing about strategic management topics to thinking, experimenting, and applying them in practical situations. You will need to draw upon your existing warehouse of experiences to examine what is in the book. Importantly you will have to search out new environments to test and evaluate your ability as a strategic manager.

THE CONTENTS OF THIS BOOK

Chapters 1, 2 and 3 aim to guide the reader through developing an initial point of view about what strategic management is, what its benefits are, and what this means for strategic managers' thinking, actions, values, etc. Chapters 4 through 13 present a review of strategic management thinking and analytical techniques. Chapters 14, 15, 16 and 17 present the specific strategic management issues and practices found in multi-businesses, small businesses, the public sector and e-businesses.

Mind maps are placed at the beginning of each chapter to help the reader make sense of the content covered. There are questions in each chapter for readers (individually or in groups) wishing to reflect on what they have read and to deepen their understanding of strategic management.

Executive exercises are also provided in some chapters for readers (working individually or in groups) to experiment with applying strategic management techniques and ideas to their own work situations. These exercises are designed primarily for people who have a number of years' management experience and who have some involvement in strategic management. We have assumed that you are able to collect data about a real organization and have practical experience you can analyse. You may be studying management on a part-time or a distance learning programme. If you work on the exercises in a group, you could perhaps concentrate on a single organization that one individual knows well and have the others in the group elicit relevant information from that person.

Readings consisting of extracts from other contemporary books on management are included at the ends of several chapters to give readers other authors' perspectives and insights. Up-to-date case studies have been provided so that readers can apply strategic thinking and analysis and reflect on strategic issues.

We should stress that the philosophical perspective of pragmatism is 'folded into' this text. We do not intend this philosophical perspective to be in the forefront. It is, however, a guiding framework that has strongly influenced what we are trying to do with this book and how we have tried to do it. This partly explains why we have offered readers opportunities at the end of each chapter to reflect on what they have been reading and thus consolidate their knowledge and understanding. We have also been motivated by this pragmatism to include the executive exercises that we hope will encourage readers to evaluate their own situations and experiences.

Finally, you will notice two other relatively novel innovations in this textbook. First, we start chapters with a story instead of a set of chapter objectives. We have done this because we think these short stories operate like the analogies or metaphors used in the synectics technique to promote creativity in strategic management. They are used to discover issues and themes by making a mental excursion. The stories are free of the detail and empirical weight of real-life strategic management situations, and thus we are freer to see a general insight that can then be looked for specifically in the knowledge and theory of strategic management.

The second relatively novel feature in writing this book is that we have made extensive use of the Internet instead of relying only on conventional library sources. You will see many URLs in the text, as well as the list of academic references in each chapter. The emergence of the Information Age built around Internet technology has occurred at an astonishing rate over the last five years. In future more and more knowledge will be sought through the Internet as well as from published journals on strategic management. We are reflecting this development in this book and to enhance its value we have built a Web site you can use with it and have also produced a CD ROM. Of course we would be glad to get your feedback on these. Have they made any difference to your experience of using the book? Please tell us what you think.

QUESTIONS

1. In the introduction we used Charles Handy's idea that there are only four basic types of manager. Thinking back to some managers you have come across, can you identify any of his types? If you were to identify yourself as one of his types, which one would it be and what reasons can you put forward for that choice? After doing this do you think Handy's classification is a useful one?

2. One theme that will crop up from time to time in the book is the tension between rationality and creativity, if you like between Apollo and Dionysus. What is your initial feeling on this tension in strategic thinking? Can you give a few examples where you felt that too much attention had been paid to one over the other?

3. Does it matter that there are so many definitions of what strategy is?

4. It is often said that the devil is in the detail. In strategy it doesn't matter so much about the grand idea but about the problems associated with implementing the grand idea. If more time were spent on getting to grips with the detail and analysing the barriers to change in the organization instead of building castles in the air, strategy would be more realistic and stand a better chance of working. Do you agree?

5. Given that strategy is not easy, most managers would be better off using Porter's generic strategies as a starting point then trying to do something different. Do you agree?

6. According to Mintzberg, by the 1990s managers were getting pretty disillusioned with strategy, but Galagan claims that because of Hamel and Prahalad it is now back in fashion. Why the disillusionment and why the renaissance?

7. Is strategy simply about persuading others to accept your vision of the future and in this getting them to commit to ambitious expectations?

8. Is the key skill of being a successful senior manager all about bringing clarity and organization to situations of fuzziness and disorganization?

9. An economist who sees something work in practice wonders whether it will work in theory. On the other hand, a pragmatist, when told something works in theory, wonders if it will work in practice. One way of seeing if something works in practice is to conduct some experiments and note the practical outcome. In 'real' life it is often difficult or impossible to conduct such experiments to see the cash-in-hand value of doing something. What alternatives are there then to actually doing the experiments?

REFERENCES

Ansoff, H I (1987) *Corporate Strategy*, Penguin, London

Ansoff, H I and McDonnell, E (1990) *Implanting Strategic Management*, Prentice Hall, London

Galagan, PA (1997) Strategic planning is back, *Training and Development*, **51**, pp 32–38

Hamel, G and Prahalad, C K (1994) *Competing for the Future*, Harvard Business School Press, Boston

Handy, C (1991) *The Gods of Management*, Business Books, London

Heymann, P B (1987) *The Politics of Public Management*, Yale University Press, London

Mintzberg, H (1994) The fall and rise of strategic planning, *Harvard Business Review*, January–February, pp 107–14

Moore, M (1995) *Creating Public Value: Strategic management in government*, Harvard University Press, London

Ohmae, K (1982) *The Mind of the Strategist*, McGraw-Hill, London

Pettigrew, A and Whipp, R (1993) *Managing Change for Competitive Success*, Blackwell Publishers, Oxford

Porter, M (1980) *Competitive Strategy*, Free Press, New York

Quinn, J B (1980) *Strategies for Change: Logical incrementalism*, Richard D Irwin, Homewood, Ill.

Rigby, D and Gillies, C (2000) Making the most of management tools and techniques: a survey from Bain & Company, *Strategic Change*, **9**, pp 269–74

Thurley, K and Wirdenius, H (1989) *Towards European Management*, Pitman Publishing, London

2

Does strategic management work?

INTRODUCTION

One of the difficulties faced by managers trying to decide whether it is worth studying strategy is that there is a widespread belief that it just does not work. This is especially true when people start to discuss entrepreneurial and innovative behaviour. Here the common sense perception is that for entrepreneurs to be successful strategy and plans are the last thing they need. These are seen as hemming them in and constricting them. Improvisation or 'off the cuff' action is what is needed. Very few of us though can be quick-witted enough to manage spontaneous and clever action. It often comes as a shock to people when they learn that many television shows are not the spontaneous events they are made out to be. In fact, in some cases, popular panel shows give the questions to the performers prior to the show to give them time to work out humorous responses. Chat shows are typically heavily scripted beforehand to make sure that they work. Leaving things to chance is just too dangerous. There are performers who are especially gifted and can literally think on their feet but many rely on hard work to memorize many hundreds, if not thousands, of jokes and stories that they can use at the right moment. Spontaneity is actually very difficult. Edison used to say that a new invention is 99 per cent perspiration and 1 per cent inspiration.

How does this link to our position in Chapter 1 urging you to become more creative and imaginative in developing strategy? Simply said, we believe that the right

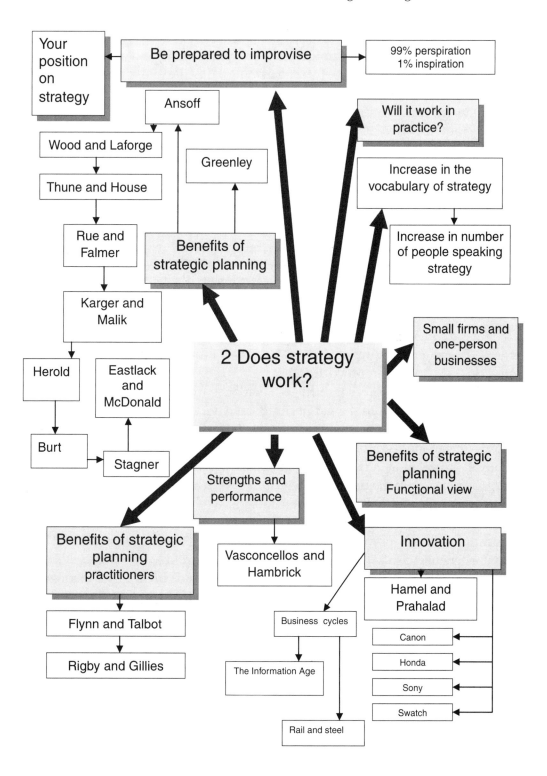

strategy very rarely just happens by accident or intuition. While strategy requires creativity, it does not mean it does not require careful planning and analysis. Even successful entrepreneurial action rarely appears out of the blue. So the point we want to make is that, while there are people who believe that strategy leeches out creativity and spontaneity leaving no room for the inspired guesses or action, in the main, strategy cannot just be left to the fates.

Apart from those who believe that over-strategizing can lead to an impoverishment of what is possible, curtailing the actions of managers, others simply do not believe that strategic management actually delivers what it sets out to achieve. Pragmatically we believe that you have to judge whether or not it works for the type of situations you will find yourself in. By reading this book you have already begun to think about strategy and may well be in a managerial role that requires you to develop strategy. You will have to decide for yourself the value of the material we have put together. In the natural and physical sciences, the truth of a proposition has quite a long shelf-life, but this is not true of strategy. You need to come to you own view on whether strategic thought and techniques deliver. It is their practical worth that counts. As mentioned in Chapter 1, when economists analyse something they often say, 'While it clearly worked in practice, will it work in theory?' We take a different tack: 'Will it work in practice?'

As we will see below, there is sufficient evidence from academic research to suggest that managers would be advised to take strategic management seriously. However, it can be said that the question of the value of strategic management is complex. We can look at studies of actual organizations and see if there is evidence that shows a correlation between strategic plans and success. Strategic management, however, is not simply the use of strategic plans. It is a way of looking at the responsibilities of management. It is a way of looking at the organization's present and future environment. It may make use of a variety of techniques. It may produce formal documents, but it may not. It is a way of generating actions, or streams of action, to provide benefits to stakeholders, to beat competitors, and to make use of the capacity of the organization. Moreover, there are different kinds of strategic management. This gives some indication of the nuances and complexity of what it is to be strategic and what it is to do strategic management. It is difficult now to think of some simple test to show that strategic management works or does not work.

It is interesting, however, that more and more managers in all sorts of organizations seem to be using the vocabulary of strategic management to frame questions about their situation and their possibilities for taking action. Strategic management appears to be a fruitful way for managers to interact with the world of the organization and its environment. We doubt whether any managers 50 years ago talked about what they were doing or intended doing using the vocabulary of strategic management. Nowadays many do use it, especially managers in large organizations where mission statements and written strategic plans are commonplace. In all sectors of the economy you will find managers now spend time devising strategies for their organizations and attempting to implement them. This change has not occurred overnight. It has been happening over the last 30 or 40 years. It has been helped by the growth of higher education business courses, especially MBAs. And each year large numbers of managers acquire or extend their vocabulary by buying the latest books on strategic management.

We take this increase in both the vocabulary of strategy and the number of people willing to have a go at speaking strategy as a good sign. It leads us to believe that there is a chance that the quality (as well as the obvious increase in quantity) of conversations taking place about strategy will improve. Of course the outcome of this increase in quality and quantity will not necessarily lead to better strategy; but an increase in the number of well-informed and articulate strategists should improve the level of strategic thought in organizations. Whether this leads to more successful strategies time will tell.

There are arguments between protagonists of different kinds of strategic management vocabulary. They may try to settle which type of strategic management is right or true, but their arguments and counter-arguments are remarkably inconclusive. Choosing between them seems to be more a matter of choosing how you like to look at management and what kinds of questions and phenomena you find interesting and want to address. The choice, then, is a personal decision based on the attractiveness of the approach rather than its scientific validity. This is not just true of strategic management. There are, in fact, lots of broad theoretical approaches in management that cannot easily be tested using a procedure in which you hypothesize, collect data, and confirm or refute the hypothesis. Here we need to stress yet again the importance of your own assessment of what is worthwhile in terms of the outcomes achieved. We do not believe it is possible to say categorically: do this as opposed to that in these circumstances; but we do believe that you have to judge the value of what you have done by its effects.

BENEFITS OF STRATEGIC PLANNING

Over the years there have been numerous studies of strategic planning and performance. Early studies measured the existence or nature of planning and looked at organizational aspects of strategic planning. One study indicated that organizations that planned performed better than organizations that did not plan (Herold, 1972). Some studies showed that organizations doing formal planning performed better than other organizations (Thune and House, 1970; Rue and Falmer, 1972; and Karger and Malik, 1975). A study by Ansoff and colleagues (1970) found that deliberate and systematic preplanning of acquisition strategies was correlated with better financial performance. In another study organizations doing comprehensive planning were found to perform better than those that were not (Wood and Laforge, 1979). Burt (1978) reported that high quality planning was associated with high performance. Eastlack and McDonald (1970) found that faster growth correlated with the involvement of chief executives in strategic management. Finally, one study found that the use of formal top management committees to develop strategy correlated with better performance (Stagner, 1969).

Overviews of such empirical studies usually conclude that there is a preponderance of evidence in favour of a link between planning and performance. However, there is also a history of studies finding no link between company performance and planning. Some studies have even found a negative relationship. Greenley (1989) reviewed nine studies based on sample surveys and decided that the research on the link between strategic planning and performance in manufacturing companies had not been definitely established.

PRACTITIONERS

While there is not total unanimity among researchers about the link between formal strategic planning and better performance, most practitioners would no doubt think even a modest level of support for the link would make it worthwhile to invest their time and effort in developing strategic plans. In fact, the evidence is better than modest. And surveys of practitioners suggest that their experience has confirmed that investing in strategic planning is a good idea. For example, a survey of the UK private sector in 1992 found a majority of companies had formal strategic planning. Many of the respondents to the survey said that strategic planning helped the organization to achieve goals and objectives, specify milestones for organizational achievement, achieve cost savings, and create a unified vision of the organization's future for staff (Flynn and Talbot, 1996). Similar benefits were reported by respondents in a survey of local government in 1993–94 (Flynn and Talbot, 1996). While there are similarities and differences between the private and public sectors, managing in either sector is challenging, and managers in both sectors obviously find strategic management useful.

As with any management tool, strategic planning benefits depend on the skill with which managers use it. Its benefits also depend on managers investing time and resources in making it work effectively (Rigby and Gillies, 2000).

A FUNCTIONAL VIEW

Even if academic research finds a correlation between strategic planning and performance it might still be objected that the case for strategic planning is unproven. It might be said, for example, that better performing organizations have the extra management capacity needed to carry out strategic planning. In contrast, organizations that are doing less well may not have the time or spare attention to think about strategic planning – they are too busy coping with the immediate problems they are experiencing. So, it might be argued, good performance causes strategic planning and not vice versa. Another argument is that good managers achieve better performance in a variety of ways and coincidentally also happen to have a tendency to carry out strategic planning. This implies that good management is the real cause of better performance and that strategic planning is just a spurious factor.

We have our own perspective on the existence of a correlation between strategic planning and better performance. This is that strategic planning has a functional relationship to performance via management attributes. We arrived at this view as a result of some recent research into strategic management in small businesses. In 1998, 513 companies in the South East of England were surveyed. Our analysis of the data on those with less than 250 employees indicated a link between strategic management processes and business health and growth. (See Table 2.1).

However, we also found that strategic management processes were more likely among organizations that were rated as very entrepreneurial, used planning to innovate, and planned for six months ahead or more. Our interpretation of these findings is that strategic management systems might reinforce or strengthen the critical management capabilities and attributes, but that these capabilities and attributes

Current Performance of Business	No Strategic Management Processes	Strategic Performance Management and / or Issue Management Systems
Rapidly Growing	4.6%	27.4%
Growing Steadily	40.3%	52.1%
Stable or Declining	55.1%	20.5%
Total	100.0%	100.0%
(no. of cases)	(305)	(73)

Table 2.1 Strategic management and business health and growth

predisposed the organization to employ strategic management processes. So, strategic planning helps managers be even more entrepreneurial, innovative, and long term in their planning. This is valuable if these attributes are direct causal conditions for organizational achievement (eg business growth). And we think they are.

STRENGTH AND PERFORMANCE

A key idea in strategic management thinking is that firms should select strategies that make use of their strengths. This idea is usually taken as self-evidently true. If it is true then the application of strategic management in ways that involves an organization making use of its strengths should pay off in better performance. There is some empirical evidence linking strengths and performance. For example, Vasconcellos and Hambrick (1989) found that organizations that rated highest on key success factors for an industry were better performers. There is also some evidence that building distinctive capabilities pays off. A survey by Bain & Company has found 'a strong correlation between financial results and a company's ability to build distinctive capabilities that serve customer needs better than the competition'. (Rigby and Gillies, 2000: 272–73.)

BENEFITS OF STRATEGIC INNOVATION

Innovation has come to be seen as the key driver of growth and profitability. In the last couple of years the United States generated more than a half of its economic growth from new industries born in the last decade. However, this is not really new. Innovation is part and parcel of the history of business cycles. Each major business

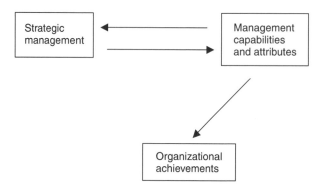

Figure 2.1 Functional strategic management

cycle is characterized by the rise of new industries. In the late 18th and early 19th century textiles and iron were the new industries. In the second half of the 19th century rail and steel industries became important. In the last century the new industries included electricity and chemicals, then petrochemicals, electronics and aviation came to the fore. The latest wave of innovation covering the present period is summed up by describing the period as the Information Age, meaning that there are new products and services clustering around digital technology, software and new media.

While innovation is a long-recognized part of the internal dynamics of market economies, what is really new is the idea that strategic management can boost levels of innovation. There has been a shift from seeing innovation as being the result of acts of pure entrepreneurial spirit to seeing innovation as something businesses make happen by looking ahead. Individual case histories have been interpreted as showing that strategic intent provides the framework for long-term efforts to develop core competencies and thus the new products or services that yield competitive advantages in the future (Hamel and Prahalad, 1994). A number of the exemplars of this type of strategic innovation have been frequently cited in the academic literature. They include Canon, Honda, Sony, and the Swiss manufacturer of SWATCH watches. This type of case study evidence is probably the most frequently cited evidence for the link between strategic management and innovation.

CONCLUSIONS

In the academic world there are arguments about whether there is proof beyond all reasonable doubt that strategic planning causes better company performance. There are even arguments about whether it is possible to prove things using surveys and statistics. However, there is a substantial amount of evidence suggesting a link between strategic planning and better organizational performance. Moreover, there is survey evidence that organizations do use strategic planning and practitioners do find it beneficial.

What if we turn the argument around and imagine an organization that has no strategy at all and no perspective on the future? For many organizations this would be unthinkable – they simply have to have strategy. So while arguments exist about the best way to produce and implement the strategy it is hard to believe that organizations should have no strategy at all. Yet, on the other hand, one of the features of modern advanced economies is the number of very small and one-person businesses. In the UK there are nearly 3 million one-person businesses (and by definition they employ no one except the owner/manager). Do they have to engage in strategic planning? Obviously the type of planning they do is different from that of the large firm but it does not follow that no strategic planning needs to take place. In fact a strong case can be made out that these firms would benefit from more of an exposure to strategic management techniques as the death rate of very small firms is very, very high. In both the United States and the UK each year thousands of new small firms are established. Each year also sees the deaths of thousands. Many new, small firms barely survive their first year of trading, and many of them fail within three years of starting up. From these statistics it can be suggested that if more thought had been put into pre-start-up and post-start-up planning, these firms would either have not started trading or would have survived longer. If planning had taken place pre-start and post-start and the firms still died, questions would need to be asked about the effectiveness of strategy and planning. So even in very small and one-person firms it is hard to see how strategy cannot confer some benefits to the organization. However, this said, it is up to the owners and managers in these firms to try strategy and planning and value them only if they produce the desired effects. If strategy and planning do not work, managers should not use them.

In our opinion strategic management is chiefly effective by reinforcing desirable management qualities. Going through the motions of strategic management is not a substitute for these management qualities – but why not use strategic planning if it can enhance these qualities?

QUESTIONS

1. What research evidence is there that strategic planning actually works?
2. Do practitioners believe that time spent on strategy is well spent?
3. How would you go about establishing the benefits of an organization engaging in strategy?
4. Innovation is just too risky a thing to leave to chance. To become a world class innovative company you have to plan extensively to make sure you have the capabilities required. On the other hand, all this planning requires masses of bureaucracy, forms to be filled, meetings to attend, reports to be written that eventually deadens even the most innovative spirit. What do you think?
5. While strategic planning is a must for large firms, there are an awful lot of very small and one-person businesses that do not really need all this jargon and mystification about core competencies and generic strategies. How would you go about persuading the owner of a small bakery employing only five people that the business would benefit from strategic planning?

REFERENCES

Ansoff, H I *et al* (1970) Does planning pay?, *Long Range Planning*, **3** (2), pp 2–7

Burt, D (1978) Planning and performance in Australian retailing, *Long Range Planning*, June, pp 62–66

Eastlack, J and McDonald, P (1970) CEOs' role in corporate growth, *Harvard Business Review*, May–June, pp 150–63

Flynn, N and Talbot, C (1996) Strategy and strategists in UK local government, *Journal of Management Development*, **15** (2), pp 24–37

Greenley, G E (1989) Does strategic planning improve company performance? In *Readings in Strategic Management*, eds D Asch and C Bowman, Macmillan, London

Hamel, G and Prahalad, C K (1994) *Competing for the Future*, Harvard Business School Press, Boston

Herold, D M (1972) Long range planning and organizational performance: a cross-validation study, *Academy of Management Journal*, **15** (1), pp 91–102

Karger, D W and Malik, Z A (1975) Long range planning and organisational performance, *Long Range Planning*, **8** (6) pp 60–64

Rigby, D and Gillies, C (2000) Making the most of management tools and techniques: a survey from Bain & Company, *Strategic Change*, **9**, pp 269–74

Rue, L and Falmer, R (1972) Is long range planning profitable? *Proceedings of the Academy of Management*

Stagner, R (1969) Corporate decision making, *Journal of Applied Psychology*, **53** (1), pp 1–13

Thune, S S and House, R J (1970) Where long range planning pays off, *Business Horizons*, **29**, pp 81–87

Vasconcellos, J A and Hambrick, D C (1989) Key success factors: test of a general framework in the mature industrial-product sector, *Strategic Management Journal*, **10** (4) pp 367–82

Wood, D R and Laforge, R L (1979) The impact of comprehensive planning on financial performance, *Academy of Management Journal*, **22** (3) pp 516–26

3

The strategic manager

INTRODUCTION

There is an old Zen story that relates the tale of an unhappy young man. This young man had for several years lived in a village that was slowly getting him down. One day he got up and thought, 'I can't stand this any more; I'm going to live somewhere else where the people are much more friendly and where there is lots to do.'

So he packed his few belongings, made his farewells to his few friends and left. On the road to his new home he met a Zen master coming from the other village. The young man asked the Zen master what the people were like in the new village as the people in his old village were so unfriendly. The Zen master looked at the young man, smiled and said, 'Strangely enough the people in the new village are just the same as those in your old village.'

The young man then asked whether there was lots to do in the new village as in his old one nothing much happened.

'You know what,' said the Zen master, 'your new village is much the same.' With this the Zen master went on his way.

As with all Zen stories you have to draw out your own meaning from this one. For us it's a reminder that the way we view people is as much about how we construct them in our own minds as it is a reflection of them. If we found the people in our last village unfriendly, the chances are that the people in the next village are going to be

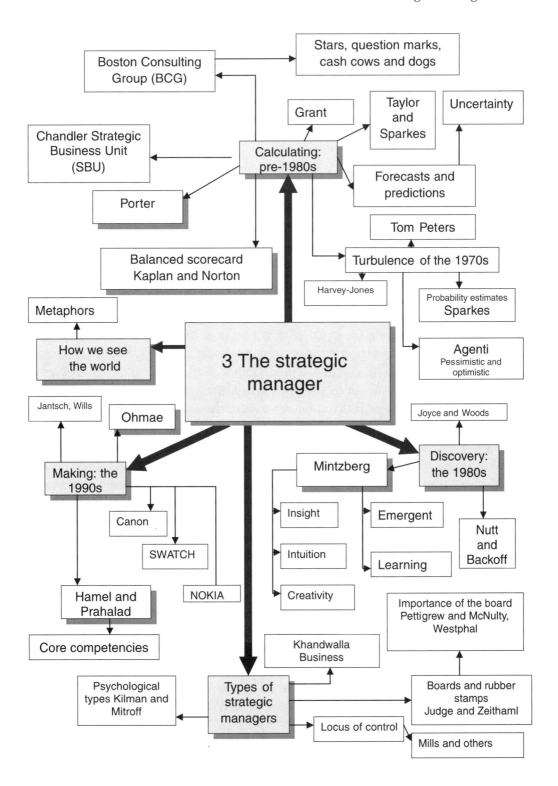

pretty much the same. It is not them that are friendly or unfriendly, it is our construction of them. In trying to write about 'typical' strategic management styles we may well have fallen into the young man's trap of constructing the style from within ourselves as opposed to something in the strategists. With this warning in mind let's continue.

There are different answers to the question of what is a strategic manager. In this chapter we will look at how strategic managers differ in the way they talk and operate, in how confident they are about pursuing innovation and risk taking, and in the formal position they occupy within the organization. We will set the scene for this examination of strategic managers by exploring three different ways of describing strategy.

DESCRIBING STRATEGY

As a way of representing a very complex history we can think of developments in strategy in the context of three descriptive terms: calculating, discovering and making. The ideas of strategy in the 1960s and 1970s might be seen in terms of calculating. For the 1980s and maybe the 1990s the idea of strategy as discovering seems most appropriate. Finally, we suggest it is now useful to think about a third description: strategy as making. Of course, we do not want to suggest that all managers moved along in sequence with this reading of history. Indeed, we often infer the character of management practices from the books and ideas that are popular. In the 1980s, books by Tom Peters were very popular. Since these stressed the crazy nature of the business environment and the importance of experimentation and innovation, we tend to assume that this was a period of strategic management in which strategy as discovering became important. Of course, it may have reflected a modest tendency in the way in which managers were managing, rather than being a sharp discontinuity from previous ways of behaving. However, there is a perception that large organizations in the 1980s cut back on the numbers of planning specialists and emphasized the responsibility of general management for strategy (see Harvey Jones in Ansoff, 1987). Such developments might be symptomatic of a decline in the view of strategy as calculating.

We would argue that all three descriptions might be applied nowadays when thinking about how managers develop strategies and plans and would by no means conclude that all managers now practise strategic management as if it were concerned with making the future. We will look at each descriptive term in turn but offer here an initial statement of their similarities and differences in terms of their consequences for the practice of strategic management. Whereas the descriptions calculating and making have a strong concern for the future, discovering accents the practice of management in the here and now. Then again, whereas calculating is often accused

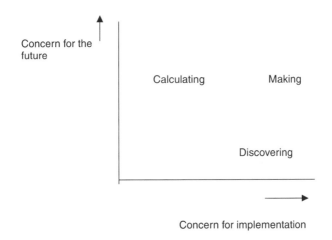

Figure 3.1 Descriptions of strategic management

of insufficient regard for strategic implementation issues, both discovering and making (although in quite different ways) have a strong concern for how strategies are implemented. See Figure 3.1.

Strategy as calculating

In the early 1960s large companies in the United States set up departments for corporate planning (Grant, 1998). Even in the second half of the 1970s it still seemed reasonable to say, as did Taylor and Sparkes (1977), that forecasting and planning was a good thing. Taylor and Sparkes said (1977: v):

> Presumably in all types of organization it is desirable to have a clear sense of purpose, commitment to agreed strategies or policies, the use of modern techniques for forecasting and planning, systems for coordinating and reviewing plans, and methods for comparing plans against results achieved.

Strategies at this time might be seen as key decisions about an organization's posture in relation to its current or future environment and forecasting techniques were accorded pride of place in the calculations of corporate planning. A forecast was a prediction. In order to make the prediction the analyst needed to identify the important forces that affected an organization. These forces were treated as variables or causal factors that would bring about changes in sales or profit or some such variable. Statistical relationships between variables were established using data from the past and these were then used to say what would happen in the future.

Of course, analysts were aware that there was a degree of uncertainty about their predictions. First, there was some guesswork involved in identifying the key variables. Secondly, relationships between variables might change over time. In other words, the past is not always a good guide to the future. Thirdly, the quality of the data used by the analyst also placed limits on the certainty of the prediction. The important point, however, was that such problems were seen as creating a tolerable level of uncertainty about the accuracy of prediction. If the procedure for predicting produced assumptions about the future that subsequent events failed completely to vindicate, then at least being a little bit wrong about the future was better than having no point of view about the future at all.

Predictions were also used in investment appraisals. In this case the analyst wanted to calculate the net benefits arising from a strategic project on the basis of predicting the future flow of costs and benefits. Based on the most likely figure for each cost and benefit expected to occur over a number of years the decision to go ahead or not was guided by the calculation of what was called the internal rate of return.

After the turbulent years of the 1970s it was clear that causal conditions could be volatile. One response to the scale of the uncertainty was to suggest that a range of forecasts might replace single figure forecasts of dependent variables (sales, profits, etc). For each forecast a probability figure would be attached (Sparkes, 1977). The basis for estimating probabilities was past data. Another response was to admit that the future could not be forecast accurately and to suggest that there was a need for both pessimistic and optimistic forecasts to cover the range of possible outcomes. Argenti (1989: 168) provides an example of an optimistic and a pessimistic profit forecast for a company over a five-year period using forecasts of turnover and margins, taking account of variables that included competition, decisions of major buyers, the age of products, productivity, and the state of the economy.

If organizations set target figures for corporate performance indicators and make forecasts for them as well, then it is possible to calculate the gap between the two. The quantified gap shows just how important it is for an organization to develop new strategies, but other matters of strategic significance might also be inferred from a gap analysis comparing targets and forecasts over, say, a five-year period. For example, gap analysis might indicate the urgency of action and the risks facing an organization (Argenti, 1989). Consider the issue of urgency. A gap analysis might indicate a sudden and adverse widening of profits gap in the fourth year showing how quickly new strategies must have an impact if this is to be avoided. Now consider the issue of risk. Pessimistic forecasts might exceed satisfactory targets; then again, optimistic forecasts might be less than even the minimally acceptable targets. The former situation might be regarded as less risky than the latter.

In the world of corporate planning, with its emphasis on calculations and forecasts, the key performance indicators were financial ones (eg profit and return on capital employed). Financial indicators are, of course, easily calculated. Of all the financial measures that might be used, profit indicators will get a large amount of attention. The aim is usually to help private businesses grow their profits.

As might be guessed, the main input to strategic planning of this kind is information. The main outcome can be a strategic plan built around a schedule providing a numerate summary of preferred strategies. Chandler (1987) indicates that this type of strategic plan schedule might include ratios such as profit/sales, return on trading capital, index of underlying market growth, index value added per employee at constant prices, and value added per £ of wages and salaries.

Chandler's numerate summary refers to strategies for a single strategic business unit (SBU). At the next level up, the corporate level, planning might have to handle a large number of SBUs. This can also be done in a spirit of calculation. Corporate headquarters can decide on strategic plans prepared by SBUs using what is known as portfolio management. The best-known technique or framework for portfolio management is the Boston Consulting Group (BCG) matrix. Portfolio management involves measuring each SBU using two dimensions. The first dimension is the strength of the SBU, which can be measured by its share of the market it serves. The second is the attractiveness of the SBU, which can be measured using an index of market growth.

Businesses that are high growth and are high share businesses are labelled 'stars'. They are considered to be likely recipients of cash within a company in order to fund the investment in growth. 'Question mark' businesses are in high growth industries but have a relatively low market share. They require cash from the company but it is not clear if they are going to turn into stars. 'Cash cows' are businesses that provide cash to other businesses in the company. 'Dogs' are in low growth markets and have a low relative market share. It is sometimes said that companies should dispose of dogs because they require cash but are unlikely to ever be stars or cash cows. The figure below shows a matrix with the four types of business. (We will look again at the use of such a matrix in Chapter 14.)

This calculating type of strategic management puts some importance, in principle, on the need to control as well as plan. The key to control within this type of strategic management is seen as monitoring, and the essence of monitoring is conceptualized as getting data to compare plans and actual figures. There is a presumption that the figures contained in the plans need to be the same as those that are monitored. The figures may be non-financial data, financial data, or financial ratios. Calculations of the gap between the planned figures and the actual figures are made and the existence of any large gaps is meant to trigger corrective action.

Porter (1980), one of the most influential writers on strategy in the 1980s, is probably best seen as coming within this calculation approach to strategy, even though he

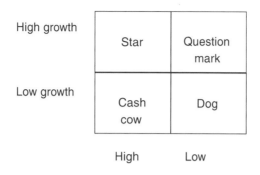

Figure 3.2 The growth/share matrix

did not focus on forecast-target gaps and strategies for closing them. He did, however, assume that the relationship between competitive forces (the independent variable) and profitability (the dependent variable) could be understood in numerical terms. He also argued that it was possible for managers to choose a business strategy having taken stock of the competitive forces in an industry. The overall tone of his approach was, therefore, a calculating one.

The idea of the balanced scorecard has been widely discussed in recent years (Kaplan and Norton, 1992). In essence, the idea is that non-financial performance measures are needed in addition to financial ones. Whereas old-style strategic planning tends to concentrate on financial measures such as sales and profits, the balanced scorecard recognizes that there are drivers of financial results that also need measuring. Consequently, the balanced scorecard requires managers to set goals and performance measures relating to customers, internal business processes, and innovation and learning, as well as goals and performance measures relating to financial results. The idea of the balanced scorecard is as much in keeping with the term calculating as was the old idea of relying on financial performance measures.

To sum up, the idea of strategic thinking as calculating involves managers in making calculations using figures. Managers are concerned about gaps between forecast and target figures, and subsequently, when monitoring, they are concerned with the gaps between target figures and actual figures. Their goal is primarily expressed in terms of better profit figures. Strategic plans can be prepared essentially as a numerate summary of strategies by calculating a set of ratios. And corporate headquarters can decide on strategic plans for SBUs by taking into account calculations of the strength and attractiveness of each of them. This kind of strategic management is aware of the limitations of calculating but prefers to work on this basis because anything else appears to be managing in the dark.

Strategy as discovering

We now look at the role of discovering in strategy. The point has been made that a pure deliberate strategy, in which a clear and precise intention is developed and then implemented as intended, is likely to occur relatively infrequently (Mintzberg and Waters, 1985). In as much as the strategic intentions were those of top managers, a pure deliberate strategy would seem to require that the managers either had total knowledge of the current and future environment or they could control the environment. In addition, a pure deliberate strategy would seem to require that the top managers have total control over the behaviour of others in the organization. We have previously considered such matters in terms of a modernist paradigm of strategic management (Joyce and Woods, 1996: 34): 'In essence, change is managed and controlled by the strategic plan, which is the fruit of analysis and choice by the strategic decision makers… the corporate future is programmable because the future and the environment are knowable and organizational change is controllable.' Mintzberg and Waters (1985) presented a range of ways in which strategies might be developed. This range of ways included ways in which strategies emerged even though they were not, initially at least, strategies formulated by top management or intended by any single group or by the whole organization. This seems to have been the basis for their proposition that emergent strategies are unintended ones. They also argued that emergent strategies are on occasion evidence that managers are flexible and willing to learn.

Mintzberg, who said that planning was a calculating style of management (1994), was keen to see thinking beyond the 'interconnected boxes' of strategic planning diagrams. Such diagrams could be found in Ansoff's (1987) classic text on strategic management. For example, such diagrams, made up of boxes and arrows, would show schematically how strategy formulation began with setting objectives, moved on to internal and external appraisal of an organization, and would lead on to decisions about strategy. Mintzberg's emphasis on the role of insight, intuition, and creativity in strategic thinking, in contrast to the emphasis on analysis in strategic planning, could be seen as an argument for managers 'thinking out of the box'. He equated strategic planning with the absence of strategic thinking, condemning it for the way in which it produced strategies that were extrapolations from the past or imitated from others. He also believed that viable strategies had to have an emergent element and that novel strategies involved some learning from discoveries and recognition of patterns in unexpected developments.

One of the main themes in Mintzberg's writing is the critique of management that splits thinking and doing. Strategic planning is seen as guilty of this. It is described as operating in a top–down way with decisions made at the top and control used to ensure implementation by middle managers and others. He argued for a committing style of management that engaged with people in the organization.

Unless creativity and intuition are seen as pure inspiration, it is probably useful to see strategic issues as the equivalent of the gap between forecast and target in strategic planning. The identification of matters that are strategic issues and then the handling of them in a problem-solving rather than analytical manner can be expected to generate more creative strategies and lead to innovations (Nutt and Backoff, 1992).

Strategy as making

The examples of stunning success by leading companies such as Canon in Japan, the Swiss company ETA that marketed SWATCH watches, and the Finnish company NOKIA were used to support the new language of strategic foresight and core competencies. Hamel and Prahalad (1994) used these cases to call into question the entire way in which strategic management had been practised and theorized. The business world responded. Corporate managers became concerned with core competencies and strategic alliances as means to make strategic foresights come true.

These new ideas were revolutionary (Hamel, 1996). They undermined the assumptions that the biggest and most powerful organizations in an industry were impregnable. They were revolutionary in academic terms too. They cast doubt over Porter's ideas of the nature of competitive forces and the creation of competitive advantage (Porter, 1980). They were suggesting that businesses compete not merely by positioning themselves correctly in relation to suppliers, buyers, and others. They drew out the way in which businesses compete by making use of their distinctive core competencies to create new products or services. So competition becomes an activity of creation as well as an activity of manoeuvring. They staked out a claim for the core importance of skills and technological expertise whereas before the pride of place in a business had been given to finance and marketing abilities. The physical products of the companies allegedly possessing core competencies – for example, car engines, printers, video cassette recorders, semiconductors, etc – gained dominance in the global market and gave a face validity to the claim that competition is now about creative learning. In putting an emphasis on strategic intent as a vision about how a company might provide benefits to customers in the future, Hamel and Prahalad set themselves apart from the strategic plans of old-style planning and the emergent strategies. That is, for them the future is something to be made – not simply predicted (as in the old-style strategic planning) nor left to take care of itself (as in emergent strategies).

There were some writers that anticipated some of the key ideas of Hamel and Prahalad (1994). For example, Jantsch (1967) drew attention to normative technological forecasting more than 30 years ago. This involved making a statement about the technology that was required and then seeing if a path to its realization was feasible.

Wills (1977) was concerned with forecasting technological innovation and implied that many managers were seeing technological change as a threat. He thought this defensiveness should be replaced by purposefulness. He wrote (1977: 75–76):

> A new technology for the mastery of technology has been spawned, not based solely on the extrapolation of existing trends in functional capabilities but on normative demands about the sort of future we wish to create... The normative approaches inherent in much of the new field of technological forecasting are equally exhilarating from the individual, social and commercial viewpoints. They provide a rigorous framework for the exploration of alternative futures and the opportunity for all to participate more meaningfully in the development of the environment in which we and our heirs shall need to live.

It is important to note that strategic planning had used forecasting based on past data (for example, extrapolating trends, building multivariate models) to predict the future, a normative approach emphasizes the articulation of a future to be created. Having identified that future, demands are made on resources, technologies and the functionalities the technologies offer. Trends and extrapolations might be taken into account, but foresight is not a forecast.

We see an even stronger anticipation of Hamel and Prahalad's ideas in the work of Ohmae (1982). Some of his views resembled the opinions of Mintzberg. For example, he suggested that strategic planning processes might flourish even as strategic thinking wasted away. Ohmae was no fan of old-style strategic planning. He put as much emphasis on creativity as he did on analysis. He wrote (1982: 277): 'Strategic success cannot be reduced to a formula.' Real strategists were imaginative, entrepreneurial and innovative.

However, in key respects Ohmae differed from Mintzberg. Often it was in these respects that he anticipated Hamel and Prahalad (1994). He placed considerable emphasis on what he called the customer's objective function, which was what the customer was looking for from a product. If, for example, the product was coffee, what did the customer look for? Was it the taste that mattered most? If so, what determined how the coffee tasted and how could a company improve the taste of the coffee for the customer? Ohmae believed that creative new products could satisfy the customer's objective function and expand the sales of the company at the same time. The result was benefits for customers and competitive success for the company.

Ohmae believed there was a pattern to be found among organizations that made assumptions about the future and succeeded in making the right decisions. He outlined the behaviour of consistently successful organizations based on foresighted decisions as follows. These organizations defined their business domain. The forces at work in their environment were extrapolated into the future on the basis of cause and effect and a logical hypothesis stated. (We should note the fundamental difference between a prediction on one hand and a hypothesis on the other.) The strategic options were considered and a choice made, and then resources (people, technology, and money) were aggressively and boldly deployed. The strategy is paced in line with resources. Finally, while the assumption holds good, the managers must stick to their strategic choices.

This pattern is quite close to Hamel and Prahalad's three step model of developing a strategic foresight, framing and acting on a core competences challenge (based on skills and technology resources), and then engaging head to head in market competition with rivals. Ohmae anticipates Hamel and Prahalad in stressing bold and aggressive deployment of resources, which they were to later discuss using the slogan 'strategy as stretch'. Ohmae believed that lack of resources (people, technology, money, etc) might be a handicap but some businesses were successful because of superb strategies. Hamel and Prahalad stressed how businesses with smaller R&D budgets had been able to take on and beat much mightier competitors. So there are lots of continuities to be found between Ohmae and Hamel and Prahalad.

It might seem plausible to suggest that different types of strategic manager flourish in different conditions. For example, organizations in the middle of environments that appear turbulent, chaotic and contradictory might be better managed by managers who use their intuition to set a strategic path and who have the political and educational skills to unify people in the organization behind their thinking. On the other hand, perhaps such conditions really require a cool and analytical head. In fact, we do not know for sure which type of strategic manager is best because there are so many contextual factors potentially at work and we do not have completely convincing evidence about the best styles of strategic manager. Case studies suggesting a link between a specific style of strategic manager and organizational success do not necessarily stand the test of time (Peters and Waterman, 1982).

	Calculating	Discovering	Making
Future Orientation	Prediction	Intuition	Foresight
Strategic Concept	Plan	Insight	Intent
Key Concern	Performance gap	Issue management	Competence challenge
Goal	Profit	Innovation	Benefits to customers
Writers	Ansoff (1987) Argenti (1989) Porter (1980)	Mintzberg (1994) Nutt and Backoff (1992)	Wills (1977) Ohmae (1982) Hamel and Prahalad (1994)

Table 3.1 Describing strategy

STUDIES OF STRATEGIC MANAGERS

The psychological aspect of how strategic managers like to work is important but not well understood. We assume that there are different psychological types. As a consequence, managers may vary in terms of how they like to relate to their world in terms of analysis, data, feelings, and so on (Kilman and Mitroff, 1976). An important psychological concept is that 'locus of control'. If a senior manager has an external locus of control then they think most things are controlled by factors outside of themselves. Whereas top managers with an internal locus of control think that, on balance, they can control things. Miller, de Vries and Toulouse (1982) found that internal locus of control chief executives were associated with innovation in products and markets, greater risk taking, and early innovation relative to competitors.

The values of top managers may also be important. Khandwalla's study (1976) of top managers in Canadian firms found variations in values and using his work it might be suggested that there is some link between environments and management values. For example, it seems that unpredictable and dynamic environments, and those containing high pressures from political, social and other forces, are correlated with top management values emphasizing risk taking and innovation as well as rational and systematic planning.

There has been relatively little work studying strategic managers in terms of their formal roles. In the case of boards of directors there has been a persistent complaint that they have been too passive in terms of strategic management and have tended to 'rubber stamp' the strategic decisions of top managers. Judge and Zeithaml (1992) looked at boards in 42 organizations and found many were not important in setting strategic direction. They reported that boards tended to go along with top management views of strategic decisions. There is some evidence showing that proactive directors are an asset. The research by Judge and Zeithaml found that board involvement in strategy processes was found among high-performing organizations. A board that rubber stamps management proposals and accepts managers' judgements on strategic investments were poorly performing companies. This link between board involvement in strategy and performance may exist because boards have expertise that improves the quality of decisions.

The importance of boards getting involved in strategy processes may vary over time (Pettigrew and McNulty, 1995). The board might be especially important in critical or transition periods. The issue here is the way in which the outside directors interact with the internal directors and thereby exercise influence. There is evidence that the dynamics within a board that is independent is different from that within a passive board (Westphal, 1998). It is not clear though that the opposite of a board that rubber stamps management decisions is a board full of internal conflict between internal and external directors. Another study by Westphal (1999) suggested a collaborative relationship is beneficial for performance. So the board should be actively monitoring the top managers but also offering advice and counselling.

CONCLUSIONS

It has been suggested that there are three different descriptions of strategy. The description of strategy as calculating was very relevant to the early days of strategic planning. Describing strategy as discovering seems most appropriate for the 1980s and maybe the early 1990s. Finally, it is now useful to think about strategy as making.

These descriptions imply different patterns of acting and talking by strategic managers. Certainly it is possible to suggest that strategic managers talk and operate in different ways. We have also looked at how psychological factors and values affect managers and correlate with innovative strategies and risk taking. Finally, we have looked at the formal positions of those involved in strategic decision making. It is still the case that chief executives play a pivotal role in strategy formulation. However, there is now more being expected of line management at all levels and an emerging view that boards should be more actively involved in strategy processes.

QUESTIONS

1. Under what sort of conditions does strategy as calculating work best?
2. Is gap analysis a viable way of dealing with possible poor performance in the future?
3. What are the key characteristics of the BCG matrix and how can they be used to formulate a strategy?
4. The balanced scorecard approach forces senior managers to address non-financial indicators as well as financial ones, while at the same time making them aware of competing stakeholder interests. This sounds great in theory but in practice the data required to draw up such a scorecard either does not exist or can only be found at some expense, so its practical applications are limited. Do you agree?
5. Mintzberg emphasizes insight, intuition and creativity in developing strategic thinking – in the common expression 'out of the box' – but this can lead to intellectual laziness, as strategists do not spend enough time understanding what is actually happening. They are more concerned with flashy creativity and futures. In doing this they lose the support of middle managers who have to implement 'mad' schemes. What steps can you take to make sure that others are on board?

How would you guard against getting out of touch with what is happening while at the same time keeping your own thinking fresh and creative?

6. Is the work of Hamel and Prahalad on strategy revolutionary or did it evolve out of what other leading strategists had been saying?

7. How useful is the slogan 'strategy as stretch' in practice? In thinking about this you might like to return to the owner of the small bakery. Do you think this person would think this was useful or would they say this is just another bit of flashy jargon?

8. How plausible did you find our three types of strategic manager? If you were forced to say what type you were, what would you answer and why?

9. Should boards be 'rubber stamps' on strategy or should they intervene more? In answering this you might like to research a few recent examples where the board has sacked the senior executive because of poor performance suggesting that the strategy pursued was wrong. The case studies on ICL and Procter & Gamble show this.

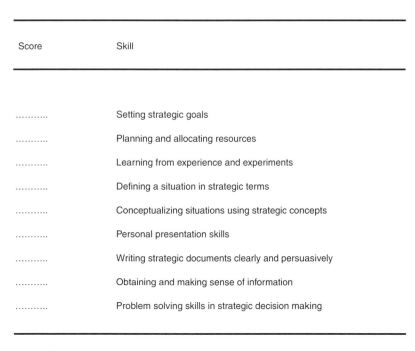

Score	Skill
....	Setting strategic goals
....	Planning and allocating resources
....	Learning from experience and experiments
....	Defining a situation in strategic terms
....	Conceptualizing situations using strategic concepts
....	Personal presentation skills
....	Writing strategic documents clearly and persuasively
....	Obtaining and making sense of information
....	Problem solving skills in strategic decision making

Note: Skill categories are based on research reported by Boyatzis, 1982.

Figure 3.3 Skills of strategic managers

EXECUTIVE EXERCISE

What in your opinion is a good strategic manager? Think about someone you believe is a superior strategic thinker and strategic manager. What skills does he or she have? Now, what about your skills as a strategic manager? How do you rate yourself on the skills listed on page 39? These skills were identified in a US study some years ago, but they still seem relevant today (Boyatzis, 1982). Score your current skills on a scale of 0 to 10 (0 = not skilled, 10 = very skilled).

Have you given yourself a low score on many of these items? Have you scored yourself low on any skills that you consider important for effectiveness as a strategic manager? Are there any of these skills you would like to develop further?

REFERENCES

Ansoff, H I (1987) *Corporate Strategy*, Penguin, London

Argenti, J (1989) *Practical Corporate Planning*, Routledge, London

Boyatzis, R E (1982) *The Competent Manager*, Wiley, Chichester

Chandler, J (1987) *Practical Business Planning*, McGraw-Hill, London

Grant, R M (1998) *Contemporary Strategy Analysis*, Blackwell Publishers, Oxford

Hamel, G (1996) Strategy as revolution, *Harvard Business Review*, July–August, pp 69–82

Hamel, G and Prahalad, C K (1994) *Competing for the Future*, Harvard Business School Press, Boston

Harvey Jones, J (1987) Introduction, in H I Ansoff, *Corporate Strategy*, Penguin, London

Jantsch, E (1967) *Technological Forecasting in Perspective*, OECD, Paris

Joyce, P and Woods, A (1996) *Essential Strategic Management: From modernism to pragmatism*, Butterworth-Heinemann, Oxford

Judge, W Q and Zeithaml, C P (1992) Institutional and strategic choice perspective on board involvement in the strategic decision process, *Academy of Management Journal*, **35** (4)

Kaplan, R S and Norton, D P (1992) The balanced scorecard – measures that drive performance, *Harvard Business Review*, **70**, pp 71–79

Khandwalla, P (1976) Style of management and environment: some findings, *Working Paper*, McGill University, Montreal.

Kilman, R H and Mitroff, I I (1976) Qualitative versus quantitative analysis for management science: different forms for different psychological types, *Interfaces*, **6** (2), pp 17–27

Miller, D, de Vries, M F R and Toulouse, J (1982) Top executive locus of control and its relationship to strategy-making, structure, and environment, *Academy of Management Journal*, **25** (2), pp 237–53

Mintzberg, H (1994) The fall and rise of strategic planning, *Harvard Business Review*, January–February, pp 107–14

Mintzberg, H and Waters, J A (1985) Of strategies, deliberate and emergent, *Strategic Management Journal*, **6**, pp 257–72

Nutt, P and Backoff, R W (1992) *Strategic Management of Public and Third Sector Organizations*, Jossey-Bass, San Francisco

Ohmae, K (1982) *The Mind of the Strategist*, McGraw-Hill, London

Peters, T and Waterman, R (1982) *In Search of Excellence*, HarperCollins, New York

Pettigrew, A and McNulty, T, (1995) Power and influence in and around the boardroom, *Human Relations*, **48** (8)

Porter, M (1980) *Competitive Strategy*, Free Press, New York

Sparkes, J R (1977) The role of forecasting and the problem of uncertainty, in *Corporate Strategy and Planning*, eds B Taylor and J R Sparkes, Heinemann, London

Taylor, B and Sparkes, J R (eds) (1977) *Corporate Strategy and Planning*, Heinemann, London

Westphal, J D (1998) Board games: how CEOs adapt to increases in structural board independence from management, *Administrative Science Quarterly*, **43** (3)

Westphal, J D (1999) Collaboration in the boardroom: behavioral and performance consequences of CEO-board social ties, *Academy of Management Journal*, **42** (1)

Wills, G (1977) Forecasting technological innovation, in *Corporate Strategy and Planning*, eds B Taylor and J R Sparkes, Heinemann, London

Reading 3.1

Taken from Chapter 1 – How persuasion works: what Aristotle taught, in *Persuading Aristotle* by Peter Thompson (1999)

The fool tells me his reasons. The wise man persuades me with my own.

Aristotle

Contra negantem principia non est disputandum.
(You cannot argue with someone who denies the first principles.)

Anon.

Everything we know about the art of persuasion today in our mass marketing era is a legacy of thinkers who lived 2400 years ago. They knew it all! The way we think and persuade today owes everything to the insights of Aristotle and his contemporaries. We are under the influence of Aristotle each time we turn on the television. Advertisers organise the text of their 30-second commercials on the basis of the structures taught at Aristotle's Lyceum. Directors and film writers structure their plots in the same way. Film actors spend years learning the same art of 'delivery' that Aristotle taught as a central element of persuasion.

In television news, politicians and other leaders seek to influence public opinion. Those who understand the power of what Aristotle called 'style' and metaphor do best. Television and radio interviews are conducted in the basic interactive framework adopted by both Socrates and modern interviewers to discover the truth.

In business, the corporate doctors known as management consultants borrow directly from Aristotle's teaching about the 'invention', which is the process of getting to the core question in the diagnosis of the ills of the company they are studying. They report to their clients using Aristotle's 'arrangement' for structuring their arguments.

At school and university, teachers and professors transfer the fundamental learning strategies of Greek logic and thought. Perhaps they teach in the Socratic style. In the social sciences, the dialectical system of Aristotle is the basis for testing the different interpretations of reality. Our courts model themselves on Greek dialectical methods as evidence is presented to prove a case. The evidence is tested by Socratic cross-examination.

So, in many different areas of contemporary life, we are still putting on Aristotle's thinking cap.

Background

Aristotle, Socrates and Plato were the three greatest minds in ancient Greece. Socrates (c. 469–399BC) left no writings but we know about him through the dialogues of Plato. His legacy is the Socratic method of reaching an answer through a dialogue of questioning or cross-examination, and arriving at the truth by discerning the differences between opposite points of view. It is, for example, the prosecution and defence method of our justice and court system, and the foundation of the method of learning pioneered at the Harvard Law and Business Schools and taught widely in Australian universities.

Plato (c. 429–347BC) was Socrates' great disciple. In the *Phaedo*, he described Socrates as 'the wisest and justest and best of all men I have ever known'. At some time in the 380s, Plato set up a school of learning and philosophy, known as the Academy. His most renowned student was Aristotle, who joined him at the age of seventeen and remained until Plato's death. Then Aristotle left Athens to become tutor to a 13-year-old Macedonian prince, later known as Alexander the Great.

Aristotle returned to Athens in 338BC and founded his own school in the gymnasium of the Lyceum in 335BC. There, for twelve years, he taught under a covered walk, known as a *peripatos*, his students becoming known as peripatetics. In the afternoons, he would teach rhetoric – which he called the art of persuasion, 'an ability in each case to see the available means of persuasion'. The Greek word *rhetor* meant public speaker and the origins of the word *rhetorike* date back to Socrates' era.

Plato was greatly disturbed by techniques which had the effect of making the weaker argument the stronger. He was convinced these means were used to build an unjust case against Socrates.

He rejected the injustice which flows from verbal trickery, blaming deceptions on the 'wise men' known as sophists, the most famous of whom, Protagoras, believed that there were no universal truths. 'Man is the measure of all things' was the belief of Protagoras, 'of things that are in so far as they are and of things that are not in so far as they are not'. If nothing is known for sure, therefore, the art of rhetoric becomes decisive in swaying the populace to arrive at conclusions and make judgments. Sophists specialised in teaching the methods of argument.

Socrates was plunged into this dubious moral context to defend his life at a trial which took place in a politically unstable interval following the conclusion of war with Sparta. Accused of blasphemy and corrupting the morals of youth through heretical teachings, Socrates became something of a scapegoat for the declining power of Athens. At his trial, arguments honed by the sophists prevailed and Socrates was condemned to death. He declined an opportunity to escape and committed suicide by drinking hemlock. In the *Apology*, Plato confronts the evil use of oratory as he records Socrates' address to the judges who have condemned him:

> Perhaps you think, O Athenians, that I have been convicted through the want of arguments, by which I might have persuaded you, had I thought it right to do and say anything so that I might escape punishment. Far otherwise: I have been convicted through want indeed, yet not of arguments, but of audacity and impudence, and of the inclination to say such things to you as would have been most agreeable for you to hear, had I lamented and bewailed and done and said many other things unworthy of me, as I affirm, but such as you are accustomed to hear from others. . . But I should much rather choose to die having so defended myself than to live in that way.

> (*Translation from Lewis Copeland and Lawrence W. Lamm (eds), The World's Greatest Speeches, New York: Dover Publications, 1973.*)

This miscarriage of justice at the trial of Socrates carried profound lessons about the use of language and emotion for purposes of evil, as well as good.

What Aristotle Taught

In Athens, learning the art of persuasion had great practical purpose. The institutions of the city functioned on rhetoric and persuasion. In Greek courts, unlike those of Rome, the accused had to defend themselves. Robust debate was also a feature of the people's assembly, or *ecclesia*, which was open to all free-born Athenian men. It was in this context that Aristotle composed *The Art of Rhetoric*, or *On Rhetoric* which appeared around 335BC. Classical rhetoric was divided into five principles or parts. Four of those principles, the elements identified by Aristotle in *On Rhetoric*, remain the foundations of modern persuasion. Another principle, which required memorisation of the text, is no longer fashionable.

The Five Principles

1 Invention

'Invention' is about identifying the central question which lies at the heart of the issue being addressed and marshalling the most persuasive arguments to answer it. The answer comes in the form of direct evidence such as witnesses and contracts, and through 'artistic' devices by which the speaker builds an argument based on *ethos* or character, *logos* or reasoning, and *pathos* or passion.

2 Arrangement

'Arrangement' is about how to structure and order an argument. What is the strongest point? What should come first, second, third and so on in the way a case is made? 'Arrangement' is the thinking and organising framework for presenting a case. It is the key to the coherence and the flow of an argument. Knowing which framework to apply is the most valuable shortcut in the preparation of any formal communication.

3 Style

'Style' involves choosing the most persuasive and evocative language to make your case. It is not just what you have to say which is important but what words you use to express your thoughts. Style is making choices about words (diction) and putting the words into sentences (composition). Grand, middle and plain styles were identified. Aristotle called metaphor – that is, expressing something in terms of something else – 'the most important thing by far'. Nevertheless, 'it will still be lacking in impact unless it is seasoned with the salt of wit'. Today we know that tapping into the imaginative power of the right side of our brain is the best way to create style through the use of metaphor.

4 Memory

'Memory' refers to the Greek–Roman habit of memorising speeches. I don't recommend memorising text beyond a few key sentences such as your opening and closing lines. When you memorise, you get too fixated with recalling what you have to say rather than putting the focus on getting your message across.

5 *Delivery*
'Delivery' is about aligning your voice and body language with your message. It is not just what you say and how you express yourself that count, but also how you express yourself non-verbally. Aristotle divided delivery into control of voice and gestures.

Non-verbal communication reveals your real emotional state. It is hard to trick an audience. If your words say one thing and your body and voice are saying something else, no one will be convinced by your words. People believe what your body and voice are saying. The great actor Jimmy Stewart recalled how, in his first feature film, *the Murder Man*, in 1935, 'I was all hands and feet, and didn't know what to do with either'. Actors train to make their act fluent. So should speakers.

Without doubt, we share one thing in common with those who lived in Aristotle's day. Speaking under performance pressure gives people the collywobbles! Speaking in the Athenian *ecclesia* must have been the same nerve-wracking experience that speaking in a presentation, to the media or in a negotiation is today. The good news is that there are techniques to help address these anxieties. They will be discussed in Chapter 5, on business presentations.

Aristotle's principles, with the exception of memory, remain the core issues in persuasive communication today. They make up much of the subject matter of this book and have equal bearing on how we make business presentations, communicate in the media and negotiate.

Artistic Persuasion
Aristotle said that you can persuade someone through direct evidence such as producing witnesses and documents, or through the use of *ethos, logos* and *pathos* – the so-called 'artistic' persuasion. An audience can be persuaded by a speaker's character (*ethos*), by the reasoning of their argument (*logos*) and by the speaker's passion (*pathos*). Like a triangle, they form a unity (see Figure 1.1). You can't succeed by applying one and not the

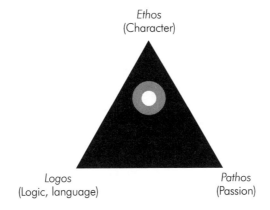

Figure 1.1   Aristotle's Rhetoric

other two principles. Being persuasive is really about speaking from your heart, your head and your soul.

Ethos or Character

Greek thinking about persuasion began with ethos, meaning character, but what is character? My father used to call it reputation. Your reputation, he said, means everything in your business. Any audience confronted by a speaker automatically wonders: Who are you? What are your values and beliefs? Why should I trust you? What qualifies you to speak on this subject? What special experience and understanding gives you 'standing' to authoritatively discuss this subject? How willing are you to share your own sometimes painful experiences in order to give authenticity to what you are saying? What 'added value' do you bring to the table or the public platform?

Ethos can build a bridge of trust and confidence with another person.

Logos or Reasoning

In Greek, logos means reasoning or argument. Homo sapiens, the wise and rational human, chooses the optimal outcome based on logical argument. Logos is the work of the head. The reasoning process is centred in the left side of the brain.

The framework of rules for building a logical, rational, persuasive and defensible argument is at the heart of Western science, knowledge and institutions. Law is supposed to be rational and logical. Bureaucracy was invented as the rational science of administration. Management consultants apply rational principles to the organisations they study. Western systems of education place overwhelming stress on developing the rational/logical faculties of students. And, in this era of globalisation, even the economy is supposedly managed on the rational principle of the 'level playing field'. Chapter 2, on thinking and organising, devotes itself to logos and its practical application in persuasive argument.

Pathos or Passion

Pathos is the feeling or passion you have for your subject. If you don't feel committed to what you say and do, you can't expect others to be committed. Pathos has made the transition from Greek to modern usage in English. It means to demonstrate feeling and sympathy or suffering. Passion will do. You don't need to demonstrate suffering for your work, but you do need to show feeling. Passion is the work of the heart. The emotional processing which takes place in the right-hand side of the brain balances the rational processing of the left-hand side.

Australia's dominant Anglo-Celtic culture distrusts passion, almost with a passion. The traditional upbringing for boys, in particular, has stressed the need for the ways of the head to dominate the unpredictable wiles of the heart. The experience of European history in this century led observers such as Freud to believe that civilisation depended for its existence on the repression of basic urges and passions.

Yet a life which lacks the yeast of emotion is dull beyond endurance. It is true that emotion starts wars, but emotion is also at the heart of the great refinements of art and culture.

Where is music without emotion? Or art? And what about poetry or human communication?

Passion changes the world and it is the people with unshakeable beliefs who make change happen. As the American essayist Emerson remarked, one person with a belief is worth 99 who have only interests. The force of their personality and convictions can influence the emotions and passions of others.

You can't fake passion – people know straight away if you try to. Genuine passion grows out of a deep-seated belief. I am sometimes asked in seminars how someone can express passion when they really don't feel it. Some public servants, for instance, tell me they feel anything but passionate about presenting a routine report. Well, maybe there is no way to be passionate about a routine report. Nevertheless, people can genuinely feel passionate about doing the best job possible on everything they attempt. They can feel a passionate belief in the value of the system in which they are writing their routine report (if they truly believe in it).

I believe that life is too short for confining your passions to home or to your activities outside work. Work takes up too much time for that. If people feel no passion for their work then they can never express passion about it. Maybe they should think about doing something else. That's what John Bell did.

John Bell

My friend, the businessman John Bell (1949–93), embodied real *ethos, logos* and *pathos* in his life and the way he communicated. John Bell was the Australian managing director of the Esprit clothing company. He once told me that no one needed to buy another T-shirt, but as a businessman he wanted to weld together his fundamental need to sell more T-shirts with doing good on a wider stage. He wanted to make a difference to the lives of vulnerable young people: unemployed kids, drug-addicted kids, abandoned kids. To do so, he began bringing his heart and soul to work as well as his head.

Late in his short life, John Bell decided that success in business should be measured by more than just profits. He began exploring how he could put more into the community than just fashion items. Those who knew him over many years say his character, wellbeing and peace of mind were transformed by the experience.

In the last year of his life, I worked with John Bell as his communication adviser. I became a sounding board for his ideas on social and environmental issues and how to communicate them. In reality, the relationship went beyond that. Not only were we good friends, but we also became joint mentors for each other.

We had met when I spoke at a business function to launch the Victorian office of a group of non-profit lawyers called the Environmental Defenders. Some time later, he called me and asked whether I would help him to communicate better. He wanted to take his message out into the community. We spent many days working on sharpening his skills. He was hungry for the knowlege. We discussed how to influence different personality styles. What was just the right way to get through to one person or another? How could a person speak with *ethos* or character? What were the most persuasive ways, *logos*, to put together an argument? What were the best ways to deliver it? What is powerful body language and how do you read the body language of the people who are listening? How could he lead his team of people to feel the same passion, *pathos*, about this mission?

At Esprit, John Bell decided to pursue a strategy of making his company stand for more than just selling clothes. It would be a business with a social conscience. His company would have two bottom lines. Neither the financial bottom line nor the social bottom line would be allowed to over-ride the other.

The Esprit Cares Trust Fund was formed to siphon off a small percentage of the turnover of the company to support community and environmental concerns. The trust gave support to homeless kids, funded the employment of young people beyond the needs of the company, and ran a farm at Taggerty in Victoria as a self-help project for children at risk. Esprit staff could take time off from work each month for voluntary community work.

John Bell was full of plans. He wanted to set up a clothing label of, by and for street kids. He was inspired by the success of the Cross Colours label in Los Angeles where kids from opposing gangs appeared to be working harmoniously on a project to produce a street label. He was confident that Australian street kids also had the potential to set up a street wear line with wide market appeal.

To get his message out, John began arranging a heavy schedule of talks and media appearances, especially on the theme of youth unemployment. He would talk to business breakfasts, lunches and dinners, to community groups and youth groups, to large groups and small. His audiences were often sceptical. They would not be swayed by emotional appeals based on *pathos* alone. Bell worked hard to deliver his message in a framework of solid reasoning or *logos*, arguing his case step by step to its logical conclusion. The frameworks which John Bell and I worked on to organise his thinking are contained in this book.

He built an evidence bank. A diary/scrapbook was his constant companion. He would paste clippings from newspapers or magazines that interested him or write out a quote he had heard which he thought might be useful some time in the future. He was always turning over in his mind how to say something more effectively or how he might enthuse other business leaders to take up social concerns.

I am often asked the question: Are great communicators born or made? My answer is that, like John Bell, they make themselves through sheer hard work. Some people have natural gifts such as easiness in company and a facility for dealing with others. But that is not enough to make someone effective in the difficult situations of communicating in a business environment in presenting or negotiating with others or in speaking on the media. A friend of mine at the Australian Graduate School of Management, James Carlopio, is fond of saying that communicating with the living is only a little easier than communicating with the dead. He's right.

The purpose of this book is to make communicating with the living a little easier still. Aristotle had it all worked out. Come join me in putting on his thinking cap.

Reading 3.2

Taken from Chapter 1 – From Shakespeare to Tom Peters, in *Shakespeare on Management* by Paul Corrigan (1999)

Management literature over the last 40 years has emphasized the importance of leadership. Book after book argues that without leadership managers and organizations will fail, and that it is this quality that is missing from the day-to-day work of real managers.

Yet leadership is not something that has only developed in the last 40 years. Shakespeare demonstrated 400 years ago the different roles a leader can take and the different skills those leaders need. His characters demonstrated very different ways in which leadership could be provided. Between them, his plays are a master class of what leaders should and should not do.

Shakespeare was writing these plays at a time of great historical change, changes that affected every aspect of society. They included shifts in the models of leadership that had dominated European society up until the end of the 16th century. Until then nearly everybody believed that great leaders were born, not made. They believed that individuals who were strong authority figures best carried out leadership. Leaders, born to rule, were born into very separate worlds from the people they expected to follow them. Once born into those separate stations of life there was little you could do but carry out your role, and followers had no alternative but to obey the direction in which leaders, from their separate world of authority, led them.

Shakespeare argued strongly against this view. Some of the leaders that he created fail precisely because they base their authority on the fact that they were born to rule. This book explores the congruence between Shakespeare's lessons on leadership with similar views of modern management theorists in the last few years of the 20th century. Both of these very different literatures argue in favour of certain leadership styles and against others. For example, the question of motivating staff is at the core of much modern management literature. How does a senior manager reach everyone in an organization with the message that links an employee's actions to the organization's vision? All managers, however large their staff group, have to struggle with the importance of communicating motivation. By now everyone recognizes this as an essential but difficult task.

Many managers see this task as a technical one. How do I ensure that every member of my staff reads the newsletter? How do I get them all to the staff meeting and to listen to the company's vision statement? But the issue of motivation goes way beyond these technicalities. For example, Tom Peters argues that leaders have to work very hard to provide meaning for their staff: 'The role of the leader is one of orchestrator and labeller; taking what can be gotten in the way of action and shaping it into a lasting commitment to a new strategic direction. In short to make meaning' (Peters and Waterman, 1982: 75). This demonstrates a much more powerful method of providing staff with motivation.

To orchestrate the different ways in which staff think about their work is to provide meaning to their work. Without that meaning, work is just a set of day-to-day activities for which staff get paid. And they don't work very hard if there is no meaning to their work. So the point that Peters is making is that great leaders make meanings for their staff, and that meaning provides them with motivation to work harder.

To demonstrate the link between Shakespeare and the tasks of the modern manager, it is difficult to think of a better example of a leader making meaning for followers than Shakespeare's Henry V's speech during the battle of Harfleur. The battle has been going on for some time. Henry with his English troops is besieging this northern French town but they are facing strong French defensive opposition and Henry's troops are beginning to falter. He rallies them with a speech that represents one of the clearest examples of a leader providing – in Tom Peters' words – a 'lasting commitment to a new strategic direction':

> Once more unto the breach, dear friends, once more;
> Or close the wall up with our English dead...
> > On, on, you noblest English,
> Whose blood is fet from fathers of war-proof!
> Fathers that, like so many Alexanders,
> Have in these parts from morn till even fought
> And sheathed their swords for lack of argument:
> Dishonour not your mothers; now attest
> That those whom you call'd fathers did beget you...
> For there is none of you so mean and base,
> That hath not noble lustre in your eyes.
> I see you stand like greyhounds in the slips,
> Straining upon the start. The game's afoot:
> Follow your spirit, and upon this charge
> Cry, 'God for Harry, England, and Saint George!'
> **Henry V,** Act 3 Scene 1 lines 1–2, 17–23 and 29–34

Why is it that nearly all the managers I know would like to deliver a speech like that to their staff? They want to make this speech, not because they want to be in a war, but because they would love to be as certain as Henry is that their people will follow them. Shakespeare's Henry leaves you in no doubt that, at the end of this speech, when he turns to charge *once more* into the battle, he is certain that his troops will follow him into danger. It is this certainty that, when asked, people will follow you, that we all want to create in our staff.

Such a relationship between leader and staff only happens when the leader has been successful in providing the staff's work with a wider meaning. The staff that Shakespeare's Henry needs to motivate are soldiers. For this wider meaning to provide the basis for motivation, it must first be understood by staff. This speech not only appeals to their skill, expertise and courage, but also imbues that courage with some very powerful meanings. Henry reminds them that, in that same area of northern France, other British soldiers have fought from 'morn to night' and only stopped fighting because of 'lack of argument'. These other soldiers were their own fathers, and Henry encourages his soldiers to demonstrate that they were their father's sons by fighting well. In this speech, Henry provides both personal and national meaning: on the personal level the soldier should fight as well as his forebears, and on a national level he should fight for his country.

As we shall see, Shakespeare demonstrates that the manager's ability to deliver such a speech springs from spending considerable time learning how to communicate and motivate staff. The ability of managers to communicate with their staff doesn't come out of thin air — it must be based upon a strong knowledge of the people with whom they are communicating. Before he became king Henry spent considerable time with young men in the bars of London, during which he found out what they were like through communicating with them. It was this communication that gave him an insight into how he could motivate them to go into a battle where they would be in great danger. If we want to be able to communicate with the strength of Shakespeare's Henry then we need to spend the time and effort understanding our staff in the way that he did.

Talk to any of Richard Branson's staff at Virgin Airways and you quickly realize how well he communicates, partly — in the early years at least — by helping cabin crew in the aircraft serve drinks and meals. This helped to build Virgin's special culture and spirit, which proved its mettle in the 'dirty tricks' allegations against its mighty competitor British Airways.

In this part of the book I underline the different reasons why Shakespeare's leaders can provide lessons for today's managers. It is important to see how Shakespeare's characters do what they do as leaders, since the issue of leadership is at the core of the concerns of most modern organizations. As we shall see, the level of uncertainty in the modern organization's environment puts a high premium on leadership, and if the organization is to chart a way through all of this uncertainty its managers have to lead. In the past you could keep a close watch on competitors with a few phone calls; now, in a global market, anything can be happening at any time and in any place. The pace of technological change may mean that an entire investment programme of millions of pounds is made redundant by a new industrial process. Change dominates the life of a business and, however much managers want it to stop, it goes on getting faster and faster.

This pace of change creates an uncertain environment for managers and makes them anxious about leading. If so many things are going to change, and you don't know what they are, how can you lead your business into such an uncertain future? In these circumstances many leaders are paralysed by the uncertainty and become immobilized. Just when their organization needs leadership it becomes much more difficult for managers to lead.

I will go on to argue that managers can only manage at all if they are prepared to take responsibility for the work of their staff. This may seem obvious, but in many organizations individual managers expend a lot of effort trying to duck that responsibility. If they succeed, then the organization is not being managed. Throughout history there are examples of what happens when senior managers fail to take responsibility for their staff, who then act on their own, without any reference to their own management. One of the most dramatic recent examples was the financial trader Nick Leeson, who plunged his employer Barings, the

Queen's 200-year-old bank, into losses of £869 million and brought it crashing to ruin. His managers in London were so pleased with the massive profits he was making in the Singapore markets that they failed to monitor how he was doing it. Consequently they missed the special account he set up to hide his losses when his luck ran out. Within Leeson's own morality, and left to his own devices, he saw himself as a brilliant operator and thought he could gamble his way out of trouble. The result of his lack of management responsibilty was catastrophic. The venerable bank went bust and the founding family was forced to sell it for a nominal £1 to a Dutch financial house.

However, as we shall see, the problem for managers is that they have to take responsibility for their part of the organization, but have to do so in a context that they can never completely control – a difficult experience. Of course, managers can attempt to get more control, but they cannot be sure of everything that affects their span of responsibility. For example, managers are responsible for ensuring that their staff come to work. A manager who fails to take this responsibility, and allows staff absenteeism to rise, will fail as a manager. So taking responsibility is vital. However, a manager cannot control all of the factors influencing staff absence. A blizzard leaving two metres of snow overnight will stop all transport, and few members of staff will get into work. The manager cannot control the weather, but is still responsible for the staff's attendance. A serious flu epidemic will also affect staff attendance – again outside the control of a manager, but still within his or her responsibility. This experience of responsibility without control is at the core of management.

Nor do Shakespeare's leaders control their world: the bad ones pretend that they can (or say that without control responsibility is impossible); the good ones tussle with the dilemma.

This book is different from most management texts in that it stresses that managers can only succeed if they recognize that if they are going to manage people successfully then they will have to engage with their emotions as managers. Given the importance of the motivation of staff in developing any organization, emotions are a vital component. As we shall see later in this chapter, I argue that emotions are as important a part of the process of management as the more rational and intellectual aspects of the work. Once we recognize how important our emotions are to management then it becomes more obvious that a playwright such as Shakespeare, who obviously works in the realm of emotions, can talk to us about management.

After dealing with the important absence of women from the contemporary productions of Shakespeare's plays and the lack of women leaders in his texts, I discuss the issue of gender in modern management. This introductory part of the book concludes with an analysis of how modern managers can learn from the different world that Shakespeare creates.

Taken from Chapter 10 – Listening to fools and knaves, in *Shakespeare on Management* by Paul Corrigan (1999)

Falstaff: a fool and a rogue to learn from

Falstaff is one of Shakespeare's greatest characters. His part in two plays (*Henry IV Parts 1* and *2*) and his posthumous part in a third (*Henry V* – a play where Falstaff is never on stage but looms large over the action throughout) make him one of the characters that most actors long to play. As we saw in Part 4 of this book, Falstaff plays a crucial role in providing Prince Hal with a close knowledge of the culture and language of ordinary people that sets Hal apart from other Shakespearean leaders. Throughout the three plays Falstaff's character develops alongside that of Prince Hal (later Henry V).

The relationship between them is one of the richest between two men in all Shakespeare's plays. The Prince Hal that Shakespeare creates over three plays listens to and learns from Falstaff even though he recognizes the considerable social distance between them. I have argued that the way in which Prince Hal learns about the language and culture of ordinary people is one of the main hallmarks of his leadership, but Shakespeare could have demonstrated Hal's learning from a wide range of very different characters. Falstaff already has a cast of friends and acquaintances from whom Hal also learns, so his necessity to learn from common people could have been supplemented by other lowlife characters without there having to be a single dominant character such as Falstaff.

With Falstaff, Shakespeare chooses to build an important character who has a strong relationship with the man who becomes Shakespeare's greatest leader. This relationship is as important to understand as the way in which Shakespeare developed his leaders themselves. We have seen that Shakespeare's fools were included in his plays to provide people of much lower status from whom leaders learn difficult lessons. They provided knowledge that cannot be found from senior members who have power. Falstaff represents another way of teaching this lesson: Shakespeare creates a character who provides Hal with a long-term relationship from which the Prince learns about real life.

Shakespeare's Falstaff is a very particular character. He is, in modern terms, middle class. His friends are of the lower orders but Sir John himself is a knight and has been an active soldier in the past. He has very little money. If one phrase were to represent his character it would be 'lovable rogue'; he is undoubtedly a rogue, but everyone through the ages loves him. He is always portrayed as a fat figure fond of his drink, juxtaposed against a strong, slim Hal.

What insights does a lovable rogue offer managers? How can a fat, drunken soldier provide modern leaders with anything useful at all? The beginning of our answer to this can be found in the very fact that he is an outsider and therefore has a different perspective upon the orthodox framework of the organization.

Here a quotation from the philosopher Ludwig Wittgenstein comes to mind. Since it might confuse us to add the third dimension of philosophy to those of Shakespeare and modern management, it is fortunate that Tom Peters has also used this quotation, with some glee, so I will quote it from his book of simple injunctions:

'If people never did silly things, nothing intelligent would ever get done'.
Right on Ludwig.
(Peters, 1994: 311)

Tom Peters' 'Right on' of agreement with Wittgenstein's recognition of the relationship between silliness and intelligence remakes Shakespeare's point about Falstaff. Throughout the two plays in which he appears Falstaff stands up for silliness, and Shakespeare, by placing him alongside the long-term intelligence of Prince Hal, demonstrates the importance of the relationship. In the above quotation Peters doesn't only like silliness for its own silly sake, but because it can often provide the boring leader with another view of how to run the organization.

Thus Shakespeare has the future king, his great leader, learning his lessons about leadership, people and life, from a rogue. Such a relationship demonstrates in great detail how leaders need very different forms of knowledge and information. Shakespeare shows how sometimes the people who provide that information may have very different moralities from those who are responsible for running the organization.

For the relationship between leader and unusual informant to flourish the leader needs to be strong and confident enough to overcome the difficulties that these different moralities can create. There is one very clear example towards the end of Henry IV Part 1 that shows how strong Hal's relationship with Falstaff has become. There has been a big battle between the loyal troops of Prince Hal's father, Henry IV, and his rebellious enemies. The battle at Shrewsbury was always going to be a difficult one for the king's troops – the sides were not only evenly matched but the rebels had one of the finest and most heroic soldiers of his time – the son of the leader of the rebels, Henry Hotspur.

Throughout the play it is Hotspur who has both the rhetoric and action of the real hero of the play. He is both a hero and a rebel. Remember from Part 4 the way in which King Henry IV worries that his son is spending too much time in taverns and not enough in court? Henry IV often compares his son to Henry Hotspur (who has the family name of Percy) and wishes he had a son of similar stature and bravery. In the very first scene of the play Henry IV contemplates the difference between Harry Hotspur (the son of the Earl of Northumberland) and, noting his high reputation and the low reputation of Prince Hal, his own son, he ends up hoping that it may be possible to prove that the two Henrys were switched at birth:

> Yea, there thou makest me sad and makest me sin
> In envy that my Lord Northumberland
> Should be the father to so blest a son,
> A son who is the theme of honour's tongue;
> Amongst a grove, the very straightest plant;
> Who is sweet Fortune's minion and her pride:
> Whilst I, by looking on the praise of him,
> See riot and dishonour stain the brow
> Of my young Harry. O that it could be proved
> That some night-tripping fairy had exchanged
> In cradle-clothes our children where they lay,
> And call'd mine Percy, his Plantagenet!
> Then would I have his Harry, and he mine.
> **Henry IV Part 1**, Act 1 Scene 1 lines 77–89

Henry the king pours praise upon the head of Harry Hotspur: he is 'the theme of honour's tongue', is the 'straightest plant' in the grove; but his own Harry has the stain of dishonour. For a father to wish his son exchanged with the son of another is a powerful set of emotions revealing disappointment, jealousy and anger. Imagine being a father and so ashamed of your son that you want to exchange him for another. This is a rejection of some power that would leave your son feeling deeply hurt.

Shakespeare writes this strong paternal emotion into his play at the very start. King Henry's speech takes place even before we have seen Prince Hal, who appears in the play a few moments later, not in the king's court but in the bad company of Sir John Falstaff.

In this scene, covered in detail in Part 4, Prince Hal tells the audience, not his father, of his intention of becoming a great king. Throughout most of the play, however, his father is left anxious and jealous of how good Henry Percy would be as a son. Given this background Prince Hal recognizes that for his father to believe in him he is going to have to take over the mantle of Henry Hotspur. To do that he is going to have to fight him and kill him, demonstrating greater honour and valour – greater heroism – than the man he is defeating. Fair and honourable personal combat is the only way of achieving this.

The Battle of Shrewsbury has two main themes. First, this is a crucial fight for the monarchy of England, between the rebels and the king, that will decide the fate of the nation. If the rebels win Henry IV's reign will be at an end and his son Prince Hal will no longer be heir to the throne. If this happens Henry Percy, as the son of the leader of the rebels, would take over as heir to the throne.

The battle is also a direct fight between Henry Hotspur and Prince Hal. Hal knows that this is his chance to prove dramatically to his father that he is as good as, and better than, Henry Hotspur. He has the opportunity to fight and kill him and in doing so not only beat his father's enemy but also to slay the ghost of the person his father is always saying is better than him. Prince Hal says as much to his father:

> I will redeem all this on Percy's head
> And in the closing of some glorious day
> Be bold to tell you that I am your son;
> When I will wear a garment all of blood…
>   for the time will come,
> That I shall make this northern youth exchange
> His glorious deeds for my indignities.
> Percy is but my factor, good my lord,
> To engross up glorious deeds on my behalf;
> **Henry IV Part 1**, Act 3 Scene 2 lines 132–35 and 145–49

Harry Hotspur comes from Northumberland, in northern England, and is therefore a 'northern youth'. Prince Hal claims to his father that all Henry Percy has been doing throughout his life through his courageous deeds has been gathering up 'glorious deeds on my behalf'. This means that when Henry Percy finally meets Prince Hal in battle, these deeds, this courage, will pass to Hal, providing he wins the fight and kills Harry Hotspur. Through this action, he tells his father, he will redeem all the slurs and anxieties about his own past behaviour on Percy's head. He has to prove himself by killing Percy. Shakespeare writes the build-up to the Battle of Shrewsbury as leading to a crescendo for Prince Hal.

In the battle Hotspur and Prince Hal meet. Prince Hal makes clear what they are fighting about:

I am the Prince of Wales; and think not, Percy,
To share with me in glory any more:
Two stars keep not their motion in one sphere;
Nor can one England brook a double reign,
Of Harry Percy and the Prince of Wales.
Henry IV Part 1, Act 5 Scene 4 lines 62–66

This leaves the audience in no doubt that this is really the decider for Prince Hal – one way or another there will no longer be two stars or a double reign in England. For Hal and country this is a crucial fight. If it is really going to eliminate one star in the sky, then the fight must be to the death.

The build-up to this fight has been developing from the king's first speech at the beginning of the play. The public prestige that would accrue to Prince Hal is enormous. Given this importance, what Shakespeare makes happen after their fight is all the more dramatic and demonstrates the power of Prince Hal's relationship with Falstaff.

The battle starts. Prince Hal has a clean fight with Henry Percy and kills him. As he makes his victorious and magnanimous speech over Harry Percy's body Prince Hal notices that there is another body on the battlefield. It is that of Falstaff. He believes him dead and, standing over the fat body, provides this kind, but distant, epitaph:

What, old acquaintance! could not all this flesh
Keep in a little life? Poor Jack, farewell!
I could have better spared a better man:
O, I should have a heavy miss of thee,
If I were much in love with vanity!
Death hath not struck so fat a deer to-day,
Though many dearer, in this bloody fray.
Embowell'd will I see thee by and by:
Till then in blood by noble Percy lie.
Henry IV Part 1, Act 5 Scene 4 lines 101–09

Hal is genuinely sad to see a friend die, and in his grief manages to allude to Falstaff's fatness several times, questioning whether 'all this flesh' could 'keep in a little life', how he will have 'a heavy miss of thee' and how he is the fattest deer struck down today. He expresses his ambivalence towards his loss by saying that he 'could have better spared a better man'. Sadly, but not sentimentally, he leaves the body of his friend next to the body of his enemy.

Falstaff, however, is just pretending to be dead in order to get out of the rest of the battle, because he is frightened and wants to save his skin. Just before the battle Falstaff had spoken one of the clearest soliloquies that Shakespeare wrote with a message that nobody could fail to understand, wherein he argues strongly against the established morality of the day. Even though his argument is subversive morality it is still compelling. He and Hal are talking just before battle commences and Falstaff starts by wishing that the day was over and he was tucked up in bed.

> Falstaff *I would 'twere bed-time, Hal, and all well.*
> Prince Hal. *Why, thou owest God a death.*
> [He leaves and Falstaff talks to the audience alone.]
> Falstaff *'Tis not due yet: I would be loath to pay him before his day. What need I be so forward with him that calls not on me? Well, 'tis no matter; honour pricks me on. Yea, but how if honour prick me off when I come on? how then? Can honour set to a leg? no: or an arm? no: or take away the grief of a wound? no. Honour hath no skill in surgery, then? no. What is honour? a word. What is in that word honour? what is that honour? air. A trim reckoning! Who hath it? he that died o' Wednesday. Doth he feel it? no. Doth he hear it? no. 'Tis insensible, then? Yea, to the dead. But will it not live with the living? no. Why? detraction will not suffer it. Therefore I'll none of it. Honour is a mere scutcheon: and so ends my catechism.*
> **Henry IV Part 1**, Act 5 Scene 1 lines 127–40

What is Shakespeare doing in writing such a speech just before a battle and at precisely the time when honour looks to be so important? Falstaff is plainly scared, but starts off thinking that 'honour pricks him' on the battlefield. He says that he has no choice, as a soldier and as a knight, but to fight in the battle. He is bound by honour. But then, in an extraordinary set of didactic questions to the audience (which he answers himself), he, from the point of view of a real soldier going into a real battle, destroys the whole notion of honour. Quite rightly he points out that honour cannot give back an arm or a leg that is lost in fighting, nor can it stop the pain of a wound, nor has it skill in surgery. For a soldier facing battle each of these is a powerful, unanswerable question.

Before a battle all soldiers worry about losing limbs and are frightened of the pain of wounds and the possibility of death. In Falstaff's time most soldiers who suffered wounds died horribly, so his is a real fear. Falstaff goes on to point out that someone who died last Wednesday may have honour, but what does that mean to him since he cannot hear and feel? He ends up saying honour is a mere scutcheon (a grave-shaped attachment for coffins), and Falstaff will have no more of this honour. Honour will not 'prick him on' to a dangerous battle.

I find these arguments very powerful, and I suspect that Shakespeare intends them to be so for every audience. I have never been in battle, but can imagine that this is what I would be thinking before it took place. Why am I doing this? How painful will it be? All the rhetoric spoken by my distant commanders will mean nothing if I am to die in pain. At this point, if I could walk away, I think I might. Falstaff's lines are delivered straight to the audience and meant to collude them into strong empathy with him and root his world-view into the audience's consciousness in a favourable way. This speech always works, and I have seen this play performed a number of times. Audiences do empathize with Falstaff and recognize that he is simply looking after his skin – most of us would do the same thing.

As the battle starts Falstaff, keeping out of the way of the dangerous fighting, comes across the body of a famous knight who had fought – with honour – on the king's side. Sir Walter Blunt had been dressed as the king to attract the opposition away from the real king and had in that disguise been killed by Harry Hotspur – a brave and honourable death. Falstaff stumbles across his corpse and immediately takes it as the final evidence of his catechism about honour. Look, he says to the audience, if you want proof about how stupid honour is, look at the dead body of Sir Walter here – 'there's honour for you!' (*Henry IV Part 1*, Act 5 Scene 3 lines 33–34).

The audience is confronted, in the middle of a battle for the monarchy of England, with two very different and indeed opposite moral codes – one of honour and one of artifice. On the one hand, most of the play underscores the importance of honour. The audience is invited to admire both Hotspur and Prince Hal and, when they fight, is thrilled by the honourable way in which they both behave. Yet just a few moments before this demonstration of honour Shakespeare invites the audience to agree with the opposite view. At this time, Falstaff persuades most into loving his dishonour. Shakespeare wants the audience to hold these two opposing views at the same time and constructs plot, character and narrative to achieve this.

To get out of danger Falstaff feigns death and, having heard Prince Hal's kind words over what Hal believes is his corpse, he rises from this pretence and comments on death and the battlefield. He expands upon this pretence of being dead and rejects it as a mere pretence because in fact it has saved his life:

> *Counterfeit? I lie, I am no counterfeit: to die, is to be a counterfeit; for he is but the counterfeit of a man who hath not the life of a man: but to counterfeit dying, when a man thereby liveth, is to be no counterfeit, but the true and perfect image of life indeed. The better part of valour is discretion; in the which better part I saved my life.*
> **Henry IV Part 1**, Act 5 Scene 4 lines 113–19

His morality is opposite to that of his friend Prince Hal, who has just met and killed his nemesis in the bravest of ways. In contrast, Falstaff gets out of danger by pretending to be dead and has a completely coherent philosophy for his actions. He cannot be accused of pretence, of counterfeiting, because real counterfeiting only happens when a man is killed. As long as someone is alive that person is a true and perfect image of life indeed. Just a few moments before there had been a classic display of heroism between the two great Henrys, Percy and Prince Hal. The reverse of this is portrayed by Falstaff but in a way that is just as understandable to the audience.

Having survived the battle by pretending to be dead, Falstaff realizes that he is next to the body of the warrior Hotspur, and that one further pretence would have a dramatic impact. Having successfully pretended to be dead, why not pretend to have killed Hotspur? 'I'll swear I killed him' (*Henry IV Part 1*, Act 5 Scene 4 lines 122–23). He carries Percy's body away, and the first people he comes across are Prince Hal and his younger brother. He presents Percy's body to the princes and claims to have fought with the dead warrior for an hour. Of course Prince Hal is surprised, since he knows he killed Percy himself, and he says as much to Falstaff and his younger brother.

Falstaff responds to this claim with vigour:

Didst thou? Lord, Lord, how this world is given to lying! I grant you I was down and out of breath; and so was he: but we rose both at an instant and fought a long hour by Shrewsbury clock. If I may be believed, so; if not, let them that should reward valour bear the sin upon their own heads.
Henry IV Part 1, Act 5 Scene 4 lines 148–54

Falstaff backs his claim by turning attention away from his own lie about Percy. He claims that the reality that both Hal and the audience know is true is in fact false.

Let's stop for a moment and see what is happening here. Throughout the play Hal has been unfavourably compared by many important people, including his father, to the bravest man in the kingdom, Hotspur. Hal meets him in mortal combat and, after a fight, kills him. By fighting and winning he has demonstrated to himself that what everyone said about him was wrong, he is brave and heroic. At this moment nobody else knows that this has happened, but a few minutes later his friend Falstaff claims that he, Falstaff, has killed Percy and, even more powerfully, accuses Hal of lying about who killed Percy for his own advantage – 'how the world is given to lying'. What would most people do in Hal's situation, having faced the demons and won, and then to be accused of lying about it? What Hal does is extraordinary. Instead of getting angry and claiming his rights over his own actions, he colludes with Falstaff's lie:

Come, bring your luggage nobly on your back:
For my part, if a lie may do thee grace,
I'll gild it with the happiest terms I have.
Henry IV Part 1, Act 5 Scene 4 lines 159–61

In public he asks Falstaff to carry Percy's body with nobility, but in private he colludes with Falstaff's lie and agrees to provide it with as much cover as he can in the happiest terms. He does this because, in Falstaff's world, a lie may do him good. Within minutes the play ends.

The fight between Prince Hal and Harry Percy is, for Hal, his real moment of truth. His personal victory over Percy is the way in which he proves himself. It is therefore startling that Shakespeare writes a scene for him where he so easily gives up something for which he has longed for most of the play. He has the proof of his own bravery and transformation in his hand. He could take Percy's body to his father, remind his father of how he always felt that Percy was better than him and say, 'Look at this body. You always felt Percy was better than me, but I killed him and I can prove that all his glory is now mine.'

Such a claim would not only be true and confirm what the audience has already seen, but would be wonderful theatre. Such an ending to a play would be very fulfilling drama, with a wonderful climax completing both the plot about who will run England and the sub-plot of the king's relationship with his son. Father could recognize how good his son was; son could become reconciled with his father. They have both defeated their enemies and can be safe in the kingdom – a great end to a great play – father and son and country united.

But Shakespeare's Prince Hal was never written to give this simple and straightforward lesson. Despite all that has gone before Shakespeare's Hal gives all of that glory and honour up to Falstaff, a man who lies and cheats. Falstaff believes that honour is a complete waste of time, and would rather duck out of battles, but he gets the honour of apparently killing the warrior – when the audience knows he is a coward who hid from the battle. Instead of there being a simple and unifying message at the end of the play something much more complex is written into it.

Why does Shakespeare do something that is so counter-productive to the main plot? Why does he throw away such a simple and wonderful ending? What lesson does this provide?

Shakespeare, as he nearly always does, chooses to tell a much more complex story. Hal, as the main character in the play, lives in two worlds, and he can switch between them in seconds. In one world, the world of court and of kings and dukes, morality is clear and of a mainstream historical nature. For that morality courage is clear and obvious. A man has to do what a man has to do, and if he does it he is admired and rises. For Prince Hal this means the necessity of a fair fight with Hotspur, the best man winning and in doing so gaining all the honour he can. Over the play Prince Hal develops great skill at this process and his honour grows. Shakespeare provides the audience with a clear picture of Hal doing this. On several occasions Hal talks straight to the audience about what he is doing and why he is doing it. The audience is meant to, and usually do, love him for it – as their hero prince.

Falstaff lives not just in a different moral world, but in an opposite world. In Falstaff's world a man pretends in order to survive, and then lies to gain advantage. As we saw from his catechism before the battle, for him honour is a dangerous joke. Shakespeare's Falstaff is good at this opposite morality and gains in competence at it as the plot of the play grows. Shakespeare has him, like Hal, talking to the audience and arguing for his morality with wit and force. These words of Shakespeare's are meant to persuade the audience that Falstaff is right. It would have been very easy for Shakespeare to have done otherwise, to have painted Falstaff as an unsympathetic character – but he didn't, because Shakespeare wants the audience to agree with him.

Therefore sometimes in the same scene, within minutes of each other, he portrays with great sympathy two very different and opposite moralities – one from Prince Hal and one from Falstaff. Even though they are opposites they exist side by side in the organization. Not only that, but Shakespeare makes sure that he and the audience give them both – even though they have opposite morality – credibility within the whole morality of the play.

In the complex conclusion over Harry Percy's body it is clear that Prince Hal has come to recognize that these two different moral worlds do live side by side and that their coexistence is a normal and necessary part of everyday life. If Hal wants to run his kingdom he needs to know that both moralities coexist in the one world; and if he wants to be a good leader he needs to be able to move between these two worlds with ease. The only way in which Prince Hal can gain this important knowledge about the organization that he is to run, the only way he can be constantly reminded of how to do it, is through the complex character that is Falstaff.

Shakespeare's Falstaff is one of the most famous comic characters ever created. He has attracted great actors and scholarship. Critics have tried to understand which real-life character he was based upon. His speed of mind and his pleasure in life are attractive characteristics, but above all it is his relationship with Prince Hal and the way that the narrative is worked out within that relationship that makes both characters so compelling. Shakespeare's Falstaff matters both in the drama and within the plot of the play because he is so closely linked to a future king. But their link makes good drama precisely because they are so very different. Time and again, as we have seen from the example above, Falstaff is not just different from the king that Prince Hal wants to be but is in contradiction to it.

For modern senior managers wanting to understand how to run their organization this is very powerful material. Shakespeare teaches them that they have to find out what is going on within their organization through unorthodox means – a lesson outlined in Part 4 of this book. He also insists that they need to recognize the strengths of certain individuals in their organizations who appear to be completely 'out of the loop' of both mainstream values and information. Many of their other senior managers, as Prince Hal's father and most of his court do, advise you to have nothing to do with these people. You will be warned that they will only teach you garbage about the organization, they will lead you astray from the crucial corporate paths that you need to tread. They will subvert those paths and will ruin your career. So stay away from them.

In fact Shakespeare shows the opposite message. If you listen to these larger than life figures in the organization, if you really get to know them as people and find out what makes them tick, even if they are against the organization, then you will gain a very great deal for your leadership. Crucially for the senior manager, Shakespeare's Hal demonstrates that you don't have to behave like Falstaff to learn from him. You can still have your own morality, one that is much more in the mainstream of the organization. You can demonstrate that you are still aiming for the cultural goals of the enterprise in the way that Hal does in his slaughter of Harry Percy. However, if you really need to know what is going on, find the awkward characters, get to know them well and listen to what they say.

In the scene over Percy's body Shakespeare's Hal leaves two more very difficult lessons for senior executives. First, the pinnacle of Hal's public success in the play, the fight and victory against Percy, is given to someone else to gain the glory and public relations success. He has killed the man, he stands over the body and could have taken it to his father or his younger brother and proved it. He could have had public plaudits – all the headlines – been paid a bigger bonus than he has ever achieved before. But he gives it up.

Having achieved the reality, which both he and the audience know he has achieved, he is less interested in the PR. The goals that he set himself looked throughout the play as if they were goals being set by the court or by his father. Once they are achieved – for himself – it matters little what his father or others think.

In organizational terms the difficult lesson for the senior executive is that on some occasions, even on some crucial occasions, the success of your actions is much more important for your own personal development as a leader than for PR purposes. This can add more to you and to the organization as private knowledge than as a part of a large fanfare. For you to achieve this it must be clear both that the goal is achieved without argument and that you know you have achieved it. If you are clear on these two issues then the organization grows both because something important has been achieved and because one of its senior executives grows with it – even if no one else knows it.

The second lesson Hal leaves us with is that when the task has been clearly achieved, when you know that you have achieved it, you can on occasion give the PR to someone else, perhaps even an ally in the organization, so that this confirms the overall goals of the organization. This is a harder lesson. Occasionally you can even give the PR success to someone who espouses a set of organizational goals that are in opposition to its mainstream goals.

Why do this? Hal, by the end of this play, knows so much about the nation that he will one day run that he understands, for example, that soldiers, real soldiers, are frightened before battle. Under these circumstances appeals to abstractions such as honour are rubbish. He knows this important fact not through his own heart but because of his relationship with this strange man. Falstaff has over the years made sure that Hal knows these difficult lessons. It is no use wanting all soldiers in the nation to be honourable. It just won't happen. You will need to appeal to real experiences of kin, of relationship, or just appeal to the nature of their work as soldiers. To become a great leader Hal needs to recognize that reality. Falstaff is the person who has made sure he understands it.

This may seem paradoxical. Why should senior managers reward a morality that goes against that of the mainstream? Shouldn't they always be bolstering the message of the mainstream corporate goals? Shakespeare's lesson shows that organizations materially are much more complex than this. If leaders want to lead them properly they not only need to know this, but must also listen to the odd people who have that different morality. This results in a real knowledge of the organization, one that you will only get by knowing someone in the organization who is your Falstaff.

In this example the organizational leader is prepared to sacrifice all the good PR of his crowning success in return for the continued relationship with the subversive person who will continue to keep him in touch with the darker morality of the organization. This is a complex message for leaders and will only be understood by those who recognize that their organizations will always be full of contradictions. This works in these plays through the characters of these two very different characters who are both, in their own contradictory way, essentially English. Pay attention to only one and you fail to understand the nation. Again Peters puts this in simple language:

Maintain one good friend who revels in telling you that you are full of hooey. When you get to the top of the heap, nothing you hear is true (or at least the whole truth). Keeping things in perspective is very very difficult. The difficulty is directly proportional to the size of the heap you are sitting atop… Quite simply no matter how hard you try, no matter how open you are, you'll end up being surrounded by 'yes people'. It's hard not to believe people who are repeating your own ideas. Resist the temptation.
(Peters, 1994: 47)

Whilst, in rejecting a 'yes-man', Peters does not go so far as to suggest that you should always make your friend a 'no-man', he does recognize that without such a figure you will inevitably end up being surrounded by 'yes-people'. It is hard to resist believing you are right.

The differences and contradictions between Prince Hal and Falstaff run through many different parts of the play. Time and again Hal has to learn some significant lessons from his fat and odd friend. As with many parts of Shakespeare these lessons are sometimes played out within a plot but they are often played out through the individual characters themselves.

© Paul Corrigan, 1999

4

Formulating missions and goals

INTRODUCTION

'To boldly go where no man has gone before' was the first example of a mission state-ment we can remember. Of course it comes from the US series *Star Trek* that has spawned over the years other series, such as *Star Trek: The Next Generation* and sev-eral films, and in the process made lots of money. At the start of each episode the mis-sion statement would be heard as the starship *Enterprise*, went about 'searching out new life forms' guided by Captain James T Kirk, assisted by Spock and Bones (the ship's doctor) and other regular characters. For those who are not fans of the series or have never seen the original, as the starship speeds across the screen we learn that it is called the *Enterprise* and it is on a five-year mission to seek out (amongst other things) new life forms. It is hard to know whether this was a clever ruse to get the commissioning television company into committing to the series for five years, an unusually long period of time for such a novel and imaginative series, or whether it just sounded good. From a business viewpoint the mission of its creator, Gene Rodenberry, might have read something like this: to create a new kind of science fic-tion series for television, that will be a world leader in its field, leading to further new products such as other series and films.

Most large organizations these days have mission statements. Usually a mission statement is defined as being a formal expression of an organization's purpose. This may be distinguished from the strategic vision, which is a description of a desired

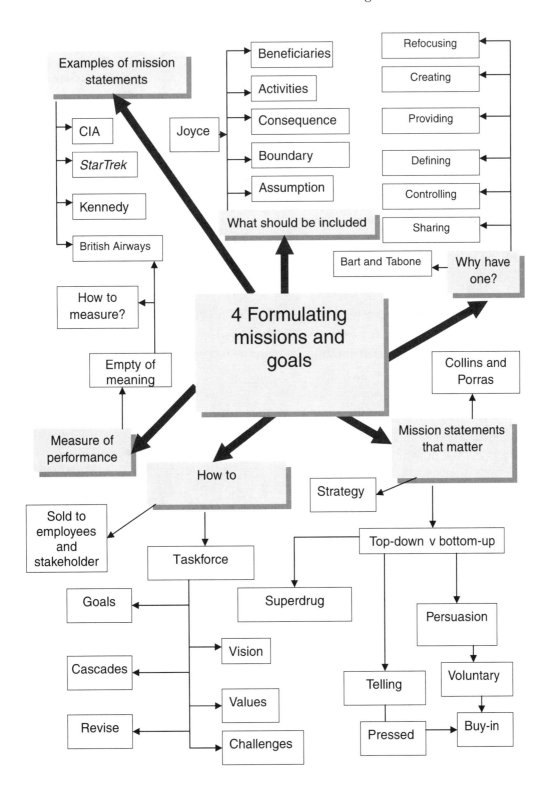

future state, and strategic goals, which are specific outcomes that contribute to the achievement of the mission in the circumstances that prevail or are emerging.

The importance of the mission statement is that it leads to focus and persistence by the organization and these things are generally assumed to be important for organizational achievement. It may also be argued that mission statements and strategic visions are important for motivating and inspiring managers and employees within an organization. The development of mission statements and strategic goals can be useful as one approach to developing systems for evaluating strategic effectiveness (see Figure 4.1).

In this chapter we will be looking at what mission statements are, why they are important, how to produce them, and their links to performance measurement and strategy.

MISSION STATEMENTS

'To be the undisputed leader in world travel.' This is the mission statement of British Airways and it clearly expresses the company's mission. With this mission statement comes values and goals. In describing its values, the company wants to be seen as:

- safe and secure;
- honest and responsible;
- innovative and team-spirited;
- global and caring;
- a good neighbour.

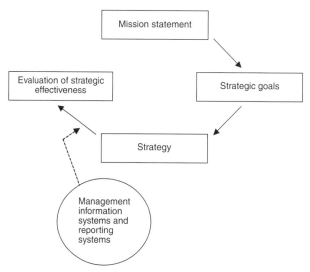

Figure 4.1 Mission statements and measurement of strategic effectiveness

The goals of British Airways are:

- (to be) the customers' choice – the airline of first choice in key markets;
- (to show) strong profitability – meeting investors' expectations and securing the future;
- (to be) truly global – (with a) global network, global outlook: recognized everywhere for superior value in world travel;
- (to employ) inspired people – building on success and delighting customers.

You can easily see what top management at British Airways wants the company to achieve and how individual employees, investors and passengers can also understand what British Airways is about. British Airways' mission statement, values and goals give shape to the company's activity making it plain what its purposes are. A mission statement, with associated values and goals, and in some instances vision, tells us what the organization is trying to do and, at a very general level, how it wants to achieve it.

A good mission statement should be clear and concise, plainly stating the organization's purpose. A mission statement that is unclear, ambiguous, or simply too verbose will fail to communicate effectively and will not be worth the paper it is written on. The scope of the organization's mission needs to be defined. If the statement is written too widely the organization may find itself caught between too many stools, unable to focus on any with enough clarity and provide the resources to achieve them. On the other hand, defining the mission too narrowly might mean that new opportunities are missed in slavish adherence to the original mission.

Here are a few other mission statements. The first one is the vision, mission and value statement of the US Central Intelligence Agency (CIA):

CIA Vision, Mission and Values

Our Vision:
To be the keystone of a US Intelligence Community that is pre-eminent in the world, known for both the high quality of our work and the excellence of our people.

Our Mission:
We support the President, the National Security Council, and all who make and execute US national security policy by:
Providing accurate, evidence-based, comprehensive, and timely foreign intelligence related to national security; and Conducting counterintelligence activities, special activities, and other functions related to foreign intelligence and national security as directed by the President.

What we stand for:
Intelligence that adds substantial value to the management of crises, the conduct of war, and the development of policy. Objectivity in the substance of intelligence, a deep commitment to the customer in its form and timing.

How we do our work:
Personal and organizational integrity. Teamwork throughout the Agency and the Intelligence Community. Total participation of an excellent and diverse work force. Innovating and taking risks to get the job done. Adapting to both a changing world environment and evolving customer needs. Accepting accountability for our actions. Continuous improvement in all that we do.

Perhaps you were surprised to see that the CIA had a mission statement but it is hard now to find any large organization without one. In fact they have become so common that you can get spoof ones done on the Internet. We had this one done at the Dilbert Web site at www.unitedmedia.com/comics/dilbert/career/bin/ms2.cgi: 'We have committed to dramatically integrate excellent data while continuing to completely leverage existing high-quality services to exceed customer expectations.' When you have finished reading this book drop us a line to tell us whether we have achieved our mission.

Mission statements exist in the public and voluntary sectors as well as in the private sector. Here are some examples of missions:

- The Salvation Army – 'to preach the Gospel of Jesus Christ, supply basic human needs, provide personal counselling and undertake the spiritual and moral regeneration and physical rehabilitation of all persons in need who come within its sphere of influence regardless of race, colour, creed, sex, or age.'
- The Foreign and Commonwealth Office of the UK – 'to promote the national interests of the UK and to contribute to a strong world community.'
- The Royal College of Surgeons of England – '...promoting and advancing the highest standards of surgical care for patients.'
- Brunel University – 'to produce high quality graduates and research which are of use to the community.'

One quick search on the Internet will reveal just how universal mission statements are now for all organizations.

The CIA mission statement contains a vision, a mission and values. The British Airways statement has a mission, values and goals. You can spend quite a bit of time trying to sort through what are sometimes quite subtle semantic differences between the various components of the mission statement and deciding whether or not the statement is actually a mission statement.

What sort of things should mission statements include? Organizations in practice vary on this. Joyce (1999) suggests an organization's mission statement may include the following:

Figure 4.2 Writing a mission statement for an organization

- who the intended beneficiaries are;
- the organization's main activities;
- the desired consequences of the activities;
- the geographical boundary the organization seeks to cover (local, regional, national, global, etc);
- any basic assumption which is seen as fundamental to its identity as an organization.

Why have a mission statement?

Bart and Tabone (1998) give three traditional reasons why an organization has a mission statement and six more that are beginning to appear. The three longer-established reasons are that mission statements:

- provide a more focused basis for allocating resources;
- motivate and inspire members throughout the organization to achieve a common goal or purpose;
- create a balance among the competing interests of different stakeholders (ie customers, society, shareholders and employees).

The more recent reasons for having a mission statement are:

- to refocus an organization during a crisis;
- to create behaviour standards;

- to provide a common purpose or direction;
- to define the scope of the business;
- to allow the CEO to assert control over the organization;
- to develop shared values or culture within the organization.

In recent years strategic management has emphasized the important role of leaders in motivating and inspiring others. As Bart and Tabone note, the desire to motivate and inspire others is also a traditional rationale for having a mission statement. The importance of this should not be lightly dismissed.

We can illustrate the mobilizing power of the well-crafted mission statement using an example from the world of politics. President Kennedy famously said in 1961 that the United States should commit itself to achieve within a decade the action of landing a man on the moon and then returning him safely to the earth. This statement is often used as an exemplar of what a good mission statement should be (that is apart from the use of the word 'man' instead of the word 'person'). It is clear and concise and embedded in it is a value – of getting the man there and back safely. It had the effect of galvanizing not only the scientists involved in the space programme but capturing the imagination of the nation. And although it was a challenge, it was achievable. But was it a mission statement or was it more like what Hamel and Prahalad term 'strategic intent'?

What Kennedy wanted was to beat the USSR to the moon. This can be seen as similar to Canon wanting to beat Xerox, and Honda wanting to become the second Ford. Americans had been startled on 4 October 1957 when the first Russian Sputnik was launched and again later on 12 April 1961 when Lieutenant Yuri A Gagarin become the first person in space.

Was Kennedy expressing a vision in his desire to beat the Russians to the moon? Vision has several meanings, it is a thing or person seen in a dream or trance or a supernatural or prophetic apparition. Or it could be a thing or idea perceived vividly in the imagination. Or it could be an imaginative insight, a statesmanlike foresight, or sagacity in planning. None of this really helps and it is probably not worth getting too involved with the possible nuances of meaning. What is important is that Kennedy provided something that excited people and set a tough but achievable challenge. His vision provided not only a strong focus for the space programme but the resources to go with it.

Kennedy captured the imagination of his stakeholders using all the power of his presidency to do so. And the threat of USSR space supremacy was sufficient for his vision to be heard and acted upon. British Airways wants to be the undisputed leader in world travel and the CIA wants to be the keystone of a US Intelligence Community that is pre-eminent in the world, known for both the high quality of its work and the excellence of its people. Both of these seem to issue a challenge – undisputed world leader, pre-eminent in the world – but in line with the ambition of the organization. Clearly, it would be folly to suppose that every mission statement needs at its centre such ambitious global goals but what every one does need are goals consistent with the organization's scope but sufficiently challenging, without being rejected as 'pie in the sky'.

The context in which the mission statement is developed is important. A mission statement constructed during a crisis will look different to one where the driving force is to motivate and inspire people.

Mission statements even in the private sector are not simply about maximizing some financial return. Look again at the British Airways statement. Strong profitability is only one of several goals. It is easy to fall into the trap of thinking that a company's goals will be all about the bottom line. Consider though one of the striking trends in recent years – the growth in self-employment and small firms in general. For these firms' owners the chief purpose of their business activity is not necessarily that of maximizing profit. Many are motivated by a desire for independence and a lifestyle that they value above financial reward *per se*.

Producing mission statements that matter

Bart and Tabone's lists are missing one reason to have a mission statement that has perhaps caused quite a few statements to be written, namely, that it is the done thing to have one. It is expected of organizations to have one irrespective of whether the organization benefits from it.

If the statement is a real one, however, the key problem for top managers nowadays is gaining agreement on its content. Unless a top manager belongs to the old school of thinking which says that mission statements are simply a step in an analytical process, he or she will want employees to sign up to it and act upon it. It is little use if it is seen as something the board, or the CEO, has cooked up which has no legitimacy elsewhere.

How to gain support for the organization's mission is a key part of the process of building the mission. It is impossible to be categorical on this as in some instances it is best for the organization to build its mission and vision up from the bottom of the organization but in others a top–down approach would be preferable. Consider for instance an organization that is facing serious challenges that requires a rethink of its mission and, on the whole, its employees do not want, for various reasons, to change strategic direction. In these cases the board or the CEO may have to act from the top to install a new mission throughout the organization, trying to persuade employees to his or her point of view. There may well come a time when persuasion and argument have to give way to telling employees that this is the new direction and mission. Clearly, it is better for employees to sign up voluntarily to the new mission than to be pressed into it, but it could well be that the survival of the organization depends on forcing a new mission through. As the old saying goes: if you cannot change people you will have to change people. In other words if employees are unprepared to sign up to the new mission then, although it may sound rather brutal, there are always other people you can employ who will support the new mission.

Superdrug, the UK high street retailer of health and beauty products, asked its employees to send in ideas when it needed to update its mission in the late 1990s. It received over 1,000 entries from which three were selected to provide the basic input into its mission. In doing this, the company was showing it was prepared to listen to its employees and gain their support in producing the mission. In doing it this way employees were less likely to see the mission as something dreamt up by head office which had nothing to do with them at all.

If employees feel that a mission statement has no relevance to their daily work it will be simply meaningless. It will not capture the imagination of employees giving them a sense of purpose and mission. There is a joke told about Kennedy's visit to NASA. On the visit the President wandered into a large hanger by mistake, where a NASA employee was sweeping up. The President asked what the employee was doing. The reply was: 'I'm helping put a man on the moon!' You might like to think about your own organization's mission statement (if you know it) and reflect on how you are helping the organization to achieve it.

We suspect that quite a lot of you either do not know what your organization's mission is, or do not feel enthused by it. It is someone else's mission and not yours. The 'buying in' to the mission is clearly not an easy thing to achieve. We have cited the way Superdrug attempted to achieve this, but there are other methods that can be considered when drawing up the mission.

A popular approach is to set up a task force consisting of employees drawn from across the organization. This task force sometimes includes board members. Other times it excludes them at this stage. In large organizations the CEO, or perhaps board members, will produce a quite high level statement about their vision or aspirations and the values they feel should be embedded in the organization. The task force is given this as a starting point. It then asks for contributions from key stakeholders, both internal and external, while at the same time conducting some preliminary environmental scan The task force then has a first stab at identifying visions, values, strategic challenges and goals. This document could include questions as well as alternative formulations of visions, mission and values. This is cascaded through the organization and comments and suggestions are requested, not only in an effort to engage employees, but also to improve the quality of the final version. At this stage the more the task force knows about what others thought of its first attempt the better. After this the task force produces another statement that incorporates as much as it feels is feasible from the internal debate. This is then circulated and further comments and suggestions invited. The task force reviews the results from this consultation and produces its final version. The final version is then accepted or amended by those who have the power to do so.

It is tempting to think that this is the process completed but the mission has to be continually 'sold' not only to employees but also to external stakeholders. It has to be reinforced not only in written form, but verbally and by behaviour. Sometimes the task force is also charged with organizing staff development for managers and other employees on the mission. Once the mission has been agreed, a broad strategy can start to be derived and goals and milestones established.

In small organizations or for the sole-trader, time is still needed for consultation with stakeholders when the mission is being developed and effort made to ensure continual 'buy-in' to it after it has been produced. Just because communication is potentially easier because of the small scale involved, it should not be forgotten in the pressures of completing everyday tasks.

Not only organizations have mission statements. Often self-help books on personal growth and achievement stress the need for individuals to have visions, missions, values and goals, so perhaps you might like to reflect on how reading this book is helping (or at least we hope not hindering) you in achieving your vision. Remember that just as organizations need to continually work on their mission, if you believe in life missions so should you.

Missions and performance measurement

If strategic goals are derivable and measurable from the mission statement then by monitoring them on a periodic basis the organization can see how it is doing in achieving its mission and vision and what, if any, corrective action is required to get back on course. However, care has to be taken when formulating a statement or strategic vision about how the organization will measure its progress. How will it know where it is at a given time in terms of this vision or mission; how will it know when the vision or mission has been achieved? While putting a man on the moon and returning him safely may be hard to do, it is pretty easy to establish whether it has been done or not. Often mission statements are poorly framed and provide major difficulties for setting up performance measurement.

It seems to us that because of the almost universal use of mission statements in all types and sizes of organizations there is a danger that in many instances statements have become vacuous, empty of meaning and having little real impact on the organization or its employees. It would be naïve to assume that every employee's values, when they are at work, align, all the time, with the mission of the organization.

Perhaps mission statements are losing their potency to enthuse employees and other stakeholders because of the temptation to couch them in terms too full of being for 'motherhood and apple pie'. Take for example the statement, 'our mission is to produce widgets of high quality for our customers'. Would anyone admit to their mission being to produce widgets of low quality for their customers?

Our random mission statement from Dilbert's Web site is an example of how easy it is to produce gobbledegook that reads remarkably like some mission statements. The statement included the words 'excellent' and 'high quality', words that often appear in mission statements and are in danger of becoming meaningless. This is not only because everyone uses them but because it is hard to derive from them measurable goals so that the organization can test how well it is doing against its mission. If the mission is to produce high quality widgets how is this to be measured?

Let's look at British Airways' goals again:

- (to be) the customers' choice – the airline of first choice in key markets;
- (to show) strong profitability – meeting investors' expectations and securing the future;
- (to be) truly global – (with a) global network, global outlook: recognized everywhere for superior value in world travel;
- (to employ) inspired people – building on success and delighting customers.

Do you think these goals are measurable and if British Airways achieved them would it have achieved its mission? Care needs to be exercised in answering these questions for it is quite easy to get muddled about the difference between missions and goals. Goals are based on judgements about the key success areas over the next few years, whereas missions are important in ensuring continuity of purpose over longer periods. It is often assumed that successful organizations combine an ability to protect their core beliefs while at the same time being open to change and evolution (Collins and Porras, 1994). An enduring mission and a more frequently changing set of strategic goals is one way to pursue an effective combination of continuity and progress in a viable synthesis.

One implication of the need to move from goals to strategic goals, to operational goals, and down to individual targets is that individual employees often have difficulty seeing how their contribution to the organization is helping in the achievement of the mission. Time and effort have to be expended in showing how individuals are, in fact, contributing to the organization's mission. If you do know your organization's mission how easy is it for you to work back from it to your own job to see how you are contributing to it? Perhaps one of the key problems with many mission statements is that it is difficult to derive from them strategic goals or objectives that can then be observed. Wanting to be 'the undisputed leader in world travel' is one thing. Working out from that the strategy to achieve it is another. As is putting a man on the moon and returning him safely.

Missions, goals and strategy

Mission statements are useful as a basis for developing strategy. If they spell out the activities of the organization and its consequences in terms of benefits for customers then non-financial goals as well as financial ones can be set. Then gap analysis can be used. As we have said before, some managers find it useful to check for gaps between projected or expected performance and desired performance. If there are gaps the task becomes one of formulating a strategy to close the gaps.

There are, though, other ways managers think about strategy. Strategy may be seen as a response to a strategic issue. Or strategy may be formulated that goes beyond the closing of a performance gap but is ambitious and challenging. It seems to us that Kennedy wanted not so much to close the performance gap with the Russian space programme but to surpass it by issuing a tough, but as we now know, achievable challenge.

CONCLUSIONS

In this chapter we have looked at mission statements. We have emphasized their importance in mobilizing organizational members. We have spent some time looking at some of the difficulties in constructing a statement, getting employees to 'buy in' to it and to 'unpack' it sufficiently for employees to see how they contribute to its achievement. We have discussed the connections between mission statements and strategy and performance measurement. If there is one message emerging from this chapter it is that developing a mission statement should be treated as a serious matter and not undertaken merely because senior managers think 'everyone else has one so we'd better have one as well'. Mission-led organizations are concerned with strategic effectiveness and this means being clear about core activities, main beneficiaries, and key benefits for customers of organizational activities.

QUESTIONS

1. Given that most (if not all) medium to large size organizations have vision/mission statements, does this suggest that they are a good thing?
2. Thinking back to the small bakery, do you think the owner needs to write a vision/mission statement?

3. What steps would you take when writing a new vision/mission statement for an organization to make sure that people throughout the organization 'buy in' to it?
4. Use the Internet to identify a couple of examples of vision/mission statements that you think are particularly interesting. Why do you think they are interesting?
5. Does it matter that it is hard to say exactly what a vision/mission statement is, as the key thing is that it gives the organization direction by letting employees and customers know what it is about?
6. Choose a mission statement to analyse. How well does it meet our criteria of what should go into a mission statement?
7. How would you know if a vision/mission statement actually makes a difference to a company? What sort of things would you want to look at and what sort of evidence would you need to collect in doing this?

EXECUTIVE EXERCISE

Think about the latest draft of your organization's corporate strategic plan or equivalent document. Formulate a short mission statement and draft it in your own words. Identify any elements that you think are missing from the mission statement. Now reflect on the mission statement you have drafted and identify at least three key performance areas. These are defined as being areas of performance that have to be effective if the organization is to deliver on the mission statement.
Mission statement:

Key performance areas:

1.

2.

3.

If possible, now discuss your conclusions about the mission statement and the key performance areas with others in a small group. Try to arrive at a consensus on the best way of expressing the mission statement and the key performance areas.

REFERENCES

Bart, C K and Tabone, J C (1998) Mission statement rationales and organizational alignment in the not-for-profit health care sector, *Health Care Management Review*, **23** (4), pp 54–70

Collins, J C and Porras, J I (1994) *Built to Last*, HarperCollins, New York

Joyce, P (1999) *Strategic Management for the Public Services*, Open University Press, Buckingham

Reading 4.1

Taken from Trick 3 – Lead from voice and vision, in *Old Dogs, New Tricks* by Warren Bennis (2000)

What's so tricky about leading from voice and vision, rather than leading from position and perceived power? The underlying issue in leading from voice is trust; in fact, I believe that trust is the underlying issue in not only getting people on your side, but having them stay there. Leading from voice is a necessary condition for movement leadership, or for any situation – such as the Girl Scouts or the Red Cross – where the leader is dealing with volunteers, free agents, and free spirits (today's work force).

Frances Hesselbein, former chief executive of the Girl Scouts and current leader of the Drucker Foundation, notes: "The challenge for leaders is to build a cohesive community both within and outside the organization, to invest in relationships, and to communicate a vision that speaks to a richly diverse workforce and marketplace."

Clarify the vision. The critical factor for success in any venture is a shared vision among associates. If you're not sure of the vision of your company, how can you tell what the advantage of an alliance would be? You must be certain you have the right map and compass before embarking on the journey.

What people want most from their leaders is vision and direction, purpose and meaning, trust and truth. Leaders create a vision with meaning – one with significance, one that puts the players at the center of things rather than at the periphery.

A vision can be shared only if it has meaning for the people involved in it. You can't be the only one making decisions. You can't be the only leader. Rather you have to create an environment in which people at all levels are empowered to be leaders, to subscribe to your vision, and to make effective decisions.

To communicate a vision, you need more than words, speeches, memos, and laminated plaques. You need to live a vision, day in, day out – embodying it and empowering every other person to execute that vision in everything he or she does, anchoring it in realities so that it becomes a template for decision making. Actions do speak louder than words.

If you think your company's vision lacks definition, you may want to address some questions that may help give it color and dimension:

- What is unique about us?
- What values are true priorities for the next year?
- What would make me professionally commit my mind and heart to this vision over the next five to 10 years?
- What does the world need that our company can and should provide?
- What do I want our company to accomplish so that I will be committed, aligned, and proud of my association with it?

Ask yourself those questions today. Your answers will be the fire that heats the forge of your company's future.

Manage the dream. Leaders manage the dream. All leaders have the capacity to create a compelling vision, one that takes people to a new place, and the ability to translate that vision into reality.

Jung said: "A dream that is not understood remains a mere occurrence. Understood, it becomes a living experience."

Jim Burke, CEO of Johnson & Johnson, spends 40 percent of his time communicating the company's credo. More than 800 managers have attended J&J "challenge meetings," where they go through the credo line by line to see what changes need to be made. Over the years, some of those changes have been fundamental. But like the U.S. Constitution, the credo itself endures.

General Electric CEO Jack Welch said: "Yesterday's idea of the boss, who became the boss because he or she knew one more fact than the person working for them, is yesterday's manager. Tomorrow's person leads through a set of shared values, a shared objective, a vision."

The single defining quality of leaders is the capacity to create and realize a vision. Yeats said, "In dreams begins responsibility." Vision is a waking dream.

The leader's responsibility is to transform the vision into reality. In doing so, they transform their dominion – whether an airline, a motion picture, or an entire industry.

Henry David Thoreau put it this way: "If one advances confidently in the direction of his dreams, and endeavors to live the life he has imagined, he will meet with a success in common hours. If you have built castles in the air, your work need not be lost. It is where they should be. Now put the foundation under them."

The times demand leaders who can manage the dream by creating a vision and then translating that vision into reality. In the course of my research, I've learned something about the current crop of leaders, and something about the kind of leadership that will be necessary to forge the future. While leaders come in every size, shape and disposition – short, tall, neat, sloppy, young, old, male and female – every leader shares a common trait: a concern with a guiding purpose, a directing goal, an overarching vision.

Managing the dream has five parts: (1) communicating the vision; (2) recruiting meticulously; (3) rewarding; (4) retraining; and (5) reorganizing. All five parts of managing the dream are exemplified by Jan Carlzon, CEO of SAS. Carlzon's vision was to make SAS one of the five or six remaining international carriers. To accomplish this, he developed two goals: (1) to make SAS 1 percent better in a 100 different ways from its competitors; and (2) to create a market niche. Carlzon chose the business traveler, because he believed that this was the most profitable niche – rather than college students, or travel agent deals, or any of the other choices. To attract business travelers, Carlzon had to make their every interaction with every SAS employee rewarding. He had to endow with purpose and relevance, courtesy and caring, every single interaction – and he estimated that there were 63,000 of these interactions per day between SAS employees and current or potential customers. He called these interactions "moments of truth".

Carlzon developed a marvelous cartoon book, *The Little Red Book,* to communicate the new SAS vision to employees. And he set up a corporate college in Copenhagen to train them. He debureaucratized the whole organization. The organization chart no longer looked like a pyramid – it looked like a set of circles, a galaxy. In fact, Carlzon's book, which is called *Moments of Truth* in English, is titled *Destroying the Pyramids* in Swedish.

One circle or segment, is the Copenhagen–New York route. All the pilots, the navigators, the engineers, the flight attendants, the baggage handlers, the reservations agents – everybody who has to do with the Copenhagen–New York route – are involved in a self-managed, autonomous work group with a gain-sharing plan so that they all participate in whatever increment of profits that particular route brings it. There's also a Copenhagen–Frankfurt segment, and so on. The corporation is structured in terms of these small, egalitarian groups.

When you lead from voice and vision, your dreams are more likely to come true.

Leading with Wisdom. Leadership has become something of a national obsession. Books almost cascade from the shelves. A recent study looked at the reasons for removing CEOs, and found ineffective leadership to be fairly high at 73 percent. Another study, at the Harvard Business School, showed that a CEO is 10 times more likely to be removed for poor performance today than 20 years ago. If you look at the major icons of American industry over the past 10 years, almost all the top CEOs have been dumped. Another study found that companies that are perceived to be well led have a much higher growth rate. Clearly, if asked to pick the factor that makes the most difference, you'd pick leadership. As Jack Welch told me: "My job is simple. I have three things to do. I pick the right people, I allocate the right resources to my 15 business units, and I transmit ideas with the speed of light. Ideas are what count. All these interactions are just building the idea pyramid."

Some people naturally seem to have that capacity to create an environment where ideas are generated. Such capacity strikes at the core of who you are. I think that core changes over time, but character means something that's not superficial. You can't put a person into a microwave and out pops the McLeader. It doesn't happen like that. Leadership is something that evolves.

What do most people want from their leadership? I think they want: meaning and direction, trust, a sense of hope and optimism, and results. These are the bottom-line issues. Great leaders provide the culture to make authentic human relationships possible. They have a sense of hardiness – an expectation of a positive outcome and some bias toward action, risk, curiosity, courage, and results. Exemplary leaders are people with conviction, commitment, resolve and passion. Yes, leadership has to do with vision, discernment and insight, but it is also about knowing not just where you're going but where you've been and where you are now. The great world leaders have all had that helicopter view.

When we consider what goes into trust in work relationships with a boss, events surrounding President Bill Clinton are instructive. Even before publication of the Starr Report, most people thought Clinton was lying about his activity in the Oval Office, and yet they still thought he was doing a splendid job, largely based on their perception of the strength of the economy.

When I talk about trust in leadership, I imagine a tripod of interdependent forces that all leaders have to some extent. All leaders have a certain degree of ambition or drive along with competence (or business literacy) and integrity or moral discernment. Most of the exemplary leaders I know seem to have these three in balance. It's hard to imagine someone with integrity but who lacks the other two qualities; maybe Hamlet fits the bill as a person with good motives but no competence or drive.

One of the most important criteria of mental health is an accurate perception of reality, but it seems to me that many great leaders have an almost unwarranted optimism — a "can-do" mentality. They have this sense of possibility. Most optimists consider themselves to be lucky and have a positive outlook. President Reagan was the perfect example, although there were times when I thought his optimism was unwarranted. Ultimately, after all the meetings and pronouncements, you've got to act — and that can be difficult. People who have brilliant ideas often need someone else to translate them into action. Leaders need managers. Without them, leaders are like lonely poets. Although strong management — too many meetings, too much bureaucracy, too much specialization — stifles innovation and intellectual capital, vision by itself means nothing. Contemplation and elegant illuminations don't mean a thing unless they are followed by action.

© Warren Bennis, 2000

5

Evaluating performance

INTRODUCTION

In the 18th century the major problem facing sailors once they lost sight of land was how to know where they were. They could easily find their latitude by measuring the height of the sun, but without accurate clocks they could not fix their longitude. In working out where they were navigators often used a method called exact reckoning that relied on estimating how far the ship had travelled and in what direction, taking into account currents, tides and wind, to arrive at their position. After a ship had been out of sight of land for a few days this method, even when used by very experienced navigators, could put the ship miles away from its true position. In fact, at times, this would lead to the ship hitting rocks and breaking up, as the sailors believed they were many miles from danger when they were not. Given the importance of this, the British Parliament set up the Board of Longitude to assess any method capable of determining with reasonable accuracy the longitude of a ship and to award a prize between £10,000 to £20,000, depending on the accuracy of the method. A watch maker called Harrison believed he could design a clock that even at sea, tossed about by heavy waves, would keep accurate time. If this were possible the problem of determining longitude accurately would be solved. Harrison tried over the years to perfect such a clock. He started with large pendulum clocks that, although an improvement on past efforts, did not reach the required degree of accuracy. Eventually he changed direction and started to work on a large pocket watch which

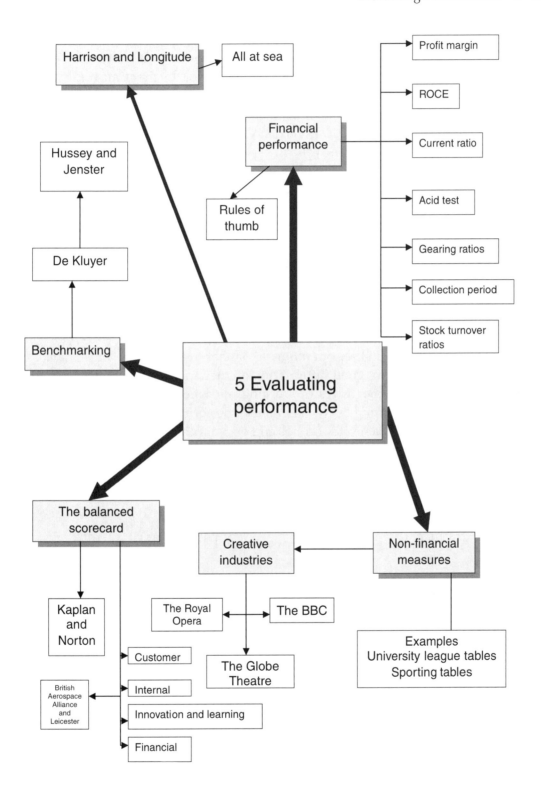

is known as Harrison Number 4. In 1761 it was ready for a sea trial and his son set sail for Jamaica. On reaching Jamaica the watch was found to be only five seconds slow. This was a truly remarkable achievement. Sailors for the first time had a way of calculating longitude accurately. After some wrangling about whether Harrison's watch had performed satisfactorily he was awarded the prize in 1773. Three years later James Cooke took a copy of a Harrison Number 4 on his expedition to the Pacific. And the rest, as they say, is history.

It is possible now through satellite navigation aids for ships to be positioned with breathtaking accuracy anywhere on the globe. And if ships' navigators know where they are, they stand a good chance of getting to where they want to be. How Harrison would have marvelled at this. Unfortunately, unlike today's ships that have complex positional and guidance equipment, organizations do not have sophisticated technology for assessing their current position in terms of performance. Nor do they have sophisticated technology for guiding them to where they want to be. Yet managers need to work out whether the organization's current situation is satisfactory or unsatisfactory and they need to be capable of assessing pretty accurately their organization's medium- to long-term performance. In the light of such assessments managers can attempt to evaluate whether operational changes are necessary or a change of strategy is required. Without good information on these matters the manager will be in the dark. One of the major ways of working out where an organization is, and where it is likely to be heading, is to use financial performance data.

This chapter mainly concentrates on helping you develop your ability to evaluate financial data. In addition, however, you will be reading about the strategy process and specific analytical techniques. At the end of this chapter you should be able to evaluate organizational performance using financial and other performance indicators.

STRATEGIC PLANNING AND PERFORMANCE

In the traditional model of strategic planning the measurement and evaluation of performance was very important. It is usually assumed that senior management will carry out evaluation, as a critical stage in the control cycle and as the basis of judgements about strategic effectiveness. However, the potential benefits of involving wider constituencies of managers and other stakeholders in evaluation should be considered. Widening participation in evaluation could, for example, increase commitment to strategic plans.

As part of a cycle of control, evaluation rests on the setting of measurable strategic goals, linked to an organization's mission. These goals can be used as the basis for a gap analysis that feeds into the formulation of a strategic plan and its execution through budgetary and operational decisions. The implementation of the strategic plan may then be followed up by measuring the impact of these decisions in terms of performance and by reporting findings up the management line. On the basis of this reporting, top managers can consider whether or not strategic goals or decisions about strategy and operational matters need revision.

David (2001) suggests there are three key questions to be asked during strategy evaluation:

- Have changes occurred in the firm's internal strategic position?
- Have changes occurred in the firm's external strategic position?
- Has progress towards stated objectives been satisfactory?

If there have been no changes in the strategic situation of the firm and performance is such that progress towards meeting stated objectives is satisfactory, then no revision of action is necessary. In all other eventualities, revision and correction of action may be needed.

Actions to follow up evaluation may be little more than fine-tuning. They could, however, involve making big adjustments in budgets, changes in the design of business processes, structural changes to the organization and culture change programmes. The follow-up may also involve improving management information systems, reporting systems and performance indicators. Financial performance indicators can be used to judge the impact of the implementation of a strategy and changes to operational activities as a result of the strategy.

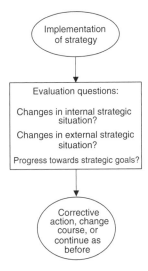

Figure 5.1 Evaluation of strategic effectiveness

FINANCIAL PERFORMANCE

Financial data is reported in the profit and loss account and the balance sheet. The former is concerned with financial performance (sales and costs) whereas the latter shows an organization's financial position (assets, liabilities) at a specific date. Over the years accountants have developed standard financial indicators that help managers make sense of financial data and decide how well their organization is doing. These financial indicators often help managers to predict future difficulties. Standard financial indicators include the following:

- **Profit margin.** Profit is sales less costs. The profit margin is profit as a percentage of sales. The profit figure can be calculated before or after interest and tax has been deducted. The operating profit is the profit calculated before interest and tax. The operating margin is therefore profit before interest and tax less costs.
- **Return on capital employed (ROCE).** This is a measure of profitability. It is defined as operating profit as a percentage of capital employed. The capital employed is fixed assets plus current assets less current liabilities. (Current assets less current liabilities are defined as working capital.) The capital employed figure can be found using the balance sheet. ROCE varies very significantly from one industry to another.
- **Current ratio.** This is calculated by dividing current assets by current liabilities. A rule of thumb suggests that this ratio should be in the region of 1.0 to 1.5. However, accountants warn managers not to treat such rules of thumb as infallible guides to the health of a company's finances.
- **Acid-test ratio.** This is calculated by dividing current assets (excluding stock) by current liabilities. According to rule of thumb, this ratio should be 1.0.
- **Gearing ratios.** Capital gearing is borrowings divided by equity shareholders' funds. If borrowings are more than 50 per cent of equity for a company there can be concern about the level of interest charges and debt repayment schedules it is meeting.
- **Collection period.** This is the value of trade debtors divided by annual sales and then multiplied by 365. It measures the days taken by customers to pay a sales invoice.
- **Stock turnover ratios.** This is the cost of sales divided by total assets.

Financial results can be laid out in charts to show how a company has performed annually on sales, profit, ROCE, and so on. This can be done over a five-year period and targets compared with actual figures.

In the case of navigation at sea, once you have found out your latitude and longitude you know where you are and can compare this to where you want to be and take corrective action if necessary. Organizations' use of financial indicators to establish the equivalent is a bit more problematic as the indicators tend to give clues to what is happening but have to be interpreted carefully. Rules of thumb exist that help in this but, as suggested below, they have to be used carefully. If an actual ratio (eg acid-test ratio) is different from the value contained in a rule of thumb then there is an indication that something could be amiss.

Financial indicators can also be used to benchmark the organization's position against its competitors. The indicators may be used in an attempt to take into account changes in organization size when comparing performance at different periods of time and between different sized organizations. You may think of comparing the indicators for one company with those of other companies in trade associations (although the data will be anonymous) or by marketing research. Unsurprisingly there are competing views on the 'best' indicators to use for different purposes and what is exactly being suggested by the results then obtained.

It is tempting to think that these ratios and rules of thumb give exact and unproblematic information about the organization. In our opinion these are the start of the process of evaluating the organization's performance and not the end. It is easy to fall into thinking that they provide the answer, instead of providing some guide to what is happening that has to be validated against other evidence. Further, strategically you might want to put them to one side temporarily to give a chance for your strategy to have an impact on performance.

NON-FINANCIAL MEASURES

Instead of focusing on the financial ratios it might make sense to start with your organization's vision and mission statements and then look at ways of assessing how well you are doing using measures that are related to these statements. For example, in the UK various league tables are published for universities and schools. Two key indicators for performance used in universities are teaching quality and research quality. A university can measure itself against its mission on these two indicators, over time to see any changes and against its competitors. It may decide as part of its mission to be excellent at teaching as measured by government. Periodically its teaching in various subjects might be assessed and the results published. From this the university can see how well it is doing against its mission and take any corrective steps required. Schools are also assessed on a variety of measures such as percentage of pupils achieving exam passes. Results from this type of assessment will inform the school of how well it is performing and indicate if any changes in strategy are required to achieve its mission.

League tables of performance are, of course, found in sport, where the teams' position in the league is published weekly. Here we do have the equivalent of a Harrison Number 4, as 'league tables do not lie' is a common expression – a team's position in the league does tell it exactly where it is! In football a bad run of results leading to a poor league position often means the sack for the manager. Unlike managers in other organizations, managers of professional sports clubs have their performance reviewed frequently and very publicly – as a glance at the sporting pages of the papers will show. If the mission of the football club is to be in the top three of the Premiership, then it is pretty obvious to everyone if this has been achieved or not, and if not what should happen.

Clearly, to stay with football for a moment, if you take your eye off the financial ball for too long then the club's financial position can soon be undermined. Again, looking through the sporting pages will show how common it is for a sporting club to drift into serious financial difficulties. Care has to be taken to maintain the financial viability of the organization, while at the same time making sure that the mission is being pursued. The organization may be brilliantly managed in financial terms but having its long-term health undermined because of poor performance on the pitch.

Organizations based in the creative industries such as theatre or opera companies often experience conflict between what the financial ratios are reporting and what the organization is trying to achieve artistically. For actors and musicians the finance side may be viewed as 'smoke and mirrors' – what they value is artistic performance and money should not get in the way of that. John Birt, while he was Director General of the BBC, became quite a controversial figure when he introduced changes to try to balance the artistic and journalistic mission of the BBC with some financial restructuring. Similar conflicts have emerged at the Royal Opera House in London in recent years. Accountants are frequently charged with knowing the price of everything and the value of nothing.

Managing a creative organization requires quite special skills to resolve the conflict between performance and money. Here evaluation of the organization's performance against mission is tricky. As part of its mission the Globe Theatre in London has the following: '… it will strive for an international reputation for performance excellence through its productions at the Globe Theatre, in performance conditions reproducing those of Shakespeare's time'. Performance evaluation measures have to be developed that give the Globe management some indication of how well it is achieving this. How is an international reputation for performance excellence measured? The Globe also aims to be self-financing: 'The activities of Shakespeare's Globe are self-financing in overall terms. Activities are therefore balanced in such a way that net income from the exhibition, box offices and donations is sufficient to cover net deficits, for example on educational and academic work.' So on the one hand the organization is striving for international excellence but at the same time ensuring that it remains financially viable. Clearly conflicts will arise between these two priorities.

Many managers are faced with such challenges during their career. Should you ease off a bit from the financial side, taking some risks to move the organization forward or should you concentrate on the financial side at the expense of the mission in the short term to guarantee organizational survival? That is for the manager to decide.

THE BALANCED SCORECARD

Kaplan and Norton (1992) argue that financial indicators of performance were more attuned to the needs of the Industrial Age but today non-financial indicators (NFIs) are needed. The Globe Theatre's aim to have an 'international reputation for performance excellence' is clearly a NFI. Here a new kind of Harrison watch is required to fix accurately the position of the Theatre on this dimension. The balanced scorecard is the idea that performance should be evaluated using a combination of both kinds of indicators – financial and non-financial.

Kaplan and Norton set out four categories of performance indicators that need to be considered in today's business environment:

- Customer perspective: how do customers see us?
- Internal perspective: what must we excel at?
- Innovation and learning perspective: can we continue to improve and create value?
- Financial perspective: how do we look to shareholders?

Many companies now provide consultancy and software on balanced scorecards. A search of the Internet revealed many such companies and the Internet addresses for some of them are shown below.

www.gentia.com/
www.balancedscorecard.com/
w3.corvu.com/
www.intrafocus.com/balanced_scorecard.htm
home.sol.no/mst/balance.htm (Norwegian site)

Some companies have used the balanced scorecard or some version of it. Two UK examples are the Alliance and Leicester and British Aerospace.

One interesting opportunity offered by the balanced scorecard approach to evaluation is the chance to study relationships between different performance indicators. It may become obvious when analysing the performance indicators over a number of years that there are cause and effect relationships between them. For instance, a rise or fall in customer satisfaction may tend to precede a corresponding rise or fall in financial performance indicators, and improvements in performance on innovation may be followed in due course by improvements in financial indicators. It does not take much imagination to see how valuable it could be for managers to have a better understanding of such relationships (if they exist) and then how this could be the basis for continuous improvement as managers learnt more and more about how to achieve better results.

BENCHMARKING

One view of benchmarking is that it consists of comparing performance ratios of a company with those of its competitors. Benchmarking might for, example, compare a firm against its major rivals in terms of the sales per employee or the percentage of headquarters staff to other staff.

Benchmarking can involve carrying out research and even doing observations on the performance of rival firms. For example, as Hussey and Jenster (1999) note, it is possible for rival supermarkets to observe the length of queues at checkouts. The consequence of this type of evaluation is possibly to focus a firm on the need for cost reduction or restructuring to increase efficiency. De Kluyver (2000) certainly suggests that cost benchmarking is relevant for comparing a company's performance with other companies. The methodology is fairly logical. A company selects the activities to be benchmarked, it identifies performance measures, it identifies key rivals, and then collects and analyses cost and performance data.

It is also possible for companies to cooperate directly for the purposes of benchmarking studies, although it has been more common to use trade associations to get anonymous data on other companies in an industry. Public sector organizations have been using benchmarking in a big way in recent years, as part of the drive to modernize the management of services and increase performance. They have been cooperating extensively to generate more valid data for performance comparisons.

CONCLUSIONS

The study and evaluation of performance tends to be neglected in contemporary texts on strategic management. Typically there is a discussion of financial ratios and the analysis of profit and loss accounts and balance sheets. We have attempted to provide a more extended consideration of the evaluation of performance. We have looked at the use of financial indicators and NFIs. We have also outlined the use of the balanced scorecard and benchmarking. However, it is important to keep in mind the way in which traditional strategic planning positioned performance measurement and evaluation as a key stage in the planning cycle, and as the basis of ensuring there was control built into the design and delivery of strategy. As well as enabling managers to make corrections to strategic implementation activities, performance measurement and evaluation can become the basis of management learning and continuous improvement.

QUESTIONS

1. While it is possible to locate with great accuracy where a ship is on the high seas we will never be able to do a similar thing for organizations. What reasons can you think of that make it hard for us to know 'where' an organization is at any one time?
2. A necessary condition for a business to be well run is for it to have excellent financial information but this by itself is insufficient. What else is needed?
3. You cannot expect creative employees to worry about costs. How do you think companies like the Globe, the Royal Opera House or the BBC square the circle between being financially sound and achieving world class creativity? Is one way of doing this by using NFIs as part of a balanced scorecard approach?
4. One useful tool strategists can use is benchmarking, as this allows them to locate their own organization against the very best. Once this has been done then a strategy can be designed to close the gap (if that is required) or even surpass what is best at present. While this sounds good it runs the danger of forcing the strategist to think conventionally as it uses existing norms and criteria as measures. What is needed is a more unconventional approach. What do you think?

EXECUTIVE EXERCISE

Find out how your own organization, or an organization you know very well, measures its strategic effectiveness. Does it use strategic goals and performance indicators? Does it have a reporting system that enables top managers to identify any gaps between actual and target performance? Are the performance indicators all financial ones?

REFERENCES

David, F R (2001) *Strategic Management: Concepts*, Prentice Hall, New Jersey
De Kluyver, C A (2000) *Strategic Thinking: An executive perspective*, Prentice Hall, New Jersey
Hussey, D and Jenster, P (1999) *Competitor Intelligence*, Wiley, Chichester
Kaplan, R S and Norton, D P (1992) The balanced scorecard – measures that drive performance, *Harvard Business Review*, January–February, pp 71–79

Reading 5.1

Taken from Chapter 3 – What you measure is what you get, in *Measuring Business Performance* by Mick Broadbent (1999)

This chapter will consider the relationships between corporate strategy, critical success factors and key performance indicators. The framework for the chapter will be that put forward by Booth (1998), who considers that any measurement framework should be the result of the mission, goals, objectives and strategies of the business. This chapter will consider other frameworks, particularly the *tableaux de bord* which is used by French organisations and is much more functional and departmental focused than the more project management approach of Booth. The role of specific stakeholders within the performance measurement framework will be considered in Chapter 4, as the focus of this chapter is on the internal processes rather than the broader environmental relationships of the business.

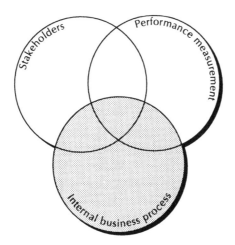

Figure 3.1: A framework for studying corporate performance measurement

In terms of our generic framework reproduced in Figure 3.1, the focus is on the internal business processes and hence links with the issues raised in Chapter 1, where the new management agendas and challenges were presented.

Otley (1997) argues that the process of performance measurement begins with the establishment of strategic objectives and the role of the business in the extended value chain. He poses three questions which should provide focus to the above abstraction. They are, firstly, what is the business attempting to achieve and why? Secondly, how does this relate to the products and services that customers will want and be willing to pay for? Finally, what factors are crucial to the success of this venture? The answers to these questions should provide a forum for the development of a set of key performance measures that would be based on objectives and provide a view of current activities.

Otley further argues that the procedures and thinking required to answer these questions is often 'fudged'. This results in a set of performance measures which are not wholly appropriate to measure the requirements specified within the objectives. Performance measures put forward may be easy to calibrate, of minor importance or narrowly financially biased rather than broader ranging.

A framework for consideration

Booth (1997) puts forward an almost Utopian world where each employee of a business fully understands the strategic objectives, takes actions which are co-ordinated and integrated to meet those objectives and that they all have adequate feedback about the business direction and performance. This world has no place for dysfunctional behaviour, self-interest, interdepartmental rivalry and empire building. Unfortunately, this is not the case. Hence a series of measures must be inaugurated that reflect strategy while also providing a framework for control that is based on company processes and reflects the particular attributes and relationships of that business.

Booth (1998) argues that the same methods for project management can be used for organisational management. He recognises the open-ended nature of organisational management and the ongoing relationship with the environment but argues that the mutual task dependencies and scheduling of finite common resources for multiple tasks provide a strong similarity. Using this idea he puts forward the model which, in a modified form, is presented as Figure 3.2.

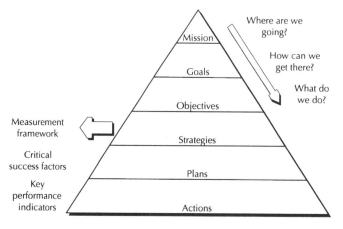

Figure 3.2: Measurement of programmes
(*Adapted from*: Booth, 1998, p.27)

Figure 3.2 is very similar to a diagram put forward by Booth in 1997, where he asked a similar set of questions to those put by Otley (1997), considered earlier in this chapter.

Booth (1998) argues that performance measurement is a framework which flows from the goals and objectives of a business (or project). Other writers use the term 'vision' in place of goals and objectives. Regardless of definitional issues, there is general agreement that higher-level issues should be cascaded down the organisation.

Because Booth (1998) adopted a more contained project management framework for considering performance measurement, he avoided the problematic debate about whether a company's mission and objectives are primary to strategy (per Drucker, 1989) or subservient to strategy (per Argenti, 1989). The pyramid of Figure 3.2 clearly takes the former view. The components in the pyramid are described below.

The mission of the company is its basic function in society and is reflected in the products or services that it provides for its customers or clients (Mintzberg, 1983). Drucker (1989) argues that the mission and purpose of an organisation is required to make 'possible clear and realistic business objectives, it is the foundation for priorities, strategies, plans and work assignments. It is the starting point of the design of managerial jobs'.

Pearce and Robinson (1985) offer a list of components that a mission statement should incorporate:

- basic product/service function;
- definition of customers and markets;
- technology;
- growth and profitability;
- common philosophy;
- social responsibility and public image.

Each is a requirement which will provide clarity for the formulation of goals and objectives.

Goals are qualitative aims for the company, whose purpose is to set the criteria whereby all decisions are taken. Mintzberg (1983) described them as 'the intentions behind [the company's] decisions and actions'. They are not precise criteria for the measurement of performance.

Objectives are goals expressed in a manner by which they can be measured. They must be specific, measurable, achievable, relevant and time-bound. The traditional objective of the firm is shareholder wealth maximisation, but since the divorce of ownership and control this maxim has often been abandoned in practice. Objectives being pursued by the head of five companies in three countries as reported by Coates et al. (1993) varied in emphasis. The UK, German and US companies all considered profitability to be important. The US companies ranked growth as being more important than cash flow and financial stability. German companies ranked cash flow and financial stability quite low, but the UK companies considered these as more important objectives. Only US and German companies included environmental factors in their objectives.

Strategy is seen as how the objectives are achieved. It is operationalised in the acquisition

Figure 3.3: Co-ordination of change activities at Abbey National Financial and Investment Services (*Adapted from*: Evans et al., 1996, p.23)

and deployment of company assets, personnel and expertise. Managers could adopt a wide range of strategies, but any selected must position the company in relation to its environment in such a manner that will work to the pursuance of the company's objectives.

Plans are the more detailed expression of future action that reflect the goals, objectives and strategies of the business. They will include the definition and structure of specific programmes which have clear mechanisms for operation and evaluation. Actions are the manifestation of the planning processes and lead to outcomes which can be measured and evaluated.

The above process should ensure that the business remains effective by meeting its objectives (doing the right things) as opposed to being merely efficient (do things right).

The measurement framework illustrated within Figure 3.2 indicates a relationship between mission, strategy, critical success factors and key performance indicators.

Critical success factors are those attributes which drive the success of the firm, focusing on the major or primary crucial factors which will have the most impact and drive accomplishments in other supporting areas (Society of Management Accountants of Canada, SMAC, 1994). The key performance indicators are those which are useful in measuring progress (or otherwise) to strategic directions required to meet overall objectives.

Evans et al. (1996) presented the manner by which change activities at Abbey National Financial and Investment Services were co-ordinated. It is presented in summarised form in Figure 3.3.

The Abbey National framework does not specify the detail of the pyramid of Figure 3.2 but it does provide the link between mission, critical success factors, performance measures and mechanisms with activities. It also highlights the manner by which performance measures and mechanisms can be used to drive change within a business's activities and the manner in which that change may lead to a revision of the mission statement.

In a similar self-learning manner, Booth (1998) has put forward an 'accountability trail', which is presented in Figure 3.4.

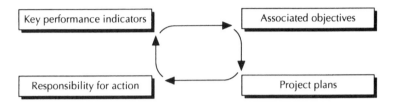

Figure 3.4: Accountability trail
(*Source*: Booth, 1998, p.28)

The accountability trail links objectives, projected plans (which should include critical success factors) and responsibilities for actions for key performance indicators in a continuous manner. The nature of critical success factors (CSFs) will be considered prior to that of key performance indicators (KPIs).

Critical success factors

Having derived the goals, objectives and strategies of the business, it becomes possible to construct measurement frameworks which are capable of evaluating progress, and influencing progress, towards meeting those goals, etc. The term 'critical success factor' has been adopted to name those factors which drive the success of the firm.

Taking a strategic rather than performance focus, Johnson and Scholes (1997) define critical success factors as 'those aspects of strategy in which an organisation must excel to outperform competition'. They go on to say that 'CSF analysis underlines this important relationship between resources, competences and choice of strategies, which is also central to the idea of balanced scorecards for assessing performance' (p.176).

Critical success factors may include:

- quality of after-sales service;
- quality and reliability of product;
- speed to market of new products;
- speed of delivery;
- prompt payment of invoices;
- efficiency of production lines;
- flexibility of product;
- development capacity of research team;
- cross-product selling.

The above does not include an exhaustive list but does provide a listing of attributes which may be combined to give a range of CSFs that a company might recognise. The CSFs for one company may be those that are recognised and valued by their customers and suppliers.

CSFs may be classified and more easily recognised by adopting Porter's value chain analysis as a framework. Porter's model (1985) recognises five primary activities of a business, and four supporting activities, which all lead to the generation of 'margin'. Johnson and Scholes (1997) adopt this framework for an information systems supplier which is presented in Table 3.1.

Table 3.1: Linking CSFs and value chain analysis

	Underpinning competences and performance targets						
CSFs	Inbound logistics	Operations	Outbound logistics	Marketing and sales	Service	Support activities	Managing linkages
Software features	Royalty payments						Customer feedback (monthly)
Customer care		Responding to enquiries (24 hrs)			Speed of response (3 hrs)	Installations database	Customer feedback (monthly)
New business opportunities				Salesforce reports (monthly)		Competitor profiling (top 10)	Customer feedback (monthly)

(*Source*: Johnson and Scholes, 1997, p. 420)

Wilson (1994) included the work of Freund (1988) who mapped the linkages between CSFs and actions for a life insurance company (Table 3.2).

Table 3.2: Critical success factors in action

CSFs	Strategies	KPIs
Ability to achieve critical mass volumes through existing brokers and agents	• Develop closer ties with agents • Telemarket to brokers • Realign agents' compensation	• Policies in force • New business written • Percentage of business with existing brokers
Be able to introduce new products within six months of industry leaders	• Underwrite strategic joint ventures • Copy leader's products • Improve underwriting skills	• Elapsed time to introduce • Percentage of products introduced within six months • Percentage of underwriters having additional certification
Be able to manage product and product line profitability	• Segment investment portfolio • Improve cost accounting • Closely manage loss ratio	• Return on portfolio segments • Actual product cost/revenue versus plan • Loss ratio relative to competitors

(*Source*: Wilson, 1994, p. 23, from Freund, 1988, pp. 2/23)

The two examples quoted above provide a range of examples of CSFs for particular companies. The CSFs for any particular company will be quite specific, reflecting the strengths, weaknesses, opportunities and threats particular to that company.

Before considering key performance indicators in detail, it may be useful to consider the links between critical success factors and those indicators put forward in the *tableaux de bord* theory and practice. This framework can operate within the traditional functional hierarchical structures, with each department or subdepartment establishing its own *tableaux de bord*. This includes key performance measures for that particular part of the organisation. Hence managers in each department decide their own critical success factors which are then converted into the measurement framework of the *tableaux de bord*.

Innes (1995) argues that the development of the *tableaux de bord* for subdepartments requires considerable effort as individual managers must consider how the role of their department contributes to organisational strategy. The process is as follows:

Define objectives of the subdepartment in relation
to the strategy of the company
▼
Decide the critical success factors of the subdepartment
▼
Select detailed performance measures for their own
tableaux de bord

The finalised *tableaux* usually contains non-financial measures, as it is not part of the formal accounting reporting system. Lebas (1993) defined the *tableaux* as 'the managerial information system that supports the achievement of performance just like the dashboard on a car allows the driver to reach his (or her) destination... These indicators are not all expressed in the same unit, their coherence comes from a model of the car operation system' (pp.6, 7). The *tableaux de bord* usually has several non-financial performance measures presented in chart form.

At first sight the *tableaux de bord* mechanism may mean that each subdepartment may pursue a series of individualistic objectives. This is not the case, however: each manager must integrate and co-ordinate both horizontally and vertically with other managers in the establishment of critical success factors. This results in a co-ordinated approach pursuing the same objectives and strategies. The *tableaux de bord* thus provides a 'mini' view of the link between strategy, critical success factors and key performance indicators.

Key performance indicators

Binnersley (1996) put forward the very simple proposition that performance measurement done correctly will help everybody in the company to focus on the right things, in the right place and at the right time. The ideas contained within this statement mean that performance indicators must consider criteria which includes the consideration of the:

- long term and short term;
- financial and non-financial;
- strategic aims translated into critical success factors;
- efficiency and effectiveness.

The long-term and short-term criteria linked to traditional financial measures of profitability, return on capital employed, earnings per share, etc., have already been considered in Chapter 2. They will be further developed in Chapter 4, when economic value analysis (EVA) will be developed to consider the role of the shareholder and performance measurement. The balance of financial and non-financial factors will be discussed in considerable detail in Chapter 6. This leaves two remaining issues. The first, the manner in which strategic issues are translated into critical success factors and then integrated into performance measures, will form the major thrust of this section. The second issue, that of efficiency and effectiveness, will be considered afterwards.

Examples of performance indicators put forward by SMAC (1994) include:

(i) *Environmental indicators*
- Hours of community service
- Hours of industry activities
- Percentage use of recyclable materials
- Amount of pollutant discharge
- Accidents and injuries resulting from products or services
- Fines/violations of government regulations

(ii) *Market and customer indicators*
- Share of market
- New and lost customers
- Customer satisfaction or dissatisfaction indices
- Quality performance
- Delivery performance
- Response time
- Market/channel/customer profitability
- Warranties, claims, returns

(iii) *Competitor indicators*
- Share of market(s)
- Customer satisfaction or dissatisfaction indices
- Quality performance
- Delivery performance
- Price performance
- New product development cycle time
- Proportion of new products
- Financial performance

(iv) Internal business processes indicators
- Product development cycle time
- Number of new products
- Manufacturing cycle time
- Inventory turns
- Order-to-delivery response time
- Sales (production) per employee
- Non-quality measures
- Reinvestment indicators
- Safety performance

(v) Human resource indicators
- Employee morale
- Applicants/acceptance ratio
- Development hours per employee
- Employee competence measures
- Employee flexibility measures
- Employee suggestions
- Turnover ratios

(vi) Financial indicators
- Revenue growth
- Market(s)/customer(s) profitability
- Product profitability
- Return on sales
- Working capital turnover
- Economic value added
- Return on capital
- Return on equity
- Cash flows

The above listings are not by any means comprehensive, but they offer a broad view of key performance indicators that provide:

- an internal and external perspective;
- a broad view of performance;
- a reflection of the human factors involved;
- a financial viewpoint; and
- a view of the complexity of the measures.

It is important that any set of performance indicators are selected to reflect a matrix of the critical success factors that are established to meet the objectives of the business. The changes in the manner in which companies will be required to operate (as discussed in

Chapter 1) will require the use of cross-team, multifunctional, performance measures that reflect cross-functional managerial processes facilitation by team working.

Evans et al. (1996) state that 'KPIs cascade corporate goals into an accountability matrix of individual management responsibilities'. This ensures that individuals understand their team's contributions to achieving targets and the interfaces which they must manage in order to jointly succeed. Figure 3.5 provides a structure which consolidates the cascading of strategy through critical success factors into a performance measurement matrix for an airline company.

The matrix outlined in Figure 3.5 provides a linking mechanism whereby processes and functions within the business are seen to be linked through the key performance measures selected. The matrix reflects the critical success factors of the various stakeholders of the business as delegated to individual teams and departments.

The top-down process articulated in this chapter and inherent within Figure 3.5 is in conflict with that of the *tableaux de bord* process which is subdepartmental led. Regardless of origin, the essential requirement is that performance measures must be integrative and strategy based. The process to deliver a mechanism will be dependent on the contingent variables impacting on the organisation.

An approach to constructing performance measures so that they reflect a balanced approach to performance measurement is now becoming more popular. The best-known framework encapsulating this view is that of Kaplan and Norton (1992) who present a 'balanced scorecard' which includes four performance measurement perspectives. The four perspectives are:

- financial performance;
- customer knowledge;
- internal business processes;
- learning and growth.

Each attempts to consolidate the strategic issues of each perspective in key performance measures, so each of the four perspectives includes sections for key success factors and performance measurement. Rather than repeat the well-known Kaplan and Norton diagram, Figure 3.6 reproduces a balanced scorecard developed for a large hotel by Brander Brown and McDonnell (1995).

As already stated the balanced approach to performance measurement will be considered in Chapter 7.

Efficiency and effectiveness

There is a growing requirement for business operations to offer value for money (VFM). Within the public sector it is a highly debated issue, as the objectives of such enterprises are often unclear and politically motivated. Within the private sector, objectives can be specified in a much clearer manner as the societal dimension is of a smaller order of importance. However, the three Es (economy, efficiency and effectiveness) do have a part to play in the performance measures of private-sector businesses. No management team would like to argue they were anything but economic, efficient and effective!

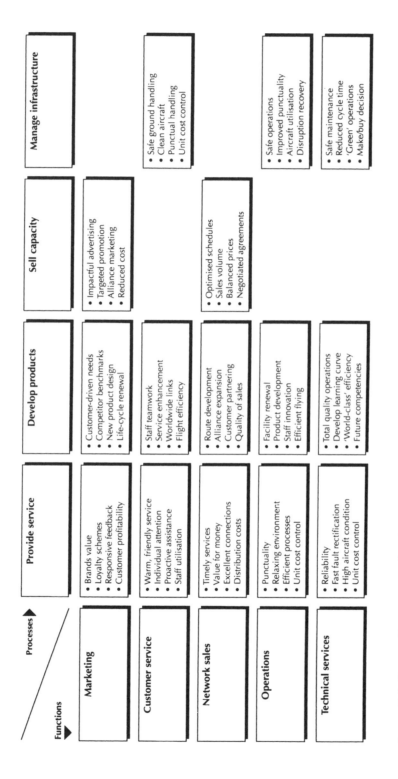

Figure 3.5: Process/function map for aligning performance measures
(Source: Evans et al., 1996, p.24)

Anthony (1965) defined management control as the 'process by which managers assume that resources are obtained and used effectively and efficiently in the accomplishment of the organisation's goals'. The definition includes two of the three Es, and by its nature assumes the third. So how do they vary, because they are often confused and hence misstated in corporate documents?

Efficiency is concerned with the ratio of outputs relative to inputs. The ratio can be improved by reducing inputs (cost cutting) or increasing outputs (increasing volume). There are, of course, measurement problems and definition problems of both inputs and outputs. Problems of this nature have already been discussed in Chapter 2 regarding the ratio known as return on capital employed. Efficiency can be compared between processes and economic units but is difficult to evaluate in isolation.

Effectiveness is a measure of how well the objectives have been fulfilled, so linking outputs with objectives. An effective organisation is one that achieves its objectives.

Wilson and Chua (1993) maintain that organisations may be:

(i)   both efficient and effective
(ii)   neither efficient nor effective
(iii)   effective but not efficient, or
(iv)   efficient but not effective.

Lowe and Soo (1980) remarked that:

> For example, if one defined effectiveness as the degree of goal achievement, then the National Aeronautics and Space Administration during the 1960s was possibly an effective but inefficient organization. President Kennedy had set a national goal of landing Americans on the moon in a decade. In 1969, after eight years of intensive research and an investment of more than 26 billion dollars, the mission was accomplished. In terms of achieving this goal, the organization was clearly effective. However, in the rush to meet deadlines and timetables, duplication was encouraged and waste inevitably occurred. But the organization was very probably not effective in the longer-run sense, since very soon after the resource flow into NASA was severely curtailed!

Since this statement was made, the spin-offs from the technological developments made during the moon programme have increased the efficiency of American industry.

Economy has a very narrow definition and is merely the less costly way of pursuing an activity. It is only input based, ignoring both outputs and objectives.

Innovation and learning perspective

CSFs	Possible measures
New markets identified	New areas/targets identified for action
Staff development	Courses completed; internal promotions made
Improvements to facilities/services	Development areas identified; new facilities/services introduced

Customer perspective

CSFs	Possible measures
Before selecting the hotel:	
Value for money	Surveys/questionnaires
Range of services offered	Surveys/questionnaires
Quality of contact/response	Third-party surveys
During stay in hotel:	
Quality of service	Guest comment cards; customer meetings
Reaction to guests' needs	Customer letters; repeat business

Internal business perspective

CSFs	Possible measures
Teamwork and co-ordination	Interdepartmental meetings (reports); interdepartmental training courses
Staff development	Courses completed; number of multiskilled staff
Cost efficiency	Gross profit percentage; net profit percentage; surpluses

Financial perspective

CSFs	Possible measures
Hotel profitability – both absolute and relative to the capital invested	Gross operating profit; net operating profit; return on capital employed; residual income
Sales achieved – with particular reference to sales mix and the volume/rate trade-off	Total sales; sales mix by department; sales mix by source
Management of working capital – especially of stocks and debtors	Average rate/occupancy; stock days; debtor days
Ability to react to changing markets	Areas for action identified

Figure 3.6: Balanced scorecard in the hotel sector
(*Source:* Brander Brown and McDonnell, 1995, p.10)

Reading 5.2

Taken from the Introduction, in *12 Ladders to World Class Performance* by David Drennan and Steuart Pennington (1999)

Becoming *world class* is on everyone's mind. As the world becomes a global market, the standards applied to 'World Class Performance' are becoming increasingly expected by customers and buyers everywhere. Global competitiveness then becomes an international search exercise as firms scan the world for best practices that will keep them ahead of the pack. And as organizations begin to focus on thinking globally while acting locally, finding new ways to stay competitive, to meet and beat ever-rising customer expectations, to compete with the best, is the talk of our time.

World class is as widely written about as any subject in management today. But by the time you have absorbed the works of Drucker, Peters, Kanter, Porter, Handy and the rest, the subject becomes confusing and clichéd to managers and workers alike.

The organizational graveyard is filled with failed attempts at culture change, total quality management, re-engineering and all the rest. Managers have become increasingly cynical about the next 'flavour of the month' fad. Experience has shown that real competitive edge is in going back to basics, and single-mindedly re-establishing focus.

This requires systematic analysis and agreement amongst the firms' stakeholders on areas where improvement is to be focused, and how such improvements are to be measured. And while the language of world class is becoming increasingly common across borders and across cultures, we believe it is critically important to make choices, ie to focus on those specific areas that will make your company truly a world class performer.

When one mentions the words 'world class' in product or business terms, people often think of the Japanese. We often ask members of our audiences: who has *not* got a Japanese product at home? Generally no hands are raised at all. When we ask why they buy Japanese products in preference to anything else, they say they are: 'good quality', 'reliable', 'value for money', and so on. In fact, in the mind of the public Japanese products have become synonymous with quality – so much so that one large UK retailer deliberately labels many of its British-made products with the Japanese-sounding brand name 'Matsui', so its customers will be automatically convinced of their quality.

But it wasn't always so. In David Drennan's boyhood days, his mother taught him to avoid Japanese products, because they were tinny, unreliable, cheap imitations of better-made Western products. These days are changed. Look what has happened. Japanese products have gone from:

tinny	to	well-made
cheap	to	good value
unreliable	to	reliable
imitation	to	innovative.

They have completely changed their image . . . but it took them nearly 40 years to get there.

Attaining world class status takes time

That's the first point to realize. There is no great tablet you can swallow that will make you world class within six months. There is no revolutionary concept that will throw out all the common-sense things you have been doing over the years, and turn you into a world class performer within the year. It takes time. It takes effort. It takes teamwork. It takes commitment. In short, it is not a technique. It is an attitude of mind. It is a way of life.

This is not a one-off event, it's a journey. But a journey where you will enjoy the stops along the way, where you will enjoy the pleasure of repeatedly breaking your own records, in which you will enjoy getting to places where you've never been before. And when you can genuinely compete with the best in the world, it brings a pride and enthusiasm among your people that is quite unique. It is hard work, but it's thrilling too.

What is 'world class'?

World class means 'being able to compete with the best in the world at what you do'. It doesn't mean winning the gold medal every time. No company manages to do that. It just means being able to compete credibly with the best anywhere. Let's look at some of those companies that we could put in the world class category. Many appear in the *Fortune* magazine Global 500 list. These companies no doubt became big by satisfying a lot of customers, and they certainly qualify as players on a world scale.

The companies in the *Fortune* Global 500 are classified on the basis of size and financial performance. Let's look at a selection from *Fortune's* 1998 list (see Table 0.1).

With few exceptions most of these companies would be categorized as world class in their field. Microsoft, Intel, Disney and Merck all appear in the top 10 of 'most admired companies' in America in 1998. More people travel in Boeing planes round the world than any other type, while British Airways have won the 'Best Airline' title 10 years in a row. Marks and Spencer, despite temporary troubles, is a legend with its customers in the United Kingdom, while Wal-Mart has taken serving customers so seriously, it has well surpassed long-time No. 1 US retailer Sears Roebuck to become the biggest retailer in the world by far.

Table 0.1 Size and financial performance of selected *Fortune* Global 500 companies

	Sales per employee ($)	Profits per employee ($)	Profit % on sales	Return on assets (%)
Intel	391,719	108,516	27.7	24.0
Microsoft	510,885	155,361	30.4	24.0
Motorola	198,627	7,867	3.9	4.3
Boeing	191,632	(744)	(0.4)	–
British Airways	233,519	12,423	5.3	3.9
Merck	439,330	85,762	19.5	17.9
Dupont	419,773	24,442	5.8	5.6
Glaxo Welecome	248,985	57,713	23.2	21.8
Disney	208,083	18,204	8.7	5.2
Sony	318,110	10,457	3.4	3.7
General Electric	329,130	29,721	9.0	2.7
GEC (UK)	143,045	15,452	10.8	11.4
Matsushita (Panasonic)	232,934	2,765	1.2	1.2
Wal-Mart	144,605	4,274	3.0	7.7
Tesco	216,941	6,660	3.1	6.8
Marks & Spencer	280,829	28,237	10.1	10.6
Federal Express	106,828	3,348	3.1	4.7
British Post Office	52,192	2,959	5.7	6.4
Procter & Gamble	337,396	32,217	9.5	12.4
Unilever	169,899	19,034	11.2	17.2

But these companies are not all world class performers in financial terms. The companies are not all directly comparable, of course, but they have been grouped into related fields. Yet look at the variability in performance of these companies. Intel and Microsoft are the exceptions – despite their 1998 stock market sufferings they win the gold medal on financial performance whichever measure you use. But would the customers of Wal-Mart class the company as ordinary because they make only a third of the profit of Marks and Spencer, or they achieve only half the sales per employee of M&S? Of course not. Would we reject Boeing because they made a loss in 1997? The users and buyers of their aircraft wouldn't say so. Would we condemn Matsushita, makers of Panasonic products, because they made only a measly 1.2 per cent profit on sales? We don't think so. In fact, the vast majority of people who buy these companies' products or use their services have no idea about their sales volume or profitability. And they don't much care either. They only know that their products and service are the best around.

What customers see as truly world class

So if it's not just financial performance that makes companies world class, what is it? Well, it doesn't mean perfection. World class is a comparative measure. It implies: is this good enough to be compared to the best in the world? And the ultimate judges on these matters are customers themselves. What makes companies world class *in the customers' eyes?* Just this.

- *The quality of the product or service.* Does the product fulfil all the requirements it promised? Does it work first time out of the box? Is it simple enough that I don't need an 80-page instruction book to work it? Is this the best service I can get for my purpose compared to what I could get elsewhere?

  In making their choices, customers are forever evaluating their alternatives. Is this the best I can get? Companies who cannot regularly meet their customers' expectations first time with their products or service have little chance of becoming world class.

- *Value for money.* Is the value I perceive in getting this product or service greater than the money I have to part with? How does that compare with the price-value I could get elsewhere? This is where perception plays a key part in the customer's decision. If the item concerned is a branded product with identical features, then price becomes the main consideration. More often than not, however, there's always 'added value' that companies can add to their product that customers will perceive as worth paying for, and will distinguish them from the competition. That's something world class companies excel at.

- *Service.* Is it a pleasure to deal with this company? Are they easy to do business with? Are they as concerned to help after the sale as before? Do they put themselves out to resolve your problems? Do they respond speedily to your problems? Are they concerned about you? Do they really put customers first?

  Or do they move you from pillar to post and let you fight your way through their system to get your problem attended to? Are you greeted by a mechanical voice on the telephone that forces you through a number-punching sequence before you get to talk to a real person? Are you compelled to listen to the eternal canned music as you hang on?

  In an age when companies catch up on each other's technology in relatively short order, quality of service may well be the key factor that distinguishes one company from another. That is something of which world class companies are acutely aware.

- *Reliability.* Here, the kind of questions customers ask themselves are: will the company actually deliver when they say they will? Will the product actually prove to be reliable in practice? Is the quality of their product or service consistent? Do they phone you back when they say they will? Do they keep their promises? Can you trust them? In that respect, are they better than all the rest?

This is an area where the Japanese are the all-time champions. They taught the rest of the world what real quality and reliability looked like. Cars are complicated products, and for a long time we all accepted that things would inevitably go wrong from time to time. Today you can buy a Japanese car that might have 10,000 parts in it, all requiring design, manufacture and assembly – and nothing goes wrong. Nothing. That's remarkable. But you can't get there without having spent years working on quality and having every employee paying attention to the detail every minute of the day. That's what it takes to reach world class standard.

- *Innovation*. What won the gold medal at the last Olympics may well not be good enough to win next time. Standards – in business as well as in sport – improve all the time. So to stay at world class standard means constant change and innovation, always trying to produce something that beats the customer's expectations. And that's quite exciting – for employees as well as customers.

One company that makes constant innovation into a cherished principle is US company Rubbermaid. They make plastic and rubber products. They work to ensure that 25 per cent of their sales in any year come from products introduced in the previous five years. In 1993, they introduced some 365 new products. That was the year they won the title of 'Most Admired Company' in America. That's world class.

World class companies are not marvellous at everything

When sportsmen aspire to Olympic standards, no one expects to win medals at the 400 metres and at weightlifting too. They know they can't be world standard at everything. They have to choose. So they concentrate on their strengths and work on them until they can compete with the best in the world. It's just the same with companies. You have to choose what you want to be best at.

Do you know what you want to be best at? What do you want to concentrate on? Market share? Operating efficiency? Customer service? How well you manage and use your employees? Below is a list of performance measures used by real companies around the world. They are divided into five categories. Have a good look through the list and choose what you think should be the priorities for your company.

Customers
- order to delivery time/waiting time;
- right first time: service and product;
- on time in full (OTIF) delivery;
- customer complaints;
- speed of problem resolution;
- phone response time;
- letter response time;
- customer survey scores.

Employees
- sales per employee;
- profit per employee;
- standard hours vs attended hours;
- absence;
- staff turnover;
- employee survey scores.

Financial performance
- return on capital/assets;
- profit percentage on sales;
- investor returns;
- share price;
- unit costs.

Market performance
- market share;
- product innovation;
- sales growth.

Internal efficiency
- sales per square foot;
- profit per square foot;
- added value time vs process cycle time;
- standard hours vs attended hours;
- stock turns;
- overall machine efficiency;
- costs of quality;
- inspection costs and delays:
    - re-work;
    - scrap;
    - customer returns;
    - costs;
    - penalty costs;
- time to market.

So, what measures would be most important to your organization? What would have the biggest impact on your performance? What would be most appreciated by your customers? Whatever you decide, remember, don't choose too many. Concentration is the key to excellence.

You may achieve results you never thought possible

When you do start down the road to world class, it looks like a daunting journey. But over time companies can reach levels of performance they never dreamt were possible. Here is one example. Back in 1979, Motorola senior management held a three-day confer- ence together in Chicago. Near the end, one of the sales managers stood up and said: 'Our customers think our quality stinks.' The audience was dumbfounded. Their measured defect rate was already good and it was something they were working on constantly. However, the company was so stung by the criticism that it decided to make quality its prime goal. And look what happened.

We'll assume their defect rate was already a pretty good 0.5 per cent to start with. But that still means:

5 parts were wrong	in 1,000, or
50	in 10,000
500	in 100,000, and as many as
5,000	in 1,000,000

That's a lot of faulty bits getting out to customers. Over the following years the company kept 'raising the bar', setting new targets. By 1992, they were into their Six Sigma quality programme. That year the target they set was 'no more than 3.4 defects in a million parts produced'. Only 0.5 per cent scrap sounds pretty good to most people, but the company's 1992 performance standard is not just 10 times better or even 100 times better. It's *1,400 times* better. Now that's world class!

That kind of achievement takes time, effort, determination and teamwork. But it has a threefold benefit. Customers soon notice and start trusting you with more of their business. Employees feel a great sense of pride and accomplishment. And the bottom line improves markedly.

World class companies are all around us

Wherever you live and work there are large international companies in operation. With their resources of management talent and global reach, these companies tend to seek out good practices wherever they can find them, and put them into operation across their organizations. And these are the companies that set the standards that everyone else has to follow.

Take McDonald's, the fast food chain, as a case in point. Wherever they go in the world, McDonald's know exactly what they want. They know the kind of locations they need for their restaurants and just how they should be laid out, decorated and furnished. They know exact- ly what kind of meat and vegetables they need, and so do their local suppliers, in minute detail. Their restaurant staff may be young, but there's a thick tome laying down in excruci- ating detail how the food should be prepared, exactly how long it should be cooked and at what temperature, when it should be thrown away if not used, how customers should be greeted, how orders should be taken, etc. They don't just hope. They rely on thorough plan- ning, preparation and training.

The indigenous population soon gets used to the new standards set by such companies. Their expectations rise. They get impatient with local companies who get stuck in their old ways. They begin to give them less of their business. The fact is, for any business who wants to thrive and survive, there is no alternative but to actively seek out these best practices and make them your own.

You don't have to re-invent the wheel

The good news is: you don't have to start from scratch. You can get a leg up by learning from the experience of others who have gone before. You can avoid some of the mistakes they made, and adopt or adapt the techniques and processes that took other companies to world class levels of performance. Of course, you won't become world class overnight. As we know, it takes time and it takes practice. But you can enjoy all your steps of achievement along the way.

And, surprising as it may seem, those companies who are world leaders in their field are not uniquely filled with exceptional people. But they do have focus, they know what they want to be good at, they seek to serve their customers better than anybody, and they involve and enthuse every one of their employees in doing it.

The 12 ladders to world class performance

To make the whole issue of progress to world class more accessible and practical, we have distilled what is a complex subject into 12 key factors, each of which we know can make significant differences to the performance of any organization. They have been composed from directly observing a great variety of world class companies, and studying what practical things they did to take themselves to that level of achievement. This is workable know-how you can put into operation in your own organization, and which fills the rest of this book.

Each of the factors has been subdivided into five levels, representing progress from ordinary performance right up to world class standard. There are good reasons for this:

- It helps you see just where you are now.
- It shows you what practical things you have to do to get to the next level.
- It recognizes that getting to world class is a step-by-step process. It is a journey, not an event.

Here are the 12 Ladders:

1. Aligning Management Objectives
2. Customer Focus
3. Organizing the Workplace
4. Visible Measurement Systems
5. Managing for Quality
6. Eliminating Waste
7. Best Operating Practices and Continuous Improvement
8. Teamwork
9. Staff Empowerment and Involvement
10. Rewards and Recognition
11. Purposeful Communication
12. Continuous Learning.

6

Analysing markets and customers

INTRODUCTION

In 1913 Russia celebrated the tercentenary of Romanov rule in a series of lavish public ceremonies. Nicholas, the Tsar, his wife, Alexandra and their family were greeted with vast, jubilant crowds throughout the celebrations yet in a little over five years, by July 1918, Nikolai Romanov, as he was then known, was executed along with other members of his family and retinue. The causes of the Russian Revolution are complex but one aspect of the demise of the Tsar concerned his view that there existed a direct bond between the Tsar and his people. The Tsar simply knew what was best for his people. He saw himself as a father figure with the best interests of every Russian always in his thinking and he thought he could reach out individually to each Russian to examine his or her very soul. He did not need to be told what his people wanted, he already knew and always acted in their best interests. Nicholas was Russia. Russia was Nicholas.

But while Nicholas and his court were busy congratulating themselves on the success of the tercentenary celebrations and perhaps unconsciously looking forward to another 300 hundred years of Romanov Rule, the reality in the outside world was far less rosy. To those outside his direct retinue the signs of impending doom were clear to see. Yet Nicholas, in the main, refused to see what was happening and was most reluctant to cede any power and to undertake a programme of reform and modernization. He believed that he knew what was best for his people.

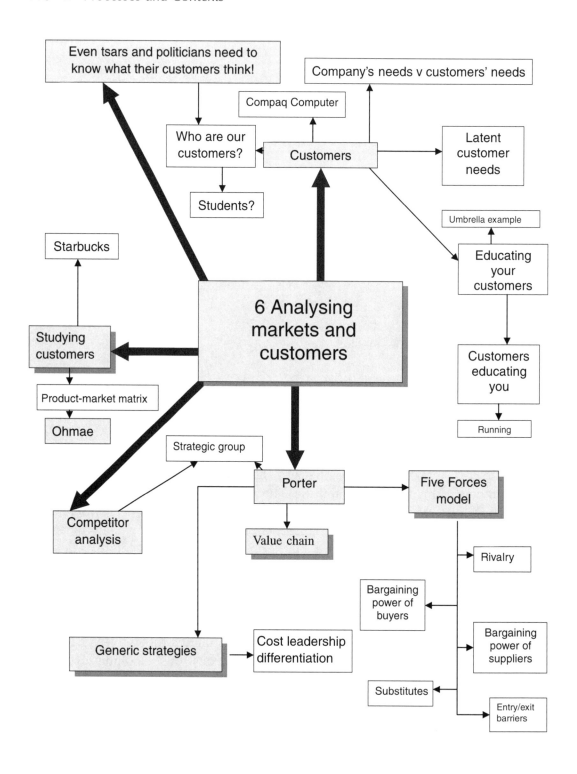

Modern politics is much more about finding out what people are thinking – particularly US politics, with British and European politics increasingly following suit. In the United States, countless polls are taken in the run up to elections for the Senate, Congress or the Presidency to assess how voters will react. Voters are split into different groups defined by gender, ethnicity, age, class and location so that different voter segments can be targeted. Candidates may vary their promotional material and speeches depending on the audience they are trying to reach. Changes will reflect what the pollsters have told them about the segment they are addressing. The candidates' teams will monitor opinion polls to see how well the candidates are doing. Policies will be changed, new ones introduced and old ones given a different 'spin' in an attempt to get the candidate elected. A classic analysis of the US presidential election can be found in a series of books entitled *The Selling of the President*. In these the president is seen as a commodity that has to be sold to the public. The person who becomes president has 'sold' his product to the US electorate more successfully than his opponent. In the 1968 Presidential Elections Richard Nixon was accused of selling himself like a product.

Would Nicholas have survived if he had rejected his view of being Russia, and instead listened and responded to his 'customers'? Should he have hired a market research company to establish what Russians wanted and then found ways of giving the people this? Who knows?

CUSTOMERS

We will be concentrating on customers in this chapter. In particular, we will be looking at how the market can be dissected using a product-market matrix. We will also emphasize the need to give a lot of importance to understanding the needs and expectations of users/customers in the development of strategy.

Concentrating on customers should be a key activity, or the key activity, of any organization, but often organizations become overly focused on production and internal issues and in the process neglect their customers. It is not infrequent for organizations to be led by autocratic figures who believe they know what their customers want. Over a period of time a company's customers drift away as its products become less attractive and other firms start to put on the market new products that customers find more appealing.

While the fate of senior managers in poor performing businesses is not as brutal as that of the Romanovs there are consequences for chief executives of poor business performance. For example, in the period up to 1998 Compaq Computer Corporation's success and growth was noted and celebrated in the media and the

Chief Executive, Eckhard Pfieffer, was given some of the credit for the success. The firm's share price had been showing a rising trend from 1995 through to 1998. But Dell and Hewlett-Packard then overtook Compaq in the retail market. Its share price fluctuated in 1999 and 2000 around a level much lower than in 1997 and 1998. The Board of Compaq dismissed its Chief Executive in 1999.

In some instances an important question to ask when developing strategy is, Who are our customers? This may appear to be obvious but two points need to be considered. First, we may be unsure or simply mistaken as to who our customers are. For example, in a university students may not be considered as customers but raw material that lecturers work with to provide a 'finished product' for firms or businesses. So the customers are the firms or businesses, consequently it is the requirements of business that should shape the production process and not the students. However, some argue that it is neither business in general nor students in particular who are a university's customers but a wider intellectual or cultural or professional community with its own values and needs. In this example, definition of the customers is contested and different groups argue according to their own interests. In devising a strategy in these circumstances attention has to be paid to who the customers are. It would make little sense to devise a product or deliver a service that while appealing to some people did not appeal to the organizations' actual customers. This problem is not just found in universities. Many businesses suffer from not being sure who their customers are.

Second, businesses may know very well who are their customers but assume that they know what their customers want. Often a business becomes production-oriented as senior managers have, perhaps unknowingly, substituted what they want for what the customer wants. For example, managers may champion a superior product in the belief that this is what the customer wants. The business's energies are consumed in building the best, irrespective of either cost or customer need. The business has drifted away from its customers. It may well be a hard lesson to learn and perhaps a cynical one but it is not necessarily true that the better produced product or service wins in the marketplace. An inferior product that is targeted more closely to customer needs could enjoy higher sales than an apparently superior one.

Finding out what customers want and giving it to them is not a bad idea but, as you will read below, customers might have latent needs that a new product or service could give them. They might be unaware of these needs until the product or service appears in the marketplace. A good example of this is the Walkman. In sectors where technology changes very quickly new products are continually appearing. Take the mobile phone, for example. As little as ten years ago few people owned a mobile phone whereas it is very common to own one now. Technological changes have occurred that could mean that your mobile phone now has many more functions – it might be able to send and receive e-mail, keep your appointments, and have a small word processor built in as a matter of course.

THE SUBJECTIVE SIDE OF VALUE

Shaping the needs of your customers and interpreting for them what your product or service does for them also needs to be considered. Instead of seeing the features of your product as fixed it might be possible for you to educate your customer to see the benefits of other attributes. This creates value in your customers' mind. In these cases there is nothing essential about what you put on the market but rather you establish in the customers' mind what to value. In its extreme form even potential defects in products can be 'spun' to become benefits. In the past the chocolate bar Milky Way was advertised as the snack you can eat between meals without ruining your appetite. Presumably what this means is about an hour after eating this you will feel hungry again. This is not a bad thing but a good thing as you can now eat a meal. In this view nothing is simply good or bad, positive or negative. Things are interpreted and have the potential to be interpreted in other ways. A friend of ours was once caught in a sudden downpour in London without a raincoat. Seeing a man selling umbrellas she went to buy one. The umbrellas were cheap and of very poor quality. She asked how long one would last. Quick as a flash came the well-rehearsed response: 'You'll have lost it before it falls to bits and as it's cheap you won't have lost much money!' She bought it. The cheapness and poor quality were a benefit as a more expensive, long-lasting umbrella would be a waste of money if it were lost.

Let's look at another example: training shoes. It might sound like a good idea to invest in R&D aimed at making a lighter, more stable, and shock absorbent shoe. This might better meet the needs of runners but might lead to a reduction in sales because training shoes are not just purchased to run in but also as fashion statements – many customers are buying the shoe because they believe it helps them in creating an identity with their peers and they would see the new shoe as less fashionable than the old one. Again, knowing what business you are in – in this case running shoes or fashion shoes – will help you plan better. Another example is the current fashion for 4×4 vehicles. These are rarely taken off-road but are used in urban areas. This is saying something about the owners. Knowing why your customers are buying your product or service helps enormously.

FIVE FORCES MODEL

As we mentioned in Chapter 1, Porter's Five Forces model can be used to analyse the external competitive environment of the organization. Porter (1980) drew attention to the construction of an industry's competitive structure by five broad types of competitive forces. He suggested a raft of specific questions that can be asked about each separate type of competitive force (buyers, suppliers, etc). The model has almost become a mantra for students of strategic management. It is often assumed that the competitive environment is the main thing that should be covered in an appraisal of the external environment. You will need to form you own views on the usefulness of this approach. It is likely to be of importance to you if you are on a course about strategy because it is a tool used extensively to analyse cases for assessment.

The five forces identified by Porter are listed as follows:

- Rivalry among competitors in the industry.
- Bargaining power of buyers.
- Bargaining power of suppliers.
- Substitutes.
- Entry/exit barriers.

Porter believed that the profit of each industry was dependent on the aggregate strength of the competitive forces. A company will have relatively low profits in an industry in which buyers and suppliers have considerable bargaining power, rivalry with other competitors is intense, the threat of substitutes is substantial, the entry of new competitors is easy, and exiting the industry is difficult. Where competitive forces are weak in aggregate – buyers and sellers have little bargaining power, competitors are not aggressive, etc – then profits will be relatively high. The idea of a negative relationship between the aggregate of competitive forces and industry profit is depicted in Figure 6.1.

Porter built on his work on techniques for analysing competitors and industries and contributed additional ideas that became very influential. He suggested that strategic choice could be looked at in terms of making a selection from one of a small number of generic strategies. Two of the strategic options – cost leadership and differentiation – involved a successful delivery of value to the customer at a level of costs that allowed companies to sustain competitive advantages. Specifically, cost leadership involved marketing products at standard prices while keeping costs relatively low. Differentiation was a strategy of offering superior value at a premium price and at costs above that possible under the cost leadership option. Either way, companies secured profit margins that could be reinvested to maintain either cost

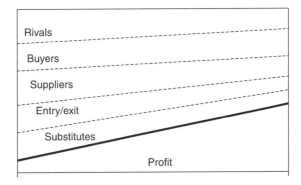

Note: This figure represents the proposition that the weaker the competitive forces (in aggregate terms), the more profit there is.

Figure 6.1 Competitive forces and profit

leadership or differentiation. Later Porter popularized the notion of a value chain. This entailed seeing a company as an assembly of activities each of which could be analysed in greater and greater detail if needed. Activities were then appraised for their contribution to value as perceived by the customers and costs. The value chain offered managers a way of thinking about how they could in practice identify changes that would move the company towards the implementation of cost leadership or differentiation strategies.

Hussey and Jenster (1999: 42) acknowledge the importance of Porter's contribution to the analysis of industries using the Five Forces model. They say: 'One main value of the Porter concept is that it broadened thinking, both about the number of forces that should be considered and the factors within each. Traditionally some thought has always been given to competitors and to customers, but Porter demonstrated that this was inadequate to fully understand the industry.' Their point is obviously that as well as competitors and customers there are suppliers, substitutes, and entry/exit barriers to consider.

While we can easily agree with their judgement, it is also possible to argue that pragmatic strategists may well find it useful to focus in the first instance on just three parties when trying to work out a strategy. If you are not careful it is easy to fall into paralysis by analysis with a detailed application of the five forces. What we mean by this is that you are forever collecting and analysing bits of data about the forces and this takes your attention away from actually doing something. Remember you might need to experiment and then adjust your strategy accordingly. Waiting until you have all the information on all the forces might mean you lose ground to your competitors who have acted more swiftly. You may well now be getting tired of us stressing the practical value of knowledge but you need to try out the five forces for yourself to see how well they work for you in the environment you find yourself in.

COMPETITOR ANALYSIS

Competitor analysis may be carried out to identify strategic issues that need handling. As with industry analysis there is a complex decision to be made about how the boundaries of the industry are to be drawn in order to identify a company's competitors. A company risks overlooking future competitive threats if the industry boundary is drawn too tightly. In any case, any decision on the exact nature of the industry needs to be kept under review these days because of the surprising twists and turns created by the pace of technological and commercial developments. At one time the UK retail banking industry seemed quite distinct from the building society industry but that has changed enormously in recent years.

The information for competitor analysis can be obtained in a variety of ways. A company might commission market research, pool internal knowledge held by its owners and monitor press reports. Once information has been collected and analysed it is possible to use strategic group mapping to make sense of the strategic issues posed by the presence of competitors in an industry. A strategic group is the group of firms that follow the same strategy in terms of the strategic dimensions used to map them. Porter (1980) outlined the use of this technique and justified it primarily in terms of the need to understand the variations found in the profitability of companies in the same industry.

One approach is to identify two variables (strategic dimensions) and then see if the data collected can be used to identify strategic groups. These two variables can be selected from the many different strategic dimensions suggested by Porter, including product quality, technological leadership, cost position, service, price policy, brand identification and choice of distribution channels. Each competitor is represented on a map (graph) using the two variables and then the graph is inspected to see if there are any obvious clusters. There may be a trial and error element in this mapping technique. Perhaps various pairs of variables will have to be tried out until the map produces something meaningful. The identification of a number of groups in a map can be used to frame a number of interesting strategic questions. For example, do the groups consist of companies with more or less the same strategy and with the same level of actual profitability? Does profitability vary mainly on the basis of which strategic group a company belongs to? Following on from this management might ask: Should the company seek to migrate from its current strategic group to another one with more profit potential? What barriers will be experienced in shifting strategic position by moving from one group to another?

This technique for analysing competitors encourages us to think of strategic choice as a choice of which strategic group to join. As Porter points out, however, in the context of a changing industry structure a company might think about seeking to create a new strategic group.

STUDYING CUSTOMERS

To paraphrase Ohmae (1982), a good strategy is the result of the company matching its strengths to the customers' needs better than do the competitors (see Chapter 1). Of course, firms have to study competitors and customers – as well as their own strengths and weaknesses. But firms have a choice about the emphasis and the order in which this is done. For example, they can watch their competitors very closely and always move quickly to match or top competitors' initiatives and then check out that this is what the customers want. Or firms can initially concentrate on understanding what customers are looking for from the product or service. Having understood what the customers want, they can plan to develop the product or service to better meet the needs of customers, and finally check out the likely reaction of their competitors in response to their own development of product-market strategy.

One way to study the company's customers is by using a product-market matrix. Ohmae (1982) recommends this as a way of dissecting a market. The matrix is composed of two factors: the set of product lines produced by the company, and the market the company operates in. Of course the products may in fact be services rather than physical products. The market is defined in terms of the different types

Types of customer	1	2	3	4	5
Product lines					
1					
2					
3					
4					

Table 6.1 Product-market matrix (Ohmae, 1982)

of customers the company has. So the market is equated to customer groups. A business may feel it has a multitude of customers and not be sure about how to group them. For simplicity the company may want to consider only 5–8 customer types or groups. These could be defined in terms of what they look for in the products they buy, ordering patterns, and their importance to the business in terms of sales. Each part of the matrix is a product-market segment. Data can be entered into the matrix to show, for example, current sales in each segment.

It is not our intention to prescribe exactly how the product-market matrix is used to generate strategy, but in deciding on the customer types or groups it is important that managers think about what each group looks for from the company's products. It may become clear during the process of getting data and completing the matrix that there are some segments that are, or could be, strategically important. It may become clear that a particular product line has not been marketed to a particular customer group. And so on.

The concept of 'what the customer is looking for from the product' is an important one and deserves serious consideration. A first important point is that customer needs may be latent, as we mentioned earlier. Hamel and Prahalad (1994) pointed out that a company should not think only in terms of what customers are currently looking for because customers may have latent needs that they are not actually aware of.

Another key message here is: do not assume a one-to-one relationship between what the customers are looking for and what the company can do to better meet this. As Ohmae (1982) suggests, customers of coffee may want a superior taste. This may be delivered through a wide range of alternative variables (the quality of the coffee beans, the water used to make the coffee, the water temperature, etc). The company may be able to influence some of the variables. Coffee shops, such as Starbucks, currently represent a fast-growing sector. Here customers are presented with not just one or two types of coffee but different ways of consuming it, cappuccino, café latte and so on, plus a wide range of toppings, not only chocolate but nutmeg, cinnamon and others. In fact for the novice coffee drinker the combinations appear formidable, but with increasingly sophisticated customers who have been 'educated' in the different combinations this concept is proving to be a winner. Starbucks run coffee education events where you can in their words, 'Discover the intriguing subtleties of coffee at an in-store coffee seminar with one of our coffee experts.' Their Web site is at www.starbucks.com/ and it's well worth a visit. I'll have a non-fat, grande, dry with hazelnut top expresso to go.

Thirdly, studying customer needs should not be a superficial exercise. One approach to ensuring an in-depth study is to take the customers' values or needs and analyse them hierarchically (Ohmae 1982). For example, if customers look for simple and quick preparation when buying convenience food, it can be asked whether they value the ease of preparation or the avoidance of having to wash pots and pans and cooking utensils generally. If it is ease of preparation they value, are they concerned about the actual time or is it the complexity that is a problem? And so on.

We do think it is extraordinarily helpful to think about the company itself, the customers, and the competitors and to study all three of them. The product-market matrix, as we have seen, can help a company better understand its market. A benchmarking study looking at the functional activities of the business (raw material sourcing, design, production, sales, servicing, etc) can show where the competitors are stronger. An internal appraisal of the company's own functional activities in the light of the key success factors of the industry may be useful for determining strengths and weaknesses. All these studies can feed into the best strategy for the company in question.

In a sense we have now returned to Tsar Nicholas and modern politicians. Nicholas refused to change, believing that he knew what was best based on his view of what a Tsar was. Today modern politics has taken up the tools of the business world with enthusiasm to monitor closely how well politicians are doing. Just as firms have products and services that are real, so do politicians. It is easy to believe that anything can be 'spun' to your advantage no matter what. Clearly understanding customer needs is important but to believe that they can always be shaped to your own ends irrespective of the actual qualities of what you are producing seems to us to go a step too far.

CONCLUSIONS

This chapter should have developed your knowledge and understanding of customers and their needs. This knowledge and understanding has been placed in relation to competitive advantage by pointing out again that successful strategy leads a company to align its strengths to form a better match with the needs of customers than that managed by competitors. We have outlined some of Porter's ideas in relation to the analysis of the competitive environment, but attention has also been given to the importance of understanding customers as the foundation of success or, if neglected, the source of disaster.

QUESTIONS

1. Consider the following organizations. Who are their customers? A university, Greenpeace, the Liberal Democrats, this book, Manchester United (see the case study on Manchester United plc).
2. Going back to the small bakery, how would you help the owner identify the bakery's customers and their needs?
3. Looking at advances in phone technology, how would you go about educating customers on some of the new features? (The case study on Vodafone may give you some idea of the changes that have happened to mobile phone technology over the past few years.)
4. Is it true that you can very nearly always recast negative product or service features as positive? For example, a glue that does not stick is sold as 'stick it' notes, a cloth that loses its dyed colour after a few washes is sold as faded denim, a cheap umbrella is sold on the grounds that it doesn't matter if you lose it. Can you 'spin' some more negatives into positives?
5. Select a product or service of your choice and apply Porter's five forces model to it. How difficult did you find this to do? What (if anything) made it hard to do?
6. Using a product or service you are familiar with, try to apply Porter's value chain analysis to it. How difficult did you find this to do? What (if anything) made it hard to do?
7. How would you reconcile the analytic and systematic approach of Porter's five forces and value chain with a more creative and intuitive approach to satisfying customers' needs?
8. How useful is the idea of industry in understanding competitors? You may like to think about the way banks and building societies have merged in recent years; or the way Nike running shoes have become fashion statements; or the way separate utilities such as gas and water have merged.
9. How easy is it for an organization to move into another industry? The ICL case study shows how it has moved from being mainly a builder of computers to an e-solution business.
10. Is strategy simply about 'a company matching its strengths to the customers' needs better than do the competitors'?
11. How do you find out about needs customers have that they are themselves unaware of? For instance, as a customer of this book how could we have gone about finding out about your latent needs? You might like to refer to the Starbucks case study on this.

REFERENCES

Hamel, G and Prahalad, C K (1994) *Competing for the Future*, Harvard Business School Press, Boston

Hussey, D and Jenster, P (1999) *Competitor Intelligence: Turning analysis into success*, Wiley, Chichester

Ohmae, K (1982) *The Mind of the Strategist*, McGraw-Hill, London

Porter, M (1980) *Competitive Strategy: Techniques for analyzing industries and competitors*, Free Press, New York

FURTHER READING

Anderson, P and Mann, N (1999) *Safety First: The making of New Labour*, Granta Books, London

Denton, R E (1994*) The 1992 Presidential Campaign*, Praeger Paperback, Westport, Conn.

Denton, R E (1998) *The 1996 Presidential Campaign*, Praeger Paperback, Westport, Conn.

Fairclough, N (2000) *New Labour, New Language?* Routledge, London

Hohenberg, J (1994) *The Bill Clinton Story: Winning the Presidency*, Syracuse University Press, New York

McGuinniss, J (1968) *The Selling of the President*, Trident Press, Simon & Schuster, New York

Newman, B I (1994) *The Marketing of the President: Political marketing as campaign strategy*, Sage Publications, New York

Popkin, S L (1994) *The Reasoning Voter*: Communication and persuasion in Presidential campaigns, University of Chicago Press

Reading 6.1

Taken from Chapter 6 – Analysis: turning information into intelligence, in *Competitive Intelligence* by Michelle Cook and Curtis Cook (2000)

Do not believe in anything simply because you have heard it. Do not believe in anything simply because it is spoken and rumoured by many. Do not believe in anything simply because it is found written in your religious books. Do not believe in anything merely on the authority of your teachers and elders. Do not believe in traditions because they have been handed down for many generations. But after observation and analysis, when you find that anything agrees with reason and is conducive to the good and benefit of one and all, then accept it and live up to it.

Buddha

The successful (person) is the one who finds out what is the matter with his (or her) business before his (or her) competitors do.

Roy L Smith (adapted by C Cook and M Cook)

It is difficult to conduct business without hearing about your competitors. You should be worried if you are able to go through a week without any knowledge about what is happening in your business environment, whether it be an advertisement you see in a newspaper, a rumour from one of your salespeople or perhaps a new customer who explains why she has opted for your product or service when two of your rivals contacted her first.

While it is virtually impossible to ignore information, it is very easy to be overwhelmed by it. Information is everywhere, and attempting to know all and see all will effectively paralyse your business. How do you strike a balance? How do you learn to recognize the value in certain pieces of information, while avoiding overload?

The answer is to shift the focus away from information gathering and focus on analysis. Most business executives will tell you that, while it may be ideal to have every piece of data required for a decision, the business world is not ideal. Waiting for that level of accuracy will result in sluggish and ineffective actions, or reactions to a more nimble competitor who has recognized a window of opportunity. These executives understand that it is better to be close all the time than to be accurate occasionally. This is the value of analysis in CI.

Analysis is the key to effective business decision-making. In the intelligence age, markets are so competitive and so connected that a technological change or a new entrant in your industry can put you out of business before you know what has happened. Keeping your finger on the pulse of your business environment is crucial to avoid this fate. No business is immune. While it is common to hear about the 'category killer' stores putting local shops out of business, it is just as common today to find a new and innovative start-up introducing a cutting-edge product that renders an industry leader's wares obsolete. All businesses ignore the competition at their peril. Failure and success have as much to do with a company's ability to manage intelligence about itself, about its competitors, about the environment in which it operates and about its ability to execute strategies based on the intelligence at its disposal as it does with deep pockets and loyal customers.

The globalization of culture and commerce has brought about dizzying changes for businesses in the last decade. It is no longer a simple task to identify rivals because the competitive environment is more dynamic, expansive and unpredictable than ever before. These factors all contribute to the difficulty in anticipating what the future holds. Toss in a heaping dose of technology, a trend towards deregulation and harmonization of international standards, increasingly sophisticated and demanding consumers in markets around the world and the creation of new business channels, and the task of remaining competitive seems daunting, if not impossible. The good news is that it is possible.

How does one go about analysing the business environment? It helps first to understand the different elements of the environment as well as the different levels of analysis that can be conducted. We break the various types of competitive analysis into three main categories: market analysis; industry analysis; and company analysis. Depending on the nature of your company, industry and competitive objectives, the analysis techniques will differ. Some of the analysis techniques can be used for more than one type of analysis. For example, patent analysis is most commonly used for company analysis so we have included it in that section; however, it also has applications in industry analysis and market analysis as well.

There are many different tools to analyse industries, companies and markets. We have selected the ones we find most beneficial. There is one integral analysis tool that has not been included in this chapter. It is competitive benchmarking. We discuss benchmarking and explain how to benchmark your organization against another in the following chapter. However, a full book on benchmarking would still not cover it completely because it is such an extensive discipline on its own. Chapter 7 gives you a good overview of it and how to get started using competitive benchmarking.

We include the following analysis techniques in this chapter: event analysis, intelligence mapping, market factor analysis, company profiling, competitor profiling, merger analysis, patent analysis, personality profiling, Porter's model of five forces, ratio analysis and SWOT analysis. More analysis techniques are being developed all the time. The ones we include will enable you effectively to conduct market, industry and company analysis, thereby gaining a better competitive advantage.

Market analysis

With the global economy becoming increasingly competitive, businesses are anxious to explore new opportunities for growth in other parts of the world. Entering new markets is not a matter of duplicating your current business practices in another geographic location. There are a number of factors to analyse when you are determining the potential or opportunity within a new market, whether that market spans a region, a country or a number of countries. We include two types of analysis that can be used to analyse markets: market factor analysis and intelligence mapping.

Market factors analysis

We have identified five broad factors that need to be addressed when conducting an analysis of a market. They are political, economic, social, technological and industry-specific. This type of analysis provides you with both a historical perspective regarding market evolution and development, and an increased ability to forecast the direction in which the market is headed.

Political analysis

How would you feel if you invested heavily in a new operation overseas and, a month after you opened your doors for business, a coup breaks out in the country? The government is overthrown, the military takes over and all foreign investment, including your operation, is seized until further notice. While this example is extreme, it illustrates the potential hardship a company can face if it has not adequately analysed and assessed the political risk when it explores new markets. A bit of advance preparation can save a considerable amount of hardship later on.

One factor to consider is the type of government and legal system. Such information is available from a number of sources, such as the CIA World Factbook. But do not stop there. Analyse the status and personality of the present leadership, from the president or prime minister to the key decision-makers in the power departments. A historical perspective of the area's political stability, and the current political issues facing the country, are necessary ingredients for a thorough analysis. It is also important to analyse the legal system or systems within the target market as well. You should examine what laws are on the books that could affect your competitiveness in these markets, find out how effectively and fairly they have been enforced in the past and determine whether changes are pending that could also affect your ability to compete. While it is often difficult to analyse the level of corruption within a political or judicial system, any information that you gather in this regard will be extremely valuable for your decision.

Governments exercise varying degrees of control in different industries in different parts of the world. In the United States, for example, businesses are relatively free from the government telling them how to operate. As long as companies adhere to well-documented laws, they are free to go forth and prosper. On the other extreme, you have China's planned economy, in which factory output for a given business is dictated and the concepts of competition, marketing and continuous improvement are non-existent. While this is changing in China, it is difficult to describe the role of government in industry as anything but oppressive. Knowing the extent to which this occurs in your target market, and the impact that might have on your ability to succeed, is crucial.

Government control or influence is exerted in other ways that affect competitiveness as well. For example, a manufacturing company may find the environmental regulations regarding emissions too onerous to consider building a factory in a specific country. To meet all the standards required in that nation would be more costly than to ship the finished product over a longer distance into that market from a factory operating under less stringent environmental restrictions.

There are still many barriers to foreign investment in certain markets. Fortunately, they are decreasing as more countries accept open markets as a key to their growth, and international agreements and membership into international trade organizations increase the likelihood of more equitable treatment when conducting international business. Yet it is important to find out the extent to which preferential treatment is still given to domestic companies, and how such treatment creates competitive advantages for those firms.

One area in which we have advised clients concerns the impact of conducting business in a country or region in which human rights abuses are prevalent. Regardless of whether these abuses are widely publicized, there is a potential for serious backlash against the firm, which can undoubtedly affect its competitiveness. This whole situation can simply be avoided if a company sets ethical guidelines for the way in which it conducts business and respects people.

Economic analysis

An economic analysis of a target market helps you understand the historical growth or decline of a particular market, as well as its potential for greater affluence in the future. There are very few circumstances in which a company would want to invest heavily into a market that is not only economically depressed, but has been on a downward spiral for many years with no sign of hope.

On a very broad level, your company will want to feel confident that the market in question has the infrastructure in place to support whatever type of business you are in. If you need roads or railways, airline routes or office space in a particular location, this type of analysis at the outset saves time and money later in the process. If the target market does not have what you need in the way of infrastructure, you can find out if there are plans for improvements, changes or additions, and whether money has been dedicated to these efforts. Competitive advantages can be gained if you, and not your competitors, are aware of an upcoming change that will make conducting business in a previously untested market much more lucrative.

Conducting this analysis requires an examination of the strengths of the various industry sectors within the market relative to other markets, and in terms of historical growth and potential. Clearly you will be more interested in sectors of the industry that seem more relevant to your business, but you also want to feel confident in the market's economic capabilities as a whole. Your consumer-product business may have very little in common with natural resources but, if the economic strength of a particular market is in mining and forestry and these industries are declining rapidly, you will have to determine whether large-scale employee reductions in these industries in future years will hinder your efforts to sell your product or service in this market.

Many governments collect and publish economic statistics, including import and export data, from their own country as well as foreign countries. These can be valuable sources of information to forecast growth trends for certain products or services. These departments also publish demographic information, such as census results and other types of surveys. This can give you insight into a number of economic factors, including the distribution of wealth and earnings within a market.

Governments also promote economic development within their borders, and often provide incentives to attract new business. The Invest in France Programme is a prime example, where the government has tried to remove as many barriers as possible to foreign firms looking to set up shop in France. Contacting economic development agencies within your target markets to learn about incentives may result in competitive advantages that you, and perhaps your competitors, did not know existed prior to your analysis. The difference is that now you know.

Social analysis

An intelligent organization never overlooks the impact of social and cultural elements on its competitiveness. Throughout this book, we discuss a number of issues relating to competing internationally, including language challenges, belief systems and general cultural differences that organizations need to understand and respect to maximize their success in foreign markets. Some of these are obvious and well documented. Others are less obvious.

Consider Canada and the United States. These two technologically advanced and highly industrialized nations share the world's longest undefended border. They are partners in the world's richest bilateral trade, and share much of the same culture. With the exception of a percentage of the French-speaking population in Quebec, who are also exposed to all things American, the two countries share the same language. So why is it so difficult for Canadians to accept and celebrate entrepreneurial effort and success? Somehow, during the development of these relatively young nations, Canadians became risk-averse and suspicious of success while people in the US became the champions of new ideas and new challenges. While this may be a generalization, it has played itself out in the business world to the detriment of Canadian businesses. An article in a Canadian business magazine featured a very innovative Canadian entrepreneur who found success only after he left Canada to build his business in Seattle, Washington. When asked why he took this approach, he indicated that Canadian investors and potential partners loved his idea but wanted to wait until he had achieved success before backing his business. In contrast, when he approached US investors for financial backing, they wanted to know how he was going to achieve his goals and objectives. Satisfied with his vision, innovative business idea and sound strategy, they decided to get involved at the critical start-up stage.

It is not always possible to gauge the level of business sophistication in any particular market, or to understand the nuances that make different people, businesses or cultures react differently from others in certain environments. A social analysis helps give you more information on how receptive a market may be to a new product or service, and how open it may be to a new business model or an untested marketing approach.

Technology analysis

We cannot overstate the impact technology is having on the way business is conducted globally. As a result, the level of technological use and the rate of adoption are key elements of a market analysis. We have seen that the level of use of technology is directly proportional to its influence in business. We call this the law of technological influence. The technological maturity of the market you enter must be analysed. The market's rate of adoption of technology will also be a factor in any decisions you make about competing in that area. For example, a business that is a low technology user will be at a competitive disadvantage if it attempts to enter a market in which competing firms are high technology users. Conversely, a firm that has embraced technology in every aspect of its business may find it disadvantageous to enter a market in which the trappings of technology do not exist or are not readily available. It may seem obvious that a company will not expand its Internet service business to a market where 10 per cent of the population have telephones, 5 per cent have cable television and 2 per cent have computers. It is less obvious when a business that has automated all of its processes and uses computers in every department establishes an office in an area where power generation facilities are unreliable and leading-edge computer hardware is difficult to procure from local sources.

Technology plays a tremendous role in an organization's competitiveness. A thorough analysis of it will increase the value of your market analysis and, ultimately, your recommendations to decision-makers.

Industry analysis

The political, economic, social and technology analyses that you have conducted set the stage for your industry analysis. This fifth market analysis factor moves your efforts from the overall market environment to your specific industry. Some of the analysis tools that can be incorporated into this stage include Porter's five forces, competitor profiling, SWOT analysis, event analysis, merger analysis and patent analysis.

Intelligence mapping

Leonard M Fuld, author of *The New Competitor Intelligence: The Complete Resource for Finding, Analyzing, and Using Information about your Competitors*, developed a valuable competitive analysis tool called 'intelligence mapping'. It is a means to map the intelligence resources you can find in a particular country. We include it as a market analysis technique but it has value for industry analysis and company analysis as well.

Fuld suggests the following technique for creating an intelligence map:

1. Identify a business event or a company.
2. Call sources (securities analysts, Department of Commerce analysts, news reporters, banks and consulates) that follow business events for that country.
3. Ask these questions, paraphrased as necessary:
- 'If you had to go to Country X to find information on private company Y, what sources would you go to first?'

- 'Which sources - local newspaper, stock analyst, bank, database or government filing - would give you the most accurate and timely information on a private company?'
- 'Which of the sources are most likely to have the information, and which are least likely? Could you rank them?'
4. Based on the answers, determine which of the sources prove to be stronger antennas and which are weaker. The stronger ones will define your intelligence map. Keep this map in mind, and you will be able to gather intelligence more quickly and more accurately (Fuld, 1995:209).

Fuld refers to antennas as part of his intelligence antennas law, which he describes as, 'Each country or region has a set of intelligence antennas that act as information magnets and are superior in picking up and absorbing information in that country or region' (Fuld, 1995:207). These antennas can be analysts, associations, banks, external traders, government, internal traders and publications.

Each country tends to be different in the collection and housing of information. That is the reasoning behind creating an intelligence map. By doing so at the beginning of a project, you potentially save yourself countless hours of research and frustration later. You can then refer to the map whenever you conduct research in that particular country.

Industry analysis
Having a strong understanding of the industry in which you are operating is the best way to position your organization for success. Thorough industry analysis gives you insight into industry profitability, success indicators and life cycle:

- *Industry profitability*: What segments within the industry are getting the most attention from competitors and why? Are these the segments your company should focus on?
- *Success indicators*: What are the areas in which your competitors excel? What are their strengths, weaknesses, strategies and relative performance in the areas in which you want to compete?
- *Industry life cycle*: Is the industry new or mature? How will your business measure up to existing competitors? Which ones are likely to be the greatest threats to your success? Is the industry in a high-growth stage or has growth slowed as rivalry intensified? Has the increase in competition and substitute products or services made buyers and suppliers more influential? What factors are likely to be important to success in this industry in the future? How prepared is your company for that future?

Porter's five forces model
In his early works on competition within industries and competitive strategies, Professor Michael Porter of the Harvard Business School developed a model identifying five forces that act on players in a competitive environment. These forces determine an industry's attractiveness and are identified below:

- competition within the industry;
- threat of new competition;
- influence of suppliers;
- influence of customers;
- threat of alternatives or substitutes.

Competition within the industry

Competition within an industry is a way of life in most markets around the world. Rivalry in the business world is viewed as economically healthy, particularly when it is supported by a mild dose of regulatory guidance to ensure fair and equitable conditions for the business community and consumers. Most businesses, large or small, recognize the direct competition within their immediate market, whether that be at the town, city, county, provincial, state or national level. They may not recognize or consider the indirect competitors that share the territory. Consequently, they may be confused about a decline in their business because they have not broadened their scope of enquiry to consider non-traditional rivals.

International companies or multinationals may recognize the other multinational businesses or strong national competitors against which they compete in various markets; however, they may fail to consider strong rivals in smaller regional markets. These 'small fish' can quickly infiltrate the 'big pond' and change the industry environment for everyone. This is becoming more common as the international markets grow and the barriers to competition shrink. Many countries that historically controlled business through government intervention and stiff restrictions on foreign investment are embracing economic reforms and opening up to the benefits of more liberal trade.

Threat of new competition

This is a double-edged sword for any business because the creation of new markets is linked to the creation of new potential competitors, which is the second force that Porter identified. If you can entertain the idea of selling your goods or services in new markets, remember that many of your competitors are thinking the same thing. In addition, entrepreneurs in these new markets are becoming aware of the opportunities in your back yard. The threat of new competition grows every day. Many businesspeople are convinced that their product or service is so fantastic that everyone will want to buy it. This is what we call the 'Field of Dreams' approach to business. The notion that 'if you build it, they will come (insert buy)' does not work in the business world. What such businesspeople tend to forget is that, if they are correct and their product or service is fantastic, the idea may be duplicated by many. Existing businesses that have built their reputation on specific functions of their organizations are now being analysed so that those areas of excellence can be introduced into other companies, including competitors.

The only real barriers to entering new industries, or new markets for that matter, are the decision-makers' perceptions of how difficult it is to do so. Is there a market for your company's product or service? Is it economically viable to enter the market? Is the regulatory environment supportive or overbearing? Does your company have the skills and resources to succeed in this area of business?

Influence of suppliers

It is rare to find a business today that is wholly self-sufficient. Outsourcing, contracting and partnering have all become part of everyday operation. This is particularly true in more mature industries. In the automotive industry, engines may be built in one factory, and the seats designed and constructed by another company at another location. Both components are shipped for final assembly to the factory where the automobile frame has been constructed. Of course, assembly can only occur if the tyre supplier, the exhaust supplier and the paint supplier, among others, have also shipped their key components at the same time. And the price the manufacturer charges must be competitive in its class while still leaving room to make a reasonable profit.

In most instances, your business is integrally linked to the fortunes and misfortunes of your suppliers. Their efficiency, greed, mismanagement or vision can all play a part in your success. It is crucial that you analyse the impact of their influence on your operation.

Influence of buyers

'The customer is always right.' True or not, this old adage does not adequately describe the ability of buyers to influence your business or an industry as a whole. Porter emphasized the customers' demand for greater quality or service, the bargaining power of large-volume customers and, of course, their ability to shop around for alternatives. Customers exert considerable force on an industry and have the power to make winners and losers. Businesses that are interested in success must analyse and act on the needs of customers and potential customers as part of their competitive strategy.

Threat of alternatives or substitutes

Why are there so many models of Sony's Walkman? The company took the position that it had to provide a portable audiocassette or CD player to match anything that a competitor might put on the market. Any new feature on a rival's product was seen as a threat to Sony's leadership and the Walkman's brand recognition. Why is the recording industry threatened by the Internet? Musicians now have an alternative for getting their music out to the masses, even if they do not have a recording contract. At the retail level, music stores are forced to compete with online vendors of CDs and audiotapes. Whether it be generic or 'no name' products in food stores, insurance services offered through banks, or Internet service offered by cable television companies or telecommunications giants, there is always the threat that your customers will be able to get the same thing you are offering or something similar in a way that they prefer. While Porter identified threats from alternatives or substitutes in his works in the 1980s, it would have been difficult accurately to determine the impact this competitive force would have in the business world today.

The industry level is where you see Porter's five forces being played out. Analysing the forces that Porter identified in his model of a competitive industry is an excellent point of departure.

Competitor profiling

One of the analysis techniques we use to determine a company's standing within an industry is to determine the company's main competitors and conduct a competitor profiling. On behalf of the company, we compile research covering each of the main functions of the company and each of its competitors' functions. These include company history, management information, strategy, finance, marketing, sales, products and/or services, distribution, employment, research and development, technology and image. After compiling data for each of these areas for each of the companies, we compare them.

An optional part of competitor profiling, but one that we find particularly valuable, is to assign each competitor a value for its functions. For example, out of a possible score of 10, where 1 is the least impressive and 10 is the most impressive, we might assign Competitor A a rating of 5 for its marketing efforts. We might give Competitor B a 7 and Competitor C an 8. We would continue to do this for each of the functions listed in Table 6.1 below. Afterward, we could very easily chart the results for an at-a-glance look at the strengths and weaknesses of the main companies within an industry.

Table 6.1   Competitor profiling chart

	Company	Competitor A	Competitor B	Competitor C
Company History				
Management				
Company Strategy				
Financial Information				
Operational Information				
Marketing Information				
Sales Information				
Product Information				
Distribution Information				
Employee Information				
R & D/Engineering				
Technology				
Image				

While this technique has some similarities to benchmarking, it is more of an overview. Competitive benchmarking is far more exhaustive.

To further your understanding of the competitive environment in which you operate, an analysis will be more valuable if it looks at the different levels within that environment – namely, further industry analysis and company analysis.

Company analysis

Company-level competitive analysis has several components: technical analyses, personality analyses and operational analyses. Technical analyses provide a statistical snapshot of a company that may help to explain its situation. Standard accounting reports and formulae, such as financial summaries, profitability ratios (return on sales, return on assets and return on equity), debt/equity ratios and cash flow help to create a technical perspective of the competitor.

Personality analyses give you a more qualitative type of information that may help explain how a competitor perceives itself and how it may react in a particular situation. By looking at the organizational structure, the ownership and key managers or board of directors, you can formulate an opinion on corporate culture. Combined with information on that organization's goals, marketing communications, policies and strategies, you have a useful view of the competitor's personality.

A competitive analysis at the operations level examines the key elements of operating a business. Areas such as research and development, manufacturing, marketing, sales, distribution and customer service are analysed to determine where competitive advantages exist.

General Electric, for example, has demonstrated considerable skill in this regard. It analyses its diverse core businesses to such a degree that it is able to maintain either first or second place in the markets for those businesses. If analysis illustrates that General Electric cannot achieve its goal, then that particular business is divested.

Technical, personality and operational analyses work best as analysis tools when they are considered together to create an image of a competitor. For example, imagine you are competing in a high-technology industry and are interested in the position of two rivals. You have already determined that Competitor A has a positive cash flow and very little debt. Financially, this company looks like a dangerous competitor. Competitor B has a negative cash flow and considerable debt, and does not seem to pose a competitive threat from a technical perspective. However, Company A has been in the industry for a long time. Its management team has not changed with the times and, like the board of directors, it has remained fiercely conservative in an industry that has begun to change rapidly. Marketing strategies have targeted loyal customers with discounts and incentives. New products are few and far between, and the upgrades of existing products have not introduced much in the way of innovation.

Company B has been around for less than two years and has amassed its debt by hiring and acquiring the best and brightest in the industry, and investing more heavily in research and development than you and Company A combined. The management team was hand-picked with the help of a successful industry insider and consultant. Company B has been aggressive in its pursuit of new business opportunities, and innovative in marketing its new product line, which according to rumours will set a new standard in the industry. Who is the threat? Without considering both the technical and personality components of the analysis, you are simply collecting data that may not provide you with the insights you need to analyse your competition effectively.

Business strategies are often developed in a framework that considers the financial position of the company and the corporate culture, which were discussed earlier, and the company's strengths and weaknesses in the key areas mentioned above.

The company analysis techniques that we discuss in this chapter include SWOT analysis, company profiling, ratio analysis, event analysis, patent analysis, personality profiling and merger analysis.

SWOT analysis
SWOT stands for strengths, weaknesses, opportunities and threats, and is a valuable tool that spans competitive intelligence, marketing and communications. It examines your competitors' strengths and weaknesses, and the opportunities and threats in your market.

There are many factors to consider for each variable in the SWOT analysis. The strengths are all the powerful attributes that an organization may possess. Some strengths to consider are:

- patents – quality and quantity;
- technology – owned or readily available;
- market share – current position (dominant or weak, for example) in the market;
- management expertise – who are the major decision-makers and what do they bring to the table?;
- financial position;
- customer loyalty; and
- quality of product or service – effective marketing, skilled employees, image.

Weaknesses are your competitors' liabilities or potential liabilities. They can take the form of:

- financial debt;
- unskilled workers;
- labour strife;
- poor image or visibility;
- inefficient production equipment or processes, or outdated technology;
- poor after-sales service;
- ineffective or minimal marketing;
- poor-quality products;
- lack of management experience or divisive management; and
- lack of customer loyalty.

There are as many different strengths and weaknesses as there are companies, but the above factors cover the major ones that should be considered during the analysis of a competitor. Analysis of strengths and weaknesses occurs at the corporate or business level, whereas opportunities and threats are analysed at the market or industry level, examining the favourable and unfavourable conditions that can impact on your organization's ability to compete.

Opportunity may take the shape of a new start-up in your industry that has innovative technology but lacks capital and business skills to take it to the next level. If the company's technology complements your line of business, perhaps a merger offer or a partnership would give your operation a competitive advantage. That same start-up, with a bucket of venture capital and a visionary management team, could be a threat to your position in the market. A regulatory change that impacts on your manufacturing process or licensing costs is another example of a threat that needs to be analysed, preferably before it is implemented.

Here are a few examples of opportunities that may affect your organization:

- government regulations or pending regulations that would aid a company;
- changing demographics that might assist a company in increasing its client/customer base;
- decreases in operating costs or materials costs;
- patent expirations (other companies').

These are examples of threats that may affect your organization:

- raw materials shortages;
- costly government regulations;
- increasing bank interest rates;
- new competitors.

There are many factors that need to be looked at to conduct an accurate and thorough SWOT analysis. These include: products; finances; technology; human resources; strategic alliances and partnerships; manufacturing or operations; marketing and sales; branding; and image.

When trying to predict the opportunities or threats that might arise, Larry Kahaner suggests that there are four main areas to look, as outlined in his book *Competitive Intelligence: From Black Ops to Boardrooms* (1996):

1. the company's public forecast;
2. industry experts' forecasts;
3. what the company's current or past actions indicate for the future; and
4. how the competitive environment will affect the company's future.

As part of the company's public forecast, mission statements are an excellent source of potentially valuable intelligence, which should not be overlooked. Often an organization creates mission statements at a time when it is in a shift or crisis. The resulting mission statement often reflects its perception of itself and its plans for the future. Typically you will also find information about company goals and philosophies contained in its mission statement as well. Always try to find out an organization's mission statement to determine where it is headed. These mission statements are often posted on Web sites or printed in annual reports or corporate capability brochures. If you are having trouble finding a company's mission statement, it may be under a different heading such as plans, vision and values, philosophies, goals or objectives. They come in many different lengths.

Kahaner also suggests following the industry analysts' predictions to learn about possible moves the industry as a whole might take. These may include stock market analysts, newsletter reporters, trade associations and labour unions.

Analysis of strengths, weaknesses, opportunities and threats in each of these departments of an organization is a valuable way to learn about a company or industry opportunities.

Company profiling
One of the most sought-after applications of competitive intelligence is a detailed description of a particular company. Due to the number of requests we had for this type of project, we developed a detailed technique, called 'company profiling', which we use to analyse a company's activities, operations or strategies. It entails examination of a company's background information, management, strategies, finances, operations, technology, marketing, sales, products and/or services, distribution, employees, R & D or engineering, and any other types of information we can dig up about a company. While conducting detailed research on a company is not new, analysing all the components of a company simultaneously creates an expansive picture of the company that might not otherwise have been obtained.

By researching all the functions of a company at the same time, we are often capable of analysing the company in greater detail. For example, if we learn that a company has a risk-taking management team that plans to implement some aggressive marketing and corporate strategies, but know that their finances are not in the best condition and that they are not very technologically astute, we may be able to deduce that this company could have difficulty in carrying out its grandiose plans.

Some of the best applications for this type of analysis include mergers, alliances, joint ventures and other partnership arrangements where companies need to know everything they can about the company in question.

See the accompanying box for a company profiling worksheet developed to ensure thorough research and analysis of each of the main aspects of the company being researched.

COMPANY PROFILE WORKSHEET

Company name
Address
Telephone number(s)
Toll-free number(s)
Fax number(s)
Web site address

Company background
History of the company (ie founding date, number of employees)
Key ownership of the company (ie company structure, key shareholders)
Key industry sector(s) the company is involved in
Perception of the company by media, customers, etc
Exchange on which securities are traded

Management information
Name and relevant background information of key corporate executives and
advisers – there are typically six levels of corporate executives and advisers to
consider in the management of a company:
1. president, chief executive officer (CEO), chief operations officer (COO),
   chief financial officer (CFO), chief marketing officer (CMO) an chief information officer (CIO);
2. senior or executive vice-president;
3. vice-president of operations, vice president of finance, vice-president of
   marketing, vice-president of informatics, etc;
4. board of directors;
5. legal adviser(s) – this may be a legal firm;
6. accounting adviser(s) – the person or company that audits the company's
   financial information.

Company strategy
Company's focus (past, present and future)
Corporate culture
New product developments
Market entry strategies/new markets
Mergers and/or alliances
Joint ventures

Financial information
Revenues
Profitability
Fixed costs
Variable costs
Debt
Captial
R & D expenditures

Operational information

Facility information
    Number of facilities
        Location
        Size
        Condition of facilities
        New/upcoming/expanding facilities
Technology used in operations
Operational output

Technology information

Types of technology used in each of the company's main functions Server and Web site information

Marketing information

Key markets served
Market share in each market
Marketing and advertising strategies
Market entry strategies
Customers/clients served in each market

Sales information

Number of people on sales force
Key sales channels
Customer service information
Sales force compensation methods
Major customers/clients

Product and/or service information

Major product lines
Minor product lines
Sales information by key product lines
Specifications on products
Suppliers of raw materials, parts, labour or intellectual capital

Distribution information

Supply chain used
Shipping methods
Suppliers

Employee information

Number of employees
Number of employees in major employment categories (ie marketing, human resources, accounting, etc)
Salaries of major employment groups
Union information/collective bargaining agreements
Subcontracting

R & D/engineering
Types of R & D
Number of R & D staff/contractors/Consultants
Types of engineering
Number of engineering staff/contractors/consultants
R & D/engineering budget

Other information
Specify

Ratio analysis

These analysis techniques are borrowed from bankers who quickly and effortlessly size up a company's financial strength and future using ratios. Some of these ratios include the current ratio, quick ratio, accounts receivable ratios, inventory turnover ratio, average days in inventory ratio, total debt to assets ratio, debt servicing ratio, debt to equity ratio and profitability ratios. Before you leave this chapter, thinking it was intended for accountants, keep reading. The ratios sound less palatable than they actually are. A general understanding of them now will be extremely valuable when you are analysing your competitors.

The current ratio indicates how liquid a company is. In other words, will it have sufficient money to pay its suppliers, contractors and other short-term debtors on time? The higher the ratio, the greater degree of liquidity a company has.

Current ratio

$$\text{Current ratio} = \frac{\text{current assets}}{\text{current liabilities}}$$

For example, if ABC Corporation has 750,000 euros in current assets and 500,000 euros in current liabilities, you would divide 750,000 euros by 500,000 euros to obtain 1.5 as the current ratio.

Quick ratio

The quick ratio (also called the acid-test ratio) is very similar to the current ratio, except that it considers that the company's inventory may be difficult to sell. It is a much stricter measure of liquidity of a company.

$$\text{Quick ratio} = \frac{\text{current assets} - \text{inventory}}{\text{current liabilities}}$$

Accounts receivable ratios

The accounts receivable ratio is an indicator of the quality of the organization's inventory – in other words, how quickly accounts receivables are collected and how quickly inventory is sold and payment received. By determining this and the average collection period a company has, you can determine how much pressure there is on the liquid position of the company and whether it will be forced to seek and rely on short-term loans.

$$\text{Accounts receivable turnover} = \frac{\text{total sales}}{\text{accounts receivable balance}}$$

$$\text{Average collection period} = \frac{365 \text{ days}}{\text{accounts receivable turnover}}$$

For example, if ABC Corporation has sales totalling 10,000,000 euros and its accounts receivable balance is currently at 1,000,000 euros, then you know that its annual sales are 10 times the amount of the outstanding receivables. This indicates that the cycle of sales and collection of receivables was repeated 10 times across the year. If you then divide 365 days in a year by 10, you can determine that it takes approximately 36.5 days to collect on each sale made by ABC Corporation, which is fairly good.

Inventory turnover ratio
Determining how quickly a company turns over its inventory is also a valuable financial indicator.

$$\text{Inventory turnover} = \frac{\text{sales}}{\text{inventory}} \quad \text{or} \quad \frac{\text{cost of goods sold}}{\text{inventory}}$$

The results of using these ratios can be very different based on the type of data you are using. Cost of goods sold is typically a more accurate representation of inventory turnover. If you further divide 365 days in a year by the inventory turnover, you can determine how many days on average inventory sits in a warehouse or store.

$$\text{Average days in inventory} = \frac{365 \text{ days}}{\text{inventory turnover}}$$

A competitor may be considering a huge inventory amongst its assets, yet if you can determine its inventory turnover to be extremely slow, then you can more realistically gauge its strength.

Total debt to assets ratio and debt servicing ratio
To determine a company's level of indebtedness, there are two main ratios to consider: total debt to assets ratio and the debt servicing ratio.

$$\text{Total debt to assets ratio} = \frac{\text{total debt}}{\text{total assets}}$$

$$\text{Debt servicing ratio} = \frac{\text{EBIT} + \text{depreciation}}{\text{Interest} + (\text{principal payments}/(1-t))}$$

where EBIT stands for earnings before interest and taxes and t stands for the marginal tax rate.

Debt to equity ratio

$$\text{Debt to equity ratio} = \frac{\text{long-term debt}}{\text{shareholders' equity}}$$

The best use for the debt to equity ratio is to get an understanding of a company's ability to generate new funds for financing its growth strategies. The larger the resulting number from the equation, the worse off the company is. The acceptable debt load to equity ratio differs between industries.

Profitability ratios
A competitor's profitability is an extremely important factor to understand to enable your organization to be more competitive. There are two main ratios used to determine profitability of a company. They are return on assets and return on equity.

$$\text{Return on assets} = \frac{\text{net income}}{\text{total assets}}$$

$$\text{Return on equity} = \frac{\text{net income}}{\text{total stockholders' equity}}$$

A healthy return on equity is approximately 20 per cent. However, these ratios vary from industry to industry, so be sure to determine the industry average before deciding if a company is reasonably profitable.

Event analysis
Monitoring the movements of a company and looking for competitively significant moves or events is an immensely valuable analysis tool, which we label 'event analysis'. It entails analysing past and current events within a company or marketplace to detect possible future events that may result in changes to your competitive position. For example, if a company signs a licensing agreement or memorandum of understanding with a foreign company, this is a 'red flag' that the company has expansion plans, either to a new market or for new technology or products. If a company purchases land, at some point in the near future it will probably build some facility or office on that property. If it acquires a company whose processes are outside the realm of its usual products or services, obviously it has plans to expand into other areas.

When a company books a significant block of advertisement space in trade or consumer publications, it might indicate a new product or service launch, or a new marketing strategy. If it advertises many new job listings, it may be embarking on expansion in a particular area of the company. For example, if a company advertises many new job listings in engineering, it probably has plans to design a new product or significantly change an existing one. If it plans to hire many new marketing people, the chances are it has a new or improved product or service already well under way and is about to promote it.

Event analysis from a historical perspective is often useful for illustrating why certain industries or industry players struggle with the changing nature of competition. Electrical utilities are a prime example. For decades, the electricity business was a relatively risk-free, stable and profitable industry. All this has changed in the last few years with concerted efforts by governments to deregulate energy markets. Competition, not surprisingly, has now become critical in developing a company's strategy. Strange as it sounds, thinking about competition was not always a vital aspect of conducting business in the electricity industry.

Deregulation is an event that creates opportunities and threats. In the case of the utilities, long-standing monopolies are being forced to compete by new rules. Strategies and motives, mergers and alliances, national and international competitors, and more demanding customers are all now key elements in business strategies. Players in the electricity industry are looking to diversify – whether it is in the form of selling off volatile power-generation operations to companies better able to manage the risk, or merging with natural gas companies. Utilities and other electricity businesses cannot ignore the increasingly competitive environment.

When analysing industries through event analysis, keep the historical perspective in mind when you conduct your competitive analysis. Where a company has come from may give you valuable insight, not only into where it is going, but how successful it may be in getting there.

Patent analysis

If you are trying to measure innovation and potential in a company, follow its patents and trademarks. Patents and trademarks can tell you which companies are assuming leadership roles or will take future leadership roles and which countries are at the cutting edge of technology. They can also tell you about strategic alliances between companies and the relationships between subsidiaries of the same parent corporation, maturity of technologies and the duration needed to exploit different types of technologies or innovations fully, where research and development funds are being spent, and individuals within organizations that are particularly innovative.

Personality profiling

Personality profiling is one of the most interesting ways to analyse a company and predict its future moves. It entails creating a profile of the key decision-makers to help predict the direction in which they will take the company. For example, it is very common to see a shift in corporate culture and priorities when a new CEO steps into the shoes of a previous leader, and is clearly looking to put his or her mark on the company.

People tend to have patterns in their attitudes and behaviours, which you can see if you look at their history and background. For example, a corporate executive who has a history of relying heavily on financial information and, more importantly, the bottom line will probably guide the company in the direction of its most profitable business units. Efforts will be directed to those units. An executive with a marketing background will continue to focus a lot of attention on the marketing of the company's products and services. Whatever has proved successful for a person will be a pattern that he or she continues. Conversely, whatever strategies failed probably will not be repeated again.

When trying to put together a personality profile of an executive, start by looking at the community newspapers of the towns or cities the person has lived in. Typically these papers include articles about their more successful residents. Each article on its own might not tell much about the personality of the person in question; however, when pieced together, they start to paint a picture and may expose some very apparent traits. Another way to start when creating a personality profile is to examine articles about the company as a whole to create a profile of its CEO or other very senior executives. Often these people make the decisions for the company, so their actions are reflected in the strategies and direction of the overall corporation.

You can gain valuable insight into someone's identity by examining his or her:

- childhood history (where the person was born, whether he or she was poor and what traits the parents might have imparted);
- education (where he or she studied, for how long and what the person has learnt outside of school);
- work history (how the person handled situations that arose in his or her previous job, what types of organizations he or she has worked for and whether it was in the private or public sector);
- current lifestyle (how the person spends his or her time and money);
- goals and objectives (what drives the person and whether he or she appears to be conservative in approach to reaching goals or whether he or she is driven by instinct).

Also consider body language and gestures when analysing a personality. These may be evident during speeches or television interviews. Some analysts also examine the handwriting of a person, using graphology to determine a person's identity.

Merger analysis
What if your organization is looking to acquire or merge with another one? What would you do? Take a few tips from the king of acquisitions, also known as John Chambers, the President and CEO of Cisco Systems. He cites five things that he looks for when analysing the prospects of acquiring a particular company, according to a recent interview in *Business 2.0*:

1. shared vision of where the industry is heading and similar or complementary roles each company wants to play in it;
2. short-term gains for acquired employees who may be uncomfortable during times of merger or acquisition;
3. long-term strategy wins for the shareholders, employees, customers and business partners;

4. similar cultures and chemistry; and
5. geographic proximity, particularly for large acquisitions.

If a deal does not meet at least three of the above criteria, Cisco will not touch it. If it even has four, there is some scepticism. For Chambers, meeting all five of the above criteria makes for a successful acquisition candidate.

Daimler's Jurgen Schrempp and Chrysler's Robert Eaton might disagree with the necessity for similar cultures and geographic proximity. Their merger to form Daimler Chrysler was an atypical union. Considered by some to be competitors and unlikely candidates to join forces, their merger has been highly successful, despite the Atlantic Ocean between them and the differing cultures between Germany and the United States, both at a social and corporate level. This merger is discussed in greater detail in Chapter 14.

The best and most successful forms of analysis incorporate more than one technique before drawing conclusions. For example, if you consider the strengths and weaknesses together with the capabilities of a competitor, you will have a picture of what that company is capable of doing. If, at the same time, you analyse the corporate culture and management personalities of the competitor, you will have an understanding of the ways the competitor will act within the industry. Not only will you know what it can do, you will know what it will do. One without the other would create an incomplete picture.

Consider the case of Pointcast, the 'push technology' that allows online subscribers to indicate the news they would like to receive from numerous sources. Users simply launch Pointcast on their computers and the application brings the news to their desks. Soon after push technology appeared in the marketplace, it was 'all the rage'. Yet the technology never took off the way 'experts' anticipated. In fact, very early in its existence Pointcast turned down a multi-million dollar offer and assistance from a much larger and wealthier firm to market the technology itself. Years later, Pointcast was bought for a fraction of the earlier bid. If you had been competing with Pointcast, it would have been critical to have examined the company's aggressive 'I'll do it alone' management style, as well as its capacity to turn the technology into the phenomenon it could have been. If you had analysed both concurrently, you would have recognized that, while Pointcast was aggressive in its approach, it lacked sufficient human and financial resources and business savvy to make push technology the household (and business) name it could have been. Your conclusion would have been not to worry about Pointcast as a threat.

Analysis is the lifeblood of competitive intelligence. Without it, there is only information or knowledge; with it, data, information and knowledge are miraculously transformed into intelligence. Companies that conduct strong analysis will see the fruits of their labours in the form of competitive advantage. In the intelligence age, strong analysis skills will be instrumental to an intelligent organization's success. Analysts who master these skills will become the intelligence innovators of this age.

Reading 6.2

Taken from **Knowledge management by Nigel Ghent**, in
The Growing Business Handbook **edited by Richard Willsher
and Adam Jolly (2000)**

The vertical leap

What does it take to compete at Internet speed? Business strategies based on calculated and gradual growth are quickly giving way to a new model – the vertical leap.

As market forces, competitive strategies and customer buying patterns become less predictable, companies are reinventing themselves to handle virtually instant growth and change. Sustained success – indeed, even survival – will come to those with the infrastructure and expertise to navigate through multiple and successive vertical leaps.

In just a year of operation, it is not uncommon for an Internet business to find itself managing more data than some of the world's largest banks have accumulated over the course of many years. To succeed, they have to leap within a few months to a fully-grown, mature and stable information infrastructure.

More traditional businesses have faced equally daunting challenges in the past. For example, the day after Citibank moved in with ATMs, banks across Japan were forced to deal with around-the-clock competition. Within 24 hours, these businesses were blind-sided by a competitive dimension for which they were ill prepared.

The ability to vertically leap multiple levels rather than move gradually through one business model change at a time rests squarely on a solid, yet agile information infrastructure with several key attributes:

- Firstly, the infrastructure must be information-centric, focusing on and ensuring that information is accessible and available all day, every day.
- Secondly, it must be virtual – omnipresent, yet unobtrusive, adaptable and capable of hiding complexity.
- Thirdly, it must be future-oriented, balancing structure and flexibility to meet unexpected and constantly changing requirements while providing a solid foundation for ever-growing information flows within and outwith the enterprise.
- Finally, it must be instant, making the access to, recovery and management of information fast and efficient.

Infusing these attributes into your company's information infrastructure will transform it from a mere blueprint for connecting existing information technologies into a dynamic web of information tying together your intellectual capital, knowledge tools, core technologies and external data sources (customers, suppliers and partners). This new information infrastructure will enable you to move away from horizontal connections, from always playing catch-up with new application requirements, from analysing what has happened, to proactively and accurately assessing future needs, to being constantly prepared, to leaping vertically and confidently into uncharted vistas.

New guidelines for selecting vertical leap-ready storage

So, where do you start? The most important decision in the creation of the new infrastructure is the storage platform – the dynamic source, the constantly flowing fountain of information, keeping the web of intellectual capital, tools and technologies alive and growing in value. These are the new guidelines for selecting storage that renders the infrastructure capable of handling the vertical leap:

- Universal connectivity to users – anywhere, anytime.
- Adaptive design.
- Embedded intelligence.
- Solution integration and support.

Case study: Jordan

The Jordan motor-racing team must take a vertical leap almost weekly.

The team generates a wealth of data for its engineers to comb through in order to evaluate both car and driver performance. Data from the limited number of practice laps allowed on the Friday before each Formula 1 race are transmitted to Jordan's headquarters at the Silverstone racetrack in England. There, engineers can continually replay laps and, based on the performance, change the parameters of the car.

'That's why on a Sunday, if you come to the Grand Prix, you'll see that our performance increases quite a few seconds per lap,' says Mark Gallagher, Jordan's Director of Marketing. 'EMC has brought us something very tangible that makes us more competitive.'

EMC is a leading player in the rapidly growing market for intelligent enterprise storage systems, software and services.

The Jordan team, like thousands of enterprises around the globe moving at Internet speed, relies on EMC for the edge it needs to move its business ahead and win.

With vertical leap-ready storage from EMC behind them, the Jordan team celebrated its most successful season ever in 1999.

The Jordan team depends on EMC to make it competitive in an environment in which every thousandth of a second counts. EMC Enterprise Storage has allowed the team to create an E-Infostructure unmatched in Formula 1 racing. The unconventional decision to put storage, not servers, at the heart of Jordan's IT infrastructure, gives the team an advantage over its rivals.

'EMC has already solved several fundamental information flow problems for us, enabling our engineers and technicians to manage more efficiently the data our cars generate while on track,' says Eddie Jordan, Chairman of Jordan Grand Prix.

Gallagher notes that speed to market is very important to Jordan. 'If our engineers come up with a technical innovation which can shave a fraction of a second per lap, then we want to see that on the Formula 1 car not in six months' time, but at the next race next weekend. If we weren't getting the right information at the right time it could lead to the wrong decisions being made and that could cost us a victory.'

And what is victory in a Grand Prix worth to Jordan? According to Gallagher the figure is in the region of $20 million to $30 million.

Case study: Mail.com

Mail.com, Inc., a leading Internet messaging provider, is building a large-scale, cutting-edge EMC Enterprise Storage Network (ESN) that will enable it to manage its rapid growth, provide streamlined management of expanding information assets and deliver exceptional web site availability and performance.

Charles Walden, Mail.com's Executive Vice-President, Technology, comments, 'Our customer base has rocketed from one million to over seven million in the last 12 months. Our EMC Enterprise Storage Network will help us maintain our high-quality service by ensuring we remain operational during this exceptional growth. With EMC Enterprise Storage Network as our core infrastructure, Mail.com can scale easily – cost-efficiently supporting large increases in online storage requirements.'

Mail.com has purchased 27 terabytes of EMC Symmetrix Enterprise Storage – the equivalent of nearly seven billion electronic mail messages – and is also implementing a suite of EMC software.

'EMC is operating on an entirely new level by providing real, open solutions that transform our vision of unsurpassed flexibility and growth into a reality,' says Walden. 'The truly centralised information management significantly reduces the complexity and costs of managing our growing infrastructure. EMC's storage management software tools let us move storage to those applications that need it the most today and change it around tomorrow if necessary.'

© Kogan Page, 2000

7

Identifying and addressing issues

INTRODUCTION

Before 1983 all vacuum cleaners worked by picking up dirt by air suction through a filter bag. The person usually credited with the invention of the vacuum cleaner is Ives W McGaffey who obtained a patent in 1869. To clean a carpet in this manner is still referred to as hoovering after W H Hoover, an early businessman associated with vacuum cleaner technology. In fact Hoover's early partner, James Murray Spangler took his version of a vacuum cleaner to Hoover, who at the time had a leather manufacturing company, to produce it. Spangler died in 1915. If he had lived longer we may well have talked about spangling instead of hoovering.

James Dyson, a British inventor, introduced a radically different vacuum machine, the Dyson Dual Cyclone. Instead of relying on air suction his machine used centrifugal force to pick up dirt. According to Dyson, his system experiences no loss of suction, whereas for conventional bag systems, as more dirt is picked up, over time suction is reduced.

Dyson have a Web site at www.dyson.com/ where you can learn more about James Dyson, and his inventions such as the Ballbarrow and the Dual Cyclone. For a brief history of the early years of vacuum cleaners the Web site www.designmaker.com/vacuums/vachist2.htm provides a good introduction.

Imagine the arguments and debate that must have taken place and still are taking place at conventional vacuum cleaning companies such as Hoover and Electrolux as

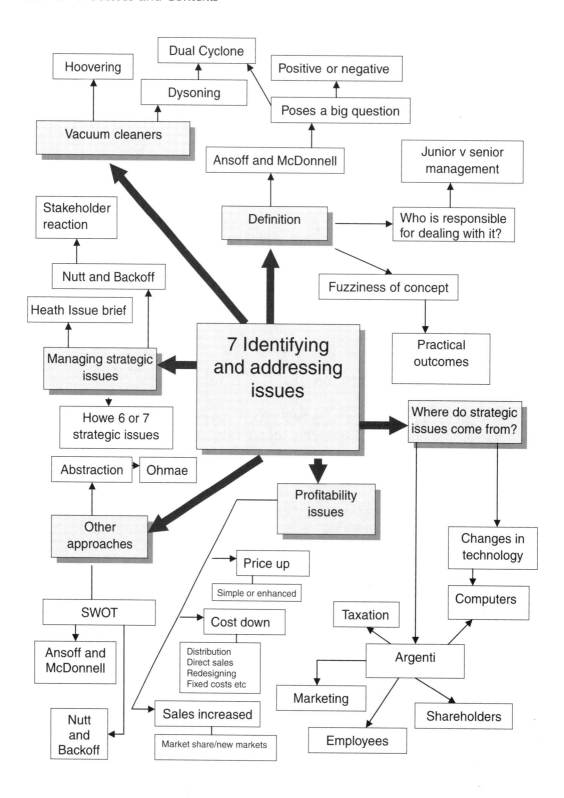

Dyson's machines capture more and more of the vacuum cleaner market. Should the other companies abandon their existing technology and go over to the new one, with all the problems of patents that Dyson holds for his system; or should they continue with their existing technology and try to improve it further? The introduction of the Dual Cyclone was a strategic issue facing them. If not successfully resolved it had the potential to seriously damage their vacuum cleaning business.

WHAT IS A STRATEGIC ISSUE?

A strategy might be linked to a performance gap, a strategic issue, or a challenge. In this chapter we focus on strategic issues. Every organization has strategic issues. Ansoff and McDonnell (1990: 369) define a strategic issue as 'a forthcoming development, either inside or outside of the organization, which is likely to have an important impact on the ability of the enterprise to meet its objectives'. An issue is not necessarily a bad thing. We cannot equate strategic issues solely with developments that are threats or represent increasing internal weakness. Strategic issues can also be developments that are opportunities or represent a growth in strength. A strategic issue is, therefore, something positive or negative that poses a big question about the organization's future level of success or even its survival. We can also say that strategic issues offer the analytical and creative bridge needed to move from an organization's strategic vision of its desired future to the courses of action selected to bring about that future.

In practice managers face the difficulty of moving from an ill-defined concern to a precise statement of the strategic issue that can be addressed by management action. However, not all concerns are really strategic issues. Organizations on a daily basis face many problems but only a few of these can be classed as strategic issues. Clearly the success of the Dual Cyclone has meant that traditional vacuum cleaning manufacturers are faced with a strategic issue. What should they do? Often changes in technology present established firms with such challenges. Before hand-held electronic calculators appeared, calculations were often done by slide rules, and unless you are now in your mid-30s or older, you will probably have little idea what a slide rule is and how it worked. Not only do technological changes challenge organizations. So do other things. Being able to filter out those problems that require a tactical, that is, short-term and immediate response and those that require a more long-term strategic response is complex. It can be quite easy to confuse mainly tactical and operational issues with strategic ones and vice versa. There is no one definition of what counts as a strategic issue but one definition would be 'a strategic issue is a problem that stands in the way of an organization achieving its strategic goals and requires action to be taken to overcome it'.

Another way to think about strategic issues as opposed to other issues facing an organization is to ask who is responsible for dealing with the issue. If the answer is senior management then the issue is much more likely to be a strategic issue. If, on the other hand, it is management at lower levels then the problem may well not be strategic in nature. Even these definitions are pretty fuzzy. It is not easy to come up with a cast-iron definition. What is important is not to worry too much about coming up with a cast-iron definition and acting upon it but to assess carefully the issue facing the organization. From this preliminary analysis it should be possible to work out who should deal with the issue and at what level. Remember it is the practical consequences of your actions that count – a typical pragmatic response to this type of definitional dilemma. You need to concentrate on the practical outcomes of considering the issue to be strategic and then weigh them up against the consequences of considering an issue not to be strategic. From this you should be able to get sufficient insight into the problem to set in motion the business of resolving it, at the appropriate level and in a suitable way.

WHERE DO STRATEGIC ISSUES COME FROM?

Technological changes can easily become strategic issues for an organization. Technology changes at an ever-increasing pace in the modern world. Above we looked at the way Dyson's invention is changing the market for vacuum cleaners and the way slide rule manufacturers were more or less completely wiped out by electronic calculators. As you read this book you might like to reflect whether the Internet will make book technology redundant and very soon you will be reading, if that is the right word, books on or via the Internet. E-commence and e-business are threatening to rewrite the rules on how commerce and business is transacted.

We have identified external technological developments as a major source of strategic issues for organizations. However, if we go back to Ansoff and McDonnell's definition of a strategic issue, then we can suggest that there are many sources of strategic issues, some internal to an organization and some external. According to Argenti (1989) the issues may be in the marketing area but they may occur in relation to the employees, shareholders, computers, tax, and so on. Some writers on strategic management have drawn attention to the way that issues once considered a matter of PR now need to be handled in a more integrated way with business planning. Heath (1997: 17) cited a survey of 400 public affairs personnel showed that many of them 'assisted in issues identification, monitoring, and analysis' and that they 'provided information for the strategic business planning group'. One PR area that seems to be steadily becoming more and more important each year is environmental management and sustainable development (Welford, 2000). Social and ethical issues of sustainable development may soon commonly be seen as marketing issues on the issue agenda of large organizations.

IDENTIFYING PROFITABILITY ISSUES

A management decision to identify the strategic issues that need sorting out might be triggered by a business becoming unprofitable. A detailed analysis of the business will probably be needed to pinpoint the real cause of the lack of profitability. The analysis can be guided by asking diagnostic questions (Ohmae, 1982). What would be the starting point for a set of diagnostic questions about a business experiencing a lack of profitability? The profitability of a business is a function of pricing decisions, cost, and sales volume. So the first set of diagnostic questions might be:

- Can the price of the product (or service) be increased?
- Can the costs of the product (or service) be reduced?
- Can the volume of sales be increased?

Depending on the answer to these questions, further diagnostic questions can be posed. If the price can be increased the questions might be:

- Can there be a simple price increase?
- Can the product (or service) be enhanced and the price increased by more than any cost increase?

If the issue is a cost issue, there are other diagnostic questions:

- Can changing the distribution channels reduce distribution costs?
- Can changing to direct sales reduce distribution costs?
- Can redesigning the product (or service) to a lower specification bring down costs?
- Can fixed costs be cut?
- Can changing suppliers reduce costs?
- Can the cost caused by poor quality work be eliminated?
- Can reducing downtime increase productivity?

A positive answer to the question of whether sales volume might be increased can lead to yet another set of diagnostic questions:

- Can we increase our share of the current market we compete in?
- Can we find a new market for our goods and services?

If it is possible to increase the company's share of a current market, the issue might be narrowed down to a very specific one:

- Can we improve customer satisfaction by improving the product (or service)?
- Can we improve our sales activities?
- Can we use advertising and PR to increase consumer awareness of our product (or service)?
- Can a change in pricing increase our market share?

Ohmae (1982) suggests that this narrowing down of the issue is extremely useful. Applying this type of approach may mean managers end up with specific ideas for action to address the profitability issue. This general approach is presumably applicable to any kind of issue – not just profitability.

OTHER APPROACHES

The use of a SWOT analysis to identify strategic issues is possibly the easiest approach – it can be very straightforward. Every item listed as a strength, weakness, threat, or opportunity may be treated as a strategic issue (Ansoff and McDonnell, 1990). For example, it is a strategic issue if there is a threat or opportunity posed by the environment. The organization needs to decide on the right strategic action either to handle the threat or seize the opportunity. Even a strength or weakness could be considered a strategic issue. If there is strength and it is not being fully exploited then this implies missed opportunities. If there is a weakness and it is not being corrected then there is an issue about when it becomes a real source of vulnerability. In each case there is an implication for the degree of success and achievement managed by the organization. If a SWOT is used to identify strategic issues there is a need to rank them in order of importance otherwise managers will be faced by more issues than they can tackle.

Ohmae (1982) has suggested an abstraction process that is useful for enabling large numbers of managers to contribute their experience and insights to a SWOT analysis. A sample of managers in a large organization, for example, can be interviewed or surveyed to obtain their perceptions of the weaknesses of the organization in relation to its main rivals. This can produce a long list of competitive disadvantages as perceived by the organization's managers. Next, grouping all the similar or related disadvantages reduces the long list to a shorter one. Finally, by studying each of the groupings of disadvantages the organization seeks to establish the precise nature of the issue. It is possible that at this stage the organization should be looking for the underlying cause of the group of competitive disadvantages.

The abstraction process lends itself to a participatory process and many managers (and employees) can be deliberately involved on the basis of it. However, perhaps all approaches might be done in a way that involved large numbers of people. For example, could workshops be held to brainstorm strengths and weaknesses, opportunities and threats? This exercise does not have to be done by analytically-minded specialists.

MANAGING STRATEGIC ISSUES

The first thing to say about managing strategic issues is that it might be best to design a separate process for analysing and addressing strategic issues alongside the strategic planning cycle. This allows the organization to react more promptly to unexpected events through its issue management system.

It is important, however, that strategic issue management is placed within the context of the strategic vision or strategic goals of the organization that are handled through a planning cycle. When issues are addressed and, in successful cases, solved this should take the organization towards its strategic vision or fulfilment of its strategic goals.

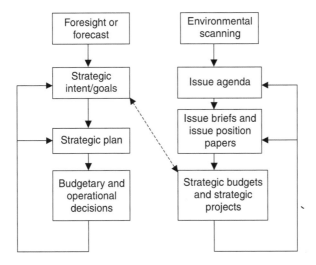

Figure 7.1 Strategic planning and issue management

Senior managers are responsible for identifying strategic issues. If they identify a large number of strategic issues facing their organization, then it becomes necessary to decide which ones will receive attention. Howe (1997) considers that six or seven strategic issues are probably the most that an organization can address, but he even suggests that concentrating on three or four might be better. This implies a key process for management – forming a strategic issue agenda by selecting the top three to eight issues to address. Consulting stakeholders and researching the impact of the issues may help managers do this. In making the final selection of issues to go on the issue agenda a management team may cast their votes and then rank the issues in order of importance by the votes cast. The point here is that management commitment and attention to strategic issues has limits and it is normally critical that the most serious issues are handled first. However, there may be occasions when management teams choose to deal with easier issues first because, for example, they are learning to work together and need some successes to gain legitimacy in the eyes of people in their organization.

Senior management may assign responsibility for strategic issues to *ad hoc* groups or operational units who are then required to report to senior management. The managers concerned are then responsible for analysing the issue and managing its resolution. The managers in the *ad hoc* groups and operational units need to use analytical skills and creativity when formulating a response to an issue. It is often a good idea for the managers to think about what particular strengths or competencies their organization has and try to exploit them to resolve the issue favourably. There are instances when managers will have to consider, though, working on a weakness to counter a threat.

Nutt and Backoff (1992) have provided probably the most thorough treatment of how to identify and solve strategic issues, and then how to plan the implementation of strategic actions to solve the issues based on links to a SWOT analysis. They advise managers to think of strategic actions that relate to the strategic issue and that simultaneously relate to a SWOT analysis. So as well as addressing the issue, the actions considered should build on strengths, or overcome weaknesses, or exploit opportunities, or block threats. Their approach emphasizes creativity and they recommend brainstorming and other techniques. This is not the place to explore implementation in any great detail, but we can note that they place great store on the politics of strategic change, drawing attention to such matters as the construction and maintenance of coalitions for change. Their techniques reflect a need to pay careful attention to, and manage, stakeholder reactions to proposals for strategic action. They suggest that stakeholders can be analysed in terms of their position and importance. Obviously important but antagonistic stakeholders are a high priority for efforts at stakeholder management.

Researching issues, analysis, and planning responses probably ought to be handled systematically. This may be achieved through the use of a system of 'issue briefs' and 'issue position papers'. The structure of an issue brief is relatively logical. The issue brief should define and explain the issue, explore the options, clarify the nature and timing of the consequences of the issue for the organization, and look at the positions of stakeholders in relation to the issue. Heath (1997) describes the issue brief as a 'thinking document'. It is the basis for an issue position paper that sets out how the organization will handle the issue.

CONCLUSIONS

Strategic issues are external or internal developments that have major impacts on the ability of the organization to achieve its strategic vision or strategic goals. Some people see strategic issues and their management as central to the process of strategic management. In analytical and creative terms, managers can use strategic issues to decide on courses of action to bring about the organization's strategic vision or strategic goals. This chapter has concentrated on the analysis of strategic issues but has also provided an introduction to strategic issue management. This has involved some references to the importance of forming strategic issue agendas, using analysis and creativity, and planning implementation so as to facilitate stakeholder management.

QUESTIONS

1. What are the strategic issues facing Nissan or J D Wetherspoon? (Use the case studies to identify and comment on each issue.)
2. What sort of questions do you need to ask to investigate why a business is performing poorly?
3. Our small bakery owner has just learnt that a large supermarket with an in-house bakery is about to open two miles away. What diagnostic questions does the owner need to ask?
4. What would be your SWOT analysis of the Body Shop? (Use the case study.)
5. Sketch out how you would organize senior management to deal with the strategic issues facing an organization. What role, if any, would issue briefs and issue position papers play in this?
6. What role should stakeholders play in strategic issue identification and resolution? You may like to think of the issues raised in the Manchester United case study. Alternatively the Shell case raises issues about stakeholder identification in relations to big environmental issues and how Shell tried to deal with them.

EXECUTIVE EXERCISE

Think about the organization where you work. Try to identify up to eight strategic issues that are particularly important. List the issues.

Issues

1.

2.

3.

4.

5.

6.

7.

8.

Now think about possible links between the issues. Are any items on the list caused by any other items on the list? Draw a map of the issues showing the cause and effect relations between issues with arrows. Does the map suggest that any of the strategic issues you have identified are of critical importance and need priority attention?

If you are working in a group, discuss your list of strategic issues with others in the group and see how much overlap there is in the group members' lists. Also discuss how top priority issues are best identified.

REFERENCES

Ansoff, H I and McDonnell, E (1990) *Implanting Strategic Management*, Prentice Hall, London

Argenti, J (1989) *Practical Corporate Planning*, Routledge, London

Heath, R L (1997) *Strategic Issues Management*, Sage, London

Howe, F (1997) *The Board Member's Guide to Strategic Planning*, Jossey-Bass, San Francisco

Nutt, P C and Backoff, R W (1992) *Strategic Management of Public and Third Sector Organizations*, Jossey-Bass, San Francisco

Ohmae, K (1982) *The Mind of the Strategist*, McGraw-Hill, London

Welford, R (2000) *Corporate Environmental Management 3: Towards sustainable development*, Kogan Page, London

Reading 7.1

Taken from Chapter 2 – Social and ethical issues for sustainable development, in *Corporate Environmental Management 3* by Richard Welford (2000)

The ethical dimension is central to doing business in a way which is consistent with sustainable development. Here it is argued that social and environmental issues are a subset of business ethics and that by considering the structures and procedures which define the ethics of a company we ought to be able to say something about the prospects and preconditions for improvement. Traditionally, business ethics were often seen as a topic which was of little concern to the day-to-day operations of business, where the emphasis was often on maximizing profits without being overtly antisocial. In the 1990s in Western economies and some developing countries a range of stakeholders began to demand greater accountability on the part of business and, more specifically, called for businesses to act in more honest, open and transparent ways.

Nevertheless an emphasis on ethical ways of doing business as a core factor in a business' strategic plans is still unusual. Moreover, the study of ethics is not even that common in the business schools which are supposed to train and educate the managers of the future. Within the social sciences we have seen the study of political economy, for example, replaced by economic science and positive economics, and this has placed an emphasis on theories of optimization rather than sustainability at the firm level. To begin to tackle the challenges of sustainable development we must begin to redress this balance. Western economies have developed along particular paths with an emphasis on industrial growth, efficiency (defined in narrow monetary terms) and performance (usually defined by profits and increases in share prices). The politics of the 1980s that were associated with Thatcherism and Reaganism led to the common cry that 'there is no alternative' and the development of a narrow, profit-centred corporate ethic. In the 1990s a few well-publicized cases of unethical practices led to a number of embarrassments for 'blue chip' companies, but in the new millennium we can expect to see businesses held more and more accountable for their actions. The information society, in which people have increasing access to both 'official and 'unofficial' information about companies and their activities, will make the internal workings of well known companies much more transparent, and this will mean that they are increasingly unlikely to be able to hide unacceptable practices in the name of profit maximization.

It seems obvious, therefore, that social responsibility and environmental considerations can no longer be ignored in the context of an ethical (and indeed efficient) approach to doing business. Hartley (1993), for example, suggests that the interests of a firm are actually best served by scrupulous attention to the public interest and by seeking a trusting relationship with the various stakeholders with which a firm is involved. In the process, society is also best served because the firm is forced to consider a whole range of competing objectives and to move away from activities which are derived from short-term performance indicators. These various stakeholders which the firm must consider are its customers, suppliers, employees, shareholders, the financial institutions, local communities and government. The stakeholder concept stresses the idea that a company has responsibilities to all these groups (even though they will have unequal amounts of power) and will be involved in balancing the often competing demands put upon it. A company's ethical stance will be influenced therefore both by internal values and by pressures exerted on it from external sources.

Defining the ethics of business

The starting point must be to provide a definition of business ethics. This is difficult, because it will depend on both the values of the individuals working in the organization – particularly on the culture created by the individual ethics of senior management – and on any codes of conduct which formally exist within the organization or standards adopted from external agencies. We do not observe one single ethical code in all parts of society, but different codes in different places and at different times, and this is replicated within any business. However, we can distinguish between 'personal value systems' which individuals will bring to the workplace and a 'formal business code' which may exist in some businesses through an explicit set of rules (Burke et al. 1993). Perhaps more importantly, however, we ought to think about the 'actual value system', which is the moral climate experienced by staff in their daily business lives and which determines the behaviour of the firm as a whole, and a 'necessary value system', which is the minimum level of ethics (often equated with legal requirements) which has to exist for the firm to survive.

In a pluralistic society, social, cultural and organizational power structures will tend to interact with these value systems. Such interaction may bring about a consensus or norm in certain areas of business activity, but it may also result in conflict where the ultimate outcome will depend crucially on the balance of power. One of the phenomena we have seen in the last few years is a shift of some of that power towards the consumer and the general public, and this has renewed the interest in business ethics and corporate responsibility.

Another issue which causes problems for those advocating stronger codes of business ethics is that not all desirable ethics are mutually consistent. In those circumstances, judgements have to be made based on valuing different ethical actions. This too is a significant source of conflict. Again though, outcomes will be determined by power structures and dominant ideologies will tend to arise. Such ideologies are nevertheless often a product of compromise and may not necessarily be first-best solutions. This is particularly apparent when we compare the conduct of those companies that are implementing environmental management strategies with the imperatives called for by the concept of sustainable development (Welford, 1993).

The study of business ethics is not new. In the 19th century Utilitarian reformers highlighted the need for ethical principles to be part of the free enterprise system. Currently, the literature on business ethics and on ethics generally is vital and growing. A key issue, however, is that there are many dilemmas where major principles, held to be moral imperatives, can be incompatible in some circumstances. There must exist therefore some sort of hierarchy which places more emphasis on one principle than on another. What we are clearly observing nowadays is the movement of social and environmental considerations up that hierarchy.

Ultimately, however, it is organization which dictates the hierarchy of different principles. The various levels of organization, from whole economic and political systems via institutions and organizations to individual relationships, suggest particular hierarchies of principles (Donaldson, 1989). These hierarchies obviously shift over time and between different economic and political systems. They can be influenced, although that, in turn, will depend on power relationships. Many principles of business ethics might be considered somewhat abstract. A key issue, therefore, is how commonly accepted principles (such as improved environmental performance at the firm level) can be translated into practice. This has to be done via codes (legal and self-regulatory), education, communication and information. But these vehicles for change are themselves open to manipulation by those with power and the best principles are not always translated into best practice. Increasingly, for example, people are agreeing with the principle of sustainable development, but the vehicles for translating that into business practice have stopped far short of real sustainable solutions.

Because language is the basis of communication, it plays a crucial part in the translation of a principle into practice. Commonly, one person's technical term is another person's jargon. Again, the whole concept of sustainable development has come to mean a number of different things to different people. Terms such as sustainability, sustainable growth, sustained growth, sustainable development and sustaining organizations have become confused. Commonly they are associated with environmentalism, and key concepts such as social responsibility, equity and futurity are sidelined. Moreover, when ethical outcomes are discussed, words such as moral, ethical, good, efficient, rational, effective, fair, best and improved, all come to mean different things in different circumstances. The meanings, connotations and overtones of words and phrases are often deployed in the conflicts and struggles for supremacy. The language of management is rich in emotive and ideological content and therefore what companies and managers say they are doing must be treated with healthy scepticism. What they are actually doing, assessed against clearly defined principles and measures, is much more important. Hence in communicating their message about environmental performance, companies must be open and honest and not be tempted along the road of self-gratification and overstatement which we so often observe.

According to Donaldson (1989) there has been a relative neglect of the systematic handling of values in business, which has been self-conscious. The consequences of the neglect can be seen both in anxiety about industrial performance in the West and a rise in concern about moral or ethical issues. A patchy awareness of the problem is to be seen in the sporadic (and at times piecemeal) nature of attempts by governments to regulate industry. This is well illustrated by the uneven growth in environmental legislation in the West and the continued growth of ad hoc codes of conduct in this area.

All organizations operate an ethical code, whether they know it or not. This may not be consistent at all times, but it is based on codes of conduct which are embedded into company culture and through the actions and decisions of senior management. Those codes will also be influenced by society's norms and in the business world by institutions and practices which stress the need to create wealth measured in quantitative financial terms. For any business which wishes to survive or avoid hostile takeover, the system necessarily pushes profits to the top of the corporate agenda and pushes other issues, such as social responsibility and environmental protection, down the agenda.

Moreover, there is no business practice, action or statement that cannot have an ethical dimension. Businesses serve a variety of purposes for different stakeholders. Therefore we might argue that as a necessary condition, business activities are justifiable only in so far as they can be shown to meet the legitimate requirements of stakeholders. However, these requirements can be and often are in conflict, and can change over time. In identifying requirements and reconciling them, we have major problems. Moreover, we have suggested that the principles, ideals and moral values upon which stakeholders' requirements are based can be in themselves contradictory. The traditional way of resolving these issues is for the firm to assume primacy over individuals, allowing it to pursue objectives which are dictated by senior management and subject to financial constraints imposed by owners and lenders. Thus firms often adopt their own identity and culture, and often exist outside the democratic framework. But we must realize that business ought to be a means and not an end, and it is a means for satisfying the requirements of all who have a legitimate claim.

It might be argued that any philosophy or course of action that does not take the public interest into consideration is intolerable in today's society (Hartley, 1993). Today's firms face more critical scrutiny from stakeholders and operate in a setting which is becoming more regulatory and litigious. The notion of public trust is also becoming more important. A clear measure of how far we have come towards a more responsive and responsible business climate is indicated by the fact that if a firm violates public trust, it is likely to be surpassed by its competitors who will be eager to please customers by addressing their wants more accurately. Moreover, while the overwhelming majority of business dealings are non-controversial, any abuses increasingly receive considerable publicity, harming the image of business. NGOs are also increasingly powerful in societies where individuals have more access to information. Media such as the Internet provide a relatively cheap means for NGOs to highlight what they might see as the abuses of power of large TNCs, for example. This phenomenon is not restricted to the West, however, and often it operates in developing countries, where NGOs have been successful in embarrassing large firms that have traditionally paid little regard to social and environmental conditions.

In order to remain economically active, firms need to learn from their mistakes or from those of other firms. They need to take care to avoid situations and actions that might harm their relationship with their various stakeholders. In the worst of all cases, where a firm faces a catastrophe suddenly and without warning, its whole market image and business strategy can be destroyed. Examples of such events are increasingly commonplace. For example, in the case of Union Carbide, when one of its chemical plants in Bhopal, India, leaked 40 tons of toxic chemicals, the event had (and still has) a profound effect on the reputation of that company. Although the company quickly rushed aid to the victims, it was bitterly condemned for complacency and the loose controls that permitted the accident to happen in the first place. Other companies such as Shell have had their image tarnished by their activities in places such as Nigeria, and have been forced to reconsider their whole approach to social, environmental and ethical issues.

Environmental considerations are only one of the many issues that might be included under the umbrella of business ethics. It is nevertheless an issue which has grown in importance. As a result of the many accidents and growing environmental damage caused by firms, there have been increasing demands from consumers for firms to operate more ethically in this area. The consumer movement has shaped and contributed fundamentally to the significant increase in legislation and regulation at all levels of government. This has been aimed at preventing abuses in the marketplace and the environment, and therefore environmental management strategies are increasingly commonplace in the leading companies around the world. To date, however, environmental considerations have not been given enough attention within the framework of business ethics because dominant ideologies are being shaped more by short-term financial considerations than by the need to do business in a sustainable way. Increasingly, it is social issues which are also being seen as important to stakeholders and, although even more difficult to define, control and quantify, these issues will be increasingly important to firms that wish to project a positive profile of their activities.

Codes of conduct and standards

Although there has been an increasing amount of regulation covering a range of environmental issues, the European Union's intent within its Fifth Environmental Action Plan has been to put more and more emphasis on market-based and voluntary measures. Coupled with this, deregulation measures, introduced by more right-wing governments to appease industry, have been seen in some European countries and have meant even more emphasis being put on voluntary codes of conduct and standards. Of course, it was industry itself which lobbied for the European ecomanagement and audit scheme to be voluntary when the first draft suggested that it might be mandatory for the worst polluting industries. Codes of conduct such as the International Chamber of Commerce and World Business Council's Charter on Sustainable Development, and standards such as ISO14001, have certainly had a significant impact on the environmental profile and practices of companies, but they too have not been without their critics. They provide a framework for businesses to implement their own systems, plans and targets, but the underlying motivations for adopting such codes and standards are not always so clear and questions have been raised as to whether they go far enough down the road of sustainable development. The design and definition of voluntary codes and standards are therefore important to consider.

Codes of conduct defined within an organization or imported from elsewhere in the form of standards are usually associated with practical sets of rules and guidelines. They tend to be expressions of mixtures of technical, prudential and moral imperatives.

They influence behaviour and therefore ethical outcomes. However, standards which are externally driven are typically expressed in a form that is well protected from discussion, expressing aims in a matter-of-fact language (Donaldson, 1989). In turn, therefore, a standard carries with it a dominant ideology which, because it is standardized, has a multiplier effect and increasing weight if the standard becomes a norm.

The adoption of codes of conduct and standards within any organization necessarily raises a number of questions. The most obvious one concerns the type of subculture which a standard brings with it. Does it represent a piecemeal attempt to placate demands from pressure groups and consumers or is it a more serious attempt at ethical behaviour? We ought also to ask how effective the codes are in promoting what they stand for. Taken together, these questions provide a measure of the extent to which the standards are genuine and operational rather than cynical and self-deluding.

Codes of conduct, and particularly standards, which become accepted across firms in an industry or even across industries are very powerful, and we often see them written into contracts between organizations. We might be inclined to think that a standard promoting some sort of environmental improvement is a huge step forward and that companies which follow others in adopting such standards should be congratulated. But rather more analysis of the content and purpose of such a standard is necessary before we can reach an answer to that question. Without suggesting that environmental standards are indeed bad, we must nevertheless consider whether, in fact, some standards push employees and customers into a set of values which verge on indoctrination. Stakeholders in those sorts of situations come to possess what Marxists see as false consciousness. In addition, the fact that a standard is widely accepted does not guarantee that the values within it are not restricted or inconsistent. Values contained in standards can also be restricted when, for example (and typically), they exclude any consideration of the impact of a company's activities on indigenous populations in developing countries.

There is very little research on the generation, operation, monitoring and amendment of codes and standards. However, it is argued forcefully by Donaldson (1989) that because codes tend to be expressions of mixtures of technical, prudential and moral imperatives, and because they tend to vary in the extent to which they are or can be enforced, they cannot be regarded as the major vehicles for identifying and encouraging the practices which will raise the level of values in business and industry. Moreover, codes and standards are defined outside the normal democratic framework which determines laws. They are constructed by agencies (often professional bodies or representatives of senior management in industry) with their own motivations, values and interests. On this subject Donaldson and Waller (1980) point to a statement of Bernard Shaw when he asserted that professions can be conspiracies against the laity; and their codes, it may be added, are widely held to be primarily aimed at the protection of the members of the profession rather than the public. Much the same accusation might be levelled against industrial standards. Moreover, the matter of the development of codes and standards is bound up with the matter of enforcement. Codes which are not enforced or fail to deliver their expected outcomes, for whatever reason, might be thought of as little more than cynical expressions of pious hopes.

Much of what has been discussed here can be illustrated by reference to the Responsible Care Programme, which in itself provides a standard for firms operating in the chemical industry to adopt. The Responsible Care Programme might be seen as one of the earliest environmental management systems standards used across companies. It is a voluntary code where performance is measured in terms of continuous improvement. Responsible Care is unique to the chemical industry and originated in Canada in 1984. Launched in 1989 in the UK by the Chemical Industries Association (CIA), the cornerstone of the system is commitment. Chief executives of member companies are invited to sign a set of guiding principles pledging their company to make health, safety and environmental performance an integral part of overall business policy. Adherence to the principles and objectives of Responsible Care is a condition of membership of the CIA. All employees and company contractors have to be made aware of these principles. The guiding principles also require companies to:

- conform to statutory regulations;
- operate to the best practices of the industry;
- assess the actual and potential health, safety and environmental impacts of their activities and products;
- work closely with the authorities and the community to achieve the required levels of performance;
- be open about activities and give relevant information to interested parties.

A company operating the Responsible Care Programme is required to have a clear company policy and the communication of this is seen as vital. The key principle being used in the Responsible Care Programme is self-assessment. However, the CIA does assess the effectiveness of the programme across all firms by collecting indicators of performance from the firms. Companies are encouraged to submit six classes of data to the association. Individual company data are not published but a national aggregate figure is published annually. This shows industrial trends and enables individual companies to assess their own placing accordingly. The six indicators of performance are:

1 Environmental protection spending
2 Safety and health (lost time, accidents for employees and contractors)
3 Waste and emissions
   - discharges of 'red list' substances
   - waste disposal
   - an environmental index of five key discharges by site
4 Distribution (all incidents)
5 Energy consumption (total on-site)
6 All complaints.

A key element of the Responsible Care system is the sharing of information and participation of employees and the local community. Local Responsible Care 'cells' operate for the exchange of information and experience between firms. Employee involvement is also encouraged and the CIA has established training programmes which set targets for appraisal. Firms are also encouraged to have community liaison groups and initiatives that recognize the continuing need to forge improved relationships with the public.

However, in its three-year report of the Responsible Care Programme (ENDS, 1993) the CIA was forced to admit implicitly that the Responsible Care Programme was not functioning in accordance with its aims. The main reason for this is that sites claiming to adhere to the Responsible Care standard were simply not adhering to its principles. Over the three-year reporting period, only 57 per cent of firms made returns for all three years and only 74 per cent made any returns at all. Even more importantly, the third indicator of performance deals with waste and emissions where firms are supposed to report an environmental index by site, designed to give a composite picture of gaseous, liquid and solid releases. Only one-third of the total firms which were supposed to be operating Responsible Care reported these data in full, and of those which reported the index, over 30 per cent reported a worsening environmental impact.

Codes of conduct are therefore nothing if they are not adhered to and voluntary approaches often slip down a list of priorities when other pressing issues arise. It is perhaps not surprising that the lack of response from the chemical industry over Responsible Care occurred during a particularly bad economic recession. However, at the core of a strategy for environmental improvement there has to be commitment, and no standard or code of conduct will survive without that commitment. While some chemical companies are clearly committed to improving their environmental performance, it seems that too many are not adhering to the spirit of Responsible Care. Indeed, while some make efforts to follow the guidelines of the programme, many more treat Responsible Care as a smokescreen. Many of those managers in the chemical industry who appear confident of their procedures to improve environmental performance are certainly either suffering from the false consciousness which was suggested earlier or are making much more cynical attempts to hide their environmental impact in an attempt to hang on to market share and profitability.

The contribution of ethics to sustainable development strategies

Ethics refers to standards of proper conduct. Unfortunately, there is often not complete agreement as to what constitutes ethical behaviour. In the case of illegal and exploitative activities, there is not much dispute. But many practices fall into a grey area, where opinions may differ as to what is ethical and what is unethical and unacceptable. Possible examples of environmental strategies which fall into that grey area relate to the ecolabelling of products and claims associated with the environmental friendliness of a product. These are examples of firms using tactics to persuade people to buy, often misleading customers into thinking that they are getting a product which will not harm the environment, and exaggerating advertising claims. Unfortunately, some business firms have decided to 'walk on the edge' of ethical practices (Hartley, 1993). This is a dangerous strategy, because the dividing line will be different for everybody. Moreover, what society once tolerated as acceptable behaviour is rapidly becoming unacceptable and firms which choose to position themselves so close to criticism will end up battling with time. To a large extent business ethics are firmly on the agenda for the new millennium. Society expects, and is now demanding, much more ethical conduct whereas it had previously regarded questionable practices with apathy or ignorance.

It is now no longer justifiable to see business ethics as directly connected with the law and 'necessary value systems' as inappropriate. The relationship between ethical conduct and the law is sometimes confusing. Naïve businesses might rationalize that actions within the law are therefore ethical and perfectly justifiable. But an 'if it's legal, it's ethical' attitude disregards the fact that the law codifies only that part of ethics which society feels so strongly about that it is willing to support it with physical force (Westing, 1968).

Many businesses assume that the more strictly one interprets ethical behaviour, the more profits suffer. Certainly, the muted sales efforts that may result from toning down product claims or refusing to buy raw materials which result in the exploitation of indigenous populations may hurt profits. Yet a strong argument can also be made that scrupulously honest and ethical behaviour is better for business and for profits. Well-satisfied customers tend to bring repeat business and it is therefore desirable to develop trusting relationships with not only customers but also with personnel, suppliers and the other stakeholders with which a firm deals. An unbending disavowal of the unethical practices such as false environmental claims and improper waste management can create, in turn, a healthier business culture for an entire industry. A firm's reputation for honest dealings and environmental action can also be a powerful competitive advantage. Ethical conduct is not incompatible with profitability but it does change timescales. It is more compatible with maximizing profits in the long run, even though in the shorter term disregard of these ethical principles may yield more profits.

Unfortunately, the perception that unethical and shady practices will yield more sales and profits still prevails in many organizations. Given the institutional setting of the modern capitalist economy, there are certain factors which can be identified that tend to motivate those less than desirable practices. These include an overemphasis on short-term performance, the dominance of competition over cooperation, expediency and indifference, and a dominant ideology towards environmental management which stresses piecemeal approaches rather than a strategy based on the principles of sustainable development. Let us examine these issues in more detail.

The overemphasis on short-term performance

In most firms, career development and higher salaries depend on achieving greater sales and profits. This is true not only for individual employees and executives but for departments, divisions and the entire firm. The value that stockholders and investors, creditors and suppliers place on a firm depends to a large extent on growth. In turn, the dominant measure of growth is increasing sales and profits. The better the growth rate, the more money is available for further expansion by investors and creditors at attractive rates. Suppliers and customers are more eager to do business. Top-quality personnel and executives are also more easily attracted.

In particular, the dominant drive would seem to be towards profits and profit maximization. This is justified by economists such as Friedman (1963), who argues that 'few trends could so thoroughly undermine the very foundations of our free society as the acceptance by corporate officials of social responsibility other than to make as much money for their stockholders as possible' (p133). Friedman's view, and that of many others, simply neglects the responsibility that all actors in society have to benefit society in terms which are wider than the narrowly based performance measures which he adopts.

The emphasis on quantitative measures of performance and on growth, in particular, has some potential negative consequences. In particular, it tends to push social and environmental issues down the corporate agenda. If growth can be achieved at the expense of marginal environmental damage, then little account will be taken of the real impact of this damage. The emphasis on growth becomes all pervading and environmental objectives (which may or may not exist) are compromised. Even where the objective is to maximize growth subject to other constraints, growth can easily be justified by devaluing the importance of those other constraints. Moreover, with a dominant growth strategy, people are not measured on the basis of their moral contribution to the business enterprise. Hence, they become caught up in a system which is characterized by an ethic which is foreign to and often lower than the ethics of human beings (Holloway and Hancock, 1968). That tends to devalue the role of the worker and of those involved further down the supply chain. It is little wonder, therefore, that when it comes to the consideration of the effect that the production and processing of raw materials might have on indigenous populations in developing countries very little weight is attached to the needs and aspirations of these peoples.

The dominance of competition over cooperation

An intensely competitive environment, especially if coupled with a firm's inability to differentiate products substantially or to cement segments of the market, will tend to motivate unethical behaviour (Hartley, 1993). The actions of one or a few firms in a fiercely competitive industry may generate a follow-the-leader situation, requiring the more ethical competitors to choose lower profits or lower ethics. Moreover, in a fiercely competitive environment the objective of the firm is dominated by the need to increase market share, to stay one step ahead of competitors and therefore to adopt isolationist and independent strategies. To succeed in the marketplace, businesses feel the need to cut costs, to downgrade other objectives which might be perceived as expensive, and to cut corners where possible.

That is not to suggest that competition is bad but that its dominance does mitigate against the opportunities which can be brought about through cooperation. Moreover, environmental issues are often overlooked because they are perceived as adding to costs, with any benefits being somewhat intangible. Cooperative strategies can lead to synergetic benefits to businesses within a region or industry and can prevent the wasteful duplication of resources in many areas (Welford, 1993). Such a strategy leads to the sharing of experiences and the sharing of the costs and benefits of research and development which, in turn, encourages all firms to adopt best practices and procedures.

Expediency and indifference

The attitude of expediency and indifference to the customer's best interests accounts for both complacency and unethical practices. These attitudes, whether permeating an entire firm or affecting only a few individuals, are hardly conducive to repeat business and customer loyalty. They are more prevalent in firms with many small customers and in those firms where repeat business is relatively unimportant. But such attitudes also have an impact on environmental issues. They tend to mean that corners are cut and due care is not taken to protect society and the environment. They tend to increase the unnecessary use of resources and generate excessive waste, and to mitigate against the adoption of systems and procedures that can prevent accidents and environmental damage. Moreover, indifference and apathy tend to mitigate against accepting the responsibility which every individual and every firm has in protecting the environment now and into the future.

The dominant ideology towards environmental management

Significant evidence exists that management trends which become popular exert a strong influence on the on-going techniques of corporate management. New concepts which are successfully implemented in certain organizations become accepted, dominant and, even when they are inappropriate, the norm (Mintzberg, 1979). DiMaggio and Powell (1983) offer three explanations for this phenomenon. Firstly, organizations will submit to both formal and informal pressures from other organizations upon which they depend. Secondly, when faced with uncertainty, organizations may model themselves on organizations that have seemed to be successful and adopt the sorts of techniques which they see being introduced. Thirdly, normative pressures which stem from a degree of professionalism among management can cause the adoption of 'fashionable' management techniques. Universities, training institutions, standard-setters and professional associations are all vehicles for the development of these normative rules.

These are precisely the trends we are seeing in contemporary approaches to environmental management, which are often piecemeal and sporadic. This approach is not consistent with the concept of sustainable development because it does not go far enough in developing strategies which will reverse the trend towards environmental degradation. But the piecemeal approach is becoming the accepted ideology because it is being adopted by leading firms, espoused by academics and legitimized by standard-setters and policy-makers.

Moreover, this trend is further reinforced by so-called benchmarking analysis, which is becoming increasingly common in industry. As a principle, benchmarking can be valuable, but it can also reinforce inappropriate general techniques. Current environmental standards are not high, and this in turn gives the impression to imitators in industry that the social and environmental challenge facing industry is actually quite weak. The reverse is true and what is needed therefore is a change in the dominant ideology.

Such a change in ideology is difficult to achieve, of course, because management standards have been set by industry itself. They have been designed to be voluntary and not to conflict with the ideology associated with profit maximization in the short to medium term.

Arguments such as the ones outlined above, suggesting that industry has not gone far enough, will therefore be treated with derision by industry and sidelined. The power which industry has in the current economic system is therefore a barrier to further development of the concepts of sustainable development. Thus the only way to bring about a change in this suboptimal dominant ideology is to challenge the very basis of that power. Without a fundamental revolution in the way we organize our society, such a challenge can only come about through a legislative process.

The pervasiveness of senior management ethics

The attitudes, values and actions of senior management will tend to form the culture in any organization. In particular, the chief executive will tend to be very important in influencing the behaviour of the next tier of executives and down the line to the shopfloor employees. We know that senior management will tend to have a contagious influence and too often they will have a vested interest that is more associated with short-term performance than in acting ethically. Acting ethically and in an environmentally responsible manner therefore often requires culture change from the top down, but if the chief executive is not keen to drive such change then we must ask ourselves who will.

Related to the top executive's influence over a company is the often mechanistic management systems and structures which so often exist in the most inflexible organizations. These are in place because they are easy to control, but such structures will often stifle creativity. Moreover, any discussion relating to values will be secondary to structure and this will too often define the firm's immediate interests in terms of short-term performance. Customer and employee safety, integrity and environmental protection will be secondary considerations.

While senior management itself may not be directly involved in unethical practices, it often promotes such behaviour by strongly insisting on short-term profit maximization and performance goals. When these goals are difficult to achieve and not achieving them can be met with severe penalties, the climate is set for undesirable conduct: deceptive advertising, overselling, adulterated products, inappropriate waste-management practices, negligence towards environmental standards and other unethical behaviour. A clear alternative to the mechanistic, management-dominated approach is to encourage the participation and creativity of the workforce and make them feel valued. This, in turn, encourages commitment to the organization, better work practices and avoids the problems associated with apathy and indifference (Welford, 1992).

Structural barriers to ethical business and environmental management

The very nature of the contemporary capitalist structure which stresses competition, the maximization of profits and the reduction of costs acts as a fundamental barrier to the adoption of ethical practices in business. In many markets, particularly where oligopolistic structures exist, we often see strategies which are based on tacit collusion where firms will follow dominant market leaders. It is often perceived that unless such a strategy is adopted, firms will be at a competitive disadvantage and their viability may even be threatened. Therefore what becomes accepted business practice by dominant firms tends to permeate a whole industry so that the dominant ideologies associated with the most profitable companies perpetuate themselves and set the tone for business strategies. In these circumstances it is market share and financial performance which come to dominate other measures of the success of the company.

On the other hand, in times when demand falls or when any firm finds itself in a very competitive situation, financial indicators remain dominant and cost-cutting often prevails. However, we know that in two major catastrophes, Bhopal and the Alaskan oil spill, cost-cutting severely affected safety measures and contributed greatly to the gravity of the problem and the consequent handling of it (Hartley, 1993). Whatever the market structure, therefore, success is measured first and foremost on principles of financial management and wider ethical considerations are sidelined. The overemphasis on money, dictated by the economic system, therefore represents a barrier to the adoption of sustainable environmental strategies.

According to Donaldson (1989), however, the most serious barriers to improvement are not in the nature of people or business and industry, but are attitudinal. There is, therefore, a need to change attitudes via a change in the culture of an organization. Central here is a commitment towards improved ethics. Many studies have demonstrated the ease with which the commitment of employees can be gained through methods associated with behavioural science (Luthans, 1985). While such techniques are sometimes criticized as being potentially manipulative, we must recognize that they hold great potential for increasing ethical behaviour. However, we are not seeking a bolt-on morality (so often common with codes of conduct and standards) but a genuine attempt at introducing real ethical improvements.

This inevitably leads us to consider whether current bureaucratic structures in society and industry are conducive to the introduction of systems which promote ethical behaviour. The stunted development of any consideration of alternative forms of bureaucracy provides us with a major challenge for the future. There is a need for more innovation and imagination on the part of management. Cooperative and participative forms of industrial organization, for example, have often been seen as appropriate only to alternative small artisan operations or have been a last-resort attempt at rescuing businesses which are due to close for commercial reasons. Ethical concerns (and particularly environmental concerns) challenge us to look more closely at developments which are associated with industrial democracy and alternative industrial arrangements. The bureaucratic habits of hierarchy and the narrow distribution of power may not be conducive in the end to a sustainable future.

Operational barriers to ethical business and environmental management

Businesses are also prevented from acting in a more environmentally friendly way by ideologies relating to product responsibility, promotional activities and international trade which are based on custom and practice rather than on any real evaluation of ethical considerations. There is an accepted code of conduct in each of these areas which, once again, stresses short-term performance, perceives change as being costly and fundamentally devalues the rights of individual human beings. It is worth examining each of these issues in turn.

Product responsibility

The traditional view of a product is that once it is sold the responsibility for its safe use and disposal passes to the consumer. That cut-off point means that firms often do not consider the environmental damage done by the use and disposal of the product which it produces. More forward-looking companies are now accepting that the product which they produce is fundamentally their responsibility from cradle to grave, and the most advanced companies have introduced product stewardship procedures to ensure that a product is used correctly and disposed of in an environmentally friendly way. However, this approach is yet to be found throughout industry, where the dominant ideology seems to stress the idea that property rights imply responsibility, so that as soon as such rights are transferred through the sale of the product, the company no longer has a duty of care against social and environmental damage.

Promotional activities

Promotional activities are designed to increase sales and are judged on the basis of so doing. The whole experience of green marketing to date has been associated with exaggeration and deception. There is often a temptation in marketing departments to exaggerate a little and to overemphasize a product's attributes. Unfortunately, moderation is not always practised. Mild exaggerations often multiply and become outright deception. With many products, false claims can be recognized by customers, who refuse to rebuy the product. But where such claims cannot be substantiated easily, false claims are harder to detect. Nevertheless pressure groups and competitors are always willing to expose unreasonable claims and that damages not only product sales but also the reputation of the firm. Advertising statements, if well presented and attractive, should induce customers to purchase the product. But if the expectations generated by advertisements are not realized, there will be no repeat business. Repeat business is the very thing most firms seek: a continuity of business, which means loyal and satisfied customers.

International trade

Many firms today do business worldwide and source their raw materials from a range of countries. Although this presents great opportunities, it also poses some problems, some ethical dilemmas and many opportunities for abuse. Unethical practices have a critical effect on the image of companies at home and abroad. Union Carbide's acceptance of lower operating standards in its operations in developing countries led to the Bhopal accident. The lesson to be learned is that standards and controls must be even more rigidly applied in countries where workers and managers may be less competent than they are in more economically and educationally advanced countries. A major ethical question also revolves around the sourcing of raw materials from parts of the world where indigenous populations are adversely affected. The drive for low-cost inputs leads to the exploitation of such people, the abuse of their land, and attacks their fundamental rights to lead their lives as they would wish.

Moving towards sustainable development through industrial democracy

It is commonly claimed that there is an inevitable trade-off between profit and ethics or morals and that the ultimate constraint to improved ethical behaviour is the need to show an acceptable rate of return on investment. The counter-claim is that behaving ethically is good business and that taking an honest and ethical approach to industrial activities will lead to satisfied customers and repeat business. There are two problems with each of these arguments. Firstly, they assume implicitly that we can measure ethics and thereby characterize 'the ethical firm', or provide lists of good or bad practices. The notion of the ethical firm is not only difficult to describe but attempting so to do is also fruitless. Secondly, both arguments assume implicitly an underlying business structure where the primary outcome is profitability, even though alternative models might be more applicable.

There is a need to look towards alternative ideas and alternative structures. Many of these actually require marginal changes but can bring about much improved outcomes. For example, key procedures are associated with reforms in the workplace which firms can adopt to push them along the path of more ethical behaviour. This revolves around issues of industrial democracy and respecting the values of everybody associated with a firm or organization. More open procedures and less hierarchical bureaucracy in decision-making could be developed within firms. This in turn needs to be linked to an ethical awareness-raising campaign both within and external to the firm, helping to raise the overall ethical profile.

The debate surrounding bureaucracy is too wide to discuss here. But one of the most important points, which is of direct relevance to the contemporary business scenario, is expounded by Argyris (1964), who argues that firms typically place individuals in positions of passivity and dependency that are at odds with the needs of mature individuals. Bennis (1972) and Burns and Stalker (1963) go further in suggesting that bureaucracies are too inflexible to be able to adapt to changes in increasingly volatile and discriminating markets. Traditional bureaucracies reserve decision-making to the top of the organization and decisions are subsequently handed down. Because of the narrow constituency involved in the decision-making process, they may not only be suboptimal decisions but may be severely at odds with the values of a workforce. Bureaucracies hold within themselves methods of controlling and channelling information. Those with power in the bureaucracy will go to great lengths to ensure conformity to internal codes and they have a great range of sanctions available to them for persuasion and enforcement. We have already argued that such codes may be at odds with more ethical behaviour. Flatter hierarchies, participative decision-making and increased self-determination by workers seem to be obvious initial steps to be taken to begin to resolve such problems. We will return to this assertion throughout the book.

If increased industrial democracy better enables firms to act in ethical ways and if the many advocates of participative arrangements (eg Welford, 1989) are right in suggesting that participation improves productivity and performance, then we need to consider why we have not seen manifestations of this form of industrial organization. Any movement towards some form of corporate democracy is taking place slowly and in a piecemeal fashion. But it might be accelerated if legislation which more freely permits different styles of participation and democratic processes was to be introduced, thus doing away with the restrictive structure of authority and responsibility required by law which often inhibits moves in this direction.

Conclusions

Companies are faced with the challenge of integrating considerations based on the key concept of sustainable development into their production and marketing plans. There is always an incentive, however, for profit-maximizing firms seeking short-term rewards to opt out of their ethical obligations towards environmental management. What is required, therefore, is a thorough re-examination of business ethics within any organization and a change in ideology towards an acceptance by industry of its ethical and social responsibilities. Increasingly in a society where there is easy access to information about the activities of business and a greater willingness to boycott the products of some businesses, managers will realize that an ethical stance is not only important, it will also make good business sense.

Perhaps one of the most important lessons which firms are beginning to learn relates to the desirability of seeking an honest and trusting relationship with customers (as well as with their other stakeholders). Such an ethical relationship requires a widely defined concern for customer satisfaction and fair dealings. Objectives should be written in ethical terms and stress loyalty and repeat business. Such a philosophy and attitude must permeate an organization. It can easily be short-circuited if a general climate of opportunism and severe financial performance pressure should prevail. Indeed, ethical stances to the wide range of issues facing businesses will be imperative if our objective is to move towards a situation which is consistent with sustainable development.

An honest and trusting relationship should not be sought with consumers or final users alone. It should characterize the relationship between sales representatives and their clients, which suggests no exaggeration or misrepresentation, greater efforts at understanding customers' needs and better servicing. It may even mean forgoing a sales opportunity when a customer's best interest may be served better by another product or at another time. The trusting relationship suggests repudiating any adversarial stance with employees, suppliers and, beyond this, with all the communities in which a firm does business. Firms need to throw away ideologies based on financial performance alone and consider their corporate relationship with society. Such a relationship requires sound ethical conduct. It should foster a good reputation and public image.

It has been argued that the competitive nature of markets is often a barrier to corporate environmental performance and creates isolationist strategies. Unethical and unilateral actions may result in an initial competitive advantage but may hurt a firm's overall image and reputation in the longer term. To have a coherent environmental strategy, firms need a consistent set of business ethics and need to measure their performance using a range of longer-term indicators. Placing environmental management within the framework of business ethics also reminds us that it is really not possible to separate broad social and environmental considerations from other more specific issues such as the treatment of women and minority groups, the treatment of animals and the protection of indigenous populations. A set of ethics alone will not necessarily lead to better business practices, however. What we also require is a fundamental re-examination of dominant ideologies in the business world and culture change which is capable of challenging accepted wisdoms.

The rise of organized pressure and interest groups makes it doubly important that managers consider the arguments of all stakeholders in a decision's outcome. Since these groups publicly promote their causes in a single-minded way and do not therefore face the competing objectives so often faced by management, they have an advantage over the traditional company in the strong message which they can convey. Decisions taken in isolation by an élite group are therefore far more likely to result in suboptimal outcomes.

The main thrust of the argument in this chapter, however, is that the major issues and arguments surrounding business ethics, and environmental considerations in particular, are not so much substantive but more associated with procedures and received 'wisdom' associated with structures and hierarchies. It has been argued that these barriers to improved ethics can be removed through the removal of such traditional structures. There needs to be a new emphasis on stakeholder accountability and a move towards new democratic forms of organization within the workplace. There is nothing in the nature of people or of businesses which makes adjustment towards ethical behaviour impossible. Vested interests held by those in power does have to be addressed though, and this is one of the major challenges which we must overcome.

8

Formulating scenarios

INTRODUCTION

Commedia dell'arte is an improvised play in two parts, the imbroglio and the scenario. It is acted out by stock characters, some wearing distinctive masks and costumes, such as Harlequin, Pedrolino, and Punchinello, who improvise a comic drama that ends happily for all. Modern day pantomime and Punch and Judy shows have their origins in this. Today's meaning of scenario as an outline of a play or a film and a possible sequence of future events is derived from *commedia dell'arte*. Future events for Harlequin and the other characters are based upon everything being resolved happily (which is not necessarily the case for today's organizations). The meaning of imbroglio as a confused situation is also apt for organizations that are faced with difficult situations. Perhaps the next time you hear someone doing scenario planning you may want to think of them as Mr Punch!

In *commedia dell'arte* the play usually revolves around four stock characters wearing distinctive masks, but variations on this are possible. The four characters are Pantalone, Dottore, Harlequin servant to Pantalone and Scapino/Brighella another servant of Pantalone. Each has a unique and, to those who know the *commedia* well, recognizable character. For instance, Dottore is a professional such as a doctor or university professor who relishes giving advice to others even when he knows nothing. He has the unfortunate habit of talking too much, often spouting complete nonsense.

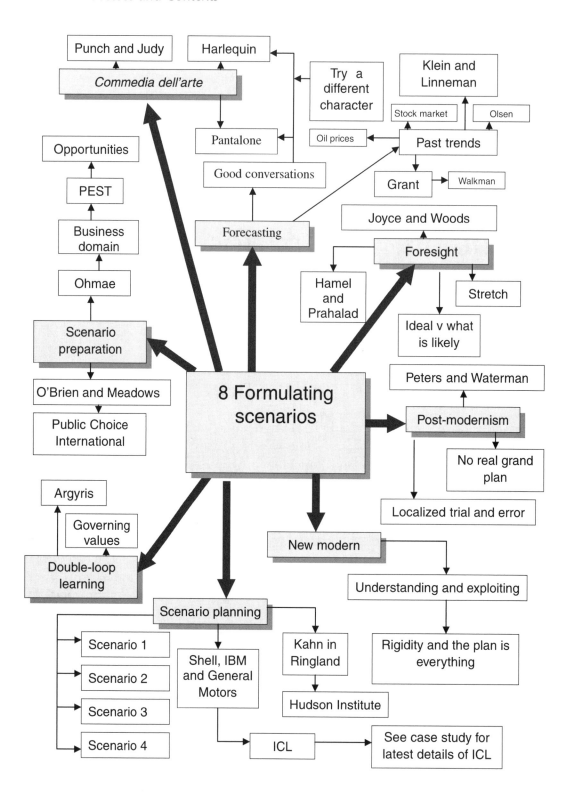

The younger members of the *commedia* take great fun in ridiculing him. Evidently, originally Dottore was portrayed as coming from Bologna and from this we get the expression to be 'full of baloney'.

Harlequin on the other hand can be viewed as a precursor of Figaro. He does not seem to spend much time doing any work for his master; instead he spends his time on his own plots and intrigues. He occasionally speaks directly to the audience. There are also many minor characters such as the Captain, Columbina, another servant, the lovers and Pulcinella from whom we get today's Mr Punch. For those of you that are interested in learning more about *commedia dell'arte* there are several Web sites to try such as www.commedia-dell-arte.com/links.htm.

One of the interesting things about the *commedia dell'arte* is that the story is produced through the use of improvisation – but improvisation carried out within a pretty precise framework. Before the actors go on stage they often agree upon the main thrust of the performance, then using their skills and knowledge of the type of things their character would do, they improvise the performance. This takes great skill and practice, especially as each performance is supposed to be new and fresh.

When we discuss and argue about problems and possible solutions all those involved (including ourselves) can have stereotyped views that are hard to move away from. In organizations you might find the Dottore equivalent: the team member who believes he has superior knowledge about everything and misses no opportunity to tell you so even if for most of the time he is talking baloney. Or are you more like Pantalone, who spends an awful lot of his time trying to bully the other characters but to no avail? Of course we are not like that. Seriously though, it is very easy to fall into the trap of having your position irrespective of the problem and being deaf to what others are telling you.

FORECASTING

In the past strategic management was often associated with forecasting. The strategist would attempt to model in some way the future and then adjust the organization's trajectory to the outcomes of the forecast. For instance, you might forecast that the demand for your product is about to decline because of new, superior products appearing on the market. Or you might predict changes in consumer income and plan actions to exploit this development to your benefit. Forecasting the future and responding to it are key activities of strategy. Scenario planning could be seen as an attempt to do just this. If the future is going to be such and such, what do we need to put in place because of this? Just like in the development of a play or a film, a scenario would be constructed to set the scenes, if you like, in which action would be required to achieve the strategic goals or strategic vision. The organization, just as in a *commedia dell'arte* play, would start with a confused and unclear situation that would be resolved in the scenario, and it would attempt to figure out a way forward to successfully resolve its present predicament. Scenario planning can be extended by modelling not just one possible future but several and then trying to work out the best way forward to maximize the organization's future irrespective of which actual future occurs. What some have claimed for this type of approach is that it gives the strategist a good way of conversing about the future. In short, it produces good strategic conversations.

When doing scenarios, take care not to fall into the trap of fixing your own creativity or way of thinking about possible futures. As we said above, the *commedia* has stock characters that act within the confines of their known personality, albeit improvising around their stock character. Often in organizational settings we do the same. Some of us concentrate on the financial part of a scenario, as we are figures people. Others stress the people aspects, others technology, and so on. So although we believe we are thinking creatively, we have a tendency to work more on one part of the scenario than other parts. You might like to recount to yourself and, if you are brave enough, to others when you engage in scenarios that you have inadvertently fallen into playing a stock character and need to shift into another role. Instead of being Dottore try being Harlequin.

Klein and Linneman (1984) found that in the early 1980s major companies were inclined to favour forecasts based on past trends. A major problem with this type of analysis is that discontinuities may arise that throw out the existing trend. A good example of this is the 1973 oil crisis when OPEC managed to engineer a steep rise in oil prices by restricting supply. Assumptions based on the past trend in oil prices would have led to a wrong forecast about the future. In 1973 the price per barrel of crude oil (OPEC official average sales price, 1995 US $) was US $10.29, by 1975 it was US $28.07 rising to US $54.94 in 1980 and by 1995 it had fallen back to US $16.84 a barrel. As we write this book the price of oil per barrel is relatively high, but it could have fallen again by the time you read this.

There are of course examples when trying to predict the future has been singularly wrong. For instance, Olsen, President of Digital Equipment Corporation, was reported to have said in 1977, 'There is no reason for any individual to have a computer in their home.' This is more an example of where the past cannot tell us much about the future as a change has occurred, or is about to occur, that makes the past out of date. Grant (1995) gives a similar example of a technological change based on the Walkman, arguing that Sony had difficulty in assessing the demand for the Walkman because it was such a new product.

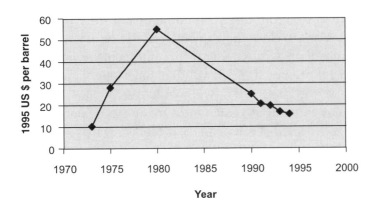

Figure 8.1 World crude oil prices

Just before the great stock market crash in 1929, the *Wall Street Journal* said in October 1929, 'Conditions do not seem to foreshadow anything more formidable than an arrest of stock activity and business prosperity like that in 1923. Suggestions that the wiping out of paper profits will reduce the country's real purchasing power seem far-fetched.' Unfortunately this was spectacularly wrong.

It is easy to find numerous examples of trend projection that has gone hopelessly wrong. However, it would be foolish to completely abandon some thinking about possible trends as without this, future planning would be a set of random decisions.

FORESIGHT

A major difficult in forecasting is that it has a tendency to become more than just a way of thinking and talking about the future but easily tempts us in to thinking we have scientifically predicted the future. So instead of using forecasting as a way of generating conversations about the future that we know are only conversations, we begin to believe we have actually predicted the future correctly. Hamel and Prahalad (1994) use the word foresight as opposed to forecast to draw attention to the difference between thinking about the future (foresight) and trying to predict the future (forecast).

Foresight is extended further to include some idea of what an 'ideal' future would be for the organization. Think about you own future to see if you can build different scenarios, including some thoughts about what would be ideal, as well as some fore-casts. Try also to shift out of your normal thinking mode into different ones. It is worth doing this for a few moments, jotting down your thoughts as you do so. You might find that there is a big gap between what your 'best' forecast of the future is and what you would like the future to be. From this you should be able to start thinking about the possibility of taking actions to close the gap between the two. We believe that you need to think of challenges that, while being difficult to achieve, would move you nearer to your ideal goal. This can be difficult as we all have a tendency to concentrate on what is likely and to feel that what we would really like is unobtainable. Organizations have similar difficulties as they are made up of people just like us. When developing strategy, organizations can also tend towards forecast and not devote enough resource to foresight and finding ways of achieving that foresight.

We have, in our earlier work, suggested that we need to shift our thinking away from worrying about whether the future is either not knowable or completely knowable (Joyce and Woods, 1996: 7) to thinking more about positive features of the present that can be projected into the future and negative features that can be eradicated or mini-mized. Spending resources on arguing about whether it is possible to predict the future or not can be diverted to constructing what the ideal future should be and finding ways of moving towards it. This seems to us to be a more positive response as it concentrates our energies on being proactive instead of reactive. It also addresses the problem of predicting the future and believing we have done this correctly. This is not to say we should be blind to trends in the environment, as we need to take account of them as we plan to reach our ideal future. In fact a major challenge is to use foresight and forecast in such a way as to give you the best chance of reaching your ideal future.

POST-MODERNISM

As a reaction to the uncertainties of the future an influential group of writers on strat-egy such as Peters and Waterman (1982) championed an alternate approach that cel-ebrated a style of strategy emphasizing localized trial and error. They argued that by the time the centre of an organization had realized what was happening and planned to cope with it, it was already too late. Managers further down the corporate hierar-chy needed to be empowered to make speedy decisions in order to cope with the speed of change. The old-style 'modernist' strategic plan was a luxury that could not be afforded. We characterized the new style of strategy as 'post-modern'. This style had the advantage that information was being produced and processed rapidly throughout the organization and acted upon. If a local manager or employee saw a market opportunity or a way of improving the quality of the product or service, they could do so immediately, without waiting for the centre to respond. Of course a lot of these initiatives would fail, but, it was argued by supporters of this view, many would not. The corporate centre would ensure the organizational framework for this to take place but would have to give up its grand plan perhaps substituting organizational values and meaning in its place. The centre would set in place mechanisms that allowed information about successful local initiatives to be spread through the organization. In so far as there was a grand plan it was to go with the flow of what was happening throughout the organization.

We believe that there is a way of combining the best features of both the 'modernist' and the 'post-modernist' approach to strategy, and we have termed this 'new modern'. Simply, new modernists need to be skilled in understanding and exploiting long-term trends without falling into the trap of rigidity and believing that the plan is everything. They have to encourage experimentation throughout the organization and find ways of communicating the results of successful experiments across the organization. They need also to have skills in foresight to give the leadership the organization requires to survive in the future. They need to be able to inspire managers and employees in their organization with their vision, continually building the commitment and competencies of their employees to succeed in the long-term goals of the organization.

A question you are probably asking yourself now is, if forecasting is so difficult doesn't it follow that foresight is just as hard being prone to just the same problems? The first point we want to make here is the one we made above, that is, forecasting is about what you think the future will be and foresight is more about what you want the future to be. We would be misleading you if we gave the impression that foresight is very easy – that all you have to do is wish for your ideal future and it will be easy to bring it about. You have to have some idea about what is possible. Foresight is certainly weighted more towards an articulation of what you want as opposed to what you think will happen. But it does not take place in a vacuum, you have to have some idea about what is going on and how to build upon possible futures and negate others. That said, the key point is thinking about what you want and trying to figure out how to achieve it. It is proactive as opposed to reactive.

The second point is about setting goals that others can and will engage with. So, in terms of your foresight, are you setting a sufficiently stiff challenge? Too easy and you have not stretched the organization enough. Too demanding may simply result in cynicism and widespread apathy to the goal as employees think it is unobtainable. President Kennedy managed to come up with a goal that was, in retrospect, achievable, but at the time looked, to say the least, challenging. His foresight galvanized NASA and the nation, and any barriers that stood in the way of landing a man on the moon and returning him safely were overcome.

SCENARIO PLANNING

For every example of brilliantly conceived foresight there are probably many, many more that we never hear about because they fail. They fail for many reasons. Perhaps circumstances change, making them, even with goodwill, unachievable. Perhaps they were always unachievable, as they were unrealistic. How then can we develop skills in foresight that steer a course between being undemanding and being unrealistic? One way is to engage in scenario planning. This allows managers the space to think about possible futures. To talk to each other about the assumptions they are making about the future. To exchange ideas and importantly to think imaginatively and creatively about what they want to happen. As we said in the introduction the characters in the *commedia dell'arte* would be set a problem in the imbroglio and then improvise a resolution of it in the scenario. As it was a comedy the play invariably ended happily. In business often the outcome is not so funny.

Herman Kahn featured prominently in Ringland's (1998) account of the early history of scenario planning. It seems he led the way in terms of the idea of producing reports as if they had been written at a future time. The reports were produced using both analysis and imagination. In the 1960s he set up the Hudson Institute and it is reported that he was concerned with breaking past mental blocks and considering the 'unthinkable' in relation to the future. Much of the respectability of scenario planning derives from its use by companies like Shell, IBM and General Motors. It is well known that scenario planning was credited with helping Shell to cope with the turbulent events of the 1970s due to oil price changes.

Scenarios allow us to think and talk about diverse possible futures. Very often this means attempting to think imaginatively about the future. This is supported by the construction of stories in which assumptions and uncertainties are combined to produce multiple scenarios. We can then weigh one scenario against the other. We can develop worst-case, best-case and most-likely-case scenarios continually testing our assumptions about the future. We can use past data to help us extrapolate into the future, while being aware of the difficulties inherent in this. At ICL in 1995 a second round of scenario planning was begun with the aim of developing scenarios for the year 2005. As part of this round of scenario planning, interviews were conducted with 50 senior ICL staff, interview transcripts were analysed, and over 60 trends and uncertainties identified. Further analysis produced two scenarios. Finally, workshops for business units were used to enable management teams to think about the scenarios and discuss future strategies (Ringland, 1998). Our belief is that the more people are involved in such ways, the more influential the scenarios will be and the more commitment there will be to acting on the basis of them.

   Below are four scenarios that illustrate just how diverse a set of scenarios might be and thus how important it would be to test any long-term strategy for robustness in each of them.

Scenario 1

Within the next 20 years the size of organizations will shrink and more people will become self-employed. Many of today's large global organizations will have disappeared, having been replaced by complex networks of smaller scale organizations. Apart from occasional local conflict, the world will be characterized by political stability, increasingly of a democratic Western type, and rising real wealth across the globe.

Scenario 2

Environmental concerns will increase over the next 20 years leading to a fundamental shift away from free market ideology towards more strictly controlled markets. This will result in less freedom for consumers in what they purchase and related loss of control for organizations in what and how they produce commodities. The global movement of resources will slow down, as local production will be favoured. Political conflicts will increase as a result of this and nation states will increase their political power over their subjects. Real wealth will start to decrease in the developed world.

Scenario 3

E-business will dominate the world of 2020. Locality will be unimportant in both the production and consumption of 'things' as people increasing live in the virtual world. The type of 'thing' produced and consumed will increasingly become 'virtual' in ways that are difficult for us to envisage today. Nation states will become less important as they will be undermined by this virtual world. In this Information Age wealth will be unevenly distributed. Many will benefit enormously from this, but others will be excluded. The economy will be increasingly volatile as organizations will have, compared to a generation ago, short life spans.

Scenario 4

E-business will not have changed the fundamental rules of the game and apart from the great e-business collapse of 2004, which saw many e-business millionaires wiped out overnight, the impact of e-business will have been remarkably minor. What will be more important in shaping the 2020s is the invention and widespread use of 'sphb' a clean and cheap substitute for petrol, costing about 95 per cent less per gallon than petrol and having only a very, very minor impact on the environment. Thinking back to the turn of the century it now seems strange that no one had thought about producing 'sphb' before, considering how easy it is to produce – so easy in fact that about half the households in the world now have their own 'sphb' production machine. While this was happening, world GNP was becoming increasingly concentrated in 30 large multinational organizations, with nearly 10 per cent of the world's workforce being employed by them. These huge organizations replaced nation states as sources of political power.

Some argue that scenario planning and the Delphi technique, where we try to envision the future, have advantages over other ways of constructing strategy. It is argued they are not so rooted in the present and require what has become known as double-loop learning as opposed to single-loop learning. Argyris (1990) has distinguished between these two types of learning. Single-loop learning is usually characterized as being reactive. An organization might be faced with a particular problem that needs attention and it reacts to this by exploring solutions to the presenting problem. The status quo is maintained. The problem is not considered to be of such a magnitude that the organization needs radical surgery. Double-loop learning is more concerned with exploring the underlying values that determine the way the organization's managers are thinking and acting. This may result in radical new strategies. Likewise, scenario planning may help to bring to the surface the governing values that shape how managers are thinking about the future and thereby open things up.

Using double-loop learning as part of scenario planning frees managers up to consider new possible futures and responses to them that are more than reacting to current problems. Another way of thinking about scenario planning is to think of it in terms of 'anticipatory learning'. Here the scenarios are used to enable managers to reflect on what skills they require to cope with possible future events as well as, in the sense we have been developing scenarios, create a future for their organization. In this, HR strategies have to be considered in order that the skill base required for the perceived future is put in place early enough for the organization to be able to reach the desired goal. Often, while financial and technical details are elaborated quite closely in scenarios, the HR part can be underplayed, particularly around the learning needs of employees. If some double-loop learning, or a shift towards anticipatory learning, is required then human resources need to be aligned with the preferred strategy.

SCENARIO PREPARATION

Ohmae (1982) outlined a very simple process for developing scenarios. First, the managers must identify their business domain. This can be done in terms of the

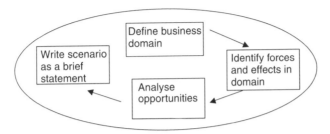

Figure 8.2 Scenario development

customers' point of view rather than in terms of the product. Hence, an organization may define its domain as concerned with helping customers get or keep their clothes clean, rather than as concerned with the manufacture of washing machines or soap powder. The next step is to identify the economic, social, technological, and political forces at work in this business domain. These forces, once identified, can be analysed for their effects. For example, a social force (trend) towards gender equality in society has the effect of increasing the number of working wives. Finally, the managers can analyse these effects for the opportunities they offer. An example of this might be the opportunity to sell more convenience and pre-prepared meals to families because of the growing numbers of working wives. The final step is to write the scenario as a brief statement about a business domain identifying the forces at work, their effects, and the consequent opportunities for new products or services.

The example of a trend towards gender equality is very plausible. However, the argument for using scenarios is that the future is highly uncertain. So we need to think about turbulence and discontinuities as well as trends. The formulation of a set of distinct scenarios which presume very different values for key factors allow managers to prepare for quite diverse eventualities.

Another approach entirely is a scenario-based approach to future visioning (O'Brien and Meadows, 1998: 39). They define a vision as 'a carefully formulated and clearly articulated statement of intentions that defines a destination or future state of affairs that an individual or group finds desirable…'. They also say that, 'Attributes of a vision include: ideality (the pursuit of excellence), uniqueness (pride in being different), imagery (vivid pictures of the future) and future orientation.'

They describe an approach to visioning scenarios developed by Public Choice International. This begins with the formation of a steering group and project group. The concerns and opinions of stakeholders are obtained (for example, by using focus groups). The project team develops a history of the organization, a summary of key issues and concerns, and a set of scenarios describing a future nature or state of the organization. The work of the project team is then discussed by as wide a range of people as possible and ideas for action generated. The ideas for action are then discussed widely and a bottom–up vision written. Finally, key stakeholders are asked to commit to implementing specific action components of the vision and a detailed implementation plan is drawn up.

CONCLUSIONS

This chapter began by emphasizing the difference between a forecast and foresight. The importance of scenarios was introduced and justified in part as a response to the uncertainties of the future. There are, however, different types of scenarios. There are scenarios that prepare managers for uncertainty by looking at alternative outcomes based on different combinations of values for key factors. There are also scenarios produced by processes for future visioning. The simple approach of Ohmae, based on diagnosing forces and their effects and then analysing them for their opportunities, was also presented.

QUESTIONS

1. How would you recognize that you had become closed to new and novel solutions to a strategic problem? In terms of the introduction to the chapter, how would you recognize that you were in danger of talking baloney?
2. While forecasts based on the past can be hopelessly wrong, what alternatives are there?
3. What do you think the price of oil will be per barrel in five years' time? What evidence have you used to come to this conclusion? Using the Toyota case study, do you think Toyota is correct in spending so much money on research into petrol alternatives?
4. What is the difference between foresight and forecast and does it matter much in practice anyway? Going back to Apollo and Dionysus, is forecasting a typical Apollo task, while foresight is more one for Dionysus? Or should both take place in a balanced manner?
5. How would you convince our small bakery owner to engage in some foresight?
6. This book is supposed to be a pragmatic treatment of strategy but halfway through this chapter you have stumbled on a philosophy class – post-modernism – surely you don't have to understand all this? What reasons (if any!) could you advance for thinking about strategy in terms of modernism, post-modernism and new modernism? Does thinking about strategy in these terms make a practical difference to how strategy is carried out?

7. What are the advantages of scenario planning? Are there any disadvantages?

8. Develop four scenarios for an organization you are familiar with or one featured in the case studies. What did you come up with? More importantly, did it allow you to have 'better' conversations about the future than you might have done without them? Also, do you think you uncovered any double-loop learning or anticipatory learning that might have to take place? Did the scenarios allow you to have 'better' thoughts about the HR implications of these scenarios? Lastly on this, to what extent can you generalize from the four different scenarios about the future?

9. Using the Procter & Gamble case study, can you see the company not through the eyes of its senior managers but of its customers? From this, use Ohmae's process to develop a couple of scenarios for the company to think about.

EXECUTIVE EXERCISE

This is an exercise in scenario planning. (Note that this will not involve the type of scenario preparation suggested by Ohmae, which we will be using for the executive exercise in Chapter 9.) Spend up to five or ten minutes by yourself trying to brainstorm answers to as many as possible of the following questions with respect to your organization and its industry (or one of its industries):

- Which of the current trends in this industry do you think will still be continuing in five years' time?
- What current trends do you think will have reversed or ceased in five years' time?
- What forecasts can you confidently make about current trends in five years' time?
- What assumptions do you think can be safely made about this industry in five years' time?
- What variables do you think are critical for the success of the businesses in this industry now? Will these still be critical in five years' time? What new variables might be critical?
- What critical variables do you think will be important but unpredictable in five years' time?

Try to arrive at a decision on the key assumptions that can be safely made about the future of the industry in five years' time. Now try to decide on the top two or three variables that will be hard to predict but highly critical for the industry. Combine assumptions and possible outcomes for the unpredictable variables to generate scenarios for the future of the industry. Build in details if you can. For example, some facts may be deduced from the assumptions or critical variables. Use the details to elaborate the scenario and make it seem convincing and plausible. Reject scenarios that seem less plausible. Decide on three scenarios (a most probable one, a worst-case scenario, and a highly desirable scenario). Use these scenarios to suggest two or three innovations that businesses in the industry should consider introducing.

If you are able to discuss your conclusions in a small group, report your scenarios and the ideas for innovations and ask others in the group to evaluate the plausibility of your analysis and ideas.

REFERENCES

Argyris, C (1990) *Overcoming Organizational Defences*, Allyn and Bacon, London

Grant, R M (1995) *Contemporary Strategy Analysis*, Blackwell Publishers, Oxford

Hamel, G and Prahalad, C K (1994) *Competing for the Future*, Harvard Business School Press, Boston

Joyce, P and Woods, A (1996) *Essential Strategic Management*, Butterworth-Heinemann, Oxford

Klein, H E and Linneman, R E (1984) Environmental Assessment: An international study of corporate practices, *Journal of Business Strategy*, Summer issue

O'Brien, F A and Meadows, M (1998) Future visioning: a case study of a scenario-based approach', in *Strategic Development: Methods and models*, eds R G Dyson and F A O'Brien, Wiley, Chichester

Ohmae, K (1982) *The Mind of the Strategist*, McGraw-Hill, London

Peters, T and Waterman, R (1982) *In Search of Excellence*, HarperCollins, New York

Ringland, G (1998) *Scenario Planning: Managing for the future*, Wiley, Chichester

Reading 8.1

Taken from Chapter 1 – Strategic planning in the greenhouse, in *Cool Companies* by Joseph J Romm (1999)

Imagine a world in which fossil-fuel use has begun a slow, steady decline. More than a third of the market for new electricity generation is supplied from renewable sources. The renewables industry has *annual* sales of $150 billion, and the fastest growing new source of power is solar energy. An environmentalist's fantasy? No, that's one of two planning scenarios for three to four decades from now, developed by Royal Dutch/Shell Group, the world's largest publicly traded oil company, widely viewed as a benchmark for strategic planning. In this future, average per capita energy consumption nearly doubles by 2060.

Imagine "a rather different world in which new technologies, systems and lifestyles would deliver continuing improvements in energy efficiency so that average per capita consumption rises by only some 15 percent by 2060."[1] A techno-fantasy? No, this is Shell's other energy scenario as described in 1997 by John Jennings, former chairman of the Shell Transport & Trading Group. "Technological advances are enabling increasing energy efficiency in many areas from industrial processes to building construction," *cutting primary energy use by up to 60 percent in the transportation, industrial, and commercial sector.* Shell bases this "dematerialization" scenario on emerging advances ranging from highly fuel-efficient "supercars" to advances in materials, miniaturization, and information technology.

Whether through cool power or energy efficiency, Royal Dutch/Shell Group, the best predictor in the energy business, anticipates a cool future for the world. It is betting hundreds of millions of dollars on its scenarios by expanding its renewable energy division. At the same time, the company is dramatically reducing its own greenhouse gas emissions. Shell projects it will reduce its total greenhouse gas emissions from the equivalent of 140 million tons of carbon dioxide in 1990 to 100 million tons or less in 2002.[2]

The key strategic planning question for any company is: How can we thrive in an uncertain future? The version of that question considered on these pages: What should we do if our core business is likely to be affected by growing concern over global warming? We will learn how big companies like Toyota, DuPont, Interface, and General Motors, as well as small ones, are changing their products and processes because of environmental considerations, including global warming. I begin with a company whose primary product—oil—is a leading cause of global warming: Royal Dutch/Shell. Shell is reinventing itself using its much admired approach to strategic planning. As you seek to help your own company change, you will find few better models than the process pioneered by Shell.

If a major producer of fossil fuels, such as Royal Dutch/Shell, can embrace the change that global warming requires, your company can, too. The key is scenario planning aimed at changing the decision-making assumptions of your managers.

All that is needed for either of Shell's remarkable scenarios to come true is for companies to adopt the cool strategies described in this book.

The planners of Royal Dutch/Shell

Throughout the 1990s, Royal Dutch/Shell has found itself leading the list of the world's most profitable companies, thanks in large part to its excellence in strategic planning. In 1997, the company had sales of $128 billion, net income of $7.8 billion, and more than 100,000 employees in 132 countries.

Yet, just as the company has reached the top, its future is in jeopardy. On the one hand, the company believes that both global warming and limited supplies of fossil fuels, particularly oil, merit serious attention. On the other hand, the company has been shaken by the public response to its practices in Nigeria and to its plans to dispose of its forty-story Brent Spar oil storage tank. These factors have driven the company's latest efforts at planning, inspiring its top managers to pursue transforming Shell into a "sustainable energy company." While it is easy to be skeptical of such a difficult goal for the world's largest oil company, Shell's track record on turning planning into reality is matched by very, very few companies.

According to the *Economist* magazine, "The only oil company to anticipate both 1973's oil-price boom and 1986's bust was Royal Dutch/Shell."[3] Correctly anticipating the future was not the hard part for the Planning Group. One of the developers of Shell's planning process, Pierre Wack, has written, "Surprises in the business environment almost never emerge without warning." Many others foresaw the oil crisis. *The hard part was getting Shell's managers to rethink their mental models.* Wack saw the same mind-set problems that scientists, for example, must overcome before they break through to novel insights. Wack came to realize that providing new information was not enough, because "novel information, outside the span of managerial expectations, may not penetrate the core of decision makers' minds, where possible futures are rehearsed and judgment exercised."[4]

Wack compares that time to the days prior to the attack on Pearl Harbor, when there was a massive volume of intelligence signals ("noise") coming in. He quotes Roberta Wohlstetter writing in 1962: "To discriminate significant sounds against this background of noise, one has to be listening for something or for one of several things…. One needs not only an ear but a variety of hypotheses that guide observation." The Japanese commander of the attack, Mitsuo Fuchida, was quite surprised that the attack on Pearl Harbor was a surprise. Prior to the Russo-Japanese War of 1904, the Japanese Navy used a surprise attack to destroy the Russian Pacific fleet at anchor in Port Arthur. Fuchida asked, "Had these Americans never heard of Port Arthur?"[5]

The approach Wack developed at Shell was "scenario planning", but a type of scenario planning entirely different from that of most companies. Wack did not merely want to quantify uncertainties—i.e., the price of oil may be $20 or $40 per barrel in 2005—because this offers little help to decision makers. Wack wanted to offer managers two or more complete worldviews or scenarios—grounded in a sound analysis of reality. One of these scenarios might be business as usual, while at least one would be a radically different, though plausible, view of the world.

Even though Wack foresaw the energy crisis and presented the results to Shell's management, "no more than a third of Shell's critical decision centers" were acting on the insights gained from the energy crisis scenario. Wack came to realize that although all managers had the new information, most were still processing it through their old paradigm or mental model, what Wack called their "microcosm".

I cannot overemphasize this point: unless the corporate microcosm changes, managerial behavior will not change; the internal compass must be recalibrated....

Our real target was the microcosms of our decision makers: unless we influenced the mental image, the picture of reality held by critical decision makers, our scenarios would be like water on stone....

Wack and his fellow planners realized they "needed to design scenarios so that managers would question their own model of reality and change it when necessary, so as to come up with strategic insights beyond their minds' previous reach." The Planning Group designed a set of scenarios early in 1973 that would force a paradigm shift. Shell managers were presented a business-as-usual scenario. They were also presented the underlying assumptions required for that scenario to hold. Those assumptions were shown to be wholly unrealistic, requiring several "miracles"—each of which was highly improbable—to occur simultaneously. The only way to delay the energy crisis would be the discovery of "new Middle East–sized oil reserves in an area that would have no problem in absorbing revenues" or "seizure and control of producers by consuming countries."

Once managers saw that their faith in the status quo was built on miracles, they were more receptive to new thinking. Wack and his fellow planners led the Shell managers through the process of building a new paradigm, showing them what was likely to happen in the future and what the implications were for the managers' own decisions and actions.

Since oil price increases were inevitable, oil demand would drop. Demand would no longer outpace GNP. Using this scenario, Wack told the refining managers to prepare to become "a low-growth industry."

The planners made clear that the energy shock would have dramatic effects worldwide, but it would affect individual nations differently. The effect would depend on whether a given country was an oil exporter or importer, whether it was free market or centrally planned, and, for importers, how much they relied on imports and how easily they could find alternatives. Therefore, one basic, rigid strategy would not be useful for operating different companies in different parts of the world. Each region would have to respond independently. As a result, Shell would "need to further decentralize the decision-making and strategic process."

Even those managers who remained skeptical at least understood the flaws in their old paradigm and the powerful implications of the new one. When the OPEC oil embargo did occur, and the underlying assumptions of the energy crisis scenario were proven correct, Shell managers were far quicker to shift their behavior accordingly. They slowed down investments in refineries. Their projections of energy demand were consistently lower and more accurate than those of their competitors. They decentralized, while their competitors were becoming more centralized—and hence more inflexible—in a world of rapidly changing events.

Shell rose rapidly from its position as the weakest of the seven largest oil companies in 1970 to one of the two strongest *only ten years later.* Anticipating the oil bust of the mid-1980s was apparently even more lucrative, helping to put the company atop *Fortune* magazine's list of the world's most profitable companies in the 1990s.

Shell developed the two scenarios described in this chapter in the mid-1990s. Predicting our energy future over the next few decades is risky, but Shell's track record on predictions is hard to beat. When such a company predicts a fundamental transition from fossil fuels to renewable energy and other advanced energy technologies—one that will have a significant impact on every aspect of our lives—smart executives pay attention.[6]

Scenario one: sustained growth (with cool power)

The first scenario, which Shell labels "Sustained Growth", entails rapid growth in renewable energy. Here is what Chris Fay, Chairman and CEO of Shell UK Ltd., said in a 1995 speech:

> There is clearly a limit to fossil fuel. I showed how Shell analysis suggests that resources and supplies are likely to peak around 2030 before declining slowly. …
> But what about the growing gap between demand and fossil fuel supplies? Some will obviously be filled by hydroelectric and nuclear power. Far more important will be the contribution of alternative, renewable energy supplies.

Fay presented a detailed analysis of future trends in oil supply and demand, noting that the fossil fuel peak in 2030 would occur at a usage level 50 percent higher than today. Shell's analysis does not rely exclusively on supply limits. After all, people have been worried about such limits for decades. What's significant is that the analysis incorporates the tremendous technological advances that have been made in renewables over the past two decades and that are projected to be made over the next two decades.

These advances in wind power, solar energy, and biomass power (discussed in Chapter 6) have been receiving only modest press attention. They have, however, been sufficient to convince Shell planners that renewables may take over the market for electricity generation in a few decades *even if electricity from fossil fuels continues to decline in costs.* Their analysis does not assume price hikes in fossil fuels. Nor does Shell assume any attempt by governments to incorporate environmental costs into the price of energy, even though every single independent analysis has found much higher environmental costs for fossil fuel generation than for non-fossil fuel generation. Indeed, the growing consensus on the dangers of global warming, as reflected in the work of the Intergovernmental Panel on Climate Change and in the Kyoto agreement, makes it almost inevitable that carbon dioxide will have a price in most industrialized countries within several years. (see Chapter 10).

This scenario is called Sustained Growth because "abundant energy supply is provided at competitive prices, as productivity in supply keeps improving in an open market context." In this scenario, energy consumed per capita worldwide rises steadily, so much so that by 2060 the global average reaches the level Japan has today. Worldwide economic growth of 3 percent per year is achieved through a 1 percent per year improvement in energy intensity (energy per unit GDP) and a 2 percent per year increase in energy production, which increasingly comes from renewable sources.

According to Shell's strategic planning group, the Sustained Growth scenario "can claim to be a genuine 'Business as Usual' scenario, since its energy demand is a continuation of a long historical trend, and the energy is supplied in the way which continues the pattern [of the last 100 years] in which energy forms rise and fall over periods of decades."

Shells' analysis projects the steady and large drops in the price of renewables of the last two decades into the next two decades, as further advances in technology combine with economies of scale as market share grows. For instance, Shell believes that by 2010 commercial energy from biomass (plant matter) could provide 5 percent of the world's power. The value of that power generation would exceed $20 billion. By the mid-2020s, annual sales of wind power plants could exceed $50 billion.

Shell expects photovoltaics (which converts sunlight into electricity), along with emerging highly efficient, low-polluting natural-gas-driven technologies, such as fuel cells (see Chapter 6), to be key drivers of the growth of distributed power systems. Such systems may increasingly be the power source of choice as opposed to the large, expensive, polluting power plants of the past. Just as smaller, more versatile personal computers trumped large mainframe computers or as cellular phones are making the grid of telephone lines obsolescent, distributed sources can obviate the need for huge power lines and other costly elements of a large electric-power grid in developing nations (aside from having superior environmental performance.) The Sustained Growth scenario projects that photovoltaics and other direct conversion of sunlight will be the most rapidly growing form of commercial energy after 2020. Annual sales in 2030 could exceed $100 billion.[7]

This is a "cool power" scenario because it anticipates greatly expanded use of both renewable energy and advanced natural gas technologies. This scenario is tantalizing not only because of Shell's reputation but because it offers the serious possibility that the world could soon realize the dream of nearly pollution-free energy. As we will see, Shell is betting a considerable amount of money on this scenario.

Scenario Two: Dematerialization (with energy efficiency)
Shell's second, "Dematerialization", scenario is "driven by convergent and mutually enhancing developments in information technology, telecommunications, materials and biotechnology which in turn could have considerable potential to change social values and with them lifestyles. If this indeed happened, we would experience a transition phenomenon as profound as that brought about by the invention of the automobile and subsequent developments in individual mobility during this century."

Shell planners, for instance, see converging technological developments having a revolutionary impact on transportation. Advances in engines (such as fuel cells), batteries, control system electronics, alternative fuels, and super-strong, light-weight materials lead to the emergence of a super-efficient car. This supercar, together with advances in information technologies that make possible extensive telecommuting, internet shopping, and the like, reduce primary energy use in transportation by 60 percent. New technologies, processes, and materials make possible similarly large savings – 60 percent – in the industrial and commercial sectors. *To achieve this level of savings would require most companies in the developed world and then in the developing world to adopt the energy-efficiency strategies described in this book.*

In this scenario, average per capita energy consumption rises by only some 15 percent by 2060. Primary energy use grows at only 1.3 percent per year until 2030 and then slows to "below one percent as greater energy productivity spreads from the more advanced regions of the OECD to the industrialized and developing countries elsewhere," says Jennings. "To support a three percent growth in GDP, improvements in energy intensity will have to reach a sustained two percent per annum – a rate which admittedly has only been seen for limited periods in the past." Indeed, the historical average of energy intensity improvements in the United States for the last 100 years has been 1 percent per year.

Scenarios are not, however, predictions. The Royal Dutch/Shell planners are not saying how the world *will* be or even how the world *should* be, only how the world *may* be. What is particularly interesting about these scenarios is thr extent to which Shell believes in them and is willing to act on them. Perhaps this is in part because these scenarios emerged at a time when the company was, in several respects, under siege.

Driving Strategic Change at Shell

In the mid-1990s, Shell was trying to decide what to do with a forty-story North Sea oil storage tank, named Brent Spar, that it no longer needed. Its giant carcass extended more than 90 feet above the surface and 370 feet below. When Shell and the British government agreed to allow the company to scuttle the platform and let it sink to the bottom of the ocean, Greenpeace organized a boycott against Shell gasoline in Europe and even landed protesters on the platform itself. Ultimately, the public outcry drove Shell to get independent scientific help to decide what to do with Brent Spar. It chose an innovative reuse proposal for the tank. Slices of the Spar's hull will be cleaned and then used to help complete a planned extension of a Norwegian landing dock. This agreement saved both money and energy that would otherwise have been spent in new steel construction.

At the same time, Shell has been criticized for its operations in Nigeria, where it has been a major oil producer for decades. Nigeria has had a history of political repression. When members of the Ogoni people began attacking the company's oil fields in the early 1990s, "Shell gave Nigeria an important pretext for violence when it specifically asked the government to send the mobile police – known locally as the 'kill-and-go mob'." *The New York Times* explained in 1996. "Shell paid for the transportation and salary bonuses of some troops – ostensibly oilfield guards – who committed the abuses."[8]

There was more. Growing concern over climate change has led to increased criticisms of Shell, both because of its emissions and for its membership in the Global Climate Coalition, an organization that opposes strong action on global warming. Far more so than in America, Europeans view strong action on global warming as essential and have been critical of companies that appear to endorse inaction.

In response to all of these issues, Shell launched a major effort to rethink its purpose and long-term goals. In the mid-1990s, the company interviewed 7,500 members of the general public in ten countries; 1,300 opinion leaders in twenty-five countries, including experts on energy and the environment; and 600 Shell people in fifty-five countries "to understand society's expectations of multinational companies" and "to explore the reputation, image, and overall standing of the Group." In a remarkable 1998 report, "Profits and Principles – Does There Have to Be a Choice?" the company reported some of the questions in sobering terms: *"We had looked in the mirror and we neither recognized nor liked what we saw."*

The result has been a series of actions to reinvent the company. For instance, in the report Shell committed to begin reporting a "triple bottom line" of economic, social, and environmental performance. Shell will continue reporting basic economic measures, such as "return on average capital employed" and economic value added. In addition, Shell will report on "environmental value added," acknowledging "we must adjust our measurements of wealth creation and profit with a charge for natural capital employed," taking into account the impact of their actions on the ecosystem and the depletion of raw materials. The third bottom line Shell will report on is "social value added," which includes benchmarks on social and ethical accountability.

Other reinvention actions involve Shell's business investments. In October 1997, the company established a fifth core business, Shell Solar, which will sit alongside its other core businesses: exploration and production, oil products, chemicals, plus gas and oil. Shell Solar brings together the company's activities in solar, biomass, and forestry. Shell says it will pump more than $500 million into renewable energy technology over the next five years, splitting the money between photovoltaics and biomass. *Shell already owns two photovoltaic companies*, one in Japan and one in the Netherlands. It plans to increase solar cell manufacturing worldwide, with the goal of capturing a 10 percent share of the photovoltaics market by 2005. It is exploring the possibility of entering the wind power business.

The company also plans to expand its existing tree plantation business, much of which is located in South America. It intends to apply its expertise in this area to development of biomass power generation, which, as noted earlier, it expects to be a rapidly growing business.

This move "underscores the Group's strategic direction," said Jeroen van der Veer, the group managing director responsible for renewables, "which is to provide energy and develop resources efficiently, responsibly, and profitably in order to help meet the world's growing needs and to do so in a way that contributes to sustainable development." Commenting on van der Veer's statement, *Oil & Gas Journal* noted in November 1997,

"Two years ago, no oil company would have risked a statement stressing sustainable development – at least in the context generally favored by environmental activists – but Shell has learned some hard lessons."[9]

Shell's vision of sustainable development is perhaps best exemplified by its idea of a "Sun Station" for self-sustaining communities:

> In operation, a Sun Station can be owned and managed by Shell Solar or by a local consortium of investors. A station manager with a small local team will operate a tree nursery, a managed wood plantation of high-yield tree varieties, tree harvesting and delivery, and power generation equipment based on a small wood gasifier-engine system. A local grid will be installed to distribute electricity to homes, health clinics, schools and commercial activities such as small workshops. Photovoltaic power will also provide backup resources for essential uses such as vaccine refrigeration. Co-generated heat supplies will be available for grain-drying, laundry, etc. Where connection to the grid is impracticable, photovoltaic panels with dedicated battery storage will provide basic lighting and other low-power applications including radio and television. A rural shop located at the power generation sites would stock goods for basic energy needs such as high-efficiency/low-energy consuming lamps or appliances, solar home systems, batteries, gas cylinders, and perhaps fuel and lubricants for two-stroke engines.

That's Royal Dutch/Shell talking – not Arthur C. Clarke or any other science fiction visionary.

Shell is also beginning to invest in the core element of its Dematerialization scenario – the hydrogen fuel cell at the heart of the supercar. Fuel cells are pollution-free electric "engines" that run on hydrogen (see Chapter 6). At the July 1998 launch of London's new Zevco hydrogen-powered taxi, Chris Fay said "we believe that hydrogen fuel-cell powered cars are likely to make a major entrance into the vehicle market throughout Europe and the U.S. by 2005."

In August 1998, Shell signed an agreement to work with a fuel cell engine company owned by DaimlerChrysler, Ballard Power Systems in Canada, and Ford Motor Company. Initially, fuel cell cars are likely to run on liquid fuels such as gasoline, if those fuels can be converted to hydrogen cost-effectively. Shell has proprietary technology for making such conversions. Running on gasoline, fuel cell cars would still have half the carbon dioxide emissions of a regular car.

In the long term, Shell believes cars will run on hydrogen that is generated from renewable energy sources. Those would truly be cool cars, since they would have no carbon dioxide emissions at all. Shell has launched a new company, Shell Hydrogen, to control all activities related to fuel cells and hydrogen research. Fay noted that "at Shell, we are convinced that hydrogen . . . represents one of the fuels of tomorrow. For us, the long-term decarbonization of fuel represents an exciting challenge. *Hydrogen could be the next logical step in the long but steady march from high carbon to low carbon to no carbon fuels.*"

On global warming, Shell's thinking extends back a decade or more. In 1989, Ged Davis, head of scenario planning for Shell International, wrote a paper for Shell titled,

"Global Warming: The Role of Energy-efficient Technologies." Today, the company's public expression of concern spans the breadth of their senior management. Shell's senior managing director, Cor Herkstroter, has said, "Despite the many remaining uncertainties about the nature and the risks of the process, I believe that there is now sufficient evidence to support prudent precautionary action." Jennings has said, "given the risks and uncertainties, it is clearly prudent to develop alternative ways of generating energy, learn to use energy more efficiently, and reduce the environmental impact of producing and burning fossil fuels."

In a February 1998 speech, Mark Moody-Stuart, Shell's chief executive, said, "For my own part, I find myself increasingly persuaded that a climate effect may be occurring . . . We believe that the nature of this risk is such that prudent precautionary measures should be taken. We favored agreement at Kyoto — provided targets were consistent with a flexible long-term global approach. And we believe the outcome was reasonable." He noted that charting a careful course of action on climate change "means not allowing real concern for economic costs and practicalities to prompt shrill opposition to any action — or even a tobacco-industry-like reluctance to admit the possibility of any problem."

In April 1998, Shell decided to leave the Global Climate Coalition.[10] It has also started a new "Sustainable Energy Solutions" fund to support projects outside the company, which will ultimately grow to $25 million a year. At the same time, it has made a high-level internal commitment to reinvent itself as a "sustainable energy company." Whether the world's most profitable oil company can, in fact, achieve as seemingly a contradictory a goal as being a sustainable energy company remains to be seen; but given their past successes, Shell should never be underestimated.

The company has also begun to address its own greenhouse gas (GHG) emissions, which include carbon dioxide as well as methane and chlorofluorocarbons. The company expects to cut its emissions sharply by curtailing the flaring of natural gas in its oil production, by making its operations more energy efficient, and by factoring in a "carbon price penalty in our investment calculations for new projects, and existing major assets, with major GHG emissions." In August 1998 Jeroen van der Veer told an International Energy Agency conference that Shell had already reduced its total GHG emissions 13 percent below 1990 levels and that emissions per unit of production had dropped by nearly 30 percent. In 2002, Shell projects its total emissions will be more than 25 percent below 1990 levels, a drop from 140 million tons of carbon dioxide equivalent to 100 million tons or less.

Shell has, as we have seen, already begun to devote considerable resources to bringing about the two scenarios described earlier, "Sustained Growth" and "Dematerialization." Both of these are, in some sense, sustainable energy scenarios because they stabilize carbon dioxide concentrations at twice the pre-industrial levels. This is still likely to result in serious climate change worldwide. Yet, it would stave off the far more brutal impacts that the models suggest the planet would experience if we triple or quadruple carbon dioxide concentrations, which is likely without strong action from both the public and private sector. Either of the goals at the heart of the scenarios —

50 percent renewable power by 2050 or decades of 2 percent per year improvement in energy intensity – will require a significant number of the companies in this country and around the world to become cool.

This book is, in one sense, a guide for how to make Shell's scenarios a reality. Indeed, I suspect the ultimate way the planet will stabilize carbon dioxide concentrations is by combining Shell's scenarios, by combining cool power *and* energy efficiency.

Now let's examine the guiding principle behind creating a cool company – the application of lean thinking to reducing your company's greenhouse gas emissions. That will explain why such reductions can be achieved together with the kind of rise in profits and productivity needed to sustain economic growth throughout the twenty-first century.

© Joseph J Romm, 1999

Reading 8.2

Taken from Chapter 1 – The next industrial revolution, in *Natural Capitalism* by Paul Hawker, Amory B Lovins and L Hunter Lovins (1999)

Imagine for a moment a world where cities have become peaceful and serene because cars and buses are whisper quiet, vehicles exhaust only water vapour, and parks and greenways have replaced unneeded urban freeways. OPEC has ceased to function because the price of oil has fallen to five dollars a barrel, but there are few buyers for it because cheaper and better ways now exist to get the services people once turned to oil to provide. Living standards for all people have dramatically improved, particularly for the poor and those in developing countries. Involuntary unemployment no longer exists, and income taxes have largely been eliminated. Houses, even low-income housing units, can pay part of their mortgage costs by the energy they *produce*; there are few if any active landfills; worldwide forest cover is increasing; dams are being dismantled; atmospheric CO_2 levels are decreasing for the first time in two hundred years; and effluent water leaving factories is cleaner than the water coming into them. Industrialized countries have reduced resource use by 80 percent while improving the quality of life. Among these technological changes, there are important social changes. The frayed social nets of Western countries have been repaired. With the explosion of family-wage jobs, welfare demand has fallen. A progressive and active union movement has taken the lead to work with business, environmentalists and government to create "just transitions" for workers as society phases out coal, nuclear energy and oil. In communities and towns, churches, corporations and labor groups promote a new living-wage social contract as the least expensive way to ensure the growth and preservation of valuable social capital. Is this the vision of utopia? In fact, the changes described here could come about in the decades to come as the result of economic and technological trends already in place.

This book is about these and many other possibilities.

It is about the possibilities that will arise from the birth of a new type of industrialism, one that differs in its philosophy, goals, and fundamental processes from the industrial system that is the standard today. In the next century, as human population doubles and the resources available per person drop by one-half to three-fourths, a remarkable transformation of industry and commerce can occur. Through this transformation, society will be able to create a vital economy that uses radically less material and energy. This economy can free up resources, reduce taxes on personal income, increase per-capita spending on social ills (while simultaneously reducing those ills), and begin to restore the damaged environment of the earth. These necessary changes done properly can promote economic efficiency, ecological conservation and social equity.

The industrial revolution that gave rise to modern capitalism greatly expanded the possibilities for the material development of humankind. It continues to do so today, but at a severe price. Since the mid-eighteenth century, more of nature has been destroyed than in all prior history. While industrial systems have reached pinnacles of success, able to muster and accumulate human-made capital on vast levels, *natural capital*, on which civilization depends to create economic prosperity, is rapidly declining,[1] and the rate of loss is increasing proportionate to gains in material well-being. *Natural capital* includes all the familiar resources used by humankind: water, minerals, oil, trees, fish, soil, air, et cetera. But it also encompasses living systems, which include grasslands, savannas, wetlands, estuaries, oceans, coral reefs, riparian corridors, tundras and rainforests. These are deteriorating worldwide at an unprecedented rate. Within these ecological communities are the fungi, ponds, mammals, humus, amphibians, bacteria, trees, flagellates, insects, songbirds, ferns, starfish, and flowers that make life possible and worth living on this planet.

As more people and businesses place greater strain in living systems, limits to prosperity are coming to be determined by natural capital rather than industrial prowess. This is not to say that the world is running out of commodities in the near future. The prices for most raw materials are at a twenty-eight-year low and are still falling. Supplies are cheap and appear to be abundant, due to a number of reasons: the collapse of the Asian economies, globalization of trade, cheaper transport costs, imbalances in market power that enable commodity traders and middlemen to squeeze producers and in large measure the success of powerful new extractive technologies, whose correspondingly extensive damage to ecosystems is seldom given a monetary value. After richer ores are exhausted, skilled mining companies can now level and grind up whole mountains of poorer-quality ores to extract the metals desired. But while technology keeps ahead of depletion, providing what appear to be ever-cheaper metals, they only appear cheap, because the stripped rainforest and the mountain of toxic tailings spilling into rivers, the impoverished villages and eroded indigenous cultures – all the consequences they leave in their wake – are not factored into the cost of production.

It is not the supplies of oil or copper that are beginning to limit our development but life itself. Today, our continuing progress is restricted not by the number of fishing boats but by the decreasing number of fish; not by the power of pumps but by the depletion of aquifers; not by the number of chainsaws but by the disappearance of primary forests. While living systems are the source of such desired materials as wood, fish or food, of utmost importance are the *services* that they offer,[2] services that are far more critical to human prosperity than are nonrenewable resources. A forest provides not only the resource of wood but also the services of water storage and flood management. A healthy environment automatically supplies not only clean air and water, rainfall, ocean productivity, fertile soil, and watershed resilience but also such less-appreciated functions as waste processing (both natural and industrial), buffering against the extremes of weather, and regeneration of the atmosphere.

Humankind has inherited a 3.8-billion-year store of natural capital. At present rates of use and degradation, there will be little left by the end of the next century. This is not only a matter of aesthetics and morality, it is of the utmost practical concern to society and all people. Despite reams of press about the state of the environment and rafts of laws attempting to prevent further loss, the stock of natural capital is plummeting and the vital life-giving services that flow from it are critical to our prosperity.

Natural capitalism recognizes the critical interdependency between the production and use of human-made capital and the maintenance and supply of natural capital. The traditional definition of capital is accumulated wealth in the form of investment, factories and equipment. Actually, an economy needs four types of capital to function properly:

- human capital, in the form of labor and intelligence, culture and organization
- financial capital, consisting of cash, investments and monetary instruments
- manufactured capital, including infrastructure, machines, tools, and factories
- natural capital, made up of resources, living systems and ecosystem services

The industrial system uses the first three forms of capital to transform natural capital into the stuff of our daily lives: cars, highways, cities, bridges, houses, food, medicine, hospitals and schools.

The climate debate is a public issue in which the assets at risk are not specific resources, like oil, fish or timber, but a life-supporting system. One of nature's most critical cycles is the continual exchange of carbon dioxide and oxygen among plants and animals. This "recycling service" is provided by nature free of charge. But today carbon dioxide is building up in the atmosphere, due in part to combustion of fossil fuels. In effect, the capacity of the natural system to recycle carbon dioxide has been exceeded, just as overfishing can exceed the capacity of a fishery to replenish stocks. But what is especially important to realize is that there is no known alternative to nature's carbon cycle service.

Beside climate, the changes in the biosphere are widespread. In the past half century, the world has lost a fourth of its topsoil and a third of its forest cover. At present rates of destruction, we will lose 70 percent of the world's coral reefs in our lifetime, host to 25 percent of marine life.[3] In the past three decades, one-third of the planet's resources, its "natural wealth," has been consumed. We are losing freshwater ecosystems at the rate of 6 percent a year, marine ecosystems by 4 percent a year.[4] There is no longer any serious scientific dispute that the decline in every living system in the world is reaching such levels that an increasing number of them are starting to lose, often at a pace accelerated by the interactions of their decline, their assured ability to sustain the continuity of the life process. We have reached an extraordinary threshold.

Recognition of this shadow side of the success of industrial production has triggered the second of the two great intellectual shifts of the late twentieth century. The end of the Cold War and the fall of communism was the first such shift; the second, now quietly emerging, is the end of the war against life on earth and the eventual ascendance of what we call natural capitalism.

Capitalism, as practised, is a financially profitable, nonsustainable aberration in human development. What might be called "industrial capitalism" does not fully conform to its own accounting principles. It liquidates its capital and calls it income. It neglects to assign any value to the largest stocks of capital it employs – the natural resources and living systems, as well as the social and cultural systems that are the basis of human capital.

But this deficiency in business operations cannot be corrected simply by assigning monetary values to natural capital, for three reasons. First, many of the services we receive from living systems have no known substitutes at any price; for example, oxygen production by green plants. This was demonstrated memorably in 1991–93 when the scientists operating the $200 million Biosphere 2 experiment in Arizona discovered that it was unable to maintain life-supporting oxygen levels for the eight people living inside. Biosphere 1, a.k.a. Planet Earth, performs this task daily at no charge for 6 billion people.

Second, valuing natural capital is a difficult and imprecise exercise at best. Nonetheless, several recent assessments have estimated that biological services flowing directly into society from the stock of natural capital are worth at least $36 trillion annually.[5] That figure is close to the annual gross world product of approximately $39 trillion – a striking measure of the value of natural capital to the economy. If natural capital stocks were given a monetary value, assuming the assets yielded "interest" of $36 trillion annually, the world's natural capital would be valued at somewhere between $400 and $500 trillion – tens of thousands of dollars for every person on the planet. That is undoubtedly a conservative figure given the fact that anything we can't live without and can't replace at any price could be said to have an infinite value.

Additionally, just as technology cannot replace the planet's life-support systems, so, too, are machines unable to provide a substitute for human intelligence, knowledge, wisdom, organizational abilities and culture. The World Bank's 1995 *Wealth Index* found the sum value of human capital to be three times greater than all the financial and manufactured capital reflected on global balance sheets.[6] This, too, appears to be a conservative estimate, since it counts only the market value of human employment, not uncompensated effort or cultural resources.

It is not the aim of this book to assess how to determine value for such unaccounted-for forms of capital. It is clear, however, that behaving as though they are valueless has brought us to the verge of disaster. But if it is in practice difficult to tabulate the value of natural and human capital on balance sheets, how can governments and conscientious business persons make decisions about the responsible use of earth's living systems?

Conventional capitalism

Following Einstein's dictum that problems can't be solved within the mind-set that created them, the first step towards any comprehensive economic and ecological change is to understand the mental model that forms the basis of present economic thinking. The mind-set of the present capitalist system might be summarized as follows:

- Economic progress can best occur in free-market systems of production and distribution where reinvested profits make labor and capital increasingly productive.

- Competitive advantage is gained when bigger, more efficient plants manufacture more products for sale to expanding markets.
- Growth in total output (GDP) maximizes human well-being.
- Any resource shortages that do occur will elicit the development of substitutes.
- Concerns for a healthy environment are important but must be balanced against the requirements of economic growth, if a high standard of living is to be maintained.
- Free enterprise and market forces will allocate people and resources to their highest and best uses.

The origins of this worldview go back centuries, but it took the industrial revolution to establish it as the primary economic ideology. This sudden, almost violent, change in the means of production and distribution of goods, in sector after economic sector, introduced a new element that redefined the basic formula for the creation of material products: Machines powered by water, wood, charcoal, coal, oil, and eventually electricity accelerated or accomplished some or all of the work formerly performed by laborers. Human productive capabilities began to grow exponentially. What took two hundred workers in 1770 could be done by a single spinner in the British textile industry by 1812. With such astonishingly improved productivity, the labor force was able to manufacture a vastly larger volume of basic necessities like cloth at greatly reduced cost. This in turn rapidly raised standards of living and real wages, increasing demand for other products in other industries. Further technological breakthroughs proliferated and as industry after industry became mechanized, leading to even lower prices and higher incomes, all of these factors fueled a self-sustaining and increasing demand for transportation, housing, education, clothing and other goods, creating the foundation of modern commerce.[7]

The past two hundred years of massive growth in prosperity and manufactured capital have been accompanied by a prodigious body of economic theory analyzing it, all based on the fallacy that natural and human capital have little value as compared to final output. In the standard industrial model, the creation of value is portrayed as a linear sequence of extraction, production and distribution: Raw materials are introduced. (Enter nature, stage left.) Labor uses technologies to transform these resources into products, which are sold to create profits. The wastes from production processes and soon the products themselves, are somehow disposed of somewhere else. (Exit waste, stage right.) The "somewheres" in this scenario are not the concern of classical economics: Enough money can buy enough resources, so the theory goes, and enough "elsewheres" to dispose of them afterward.

This conventional view of value creation is not without its critics. Viewing the economic process as a disembodied, circular flow of value between production and consumption, argues economist Herman Daly, is like trying to understand an animal only in terms of its circulatory system, without taking into account the fact it also has a digestive tract that ties it firmly to its environment at both ends. But there is an even more fundamental critique to be applied here, and it is one based on simple logic. The evidence of our senses is sufficient to tell us that all economic activity – all that human beings are, all that they can ever accomplish – is embedded within the workings of a particular planet. That planet is not growing, so the somewheres and elsewheres are always with us. The increasing removal of resources, their transport and use, and their replacement with waste steadily erodes our stock of natural capital.

With nearly ten thousand new people arriving on earth every hour, a new and unfamiliar pattern of scarcity is now emerging. At the beginning of the industrial revolution, labor was overworked and relatively scarce (the population was about one-tenth of current totals), while global stocks of natural capital were abundant and unexploited. But today the situation has been reversed: After two centuries of rises in labor productivity, the liquidation of natural resources at their extraction cost rather than their replacement value and the exploitation of living systems as if they were free, infinite and in perpetual renewal, it is people who have become an abundant resource, while *nature* is becoming disturbingly scarce.

Applying the same economic logic that drove the industrial revolution to this newly emerging pattern of scarcity implies that, if there is to be prosperity in the future, society must make its use of *resources* vastly more productive – deriving four, ten, or even a hundred times as much benefit from each unit of energy, water, materials, or anything else borrowed from the planet and consumed. Achieving this degree of efficiency may not be as difficult as it might seem because from a materials and energy perspective, the economy is massively inefficient. In the United States, the materials used by the metabolism of industry amount to more than twenty times every citizen's weight per day – more than one million pounds per American per year. The global flow of matter, some 500 billion tons per year, most of it wasted, is largely invisible. Yet obtaining, moving, using and disposing of it is steadily undermining the health of the planet, which is showing ever greater signs of stress, even of biological breakdown. Human beings already use over half the world's accessible surface freshwater, have transformed one-third to one-half of its land surface, fix more nitrogen than do all natural systems on land and appropriate more than two-fifths of the planet's entire land-based primary biological productivity.[8] The doubling of these burdens with rising population will displace many of the millions of other species, undermining the very web of life.

The resulting ecological strains are also causing or exacerbating many forms of social distress and conflict. For example, grinding poverty, hunger, malnutrition, and rampant disease affect one-third of the world and are growing in absolute numbers; not surprisingly, crime, corruption, lawlessness, and anarchy are also on the rise (the fastest-growing industry in the world is security and private police protection); fleeing refugee populations have increased throughout the nineties to at least tens of millions; over a billion people in the world who need to work cannot find jobs, or toil at such menial work that they cannot support themselves or their families;[9] meanwhile, the loss of forests, topsoil, fisheries and freshwater is, in some cases, exacerbating regional and national conflicts.

What would our economy look like if it fully valued *all* forms of capital, including human and natural capital? What if our economy were organized not around the lifeless abstractions of neoclassical economics and accountancy but around the biological realities of nature? What if Generally Accepted Accounting Practice booked natural and human capital not as a free amenity in putative inexhaustible supply but as a finite and integrally valuable factor of production? What if, in the absence of a rigorous way to practice such accounting, companies started to act *as if* such principles were in force? This choice is possible and such an economy would offer a stunning new set of opportunities for all of society, amounting to no less than the *next industrial revolution*.

Capitalism as if living systems mattered

Natural capitalism and the possibility of a new industrial system are based on a very different mind-set and set of values than conventional capitalism. Its fundamental assumptions include the following:

- The environment is not a minor factor of production but rather is "an envelope containing, provisioning and sustaining the entire economy."[10]
- The limiting factor to future economic development is the availability and functionality of *natural capital*, in particular, life-supporting services that have no substitutes and currently have no market value.
- Misconceived or badly designed business systems, population growth, and wasteful patterns of consumption are the primary causes of the loss of natural capital, and all three must be addressed to achieve a sustainable economy.
- Future economic progress can best take place in democratic, market-based systems of production and distribution in which *all* forms of capital are fully valued, including human, manufactured, financial and natural capital.
- One of the keys to the most beneficial employment of people, money and the environment is radical increases in resource productivity.
- Human welfare is best served by improving the quality and flow of desired services delivered, rather than by merely increasing the total dollar flow.
- Economic and environmental sustainability depends on redressing global inequities of income and material well-being.
- The best long-term environment for commerce is provided by true democratic systems of governance that are based on the needs of people rather than business.

This book introduces four central strategies of natural capitalism that are a means to enable countries, companies and communities to operate by behaving as if all forms of capital were valued. Ensuring a perpetual annuity of valuable social and natural processes to serve a growing population is not just a prudent investment but a critical need in the coming decades. Doing so can avert scarcity, perpetuate abundance and provide a solid basis for social development; it is the basis of responsible stewardship and prosperity for the next century and beyond.

    1. Radical Resource Productivity. Radically increased resource productivity is the corner stone of natural capitalism because using resources more effectively has three

significant benefits: it slows resource depletion at one end of the value chain, lowers pollution at the other end and provides a basis to increase worldwide employment with meaningful jobs. The result can be lower costs for business and society, which no longer has to pay for the chief causes of ecosystem and social disruption. Nearly all environmental and social harm is an artifact of the uneconomically wasteful use of human and natural resources, but radical resource productivity strategies can nearly halt the degradation of the biosphere, make it more profitable to employ people and thus safeguard against the loss of vital living systems and social cohesion.

2. Biomimicry. Reducing the wasteful throughput of materials – indeed, eliminating the very idea of waste – can be accomplished by redesigning industrial systems on biological lines that change the nature of industrial processes and materials, enabling the constant reuse of materials in continuous closed cycles and often the elimination of toxicity.

3. Service and Flow Economy. This calls for a fundamental change in the relationship between producer and consumer, a shift from an economy of goods and purchases to one of *service* and *flow*. In essence, an economy that is based on a flow of economic services can better protect the ecosystem services upon which it depends. This will entail a new perception of value, a shift from the acquisition of goods as a measure of affluence to an economy where the continuous receipt of quality, utility and performance promotes well-being. This concept offers incentives to put into practice the first two innovations of natural capitalism by restructuring the economy to focus on relationships that better meet customers' changing value needs and to reward automatically both resource productivity and closed-loop cycles of materials use.

4. Investing in Natural Capital. This works toward reversing world-wide planetary destruction through reinvestments in sustaining, restoring and expanding stocks of natural capital, so that the biosphere can produce more abundant ecosystem services and natural resources.

All four changes are interrelated and interdependent; all four generate numerous benefits and opportunities in markets, finance, materials, distribution and employment. Together, they can reduce environmental harm, create economic growth and increase meaningful employment.

Resource Productivity

Imagine giving a speech to Parliament in 1750 predicting that within seventy years human productivity would rise to the point that one person could do the work of two hundred. The speaker would have been branded as daft or worse. Imagine a similar scene today. Experts are testifying in Congress, predicting that we will increase the productivity of our resources in the next seventy years by a factor of four, ten, even one hundred. Just as it was impossible 250 years ago to conceive of an individual's doing two hundred times more work, it is equally difficult for us today to imagine a kilowatt-hour or board foot being ten or a hundred times more productive than it is now.

Although the movement toward radical resource productivity has been under way for decades, its clarion call came in the fall of 1994, when a group of sixteen scientists, economists, government officials, and businesspeople convened and sponsored by Friedrich Schmidt-Bleek of the Wuppertal Institute for Climate, Environment and Energy in Germany, published the "Carnoules Declaration". Participants had come from Europe, the United States, Japan, England, Canada and India to the French village of Carnoules to discuss their belief that human activities were at risk from the ecological and social impact of materials and energy use. The Factor Ten Club, as the group came to call itself, called for a leap in resource productivity to reverse the growing damage. The declaration began with these prophetic words: "Within one generation, nations can achieve a ten-fold increase in the efficiency with which they use energy, natural resources and other materials."[11]

In the years since, Factor Ten (a 90 percent reduction in energy and materials intensity) and Factor Four (a 75 percent reduction) have entered the vocabulary of government officials, planners, academics, and businesspeople throughout the world.[12] The governments of Austria, the Netherlands and Norway have publicly committed to pursuing Factor Four efficiencies. The same approach has been endorsed by the European Union as the new paradigm for sustainable development. Austria, Sweden and OECD environment ministers have urged the adoption of Factor Ten goals, as have the World Business Council for Sustainable Development and the United Nations Environment Program (UNEP).[13] The concept is not only common parlance for most environmental ministers in the world, but such leading corporations as Dow Europe and Mitsubishi Electric see it as a powerful strategy to gain a competitive advantage. Among all major industrial nations, the United States probably has the least familiarity with and understanding of these ideas.

At its simplest, increasing resource productivity means obtaining the same amount of utility or work from a product or process while using less material and energy. In manufacturing, transportation, forestry, construction, energy and other industrial sectors, mounting empirical evidence suggests that radical improvements in resource productivity are both practical and cost-effective, even in the most modern industries. Companies and designers are developing ways to make natural resources – energy, metals, water and forests – work five, ten, even one hundred times harder than they do today. These efficiencies transcend the marginal gains in performance that industry constantly seeks as part of its evolution. Instead, *revolutionary* leaps in design and technology will alter industry itself as demonstrated in the following chapters. Investments in the productivity revolution are not only repaid over time by the saved resources but in many cases can *reduce* initial capital investments.

When engineers speak of "efficiency", they refer to the amount of output a process provides per unit of input. Higher efficiency thus means doing more with less, measuring both factors in physical terms. When economists refer to efficiency, however, their definition differs in two ways. First, they usually measure a process or outcome in terms of expenditure of money – how the market value of what was produced compares to the market cost of the labor and other inputs used to create it. Second, "economic efficiency" typically refers to how fully and perfectly market mechanisms are being harnessed to minimize the monetary total factor cost of production. Of course it's important to harness economically efficient market mechanisms and we share economists' devotion to that goal. But to avoid confusion, when we suggest using market tools to achieve "resource productivity" and "resource efficiency", we use those terms in the engineering sense.

Resource productivity doesn't just save resources and money; it can also improve the quality of life. Listen to the din of daily existence – the city and freeway traffic, the airplanes, the garbage trucks outside urban windows – and consider this: The waste and the noise are signs of efficiency and they represent money being thrown away. They will disappear as surely as did manure from the nineteenth-century streets of London and New York. Inevitably, industry will redesign everything it makes and does, in order to participate in the coming productivity revolution. We will be able to see better with resource-efficient lighting systems, produce higher-quality goods in efficient factories, travel more safely and comfortably in efficient vehicles, feel more comfortable (and do substantially more and better work)[14] in efficient buildings, and be better nourished by efficiently grown food. An air-conditioning system that uses 90 percent less energy or a building so efficient that it needs no air-conditioning at all may not fascinate the average citizen, but the fact that they are quiet and produce greater comfort while reducing energy costs should appeal even to technophobes. That such options save money should interest everyone.

As subsequent chapters will show, the unexpectedly large improvements to be gained by resource productivity offer an entirely new terrain for business invention, growth and development. Its advantages can also dispel the long-held belief that core business values and environmental responsibility are incompatible or at odds. In fact, the massive inefficiencies that are causing environmental degradation almost always cost more than the measures that would reverse them.

But even as Factor Ten goals are driving reductions in materials and energy flows, some governments are continuing to create and administer laws, policies, taxes and subsidies that have quite the opposite effect. Hundreds of billions of dollars of taxpayers' money are annually diverted to promote inefficient and unproductive material and energy use. These include subsidies to mining, oil, coal, fishing and forest industries as well as agricultural practices that degrade soil fertility and use wasteful amounts of water and chemicals. Many of these subsidies are vestigial, some dating as far back as the eighteenth century, when European powers provided entrepreneurs with incentives to find and exploit colonial resources. Taxes extracted from labor subsidize patterns of resource use that in turn displace workers, an ironic situation that is becoming increasingly apparent and unacceptable, particularly in Europe, where there is chronically high unemployment. Already, tax reforms aimed at increasing employment by shifting taxes away from people to the use of resources have started to be instituted in the Netherlands, Germany, Britain, Sweden and Denmark, and are being seriously proposed across Europe.

In less developed countries, people need realistic and achievable means to better their lives. The world's growing population cannot attain a Western standard of living by following traditional industrial paths to development, for the resources required are too vast, too expensive, and too damaging to local and global systems. Instead, radical improvements in resource productivity expand their possibilities for growth and can help to ameliorate the polarization of wealth between rich and poor segments of the globe. When the world's nations met in Brazil at the Earth Summit in 1992 to discuss the environment and human development, some treaties and proposals proved to be highly divisive because it appeared that they put a lid on the ability of nonindustrialized countries to pursue development. Natural capitalism provides a practical agenda for development wherein the actions of both developed and developing nations are mutually supportive.

Biomimicry

To appreciate the potential of radical resource productivity, it is helpful to recognize that the present industrial system is, practically speaking, a couch potato: It eats too much junk food and gets insufficient exercise. In its late maturity, industrial society runs on life-support systems that require enormous heat and pressure, are petrochemically dependent and materials-intensive, and require large flows of toxic and hazardous chemicals. These industrial "empty calories" end up as pollution, acid rain and greenhouse gases, harming environmental, social and financial systems. Even though all the re-engineering and downsizing trends of the past decade were supposed to sweep away corporate inefficiency, the U.S. economy remains astoundingly inefficient: It has been estimated that only 6 percent of its vast flows of materials actually end up in products.[15] Overall, the ratio of waste to the *durable* products that constitute material wealth may be closer to one hundred to one. The whole economy is less than 10 percent – probably only a few percent – as energy-efficient as the laws of physics permit.[16]

This waste is currently rewarded by deliberate distortions in the market place, in the form of policies like subsidies to industries that extract raw materials from the earth and damage the biosphere. As long as that damage goes unaccounted for, as long as virgin resource prices are maintained at artificially low levels, it makes sense to continue to use virgin materials rather than reuse resources discarded from previous products. As long as it is assumed that there are "free goods" in the world – pure water, clean air, hydrocarbon combustion, virgin forests, veins of minerals – large-scale, energy- and materials-intensive manufacturing methods will dominate, and labor will be increasingly marginalized.[17] In contrast, if the subsidies distorting resource prices were removed or reversed, it would be advantageous to employ more people and use fewer virgin materials.

Even without the removal of subsidies, the economics of resource productivity are already encouraging industry to reinvent itself to be more in accord with biological systems. Growing competitive pressures to save resources are opening up exciting frontiers for chemists, physicists, process engineers, biologists and industrial designers. They are re-examining the energy, materials and manufacturing systems required to provide the specific qualities (strength, warmth, structure, protection, function, speed, tension, motion, skin) required by products and end users and are turning away from mechanical systems requiring heavy metals, combustion and petroleum to seek solutions that use minimal inputs, lower temperatures and enzymatic reactions. Business is switching to imitating biological and ecosystem processes replicating natural methods of production and engineering to manufacture chemicals, materials and compounds and soon maybe even microprocessors. Some of the most exciting developments have resulted from emulating nature's life-temperature, low-pressure, solar-powered assembly techniques, whose products rival anything human-made. Science writer Janine Benyus points out that spiders make silk, strong as Kevlar but much tougher, from digested crickets and flies, without needing boiling sulfuric acid and high-temperature extruders. The abalone generates an inner shell twice as tough as our best ceramics and diatoms make glass, both processes employing seawater with no furnaces. Trees turn sunlight, water and air into cellulose, a sugar stiffer and stronger than nylon and bind it into wood, a natural composite with a higher bending strength and stiffness than concrete or steel. We may never grow as skillful as spiders, abalone, diatoms or trees, but smart designers are apprenticing themselves to nature to learn the benign chemistry of its processes.

Pharmaceutical companies are becoming microbial ranchers managing herds of enzymes. Biological farming manages soil ecosystems in order to increase the amount of biota and life per acre by keen knowledge of food chains, species interactions and nutrient flows, minimizing crop losses and maximizing yields by fostering diversity. Meta-industrial engineers are creating "zero-emission" industrial parks whose tenants will constitute an industrial ecosystem in which one company will feed upon the non toxic and useful wastes of another. Architects and builders are creating structures that process their own wastewater, capture light, create energy and provide habitat for wildlife and wealth for the community, all the while improving worker productivity, moral and health.[18] High-temperature, centralized power plants are starting to be replaced by smaller-scale, renewable power generation. In chemistry, we can look forward to the end of the witches' brew of dangerous substances invented this century, from DDT, PCB, CFCs and Thalidomide to Dieldrin and xeno-estrogens. The eighty thousand different chemicals now manufactured end up everywhere, as Donella Meadows remarks, from our "stratosphere to our sperm". They were created to accomplish functions that can now be carried out far more efficiently with biodegradable and naturally occurring compounds.

Service and Flow

Beginning in the mid-1980s, Swiss industry analyst Walter Stahel and German chemist Michael Braungart independently proposed a new industrial model that is now gradually taking shape. Rather than an economy in which *goods* are made and sold, these visionaries imagined a *service economy* wherein consumers obtain *services* by leasing or renting goods rather than buying them outright. (Their plan should not be confused with the conventional definition of a service economy, in which burger-flippers outnumber steelworkers.) Manufacturers cease thinking of themselves as sellers of products and become, instead, deliverers of service, provided by long-lasting, upgradeable durables. Their goal is selling results rather than equipment, performance and satisfaction rather than motors, fans, plastics or condensers.

The system can be demonstrated by a familiar example. Instead of purchasing a washing machine, consumers could pay a monthly fee to obtain the *service* of having their clothes cleaned. The washer would have a counter on it, just like an office photocopier, and would be maintained by the manufacturer on a regular basis, much the way mainframe computers are. If the machine ceased to provide its specific service, the manufacturer would be responsible for replacing or repairing it at no charge to the customer, because the washing machine would remain the property of the manufacturer. The concept could likewise be applied to computers, cars, VCRs, refrigerators and almost every other durable that people now buy, use up and ultimately throw away. Because products would be returned to the manufacturer for continuous repair, reuse and remanufacturing, Stahel called the process "cradle-to-cradle".[19]

Many companies are adopting Stahel's principles. Agfa Gaevert pioneered the leasing of copier services, which spread to the entire industry.[20] The Carrier Corporation, a division of United Technologies, is creating a program to sell coolth (the opposite of warmth) to companies while retaining ownership of the air-conditioning equipment. The Interface Corporation is beginning to lease the warmth, beauty and comfort of its floor-covering services rather than selling carpets.

Braungart's model of a *service economy* focuses on the nature of material cycles. In this perspective, if a given product lasts a long time but its waste materials cannot be reincorporated into new manufacturing or biological cycles, then the producer must accept responsibility for the waste with all its attendant problems of toxicity, resource overuse, worker safety and environmental damage. Braungart views the world as a series of metabolisms in which the creations of human beings, like the creations of nature, become "food" for interdependent systems, returning to either an industrial or a biological cycle after their useful life is completed. To some, especially frugal Scots and New Englanders, this might not sound a novel concept at all. Ralph Waldo Emerson once wrote, "Nothing in nature is exhausted in its first use. When a thing has served an end to the uttermost, it is wholly new for an ulterior service."[21] In simpler times, such proverbial wisdom had highly practical applications. Today, the complexity of modern materials makes this almost impossible. Thus, Braungart proposed an Intelligent Product System whereby those products that do not degrade back into natural nutrient cycles be designed so that they can be deconstructed and completely reincorporated into *technical nutrient* cycles of industry.[22]

Another way to conceive of this method is to imagine an industrial system that has no provision for landfills, outfalls or smokestacks. If a company knew that nothing that came into its factory could be thrown away, and that everything it produced would eventually return, how would it design its components and products? The question is more than a theoretical construct, because the earth works under precisely these strictures.

In a *service economy*, the product is a means, not an end. The manufacturer's leasing and ultimate recovery of the product means that the product remains an asset. The minimization of materials use, the maximization of product durability and enhanced ease of maintenance not only improve the customer's experience and value but also protect the manufacturer's investment and hence its bottom line. *Both* producer and customer have an incentive for continuously improving resource productivity, which in turn further protects ecosystems. Under this shared incentive, both parties form a relationship that continuously anticipates and meets the customer's evolving value needs – and meanwhile rewards both parties for reducing the burdens on the planet.

The service paradigm has other benefits as well: It increases employment, because when products are designed to be reincorporated into manufacturing cycles, waste declines and demand for labor increases. In manufacturing, about one-fourth of the labor force is engaged in the fabrication of basic raw materials such as steel, glass, cement, silicon, and resins, while three-quarters are in the production phase. The reverse is true for energy inputs: Three times as much energy is used to extract virgin or primary materials as is used to manufacture products from those materials. Substituting reused or more durable manufactured goods for primary materials therefore uses less energy but provides more jobs.[23]

An economy based on a service-and-flow model could also help stabilize the business cycle, because customers would be purchasing flows of services, which they need continuously, rather than durable equipment that's affordable only in good years. Service providers would have an incentive to keep their assets productive for as long as possible, rather than prematurely scrapping them in order to sell replacements. Over-and undercapacity would largely disappear, as business would no longer have to be concerned about delivery or backlogs if it is contracting from a service provider. Gone would be end-of-year rebates to move excess automobile inventory, built for customers who never ordered them because managerial production quotas were increased in order to amortize expensive capital equipment that was never needed in the first place. As it stands now, durables manufacturers have a love-hate relationship with durability. But when they become service providers, their long- and short-term incentives become perfectly attuned to what customers want, the environment deserves, labor needs and the economy can support.[24]

Investing in Natural Capital

When a manufacturer realizes that a supplier of key components is overextended and running behind on deliveries, it takes immediate action lest its own production lines come to a halt. Living systems are a supplier of key components for the life of the planet, and they are now falling behind on their orders. Until recently, business could ignore such shortages because they didn't affect production and didn't increase costs. That situation may be changing, however, as rising weather related claims come to burden insurance companies and world agriculture. (In 1998, violent weather caused upward of $90 billion worth of damage worldwide, a figure that represented more weather-related losses than were accounted for through the entire decade of the 1980s. The losses were greatly compounded by deforestation and climate change, factors that increase the frequency and severity of disasters. In human terms, 300 million people were permanently or temporarily displaced from their homes; this figure includes the dislocations caused by Hurricane Mitch, the deadliest Atlantic storm in two centuries.)[25] If the flow of services from industrial systems is to be sustained or increased in the future for a growing population, the vital flow of life-supporting services from living systems will have to be maintained and increased. For this to be possible will require investments in natural capital.

As both globalization and Balkanization proceed, and as the per capita availability of water, arable land, and fish continue to decline (as they have done since 1980), the world faces the danger of being torn apart by regional conflicts instigated at least in part by resource shortages or imbalances and associated income polarization.[26] Whether it involves oil[27] or water,[28] cobalt or fish, access to resources is playing an ever more prominent role in generating conflict. In addition, many social instabilities and refugee populations – tens of millions of refugees now wander the world – are created or worsened by ecological destruction, from Haiti to Somalia to Jordan. On April 9, 1996, Secretary of State Warren Christopher gave perhaps the first speech by an American cabinet officer that linked global security with the environment. His words may become prophetic for future foreign policy decisions: ". . . [E]nvironmental forces transcend borders and oceans to threaten directly the health, prosperity and jobs of American citizens. . . [A]ddressing natural resource issues is frequently critical to achieving political and economic stability and to pursuing our strategic goals around the world."

Societies need to adopt shared goals that enhance social welfare but that are not the prerogatives of specific value or belief systems. Natural capitalism is one such objective. It is neither conservative nor liberal in its ideology, but appeals to both constituencies. Since it is a means, and not an end, it doesn't advocate a particular social outcome but rather makes possible many different ends. Therefore, whatever the various visions different parties or factions espouse, society can work toward resource productivity now, without waiting to resolve disputes about policy.

The chapters that follow describe an array of opportunities and possibilities that are real, practical, measured and documented. Engineers have already designed hydrogen-fuel-cell powered cars to be plug-in electric generators that may become the power plants of the future. Buildings already exist that make oxygen, solar power and drinking water and can help pay the mortgage while their tenants work inside them. Deprintable and reprintable papers and inks, together with other innovative ways to use fiber, could enable the world's supply of lumber and pulp to be grown in an area about the size of Iowa. Weeds can yield potent pharmaceuticals; cellulose-based plastics have been shown to be strong, reusable, and compostable; and luxurious carpets can be made from landfilled scrap. Roofs and windows, even roads, can do double duty as solar-electric collectors, and efficient car-free cities are being designed so that men and women no longer spend their days driving to obtain the goods and services of daily life. These are among the thousands of innovations that are resulting from natural capitalism.

This book is both an overview of the remarkable technologies that are already in practice and a call to action. Many of the techniques and methods described here can be used by individuals and small businesses. Other approaches are more suitable for corporations, even whole industrial sectors; still others better suit local or central governments. Collectively, these techniques offer a powerful menu of new ways to make resource productivity the foundation of a lasting and prosperous economy – from Main Street to Wall Street, from your house to the White House and from the village to the globe.

Although there is an overwhelming emphasis in this book on what we do with our machines, manufacturing processes and materials, its purpose is to support the human community and all life-support systems. There is a large body of literature that addresses the nature of specific living systems, from coral reefs to estuarine systems to worldwide topsoil formation. Our focus is to bring about those changes in the human side of the economy that can help preserve and reconstitute these systems, to try and show for now and all time to come that there is no true separation between how we support life economically and ecologically.

9

Suggesting new business opportunities

INTRODUCTION

What connects Paul Nipkow, John Logie Baird, Boris Rozing, and Vladamir Zworykin? Any ideas? Could it be space travel, nuclear weapons, motor cars? In fact, the answer is television. Nipkow, a German, in the 1880s is credited with producing a mechanical system that was capable of transmitting a simple picture. John Logie Baird, a Scot, developed his mechanical system that was first shown to the public in 1926 consisting of a 30 line image. Boris Rozing, a Russian, had in the early years of the 20th century made important advances in vacuum tubes which made obsolete the mechanical system of transmitting and receiving pictures replacing it with an electronic system. In the United States in the late 1920s one of Rozing's students, Vladimir K Zworykin, made further advances in cathode tube technology. The moment that the first regular television broadcasts started in the UK in 1936 was the culmination of over half a century's developments, with many individuals making important contributions.

While the technical side of the story of the early years of television is quite difficult to chart, the business insights required to turn inventions into innovations and then into a product is perhaps harder. We know a lot about the establishment of individual

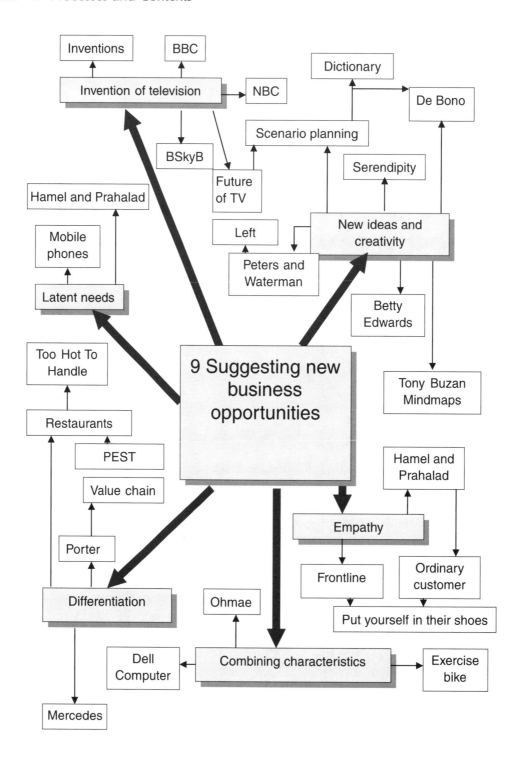

companies to produce cameras and television sets. We know about businesses such as the British Broadcasting Company, later the British Broadcasting Corporation (BBC), and in the United States, the National Broadcasting Company (NBC), that commission and broadcast programmes. We do not know quite so much about how the business side was developed in terms of strategy, especially in the development of new markets.

One important difference between UK and US television was the way it was funded. In the UK the BBC was funded by a licence and in the United States advertising was used. In the UK it was not until 1956 that a commercial channel, ITV, was established that relied on advertising for its revenue. Nowadays the satellite firms such as BSkyB receive money both from advertisements and channel subscription.

The range of channels has increased enormously over the past 25 years with the advent of new terrestrial, cable, and satellite ones. With the introduction of digital technology hundreds of channels are now available, with a vast range of content, unthinkable only a few years ago. What we are now seeing is the convergence of computer technology and television technology.

When you sit down tonight to watch your favourite soap, or sports channel, or movie channel, delivered by digital satellite to your wide screen, nicam stereo TV you might like to think how far from the early mechanical devices of the 1920s we have come. This is not only in terms of technological advances but also in content. If you were now to project what the next 70 years will bring, in terms of technology and content, what would you come up with?

As we saw in the previous chapter, scenario planning allows us to clarify our thoughts about possible futures and develop strategies. Imagining scenarios is often a good way of coming up with ideas for new business opportunities but there are others.

NEW IDEAS AND CREATIVITY

There is a strong presumption that creativity and imagination are powerful ingredients in the making of new ideas for business opportunities. There has been a little speculation that the individual dimensions of creativity are linked to the functioning of the two halves of the brain. For example, Peters and Waterman (1982: 59) reported that: 'Research on the functions of the brain show that the left and right hemispheres differ substantially. The left half is the reasoning, sequential, verbal half; it is the "logical" and rational half. The right half is the artistic half; it is the half that sees and remembers patterns, recalls melodies, waxes poetic.' They suggested that successful companies recognized and nurtured the intuitive and creative work associated with the right half of the brain. They argued that companies can suppress or enhance creativity among managers and employees by the way they practise management. If management practices presume the left half of the brain's traits of logical and rational thought, then the intuitive and creative component of people is partially suppressed. Of course it is also possible to argue that some individuals are naturally more creative than others. In this case it might be assumed that creative individuals are blessed with an abundance of right hemisphere thinking, while others are restricted by boring, mechanical, logical left hemisphere thinking.

Serendipity (the faculty of making happy and unexpected discoveries by accident) is also important in coming up with new ideas. Again some people do seem to have this knack, while most of us do not. Whether or not we are all differently endowed with creativity and imagination, just as some of us can run very fast or master a musical instrument with relative ease, is not quite the point here. We believe it is possible even for the most unimaginative of us to become reasonably good at this. Of course it would be naïve to think that all of us with good coaching could run fast enough to compete in the Olympics or play in an orchestra, but we do believe that we would be able run a bit faster than we do now or learn to play an instrument with the right kind of help.

There are many simple techniques that can help us in freeing up our creativity and imagination. One technique suggested by Edward de Bono is to use a dictionary. When you hit a brick wall in your thinking and cannot make any more progress, he suggests you open a page of a dictionary at random and with your eyes closed pick a word. Then using this word think how it will help you solve the problem you have. This is a way of shutting down the left side of your brain and letting the right side take over. For such a simple technique it is remarkably effective. More about de Bono and his ideas on thinking can be found on www.edwdebono.com/debono/ where, amongst other techniques, you can learn about using his six hats and six shoes.

Many of us believe we cannot draw, as we are just not artistic. An interesting technique developed by Betty Edwards is to turn the picture we are trying to draw upside down. This defeats the logical, left part of the brain and forces the right to take charge. Believe it or not, it works. Again, if you are trapped in your logical mode and need to get into right brain thinking, spend 15 minutes or so using her techniques and you will move into right hand mode. If you want to know more about this, the Web site is at www.drawright.com/.

Another way to free up your creativity is to use mind mapping, a technique advocated by Tony Buzan. (We have provided a mind map to guide you through the material in each chapter.) Mind mapping also gives you the chance to make new connections and to see things differently. More about this can be found at www.buzancentre.com/.

EMPATHY

Now we want to concentrate more on ways of looking for new products or services. Firstly we are going to look at a method derived from Hamel and Prahalad (1994: 103) who have suggested that industry foresight 'comes when senior executives in a company are able to empathize with basic human needs'. They also say (1994: 104): 'If senior management isn't capable of empathizing with the needs of "ordinary" customers, it will be incapable of meeting those needs ahead of competitors.' We call this the empathy method.

It is remarkably easy for senior executives to get out of touch with what their customers want. Often the lifestyle of the executive is very different from that of the customer. It requires quite a feat of imagination to get back in touch with them. Businesses often have schemes whereby senior executives are sent back to the 'shop floor' just so they can get back in touch. A recent UK television programme exploited this idea. The format was for a board level executive to be sent back to the 'front line' to see what was actually happening. Invariably the programme ended with the executive telling the board how things had to change because they were out of touch with their customers. In short they were not empathizing with their customers.

It is pretty easy to say that we should empathize with customers but how can we actually do this? One way is to put oneself in the position of the customer. If your lifestyle is very different from your customers' you may find it difficult to imagine yourself in their position. You may simply not have the imagination to do this. If so, you might want to consider actually experiencing a typical customer's lifestyle. Clearly, using market research techniques such as focus groups will help you gain an understanding of your customers' needs, but perhaps a more radical thing to do would be to try their lifestyles. In doing this you may well be able to foresee new business opportunities. At the heart of this approach is an attempt to put yourself in the shoes of your customers to figure out what will make a difference to their quality of life.

COMBINING CHARACTERISTICS

The second method we will look at is the combination method. Ohmae (1982) proposes that we take different combinations of the characteristics of a product or service assessing each combination in terms of market potential. Through this a new product or service may appear. An actual example may help you see how this can be used. A company sells three types of exercise bike: the Mark I at £200, the Sports at £250, and the Professional at £350. It also produces three types of heart monitor: a

	Ear Lobe	Transmitter with no memory	Transmitter with memory
Mark I	Already sold	Medium market potential	Low market potential
Sports	Low market potential	Already sold	High market potential
Professional	Low market potential	Already sold	Already sold

Table 9.1 The combination method

basic earlobe monitor at £70, a belt transmitter with no memory at £100, and a belt transmitter with memory at £190. It already sells its exercise bikes with a heart monitor attached (see Table 9.1). It assesses the market potential of selling other combinations and comes up with the idea of the Sports being sold with the transmitter with a memory.

Modern manufacturing technology often allows for hundreds if not thousands of unique combinations to be made. Some computer companies specialize in building from basic components a computer just for you. By using the latest technology they can easily build a unique computer for you once you have specified the hard disk size, memory, screen, etc. Interestingly, though, very few computer companies will supply you with a computer of a colour other than beige. Henry Ford would have approved of this. Dell Computer Corporation will let you customize the computer you want to purchase. At the company's Web site we counted 15 components that can be specified including a hard disk, monitor, speakers and memory. There are 12 memories and 8 hard disks available. This alone gives 96 different configurations. We could not specify colour. The Dell site is at www.euro.dell.com/countries/uk/enu/gen/default.htm.

DIFFERENTIATION

The next method is called differentiation. Porter says (1980: 37):

> The second generic strategy is one of differentiating the product or service offering of the firm, creating something that is perceived industry-wide as being unique. Approaches to differentiating can take many forms: design or brand image (Fieldcrest in top of the line towels and linens; Mercedes in automobiles), technology (Hyster in lift trucks; MacIntosh in stereo components; Coleman in camping equipment), features (Jenn-Air in electric ranges); customer service (Crown Cork and Seal in metal cans), dealer network (Caterpillar Tractor in construction equipment), or other dimensions.

The key to successful product or service differentiation is one that creates value in the customers' mind which they are prepared to pay more for than it cost you to make or provide. It makes little sense to differentiate your product, at great expense, if the result is not something that customers are willing to pay for. This is clearly linked into Porter's idea of the value chain. In this the steps taken to produce the product or service are costed and measured against the value the customer places upon them. If you are not creating value for your customer when differentiating the product but are incurring costs in doing so you are wasting resources.

The list of businesses Porter gives above contains large well-known for-profit firms but differentiation can equally well apply to a whole range of public and voluntary firms of differing sizes. In some ways it might be easier for the smaller organization to apply a differentiated strategy to its product or service as it is closer to its customer base and changes can be made easily.

Looking at restaurants is a good way of seeing differentiation at work. We are writing some of this book in West London, where there are numerous restaurants. How does an individual restaurant differentiate itself from all the others? Firstly, around here, by type of food. We have a remarkable range of world food including the common Chinese, Italian, Indian (traditional curry and Balti), and Greek. There are also several traditional British cafés, some more upmarket cafés, and fish and chip shops. There are Kebab takeaways, pizza eat-in and takeaway restaurants. The following types of food are also available: Thai (increasingly popular especially in pubs), Caribbean, Tapas (Spanish food), Tex –Mex (hot food from Texas and Mexico) French, Japanese, Dutch pancakes, US fast food, Mongolian (barbecued), and Sri-Lankan. Next, the different types of food are differentiated by price. Again around here, there are several Chinese restaurants, falling mainly into three price ranges, from quite cheap to up-market. Next, even within the nationality of the cooking, restaurants differentiate themselves; for example, there is North Chinese, traditional Chinese etc. Another differentiation is to do with the little extras offered such as chocolates with the bill or hot towels. Some restaurants have introduced 'eat as much as you like menus' at certain times in an attempt to differentiate themselves.

Changes in technology, social patterns, the economy and other structural things will affect the restaurant business. Technological changes in food cooking such as freezing and microwaves have transformed the type and quality of food available. By monitoring these changes a restaurant might be able to steal a march on its competitors by being able to offer a new range of dishes at a low price. Changes in social patterns such as more gay couples eating out has offered business opportunities for restaurants by becoming 'gay-friendly'. In fact, in most major metropolitan areas there are clusters of firms catering for the 'pink' pound or dollar. The growth of single people living alone in the UK provides a business opportunity to cater for them as most restaurants target couples and groups. Changes in the economy might mean that there is more money for eating out and people are prepared to pay more for food. This could be exploited by going up-market. By being relatively small and close to their customers restaurants should be able to differentiate themselves from their competitors.

LATENT NEEDS

Customers and their needs evolve. Firms should not only be trying to understand the needs of their current customers. They may also find it important to be interested in the needs of people who may not yet be customers. And the needs that matter in 10 or 20 years' time may not exist now. Few people 30 years ago thought that they needed a mobile phone or access to the Internet. Access to both is now needed by large and rapidly growing numbers of people around the world. Therefore it is important to consider latent as well as currently known needs. Identifying the latent needs of customers is difficult but potentially highly important.

If you could establish some latent needs and then provide products or services that supply them at a price people were prepared to pay you would be on to a winner. If you want to be an industry leader in 10 or 20 years' time you may need to be already developing new products or services that will one day put your firm in that position. It is often no use asking current customers hypothetical questions about their needs in a future that may be radically different from the present. As Hamel and Prahalad (1994: 291) express it, 'No firm is going to find the future first if it waits around to get directions from existing customers.' Responsiveness to customers is not enough.

This discussion of latent needs has implications for the development of strategic management. Hamel and Prahalad (1994) have warned that much conventional strategic planning fails to address latent and currently unarticulated customer needs. They argue for a strategic process that is more exploratory and less ritualistic.

We can illustrate the more exploratory and less ritualistic thinking needed by taking the restaurant industry. We tried to think in an exploratory and creative way to see if we could come up with something. Our idea is to open restaurants where you learn to dance then have a meal and then continue dancing. There is a current fashion for learning dances – salsa, jive, tango and others. Usually people learn to dance in town halls, church halls, or school halls, not places with great ambience, but the classes are very popular. When those learning are reasonably good at the dance they can go to a large dance hall. So once they have passable skills there are lots of venues to go to. Our idea is for people to do the learning not in a cold church hall but in a restaurant with a meal or buffet thrown in.

Salsa food for Salsa dancing
Learn to Salsa and experience hot Salsa food
At London's top Salsa dance restaurant

Too Hot To Handle

In a way we are back to using empathy and the combination method so as to successfully differentiate a new service. Perhaps many new product ideas are based on an empathic understanding of customers' actual and latent needs plus a design based on a combination of attributes to produce new products and services. The way television has changed and will change in the future has all these elements embedded in it.

CONCLUSIONS

This chapter has assumed the importance of innovation as a route to success. It has been stressed how critical it is to understand the needs of customers. Perhaps price-cutting wars are important at some moments in the history of a particular industry, but we have assumed that generally speaking these days the successful firms are ones that grow because of innovative product-market strategy. Practical ideas for thinking up new ideas have been considered. We have stressed the dynamic nature of customer needs and therefore the potential pay-off for firms that identify latent or unarticulated needs.

QUESTIONS

Instead of us setting you a set of questions for this chapter the task is for you to come up with at least six and answer them. We are doing this as this chapter is all about being creative. If you have internalized the lessons of the chapter this will be a really easy task. On the other hand… .

In our experience as teachers of strategy this exercise is what excites students about the subject. It gives you a chance to 'think out of the box', to be creative, to be less like Apollo and more like Dionysus. But to do this well requires a lot of hard work! Best of luck.

EXECUTIVE EXERCISE

In this exercise we want you to experiment with using empathy to generate ideas for providing your organization's customers with new kinds of benefits. What latent or future needs of your customers could your organization meet? We suggest you follow Ohmae's methodology for scenario planning. Begin by thinking about any major trends or developments that have been occurring over a number of years and are still underway. These could be political, economic, social, environmental, or social. Write down the six most important ones.

Much depends on whether your customers are consumers or other businesses. If your customers are consumers, try to identify any effects these trends or developments might have on how your customers live. If your customers are other businesses, try to identify any effects on how businesses operate. Note the three most plausible trends or developments and their effects.

Now assume that these effects are creating business opportunities. Brainstorm some ideas for new products or services. Note the three best ideas.

Trend/Development   Effect   Opportunity: ideas for new
                                     products or services
1. _____   _____   _____

2. _____   _____   _____

3. _____   _____   _____

If you are able to discuss your ideas in a group, present your ideas to the other group members. Ask them to evaluate the plausibility of your ideas.

REFERENCES

Hamel, G and Prahalad, C K (1994) *Competing for the Future*, Harvard Business School Press
Ohmae, K (1982) *The Mind of the Strategist*, McGraw-Hill, London
Peters, T and Waterman, R (1982) *In Search of Excellence*, HarperCollins, New York
Porter, M (1980) *Competitive Strategy: Techniques for analyzing industries and competitors*, Free Press, New York

10

Evaluating strategic options

INTRODUCTION

In Greek mythology the stories about Prometheus concern the stealing of fire from the gods. In one story Prometheus deceives the great god Zeus and as a punishment Zeus takes fire away from mankind. But then Prometheus finds it. This really upsets Zeus. He creates Pandora and when she opens the jar she always carries, evil and disease are let loose on mankind. The other story is how Prometheus is bound to a rock and, as punishment for stealing fire from Zeus, an eagle eats his liver.

This mythology appears to have inspired some intellectuals in the midst of the start of the Industrial Revolution. First, Mary Shelley (née Wollstonecraft), in 1818, wrote *Frankenstein, or, the Modern Prometheus*. In this a scientist, Frankenstein, creates an artificial man using parts of corpses and electricity. Eventually the creature kills Frankenstein. This is a pretty pessimistic view of science. The overt message of *Frankenstein* seems to be that usurping the power of god(s) by creating life inevitably leads to disaster. Many meanings can be attached to the story. Another reading of the meaning is that scientific knowledge has its price, which has echoes of the original stories of Prometheus stealing fire.

Secondly, in *Prometheus Unbound*, a play written in 1819, Mary Shelley's husband celebrates both the power of the imagination and the power of science for understanding the world. The young Shelley's heroes were the scientists such as Newton,

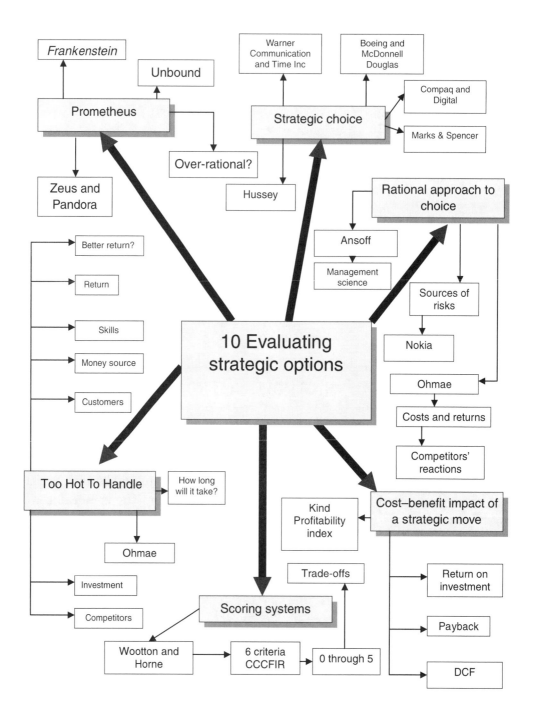

who had laid bare the world through reason and scientific endeavour. Shelley's logic is something like this: Prometheus gave us speech (he equated fire with speech), which gave us thought (reason), which leads to science. This could at least question traditional authority both on earth and in the heavens. Shelley's *Prometheus Unbound* is not an easy play to understand and interpret but we take it to be relatively optimistic about the application of science and reason to the world.

In the 19th century the potential dangerous consequences of science and reason as the way of understanding and acting in the world, as opposed to the importance of feeling, continued to concern intellectuals. Shelley in his later works moved away from science. What the Shelleys, and others such as Wordsworth and Coleridge, were reacting against was the coldness of science and reason in explaining our experiences. So in a way we are back to the tension between Apollo and Dionysus, between reason and feeling.

This seems a long way from strategic management but it is not that far. Let us see if we can persuade you. In the last chapter we explored creative ways of thinking up new products or services. While some of this can be done in a pretty routine and reasoned or scientific way, the danger is to get over-rational, too much 'left hemisphere', and not use enough imagination and feeling, 'right hemisphere'. It is not that reason and a scientific approach are wrong. They just leave out the creative and imaginative part. You may not want to ask for Divine intervention but you need to guard against too much rationalism. Too much Apollo and not enough Dionysus. If you have too much of Dionysus though, while you may be having a great time, you can wake up with a terrible hangover and nothing achieved. As always it's about getting the balance right. Our aim in this introduction is to get you to think about this in a novel, innovative way.

In this chapter paradoxically we have to emphasize a more reasoned and scientific approach to balance, perhaps, than the exciting creative work of the previous chapter. Sometimes you may well have to go with your feelings but it will still take a lot of hard work to get results. It is one thing to say you want to put a man on the moon; doing it is another.

STRATEGIC CHOICE

Firms are making big choices all the time. In 1989 Warner Communications and Time Inc merged. In 1997 Boeing and McDonnell Douglas merged. In 1998 Daimler-Benz and Chrysler announced they were merging. In all these cases the two firms that were merging would have had to think about a number of factors. What synergy would be possible from the merger? How would their respective assets complement each other? How integrated would the new firm need to be? How could the different cultures of the two firms be handled within the new merged firm?

In 1998 Compaq Computer Corporation bought Digital Equipment Corporation, a company that employed twice as many people as Compaq did. Was this a good strategic choice? Compaq sales had been growing rapidly and its share price had been climbing fast. Compaq was a PC maker, and buying Digital could offer access to another computer hardware market. Would this purchase of Digital really give Compaq new strategic choices? Could Compaq integrate the purchased firm into its structure? Had it the skills and pre-acquisition planning capability needed to make the purchase a success?

In the 1990s Hewlett-Packard was primarily a maker of PCs, servers, printers and scanners. In the late 1990s sales growth of the firm was slowing. The organization needed to ask: Should it continue with its current product-market strategy, or was the time ripe for a new strategic direction? Should it shift from products to services? Should it migrate to the markets being created by the Internet?

Cadbury-Schweppes can trace its history back to the early 19th century. It is now an international business and had sales in excess of £4 billion in 1999. However, the food and drinks industry continues to evolve. Should the firm concentrate on its current products and markets, or should it be taking measures to increase its market share in markets where it is currently weak? Should it seek a merger partner? Should it develop new products?

As is well known, Marks & Spencer hit a bad patch in the late 1990s and it is still not clear if it will regain some of its former glory. Falling profits, job insecurity, and problems in the boardroom were symptoms of malaise at this previously excellent firm. What should it do now? Concentrate on turning around its profitability problem through revamping its UK stores, or take some new course of action?

We often wonder if strategic choices are victims of fashion. By this we mean that decisions about strategic choices might be made on the basis that they must be right because other companies are making the same choices. Strategic moves such as forming strategic alliances or mergers and acquisitions seem to go in waves. For example, cross-border mergers and acquisitions appeared to increase very rapidly in the years from 1991 through to 1995. Was this because each individual decision had been thoroughly evaluated and the evidence of net benefits to the firms was compelling? Or was it a case of imitation? The possibility of decision making by joining a bandwagon cannot be ruled out. We take the view argued by Hussey (1999) that there should be an attempt to evaluate a strategic option even when there is general enthusiasm for choosing the option.

A RATIONAL APPROACH

Strategic projects will either be allocated by senior management or will have to be considered by a board or management committee before approval is given. In either case it is likely that in big organizations the evaluation of strategic options will be presented formally in a report. The quality of such reports will naturally depend on the quality of the data and the quality of the thinking; but what is their content?

Ansoff (1968) points out that formally speaking the logical basis for a decision about strategic action is quite simple. A firm should choose from the alternative possible options the specific one that looks as though it will offer the best performance in relation to key objectives. In practice he recognized that this is a complex and imprecise decision. Ansoff took the view that what he called management science can help clarify the choices, but the final responsibility for making a choice is that of the managers.

In making a choice, however, he drew attention to the importance of considering the risks that exist. He noted that there could be events that were currently unforeseeable. He also noted that decisions taken in the light of foreseeable events carried risks. Decisions would be based on projections of future business conditions but these might be wrong or at least not completely right. Even if conditions were accurately forecast, judgements about the success of the firm in those conditions could be wrong. Then again there were risks brought about by the possibility that competitors would react to strategic actions taken by the firm, and these reactions would possibly impinge on the effectiveness of the strategic actions taken.

While Ansoff's analysis of sources of risk in relation to strategic choice dates back a quarter of a century, it continues to be sound in business terms. Take the case of Nokia, the company that has almost a third of the global market in mobile phone handsets. When Nokia decided to bring out WAP (wireless application protocol) handsets, what risks were being run? One risk must have been the possibility that the consumer demand conditions in the industry would deteriorate, possibly because the market is nearing saturation. A second risk might have been that Nokia products would be less successful in future if it failed to acquire capability in the new technology incorporated in the latest handsets. Yet another risk was that Japanese handset makers might react more quickly to new opportunities placing Nokia under more competitive pressure in its European markets.

Ansoff followed up his analysis of risks by referring to decision theory and the comparison of the risk-reward characteristics of strategic alternatives. The rules that might be applied in making comparisons include setting a minimum acceptable performance level. So, if a strategic option looks likely to produce results below a specified acceptable level it is rejected. Among other approaches he discusses there is the expected value approach, which consists of taking account of the probability of success while evaluating the value of the performance in terms of the various objectives of the firm.

Ohmae (1982) offers something similar to the Ansoff account of decision making. He advises managers to calculate the costs and returns of various possible strategic moves. He suggests (Ohmae, 1982: 72): 'Our calculations will soon tell us that depending on the different product and production facility development efforts involved, each of our strategic moves would have a different incubation period, a different cost-benefit impact, and a different point of diminishing returns against the investment required to implement it.'

The next step in his approach to strategic appraisal involves taking account of competitor reactions. So the strategic moves of competitors have to be forecast. The cost-effectiveness for the competitors of their moves, the impact of the competitors' moves on the firm, and the time needed by the firm itself to make a strategic move are all identified by him as factors. In the light of the calculations and the evaluation of competitors the firm can then decide on its own strategic moves, including their sequence.

COST–BENEFIT IMPACT OF A STRATEGIC MOVE

The most formally rational methods of evaluating strategic options are probably financial methods of project appraisal. There are several such methods covered in management books. The most commonly mentioned are return on investment, payback method, and discounted cash flow and net present value.

The calculation of return on investment requires forecasts of the initial investment cost and annual profits over a period of time. An average annual profit is estimated and divided by the initial investment, and then multiplied by 100. This yields a percentage for the average rate of return.

The payback method also uses forecasts of initial investment and the annual profits over a number of years. However, in this case, the point is to identify how many years it will take before the cumulative profits will equal the initial investment.

The discounted cash flow method looks at the cash outflow and inflow over, say, the first 10 years of a strategic project. The cash outflow or inflow for each year is discounted by an appropriate factor to determine the present value of that flow and then an aggregate figure is found over the 10 years. This is the net present value. Firms could choose between projects on the basis of their net present values.

The discounted cash flow method is based on the idea that a certain amount of money now for immediate spending is worth more than having the same amount of money to spend next year. Consequently, if we were to lend some money for a year we might expect some financial return for not being able to spend the money immediately. The amount of money we might require in compensation for not being able to spend it immediately could be used to work out a rate of return. Likewise the same amount of money in ten years' time would be worth much less than it is now. So the further away in time the cash outflow or cash inflow is, the bigger is the discount factor. Tables of discount factors may be consulted to identify the appropriate factor for different rates of return and different years.

Project appraisal can also be carried out using the profitability index (Kind, 1999). This index requires that the cost of capital be calculated. The cost of capital can be found using a combination of the percentage rate of return that shareholders would like and the percentage interest on borrowing. These two elements can be weighted to reflect the debt–equity ratio. Then the profitability index is simply the present value of the initial investment added to the net present value of the project at the cost of capital and divided by the present value of the initial investment. Strategic projects with a high profitability index score should be preferred over projects with a low score.

SCORING SYSTEMS

In practice there may be hundreds of evaluation criteria used to evaluate alternative courses of action. And in practice evaluation may be quite unsystematic with arguments and counter-arguments offered in meetings until an opinion emerges. A simple and systematic approach to evaluation, however, can use a table with all the options being considered shown at the head of the columns and a small number of evaluation criteria shown on the left hand side of the table at the start of each row. Wootton and Horne (2000) suggest six criteria that can be used to evaluate strategic options:

- competitiveness;
- controllability;
- compatibility;
- feasibility;
- impact;
- risk.

Each criterion needs to be operationalized. For example, what is meant by feasibility? According to Wootton and Horne (2000) this refers to resources, resistance and constraints. So an analysis of the importance and availability of different types of resources would be important before scoring this item. A stakeholder analysis would also be needed to evaluate how different stakeholders are likely to react to each specific option and then how important or powerful they are. Likewise some analysis of constraints would be undertaken. Finally, taking account of these analyses, a judgement on the score for feasibility would be made and recorded in the table.

If each option is scored (say, on a scale of 0–5) against each criteria then the total score for each strategic option can be calculated. The results of the evaluation should be used to prompt some key questions about the alternatives. For example, two alternatives might have the same total score but might show quite different profiles in respect of the six criteria. This ought to lead managers to think through the trade-offs they might be making in selecting one of strategic options. It is possible that one strategic option appears to offer a high impact in terms of profits but also to entail a high level of risk. In comparison, another one of the strategic options might offer more modest results in terms of profits but carry relatively little risk. Since both have the same total score this clearly requires managers to think through the circumstances of the organization and then make an informed decision. In other words, scoring systems should not relieve managers of the final responsibility for taking decisions.

TOO HOT TO HANDLE

We concluded the last chapter with our big idea being Too Hot To Handle, a restaurant serving Salsa food and offering Salsa classes and dances. There are several pretty obvious things we need to do to see if this is a workable idea. Using Ohmae's ideas (1982), as well as being aware of the concern of financial appraisal methods with investment costs and cash flows, we can ask:

- How much will we have to invest to do this?
- Where is the money for the investment coming from?
- What do potential customers think of the idea?
- What skills do we need to do this and do we need to acquire new ones?
- What return will the investment make?
- If we were to use the money for something else would we get a better return?
- What will our competitors do?
- How long will it take to launch the restaurant?

There's a lot of hard work to do before we open for business. We need to undertake some detailed business planning. First of all we have to work out what we need to do to start our salsa restaurant. There are many commercially available programs that help you in working out your idea further and costs involved. Word 97 comes

TOO HOT TO HANDLE

General Overview
TOO HOT TO HANDLE is a restaurant serving hot Salsa food. To go with the food we offer Salsa classes and dances.

Mission Statement
We aim to provide the best Salsa food in town, with the best Salsa teachers and music.

Objective of Profile
We are looking for partners to help us achieve our mission.

Product/Service Overview
Salsa food, Salsa teaching, Salsa dancing

Marketing Overview
We aim to serve the existing salsa dancing community and introduce people to the excitement of Salsa

Human Capital

Financial Situate

Financing/Exit Strategy

Use of Proceeds

Summary - Call to Action

As you can see we have only filled in part of the template but it does give you some idea of how you can start to add a little more flesh to an idea. The template below has serveral interlocking sheets that let you plan ahead. This one is in dollars. It gives the general idea of what is possible.

	2000	1st Qtr	2nd Qtr
Days sales in accounts receivable			
Days materials cost in inventory			
Days finished goods in inventory			
Days materials costs in payables			
Days payroll expense accrued			
Days operating expense accured			

Figure 10.1 Too Hot to Handle

Direct labor as % of sales		of sales	$0	$0
Other payroll as % of sales		of sales	$0	$0
Payroll taxes as % of payroll		of payroll	$0	$0
Insurance as % of payroll		of payroll	$0	$0
Legal/accounting as % of sales		of sales	$0	$0
Office overhead as % of sales		of sales	$0	$0

Sales

Sales		
Cost of sales	$0	$0

Gross profit	$0	$0

Figure 10.1 (continued)

with a template that asks a series of questions to help clarify your thoughts. For Too Hot to Handle we have included part of the output from this. See Figure 10.1.

CONCLUSIONS

In the last chapter we went through various methods you can use to be creative and come up with possible new products or services – if you like, the 'big idea'. In this chapter we have discussed how you can go about evaluating strategic options. We looked at the questions that need to be asked about strategic options. We drew attention to factors such as investment costs, risk and feasibility. We also looked at how the different considerations can be combined in arriving at a final decision about the strategic option to select. We have given some attention to analytic techniques.

QUESTIONS

1. As we write this, Marks & Spencer is still having a tough time in the market even though it has revamped its clothes and embarked on an ambitious plan of shop refurbishment. We (at present) do not know how successful this will be but if there is a Marks & Spencer near you spend some time looking around the store to see if you can work out what the company is doing strategically. Do you think the strategic choice(s) it is making are having the desired effect?

2. Using the Glaxo-Wellcome case study can you evaluate what risks are present in its merger?

3. The 3G licence auctions around the world have forced the major mobile phone companies to evaluate how much they are prepared to pay for access to the new frequencies. What risks were involved in formulating a strategy for 3G access? How do you take into account the response of other mobile phone companies to your strategy given that they are also analysing your responses? You might like to look at the Vodafone case to help you answer this.

4. What financial methods are available to evaluate strategic options?

5. How feasible is it to use the criteria set out by Wootton and Horne to evaluate strategic options? The owner of the small bakery is thinking of buying another retail outlet but is unsure how to evaluate whether to do it or not. Would you suggest the owner uses the criteria set out by Wootton and Horne? Give reasons for your answer.

6. Too Hot to Handle seems a great idea but the list of things we would need to do before deciding on whether to open it looks pretty daunting. How do we keep our creative enthusiasm going while we plough through all these questions?

7. No matter how much time and effort has been put into making the business case, using accounting information and financial analysis, the decision on the 'big' strategic thing is down to it feeling right. Do you agree?

EXECUTIVE EXERCISE

Review your work in previous chapters' executive exercises. Select two or three of the most plausible ideas for strategic action. These should be ideas you think are likely to be feasible in the case of your own organization. Then evaluate them. Finally, generate a performance indicator relevant to the strategic action you have selected.

Now review the methods or approaches you used to evaluate the ideas for strategic action. How satisfied were you with the evaluation? What were the biggest barriers to effective evaluation of the strategic actions?

REFERENCES

Ansoff, H I (1968) *Corporate Strategy*, Penguin, Harmondsworth

Hussey, D (1999) *Strategy and Planning: A manager's guide*, Wiley, Chichester

Kind, J (1999) *Accounting and Finance for Managers*, Kogan Page, London

Ohmae, K (1982) *The Mind of the Strategist*, McGraw-Hill, London

Wootton, S and Horne, T (2000) *Strategic Thinking: A step-by-step approach*, Kogan Page, London

11

Key factors for success (KFS) and core competencies

INTRODUCTION

After World War I it became apparent to German Intelligence Officers that the British had been able to decode German encrypted messages and had gained a distinct advantage in the war. The Germans needed to find better ways of encrypting material so that it could not be read by other countries. In 1926 the German armed forces started to use the Enigma machine. This was an electrical–mechanical device that automatically encoded messages using a series of discs and wiring. This device was believed to give excellent protection against other people decoding German secret messages. Existing methods of decoding secret codes were useless. British code breakers were mystified. With German military build-up accelerating in the 1930s and Hitler increasing his demands on neighbouring nations such as Poland and Czechoslovakia it was becoming apparent that the Enigma code needed to be broken. For the time being, however, the advantage was with the Germans.

The first small chink in the Enigma code's armour was uncovered by a group of Polish cryptologists led by Marian Rejewski. He was able to work out each of the 105,456 possible starting combinations of the Enigma. The code was still not broken. The Enigma machine also had a set of plugs that increased the possible combinations.

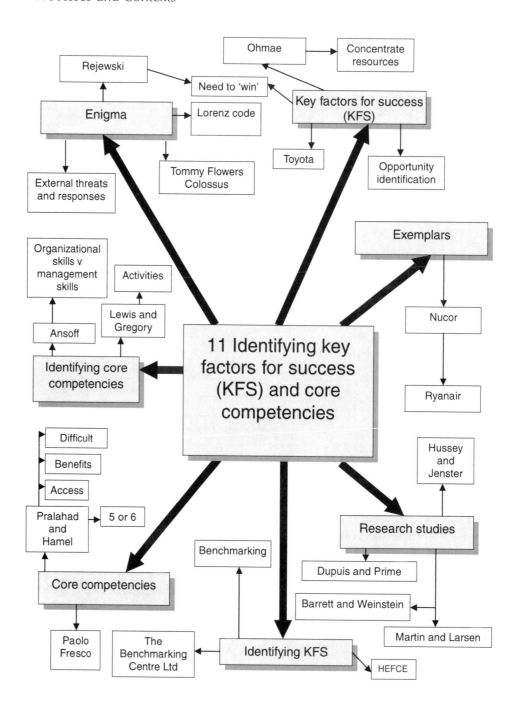

Further work, however, was successful and the Poles were able to decode all the Enigma messages they intercepted. The advantage was now with the Poles.

But in 1938 the Germans introduced improvements to the Enigma system that made it impossible for Rejewski and his team to break the code. The advantage was back again with the Germans. With a German invasion of Poland becoming likely in 1939, the Poles decided to give to the British all they knew about Enigma, and an actual machine. The Enigma machine only reached England days before Poland was invaded on 1 September 1939. It took the British a year to break the code. However, different parts of the German Armed Forces used variants of the Enigma. So while the British might be able to read a fair proportion of the Luftwaffe's messages, messages from the German Navy could not be read. This gave the Germans a real advantage especially in submarine warfare. As it looked likely that the Navy code would never be broken it was decided that actual German navy codebooks were needed. In a series of attacks on German navy vessels codebooks were secured. This gave the British an advantage.

Hitler communicated with his generals in an even more complex code than the Enigma, the Lorenz. What was needed was a fast electrical–mechanical way of decoding the Lorenz. Colossus was conceived. Colossus was arguably the first computer in the world as it was programmable and used values. This remarkable machine was constructed by Tommy Flowers, an engineer working for the British Post Office. Just before Christmas 1943 Colossus started work. The advantage had settled on the British side.

The Enigma story shows advantage first going one way, then the other, and then back. These swings and the way external threats (in this case invasion and war) can spur people on is a good illustration, albeit an extreme one, of how organizations compete against each other and exploit internal resources to gain advantages. In this chapter we look at two related ideas – key factors for success (KFS) and core competencies – as ways of securing advantages over competitors.

KEY FACTORS FOR SUCCESS (KFS)

Ohmae (1982) stressed the importance of firms focusing their resources on developing functional competencies in order to achieve advantage over competitors. Ohmae argued (1982: 49): 'Interestingly enough, the most effective shortcut to major success appears to be to jump to the top rank by concentrating major resources early on a single strategically significant function, become really good and competitive at it, and then move to consolidate a lead in the other functions by using the profit structure that early top status has made possible.' He was concerned here with the costs and performance of functions such as purchasing, design, engineering, sales, servicing, and so on. In other words, he considered the issue to be one of functional competence.

Strength in a specific function (eg design or servicing) could be decisive in an industry. This is the idea of KFS in the particular industry or business. For example, Ohmae (1982) claimed that Toyota gained market share in its forklift truck division by building up a strong and effective service network. So a firm should first identify its industry's KFS and then, secondly, should prioritize improving particular functions and concentrating its resources on developing strategic advantage over its competitors in these functions. Ohmae suggested that outstanding organizational achievements could result from this method of business strategy based on KFS.

Behind this is the idea that if you can identify an opportunity, even if you have in general inferior resources to your competitors, you can by targeting them carefully achieve a strategic advantage. Just as in the Enigma story Rejewski and his team managed to defeat the German Enigma code by deploying their limited resources to concentrate on the problem intensively. In fact, military strategy and tactics are full of examples of generals who have concentrated their resources in such a way as to achieve a remarkable victory against superior forces. In some instances the drive to 'win' is so strong that inferior resources can defeat superior ones. In business, while we sometimes use war metaphors to describe business situations, we are clearly not at war in the military sense. We are faced with challenges and threats that if not dealt with would mean the end of the business. These situations may give us the motivation to achieve startling results. We are more concerned here with the run of the mill strategic development where we scan the environment to check for not only possible threats but also opportunities. In doing so we may encounter a situation where normally our resources would not be sufficient but by targeting them carefully success could be achieved.

Exemplars

So, at the centre of the thinking on KFS is the notion that the key factors can be identified and resources concentrated in them. In this way a firm with inferior resources might by better allocation and focusing of its resources outperform a competitor with superior resources. This is a tough task for most firms to undertake; however, the experiences of Nucor in the United States and Ryanair in Europe suggest that it is possible.

Nucor is a US steel company. In recent years it has frequently been held up as a remarkable success story. The essence of its story is how it went from being a very small company to being a low-cost and large-scale steel producer. Nucor concentrated its resources on the exploitation of minimills technology located away from big cities. This technology was seen as only suitable for low-grade steel and yet the siting of the minimills made a lot of sense in an industry characterized by buyers in local markets. Industry giants, such as US Steel, with their more capital-intensive structures appeared to have been defeated by Nucor's competitive strategy.

Ryanair offers another example of a business minnow that has managed to achieve success despite its meagre resource base compared to industry leaders. Throughout most of the 1990s Ryanair enjoyed a high rate of growth, becoming a highly profitable airline in the low-fare segment of the industry. Ryanair appears to have achieved its success by concentrating on keeping operating costs low. This involved using cheaper airports, using fewer flight attendants, getting savings in maintenance costs by using a single type of aircraft, and cutting down on idle time in airports.

Research

We have found some research on the importance of KFS. However, it looks as though much of the research was generally not really concerned with the functional areas that had interested Ohmae (1982).

Hussey and Jenster (1999: 79) report a study of 128 manufacturing firms that found superior returns were achieved by firms that monitored their KFS and took remedial actions when required. Dupuis and Prime (1996) looked at KFS in global retailing using French hypermarkets in the United States and Asia. They concluded that there were three KFS, namely: maintaining the innovativeness of the concept and the retailing mix through either adaptation or globalization; creating harmonious relationships between investors and the different actors in the channel; and developing an adjustment capacity to different cultural environments. Barrett and Weinstein (1998), in a study of nearly 200 US firms, tested whether corporate entrepreneurship, flexibility, and market orientation were KFS. Their results supported the view that superior business performance was positively associated with these three factors. In an article in the *International Journal of Retail and Distribution* (1997: 227) three KFS for retailing were identified. These were, 'striving to achieve effective leadership, constant improvement of products and services and the establishment of a system of employee empowerment and reward structures'. Lastly Martin and Larsen (1999: 209) claim that the KFS for successfully trading in China include 'business etiquette, comprehension of Chinese advertisements and a sufficient knowledge of the Chinese language'.

On the whole we think these studies only contribute a little to our understanding of KFS. This is mainly for two reasons. Firstly, as we said above, the studies were not really exploring functional areas such as engineering, sales, servicing, etc. Secondly, at the methodological level, it is quite difficult to design research that can actually isolate KFS.

Identifying KFS

What can you do if you need to find KFS for your industry? One approach is to examine some successful firms and some unsuccessful firms in your industry to see if any particular things stand out. Benchmarking may well help in doing this. Increasingly companies are using benchmarking to measure themselves against the best not only in their industry but also in general. Information on benchmarks is available commercially. For instance, Financial Services and Banking Benchmarking Association provide benchmarks for financial and related services for the United States. Their Web site is at www.fsbba.org. In the UK there are many benchmarking services on offer, for example, The Benchmarking Centre Ltd. They can be contacted on www.benchmarking.co.uk. This Web site provides free information on benchmarks in the hospitality industry: www.cateringnet.co.uk/monthly/month0298/experia1.htm. All the major accounting firms and consultants offer benchmarking services. See, for example, KPMG at www.kpmg.co.uk/.

Examples of benchmarking can also be found in the public sector. In England the Higher Education Funding Council (www.hefce.ac.uk) provides detailed information on the institutions it funds and allows universities to compare themselves. Information is available on learning and teaching, research and wealth generation, and other activities.

Is the importance of KFS declining?

There are a number of writers who have in recent years underlined the increasing complexity and dynamism of the world confronting top managers. Bryson (1995: 3) suggests, for example, that change is being aggravated by 'increased interconnectedness', which is 'most apparent in the blurring of three traditionally important distinctions – between domestic and international spheres; between public policy areas; and between public, private, and nonprofit sectors'.

Within the private sector there are rapid rates of change, technological convergence and discontinuity. Hamel and Prahalad (1994) made a powerful argument for rethinking the traditional emphasis on analysing industry structures in strategic analysis. They said (Hamel and Prahalad, 1994: 37), 'Unpredictable and turbulent change can come to any industry today... More and more industries, by their very nature, seem to be perpetually underdefined, or even undefinable.' They suggested, for example, that the digital industry is a collection of industries that are converging and disintegrating all at the same time. But it was not just this highly technological industry they had in mind. 'Deregulation, globalization, fundamental breakthroughs in science, and the strategic importance of information technology are blurring boundaries in a wide variety of industries' (Hamel and Prahalad, 1994: 39).

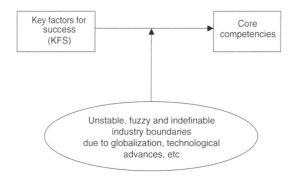

Figure 11.1 The shift from KFS to core competencies

Convergence and disintegration and the blurring of boundaries not only reduce the value and importance of Porter's (1980) techniques for industry analysis (especially the Five Forces model), they also undermine the usefulness of KFS. One implication of this changed state of competition in the new global world of fuzzy and unstable industry boundaries was the increasingly misleading nature of measuring organizational performance using market share. Successful firms might develop strengths (core competencies) that were used in a range of end products that yielded revenue in a whole range of different industries. While growth and profitability demonstrated these firms' success, this success need not show up as high share of the market in any individual industry.

In fact, Hamel and Prahalad were not arguing that industry structures had completely disintegrated, but rather that competition took place through positioning businesses within industries and also for dominance in the industry structures of the future. Positioning a business using the kind of strategic thinking made popular by Porter was no longer enough. Likewise we might argue that KFS continue to be important even in the new competitive conditions because there are still industries which for the time being have clear boundaries. However, it is important that KFS are supplemented by strategic moves based on core competencies that are not industry specific in the same way.

CORE COMPETENCIES

Paolo Fresco joined the board of Fiat in 1996 and became its Chairman in 1998. He is reported to have said (2000) that Fiat should be seen 'as a set of related businesses built around a shared platform of skills' and that 'we intend to build on our core competences'. (Source: *The Economist*, 3 June 2000: 91–92.)

In recent years many managers have shown interest in the ideas of seeing their companies as based on skills. Many have even used, as Paolo Fresco did, the language of core competencies. What are core competencies?

Core competencies, as proposed by Pralahad and Hamel (1990), can be seen as a continuation of Ohmae's thinking on KFS. Prahalad and Hamel argued that at most any firm is likely to have about five or six core competencies. These core competencies may relate to management activities, but can also be based on complex fusing together of production skills and technology. For example, firms may be said to have core competencies in technological areas such as optics, or miniaturization, or engines. Prahalad and Hamel lay particular emphasis on the role of these core competencies in relation to competitive advantage, and hence they propose three tests to establish whether a competence is, in fact, core. The tests are:

- Could the firm gain access to several different markets by using the competence?
- Does the competence contribute significantly to the perceived customer benefits of the end product or service?
- How difficult is it for other companies to acquire the competence?

Prahalad and Hamel (1990) suggest that skills and technologies are the basic elements of a core competence. They indicate that core competencies are embedded in core products that are then used in a range of different end products. Perhaps firms that can organize and nurture linkages between skills, technologies, core products and end products are better at coping with dynamic competitive situations that demand high rates of innovation. This model of the successful corporation is often identified as an example of the resource-based view of strategic management, in which the firm is conceptualized as a portfolio of resources rather than a portfolio of products or strategic business units.

Identifying core competencies

Just as with KFS, the idea of core competencies is intuitively appealing but how do we actually go about finding what core competencies are for a particular firm? Ansoff (1968) outlined an approach to capability profiling that may be seen as a suitable framework for identifying core competencies. He saw capability profiling as a process of mapping the skills and resources in the main functional areas, and suggested analysing skills and resources in terms of facilities and equipment, personnel skills, organizational capabilities and management capabilities. Ansoff speculated that successful firms in different groups of industries would share sets of capabilities. This anticipates the KFS idea of Ohmae. Some of Ansoff's categorizations seem to have been carried through into the work of Prahalad and Hamel (1990). In particular, Ansoff's distinction between organizational and management skills reflects, in our view, a later distinction between types of core competence.

Klein and Hiscocks (1994) provided a useful starting point for practical approaches to identifying core competencies through their discussion of skill mapping. They recommended organizations develop skill maps tailored to them specifically (see Figure 11.2). They suggested four ways of identifying specific skills:

1. Examine the organization structure.
2. Carry out interviews with members of the organization.
3. Examine the organization's products or services.
4. Ask customers and market watchers.

The organization's structure can be examined to see if particular departments or units of the organization might be centres of specific skills (eg a market research unit). Asking managers and staff what they think are the skills possessed by the organization is a fairly straightforward way of acquiring information. The examination of products or services – product analysis – can be very useful, especially if compared with the results of examining the products or services of rivals. If, for example, a product has a superior performance to a similar product made by a rival company then it is important to understand how it is made and to identify any aspects of the production methods used or the components used that might be responsible. Ultimately this examination would need to pinpoint the specific skills embodied in the methods or the components. Finally, it may be that customers who consume the products or services will have definite opinions on the features that create value for

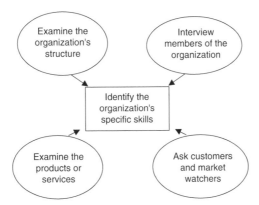

Figure 11.2 Klein and Hiscock's skill-mapping approach

them as consumers. For example, drivers of a particular make of car might identify the reliable performance of the car's engine or the styling.

Lewis and Gregory (1996) suggest a method of identifying core competencies that could be used by top management to think through the business's core competencies. They suggest that top managers are asked a series of questions about the activities of the business. The managers are encouraged to map the interdependencies and linkages between the main activities. Each of the main activities must be rated using criteria that reflect the kinds of tests suggested by Prahalad and Hamel (1990). Issues covered, for instance, would be, how well the activity is done, its contribution to customer satisfaction, and the possibility of imitation by rival firms. Prahalad and Hamel also consider it useful to break down into more detail the top-rated main activities and then to rate the more detailed activities too. Finally they suggest there is a need to identify the requirements of the top-rated activities in terms of equipment, machines, software, people skills, technology skills and management. These requirements closely resemble the categories Ansoff suggested for analysing skills and resources.

Any such method has to be applied in the context of organizational politics. To be unkind, there is often a degree of partisanship as functional specialists or particular technological groups attempt to persuade others that their particular specialization is central to the well-being of the firm. For example, HR management is seen in one organization as its particular strength, in another it is the R&D function that is seen this way, in others it is distribution or marketing or purchasing. Perhaps in some firms it is the holding of patents that stop others using the technology. So a challenge for any management team seeking to identify core competencies is cutting through all the noise of organizational politics to see where competencies really exist.

CONCLUSIONS

This chapter has turned the spotlight on the importance of KFS and core competencies, and has suggested that these can be used in strategic thinking. There has been some attention to the ways in which KFS and core competencies may be identified.

Using KFS or core competencies in strategy is a pretty common sense thing to do. If you can identify the factors or competencies, that is. The issue is not so much in agreeing with the importance of using them but of identifying them for your firm. Accounts of why an individual firm has done so well often include comments on such factors or competencies. Sometimes it is a particular technology that the firm owns, or it is to do with internal organization of resources, or a particular charismatic personality, the designs the firm uses, or its marketing. We need to go beyond individual accounts to try to discern industry patterns as from these it might be possible to isolate key factors or competencies that are crucial in a given set of competitive conditions. If this is possible, a concentration of resources should provide significant advantage for a firm even if the firm has, in the round, inferior resources. There is no assumption that these factors or competencies are stable over time or across industries. A firm may well be able to gain advantage over its competitors by picking up new factors or competencies that other firms have missed or under-emphasized.

This chapter has highlighted issues that have come to the forefront in the last decade of strategic management thinking. We have suggested that KFS are giving way to core competencies as useful for competitive advantage because of globalization, technological advance, and other changes. However, both KFS and core competencies are important as internal resources and strengths of the firm. The challenge in both cases is how to make good use of them to be innovative and provide superior benefits to customers. This contrasts with the previous decade when the emphasis was on positioning the firm in its external competitive environment and thus beating its competitors.

QUESTIONS

1. Can Ohmae's idea about focusing resources on developing functional competencies in order to achieve advantages over competitors explain Starbucks's success? (See case study.)
2. What KFS can be used to explain the growth of J D Wetherspoon? (See case study.)
3. How plausible do you find the argument that it often takes a major crisis for a firm to engage in strategy in a big way? You may find it helpful to think about Marks & Spencer or Nissan in answering this, as well as Nucor and Ryanair (discussed above).
4. The owner of the small bakery is trying to figure out what factors lead to it being successful. How useful do you think the findings reported in the *International Journal of Retail and Distribution Management* will be?
5. Using some of the Web sites given in the text on benchmarking, write a proposal to senior management about the desirability or not of using such services.
6. What are core competencies? How easy are they to identify in an organization? How useful is the method outlined by Lewis and Gregory in identifying them?
7. In designing a strategy, as it is pretty difficult to work out and then act upon the ideas behind core competencies or KFS, it is best just to use one of Porter's generic strategies. Do you agree?

8. Looking at J D Wetherspoon, is it not simply a low-cost strategy that has done the trick for the company? What other factors have contributed to its success?

9. While the past was all about positioning the firm in its external environment, today it is all about the development of internal resources aimed at providing superior benefits to customers. Is it that simple?

EXECUTIVE EXERCISE

Please select one of the ideas you have generated in a previous executive exercise. This idea should be selected on the basis that it is an idea your own organization could develop and market. The task now is to assess the gap between the current core competencies of the organization and those that would be needed to create and market a product or service based on this idea. You could use the following questions when seeking to identify the organization's current core competence:

1. Has the organization got a core competence in one or more of the following activities:
   - procurement/sourcing;
   - design;
   - specific production technologies (eg engines, miniaturization, sticky tape, optics);
   - sales;
   - distribution;
   - servicing;
   - anything else?
2. Would it be more accurate to say that the core competencies consist of sub-activities of the activities? What are they?
3. How do you know that this activity is a capability that produces a relatively large amount of the benefits experienced by customers?
4. How easy or difficult is it for competitors to imitate these core competencies? If competitors chose tomorrow to set out to imitate them, how easy or difficult would it be for them?
5. Has the organization managed to use and reuse the core competencies in a range of different products and services?
6. Could the organization market the new product or service using existing core competencies? If not, what new core competencies would be needed?

List the core competencies that in your opinion would have to be improved, augmented, or acquired. Finally, please review the exercise and decide answers to the following three questions:

- What did you like about the above approach to identifying core competencies?
- What didn't you like?
- What was missing from this approach?

If you are able to discuss this exercise in a small group, please compare answers to these three questions.

REFERENCES

Anon (1997) Key success factors from leading innovative retailers, *International Journal of Retail and Distribution Management*, **25** (6–7), pp 227–28

Ansoff, H I (1968) *Corporate Strategy*, Penguin, London

Barrett, H and Weinstein, A (1998) The effect of market orientation and organisational flexibility on corporate entrepreneurship, *Entrepreneurship: Theory and practice*, **23** (1)

Bryson, J M (1995) *Strategic Planning for Public and Nonprofit Organizations*, Jossey-Bass, San Francisco

Dupuis, M and Prime, N (1996) Business distance and global retailing: a model for analysis of key success/failure factors, *International Journal of Retail and Distribution Management*, **24** (11) pp 30–39

Hamel, G and Prahalad, C K (1994) *Competing for the Future*, Harvard Business School Press, Boston

Hussey, D and Jenster, P (1999) *Competitor Intelligence: Turning analysis into success*, Wiley, Chichester

Klein, J A and Hiscocks, P G (1994) Competence-based competition: a practical toolkit, in *Competence-Based Competition*, eds G Hamel and A Heene, Wiley, Chichester

Lewis, M A and Gregory, M J (1996) Developing and applying a process approach to competence analysis, in *Dynamics of Competence-Based Competition: Theory and practice in the new strategic management*, eds R Sanchez, A Heene and H Thomas, Pergamon, Oxford.

Martin, B and Larsen, G (1999) Taming the tiger: key success factors for trade with China, *Market Intelligence and Planning*, **17** (4–5) pp 220–29

Ohmae, K (1982) *The Mind of the Strategist*, McGraw-Hill, London

Porter, M (1980) *Competitive Strategy*, Free Press, New York

Prahalad, C and Hamel, G (1990) The core competence of the corporation, *Harvard Business Review*, May–June, pp 277–99

12

Identifying creative strategic options

INTRODUCTION

In *King Richard II* a scene takes place between Bushey, a servant to King Richard, and his Queen. Richard has just left to fight in Ireland and his Queen is grief-stricken, so Bushey tries to comfort her. Basically what he says is if you view his departure straight on you will be upset but look at it from a different angle and you will see it more clearly and not weep. The trick Bushey suggest is to look at it awry.

Act 2, Scene 2
BUSHEY:

> Each substance of a grief hath twenty shadows,
> Which shows like grief itself, but is not so;
> For sorrow's eye, glazed with blinding tears,
> Divides one thing entire to many objects;
> Like perspectives, which rightly gazed upon;
> Show nothing but confusion, eyed awry
> Distinguish form: so your sweet majesty,
> Looking awry upon your lord's departure,
> Find shapes of grief, more than himself, to wail;
> Which, look'd on as it is, is nought but shadows
> Of what it is not. Then, thrice-gracious queen,

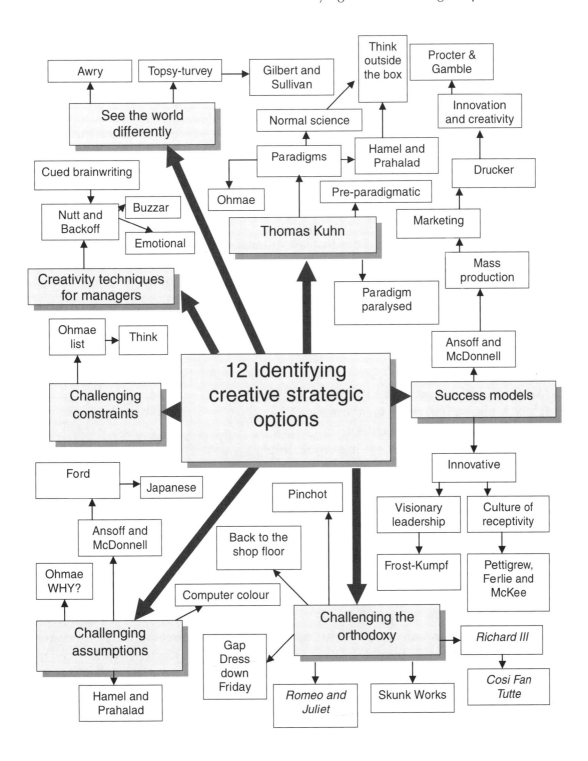

More than your lord's departure weep not: more's not seen;
Or if it be, 'tis with false sorrow's eye,
Which for things true weeps things imaginary.

What has this to do with the chapter? Let's move on to Gilbert and Sullivan operettas. In Mike Leigh's film of Gilbert and Sullivan, Gilbert is referred to as the master of topsy-turvy. When writing a story for Sullivan to set to music Gilbert would take a reasonably believable situation and change a few things, and set the world topsy-turvy and see what his imagination could come up with. What happens if someone instead of being apprenticed to a pilot is apprenticed to a pirate – as in *The Pirates of Penzance*. Add more confusion by making the birthday of the apprentice February 29, so his birthday is every four years instead of each year. His apprenticeship to the Pirate then lasts not 7 years but 28! And so on. By imagining a few changes Gilbert was able to supply Sullivan with the comic story he could set to music.

Evidently Shakespeare was familiar with the idea of topsy-turvy, as evident from this quote from *Henry IV Part I* Act 4, Scene 1:

HOTSPUR:
    You strain too far.
    I rather of his absence make this use:
    It lends a lustre and more great opinion,
    A larger dare to our great enterprise,
    Than if the earl were here; for men must think,
    If we without his help can make a head
    To push against a kingdom, with his help
    We shall o'erturn it topsy-turvy down.
    Yet all goes well, yet all our joints are whole.

So look at the world awry or at an angle. Change a few things, like pilot to pirate. What next? Thomas Kuhn in a highly influential book (1970), developed the idea of scientific paradigms. One way of understanding a paradigm is to think of it as a way of seeing the world. In the paradigm are 'tools' we use to see and interpret the world. These paradigms can be very powerful. Kuhn gives the example of the non-recording of sunspots before Copernicus. Evidently the view in the Western World prior to Copernicus was that the heavens were unchanging; therefore, by definition sunspots could not exist, and so they were not observed. Let the heavens change and the earth rotate then sunspots appear. According to Kuhn, Chinese astronomers had observed sunspots for quite some time. Amazingly sunspots could not be seen in the West because the dominant paradigm said they could not exist.

Kuhn coined the term normal science to describe periods when the dominant paradigm was answering most questions thrown up by observation using the tools of the paradigm. Even in periods of normal science troublesome facts do emerge that are difficult to reconcile with the existing paradigm but often they can be 'swept under the carpet' as the existing way of seeing the world is still providing useful output. Think of Newtonian v Einsteinian physics. For centuries the laws formulated by Newton on motion were sufficient to explain the observations being made. Slowly difficult observations emerged that were hard to fit in. Eventually Einstein's model replaced Newton's but Einstein also suffered as his strong belief in God made it hard for him to accept quantum mechanics – God would not have allowed the implication made by quantum mechanics that cause and effect were so strange.

PARADIGMS

We think it is pretty easy to extend Kuhn's argument about science into strategy development. Kuhn pointed out that students learn from experienced practitioners and teachers, who have also received a similar training; and established texts. A strong paradigm emerges about the discipline and tools required to solve problems that appear. The way of seeing the world binds us together. But for strategy we may be at what Kuhn labels the pre-paradigmatic stage. In this stage several competing views are around and none are completely dominant. The point we want to make is that an individual organization in our field may have its own paradigm for strategy that constrains managers to look at strategy in a particular way. Compare this to the technology the firm may use. This is derived from the dominant scientific paradigm and subscribed to by most if not all of the scientists in the firm. Scientists on leaving a company will not have to change their scientific paradigm when they move to another firm, but a manager involved in strategy may well have too. For example, they may be told when they join a new firm, 'We don't use core competencies here.'

'Paradigm paralysed' is where you are so bound into your worldview that even serious anomalies are ignored until it is too late. The history of business is littered with successful firms that had found the way and then the world moved on and they did not. They were stuck in the mud of their own way of doing things.

The point of all this is to encourage you to occasionally look at the world awry when you are thinking about strategy. Try another angle, don't look at the problem straight on but at an angle and like the Queen you may see a much better picture. Secondly, try a few topsy-turvy ideas, be like Gilbert and wonder what would happen it you changed pilot to pirate, or changed one year to four. And become reflexive about the strategy paradigm you use to see through. Worry about whether you are missing the sunspots because your model of the business you are in does not let you see them. One more story might bring this home. What has '10–22–38 Astoria' to do with trying to think outside of your paradigm? When you find out perhaps you can let us know.

Hamel and Prahalad are strong believers in thinking outside of your paradigm or even 'out of the box'. As they say foresight often comes not from being a better forecaster, but from being less hide-bound. 'To discover the future it is not necessary to be a seer, but it is absolutely vital to be unorthodox' (1994: 99). They stress that companies should develop skills in thinking the unorthodox and encourage the rebellious; as it is from these that the future will be created. As George Bernard Shaw said, 'The reasonable man adapts himself to the world: the unreasonable one persists in trying to adapt the world to himself. Therefore all progress depends on the unreasonable man.' Ohmae argues a very similar line when he talks about strategists needing to test the conventional. We need to get used to questioning the conventional and orthodox. While it's a terrible mouthful to say, we need to move from orthodoxy to heterodoxy, to be more rebellious and unreasonable.

THINKING 'OUT OF THE BOX'

This is all well and good, you are probably thinking, but how about some concrete examples? Let us throw this back at you. What is there about your current situation that you feel you cannot change because it's deeply embedded in your worldview? It might be the job you really want you cannot get because you lack the skills, qualifications, and contacts for it – whatever. Can you now think 'out of the box' to figure out how you could achieve your job goal? How easy is it to look at your position awry? To turn the world topsy-turvy?

It's not easy is it? Try to be unorthodox, unreasonable, and rebellious. Have a go at using some of the techniques we have suggested previously to free up your thoughts. We hope you have had a go at this to see how difficult it can be. When people try to do this they often say reality breaks in and while this is OK in theory, in real life it's nonsense. For instance, how can a small firm compete against a large one? How can one firm compete in a market where its rival owns the patents for the technology? All we can say is in these situations it's all about developing the mindset that challenges the orthodox. Of course conventional wisdom says small firms cannot compete against large ones but is that true in all cases? No. In fact, you could argue that given the growth in small firms, it is large firms that have more problems in competing, as they are too impersonal and inflexible. Look at the growth of dotcom companies; some of these started out with one or two people, yet within a few years were themselves large.

SUCCESS MODELS

Ansoff and McDonnell (1990) present an outline of business history containing two transition periods. The first was early in the 20th century when mass production became important, in which efficiency of production, specialization, and economies of scale were critical success factors. They suggest (1990: 62) that, 'As a result, entrepreneurs with strategic and creative mentalities were replaced by managers who had what came to be known as the production mentality.'

The second transition period, in the 1930s, ended up with the marketing function becoming dominant. The marketing mentality was based on the need to respond to the market, and thus on the importance of identifying what the market needed, rather than what the firm wanted to produce.

It looks as though there has been another transition. The old-style marketing orientation is no longer enough and there is a new concern with creativity and innovation. Indeed, there may even be a new concern for entrepreneurship (Drucker, 1985). In the last decade firms are increasingly embracing a success mentality based on the fruits of exploiting new technologies (eg the Internet) and the importance of creativity and innovation. The firms that are growing fastest and have the best financial results are innovative companies.

Creativity and innovation are the critical success factors in this dynamic and complex global business phase, but firms in the grip of old-style production or marketing mentalities are apparently finding the changes occurring around them threatening. Famous companies such as Procter & Gamble, Rubbermaid and Gillette have all been reported in the business press as being concerned about their capacity for successful innovation. Large companies may seek to respond by using an acquisition strategy to ensure that they can access innovative products or services, but many are also trying to reinvent themselves as more innovative companies.

In 1999 Durk Jager became the Chief Executive of Procter & Gamble, a company employing over 100,000 people around the world and with sales close to £40 billion. He was in charge of a firm that had been slipping in terms of competitiveness. It had lost 10 per cent of its share of the global market since the mid-1990s. He appeared to have very quickly diagnosed the firm's problem as one of a lack of innovation. This is despite the fact that Procter & Gamble had been spending relatively large amounts of money on R&D. Within six months of taking on the job of Chief Executive he had set up innovation teams to get new ideas to market speedily and he had put new business managers in charge of new ideas. Procter & Gamble also intended to take more risks in getting the product to market quickly. This implies that Jager saw organizational and cultural factors as important in getting a better record of innovation. It is tempting to see Procter & Gamble as a mass marketing firm with a marketing mentality seeking to become a new generation firm that is creative, innovative and suited to the dynamic and 'surprising' conditions of global business. For an update on how successful this has been, see the case study on Procter & Gamble.

Two answers for firms that want to be more innovative are to develop the right type of visionary leadership and to foster a culture of receptivity. A visionary leadership creates a strategic vision that provides a language or vocabulary that opens up new lines of action and provides numerous opportunities for others in the organization to be included in actions and programmes that are innovative (Frost-Kumpf *et al*, 1993). Organizations in more or less the same environmental conditions respond with varying degrees of strategic change. One factor in this is the receptivity of the culture found in these organizations (Pettigrew, Ferlie and McKee, 1992). So, however much pressure for innovation is created by the new global business conditions, the actual amount of innovation is mediated by the receptivity of people in the organization.

CHALLENGING THE ORTHODOXY

How can a culture of receptivity be increased? Some organizations have sought to create this in terms of a spirit of intrapreneurship, which is where receptivity to the environment and its opportunities is based on entrepreneurial processes that have been fostered, sponsored, and rewarded within organizations (Pinchot, 1985).

One difficulty in creating intrapreneurship is that most of us are reluctant to waste energy and time on doing something we feel will not work. Few innovations are successful. Many new products or services are obvious failures within a short time of being launched. Encouraging employees to spend time in doing this does meet resistance. One way around this is to create a special place where employees are allowed to think this way and actively discouraged from thinking negatively. Looking at the world awry is not easy so we all need help in doing so. Skunk works are places in firms where secretive and unconventional projects are hatched. The most famous of these is Lockheed's Skunk Works. It takes its name from the Skunk Works in Al Capp's comic strip Li'l Abner. These works are places where employees are encouraged to think differently. The Lockheed Skunk Works has become so famous that you can buy on the Web baseball caps, sweat shirts and other things bearing their logo. The home page is at www.skunkworks.net and the shop is at www.lmsw.external.lmco.com/lerc/index.html. At Lockheed's Skunk Works the company developed a plane capable of spying on the Soviet Union. In this sense it was a secretive project for obvious reasons. Skunk works are used not only for secretive projects but also for unconventional ones.

Some firms have gone in this direction of freeing up employees to think hetrodoxically by instigating dress down days. The idea is that by changing the conventional clothes we wear to work from time to time we can change our thinking. Business executives in their suits think differently when dressed casually. Presumably the often casually dressed student thinks differently when dressed in a suit. Performances of old plays often use change of period costume to more modern costume for a similar effect. There is a film of *Richard III* where instead of period clothes the actors wear clothes of the 1930s to exploit our own recent history. The scheming Richard is portrayed as a fascist dictator to bring home to us the core nature of Shakespeare's play. A recent production of Mozart's *Cosi Fan Tutte* started with the actors on a beach in swimming costumes. Baz Luhrmann's version of *Romeo and Juliet*, with Leonado di Caprio as Romeo, Claire Danes as Juliet and a sensational performance by Harold Perrineau as Mercutio, is in modern dress. There are of course lots more examples but the director's idea is for us, the audience, to think about the play differently. Getting employees to change clothes is after much the same thing. Changing clothes might just set your world topsy-turvy.

It may seem far-fetched to say that by changing what you wear to work you can slip into another paradigm, and challenge any paradigm paralysis you are suffering. But dress-down days do exist and in some pretty conventional places. The conventional thinking was that business clothes are dark suits for men and women with ties for men. What is the thinking now? Look around you to see how things are changing and how companies like Gap are benefiting from the fact that casual dressing is in. Gap exploited this trend in casual dressing on Friday 26 September 1997 when the New York Stock Exchange had its first casual dress day. The signal to start trading is given by a bell. On this day the CEO of Gap along with another senior Gap executive were allowed to ring the bell. Gap's Web site tells you more about this trend in business wear: www.gapinc.com/.

Firms do other things to free up thinking. One thing is to send groups of employees on 'away days'. Getting people away from the normal place of work isolates them from routine interruptions but also places them in novel environments. So, it seems that firms act in accordance with the pragmatist's idea of learning being encouraged by changing the environment. Putting staff through an outward-bound experience will enhance learning by changing their normal environment. Clearly other things are learnt, especially about team working, but by carefully structuring the new environment people are helped to think the unthinkable. Questions about the fundamental assumptions of the business can be asked. A recent head of a large motor manufacturing company recalled to us the success of inviting employees from across the company to such an event. Executives were present but so was a range of staff from all areas of the business. He was impressed by the new thinking that emerged from this event, often originating from employees that had no say in the direction of the business. We have already written about the need for senior executives to put themselves 'back to the shop floor' to see the business differently; this is another way that new, unconventional ideas can emerge that challenge the orthodoxy.

CHALLENGING ASSUMPTIONS

Hamel and Prahalad claim that while people in every firm believe that their firm and sector is complex, in fact there are five or six basic things that form the framework for the industry. Hamel and Prahalad (1994: 99) briefly outline one method of challenging assumptions. Their succinct explanation is as follows:

> Executives often like to believe that their industry is complicated and unique. On the other hand, we always tell senior managers, give us a couple of days to poke around your industry and we'll find the five or six fundamental conventions that underpin the industry... Once one discovers the conventions, then one can ask if there is any value in ignoring them... Contrarians find these conventions and use them as weapons against orthodox-ridden incumbents.

Once you have identified these conventions ignore them and see what happens. For example, nearly all PCs are the same colour – why? What would happen if you made them in a range of colours? The Apple Macintosh comes in a range of colours! Hamel and Prahalad (1994: 99) provide their own illustration: 'In the airline industry, conventional thinking held that a hub-and-spokes route structure was far superior to a point-to-point network... Southwest Airlines became the most profitable in the United States by ignoring the hub-and-spoke convention.'

Ohmae (1982) suggested that the strategist's method of challenging assumptions is to keep putting the same question: Why? In the case of stalemated situations where companies are stagnating, drifting or even deteriorating, the problem may be that the companies are all pursuing the same KFS. In other words, one company pursuing KFS may bring it success initially but if all companies in the industry follow this example and also pursue the same ones equally, the key factors may cease to be effective in bringing success. They are now the common sense of the industry. So, in this case, challenging the accepted common sense of the industry means challenging the current set of key factors. So the method in this case would be to identify the KFS and ask whether some new factors matter.

Challenging the assumptions of an industry is not easy because of the powerful hold that existing mindsets have on experienced managers. Management mindsets have both a positive and negative result. Managers develop their mindsets in part on the basis of their own experiences of success and failure in the industry. The mindset becomes a set of convictions about what works and what does not work in this industry. It often helps managers to deal with complexity and development. 'When complex information comes in, an experienced manager uses the [mindset] to reduce the complexity of signals, and to select appropriate responses. An inexperienced manager… becomes swamped by the volume and complexity of the information that comes in.' (Ansoff and McDonnell, 1990: 61). Unfortunately, if there is a discontinuity in the development of the industry, then the mindset becomes a problem. The experienced manager fails to recognize or fails to notice important information that does not fit the mindset. Ansoff and McDonnell (1990) point to Henry Ford's refusal to recognize in the 1930s the end of the single model strategy in the car industry. They also point to the failure of US firms to recognize the growing importance of Japanese competitors.

CHALLENGING CONSTRAINTS

Challenging assumptions may lead on to managers having to challenge constraints. Managers in a company may be unenthusiastic about taking drastic action. They may feel that there is little that can be done. They are too constrained by their situation to change. Ohmae (1982) suggests this can be handled by asking managers to identify the constraints and to list them. Then the managers are asked what might be possible if the constraints were removed. This hypothetical question can get the managers thinking of what can be tried. Finally, the managers are asked to concentrate on removing the constraints they have identified.

Ohmae (1982: 88) provided the following encouraging assessment:

> Problems vary as much as fingerprints, and so do the solutions… However – and this is my point – a change in the attitude of those who must confront the problem can work wonders. The secret lies in making people think, from the very start, what can we do? Instead of what can't we do? and then striving doggedly to strip away one by one the constraints that have turned the possible into the seemingly impossible.

CREATIVITY TECHNIQUES FOR MANAGERS

The creativity of management strategic thinking can be enhanced using some very specific techniques. These include the nominal group technique, cued brainwriting, and synectics (Nutt and Backoff, 1992). These are briefly outlined here but they represent just an illustration of a large and expanding set of techniques available for boosting creativity in strategic management decision making.

266 Processes and Contexts

The nominal group technique can be used to good effect with a team of managers engaged in strategic planning. Each member of the team works in face to face contact with the others but produces ideas without discussion. These ideas may concern the contents of a SWOT analysis, the identification of strategic issues, proposals for strategic actions, and so on. The individuals note their ideas for later discussion with others in the group. This production of ideas without discussion is meant to encourage silent reflection. The advantages of silent reflection have been concisely summed up by Nutt and Backoff (1992: 226) as follows:

> The process of silent reflection has been developed to overcome the barriers to full group participation and to encourage the development of innovative ideas. During the silent reflection phase, the SMG [strategic management group] members feel a certain tension that promotes a form of competition for good solutions. This helps the group avoid superficial arguments, tired diagnoses, and pet ideas that stifle innovation.

This period of nominal group working can be followed by discussion in order to evaluate the ideas that have been produced during the silent reflection of the nominal group phase. It is argued that this way of working generates many more ideas and prevents hasty rejection of potentially good ideas.

Cued brainwriting requires those involved in a strategic planning session to produce ideas while sitting around a table which has several sheets of paper containing a written cue (eg a question). For example, there might be four sheets of paper with questions such as:

- What are the most important strategic issues?
- Why are these strategic issues important?
- How could the firm take action to address these strategic issues?
- What assumptions have you made in suggesting strategic actions?

Each person takes a single sheet and writes ideas in response to the question until he or she cannot think of anything more to add. Then each person takes another sheet with a different question and again writes some ideas on the sheet. This continues until all participants have contributed ideas in relation to all the sheets. This is all done using silent reflection.

Synectics is the use of analogies and metaphors to stimulate creativity. As with brainstorming, synectics requires participants to refrain from criticizing ideas. Nutt and Backoff (1992: 239) say, The process of innovation is both emotional and intellectual. The synectics process seeks to engage a person's preconscious and unconscious to draw out emotional or nonrational linkages through the use of metaphors.

A synectics session may last several hours. In it metaphors and analogies may be used 'to make the strange familiar or to make the familiar strange' (Nutt and Backoff 1992: 241). There is a range of procedures available for use in a session. Direct analogy may be used. Apparently the flight of a buzzard was an inspiration for a stabilizing system used by the Wright brothers on an airplane. But other types of analogies may be used, including personal, symbolic and fantasy analogies.

CONCLUSIONS

We have looked at how managers in an organization can challenge technological, marketing and other industry assumptions in order to develop a successful and innovative new business. We have looked at the simple techniques and questions that can be used by any management team wishing to challenge the assumptions of their industry.

While managers may challenge industry assumptions in order to think up a product or service that is innovative, perceived constraints on change may also need to be overcome.

QUESTIONS

1. Wherever you are reading this now attempt to see the world awry. What did you notice that you have never seen before looking at the world normally?
2. What has '10–22–38 Astoria' got to do with changing paradigms?
3. Why do strategists have to be unorthodox and unreasonable?
4. While it is OK for large companies to have a few people thinking funny thoughts, for most organizations this is just not on. How would you persuade the owner of the bakery to think differently about his or her business?
5. Use the Procter & Gamble case study to answer the following. To what extent is Procter & Gamble's present difficulty due to its paradigm of how to innovate needing changing?
6. How would you sell the idea of setting up a skunk works or dress down Fridays to sceptical senior managers who believe such things are typical management fads dreamt up by ivory tower academics?
7. The best way to improve strategy is to simply ask why? Why?
8. Use the Ford case study to answer the following. What assumptions about the way Ford is going to do business in the future are present? How plausible do you think they are?
9. What methods are available to enhance creativity in strategic thinking? You have been asked to plan a day's course to help 'free up' strategic thinking. How would you organize the day?
10. If strategy were a car it would be a (fill in space). Why did you choose that car?

REFERENCES

Ansoff, H I and McDonnell, E (1990) *Implanting Strategic Management*, Prentice Hall, London

Drucker, P (1985) *Innovation and Entrepreneurship*, Butterworth-Heinemann, Oxford

Frost-Kumpf, L *et al* (1993) Strategic action and transformational change: the Ohio Department of Mental Health, in *Public Management*, ed B Bozeman, Jossey-Bass, San Francisco

Hamel, G and Prahalad, C K (1994) *Competing for the Future*, Harvard Business School Press, Boston

Kuhn, T S (1970) *The Structure of Scientific Revolutions*, University of Chicago Press, London

Nutt, P C and Backoff, R W (1992) *Strategic Management of Public and Third Sector Organizations*, Jossey-Bass, San Francisco

Ohmae, K (1982) *The Mind of the Strategist*, McGraw-Hill, London

Pettigrew, A, Ferlie, E and McKee, L (1992) *Shaping Strategic Change*, Sage, London

Pinchot, G (1985) *Intrapreneuring*, Harper and Row, London

Reading 12.1

Taken from Step 7 – Creating more options, in *Strategic Thinking* by Simon Wootton and Terry Horne (2000)

CREATING MORE OPTIONS

Now that you are clearer about what you wish your organisation to achieve, it is time to consider your options.

The strategic options on the following page are elaborated in the prompt sheets. If you would like some help on how to come up with new ideas, turn to the prompt sheets on creative thinking.

Once you have so many options that you need to become selective, you are probably ready for Step 8, in which you will be able to evaluate each option, using six strategic criteria. You will then be able to see which of the options you generated during this step, Step 7, will best achieve the desirable objectives that you established during Step 6. In the final step, Step 9, you will plan the implementation of the options you will have selected during Step 8.

Identifying Strategic Options

Strategic options	What might you gain from this option?	What are the problems with this option?	Examples of this option
Change nothing			
Concentration			
Product development			
Market development			
Innovation			
Horizontal integration			
Vertical integration			
Concentric diversification			
Retrenchment			
Turnaround			
Divestment			
Liquidation			

Prompt Sheet on Strategic Options

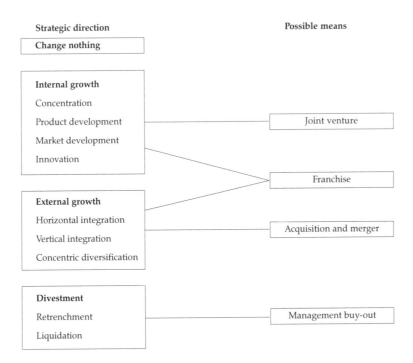

(Developed with permission from Thompson, J L (1990) *Strategic Management: Awareness & Change*, p 430, Figure 17.1 'Strategic alternatives', Chapman & Hall.)

Change nothing

The 'change nothing' option is the one in which your organisation continues to follow, in broad terms, its current direction. As most organisations are confronting both internal and external changes, this option is sometimes not a good one to follow in the long term, but since the disruptive costs of change can be very high, the 'change nothing' scenario should always be considered seriously. In any event it provides a common point of comparison for other options.

Strategies for internal growth include:

Concentration

Resources can be focused towards the continued and profitable growth of a 'single' product or service in a 'single' market. This can be achieved by attracting new customers or by increasing their usage rate, or, where feasible, by attracting customers away from competitors. The advantage of this approach is that it uses the current skills in the organisation. Growth is not likely to be dramatic.

Product Development

An organisation can think about what modified products or services it could offer to its existing customers. This is generally less risky than trying to find new customers for existing products or services.

Market Development

An organisation can build on its existing strengths, skills and capabilities in order to market its present products or services to new customers, in related market areas. This often involves a new or renewed approaches to advertising, promotion and selling.

Innovation

This implies the development of products or services that are new, as opposed to modified. Innovative organisations can keep ahead of their competitors by introducing new products or services. Constant innovation requires new finance. If the new products will need to be sold to new customers, the risks associated with the new product's development will rise markedly.

Strategies for external growth include:

Horizontal Integration

This is integration that occurs when an organisation acquires or merges with a major competitor. Market share should increase and the organisation should be looking for situations in which the pooled skills and resources can generate a synergistic effect. These will be situations in which combined efforts should produce results that are greater than the mere arithmetic addition of previous market shares.

Vertical Integration

This is integration that occurs when an organisation acquires one of its suppliers or one of its customers. In this case the benefits looked for are not primarily in market share. Efficiency gains are sought through either better prices and delivery of components or through a better planned pattern of demand.

Concentric Diversification

Here the aim is to utilise the current marketing and research skills for one product or service, in order to develop a different or new product or service in another market. What is being sought here is a wider market for your organisation's knowledge, expertise or skill in carrying out certain processes, eg, research and development or product testing.

Strategies for divestment include:

Retrenchment

This may be required when an organisation experiences declining profits as a result of economic recession, production or service inefficiency, or through the activities of competitors that are innovating faster than it is. In these circumstances, the organisation will need to concentrate only on activities in which it has distinctive competencies. The aim is to reduce its operations to those in which the organisation has advantages over its competitors. Ideally, it will have further strategies to sustain those advantages in the face of anticipated changes and the actions likely to be taken by its competitors.

If an organisation fails to recover, there may be a need to sell off (or divest) part of the business. A management buy-out can be one way to do this. It is often associated with the need to raise finance, or is prompted when one part of the organisation is dragging down the rest.

Liquidation

This approach involves the sale of a complete business, either as a going concern or on a piecemeal basis. This may not necessarily be an admission of failure. It will sometimes be in the best interests, in the long term, of the stakeholders.

Prompt Sheet on Techniques to Aid Creativity

Everyone is creative. Some people can access their creativity more easily than others. Rapid change forces managers to think about the need for creativity and innovation in their organisations. Certain conditions can benefit this process:

- Providing copious facilities
  for writing, drawing and display. Unrecorded ideas get lost easily
- Using secluded locations
  helps to produce freedom from distractions
- Setting tight time limits
  helps to prevent over-elaboration and inhibits evaluation
- Raising energy
  creativity works best when people are aroused and enthusiastic.

1. Attribute Listing

This is a very simple method and is most useful when managers might be looking for the development of basic ideas, such as spin-offs from existing products or services:

A. Identify and pick out the major attributes of a product or service.

B. Suggest as many variations of each attribute as possible. Each combination of variations creates a potentially different product, service or idea.

C. List all the combinations. Evaluate them later.

As an example, consider you have been employed as a consultant by a Christmas novelty company to come up with new ideas for balloons. After discussions with the company, you decide that the major attributes for the novelty balloons are: colour; size; shape; price; durability. Using the above A, B, C approach:

A – *Major attributes*; we could have:
size, shape, price, durability.

B – *Possible variations*; we could have:
colours – red, purple, polka-dot, etc
size – 1 cm, 1 metre, 3 metres
shape – banana, star
price – 10p each, £1 each, £25 each
durability – 5 minutes, 1 year, 10-year guarantee

C – *Possible combinations*; we could have:
3-metre polka-dot banana, £25, ten-year guarantee.

(Adapted from Cooke and Slack (1991) *Making Management Decisions*, 2nd edn, by permission of the publisher, Prentice Hall International, Hemel Hempstead.)

You would then need to decide which of the potential products you think might be worth taking further as possible new balloon products.

2. Brainstorming

This is useful in tackling 'how to do' problems, or those where a new broad idea or direction is needed. The process involves presenting the problem or the opportunity and then generating as many ideas as possible, in a limited time, preferably using a large (6 to 16) group of people.

Every possible idea is recorded in a way that everyone can see. Flipcharts are commonly used. Someone usually keeps a note of all suggestions and feeds them through to the flipchart

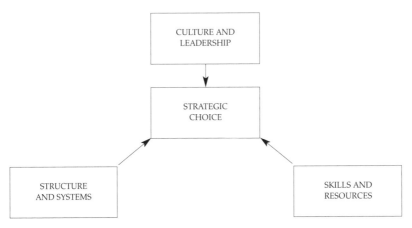

(Figure adapted from Bowman (1990), *The Essence of Strategic Management,* by permission of the publisher, Prentice Hall International, Hemel Hempstead.)

in a steady stream, acting as a kind of reservoir or 'header tank' of ideas, so as to keep the flow of ideas going. Zany ideas are encouraged, as is humour. Such ideas may be 'planted' in the audience to create a permissive atmosphere. Negativism, realism, scepticism and in particular cynicism are not allowed and must be quickly squashed by the person facilitating the brainstorming sessions. Pauses are filled by reading back the ideas already recorded on the flipcharts. The flipcharts should be torn off and displayed around the room. Ideas can be short-listed and evaluated later, using some of the techniques described in Step 8.

3. Forced relationships

This is based on the establishment of new relationships between normally unrelated objects or ideas. In a forced linking process, new applications are sought for existing products or services. One object is fixed; the other is chosen at random.

You then have to find as many ways as possible to relate the fixed object to the one chosen at random. As an example, consider you are a manager of a doctors' surgery with, say, six doctors. The declining number of patients on your surgery list has placed your future as a large practice in jeopardy. Your workforce is highly skilled and flexible. You have been asked to think up new ideas for diversifying your services. First you brainstorm list A – a list of all the things your staff can do, for example:

Possible services

A1. Medical diagnosis

A2. Minor surgery

A3. Health education

A4. Blood tests

A5. Bed baths, etc.

Tear the lists into strips and put them in a hat. Next you brainstorm list B – a list of possible areas in which you could provide services, for example:

Possible areas

B1. Schools

B2. Houses

B3. Insurance companies

B4. Football clubs

B5. Supermarkets

B6. Chemists

B7. Charities.

Again, tear the list into strips and put them in a separate hat. Next you draw one strip from each hat and in five minutes you have to write down as many uses as possible for the service chosen from list A, eg, medical diagnosis, in the area chosen from list B.

Prompt Sheet on Considering Strategic Options

A choice between the options in your table may not be a real choice. A particular strategy is only an option if it could be implemented. A number of factors will need to be considered:

Consider the external appraisal in Step 1 and the opportunities that are present for your organisation. If they fall within the organisation's mission, they will affect your decision. Then consider the internal audit that you did in Step 2 and any opportunities or abilities to obtain resources that it revealed. On the other side of the coin, discovered problems, either internally or externally, may well constrain your choice. Your personal aspirations will also influence your choice. This is demonstrated in the figure below:

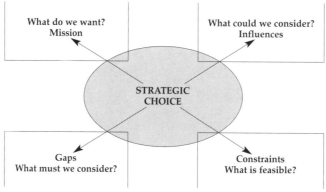

© Simon Wootton and Terry Horne, 2000

13

Planning implementation

INTRODUCTION

A car carrying a company's chief executive, chief engineer, its computer director and a consultant was travelling along a mountain pass. Suddenly the car went out of control and hurtled off the road, down a steep incline, coming to rest balanced on a ledge overlooking a steep ravine. Any movement might topple the car and its occupants into the ravine. The chief engineer was first to speak.

'We need to carefully reposition ourselves in the car, redistribute our weight slowly, see what happens, then go from there. After a few small moves we should be able to get out. Let's try a few small moves to see what will happen.'

'No,' said the computer director. 'Let's roll the car down the hill again to see if the same thing occurs. This might just be a one-off as there is nothing really wrong with either the car or our driving.'

The chief executive then said, 'I think we need to think about our shareholders and the effect this will have on the share price and the dividend. Let me jump out to check the stock market. It won't take more then a few minutes, and then we'll be able to see if it's worth trying to escape or whether the share price would be higher with us gone.'

The consultant looked at them sadly. 'Clearly what we must do is construct a vision and mission statement, and from this our strategy. Discuss this among us to gain a consensus and then decide on how to implement the strategy. Without this we are surely all doomed.'

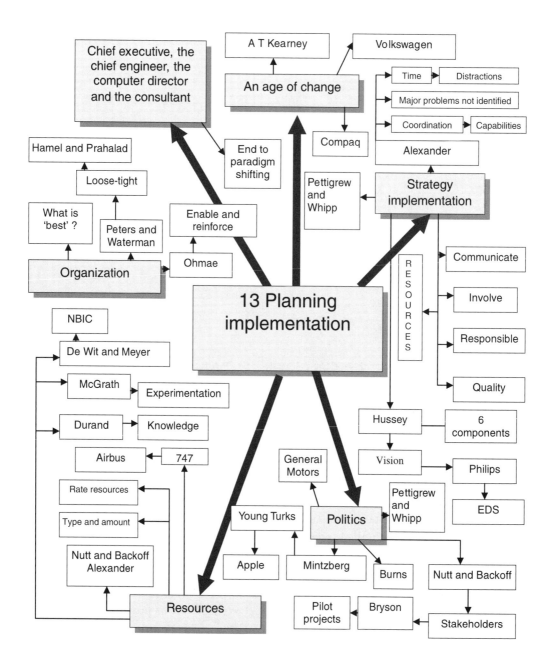

Meanwhile the car continued to balance precariously on the ledge. The engineer in desperation shouts at the consultant. 'Look we are all going to die if we don't do something. The car is balanced on a ledge. It's a drop of over 1000 metres and all you want to do is talk! We need action not words!'

The consultant says, 'Let's look at the situation awry.'

'Oh no,' says the engineer. The car tilts forwards.

'No,' the consultant says, 'we need to change our paradigm, turn the world topsy-turvey and everything will be fine.' The car shifts again.

We cannot think of a suitable punchline for this but instead we will try to expand on what's in it and how it relates to the contents of this chapter.

First, let's look at the chief executive: he is worried about the effect the crash and the car's position will have on shareholders and the stock value. It might well be a 'good' thing for the occupants of the car to perish in the fall as investors would see this as a possibility of a new management team coming in to revitalize the company. Alternatively, they could all escape, and again investors might see this as a good thing leading to higher share evaluation. He sees his job of creating shareholder value.

The computer director is a bit of a distraction in the story, as we just wanted to have a small joke about what happens when computers crash. The computer people typically want to see it happen again before committing themselves.

The engineer wants to do something practicable. He wants to try a few small things to see what happens. The material reality of the situation is obvious. Something has to be done – now.

The consultant, of course, wants to make sure that the vision and mission are in place before doing anything. But he also wants to downplay the material reality of the circumstances and deal more with how those involved perceive their situation. The consultant is more interested in foresight than forecast. Also the consultant wants to change what is being perceived, turn the world upside-down, even though the car is about to fall into the ravine.

In the previous chapter we spent some time in exploring ways in which we can attempt to rethink things to our advantage. This story perhaps redresses this to a small degree. Perhaps there are times when the reality of the situation is such that no amount of paradigm shifting, creative thinking will change the situation. Further, there comes a time when the bullet has to be bitten and whatever strategy has been agreed upon it has to be implemented. You cannot stay on the ledge forever. We are going to look at what has to be done once the strategy has been conceived to make something happen. Also there are material facts that cannot simply be imagined away.

AN AGE OF CHANGE

While it is now a truism in business circles that organizations must be continually changing, adapting, and even transforming themselves, there are few studies showing the success rate of management efforts at strategic change, or the conditions and strategies that favour successful strategic change. The consultancy firm A T Kearney surveyed 294 senior executives in medium and large European companies during 1999. It appears that nearly two-thirds reported a temporary improvement as a result of their change programme but that they had failed in terms of sustained improvement. Only one in five change programmes were considered successful (Source: *The Economist* 15 July 2000: 87).

So, successful change is hard to achieve. We also know this from individual cases. For example, there are criticisms of the quality of Compaq's implementation of its take-over of Digital Equipment Corporation in June 1998, which might be part of the cause for the subsequent fall in its share price, its losses, and the departure of its Chief Executive in 1999.

However, there are also success stories. Although it had been losing money only three years earlier, Volkswagen was very profitable and had captured over 17 per cent of Western Europe's car market by 1996. This result was partly attributed to increased efficiency, cuts in capacity, investment, and attention to image. By 1999 Volkswagen had increased its share of the Western Europe car market to 18.7 per cent and was the third largest car company in the world.

STRATEGY IMPLEMENTATION

Alexander's (1985) study of 93 private sector firms suggests some of the reasons why strategic changes are often not successful and fail to result in sustained improvements. The following strategy implementation problems were all identified by a fifth or more of the firms surveyed as being substantial:

- Implementation took more time than originally allocated.
- Major problems surfaced during implementation that had not been identified beforehand.
- Coordination of implementation activities was not effective enough.
- Competing activities and crises distracted attention from implementing the decision.
- Capabilities of employees involved were not sufficient.

These same problems, albeit of a minor nature, were widespread in the rest of the sample.

What can be done about such problems of implementation? Research findings point to some rather obvious measures to improve strategy implementation (Alexander, 1985; Pettigrew and Whipp, 1993). Drawing on this research we can suggest at least five measures.

First, top managers should communicate clearly with all employees about the strategic decisions and build receptivity to change. This involves describing the implications of strategic decisions and justifying change. Second, top managers should involve managers and employees in strategy formulation or creation and not just in the process of strategy implementation. Third, there is a need for an implementation plan detailing responsibilities and the timing of specific actions. This needs to be supported by systems for communication, targets and rewards. Fourth, the strategy itself needs to be a good quality one, partly so as not to undermine good strategy implementation, and because it is important as an ingredient in ensuring coherence in the management of change. Fifth, resources of money, people and time need to be sufficient and HR management should ensure there is the necessary organizational capacity for a strategy in terms of knowledge, attitudes and skills.

These factors fit reasonably well with the advice Hussey (1999) gives for implementing strategic implementation. He suggests six components for managing strategic implementation:

- Provide a vision statement of what the business will be like after change.
- Involve others to get commitment to the changes; and do this by holding meetings to explain the vision and plan the detail of the change.
- Give support through training and coaching.
- Plan and manage the actions needed to implement the strategy, and align budgets and measure progress.
- Monitor and control and set up special systems to do this.
- Recognize those who make implementation successful by rewarding and thanking them.

Hussey's suggestion that there is a need for a vision statement is particularly worth noting in these days of intense competition for market share and profitability. Boards will sometimes hire a new chief executive when a firm's performance has been stagnating and the board members want someone to come in and shake things up. Consequently, the new chief executive arrives and immediately launches changes to restore profitability. These may include downsizing to cut costs and restructuring and upheaval in the organization generally. This is exactly what happened when Cor

Boonstra took over as the President of Philips, the Dutch electrical and electronics firm, in late 1996. Philips had lost a lot of money in 1990 and bankruptcy had been on the cards. When Boonstra arrived he disposed of many of the firm's businesses and the workforce was reduced by over 25,000. His plan was to restructure so that Philips could concentrate on core businesses. He also moved the headquarters to Amsterdam and away from Philips' main research laboratories – a deeply symbolic act.

The pattern of a new chief executive arriving and shaking things up also occurred at Electronic Data Systems (EDS), a major computer services firm. Dick Brown was appointed Chief Executive after a period in which EDS had failed to match the growth in the market for computer services and its profits' trend had been flat. There were indications that the new Chief Executive was having an impact in his first year. Some 5,000 people left the firm bringing the total number of employees down to about 130,000, reductions in costs were made, and the organization was restructured into four global businesses. New orders for business were expected to increase in 2000 compared to 1999, and EDS's share price improved significantly in 1999. But was the new Chief Executive able to sustain the improvements in the longer term? Despite the successes already achieved, did he have a convincing vision of what the company would look like in the future?

> Yet what may be lacking is a sense of vision emanating from Mr Brown himself... When pressed on how EDS will be seen in five years, he says he would like it to be "the information utility". It is a reasonable answer, but any number of rivals might say the same. To prove he is not just a shaker, but a mover too, Mr Brown will need to channel his huge energy and self-belief into defining what is special about EDS. Mr Brown's appetite for action is not in doubt; less certain is whether he has the imagination and capacity for reflection that marks out the greatest managers.
> (Source: *The Economist* 8 January 2000: 78.)

A number of the factors emerging from research and from advice on change management look designed to help improve coordination and the capacity of employees. But it is by no means clear that the measures answer all the problems of strategy implementation. Perhaps there is also a need to pay attention to political and organizational conditions. Perhaps more attention is needed on planning how to get the necessary resources for change to occur.

POLITICS

Top management has to deal with the politics of change as well as ensure there is a vision and the necessary logistics. Take the case of General Motors. It has had a troubled history since the mid-1980s even though it has the biggest share of the global car market. The firm suffered an attempted reorganization in the 1980s and losses in the early 1990s. More importantly here, however, the top management in the late 1990s had to steer General Motors through a period of adjustment that required considerable political skills. Not only did the managers have to handle a major strike by the United Auto Workers in the summer of 1998 that inflicted heavy losses. They also had to reduce the firm's dependence on Delphi Automotives, which was a subsidiary making car components. Then there were organizational changes, including important alterations to the functioning of the divisional structure. There were also problems of internal politics in the firm's European operations that had to be sorted out. The firm is currently adjusting to the evolving global industry environment and is still perceived as a challenging organization to run. It has a series of strategic alliances and these, plus the difficulties of managing General Motors on a more integrated basis, will continue to require high order political skills from the firm's top managers.

Pettigrew and Whipp (1993) claim at one point that the management of strategic and operational changes involves coping with the 'political dimensions' of the process. The issues of organizational politics are rarely considered in any depth in strategic management theory and research. However, Mintzberg is an exception to this general observation. He argues (1998: 772) that politics 'represents the force for competition in an organization, for conflict and confrontation. People pull apart for their own needs'.

This conflict element in business life has long been recognized. Burns (1969: 232) put it briefly when he wrote, 'Thus, members of a business concern are at one and the same time cooperators in a common enterprise and rivals for the material and intangible rewards of successful competition with each other.' As Burns pointed out though, this is not simply competition between individuals. Groups emerge to which most individuals attach themselves and through which they pursue their individual interests.

Individuals and groups within an organization (and outside it) will take up positions on proposed strategic changes depending on how they expect their interests to be affected by them. Change, consequently, is often about the relationships between coalitions of interests favouring the status quo and coalitions favouring change (Nutt and Backoff, 1992). Similarly, Mintzberg (1998: 768–69) argues that periods of change involve a 'good deal of conflict. Two sides battle, usually an "old guard" committed to the status quo challenged by a group of "Young Turks" in favour of the change. As Apple Computers grew large, for example, John Scully intent on settling it down confronted a Steve Jobs who wished to maintain its freewheeling style of innovation.' In Chapter 9 we considered at length how new business opportunities were identified, but we never really gave much thought to the conflict aspects of innovation. But, as the Mintzberg reference to Apple Computers indicates, there are forces for change and forces for settling things down. Also as Mintzberg indicates, the dialectic between these two forces involves real people, in the Apple Computers' case it involved Scully and Jobs.

The existence of potential conflict during strategy implementation strongly indicates the need for stakeholder management. One approach to this is to assess the feasibility of strategic action in terms of likely stakeholder reactions and then to assess the possibilities to influence the size and nature of opposition to the proposed action.

The assessment of stakeholder reactions is a relatively simple process in principle, although the judgements themselves and their confirmation may be difficult (Nutt and Backoff, 1992). So first it is necessary to identify the stakeholders in relation to the proposed strategic action. It should be borne in mind that the list of stakeholders might well vary substantially from one proposal for strategic action to another. A stakeholder, after all, is any individual or party that will be affected by or can affect the proposed strategic change. It is also important to recognize that the total number of stakeholders identified can vary a great deal according to how far you recognize the need to identify subgroups. For example, it may be adequate to identify middle management as a stakeholder; on the other hand, because of the specific nature of the proposed strategic action, it may be necessary to identify middle managers in different departments as being different stakeholder groups. The rule of thumb is to subdivide stakeholder groups if there are likely to be significantly different reactions to the proposals within them.

Logically the next steps are to estimate the nature of stakeholders' reactions to the proposals. In the first instance it may be a good idea to estimate it as either favourable to the proposal or hostile to the proposal. Then there should be some estimation of the reasons for stakeholders being favourable or hostile. This is useful later when you consider how favourable reactions can be reinforced and hostile reactions can be neutralized or reversed. Finally, it is important to estimate the importance of stakeholders. This, again, might be done on a simple basis, allocating each stakeholder to either an important or not important category. This should be followed up by an estimation of why stakeholders have been assigned to the important or not important categories. Is it because of the power they wield? Is it because the organization feels a duty towards them?

The process so far places you in a good position to decide which stakeholders require attention. Stakeholders who are important because of their power and are likely to be very hostile to proposals for strategic changes obviously merit close attention. One obvious option at this stage is to consider modifying the proposals to see if they can be made more acceptable to powerful but potentially hostile stakeholders. It may even be possible to negotiate with these stakeholders to find a suitable compromise between their interests and what you are trying to achieve through the proposals.

Stakeholders who are powerful or influential and likely to be in favour of the proposals require quite different handling. In their case you might consider how they might be persuaded to use their power or influence to support the changes being proposed.

Stakeholder management may also lead to a consideration of the uses of pilot projects to deal with resistance to proposed changes. Pilot projects can be very useful as demonstrations that proposals are feasible, although if there is widespread and strong resistance to change then a pilot project may backfire as a tactic for stakeholder management (Bryson, 1995).

RESOURCES

The feasibility of proposed strategic changes depends on resources as well as on stakeholder reactions (Nutt and Backoff, 1992). A factor in successful strategy implementation is having sufficient resources such as money, people and time (Alexander, 1985). It has also been noted that HR management can play an important role by ensuring that the skills, attitudes, and knowledge needed by people in the organization to implement a strategy are developed.

The main analytical steps in preparing a plan for acquiring the necessary resources are very straightforward. First, the types and amounts of resources required by a proposed strategic action are estimated. Second, there is a need to establish their importance for the proposed action. Some resources may be indispensable. Others may be desirable rather than essential. The various resources can therefore be rated in terms of their importance for the strategic action. Third, the current availability of the resources and who owns or controls them is determined. Obviously, the plan for acquiring the resources will need to pay attention to resources that are both important and currently unavailable. This represents a problem for the feasibility of the strategic action. Ideas will need to be generated for the solution of the problem. The estimates of resource requirements and the proposals for obtaining important but unavailable resources form the kernel of a resource plan for strategy implementation.

The issues around getting the necessary resources for a strategy are, however, much more challenging than this outline of the planning of resources would suggest.

When Boeing developed its successful 747 jumbo it invested US $2 billion in it. This was more than the value of the firm. Airbus, a European consortium, has plans for a super-jumbo. It is estimated that it will cost US $10 billion. Obtaining the money for this project might involve getting a third in government loans and a third from other companies. Planning the finances for the Airbus project probably has to take account of factors such as international agreements on government subsidy, commercial interest rates and projected income from sales. It should also take account of likely reactions of European governments to providing subsidies, and fluctuating optimism on the part of airlines about levels of demand for, and changing patterns of, air travel which might impact on projected sales revenue.

Of course strategic projects are not all on the scale of the super-jumbo or so complex in their structure. But it is not only obtaining sufficient money for a project that can be challenging. Under a new Chairman Fiat has decided to make servicing an important skill. This raises the whole issue of how an organization acquires new skills and core competencies. Can a management plan for obtaining the necessary resources for strategy implementation build in anything meaningful on the acquisition of skills and core competencies?

Core competencies are partly based on knowledge. Knowledge can be articulated or tacit (Durand, 1998). If knowledge is tacit it may have to be gained experientially, by learning. Perhaps this can be done by means of experimental strategic projects. McGrath (1998) suggests that engaging in discovery-driven experimentation can provide information, experience and resource combinations that are available only to the firm engaged in experimentation because they are experientially acquired.

Does this sound far-fetched? The case of the National Bicycle Industrial Company (NBIC) in Japan may be seen as suggesting the role of strategic projects in developing core competencies (De Wit and Meyer, 1998). While NBIC developed a process for making truly customized bicycles, other companies found it difficult to imitate the company's achievement. It may be significant that NBIC had an implementation strategy with a project team and based on a definite pilot phase.

ORGANIZATION

Organizations by their very nature have to have structure. Choices have to be made about what structure is appropriate. Would a hierarchy be better than a flat structure? Should we go for a matrix structure or not? Should we merge these two divisions or create a new one? Do we need a skunk works to improve non-conventional and out-of-the-box thinking? Should we form an alliance with another company?

Ideas about what structure is 'best' change over time. Fashions in structure come and go. A little while ago decentralization was in. Nowadays chaordic structures are becoming fashionable. A chaordic structure is a mixture of chaos within a well-defined overall framework. It is a bit like an extension of loose–tight thinking (Peters and Waterman, 1982) with some power devolved downwards but in a well-defined manner. Dotcom firms often give the impression of this type of structure with the pace of change in the sector being so fast that more conservative control and command type structures are thought to be inappropriate.

There are different ways you can think of structural design. One way is to see it as being derived from the strategy of the organization. Once the strategy has been decided upon a suitable structure needs to be implemented to support that strategy. However, some people believe that structure does not matter all that much (Peters and Waterman, 1982) or that structure evolves over time fitting the needs of the organization.

Larger companies may want a lot from their organizational structure. They may want one that supports effective competition, sensible business planning, synergy between parts of the company, corporate goal setting, and long-term planning and investment. Some organizations like matrix structures. Ideas about how to find the best structure change over time.

Hamel and Prahalad (1994) perhaps more than anybody else have challenged the polarized positions on corporate structures. They reject both the centralized and decentralized forms of management structures found in large organizations. They place great emphasis on the ability of a company to orchestrate the development and use of core competencies and thus warn against strategic business units operating too autonomously. But while they see the importance of a corporate approach they do not favour heavy-handed corporate processes, arguing that horizontal linkages between line managers across a company are important.

The tide in business throughout the 1980s and 1990s was to make corporate centres leaner. This was the case in a number of countries. There is some evidence that the 21st century is opening with large corporations in the United States reversing this trend (Source: *The Economist* 6 May 2000: 96). There is an expectation in the United States that headquarters staff will increase, whereas expectations in Germany, Britain, France and Japan are that there will be less headquarters staff. Perhaps this reflects a more proactive role for corporate headquarters in the United States. Perhaps they are involved in developing core competencies, forging strategic alliances, as well as in handling information systems and telecommunications. This would be consistent with the sort of corporate model that Hamel and Prahalad advocated and would not necessarily indicate a turn towards very centralized command and control structures.

We are mainly concerned with looking at the matter of designing an organizational structure as an implementation issue. However, while much of the design of organizations might be seen as largely a matter of fashion, it is important to search for the principles by which organizational design can be put on a rational basis in order to make strategy more successful. After many years of strategic management research it is surprising how little has been learnt about the principles of design. We are still largely gripped by fashion. However, we might mention here two key principles when designing an organization structure (Ohmae, 1982). First, design structures that enable management commitment and attention to be given to the right things. Some structures cause muddle and lead to managers losing sight of the activities or units that require their commitment and attention. Second, design structures that reinforce and do not dissipate synergy between parts of a company. Sometimes strategic business units are lumped together when they have no real linkage. This can be highly dysfunctional.

CONCLUSIONS

This chapter has looked at factors in making implementation processes more successful, the political aspect of implementation, the planning of resources, and designing structures to implement strategy.

Factors important for successful implementation include top management communications, involving managers and employees, implementation plans, the quality of the strategy, and proper planning of resources. The political as well as visionary and logistical aspects of change were stressed. The role of stakeholder management and pilot projects in handling resistance to change was highlighted. The assessment of resource requirements and planning their acquisition was outlined fairly schematically. It was also noted that it might be necessary to suggest changes in organizational structure. Deciding an appropriate organizational structure and justifying it is generally harder than might be at first assumed – at least if management is interested in selecting a strategy on the basis of the need to implement strategic action. The trend towards larger corporate headquarters in the United States was noted and a possible link to a more proactive role for central staff was suggested.

As a result of this chapter you should understand simple approaches to planning stakeholder management and resource acquisition to support strategy implementation.

QUESTIONS

1. Why is it so difficult to successfully implement strategic change?
2 . What things can you do to increase the chances of successfully implementing strategic change?
3. How important is it to have an inspiring vision when implementing major strategic change?
4. To be good at strategy you need to be good at politics. What evidence can you provide to justify this statement?

5. In the summer of 2000 ICL finally gave up trying to become a publicly quoted company on the London Stock Exchange. What stakeholders' interest had to be considered in this change of strategy? (Use the case study.)
6. Write a briefing paper to answer the following. What steps need to be taken to acquire the necessary resources for the implementation of a strategic plan?
7. Using the Nissan case study, answer the following question. What problems do you envisage Nissan will have in successfully implementing its alliance with Renault?
8. Why have Hamel and Prahalad challenged the polarized positions on corporate structure?
9. What two key principles does Ohmae suggest when thinking about organizational structure?

EXECUTIVE EXERCISES

In this exercise we would like you to practise drawing up an action plan to implement a strategic action in your own organization. Refer back to a previous executive exercise and select an idea for a strategic action. Draw up a plan using the following questions:

- What is the name of the organizational unit or units involved?
- To whom should reports of progress on implementation be made?
- What is the overall strategy of which this specific action is a part?
- What is the strategic action, its objectives, and the details of how it will be carried out?
- What support or resources are needed?
- Who is responsible for the strategic action and its component parts?
- Who else needs to be involved?
- When does strategic action need to be started and completed?
- What is/are the performance indicator/s?
- Does the data/management information system currently exist to measure performance and identify performance gaps?

When you have completed the preparation of this plan, prepare some ideas for how this would be best presented to top management of your organization for approval.

REFERENCES

Alexander, L D (1985) Successfully implementing strategic decisions, *Long Range Planning*, **18** (3) pp 91–97

Bryson, J (1995) *Strategic Planning for Public and Nonprofit Organizations*, Jossey-Bass, San Francisco

Burns, T (1969) On the plurality of social systems, in *Industrial Man*, ed T Burns, Penguin, Harmondsworth

De Wit, B and Meyer, R (1998) *Strategy: Process, content, context*, Thomson, London

Durand, T (1998) The alchemy of competence, in *Strategic Flexibility*, eds G Hamel, C K Prahalad, H Thomas, and D O'Neal, Wiley, Chichester

Hamel, G and Prahalad, C K (1994) *Competing for the Future*, Harvard Business School Press

Hussey, D (1999) *Strategy and Planning: A manager's guide*, Wiley, Chichester

McGrath, R G (1998) Discovering strategy: competitive advantage from idiosyncratic experimentation, in *Strategic Flexibility*, eds G Hamel *et al*, Wiley, Chichester

Mintzberg, H (1998) Beyond configuration: forces and forms in effective organizations, in *The Strategy Process*, eds H Mintzberg, J B Quinn and S Ghoshal, Prentice Hall, London

Nutt, P C and Backoff, R W (1992) *Strategic Management of Public and Third Sector Organizations*, Jossey-Bass, San Francisco

Ohmae, K (1982) *The Mind of the Strategist*, McGraw-Hill, London

Peters, T and Waterman, R (1982) *In Search of Excellence*, HarperCollins, New York

Pettigrew, A and Whipp, R (1993) *Managing Change for Competitive Success*, Blackwell Publishers, Oxford

Reading 13.1

Taken from Chapter 3 – Plan to implement, in *Successful Strategy Planning* by Stephen G Haines (1998)

Phase D: implementing change successfully

Proper planning prevents poor performance

This phase does not concern strategy planning, but rather the beginning of successful implementation (Goal 2). However, in using the system's thinking model and process, it is clear that there are two goals to accomplish. Now is the time to focus exclusively on the second of these: ensuring successful implementation of your strategy plan. None of the various strategy planning models mentioned earlier have the following step.

Step 8: plan to implement

This step focuses on the process of educating and organizing to manage the implementation of the strategy plan. Thus, it deals with that difficult subject – change.

Educational briefing on change

The first thing to appreciate is how we experience change. The 'roller-coaster of change' diagram as shown in Figure 3.1 simplifies and clarifies the basic psychology of individual and organizational change.

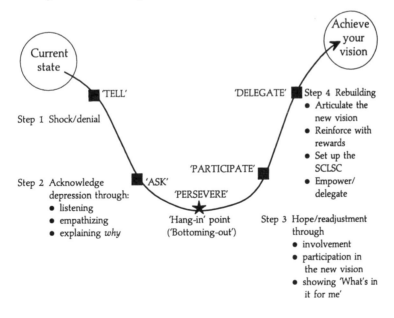

Figure 3.1 *Roller-coaster of change*

Action: Study this model's four basic steps, keeping in mind that the reality of change is much more complex. Each employee goes through this at his or her own pace and depth in a process that must be managed. We often undergo a number of different changes at the same time (personal, professional, social and spiritual). Focus on the bottoming-out point, where success or failure is often decided. When times get tough, perseverance and discipline in your thinking and acting are needed.

Questions to address

There are major questions that you should keep in mind when implementing your changes in the core strategies.

1. Not 'if' but 'when' will we start to go through shock/depression?
2. How deep is the trough? Is it different for each person? What are the implications?
3. How long does the trough take? Are employees and management at the same stage of change at the same time?
4. How do we manage change proactively?
5. Will we rebuild and fully achieve our vision?
6. At what level will we rebuild?
7. What new skills do we need to accomplish this?
8. How many different roller-coasters will we experience in this change?
9. Are there other changes occurring at the same time for people?
10. Will we hang in and persevere at the bottom? How?
11. How will we deal with normal resistance?
12. How will we create a critical mass to support and achieve the desired changes?

Action: Discuss these questions of change fully among a subgroup, the full planning team, and your other key stakeholders.

Action: Make a list of the agreed-upon key points on change that will guide your implementation.

Key points on change

1. _____
2. _____
3. _____
4. _____
5. _____

Organizing for implementation

> *What we think, know or believe is, in the end, of little*
> *consequence. The only consequence ... is what we do*

Action: Use the prototype below to review and finalize your strategy planning document for use in a practical day-to-day fashion.

Strategy planning document

<table>
<tr><td colspan="3" align="center">Sections/documents</td></tr>
<tr><td>I.</td><td>Introduction</td><td>3–6 pages</td></tr>
<tr><td>1.</td><td>Cover sheet</td><td></td></tr>
<tr><td>2.</td><td>Executive summary history</td><td></td></tr>
<tr><td>3.</td><td>Strategy planning model</td><td></td></tr>
<tr><td>4.</td><td>Acknowledgements</td><td></td></tr>
<tr><td>5.</td><td>Table of contents</td><td></td></tr>
<tr><td>6.</td><td>Environmental scanning and strategy issues</td><td></td></tr>
<tr><td>II.</td><td>Ideal future vision and strategies</td><td>12–15 pages</td></tr>
<tr><td>1.</td><td>Vision/back-up elements</td><td></td></tr>
<tr><td>2.</td><td>Mission</td><td></td></tr>
<tr><td>3.</td><td>Core values/back-up elements</td><td></td></tr>
<tr><td>4.</td><td>Key success factors/first year action plan</td><td></td></tr>
<tr><td>5.</td><td>Current-state assessment</td><td></td></tr>
<tr><td>6.</td><td>Three-year business plan (if applicable)</td><td></td></tr>
<tr><td>7.</td><td>Core strategies and top priority actions</td><td></td></tr>
<tr><td>8.</td><td>Annual plans and strategy budgeting</td><td></td></tr>
<tr><td>III.</td><td>Implementation</td><td>2–4 pages</td></tr>
<tr><td>1.</td><td>Summary of the leadership steering committee</td><td></td></tr>
<tr><td>2.</td><td>Year 1 task checklist and schedule of implementation</td><td></td></tr>
<tr><td>Total</td><td></td><td>17–25 pages</td></tr>
</table>

Now decide how you will communicate your plan to all your key stakeholders.

Ideas for initially communicating the strategy plan
- Print the plan and distribute it with a simple cover letter.
- Develop hand-outs/overhead slides for standardized use by all executives.
- Hold an organization-wide managers' meeting to hear directly from the managing director and other members of the planning team (thank them for their help).
- Organize divisional/departmental all-employee meetings to ask questions about the plan and to pose concerns.
- Set up stakeholder meetings to review results and thank them for their help.
- Hold two-day workshops to learn about strategy planning, to discuss the plan and to build supporting plans at a unit/site or individual level.
- Implement a mini strategy planning process for units.

- Display posters with planning themes.
- Hand out individual (plastic) cards with values, mission and key success factors.
- Produce videotapes of the managing director (or others) explaining the organization's vision strategies to achieve that vision.
- Publish an internal newsletter, memo or letter to introduce the plan (overall and in detail).
- Publish external news releases and special public feature stories.
- Give out report cards each quarter – shared with all stakeholders.

Now, how do we keep the plan alive over the next 3–5 years?

Action: Use this set of ideas as a guide to develop your communications game plan:

Communications to do	By whom?	By when?

To achieve your desired changes, each leader must also manage two common problems. First, changes must be nurtured, protected, encouraged and rewarded in order to be achieved. Second, despite good intentions, the crises of day-to-day living and working drive out the focus on change, so that it is often never fully implemented.

Action: Set up a strategy change leadership steering committee to combat these problems by guiding the changes dictated by the plan and establishing a yearly map to manage the change and implementation processes over the life of the planning horizon.

The leadership steering committee: the key to success
Changing behaviour always requires deep feelings
The strategy change leadership steering committee is essential in successfully and profitably implementing your strategy plan. Implementation will fail without it. We have to manage change before it manages us.

Steering committee guidelines
A *new way to run your business*, giving equal weight to changes and to the ongoing daily management of the organization.

Purposes
1. To guide and control the implementation of any large-scale organization-wide strategy planning/change undertaken.
2. To coordinate any other major performance improvement projects going on at the same time; to ensure fit with the time and energy demands of ongoing daily business activities.

Committee meeting frequency
1. Monthly or bimonthly as the process begins.
2. Quarterly once the process is functioning smoothly (but more frequently the faster you want to implement).

Criteria for membership
1. Senior management leadership teams for today and the future.
2. Informal or formal leaders from parts of the organization that are essential to implementation.
3. Core steering group members including the coordinator managing change, the key success factor coordinator and internal facilitators.
4. Credible staff who understand the strategy plan developed.
5. Key stakeholders who share your vision and are willing to actively support it.

In addition to the committee, itself, you also need to define a core steering group to manage the implementation process on a weekly and day-to-day level. One of the things the group can do is compile a list of the top priority actions under each strategy for this current year and manage them closely.

In other words, it should become 'the new way to run your business and life day to day'.

Action: Define your strategy change leadership steering committee parameters below.

1. Committee purpose: _____

2. Committee membership:

    _____   _____
    _____   _____
    _____   _____
    _____   _____
    _____   _____

3. Steering group core members: _____

    _____
    _____

4. Specific involvement of your middle- and first-line supervisors (and other key players):

_____

_____

_____

_____

_____

_____

5. Meeting frequency/length: _____

6. Meeting location off site: _____

7. Communications to and involvement of other stakeholders:

_____

_____

_____

_____

The leadership steering committee and the planning team are very similar, their guidelines being almost alike:

- led by top management
- about 80–90 per cent same membership
- size normally 15 or fewer members
- use of the consensus process and written communications after every meeting.

The frequency and intensity of the steering committee meetings are less than those of the planning team. You should be putting all your energies into implementation tasks rather than meetings.

Steering committees typically hold one-day meetings in medium- to large-size departments, business units and organizations. Such meetings must be held regularly in order to pull back from the day-to-day activities, scan the landscape and status of the strategy plan and replan its implementation as necessary.

You should institute a steering group to manage the implementation process on a weekly and day-to-day level. The group can compile a list of the top-priority actions under each strategy for the current year and manage them closely.

Summarize the parameters of the steering committee and insert it at the back of your formal strategy planning document. Use the following minimum agenda of mandatory items as a template for your meetings:

- continually scan the changing environment for plan implications
- track, report and problem-solve key issues concerning key success factors
- report and problem-solve any issues concerning the core strategies and their top-priority actions.

Finally, the steering committee should establish a task checklist to ensure implementation of the plan, particularly until the first year's new changes are completed.

Action: As a group, complete the first year's task checklist and add to it a month-by-month schedule of implementation meetings and activities to occur during the first year.

Year 1: task checklist
- Finalize the strategy plan and develop an initial communications plan. ☐
- Establish an organization-wide annual plan reflecting the action priorities for each core strategy. ☐
- Align the budget to reflect the annual priorities (to be at least 33 per cent effective in the first year – ie, strategy budgeting). ☐
- Build all department/division/unit annual plans around the organization-wide annual priorities/goals. Hold a peer review of them. ☐
- (Optional) Implement three-year business plans for each strategy business unit/ master support division/executive via mini strategy plans (over the next 12 months?) to verify, extend and integrate the organization-wide plan. ☐
- Set up an ongoing leadership steering committee to manage the change process (meet bimonthly at first, then quarterly). ☐
- Establish a task checklist for implementation and follow-up (month-by-month schedule). ☐
- Establish a system/coordinator to monitor, track and report key success factors. ☐
- Revise the performance management/appraisal and reward systems to support the desired vision. ☐
- Examine your organizational structure as well as staff/succession planning to support the desired vision. ☐
- Implement the desired change(s) in both the headquarters' departments and in units/sites/field locations. ☐
- Put in place an environmental scanning system. ☐
- Establish senior management's personal commitment to a set of tasks to lead to implementation of the strategy plan. ☐
- Set up internal staff to build your internal expert group with the skills (not just knowledge) to carry out your vision and core values. ☐
- Ensure that key cross-departmental 'strategy change projects' are set up with clear accountability. ☐
- Establish a critical mass for change (rational, political, cultural). ☐
- Put teams in place to sponsor each core strategy. ☐

- Direct resource allocation to fund the change process.   ☐
- Have two absolutely key training and development programmes in place with a top-down fashion (a) mastering strategy change and (b) visionary leadership practices and skills.   ☐
- Set up the dates for the annual strategy review (and update).   ☐
  Add this schedule to your strategy planning document.

Obviously, not all of these steps must be included in everyone's game plan. However, everyone should have a game plan to combat the failure to live up to their good intentions.

Teams, departments, business units and organizations should be careful not to be 'penny wise and pound foolish'. Don't fall prey to the tendency to put all your time, energies and resources into planning and assume that the implementation will naturally follow. The failure to bridge the gap between planning and implementation can be a major problem. If your plan truly represents your top priorities, then use it, don't abandon it.

Step 9: strategy implementation and change

People do what we inspect ... not what we expect
(Stephen Haines)

To be successful, a strategy plan must be transformed into hundreds of positive individual plans and efforts, with rewards and recognition system. This level of team, department and organization integrity in support of your vision is difficult to achieve. It takes leadership and focus. Your belief that you can do it will lead to actions, which is the bottom line of strategy planning.

The leadership steering committee must lead the implementation by following up and correcting mistakes, and by bringing disciplined persistence and integrity to the plan.

Some people may not like the preceding quote on inspect versus expect. It *is* quite harsh, but the failure to understand this is a sickness of management today, in all types of organizations. While high expectations are nice, many managers are afraid to inspect and hold people accountable for performance.

Note: When companies choose not to establish a steering committee to ensure follow-up and inspection, they usually later need assistance conducting the last step in planning – an annual strategy review. They find that they need to install a steering committee and restart their stalled implementation after all. Once these meetings are organized and held, implementation, follow-up, inspection and results pick up speed.

Step 10: annual strategy review (and update)
This is similar to a yearly independent financial audit. It has two goals:

- assess the status of how well your strategy plan has been achieved
- assess the implementation of your system of managing change.

This review has three main tasks:

- reacting to changes in the environment and their implications for updating your core strategies
- update annual action priorities for the next 12 months for each core strategy and hold the annual large-group review meeting
- update your leadership steering committee's plan for success and its system for managing change.

At this point you should have developed an excellent strategy plan for your entity. Now, your main 'planning task' is to review and update it annually only as necessary, not redo it.

The annual task is now one of verifying your vision, mission and core values, as well as checking your key success factors and core strategies, while completely redoing your current state assessment yearly plans, priorities and budgets. It is crucial to strategically manage the plan you have created.

Annual review and update

Instructions: Based on the framework (1 and 2 in Figure 3.2), each organization needs to conduct a yearly follow-up and diagnosis on how they are performing. This is key to 'learning to be a high-performance organization'.

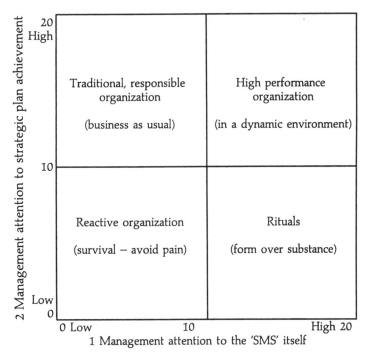

Figure 3.2 *Strategy management system (SMS)*

Summary

It is important for people to develop strategy plans for their teams, departments and businesses. However, once these plans are developed, it is crucial to have a system of managing strategically from these plans. Hence, the last piece of successful strategy planning goes by the same name: strategy management system (SMS). All your prework, planning, implementing and updating steps are what we mean by the two-part strategy management system as the new way to run your business.

For a visual representation of this strategy management system and its annual strategy review (and update), see the diagram below.

Two-part strategic management systems solution

Part I: Goal

Phases A, B, C: Develop a strategic plan/document

STEP 1: Plan to plan (educate and organize for planning)
- organizational diagnosis
- executive briefing
- plan-to-plan tasks
- visionary leadership
- team building

STEPS 2–7: Strategy design
- conduct strategic planning
- competitive strategies
- customer-focused
- annual plans/strategic budgets

STEP 8: Plan to implement (educate and organize for change)
- bridging the gap

Part II: Goal 2

Phase D: Ensure successful implementation

STEP 9: Build changes
- implementing strategic change
- leadership steering committee

STEP 10: Sustain performance
- annual strategic review (and update): independent evaluation
- increased team building
- increased leadership development

Bottom line: create and sustain a customer-focused high-performance organization

© Crisp Publications Inc, 1998

Reading 13.2

Taken from Chapter 5 – Working through the change process,
in *How To Be Better at Managing Change* by David Hussey
(1998)

In the previous chapter we looked at Kevin's situation and the meeting at which the manager of his department announced a number of changes. Regardless of whether or not the
appropriate style was chosen by the manager to announce this change, it is possible to see
how the conduct of this meeting contributed to Kevin's feelings of resistance. No good reason was given to explain the need for change, and this would only be excusable if previous briefings and communications had ensured that everyone already knew that a cost
reduction was imperative and why. No vision of what the department would achieve or be
like after the change was provided, and the mention of additional computers seemed to
be more of a random event than part of a thought out manifestation of how the department would be different. At the stage the manager seemed to have reached, the new structure should have been known and many concerns could have been removed by either
giving the details at the meeting or having smaller meetings with those concerned immediately afterwards, so that the details could be explained. Kevin might have found that he
was still in the same work group, for example. The way the meeting was conducted gave
no opportunity for two-way communication, and even a directive approach should have
allowed people to seek clarification by asking questions. There is much more about the
meeting that could be criticized, but we will have to leave Kevin to his problems.

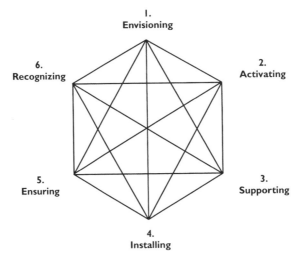

Figure 5.1 The easier approach to managing change

The EASIER approach offers a six-step change management process that, if followed, will help the change to be managed more effectively. After the approach has been described, we will test it in the next chapter by applying it to the new manager situation mentioned in Chapter 1. This situation has been chosen because it is typical of many changes that a manager will handle during a normal career. If you want to work through a complicated fundamental change situation, you might like to spend a few minutes thinking how you would apply the model if you were managing the change in the lift company. Some clues have been provided in previous chapters, and occasional mention will be made of the lift company as the model is described.

Figure 5.1 shows the six steps of the model, called EASIER after the initial letters of each label on the figure. The mnemonic aids the memory, but the connecting lines in the diagram are important because none of the steps can be said to be complete until the whole change is implemented. This is partly because with a complicated change there may be some elements of phasing. We saw, for example, how Bill in the lift company wanted to ensure that his management team was committed to his vision before trying to share it with the rest of the organization. It is also because a successful change manager has to eat, sleep and breathe the change. Building commitment to the vision, for example, is an ongoing process that does not stop because the first elements of the change have reached a point when they can be monitored. Almost every action of the manager throughout the whole process should communicate the importance of the change.

The EASIER model contains two types of actions. The first three steps are the motivational and leadership elements of the process, which aim to inspire people, reduce resistance and ensure everyone is working to make the change a success. We could call these the leadership elements of the task. However, they will rarely succeed unless attention is also given to the second half of the model, which might be termed the administration of the change – the system and analytical tasks that clarify what has to be done and measure whether or not it has been achieved. Similarly, the administrative elements will usually fail to achieve change unless they are accompanied by the leadership elements. Even when the style is coercive – as in the newspaper company situation – some element of visionary leadership is required to inspire those who are not resistant to the change.

Let us now look at each of the steps in the EASIER model in turn.

1 Envisioning

There is widespread agreement that change management is more effective when the leader demonstrates a clear vision of the desired future. This need for a vision is not restricted to organizations. Many will remember Tony Blair in the run up to the 1997 general election talking frequently about his vision for the UK, as well as his vision for New Labour. A vision is much more than a statement of the change. 'We are going to downsize by 20 per cent' may be an accurate description of the change, but it is not a vision. What is needed is a view of what the organization will be as a result of the action and clarity about why the change is necessary to take the organization towards achieving that vision.

A vision is important for a number of reasons:

- it forces the change manager to think carefully not only about the course that is being set, but also about the destination and the time it will take to reach it;
- by defining the vision, further actions may be revealed that support the change, but might otherwise have been overlooked;
- the vision becomes a beacon that can be followed even though crises and other events requiring decisions occur on the way;
- it can help shape the expectations of the people affected by the change;
- it explains why the change is important;
- a sound and clear vision has the power to motivate others.

It is easy to see why vision is important for the large, complicated changes that affect the whole organization. However, it is just as important for the smaller changes, and both the toiletries company and the innovation situations described in Chapter 1 depend heavily on a clear vision if they are to succeed. Even for changes that affect only a unit of an organization, the change is likely to be more effective if the leader is clear about the desired destination.

A vision must be:
- *credible* – it must relate to the situation the organization is in and the resources it can command;
- *challenging* – it must paint a picture that people will want to strive to achieve;
- *clear* – if it cannot be plainly set out, it is unlikely to be understood;
- *logical* – all the elements of the vision must fit together;
- have the *total commitment* of the manager leading the change – if this appears to be absent, there is no reason for anyone else to believe in it;
- *robust* – it has to be able to withstand challenges from within and without the organization.

2. Activating

The next step shown in Figure 5.1 is the process of making sure that those affected by the change are aware of the vision, understand it and, ideally, share the vision and are committed to its fulfilment. As we have seen, there may be circumstances when we have to settle for knowledge and understanding as urgency or the strength of resistance make it almost impossible to proceed with anything other than a directive or coercive style. It is true that in a crisis everyone recognizes as being urgent, it may be possible to reach a shared vision by directive means. Normally, a shared vision will only be achieved in the short term by means of a more participative style, although it is sometimes sensible to vary the style to meet the situations of different groups or levels of those affected by the change.

If it is hard to define a vision, it is even harder to activate others so that they share the commitment to it. When the situation allows, a shared vision can be very powerful in making the change more effective:

- it provides a focus so that everyone pulls in the same direction, which makes it easier to empower people in a way that aids the change process;
- resistance is minimized by means of the process of involvement;
- the adverse consequences of change may be more readily accepted because the expectations of people are shaped by the acceptance of the common cause;
- after the change, people are more likely to integrate the vision into their day-to-day work and, therefore, continue acting in a way that supports the vision;
- a well-accepted vision can become a powerful motivational force in the organization.

One of the tasks of the change leader is thus to build a bridge from the vision that they have defined to others affected by the change. Obviously the task is simpler when the change occurs in a small unit of four or five people than when it applies to the whole of a major multinational organization, but the principles by which it may be achieved are the same:

- The change manager must live the vision and be seen to be a perpetual demonstration of what it is and what it means. Actions – the music – speak louder than words – the song – and it becomes clear very quickly when the lyrics have little to do with the tune.
- Words are important and one-to-one, often informal, ways should be found of repeating the message, checking how people are responding and demonstrating its importance.
- There is a place for the explanatory meetings that describe the vision and all the supporting documentation, but these should be seen as only a small element of the process.
- Ensure that those who report to you are charged with the duty of building commitment to the vision among those who report to them.
- Continuously seek out and disseminate evidence of success. Most changes are achieved by means of numerous small actions as well as a few large ones. Evidence of the results of the sort of behaviour and actions that you want to see should be occurring all the time, and can be used to show what the vision means.
- Make sure that the vision is made relevant at the level of each job. In a large organization, this is too large a task to do single-handed and is another reason for getting some key people involved in the process very early on. However, this should not stop the change manager from continuing to talk to people about the vision at all levels of the organization.
- Learn from the things that do not appear to be going as well as expected. If the problem is caused by pockets of resistance, take special steps to try to reduce them. In extreme situations this may mean sidelining or even dismissing someone who is using guerilla warfare tactics to frustrate the change.
- Use routine management meetings to emphasize the message.
- Where it is possible, set up a series of workshops to enable a wide range of people to help determine how the vision will affect their departments and jobs.

- Ensure that there is a communications strategy (see Chapter 4).
- Exude absolute confidence about the change and the future that it will lead to.
- Be sure that the vision is reinforced by the systems and procedures of the organization (see Chapter 3).

3. Supporting

Change may put great pressures on people. One of the change manager's key tasks is to help subordinates to cope. Much of the support may be psychological, giving encouragement and empathizing, but sometimes it is necessary to give more practical help, by rearranging responsibilities or adding new resources, for example. The change manager has to ensure that the people have the necessary skills and competencies to undertake the new roles and activities that are required by the change.

As we have seen, people may resist change because they fear that they lack the abilities to take on the different challenge. Even supportive people may find that the change is making them less effective if it is causing them to neglect other aspects of their work that have not changed, say, or increases stress to danger levels or because they simply lack the knowledge and experience to do what is expected of them. The support step in the EASIER model is thus critical for success and, because it is bound up with the activating step, may also aid the process of building commitment to the vision.

Actions that should be taken by the change manager include:

- Making sure that the way you have allocated tasks is with an awareness of the individual strengths and weaknesses of your subordinates, and that thereafter you regularly demonstrate your confidence in them to deliver what is expected.
- Where it is needed, providing training at an early stage to provide missing skills and build confidence.
- Making coaching a regular part of your activity, so that you are not only listening to what you are being told, but are actively helping people by giving them suggestions, advice and encouragement. Make coaching a positive experience.
- Never treating their concerns as trivial, but always empathizing with their problems and trying to help them find ways of overcoming them.
- Empowering people to fulfil the tasks you have asked them to do. Part of the challenge the change manager faces is that of leaving a feeling of total confidence in the person, while at the same time having regular contact to give the necessary support. This tightrope is not easy to walk as badly handled discussions can be construed as an attempt to control, and inept coaching may be seen as preventing the person from being empowered.
- When there are real problems, such as inadequate resources to implement the change, offering real solutions. The skill here is to separate the roadblocks erected by those resisting change from the genuine issues of those who are trying to do the right things.
- Praising people when it is justified. If someone has done something that should be shared among others working on the change, either get that person to pass on details of it to the others or ask if you may do so.

4. Installing

Installing is perhaps not the best description of the next step in the model, but none of the better words begin with an 'I'! It is the first element of the system and analysis part of the EASIER model, and is critical to success. In essence, it is the development of a thoughtful plan for the change. A broad vision of the change is important for all the reasons discussed so far and provides a context for the change, but little will happen unless the vision is converted into strategies, and the strategies into actions. In this context, the term 'strategies' is used very broadly to cover the means by which the vision is attained. It may have its normal meaning when the change is complicated and corporate-wide, and the change is about reshaping the whole organization to meet the challenge of the future. However, it is also an appropriate word to use to describe the means by which even the simplest of changes is converted from an idea into action. It covers questions such as what are the main strands that have to be followed and, under each of these, what are the actions that have to be undertaken? This is a way of thinking that is appropriate in every change situation and, of course, would include not only the many physical things, such as the new layout of the factory in the lift company situation, but also the many things we have already discussed that facilitate the change process, such as the communications strategy.

The process that has been followed so far will have provided you with many of the building blocks you need to make a detailed plan – from an assessment of the implications of the change, which was described in Chapter 2, to defining the vision and describing the change and the reasons for it, which were discussed under the heading of envisioning earlier in this chapter.

The installation step can be undertaken by the change manager alone, with the support of one or two specialists, or as part of a more participative process. If you have adopted a directive style, the choice is almost certain to be restricted to the first two. For a more participative style, it is often desirable to involve more people in the planning process, although the nature of the involvement may vary with different groups or at different levels of the organization. For example, in the lift company situation, we saw that Bill was involving his senior managers in thinking through everything that needed to be done to implement the change, and was doing this initially in a workshop-style meeting. In another situation, or possibly even at a later stage in the lift company's change process, it might be desirable to have someone visit all those people at any level who can contribute insights into what the change would mean, to identify all the steps in much greater detail. Where the change involves only a few people and is contained within the responsibility of a unit or department, it may be that the manager already possesses all the knowledge needed to prepare a detailed plan without involving anyone. Whether the plan is put together in this way or by means of a process that involves more people depends on the style chosen for the change management, and if the plan offers an opportunity to involve others if it is sensible in the circumstances.

There is a caution that we need to make known here about who to involve in preparing a detailed plan. If the unit is very small, it is possible to include everyone, if this is appropriate. In most change situations, however, it is not desirable to involve everyone in the same way. For example, in the lift company situation, it would frustrate the change if, immediately after the management meeting that examined the implications of the change, the whole factory was called together and everyone asked to work on the detail before the changes had been agreed with the worker's representatives: it is simply an inappropriate type of change to throw out to the shop floor like this. However, a more local change could well involve people in this way. For example, a problem of high material wastage might be discussed with the people who use the material and, ultimately, a plan to correct it worked out with their participation.

Whatever the choice of process, the aims of this step in the change model are the same:

- as far as is humanly possible, to think through everything that has to be done to implement the change;
- to assign responsibilities so that those who have to take actions know what is expected;
- clarify all the detailed goals of the plan so they can be communicated to all concerned;
- provide a basis for monitoring progress;
- ensure that the necessary resources of people, facilities and money are determined and made available so that the plan can be implemented.

This last point deserves further comment. A change can be frustrated if resources are neglected, and the time to provide for those resources is *before* the organization commits itself to the change. An example is offered by the lift company case, where there is a need for some building work and costs will be incurred in changing the layout of the shop floor. The resources for this have to be agreed up front for without them it will not be possible to make the change. A more subtle example is the need to train managers and those they manage in the new methods of working that need to be adopted after a downsizing operation.

Part of the change management task is to see that the right training is provided, and quickly, and this will not happen unless the right provisions are made. Downsizing may prove to be futile without the training, so it is essential that it happens. To be told by the human resources department that the budget for the year is already committed or that this is not a priority or that training can only be given over a two-year period is to set the change on the path to failure.

Not all changes require the same planning tools and some thought should be given to selecting what is appropriate to a particular situation:

- *Simple actions plans*
  Where the situation is straightforward, involves only a few people and requires no additional resources, it may be enough for a plan to take the form of a simple listing of the actions that have to be undertaken, dates for start and completion and the name of the person responsible. This should be written down, but is not difficult.
- *Short-term plan and project budget*
  This is a combined action plan and worked budget. This should list all the actions to be taken (in much the same way as the simple plan), provide time commitments and short-term goals so that progress can be monitored and provide a budget that shows

both the expenses and the financial consequences of the change. The project budget may well cut across the normal responsibility centres, so it is advisable to ensure that the accounting system can report against this budget, which is likely to fall outside the normal budgetary process. Some special provision may need to be made so that regular reporting is possible. The timespan of the budget has to be capable of being divided into normal accounting periods, but should encompass the whole of the change project. It may span more than one accounting year, and may be for longer than the 12-month period of the normal budget.

A refinement of the short-term plan would be to also show the actions and responsibilities on a Gantt chart, which lists all the actions against a calendar and shows by means of lines when each will start and finish. This is helpful in that it is easier to discuss with others than a long action list, and it does begin to indicate where a delay in one action may cause delays in others.

- *Network analysis*
  Some change projects may involve thousands of actions and change may be frustrated if critical tasks are delayed, while others can be allowed to drift within a wider tolerance as this will not delay the whole project. In a change such as that in the lift company, it would be difficult to estimate how long the whole change would take just by listing the actions, as some can be tackled simultaneously while others have to be done in strict sequence. What is needed is a tool that not only pulls all this information together in a way that can easily be communicated, but also enables those planning the change to see where things might be done quicker if more or different resources were used. Carrying out one of the simultaneous actions earlier than planned would probably have no impact on the overall length of time it would take to complete the change project. However, allocating extra resources to one of the critical actions could reduce the overall time period for the whole project. Network analysis tools, such as critical path analysis, can be used in simple situations, although this may be taking a sledgehammer to crack a nut. They become essential, however, for the complicated projects, where actions can otherwise be easily overlooked or critical actions allowed to run late simply because there are so many things to do. Used in conjunction with a project budget, they enable every action to be closely monitored.
- *Scenario planning, sensitivity analysis and contingency planning*
  The really large projects can benefit from an analysis that helps the manager to react more flexibly in the event of unexpected obstacles. They are of limited value in all but the largest of change projects.

  Scenario planning is the development of alternative project plans based on different scenarios of the future. It is especially helpful when there are serious uncertainties about the likely outcomes of the change. It enables the organization to take action more quickly when events are not working out exactly as intended.

  Sensitivity analysis is a means of looking at what issues could cause the project to go wrong, and what the impact might be. Whereas scenario plans, in effect, look at whole different futures that could occur, sensitivity analysis examines only the impact of particular issues.

Contingency plans are fully worked out alternative plans to be put into effect if something goes wrong. In the lift company situation, there might be a contingency plan for how to proceed with the change if the shop stewards recommend rejection to their members.

5. Ensuring

If a change takes only days to fully implement, and it can be seen very easily that it has worked, the 'ensuring' step is not needed. There are changes like that, but they are probably not the sorts of changes that will tax management skills. Most changes, however, take some time to be implemented, require constant coordination and depend on things being done at the appropriate time. There may also be expenditures of either a capital or revenue nature that have to be managed.

The ensuring step in the EASIER model is about monitoring and controlling progress. There really is little point in making a detailed plan unless there is also a mechanism to measure its progress. Monitoring is the process of collecting information that shows what progress has been made, while controlling is the management task of taking whatever actions are needed when the results deviate from the plan, and congratulating people when a difficult stage has been successfully completed. The following points should be borne in mind regarding these means of measuring progress:

- Monitoring requires a system for the collection and feedback of information on actual results compared to those planned. It may be necessary to make special arrangements to obtain this information where it does not emerge as part of normal accounting system reporting.

- In any case, some data will be required that does not come out of normal systems, such as the actual progress of actions against what was planned, information from special surveys or customer reactions to a new approach. Some means have to be devised to capture such information on a regular and formal basis.

- There should be regular feedback reports, some of which, such as those for time-critical things, may be more frequent than others. Thus, it may be appropriate to have a report of expenditure against budget at monthly intervals, but critical to know immediately whether or not a key action has been started or completed on the dates set.

- Modern communication methods, such as e-mail and voice mail, should be considered as a means of collecting information.

- Regular performance meetings should be held so that key members of the management team can assess progress, and take such actions as are necessary. These meetings should also be used to collect 'soft' information that does not fit easily into more formal reports and reinforce the vision and the importance of the change.

- The style of the control meetings should fit with the style for the whole change project. It would be wrong to have a collaborative style up to and including the installation step, for example, only to switch to a coercive style in the control meetings.

- The best control is self-control, which is when you have reached a stage when every manager knows their role is critical and is always self-monitoring against the appropriate part of the plan.

6. Recognizing

The final step in the model is recognizing the parts played by others in the change process. It is very rare that a complicated change is accomplished without others besides the change manager playing an important part.

Recognition may be connected with career development and monetary incentives, but this is only one aspect. It may, in fact, be more productive to use recognition as a way of acknowledging what others have done and expressing thanks for this. The simple process of demonstrating that their role has been valued can mean a great deal, when the recipients see it as a sincere gesture.

There may be a place for team recognition. One multinational food group, for example, has an annual chairman's award for the initiative that has had most impact on the company. One year this was given to the team that had initiated and introduced across the whole organization an approach that enabled management development to be a weapon of competitive advantage. The effect on the team was to increase its already high level of motivation because its efforts had been acknowledged to the whole organization. Obviously if the annual award had been seen as a joke, the impact would have been negative. In this case, however, it was highly prized.

Although it is the last step in the EASIER model, recognizing people's contributions does not have to wait until the change has been completed. It may, in fact, be part of the ongoing process. There are several things to consider:

- Make the change part of the performance management process. Also, where the change extends over a long period, ensure that you have several review meetings with your subordinates and that they repeat this process for key people who report to them. This not only helps to reinforce the vision and the importance of the change, but gives the manager a chance to recognize what the others have contributed or take action when performance in relation to implementing the change has been less than satisfactory.
- Recognition has to be genuine, which means that praise should only be given when it is due and should be sincerely expressed. Thanking someone for their help when both parties know that more effort has gone into frustrating the change than to making it effective, would turn the process into a travesty. Equally unproductive is a murmur of thanks that is no more than a social pleasantry as this will be taken to have little meaning and may leave the person concerned feeling that the change manager is ignorant of the important role they have really fulfilled.
- It is usually better to be very specific in one-to-one meetings. 'Thank you for your support' is a bland statement that has much less meaning to the receiver than 'It was the way you got down to it and came back quickly with those stories of how positive the customers were that got all the doubters on board. We never looked back from that

moment'. The latter does not have the word 'thanks' in it, but shows that the change manager knows what the contribution was and is making a sincere acknowledgement of it.

- Public acknowledgement may sometimes be a powerful tool, but can cause embarrassment if it is not handled carefully, and it can come across as insincere (even when it is sincere). Think for a moment of some of those acceptance speeches made by film stars when they have been given an Oscar. So many seem to rattle off acknowledgements to every other person concerned in the film – 'I could not have done it without …' – when everyone listening knows that what they really mean is 'I've got to say all this, but really it was all down to me and at least I have the award that I have long deserved'.

- Often more important than public recognition is making the part played by someone who has been important in making the change work known to the change manager's boss. It is probably best to say this to the boss in the presence of the person acknowledged. If the acknowledgement is of a team, then it may be better to ask the boss to come to meet them, and make the comments there. In both cases, giving specific examples of what others have done may be more meaningful than making a generalized statement. There is real value in the change manager making it clear to the team that credit for the change is being shared. Unfortunately, the change manager can rarely spread responsibility for a failure in the same way, which is another very good reason for making every effort to ensure that the change is effective.

Knowing when to call a halt to the change process

All things come to an end and there will come a time when the change can be safely declared to have been implemented. With some change projects this point is not difficult to identify. For others, however, it may be very difficult to decide where the halting place should be. In the lift company example, is the change completed when people have agreed to it, the factory has been laid out according to the new requirements, all the capital needed for the change has been spent and any initial training has been completed? This would be the stopping place for many change managers, but it is too early. The change can only be declared to have been effective when the new ways of managing have bedded down, employees have developed a strong affinity with their focused groups and the product quality, cost and delivery objectives have been achieved. The threat of closure is not removed until the factory is delivering products that can sustain their competitiveness relative to the competing plants in the group.

Determining the cut-off point requires an ability to think beyond the immediate future and develop an understanding of all the implications of the change (see Chapter 3). Failure to do this may help explain the persistent failure rates for acquisitions, where inadequate attention is given to what happens after the shares have been acquired and top management switches attention after signing the deal. This does not explain all acquisition failure, but accounts for a great deal of it. The change has to be managed to the point where the acquisition is integrated and able to deliver the vision that lay behind the purchase.

Once the right cut-off point has been determined, the change manager's final task is to ensure a smooth transition from the change situation to normal management. Often this means reshaping processes such as performance management, changing the selection criteria for promotion or recruitment and ensuring that the key managers continue to sustain the vision behind the change. Once again, for many changes, it is a question of thinking beyond the immediate future.

The sad thing is that a successful change can be thrown into reverse almost by accident unless management continues to sustain it.

© David Hussey, 1998

14

Multi-businesses

INTRODUCTION

In a famous short story about the Emperor of China's zoo the writer Jorge Luis Borges explains how the animals in the zoo were divided up. Instead of the divisions you would expect from zoos in the West, such as reptiles, fish, insects, mammals and so on, this particular zoo had its animals classified in a completely different way. Categories mentioned are embalmed, tame, sirens, frenzied, drawn with a very fine camelhair brush. This looks pretty strange to us with our taxonomy of animals. But, and here we hope you will find this illustrative, how do you go about classifying the units of a multi-business? The Emperor and his advisers came up with a scheme (in this admittedly fictional zoo) that suited well their purpose. If you imagine the Emperor walking about his zoo perhaps this all made perfect sense. Some of his animals did look very much as if they had been drawn with a very fine camelhair brush. So it made sense to him to categorize the animals as such.

We have used the word zoo, short for zoological gardens, in this introduction. Now a zoo was a place with a collection of animals to be seen and studied. Whereas we might have been better off using the word menagerie, which is a collection of wild animals to be looked at. The studying and classification part is not normally associated with a menagerie. Perhaps this is splitting hairs. But what we are trying to get at is how do you go about structuring a multi-business? Are there taxonomic rules

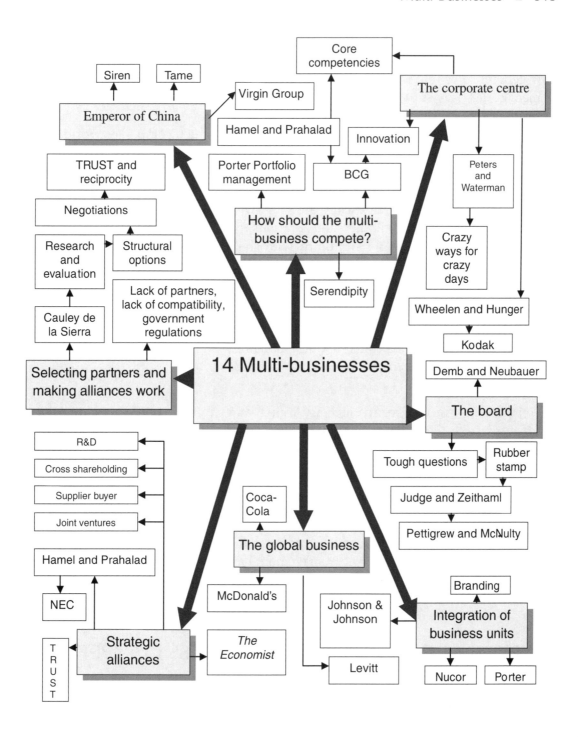

that allow us to say this goes with this, similar to 'this animal belongs in this group of animals which by and large is now agreed throughout the world'? Or are there now general rules that can be used and each multi-business is its own separate zoo or menagerie? Let's start with Virgin Group to see what sense we can make of multi-businesses.

Branson's Virgin Group of companies consists of over 200 companies worldwide, employing over 25,000 people generating revenue of £3 billion in 1999. His philosophy of running a multi-business firm is relatively unusual. Branson's business philosophy is neatly summed up on his group site as, 'Our companies are part of a family rather than a hierarchy. They are empowered to run their own affairs, yet other companies help one another, and solutions to problems come from all kinds of sources. In a sense we are a community, with shared ideas, values, and goals. The proof of our success is real and tangible.' Web sites for some of his companies can be found below.

> Main site: www.virgin.com/
> Airline: www.virgin-atlantic.com/
> Trains: www.virgintrains.co.uk/about/f_abo.htm/
> Mobile phones: www.virginmobile.com/mobile/
> Music: www.virgin.net/

Given the complexity of groups such as Virgin, what strategic concepts and tools can strategists use to think about the issues these groups face and what decisions they might take? We begin by looking at how those in corporate headquarters might conceptualize the nature and challenges of managing a multi-business organization.

Then we look at the debates about the role of the corporate centre itself and what contribution is expected of its managers. We briefly examine the role and significance of the board in strategic processes. Then we turn to the question of how integration of business units is best approached, including within the global business. Finally, we explore the way in which strategic management has been experimenting with strategic alliances and ask whether it is a passing fashion or how much longer it might be expected to survive in its present form.

HOW SHOULD THE MULTI-BUSINESS COMPETE?

In the mid 1980s portfolio management was described by Porter (1987) as the concept of corporate strategy most in use. The most famous concept of portfolio management was the Boston Consulting Group's (BCG) growth share matrix. BCG's home page can be found at www.bcg.com/home.asp.

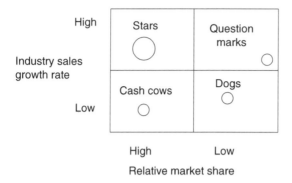

Note: The circles represent strategic business units within a firm and the size of the circles indicate the relative contribution to corporate revenue.

Figure 14.1 The BCG matrix

As outlined in Chapter 3, the BCG matrix classifies businesses or products as stars, dogs, cash cows and question marks, which are characterized using two dimensions, market growth rate and relative market share. Using this a company with several businesses (or products) can plot each in the matrix. Businesses are identified as either in high growth markets or low growth markets. They are also classified as having a high or low relative market share. The cash cows are defined as in low growth markets with a high market share, while stars are in high growth markets with high market share. Dogs have low market share and are in low growth markets and lastly question marks have low market share and are in high growth markets. From this simple classification any company with a range of businesses (products) could assess its overall portfolio and start to make judgements about what broad strategy to adopt for each. For instance, if the company invests in stars it may be rewarded by making more profit. On the other hand, cash cows, as the name suggests, can be used to generate money for investment in other businesses. If the company has some dogs it may well decide to get out of those particular businesses in order to concentrate resources on more profitable lines or may decide to try to turn them around by investment. Question marks also require investment but a pay-off in terms of profitability seems less likely because of their low market share.

A key point here is that the classification gives a firm a systematic way to describe and talk about its businesses. It does highlight some of the key parameters that have to be considered. The firm may not necessarily follow the strategy suggested by the classification but it has created the framework for formulating decisions. Strategists are alert to new ways of thinking about what to do. As we have said, the thing to do as a strategist is to try out tools to see if they work in a particular environment. The

Boston Matrix is just such a tool that needs testing. If it works for you, great. If it does not, try something else.

Another benefit of the matrix is that it may help top managers become aware of and understand important information about their business that they have over-looked. Often a business will be based on one product or idea. Over the years the business will grow, new products will be introduced with the importance of the original product diminishing. The founders of the business may have an emotional attachment to the original product, which make it hard from them to see the prod-uct's poor or even negative contribution to the overall business clearly. Using the matrix will highlight the contribution the product is making to the overall prof-itability of the business, helping the top managers make a more informed, less emo-tional decision on its future. This is not to argue that the product will be dropped, as the emotional attachment might be very high, leading to the retention of the prod-uct for 'old times' sake'. If this is the case at least the reason for retaining it will be out in the open.

A similar use of the matrix can be made when a business is being transferred from one generation to another as this presents a good opportunity for the whole business to be examined with decisions on future investment and disinvestments being made. Again, an emotional attachment to a certain product may have made it difficult for the managers to act but now there is the possibility of reappraisal.

There are of course problems with the matrix. Firstly, as usual, there is a problem of getting reasonably accurate data on where businesses are in the matrix. Secondly, it is quite possible for the data used to construct a matrix to be out of date by the time the top managers use it to make decisions.

Hamel and Prahalad's ideas (1994) suggest another difficulty of the matrix. A firm may make a range of products across several markets based on the firm's core com-petencies. Each product may have quite a modest market share but overall they are profitable. Consequently, it may not be true that low market share is incompatible with high profits. (We made this point in Chapter 11.) Perhaps the common way of thinking about markets is wrong for some businesses as their products are spread across a range of industries.

Another potential difficulty with the matrix is that it might inhibit top managers from thinking about innovation. Fast growth firms are usually characterized by the energy, imagination and resources they plough into being innovative. BCG, in a study of shareholder returns in over 5,000 companies, found that Dell Computer Company and America Online in the five years from 1993 easily outperformed all other companies in the study. Also in the top ten were Nokia, Microsoft and Cisco Systems. These are just the companies where innovation is in the centre of their business strategy. According to Deloitte and Touche, the Character Group plc had a compound growth rate on average of 95 per cent per year over the last four years ranking it number one in their survey of firms in the South East of England. Next on their list for 2000 was the Vindus Group Ltd, a car dealership that achieved an average compound growth rate of 91 per cent per year. More details of the firms can be found at www.deloitte.co.uk/growth/.

There has been a change in the way businesses pursue high growth strategies. They have moved away from a concentration on operational measures such as business process re-engineering and TQM towards a realization that innovation is at the centre of achieving high growth. This is not to say companies should not look at such things as operational efficiencies, cash cutting and use of information and communication technology (ICT). Innovation may well require a change in mindset for strategists who have been used to looking at doing existing things more cheaply or more effectively. It is not uncommon to hear senior executives of large companies worrying over how to introduce more creativity and innovation into their organizations in a way that is not bureaucratic and ultimately does not defeat the purpose of doing so in the first place. They talk about introducing some areas of chaos and unpredictable change to see what will happen realizing that over-formulation of the structures for innovation might well stifle the whole process. They are also increasingly worried about the drain of young, energetic high flyers that in the past would have made a career with them, leaving to work for or set up new emergent business sector economies. These are the people who given the right environment would flourish, producing the new products and services for the future success of the business.

Associated with the emphasis on innovation comes an emphasis on core competencies (see Chapter 11). These are seen as building blocks for successful innovation. For this to happen across the multi-business, core competencies have to be seen as a corporate resource not a local one. Often pockets of competency exist in individual business units that the business unit feels it owns. The competencies can often be guarded closely by the business unit, making it hard for the organization as a whole to leverage it into other business units. Even if there is no sense of ownership at the business unit level the centre may be unaware of what it actually has and how to exploit it across other business units. While it is a sensible thing for the centre to allow the business unit freedom to nurture its own core competencies, it must be constantly assessing whether another business unit could benefit from the competence. It must also seek to build more horizontal linkages. One way to do this is to move managers around from time to time to other business units. Serendipity (the faculty of making happy and unexpected discoveries by accident) will probably happen as managers see new opportunities as they move through the business.

THE CORPORATE CENTRE

Large organizations may have many different business units producing numerous products, often in different countries. At the centre is the corporate headquarters where the overall strategy is decided. One of its key tasks is to make sure that the company is bringing to the market a stream of new, creative, and innovative products that its customers value. There are many ways to achieve this. In markets the corporate centre may be scanning the marketplace for potential new acquisitions. When a business has been purchased great skill is required to ensure that the expertise and innovation embedded in the new company is made available across the company. This is not easy as newcomers might be resented and not given the resources they need to realize their potential. The firm's culture may be unwelcoming making the newly acquired business's employees feeling like outsiders and sidelined. The core competencies brought with the acquired firm may prove very hard to integrate in other business units.

Another approach for the corporate centre in its search for innovation is to encourage intrapreneurship. This is basically trying to encourage employees to act more like entrepreneurs but within the organization. This may require the setting up of special units where employees are given the time and resources to follow creative and even perhaps wacky ideas. Peters and Waterman (1982) advocated such an approach, arguing, in part, that bureaucracy stifles innovation and the more you try to plan innovation at the centre (or at the top), the less chance that it will happen. And anyhow you haven't got the time to wait for the centre's plan. You need to empower employees down the line to use their own innovatory skills. You need to find ways of encouraging hundreds of small, localized experiments and change – crazy ways for crazy days.

Eastman Kodak Company has been criticized for its performance in the late 1980s and early 1990s. 'Top management made strategic decisions based on protecting current products instead of developing future ones' (Wheelen and Hunger, 2000: 25). The new Chief Executive appointed in 1993 was expected to focus on cost cutting, but soon after joining the company he announced that the solution lay in divesting non-core businesses and pursuing growth opportunities.

THE BOARD

The board has responsibility for the vision and mission of the organization and approving the main strategic direction of the company. The board also has responsibilities for monitoring and controlling top managers and approving the use of resources (Demb and Neubauer, 1992). The board of directors plays an important role in protecting shareholders' interests.

The board of directors needs to be able to stand up to its chief executive. Its job is to ask the tough questions that no one else wants to ask or that people are afraid to ask. One criticism often made about boards is they are too passive, weakly accepting the chief executive's views and explanations. They appear in many instances to be little more than rubber stamps for the strategy of the chief executive. For instance, one study of large organizations found that 40 per cent of boards merely ratified management's strategic proposals (Judge and Zeithaml, 1992). While it is only fair to give the chief executive time for his or her strategy to take effect, it is important to be critical at an early stage when things start to go amiss.

Rubber stamp boards may appear to be involved but they may be very poor at protecting the shareholders' interests. Apparently the Non-Executive Directors at IBM at the time of the company's profitability crisis admitted they were not able to properly evaluate management because they lacked the relevant knowledge.

The board of directors is responsible for making sure that its chief executive is providing the strategic leadership required for the future success of the business. There are times, as Bob Ayling found, when the chief executive loses the confidence of the board, and is sacked. On 9 March 2000 he was Chief Executive of British Airways and Chairman of the London Millennium Dome's operating company. By 23 May 2000 he was neither, having been removed form both positions due to the perceived failure of his leadership.

Bob Ayling's experience is not that unusual. Chief executives are often fired by boards. Indeed, this reason for leaving has become even more common in the last 10 years or so. Boards of firms such as IBM and AT&T fired top managers in the 1990s, reflecting a greater tendency for poor management or poor results to be unacceptable than in the past.

There has been some concern about the balance between the executive and non-executive directors on boards. There has also been concern about the capabilities and the limited time given by the non-executive directors to their duties. But as Pettigrew and McNulty (1995) have suggested, the focus needs to be on processes at board level rather than variables such as the proportions of different kinds of directors.

Many organizations arrange for the board to hold a yearly strategic away day where they can review, evaluate and, if necessary, change the strategic direction of the organization. On a positive note, there is evidence that the more boards of directors are involved in strategic management the better the financial performance of the company (Judge and Zeithaml, 1992).

INTEGRATION OF BUSINESS UNITS

Organizations with many separate business units, perhaps scattered around the world, have a problem in deciding on the best way to control the company. Should they go for a large corporate centre, with decisions flowing out from that to the various business units? Or should they have a small and lean centre, with a highly decentralized structure?

Johnson & Johnson is a large and complex organization. It has nearly 100,000 employers, nearly 200 companies in over 50 countries with markets in over 170 countries. Its headquarters is in New Brunswick, New Jersey. From here it reaches out around the globe. The company's management structure consists of a Chairman, who is also the CEO and a Vice-Chairman. The board is made up of 13 members. The principal management group is made up of a team of ten executives. The international companies are run usually by natives of the country. Its Web site is at www.johnsonandjohnson.com/home.html.

Johnson & Johnson has been well known for its very small headquarters and its very decentralized structure. This type of structure works very well for some firms but for others it might not be so good as synergies between the relatively autonomous business units are difficult to achieve. It may be the case that, for example, one business unit has found a particular product line that is doing very well but the company has difficulty in replicating this across business units because of the separate nature of individual units. Further, head office may well find it difficult to impose a corporate view across its business units as it has ceded a relatively large amount of power to them.

Increasingly in the 1990s companies were looking for more synergy between their businesses often in the form of shared activities. The corporate headquarters could identify possible company-wide initiatives that could be exploited successfully at the business unit level. Also attempts could be made to export good practice from one business unit across the company or to grow core competencies throughout the business. In Chapter 13 we noted that there was evidence of a trend for US firms to expand their headquarters in terms of numbers of staff.

Nucor, a US steel firm, is reported to have only about 30 headquarters staff. This is a firm with sales of US $4 billion and over 7,000 staff. Although well known for its small headquarters and decentralized management, Nucor added a new layer of management to its corporate headquarters in 1999.

As firms have been challenged to show that headquarters do add value, there has been more talk about the need to foster linkages between strategic business units (Porter, 1987). For example, can the results of R&D funded in one strategic business unit be reused in another one? Likewise can skills, technologies, and core competencies being used in one business be transferred to and reused in another? And what about businesses in the firm sharing activities? Porter (1987) reported that Procter & Gamble's businesses had a common physical distribution system and salesforce in two instances. The corporate headquarters can obviously add value to the activities of its businesses, then, by identifying and facilitating the horizontal relationships between businesses such as transferring skills, technologies and core competencies and sharing activities. This represents a fundamentally different concept of corporate strategy from that offered by portfolio management, and may account for US trends towards larger headquarters staffs and away from old-style decentralization.

There are firms where there are few linkages between businesses. Successful branding of the company image can do a lot for individual business units as Branson has shown with his Virgin Group. While the separate activities frequently have very little in common the Virgin brand unites them in the consumer's eye, allowing dissimilar business units to gain customer awareness through the total company brand.

THE GLOBAL BUSINESS

When we look at global businesses an interesting problem emerges. How should it respond to local culture? One way is to adapt the offering to suit local tastes. This can be a costly and commonly ill-fated experience. What works well in the United States might flop in Europe. What is effective in supplying customer value in the UK might be a disaster in Japan. But by trying to respond to local needs the company, lacking the experience of the foreign market, fails. An alternative to this is to ignore local culture and force the product onto other markets.

McDonald's is a good example of a global company that tries with a great deal of success to keep its offering much the same, only occasionally bowing to local needs. In fact it has been so successful in this that we now talk about the McDonaldization of society. By this is meant that a global homogenization of culture is taking place, leading to the experience of everywhere being much the same. Think of US films and British pop music – the Spice Girls!

It is confusing because homogenization appears to be taking place along with a celebration of local culture. The smart global firm somehow finds its way through these two extremes to be able to function effectively in numerous markets throughout the world.

Levitt (1983) saw the forces of homogenization as ultimately triumphant. He saw the modern global firm offering high quality products at low prices, and reaping economies of scale from more or less standardized products. The global businesses would achieve expanded markets and profits. Other firms would be the victims of the modern global firms. Did he underestimate national and cultural differences? Levitt referred to the popularity of Coca-Cola, a globally standardized product that sold everywhere. However, less than 20 years later, in 1999, Coca-Cola's share price and profit performance were both poor. (Source: *The Economist* 12 February 2000: 92). The firm's difficulty triggered the appointment of a new Chairman for the company and a substantial cut in the firm's workforce. Early indications suggested that there was to be new management ideas about the future. The new Chairman had plans to decentralize management and he wanted the firm to adapt global brand marketing to local tastes. Local managers were to be given more responsibility for decision making and local brands would become more important. It had also been decided to open four innovation centres. It seems that standardization and economies of scale were giving way to local tastes and innovation in one of the icons of globalization based on a standard product!

STRATEGIC ALLIANCES

This may be just a phase business is going through, but recent estimates of the scale of strategic alliances suggest that, for the present anyway, they are very important. More than 20,000 alliances might have been made throughout the world in 1996–98 and as much as a fifth of sales of US's largest firms are attributable to alliances. (Source: *The Economist* 15 May 1999:109). The airline industry has a hugely important set of strategic alliances. The telecoms industry also features strategic alliances. AT&T recently formed an alliance with Microsoft. The pharmaceuticals industry has seen a doubling of biotech alliances over the past 10 years.

Alliances may be used for a variety of reasons. One reason is to offer help with entry to new markets. Partners can provide useful local knowledge of new markets. Another reason is to help with the costs of R&D. A third reason is to help firms acquire core competencies. Prahalad and Hamel (1990) and Hamel and Prahalad (1994) pointed, for example, to the use of strategic alliances by NEC to acquire and build core competencies.

The alternative to forging a strategic alliance is to acquire other firms but in many instances it is not necessary to go through the time and trouble of acquisition when a strategic alliance delivers what you and the other company need. It might also be that the other firm cannot be bought but would be open to an alliance leading to a potential win–win relationship.

Strategic alliances are sometimes perceived as a better option than acquiring companies. Alliances are sometimes based on an aggressive attempt to set industry standards, for example by licensing the manufacture of products complementary to the company's own (as with the struggle between JVC, Sony and Philips and their different video recorder formats).

Strategic alliances can be:

- joint ventures;
- cooperative supplier–buyer relationships;
- cooperation based on cross shareholding;
- agreements to cooperate on R&D.

Strategic alliances have to be managed carefully. Some companies enter into an alliance as an alternative to an acquisition strategy. In the European telecoms industry alliances were more acceptable than acquisitions. Britain's BT formed alliances with a range of European partners. But an alliance may turn into a move to acquire a partner. For example, Wal-Mart, the US retail firm, began working with Cifra in Mexico at the beginning of the 1990s but then obtained control of it in 1997.

It is no good assuming that without work strategic alliances will produce the benefits the partners hope for. Conflicts do emerge as partners start to feel they are getting the worst of the arrangement. Mutual trust is important but this is hard to maintain in the long run, as it is not uncommon for all partners to believe they are giving more than they are receiving. Rover's partnership with Honda ended on a sour note and, of course Rover's purchase and subsequent sale by BMW added to its woes. Generalizations about strategic alliances are hard to make – for some firms it provides just what they and their partners are looking for and everyone appears to have benefited, for others it just doesn't work. How then should a firm go about finding suitable partners?

SELECTING PARTNERS

Cauley de la Sierra (1995) has identified principles of selecting partners from a review of cases of strategic alliances. She picks out for special mention the importance of compatibility, an equality of commitment to the partnership, and partners who have complementary strengths that compensate for a company's weakness. Others have added to this the importance of mutual trust. Trust is established by social contact.

There is a need for careful research and evaluation to select partners. A company's management could use trade directories, company reports, market surveys, online searches, newspaper reports, press releases and knowledge held in the heads of managers about other companies. The data obtained from the research can be organized so that the companies can be compared with a desired partner profile.

The dimensions of the profile might include size, products/services, market position, technological capabilities, style and strengths of management, production capabilities, and other factors. Providing the desired profile is constructed first, the research and evaluation should provide a rigorous basis for short-listing possible partners.

MAKING STRATEGIC ALLIANCES WORK

Having carefully selected partners, the next step is to select one of the several possible structural options (eg joint ventures, cross share holding, agreements and broad pacts). Preparing for negotiations comes next. This involves the usual work of identifying goals and negotiating positions. Negotiations produce agreement on matters such as the objectives of the partnership, the legal and management arrangements, financing, contributions, benefits and decision-making procedures. All along, for the alliance to succeed there has to a champion for it. Without a powerful champion negotiations can drift, opportunities can be lost, and eventually months of hard work wasted.

Implementing a strategic alliance agreement presumably requires the usual management infrastructure. So continued sponsorship of the alliance by top management will no doubt be essential. The other ingredients will be monitoring of the strategic alliance against specified milestones; training and briefing of managers and employees; conflict-handling mechanisms; as well as a capacity to debug and improve the arrangements for partnership working. There is always a tension in a strategic alliance as you have to give something valuable to your partner who might just run away with it, and the partner feels the same – you might run away with the jewels exchanging them for paste!

It seems to us that trust and reciprocity are the key to a successful relationship but even this might not be enough, as the fit might not work. You have to then walk away from the alliance. Above all, the alliance has to be helping you achieve your competitive goals. If it is not then it needs to be terminated.

We have stressed the dangers of strategic alliances. It should also be appreciated that there are very real barriers to forming strategic alliances. A lack of suitable partners is one. This may be the result of a lack of compatibility. Then there are, in some industries, constraints posed by government regulations and agreements. The barriers that emerge in the negotiation stage may be linked to tough bargaining styles or even a mismatch of national cultures that lead to misunderstandings during negotiation.

CONCLUSIONS

Theories of corporate strategy for multi-business companies have certainly changed over the last 30 years. Currently the general wisdom has moved towards focusing on innovation by companies that operate as integrated wholes and even act in partnership with other companies. The internal integration of businesses within a company is matched externally by the formation of linkages between companies as strategic alliances. At the same time it has become fashionable to see the corporate headquarters as orchestrating the businesses and adding value through directing and leveraging resources and creating internal integration. The role of the board of directors is also being subjected to a rethink. Put rather bluntly, it is now being perceived that boards should not rubber stamp management decisions and that the more proactive they are in strategic management, the better the company will do.

QUESTIONS

1. What are the strategic lessons that can be learnt from the way Branson has structured his group?
2. How useful is the BCG matrix in devising and monitoring a strategy for a multi-business? How easy would it be to apply it to the Virgin Group?
3. Why may it be hard for the centre of a multi-business to gain the full benefits of a core competency that a single unit or cluster of units have in the group? What sort of things could the centre do to try to leverage these benefits across the organization?
4. How can the centre ensure that when new expertise and competencies are acquired they can be cascaded throughout the organization? Are there any particular problems the centre must plan for and how may they be overcome?
5. To be successful the centre must make sure that things are being run well throughout the company. This implies the establishment of routine practices and reporting structures across the organization. The centre cannot simply let the units do what they like and how they like. On the other hand to be successful intrapreneurship, innovation and creativity have to be taking place throughout the company. How does the centre ensure both things are happening?
6. What role should the board play in developing and monitoring strategy of a multi-business? You might like to use the case studies of ICL and Procter & Gamble to explore this further.
7. Using Johnson & Johnson's and the Virgin Group's Web sites, compare and contrast the way the two businesses are managed strategically.

8. In what ways are McDonald's and Madonna the same? If you were the manager of Madonna are there any strategic lessons you could learn from McDonald's?
9. Why do organizations join strategic alliances? You might like to use the Ford, Toyota and Nissan case studies as examples.
10. What factors should you take into account when searching for an alliance partner? How is trust established?

REFERENCES

Cauley de la Sierra, M (1995) *Managing Global Alliances*, Addison-Wesley, Wokingham

Demb, A and Neubauer, F F (1992) The corporate board: confronting the paradoxes, *Long Range Planning*, June

Hamel, G and Prahalad, C K (1994) *Competing for the Future*, Harvard Business School Press, Boston

Judge, W Q and Zeithaml, C P (1992) Institutional and strategic choice perspectives on board involvement in the strategic choice process, *Academy of Management Journal*, October, pp 766–94

Levitt, T (1983) The globalization of markets, *Harvard Business Review*, May–June

Peters, T and Waterman, R (1982) *In Search of Excellence*, HarperCollins, New York

Pettigrew, A and McNulty, T (1995) Power and influence in and around the boardroom, *Human Relations*, **48** (8), pp 845–73

Porter, M (1987) From competitive advantage to corporate strategy, in *Strategy: Seeking and securing competitive advantage*, eds C A Montgomery and M E Porter, Harvard Business School Press, Boston

Prahalad, C K and Hamel, G (1990) The core competence of the organization, *Harvard Business Review*, May–June

Wheelen, T L and Hunger, J D (2000) *Strategic Management and Business Policy*, 7th edn, Prentice Hall, New Jersey

Reading 14.1

Taken from Chapter 2 – Strategy and tactics, in *The Warlords* by Jorge Vasconcellos e Sá (1999)

This chapter will *apply to business administration* the concepts of strategy and tactics illustrated in the previous chapter by Hannibal's campaign. It will define some *fundamental* aspects of the use of the concept of strategy, such as:

- the basic *criteria* on which a strategy should be selected for any institution;
- the *unit of analysis* of strategy which in case of demand is the market segment, and in the case of supply is the strategic group;
- the *impact* of modifications of strategy on the alterations of tactics;
- *how to define a market segment* (one must indicate the product, geographical area, the need and the client);
- the *difference* between current strategy and future strategy;
- the *organization objective(s)* prior to defining a strategy;
- the concept of *strategic movement*;
- the *relation* between strategy and other concepts such as global service;
- how to use the concept of *strategic groups* to make inferences regarding the synergy and attractiveness of industries;
- examples of strategic and tactical *decisions*.

Strategic decisions are broken down into their three essential elements:

1. choice of *geographical* area of activity for the company (eg Portugal, Catalonia, the United States, Canada);
2. within a geographical area the choice of *industry* (eg textiles, footwear, hotel, wine, paper pulp);
3. choice of the *segment(s)* in which the company will focus within each industry and within each geographical area. For example, in textiles and garments a firm can choose from among hats, sports clothes, decorative materials, T-shirts, polo necks and so on.

The best battle plan is to win it beforehand through strategy.
SUN TZU

All men can see the tactics I use to conquer, but no one can foresee the strategy on which my victory is based.
SUN TZU

THE CONCEPTS OF STRATEGY AND TACTICS

Hannibal's campaign clearly illustrates the difference between strategy and tactics.[1] In precisely the same way as soldiers use the terms, *strategy* is the decision referring to the place, time and conditions of the battle, while *tactics* are connected with the grouping and movements of the forces during the battles (cavalry, infantry, artillery, etc). That is, strategy is decided prior to the battle but tactics are used during the battle. Strategy refers to *where* to fight the enemy (competition), tactics *how* to do it. Both are important and necessary conditions for victory, but they are well-defined and distinct from one another.

In Hannibal's campaign, his strategic decision is his choice between four alternatives: to stay *where* he was and await the Roman disembarkation in Iberia (maintenance), retreat to North Africa, fight the Roman fleet on the Mediterranean Sea or fight in Italy. After he opted for this last strategic alternative, his tactical decisions are connected with *how* Hannibal fought the successive armies sent by Rome. In Cannae in one way, in the Battle of Ticino in another, in Trebia in yet another, and so on. Victory in a military campaign (business) depends on both things, but they are conceptually different. Both good strategy and good tactics are necessary conditions; one of them alone is insufficient.

The distinction between strategy and tactics is also illustrated by Marshal Joffre, a French First World War hero. On one occasion he was asked to define strategy in simple terms. He went to a blackboard, drew an X somewhere on it and said: 'Strategy is the decision to fight here and not there, or there.' Tactics (after having made that decision) is how to fight in that place (the grouping and movement of the forces during the battle) – see Figure 2.1. As Karl von Clausewitz, one of Napoleon's great interpreters, said briefly, 'Strategy is where you are and with what strength.'[2]

Having arrived here there are some important aspects to analyse. First of all, why use the concepts of military strategy and tactics in business? Second, why are the concepts of strategy and tactics superior to the other concepts of strategy found in business literature, ie strategy as being that which is important and strategy as applying to the long term? Finally, how should these concepts of strategy and tactics of military art transplant in detail to business, and what are the implications of this? Let us consider each one of these points.

Figure 2.1 The concept of strategy according to Marshal Joffre

SUPERIORITY OF CONCEPT

As mentioned in the last chapter, there are three reasons for using the concept of military strategy in business:respect, simplicity and utility. There should be respect for the earliest concept of a word, originally developed in another area of knowledge. In fact, unlike some other words and concepts used in the world of business, the word 'strategy' was not invented by students of management (see Table 2.1). Therefore, before we start to give certain meanings to the word, it makes sense to ask ourselves what it meant in the area in which it was originally developed.[3] Another meaning should only be given to a word or phrase used in the area of business if it brings some added advantage. That is not the case with 'strategy'.

The second advantage of respecting the original concept of the word 'strategy' is simplicity in the language. Communication is facilitated whenever a word has only one single meaning. Facility of communication results from a one-to-one relationship between word and concept. Therefore when hearing the word 'strategy', the listener immediately associates this with a sole idea (where) and does not need to ask anything more, nor does the speaker have to give any additional explanation about the meaning of the word.

Finally, the concept that strategy corresponds to where (by contrast, tactics corresponds to how) is more useful than other ways in which it has been used in business literature; for example, using 'strategy' to refer to important decisions (and 'tactics' for the remainder), or 'strategy' referring to the long term and 'tactics' to the short term.

In fact, using the military and original definition two types of decisions can be clearly distinguished: those which involve the strategic choice of *where* the business will be (to invoice, to acquire clients), including decisions referring to the *geographical areas*, *industries* and *segments*, and those which are the tactical decisions then needed, such as publicity, how to

Table 2.1 Concepts used in management

Originating in Management	Originating from Other Areas of Knowledge
1. Critical factors of success 2. Segmentation 3. Fit between Strategy and Structure 4. Life cycle of the product 5. Unit of strategic business 6. Strategic group	
	1. Optimization 2. One-to-one relationship 3. Job involvement 4. Satisfaction (in the job) 5. Strength 6. Strategy

Table 2.2 Strategy and tactics

2. 2. 1	Strategy	Tactics
Where	Yes	
How		Yes

2. 2. 2	Strategy	Tactics
Where	Geographical area(s) Industry(ies) Segment(s)	
How (Functional departments)		Financial management Accounting Personnel management Marketing Management informations systems Production Organization and control

establish communication channels, how to organize the analytical accounts, which suppliers to choose, what machines to buy, etc. Thus tactical decisions in business include everything referring to the functional departments: marketing, accounts, production, etc – see Table 2.2. *If strategy is that which is important and tactics what is unimportant*, companies would only have strategic planning departments and no functional departments (finance, personnel, marketing, etc). Why waste time and money on what is unimportant? Similarly in the curriculum of management courses (eg the MBA), instead of marketing, general accounts, production, etc as subjects, there would only be strategy 1, strategy 2, complements to strategy, advanced topics of strategy, more (seminars) on strategy, strategy of internationalization, etc. Obviously this does not happen for the simple reason that both strategy and the functional areas (tactics – the how) are important.[4] It should be added that in day-to-day life both strategic or tactical decisions of great or little importance can occur – see Table 2.3.[5]

Table 2.3 The importance of decisions

	Very Important	Not Very Important	Long-term	Short-term
Strategy	Entry into a new industry	Quitting a segment and entry into a similar one in the same industry	Entry into a new geographical area	Quitting one segment
Tactics	Substitution of advertising on TV by radio or newspaper	Change of publicity from programme X to Y on CNN	Construction of a new factory	Merchandising campaign

Development date / Area of business administration	End of the 19th century	Start of the 20th century	End of the 1930s	End of the 1950s	Start of the 1960s	End of the 1960s	Start of the 1970s	End of the 70s and start of the 80s
Administrative	✓							
Accounting	✓							
Production Management		✓						
Human Resources			✓					
Finance				✓				
General Management					✓			
Management Information System						✓		
Marketing							✓	
Strategy								✓

Figure 2.2   Development dates of knowledge in management

The idea in some literature that strategy refers to the long-term and tactics to the short-term is neither useful nor correct. It is not useful because it is never clear how to differentiate between short- and long-term. Where does 'long-term' begin? After a year? Eighteen months? Two years? The idea is not correct; strategic decisions can be short-term (to be implemented immediately) or acted upon later, as shown in Table 2.3. Similarly, tactical decisions can last for a long or short time.

Thus the concept of strategy used as a synonym for *where* and the concept of tactics as a synonym for *how* makes more sense, is simpler and more useful. However, it is not surprising that certain confusion exists in management literature regarding the meaning of the word 'strategy', as strategy is the most recently developed area of knowledge within management (end of the 1970s and beginning of the 1980s).[6] Other areas, such as accounting, production and finance, started and developed earlier (see Figure 2.2).[7]

APPLYING THE CONCEPT OF STRATEGY TO BUSINESS

How can these concepts from military art be transferred to business? Which decisions correspond to strategy and which correspond to tactics? As tactics refer to the functional departments, there are three types of strategic decisions in business, as shown in Figures 2.3 and 2.4.

1   In which geographical areas will the business venture to operate (attempt to invoice, attract clients): Mexico? Catalonia? United States? Canada? Belgium? etc.

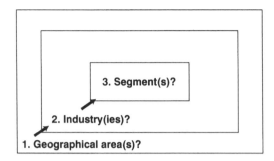

Figure 2.3 The three aspects of the strategic 'where' in management

2 In which industry(ies) in each geographical area will the business venture to operate: Textiles? Footwear? Hotels? Crystal? Wine? Paper pulp? Distribution? etc.

3 In which segment(s) in each industry and each geographical area will the business venture to operate? If the chosen industry is textiles and clothing, will it go into hat making? sports clothes? Swimwear? Underclothing? Furnishing materials? T-shirts? Polo necks? Carpets, Fitted carpets and runners? Trousers and shirts?

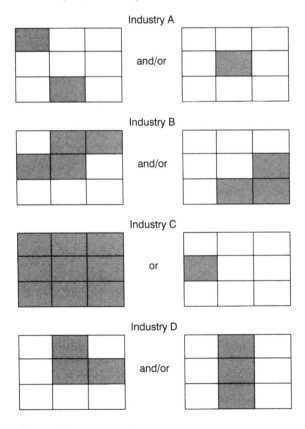

Figure 2.4 Choice of segments and areas

As Figure 2.4 shows, the alternative strategies a company might choose to follow are innumerable (N geographical areas × Y industries × K segments), but in practice they always involve one (or more) of three kinds of decisions:choice of the geographical area; choice of industry; choice of segment.

Therefore, when Philip Morris bought Miller, then Seven Up and then sold this division to Pepsi Cola, three strategic decisions were involved. The first two are the entrance into two new industries (from tobacco into beer and soft drinks) and the last is the departure from the second new industry. Philip Morris altered the *where* in terms of industry on three occasions.

Similarly, when at a certain time in the history of General Electric it entered the computer industry and then sold its manufacturing division to Honeywell, two strategic decisions were taken, both referring to industry (but not to the geographical area nor the segment). However, when Porsche stopped making the economic Porsche (Volks-Porsche) and when

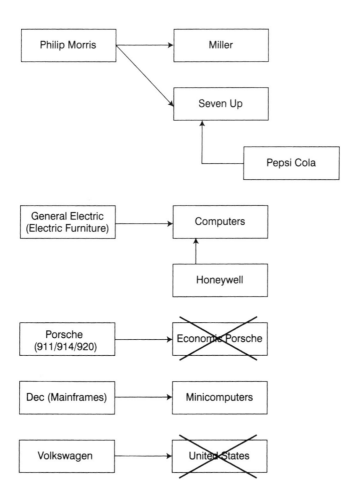

Figure 2.5 Examples of strategic moves

Dec launched minicomputers these were two strategic decisions but here they refer to segments of the market.[8] Finally, when Volkswagen announced some years ago that it was going to abandon the US market that was also a strategic decision, but was connected with the geographical area (see Figure 2.5).

As Figure 2.6 illustrates, examples can always be found of the three kinds of strategic decisions when looking through a newspaper or magazine referring to any industry. Examples referring to geographical areas include alliances between Banco Comercial Português (BCP) and Cariplo, Bital and the Banco Popular Español (later substituted by the Central-Hispano) in order to use the networks of these banks' agencies to sell financial products to Portuguese emigrants in France. Similar instances are the entry of the German bank, Dresdner Bank, to trading in the United Kingdom when it acquired Kleinwort Benson; and the acquisition of another British bank, Warburg, by the Swiss Bank Corporation (SBC).

Figure 2.6 also provides examples of strategic moves in the financial area: concentration in their original *industry* as a result of Prudential leaving real estate; the entry of both Sears and Kroger to the market. The last two examples in Figure 2.6 refer to *segments*.

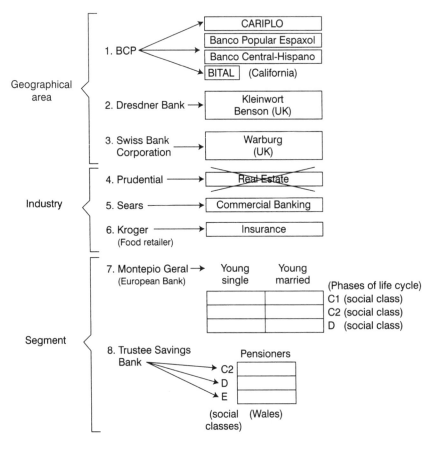

Figure 2.6 The three types of strategic decisions

Social class \ Phase of life cycle	Young single (YS)	Young married (YM)	First home (FH)	Full home	Empty home (EH)	Old single (OS)	Pensioners (P)	Survivors (S)
A								
B								
C1								
C2								
D							WALES	
E								

Note: Young single – not married
Young married – married and no children
First home – first child is below four years old
Full home – oldest child is above four years old
Empty home – when first child leaves home
Old single – divorcees or people who have never married
Pensioners – one or both people are retired
Survivors – only one of the pensioners lives on

Figure 2.7 Trustee Savings Bank strategy

The case of the Trustee Savings Bank illustrates the flexibility of strategic moves within these segments. This bank decided to concentrate on one geographical area only: Wales. Within this area it concentrated on retail banking and not on corporate banking. Finally, within the retail banking it focused on the segment consisting of retired people in classes C2, D and E. The Trustee Savings Bank has almost 90 per cent of its invoicing there (see Figure 2.7).[9]

TEN IMPORTANT ASPECTS OF STRATEGY

At this point, it is important to note ten particular aspects of the concept of strategy in business. First of all, in a company, what is the objective that underlies the definition of strategy? Very simply it is the maximization of profit. William McGowan of MCI was asked what MCI stood for; he said, 'Money Coming In'. Everything else – choice of segments, industries, geographical options – contributes to this objective.[10]

Second, what are the basic criteria according to which strategy is defined? There are two main types of criteria. One is attractiveness (margin of profit, size and foreseeable growth rate). The other is competitive advantage in its two aspects: synergy between segments (the same or different industries and geographical areas) and the degree to which the strong points are the same or different from the critical factors of success (see Figure 2.8).

Third, what is the relationship between this concept of strategy and the typologies of strategy presented in the literature, such as: maintenance, concentration, extension, geographical

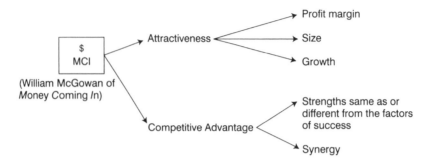

Figure 2.8 Criteria defining strategy

diversification, related diversification (further subdivided into technological and market) and unrelated diversification? The usefulness of the military concept of strategy is illustrated by the simplicity of the relationship of this concept to these typologies. 'Maintenance' refers to the decision of a company to remain in the *same* segments, industries and geographical areas. The strategy will be the same in the future as in the past. 'Concentration' refers to the decision of a company to remain in *fewer* segments and/or industries and/or geographical areas. 'Extension' refers to the situation in which a company enters into *more* segments of the same industry. 'Diversification' can refer to the industry or geographical area. In the former it can be for similar or different industries. If they are similar they can be alike in technological or market terms.

What some literature defines as strategies of increase or reduction of the market quota is connected with a later phase in strategic planning, ie with the establishment of concrete objects and time limits for the company's business units which are dedicated to the various segments. The establishment of objectives is another matter involving market quota, anticipated profit, etc.[11]

A fourth aspect is linked with the *strategy analysis unit*, which in the case of *demand* is the *market segment* and in the case of *supply* is the *strategic group*. Market segment has implications in terms of what the tactics should be (organization and operation of the functional departments). The strategic group allows certain conclusions to be drawn regarding industry. Each one of these aspects will be looked at briefly.

A segment is a sub-group of clients with like needs but distinct from other sub-groups of clients. They give importance to one aspect (eg price) when acquiring a product, while other sub-groups of clients are more concerned about such things as durability, rapid delivery, design, comfort or size. A critical factor of success is the importance given to an aspect by a segment of clients. Thus the critical factors of success vary from segment to segment within an industry. The market segment is the analysis unit, the strategic decision cell.

In the beer-brewing industry, Lone Star adapted its taste and packaging to the preferences of the population of Texas. Michelob aimed at the upper segments of the market,[12] Miller went for the blue collars, Coors for the admirers of the life style and traditional image of the Midwest.[13]

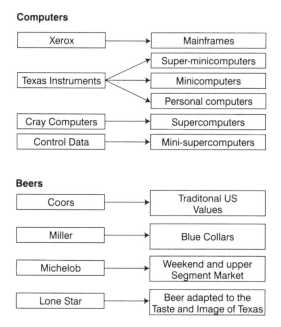

Figure 2.9   More examples of strategic moves

In the computer industry, Cray Computers specializes in supercomputers. It examined the possibility of manufacturing mini-supercomputers but opted not to do so. The supercomputers segment was abandoned by Control Data some years ago. At the present time Texas Instruments makes personal computers and stopped manufacturing minis and super-minicomputers, Xerox started making mainframes, and so on (see Figure 2.9).

In fifth place, it is important to note that the tactics to follow (ie the organization and operation of the functional departments) depend on and vary with the chosen strategy. The strategy determines the tactics. The option for one or another segment (industry/geographical area) has implications for the functional departments. Let us look at some examples.

Figure 2.10 illustrates the case of a European bank, the Montepio Geral, which started a strategic movement in 1991 to attract younger clients (from the same social classes as previously: C1, C2 and D). As a result of this strategic movement which began in 1991, the Montepio Geral had 87 per cent of its invoicing in the first five phases of the life cycle in 1993 (and 81 per cent in the above-mentioned social classes). To attract the younger type of client, the Montepio Geral developed a series of new marketing activities (eg sponsorship of concerts given by the Rolling Stones, David Bowie and Michael Jackson, as well as several marathons and awarded prizes to the best students of management degrees in various universities). New products were launched, such as debit cards and accounts for specific purposes (eg student accounts, accounts for the acquisition of cars). The service level speculated more on the automated teller machines (ATMs), sales terminals and on giving autonomy to the branches. That is, the venture into new

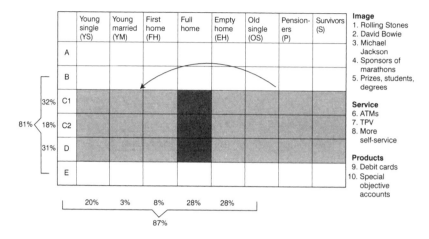

Figure 2.10 Strategy adopted by the Montepio Geral Bank

segments (alteration of strategy) implied alterations in marketing and production (ie in the functional/tactical departments).

It should be noted that the tactical level of alterations occurred in spite of the fact that the alteration in strategy was not very profound as:

1 The geographical area is the *same;*
2 The industry *remained the same;*
3 The previous segments *were not abandoned* (new ones were added);
4 The new segments were *similar* to the previous segments as the size of the segmentation matrix – the social class – remained constant.

Another example of the impact of strategic alterations in tactics, even when the alterations are small, can be found in the car industry. Figure 2.11 shows a possible matrix of industry segmentation. BMW, which initially focused on the luxury segment of less than US $40,000, later also entered the luxury segment of US $40–70,000.

Although BMW were dealing with two of the most similar segments in the industry, various modifications had to be made in the tactics (ie operation of the functional departments). For example, let us look at three modifications in marketing which took place in the areas of sales promotion, public relations and publicity.

In sales promotion terms, the New York showrooms moved to one of the best sites in Park Avenue, to try to capitalize on the prestige of the area, for the sake of the prestige of the product. With reference to public relations, in addition to the already existing tennis and squash tournaments, sponsorship of polo and skiing was initiated, as these activities were patronized by the new clients BMW wanted to attract.[14] In terms of publicity, the slogans in the luxury segment of less than US $40,000 emphasized: durability, credibility and value for money (including the second-hand market). Now, for the cars in the US $40–70,000 segment, the publicity slogans were altered to emphasize security, sophistication and luxury.

It should be noted (in sixth place in the list of strategies) that strategy always has an impact on tactics, regardless of however small the modification of the former might be. The above

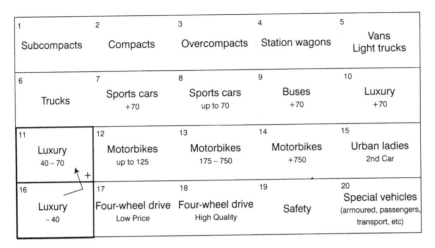

Figure 2.11 Matrix of the segmentation of the car industry

examples illustrate tactical modifications even when the new segments (strategic alterations) are similar to the old. Tactical changes are also needed when the segment remains the same but the *niche* (area within *different* segments) is altered. Figure 2.12 represents private banking within the retail bank. Within private banking two niches can be seen: the so-called old money (traditionally rich people) and new money (*nouveaux riches*). Although both niches share a passion for sophisticated financial products (common in the private banking segment) they also differ from one another: the old money favours saving time and therefore the instruments allowing it, while the new money favours aspects conferring status and prestige. The *nouveaux riches* enjoy luxurious decoration, publicity-invoking prestigious figures who were clients in the past – such as Oliver Cromwell and the Adams & Co Bank, golden and platinum-coloured cheques, etc (see Figure 2.13).[15,16]

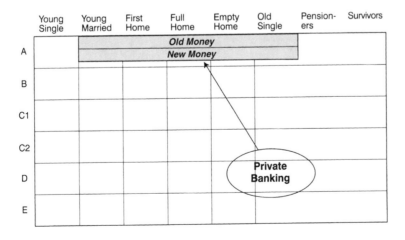

Figure 2.12 Private banking

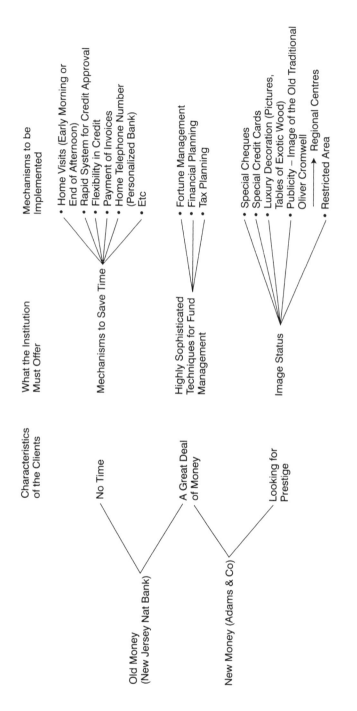

Figure 2.13 Financial products

A B E		E		E
	A		A B	
C D	B E		A B	
		C D		
		C D	C	C

Figure 2.14 Examples of strategic groups in an industry

A seventh aspect of strategy worth noting is that the segment must be precisely defined. To do that four elements must be indicated:

1 The product;
2 The geographical area;
3 The need;
4 The client.

The product itself defines the industry (financial services and cars, footwear, etc). By adding the geographical area the location of the industry is defined, which is important as at times adaptations have to be made to local tastes.[17] By defining the need, an indication is given of the critical factors of success characterizing the segment (luxury, comfort, durability). By indicating the clients, the sub-group of clientele is revealed to which the product is directed. A segment of the market is a sub-group of *clients* with specific *needs*, buying a *product* in a certain *geographical area*. When defining a segment of the market these four elements must be indicated.[18]

In eighth place, if in strategy the analysis unit on the side of demand (clients) is the market segment, on the side of supply (companies) the analysis unit is the *strategic group*. The strategic group is an important concept from which various assumptions can be made about an industry. Figure 2.14 shows a hypothetical industry with 30 segments and five companies in it (A, B, C, D and E) and the strategic positions of the various companies in the industry. Some segments are empty (for the time being companies do not take up a position for reasons of attractiveness or other factors). A strategic group is a group of companies which occupy approximately the same segments, that is, they follow very similar strategies. Companies A and B share three of the five segments in which they operate. Companies C and D also share three of five segments but as there are no segments in which company D is and in which C is not present, C and D form a more similar strategic group than A nd B.

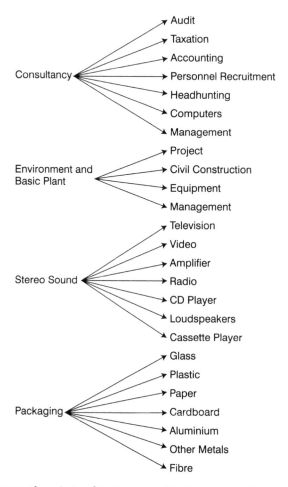

Figure 2.15 The relationship between global service and strategic decisions

Company E is a group on its own, as there is no other company with a similar strategy.

The concept of strategic group is important because, when an industry is taken and the strategic groups existing in it are defined, very interesting conclusions can be reached about the industry; for example, with reference to synergy and possible future strategic moves of the companies belonging to it. Synergy between the segments is much *greater* when both the number of groups is *lower* than the number of companies in the industry[19] and the number of segments common to all the companies of the strategic groups is greater than the number of segments in which only some of the companies of the various strategic groups are present.

By looking at the strategic groups in an industry it is also possible to foresee the future strategic movements of its companies. For example, it is very natural that as soon as company D has resources to enter other segments, it will enter the segments where company C is alone at the moment, as they should be the most synergetic.[20]

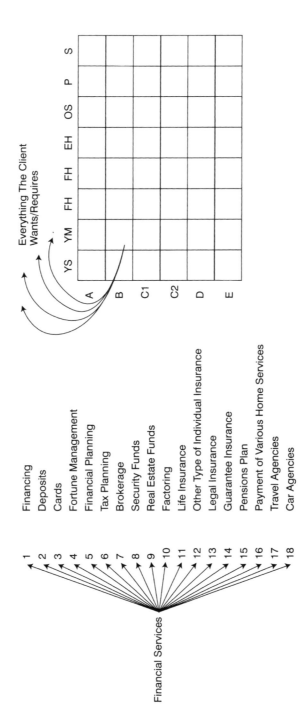

Figure 2.16 Financial services: global services and strategic decisions

A ninth important aspect of strategy is the clarification between strategic option (decision) and global service. Nowadays in many industries (auditing, environment, electronic equipment, packaging, banking, etc), there is a tendency to offer global service; that is, to define the service in terms of need, not product (see Figure 2.15 and Figure 2.16).[21] This is *to avoid losing a client* to a competitor for not offering a certain product that could be supplied by the competitor and to provide the client with *greater satisfaction and loyalty* by saving time. This is different from the strategic decision concerning the option to favour certain types of clients to the detriment of others. In other words, one possibility is to opt for a certain type of client (market segment); another is, having opted to cater for a certain type of client, to give them everything related to a certain need in order to satisfy them, keep their loyalty and provide a high degree of satisfaction.

Finally, a tenth and last aspect. In strategy there are two things which are distinct: present strategy and future strategy. Present strategy is not a matter of subjective opinion but a question of objective fact. In order to know the present strategy of a company it is not necessary to ask anyone anything – but just look where it invoices (in which segments, industries and geographical areas). The determination of the present strategy is simply a matter of the list of clients.[22]

Whether that is the desired strategy or not is another question. That is the reason for making a strategic plan – to evaluate the present strategy and see if it should be kept or if there is another one which is better, to define the future strategy.

Therefore a strategic plan is a document like any other (organizational chart, financial budget), which must be made according to certain rules. A financial budget indicates: income, outgoing cash and its source, while a specific organizational chart shows the hierarchical and functional relationships within the company. Similarly, a strategic plan is a simple document which must indicate three things: the *geographical areas* in which it is going to venture; within these geographical areas, the *industries* in which it will advance; and within these industries, the *segments* which it will back. How to prepare a strategic plan is the theme of the next chapter.

Reading 14.2

Taken from Chapter 2 – Trends, in *Managing International Joint Ventures* by Clifford Matthews (1999)

The business world is full of so-called trends. Some are more imagined than real but there is undeniably a set of real ones in force at any time. Some trends, such as the existence of macroeconomic cycles, can be considered more or less permanent features; they are part of the landscape of business. Others are more temporary, dictated by circumstances and pressures, and some are absolute passing fads, the product of little more than fashion.

All these trends, real or imagined, act together to affect the business world of which they are part. There is little doubt that these trends do have cumulative effect, but their net impact is not always easy to predict and quantify, for example:

- The significant investment programmes of the late 1960s had the expected effect of stimulating general economic activity but overall growth was still constrained by other, less tangible economic factors.
- Few would disagree that the ethos of privatization and share ownership of the 1980s had an important influence on the social responsibilities of business – but did it produce other, perhaps less obvious, business trends? Some would argue, for instance, that it had an irreversible effect on the fabric of employee–employer relations, changing for ever the unwritten commitments of both parties.

There is a wide scope and variety of business trends. Many are complementary, helping each other along, even spawning families of related 'sub-trends'. Others have exactly the opposite effect, acting to counteract or contradict each other. Many economists view the business world like this – as an uneasy liaison between complementary and conflicting trends. It is indeed a complex picture. Thankfully, there is not much doubt about the two key points: that business trends do exist and that they combine to affect the values and practices of the business world in a largely predetermined (but rather unpredictable) way. Figure 2.1 lists nine current visible business trends. We will look at each briefly, with particular reference to the way in which each trend is likely to influence or encourage the conditions for co-operative or 'joint venture' working.

ECONOMIC CYCLES

It is one of the great paradoxes that business organizations are perceived as being stable. They are best thought of as being in a state of flux, reacting continually to their business environment. At the highest 'macro' level of this environment, nothing is static – there is always an underlying groundswell of change. It is generally accepted that the overall nature of these changes follows a cyclic pattern. The cyclic form manifests itself

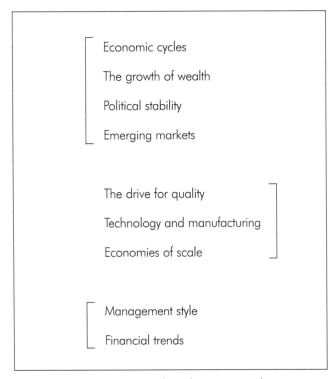

Figure 2.1   Today's business trends

at all levels of analysis, so a study of economic trends by country, business sector or industry will show a similar pattern of results. The cyclic pattern is particularly well proven at the very highest level of economic analysis; just about everyone agrees about the existence of economic cycles.

The effect of this cyclic nature of the business environment means that organizations need an almost limitless range of behaviour if they are to be capable of responding rapidly and effectively to the resulting changes and challenges that present themselves. This causes uncertainty because organizations do not have limitless capability. The overall effect can perhaps be best summarized as follows: economic cycles affect:

- the *performance* of business;
- business *confidence* (in its most general sense);
- the *expectations* of organizations and people.

These are important common denominators. Organizations are driven by the expectations and confidence of their people – once these start to suffer, then the formal 'downstream' business activities of labour markets, capital markets, competitive strategy etc suffer from a lack of impetus.

The effects of economic cycles are, of course, never absolute. Some cycles have had surprisingly little effect on particular areas of business, and it can be argued that cycles may

An increasingly cyclic business environment

CREATES

- a more risk-averse approach to business;

- a tacit acceptance of uncertainty;

- diversification – as a defensive rather than offensive strategy.

Figure 2.2   Effects of a cyclic environment

even act as a stimulus to certain types of economic activity. Whether economic cycles promote predominantly certainty or uncertainty, one trend is clear – these cycles are getting shorter. There is firm evidence for this in the records of many of the published economic indicators and more colloquial evidence in the overall 'feel' of the business world.

Shorter, steeper cycles mean more uncertainty, and the strategy of businesses has to react accordingly. Businesses (and governments) become more risk-averse, desiring quicker, less risky strategies for growth and expansion. At the other end of the strategy scale, the onus shifts towards risk *sharing* and diversification – both mechanisms intended to provide a measure of insulation from an increasingly cyclic environment. Figure 2.2 summarizes the situation.

CASE STUDY 2.1
The retail business: cycles of expectation
The retail business is one of the best examples of a cyclic environment. There is no logical reason why the consumers should want more, or fewer, retail goods this year than they did last year, apart from the influence on their decision-making of uncertainty about the future. Worries about future economic conditions such as interest rates and employment prospects affect sales of retail goods in advance of the conditions actually occurring. All sectors of the retail business, from manufacturing to distribution, sales and financing of the goods are therefore cyclic. This owes as much to the risk-averse nature of people as to the cold and impersonal rules of economics.

The net result of Figure 2.2 is a business environment with an increased trend towards co-*operative working*. Co-operation is seen as an efficient way in which risk can be shared, with even the most temporary and tenuous co-operation between organizations seen as being better than one organization shouldering all the risk itself.

THE GROWTH OF WEALTH

On balance, we are all getting richer. Does this promote an ethos of co-operation and sharing? No-one would deny individuals or businesses the objective of maximizing their own wealth. The problem with wealth is not the question of propriety, but the problem of measurement. There are numerous ways to measure wealth. At the upper level of analysis, key indicators such as Gross Domestic Product (GDP) are an attempt to quantify 'how rich' a country is. Businesses rely on traditional indicators such as Return on Investment (ROI) or capitalization value as their measure, while, at the level of individuals, it is net disposable income that really matters. These are all aberrations of sorts. Perhaps the least imperfect measure is that relevant to the individual – it is the individual who feels the economic need to work, and in doing so creates the need for businesses and organizations of all types.

Individuals world-wide are getting richer. In the developed countries of the world the personal wealth of the individual has increased steadily over most of this century with the 'survival' pressures of 50 or even 20 years ago being gradually reduced, to be replaced by more comfort-orientated pressures. Many of the richer societies of the world are becoming intensely consumerized, with individuals striving for ownership of products that can truly be considered 'luxuries'. In such an environment, there is always the tendency for risk-aversion – it is understandable that relatively wealthy people do not want to lose what they already have. The result is that individuals themselves exhibit more risk-aversion which feeds forward into the strategy of the organizations on whose behalf they make strategic decisions – the trend of risk-aversion therefore compounds itself.

The situation is mirrored at higher corporate levels. The past 20 years have seen the rise of many genuinely global businesses for oil products, foodstuffs, motor vehicles, medicines and a vast range of consumer goods made by high volume mass production methods. These global corporations are highly profitable and successful – it is fair to assume that they *enjoy* their present position. Again, the result is a type of risk-aversion, with the avoidance of too much risk taking precedence over the unfettered drive for profit.

POLITICAL STABILITY

There are three political occurrences that have caused major societal effects over recent years:

- the virtual end of the 'cold war' in Europe;
- the opening up of relations with China and the Far East;
- the downfall of communism.

These have spawned a series of more localized political trends within countries, as well as across traditional international boundaries. The consequence has been a more relaxed view of political differences. Ideological disagreements no doubt remain, but their effect as trade or business constraints has weakened, particularly in the past 10 years. While it is easy to dismiss this as merely a respite from old differences, soon to return, the fact remains that barriers to international business co-operation are far fewer than they were.

The result is a genuinely more international 'flavour' to business. Access is now possible to the manufacturing skills and lucrative markets of the world's developing countries. There is evidence that global co-operation is at last seen as being *possible*, if that is what businesses want. With the mechanics of co-operation has come the gradual realization of global interdependence – the understanding that companies in different continents have a mutual effect on the fortunes of each other.

EMERGING MARKETS

The emerging markets of the world have always provided a fertile source of business opportunity. Viewed globally, the overall industrial strategy of the world follows the broad pattern of Figure 2.3. New and developing countries start by developing a concentrated manufacturing base – initial impetus being towards those industries which are low-technology and labour-intensive. As the economy develops, industries start to shift away from primary manufacturing to lighter, more technology-based manufacture and assembly. This is accompanied by a rapidly developing technological base in which disciplines such as research and development and advanced design start to predominate. This stage is also characterized by an increasing amount of subcontracting of manufacture back to less well-developed countries. There is still plenty of room for wholesale shift of this type in the developing world. The next (and perhaps the final) stage is the move out of manufacturing-based industry altogether, into the field of pure service industries such as banking and financial services. Examples can be seen in countries such as Switzerland and the richer economies of Northern Europe which are already some way down this path.

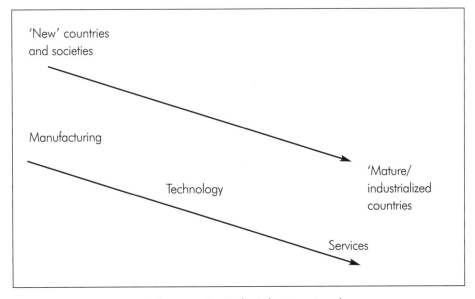

Figure 2.3 Today's business trends

The current developing countries of the Far East, Latin America and Eastern Europe are positioned at the 'manufacturing' stage, with Western Europe and the United States well into the technology-based stage. The relative positions vary with (among other things) economic cycles, but the overall trend remains. This shift of industrial structure between areas of the world is a provider of opportunity. It creates an environment in which new business concepts and ideas can take root – in short, it provides the space for businesses to grow, change, or develop their strategy in a way that they think fit. There is no single and concrete reason why the existence of emerging markets should *cause* the formation of alliances, joint ventures or other co-operative ways of working, but it provides the type of business environment in which these organizational forms can flourish.

THE DRIVE FOR QUALITY

Quality has been one of the buzzwords of recent years. There is now hardly an organization left that does not profess to recognize 'quality' as one of its competitive advantages. This has been ably assisted by the wide promotion of the ISO 9000 quality standard as a successful model of quality management. The net effect of this 'drive for quality' has been twofold: more management systems and increased requirements for product conformity.

The ISO 9000 philosophy is built on the idea of installing management systems to control and monitor those parts of an organization that are deemed to have an influence on quality (in practice, virtually all of it). Its disadvantage is that it is not directly related to the issue of product conformity. This has been addressed by a parallel, and equally strong, trend towards mechanisms that do purport to control the final quality of manufactured goods, such as standardization and the use of more prescriptive product specifications. Most product conformity requirements are consumer-driven – consumer products (electrical goods, motor vehicles, etc) that would have been acceptable to the consumer 20 years ago would today be classed as sub-standard or shoddy. Many commercial services, as well as manufactured goods, would fall into the same category.

The effect of the drive for quality has been a tightening of customer requirements in all spheres of business. Some businesses have become very proactive – continually improving quality levels on their own initiative, thereby leading customers to *expect* better quality goods and services. The overall trend resulting from this has been that manufacturers and service-providers have had to increase their efforts to retain their customers. The economic recessions of recent years have weeded out those whose quality of goods or services are poor. At the business level, the drive for quality has also provided impetus for co-operation between companies that possess top-notch skills – business alliances have taken place specifically to exploit complementary skills of technology and high quality manufacture.

TECHNOLOGY AND MANUFACTURING

As we approach the millennium, the world has a thirst for technology. A continually expanding range of products from basic comfort needs to commercial products seems to be in ever-increasing demand. This march of technology provides the businesses of the world with a valuable source of economic activity – producing business opportunities for sellers, buyers, those who develop the technology, and those who take the role of facilitators and 'enablers' in the chain of commerce. The more dynamic the rate of technological development, the greater the level of opportunities for all. There will always be open questions about whether the rate of technological change is greater now than it ever has been, or conversely, whether it peaked at some (indefinable) time in the past and we are heading for a future of technological stagnation. Despite opposing extreme views, common-sense observation seems to suggest that technology is still moving forward at a fairly constant rate. This rate varies between commercial sectors, and with time, and, of course, is always subject to the pressures, checks and balances of the market.

With the advance of technology comes the attendant problem of technological complexity. In vying with each other for competitive position in the market, goods and services become more complex. This trend is almost universal – look at the complexity of today's motor vehicles, electrical goods or financial service products compared to those of ten years ago. The effect of such complexity-increase results in a *multidisciplinary* approach to the provision of goods and services. Previously simple manufactured products now have designers to design them, consultants to advise on shape and styling, and innovative packaging and marketing techniques to present them to customers in the most appealing way. Services follow similar lines. This has encouraged an ethos of joint working between specialist companies, the objective being to produce the very best product or service with the skills and resources available, even if it does mean sharing the profits. This interdependence between skill groups has been an important structural shift in the way that technology and manufacturing coexist; single-discipline specialists still exist, but they have to work with others across technological, regional and probably cultural boundaries as well, if they want to sell to the market.

CASE STUDY 2.2
Technology trends: the entertainment business

It is not only manufacturing industry that has undergone structural shifts due to technology trends. Services such as the entertainment business have undergone major changes eg:

- *Multi-channel digital television*: this is a business driven by the march of technology, rather then consumer demand for more channels. There is a growing interdependence between communications network companies and the sports clubs and programme-makers that produce attractive material for broadcast.
- *Theme parks*: these are no longer the domain of single-discipline operators. They are now a technological mixture of advanced engineering, sound and vision experiences and computer simulation.
- *Film special effects*: the content of many films is now driven more by the capabilities of special effects and computer graphics than the storyline. This is an example of technology 'push'.

ECONOMIES OF SCALE

As well as increasing in complexity, the volume of manufactured goods (and services) is increasing as well. The increases apply not only to 'products' like motor vehicles, consumer goods or foodstuffs, but also to the project and civil construction-related aspects of industrial development such as bridges, airports and roads. This has caused an increase in the use of mass production as a general means of manufacture. Production philosophies which were once restricted to the manufacture of motor vehicles or televisions are now in widespread use for furniture, building materials and a raft of prefabricated and pre-assembled parts for the developing world. Mass production has become the ethic of industrialization.

This trend in manufacturing has not, however, just been 'more of the same'. There has been a clear trend from the labour-intensive mass production techniques of the past to a much more capital-intensive regime. The products of production lines are now made by expensive robots rather than people, with the basic economies of scale of mass production reinforced by a swing to capital-intensive methods. These pressures all push towards an increase in manufacturing volume, in order to fulfil the payback or returns on investment required. Manufacturing support techniques such as flexible manufacturing systems (FMS), just-in-time (JIT) supply, and statistical process control (SPC) have proliferated to try to improve the efficiency of the end process – evidence in itself, that the volume and complexity of the manufacturing world are increasing all the time. Practical considerations apart, the economies of scale of mass production remain as lucrative as when they were conceived nearly one hundred years ago. More products means more profit – if you can get it right.

MANAGEMENT STYLE

It is common now to hear a lot of informed (and sometimes uninformed) opinion about trends in management style. Everyone seems happy to vouch an opinion as to whether management is becoming more or less democratic, or authoritarian, and whether this is somehow 'deserved' or not. The picture is further confused by the almost weekly emergence of newly-discovered techniques and acronyms – each claiming to hold the answer to the Pandora's box of day-to-day management problems. Most turn out to be little more than fashion or, at best, capable of producing only short-term solutions. Confusion reigns.

SHOULD OUR COMPANY

1. Be authoritarian or democratic (consensual)?

2. Model itself on co-operation or conflict?

3. Value its independence or accept its *inter*dependence?

Figure 2.4   Three perennial issues of management style

Thankfully, it is possible to identify a number of management trends that are less affected by 'management fashion' diversions and which keep reappearing as salient management issues that warrant serious discussion. The three most common ones are shown in Figure 2.4. These trends follow the basic cyclic pattern discussed earlier with the timescale of the cycle dependent, as always, on a matrix of outside influences.

One of the predominant trends is the way in which company management perceives the value of organizational *independence* in its business activities. At some time in the business cycle there is a forthright view that 'the company' is a valuable but, nevertheless, limited part of the world of business and commerce and that its role is to play its true part in the interdependence of all other (nominally competing) companies in the chain. At such times, the search for extreme profit is sacrificed for the easy ambience of coexistence and co-operation. At other times, the cycle produces the opposite – the platitudes and ethos of co-operation disappear, to be replaced by the viewpoint that; 'it's us against all the rest' and that it is competition that reigns supreme, not co-operation.

Whether the prevailing management strategy, at any point in time, values interdependence or independence (these are quite neat summary terms of what the strategies are) depends upon the compounded result of many outside influences. There is a valid, if controversial, argument that this fundamental strategic issue is not actually the product of conscious strategy at all, but is simply the enforced result of outside events and constraints. It is as if company strategy in this area is almost predetermined by the course of events over which management have no control. Within this framework of constraint and speculation, the management style of any sector of business – and probably that of the business world as a whole – is, once again, broadly cyclic. It swings from being predominantly based on *independence* to a condition of relative *interdependence*, and then back again. Opinions vary as to the length of the cycle but the average seems to be between 20 and 25 years, depending on which sector you look at.

The late 1980s and 1990s were a period of *interdependence* in almost all sectors. The principle of co-operative working flourished, paving the way for strategic alliances and joint ventures. It is fair to say that this trend has been helped along by other concurrent world trends, but the result is the same – co-operation is king (at least for the moment).

FINANCIAL TRENDS

The underlying rationale of any commercial business is the quest for profit – there can be little doubt about that. What can be questioned, however, is whether this profit motive is a permanent, preset factor of the business landscape or whether it itself is cyclic, like so many of the other driving forces we have seen.

Is the profit motive cyclic?

In times of economic growth the search for profit takes priority. People and business will take whatever steps are necessary to obtain their rightful share of economic cake – and are not ashamed to admit it. This is profit as a motivator, slicing through the need for other, less important, corporate objectives. Now consider what happens when the cycle turns and the growth period ends (as we know it must). The quest for profit is magically replaced by the pursuit of stability; it is the survival of the business that suddenly becomes important. At this stage, the eyes of management strategy rotate inwards, looking for methods of cost-cutting and rationalization. Words such as 'consolidation' and 'downsizing' make their unwelcome appearance in the minutes of management meetings. The result, in summary, is that the incentive to make profit takes second, or even third place to issues that are more concerned with avoiding risk than taking it. The profit motive has not of course gone away (it would take a fundamental shift in human nature to do that), it is merely in recession.

The existence of risk is what causes many of the traditional ways of the financial objectives of business to sometimes feel a little unreal. A return on capital employed of 20 per cent may sound good, but, if a business feels that the sheer risk of financing an asset to produce this return is too great, the return will never happen – it will be little more than illusion. So, while risk is not in itself a tangible business 'parameter' (you won't see it quantified in anyone's annual report), it is a real and overriding constraint on the financial objectives of a business. The inherent level of risk present in any business environment is difficult to quantify – about the only thing you can guarantee about it is that it is *cyclic*. This is a long-winded way of saying that what looks like a good deal today might look worse (or even better) tomorrow.

It is fine, if a little distracting, to talk about risk in this general and abstract way. It is not, however, very productive. We can learn more by looking at the more tangible parts of the financial territory of business – remember we are looking for those that are subject to *trends*. These are shown in Figure 2.5.

Investment criteria

The central tenet of business investment is the concept of return. The three main interpretations: return on sales (ROS), return on capital employed (ROCE) and return on investment (ROI) are all valid indicators, in their own way, of the financial efficiency (or otherwise) of the business.

The key criterion is of course the return that is anticipated by the management of the business activity, ie the *expected return*. It is a tangible business indicator but, because it is based on expectation (in reality it is little more than a mental construct of managers), it will vary in a way which reflects the relative amount of risk and confidence that is around in the business environment. It is also closely linked to its opposite: the cost of capital – heavier costs of accessing capital result in high expectations of the performance of that capital, once the step has been taken to acquire it. The rational economic view places the value of the expected return higher than the prevailing cost of capital. It is difficult to specify how much higher it should be – it all depends on other factors such as the personal attitude to risk of the involved managers. In practice, the ratio of expected return/cost of capital is itself cyclic, varying from perhaps 25–30 per cent down to 5 per cent during periods when corporate expectations are low for whatever reason. The unavoidable existence of low expectations for some of the time during the business cycle is one of the reasons why companies sometimes feel encouraged – or, conversely, constrained – to take part in certain ways of working at various times in their business life. This means that a business's attitude to financial return

---

**All these aspects of financial management
are subject to *trends*:**

- investment criteria (How much return for how much risk?);

- project appraisal (should we do this project or not?);

- funding strategy (availability of equity or debt);

- capital structure;

- the absolute cost of capital.

Figure 2.5   Trends in financial management

(remember, it sets this attitude itself) is a strong determinant of the organizational form or structure that it will adopt. We will see later how this has particular relevance to the expected financial returns from those organizational structures that involve co-operative working, in the form of alliances and joint ventures with others.

Funding options

The funding options available to a business determine what it can and cannot do. It is of little use being dedicated to the ideology of global expansion if you don't have access to any money.

The types of funds available to a business are the same as they have always been – the simple choice between debt and equity. Despite the imaginative ways in which the financial industry manages to present these in user-friendly packages, this does not change the fundamental nature of these financial sources – you either sell equity to raise funds or you borrow. The costs of equity capital and debt are quantified and well documented at any point in time, and can be considered a known variable of the corporate financial equation. Although sometimes amalgamated together into the well known weighted average cost of capital (WACC) to a business, the variations in costs of equity and debt are frequently identified separately. Not surprisingly, both have a tendency to follow a cyclic pattern. The cycles for equity and debt rarely coincide exactly, either with each other or with the overall variation in the global economic cycle, but the approximation is close.

The relative availability and cost of equity and debt have a well-defined effect on the way that businesses organize their financial structure. In good times, the basic rule that debt is cheaper than equity holds good and a business can increase its expected return by levering its financial structure to contain more debt. When a recession hits, however, firms tend to lean heavily on equity – everyone wants equity-investors who don't want their return 'just yet', and are prepared to wait until things improve.

These features of the nature of finance mean that the prevalent financial structure of businesses changes with the rise and fall of other cycles – some predetermined and some not. There is nothing new about this finding, it fits neatly with the traditional economists' view (well one of them anyway) of the financial world as an 'uncertain disequilibrium', rather than an ordered and stable equilibrium. The effect of financial structure is almost absolute because it acts as a constraint on the motives of the managers of a business; there is nothing better at tempering the excesses of entrepreneurial spirit then the spectre of having to pay crippling dividends or debt repayments long after a project or venture has gone badly wrong. Taking a more positive view, you can think of the debt/equity structure of a business as an independent balance on the activities of the business, almost a self-checking function, restricting the projects and ventures that the business can enter, and curbing some of its over-zealous decisions. There is not much emotion in the world of equity and debt finance.

SUMMARY

We started this chapter by concluding (or was it a proposition?) that the business world is crammed full of trends, many real but some mainly illusion. In looking at them in a little more detail, there is clearly a cyclic nature to them: business fortunes go up and down, as economists and common-sense managers know that they must. So what? The main message of this chapter is that the cumulative effect of business cycles is to form, at certain times, conditions under which methods of joint working and strategic alliance between business are acceptable and *desirable*. This in no way devalues traditional economic or management theories of the business world, it is simply a manifestation of one of its many forms. Strategic co-operation is (and always has been) in the repertoire of all businesses – it just needs the right conditions in which to appear.

The scene is set. The following chapters of this book explore, in detail, the nature and character of this strategic co-operation with particular emphasis on the joint venture across international boundaries, perhaps the most difficult form of them all. We need to start with the first step: the different forms of co-operation.

TRENDS: KEY POINTS

Trends are a feature of the business world. Some are based on fashion or illusion but many are real.

1. *Economic cycles* are well defined and documented, they affect the performance, confidence and expectations of businesses.
2. *Wealth* influences businesses' views on risk: the trend is for wealthy companies and countries to become more risk-averse.
3. *Quality and technology* are influential trends which encourage the search for complementarity and economies of scale between businesses.
4. *Financial management* is affected by unavoidable changes and trends in the cost of equity and debt.

Trends have a cumulative effect on a business. Under some conditions they provide strong pressure for companies to co-operate rather than compete with each other.

15

Small businesses

INTRODUCTION

British television comedy has had several situational comedies based around small businesses. *Steptoe and Son*, based around a father and son's 'rag and bone' business, *Fawlty Towers*, featuring a small hotel run by a husband and wife, *Only Fools and Horses* with two brothers and an aged relative, and, of course, *Minder*, with a modern day 'spiv' and his 'minder' are examples. For more information on British television comedy the following site is excellent: www.phill.co.uk/comedy/index.html. These programmes exploited the stereotypes of small business and their owners with great comic effect. They also set up in the viewers' mind a picture of what small businesses are like.

Take, for instance, a typical episode from *Fawlty Towers*, 'The Gourmet Night', first shown on 17 October 1975. In this episode Basil Fawlty (played by John Cleese), the joint owner of the hotel with his wife Sybil (played by Prunella Scales), embarks on a new strategy to increase profits. He decides on a Gourmet Evening where a select number of diners will enjoy high quality food. He aims to charge them more for this and make more money. Also he is a bit of a snob and sees this as a way of attracting a better class of guest to his hotel. Unfortunately everything that can go wrong does go wrong. Firstly, Basil's chef gets so drunk that he cannot prepare the required food. Basil rings up a friend who runs a restaurant to arrange for the food to be cooked

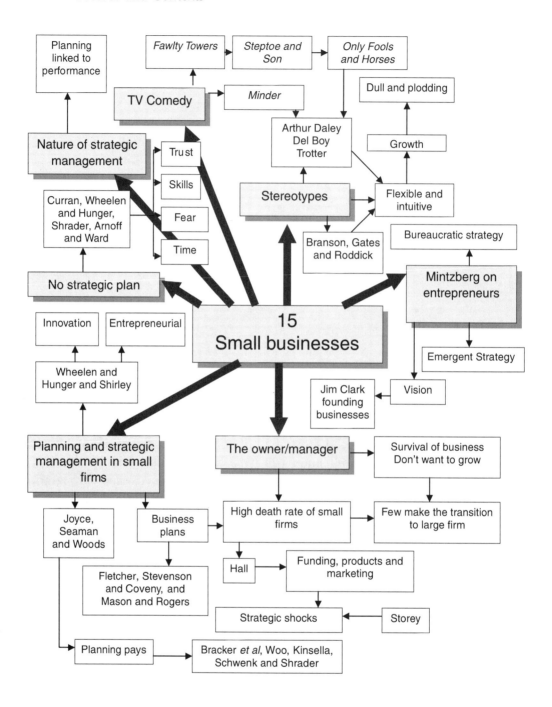

there. Basil sets off in his car to collect it. Basil's car is in urgent need of repair but Basil had decided not to get the car repaired professionally. He could not afford it, so repaired it himself. Of course the car breaks down and in a hilarious scene Basil attacks the car with a tree branch and after a series of other mishaps arrives back at the hotel on foot with the wrong dish.

In the last episode of *Only Fools and Horses*, 'Time on our Hands', Del and Rodney Trotter, the two main characters, are clearing out the garage in which they keep odd bits of furniture and other odds and ends. Rodney, looking through the junk they have collected over the years, happens upon an old watch. Instead of throwing it away he looks at it closely realizing it could be quite valuable. He does not realize quite how valuable it is. It turns out to be a watch made by Harrison of longitude fame. The watch sells at auction for a vast amount making Del and Rodney millionaires. After all those years of 'ducking and diving' trying to make a living they have finally done it. The episode ends with them walking into the sunset. Ironically the watch had been in their possession for years but they did not know it. They could have been rich, in fact very rich, years ago.

STEREOTYPES

We could have chosen almost any episode from these comedies to illustrate two stereotypical views of small business. According to one stereotype, small business owners are 'ducking and diving' individuals, always trying to find the right deal to make them rich and always failing. *Minder* with Arthur Daley or *Only Fools and Horses* with the Trotters illustrate this. According to the other stereotype they are complete incompetents like Basil Fawlty, stumbling from one potential disaster to another.

How far away are these comic representations from the truth? As a generalization we do tend to think of the smaller business, either the sole trader or the small firm employing less than 10 staff, as being managed in a pretty straightforward way with little knowledge or interest in strategy or for that matter other aspects of modern management practice. We tend to think of them as no-go areas for managers who believe in long-term planning and sophisticated strategic concepts. Apart from the lack of management skills we also have a picture of small-business managers as rugged individualists, as people who like the independence of being in charge. They are seen, perhaps cruelly, as being the king or queen of their own castle. And in the extreme version of this, played on in the comedies, they are opinionated amateurs that survive more by luck than good management.

A common view of management in the small business is that it is flexible, intuitive and based on the personal energy and acumen of the owner/manager. These qualities are used, firstly, to make sure the business survives and, secondly, to grow the business. When the business does grow, the intuitive style of management has to be replaced by a more systematic one including some formalization of strategy. Other managers may well have to be hired to cope with the increased demands being placed on the owner. They are needed to run the business both on a day-to-day basis and to plan ahead. The romantic image of small businesses pictures owners in total charge, relying on their own judgements to make things happen. Some may regret the growth of a business because they perceive it as a loss of creative turmoil and entrepreneurial spirit which is replaced by a dull and plodding but well-run business approach.

So we have various stereotypes of the small business and its owners. We have those from comedies and then others from our general understanding of them. How accurate are they? One thing that you soon learn about small businesses is their variety. It is very, very hard to make general statements about them as they are such a heterogeneous group only defined as being similar by their scale, either measured in employment terms or turnover. Consider a three person hi-tech Internet company – what will it have in common with a three person building firm apart from its size in terms of employees?

ON ENTREPRENEURS

Mintzberg has been very critical of what we might call bureaucratic strategic planning. He argued that, in reality, much strategy is emergent. He believed that managers often deluded themselves into believing that change was programmable from the top. He further felt that at certain stages in a business's life, usually at the start-up stage, the business was at its most entrepreneurial. People who are tired and fed up with the constraints of larger bureaucratic ones frequently start new businesses. These people feel hemmed in by the rules and regulations imposed on them by the firm stopping them from making imaginative and potentially risky decisions and consequently they want to escape to fulfil their own entrepreneurial vision. He has emphasized that it is the vision of these potential entrepreneurs that is important – not the detailed planning found in the more bureaucratic organization (Mintzberg, 1991).

Of course, entrepreneurs exist in larger organizations, sometimes referred to as intrapreneurs to distinguish them from entrepreneurs. One thing we have been at pains to stress in this book is the need for strategists to be creative and imaginative people, with the ability to balance forecasting with foresight in order that the rigidity imposed by the bureaucracy and stodginess of the larger organization can be overcome. But it is in the small organization that many see the natural habitat of the entrepreneur.

Once the business has been established the entrepreneurial energy of the original founder can easily be dissipated. The entrepreneur may get bored and leave to start another venture. He or she may be drawn into the running of the business with his or her entrepreneurial skills no longer so evident. It is obviously quite hard for 'natural' entrepreneurs like Richard Branson, Bill Gates or Anita Roddick to keep being entrepreneurial as their businesses grow and become bureaucratic.

An interesting development in the literature on small firms is the notion of serial entrepreneurs who take particular pleasure and pride in starting up a business, growing it, then embarking on another new venture. Presumably they feel instinctively that once the business reaches a critical mass their skills are better suited in a new venture as opposed to running an existing one. Jim Clark is an example of someone who appears to be good at founding but not at running businesses. He established Silicon Graphics, which really took off in the early 1990s. Then in the mid-1990s he set up Netscape, but Jim Barksdale was recruited as the Chief Executive soon after it was established. Just after starting Netscape, Jim Clark established Healtheon and recruited Mike Long to be its Chief Executive.

There is, though, a major difficulty with the notion that all start-ups, and for that matter all small businesses, are entrepreneurial. It is possible to define an entrepreneur as someone who starts and runs a small business. *The New Shorter Oxford English Dictionary* defines an entrepreneur as 'a person who undertakes or controls a business or enterprise and bears the risk of profit or loss', but for us being an entrepreneur is more than this definition indicates. An entrepreneur, in our view, is creative, interested in innovation and willing to take risks to bring about innovation and business growth. In the case of many owners of small businesses these attributes are largely lacking. Many owner-managers say they do not want their business to grow beyond its present size. Many small firms stay about the same size for most of their lives with the owner-manager unwilling to take further risks to grow the business. This may well be a sensible and quite clever strategy as the death rate of small firms is very high, so risking growth could well result in failure. The very fact that so few small firms manage to make the transition into larger ones and so many cease trading within a few years of being founded could be taken as evidence of the wisdom of a non-entrepreneurial approach.

THE VULNERABILITY OF SMALL FIRMS

The central fact about small business, however large their role in a modern economy, is their vulnerability. As the VAT figures show for the UK, if 100 businesses register for VAT today, within three years 33 of them will have de-registered. Clearly VAT de-registration is only a proxy for firm failure and what exactly constitutes failure is disputed. Compulsory liquidations will be most likely to hit a business before it has even reached the tender age of six years. Hall's (1992) study of involuntary liquidations among small firms found predictable problems of funding products and marketing. However, among those that survived slightly longer, he found problems caused by strategic shocks (quoted by Storey, 1994: 105).

PLANNING AND STRATEGIC MANAGEMENT IN SMALL FIRMS

An argument can be put forward that both cultural changes – the so-called 'enterprise culture' – and regulatory changes have made it too easy for people to start a business. A business plan is invariably requested by a bank or some other institution when a firm is trying to borrow money (Fletcher, 1996; Stevenson and Coveny, 1996; and Mason and Rogers, 1996) or it is the 'thing' budding business owners are taught to produce on training courses. How effective are these plans in screening out the potential failures and stopping them from starting? How many people complete a business plan and then decide not to start up as the plan shows the business to be non-viable? Given the high failure rate of young firms it might well be that too many people are being tempted into small business ownership without being able to assess reasonably well the chances of success even after completing a business plan. Perhaps there is a need for more realistic business plans prior to start up?

Given the rather gloomy picture of the life cycle of many small firms – birth followed pretty quickly by death – presented above, is there any evidence to suggest that better planning would help? Small firms that plan ahead and have a formal business plan do appear to have a superior performance compared to those that do not (Joyce, Seaman and Woods, 1996). The general link between planning and small firm performance has been investigated by several researchers. For instance, Bracker, Keats and Pearson (1988) looked at the link between a firm's financial performance and its planning and found a positive link. Both Woo and colleagues (1989) and Kinsella and colleagues (1993) found that the growth of small firms was linked positively to planning.

Some studies have used meta-analysis to examine the role planning plays in small firm performance. Schwenk and Shrader (1993) concluded that planning was positively associated with growth. There appears to be quite a weight of evidence pointing towards the beneficial effects of planning on performance.

It is important to go beyond the simple correlation of planning and performance, to identify the functions of strategic planning in small firms. One suggestion is that strategic planning is a way of fostering entrepreneurial and innovatory behaviour in the small firm. Beaver and Ross (2000) report the findings of a survey of 87 small businesses in the UK Midlands. They observed (2000: 27):

> Simplifying greatly, a central finding in this enquiry was that the principal value of strategic planning to those firms that practised and valued it, was that they had a framework for their assessments of overall performance, bearing in mind that assessment often triggers the managerial will to improve... planning facilitates comparisons with alternative futures and opportunities... In essence, it was found that the most dynamic and progressive firms embraced strategic management... as a way of nurturing their own entrepreneurial motivation.

This is consistent with the view held by Wheelen and Hunger (1995) and Shirley (1989), amongst others, that to be an entrepreneur requires strategic planning. In fact Wheelen and Hunger go as far as arguing that as an entrepreneurial business is more oriented towards growth and innovation than other small businesses it requires strategic planning to realize its ambitions more than other small firms do. So, far from seeing strategic planning as an impediment to entrepreneurial and innovatory behaviour, they see it as a necessary part of it.

Planning may be functional in fostering innovation and entrepreneurial activity, but this does not mean that the typical owner-manager of a small firm will be keen on planning. As Curran (1996: 4513) points out, 'All decisions revolve around the entrepreneur with little reliance on formal planning techniques, except where these are harnessed to the entrepreneur's vision. Decisions can be swift, opportunistic, instinctive and bold and are rarely committed to paper.' Wheelen and Hunger (1995) support this view. They point out many small firms do not plan strategically. They give four reasons for this, drawing on research (eg Shrader, Mulford and Blackburn, 1989; Aronoff and Ward, 1990):

- Not enough time. It is a common observation that 'fire-fighting' consumes the time and the energy of managers in small firms leaving little spare to engage in strategic planning. For many the end of the week is a long time ahead when survival is the name of the game. There is strong evidence to show that business owners work longer hours than is the average for full-time employees (Curran and Burrows, 1988; and Storey, Watson and Wynarczyk, 1989). It may well be a problem of lack of time, but it might also be a combination of poor time management and low priority given to planning arising from doubts over its effectiveness.

- Fear that planning hems you in, stopping the firm responding flexibly and quickly to new opportunities and threats. This echoes what is said above, in part, about entrepreneurial behaviour and planning. Many owner-managers like to believe that they are quick on their feet, ducking and diving to survive and prosper in hostile environments. In this climate strategic planning is seen as a waste of valuable time. This fear of being hemmed in by the plan may well have its roots, in part, in the role strategic planning played in the 1960s. As a broad generalization strategic planning then was seen as involving top management as a decision-making élite, based on planning as the core activity, with change defined as programmed in advance, and the management of change treated as identical to the concept of strategic implementation. This type of approach to strategic management may be described as modernist (Joyce and Woods, 1996). One of the key assumptions of a modernist approach was that to a great extent the future was knowable and the firm could thus be programmed for success. This model of strategy increasingly came under pressure by events such as the emergence of the Japanese and other new competitors. It was also challenged by writers such as Mintzberg and Peters and Waterman, who in a series of articles, books and interviews poured vast amounts of cold water on this way of doing things. It can be argued that, while a more careful reading of the critics of the old style still gave some weight to planning, this got lost in the noise, and plans were seen as being too rigid, lacking the flexibility for the swiftly changing 1970s and onwards. Planning was a waste of time in these crazy days. While you were planning, your competitors were taking your business away. Fast, intuitive, spontaneous action was required, not ponderous planning that by the time the plan had been conceived, was already out of date. We argue throughout this book that while a rigid, modernist notion of strategic planning might inhibit innovation and entrepreneurial behaviour, forms of strategic planning are in fact necessary.

- Lack of skills in strategic planning. Owner-managers in small firms may never have had the opportunity or time to acquire the necessary skills for strategic planning. Buying in consultants to do part of the work for the business can be too expensive and the perceived benefit of using consultants anyway might be quite low to the owner-manager.

- Lack of trust and openness. Owner-managers often keep information to themselves, making it hard to involve a wider group of people in the design of a plan. The owner-manager thus might find it difficult to get an objective view about the business and its direction, relying more on managing by the 'seat of the pants'.

THE NATURE OF STRATEGIC MANAGEMENT IN SMALL FIRMS

Given that there is some evidence to indicate that planning is linked to better business performance, do we know much about how this planning takes place? In a recent survey we found strategic processes in about one-fifth of the businesses that employed less than 10 people. About half of these had what we call strategic performance management systems. This means they had strategic documents that contained strategic goals. The strategic goals were quantified or measurable. They had annual performance targets derived from the strategic goals. They even had performance reporting systems linked to a system or process for planning performance improvements. This degree of development of strategic processes is very impressive for such small businesses. This reinforces a point we made at the beginning of the chapter on the diverse nature of small firms. Just because a firm employs only a few people it does not necessarily make it similar to another.

Of course we also found four-fifths of such small businesses lacked strategic processes. Even among businesses employing between 10 and 49 employees, over half of them lacked any strategic processes.

Types of Strategic Management	1–9 Employees	10–49 Employees
No Strategic Management Processes	78.9%	56.5%
Strategic Planning used for Innovation	9.6%	14.1%
Strategic Performance Management System in place	10.4%	23.9%
Strategic Performance Management and Issue Management in place	1.1%	5.4%
Total (no. of cases)	100.0% (280)	100.0% (92)

Table 15.1 Strategic processes in small firms

While some small businesses might have well-developed strategic management, the usual assumption is that strategic management in small businesses typically needs to be a simplified version of that in a large business. Small firm managers, it is assumed, lack the skills and time to do what their counterparts in large organizations do. In the survey we mentioned above we also looked at the type of strategic tools owner-managers and other managers in small firms had heard of and whether or not they had used mission statements or business and strategic plans. As can be seen in Table 15.2, owner-managers were less likely to have heard of, or used, the specific tools as against the other managers. For instance, nearly 20 per cent of the owner/managers questioned as against 5 per cent of the other managers had not heard of competitor analysis. Similarly about 80 per cent of owner/managers as against only 54 per cent of other managers had not heard of SWOT. Nearly 90 per cent of the owner/managers had not used a mission statement as opposed to only 60 per cent of other managers. About four-fifths of owner-managers had not used strategic plans as against just over half of other managers.

Percentage of respondents who had not heard of the strategic tool or not used a mission statement, business plan or strategic plan.

Strategic tool	Owner-manager	Other manager
Market Research	0.00	0.00
Competitor Analysis	18.80	5.30
Risk Analysis	25.80	9.00
Benchmarking	42.20	16.90
Resource Analysis	46.90	25.70
Scenario	52.30	24.60
Business Plan	59.40	29.80
Core Competency	75.80	41.80
SWOT	80.50	54.00
Strategic Plan	82.00	54.40
Gap Analysis	87.70	60.80
Mission Statement	88.30	59.90
Blue-skying	89.90	69.00
PEST	90.60	67.50

Table 15.2 Strategic tools

This evidence seems consistent with the idea that owner-managed small businesses either do less strategic planning or do it very informally or unconsciously, whereas more professionally managed small firms are more likely to carry out intentional and deliberate strategic planning. And as we have pointed out in Chapter 2 and in this chapter, there is evidence that strategic management processes – including strategic performance management type processes – are correlated with better business performance.

CONCLUSIONS

Small businesses that want to be entrepreneurial and grow should introduce strategic management processes. These might be quite sophisticated ones and need not be inferior or simplified versions of those found in larger organizations. It does pay to set strategic goals, annual performance targets, and to create reporting systems and processes for planning improvements in strategic performance. It might also be worthwhile for small businesses to develop strategic issue agendas and set up projects and special budgets for tackling strategic issues. Even the smallest of businesses appear to benefit from such developments in strategic management.

QUESTIONS

1. We started the chapter by looking at some 'typical' television representations of small businesses. In what ways, if you strip away the comedy, are they reasonably accurate pictures of what running a small business is like?
2. What, according to Mintzberg, motivates people to start up their own businesses? Are there any other reasons?
3. How useful is the concept of a 'serial entrepreneur' in explaining the business activity of people such as Richard Branson?
4. The owner of our small bakery asks: Why does the business need to plan? What explanation would you give?
5. How persuasive is the evidence presented in the chapter that strategic management processes are correlated with better firm performance?
6. What techniques of strategic management would be useful for the small firm?
7. Are entrepreneurs strategic planners without realizing it?
8. Why is it important before developing a strategy for a small firm to understand the motivation of the owner(s) and principal stakeholders?
9. How do the management, ownership and competitive environment between a large and small firm compare and contrast?
10. Where does competitive advantage arise in small firms and how is this different from competitive advantage found in large firms?
11. In small firms, strategy, like all other areas of the business, is an extension of the owner's ability and personality. If the owner does not think it necessary to engage in strategic thinking he or she will not. Furthermore, informality will characterize all aspects of the business. Is this so wrong?
12. Is Porter right when he says, 'There are no substitutes for strategic thinking. Entrepreneurship unguided by strategic perspectives is more likely to fail than succeed'?

EXECUTIVE EXERCISE

This exercise is a simple one for executive students who are owners and managers of small businesses. It is based on the idea of cognitive mapping and can be done using several sheets of blank paper and a pen.

First, brainstorm your current top concerns about your small business. List these on a sheet of paper, and then rank them in order of seriousness. You can do this on a subjective basis. Next, take your top-rated concern and ask yourself why it is important to do something about this concern. You can cue your answers to this by saying 'It is important to take action to deal with this concern in order to...' Your answers should indicate what goals or outcomes might be achieved, or better achieved, as a result of taking action to deal with the concern. There may be several reasons why any particular concern needs to be addressed. Repeat this step for further concerns, taking them in the order of seriousness, until you have done the same for up to five to eight of the concerns. This may generate a long list of reasons why it is important to address your most serious concerns. Alternatively, you may find that the same reasons come up for each of the concerns. Make a note of the five to eight most important reasons you identify. Again this can be done subjectively.

Now, having established there are good reasons for doing something about your concerns, do some more brainstorming to generate ideas for action to deal with each of the five to eight top concerns in turn. This brainstorming may be cued by saying, 'This concern can be dealt with by...' You may think of several different options for handling each of your concerns. List all of them on a sheet of paper. When you have done this for all the concerns assess them for their feasibility. This can largely be done on the basis of checking whether your business has the resources required to implement an idea and on the basis that there will be sufficient support inside or outside the business to give the idea a reasonable chance of being implemented. Identify the top five to eight ideas in terms of their feasibility, and note these down.

Examine each of the five to eight ideas you consider most feasible and in each case ask yourself if there are any critical assumptions underpinning the idea. For example, you might cue answers to this by saying 'This idea can be implemented if...' Note the most important assumptions.

Finally, increase your understanding of your concerns, goals, actions and assumptions by mapping their interrelations on a fresh sheet of paper divided horizontally into four sections. As shown in Figure 15.1, the top five to eight goals are placed in the top section, the top five to eight concerns are placed in the section immediately below, then the actions in the section below that, and the assumptions are recorded in the bottom section. Wherever you can, based on your experience and intuition, draw connecting arrows between assumptions and actions, between actions and con-

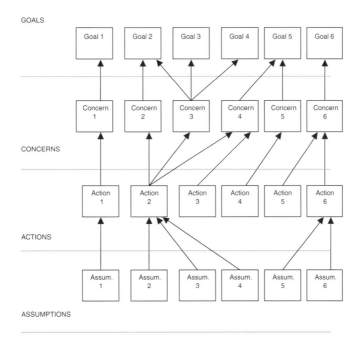

Figure 15.1 Cognitive mapping

cerns, and between concerns and goals. It is possible that this will be a complex map with, for example, individual actions being linked to several concerns, and several concerns being linked to a single goal. Studying this map may suggest new information about what actions might have the biggest pay-off in terms of important goals, how strategic goals can be better achieved, or maybe even how to package the action. Make a note of any conclusions you formulate on the basis of the mapping exercise.

REFERENCES

Aronoff, C E and Ward, J L (1990) Why owners don't plan, *Nation's Business*, pp 59–60

Beaver, G and Ross, C (2000) Enterprise in recession: the role and context of strategy, *International Journal of Entrepreneurship and Innovation*, February, pp 23–31

Bracker, J S, Keats, B W and Pearson, J N (1988) Planning and financial performance among small firms in a growth industry, *Strategic Management Journal*, November–December, pp 591–603

Curran, J (1996) *International Encyclopaedia of Business and Management*, **5**, Thomson Business Press, London

Curran, J and Burrows, R (1988) *Small business owners and the self employed in Britain: a secondary analysis of the general household survey, 1979–84*, A Report for the Economic and Social Research Council

Fletcher, M (1996) How bank managers make lending decisions to small firms, in *Small Firms: Contributions to economic regeneration*, eds R Blackburn and P Jennings, Paul Chapman Publishing Ltd, London

Hall, G (1992) Reasons for insolvency amongst small firms – a review and fresh evidence, *Small Business Economics*, **4** (3), pp 237–50

Joyce, P and Woods, A (1996) *Essential Strategic Management*, Butterworth-Heinemann, Oxford

Joyce, P, Seaman, C and Woods, A (1996) The strategic management styles of small businesses, in *Small Firms: Contributions to economic regeneration*, eds R Blackburn and P Jennings, Paul Chapman Publishing, London

Kinsella, R P *et al* (1993) *Fast Growth Firms and Selectivity*, Irish Management Institute

Mason, C and Rogers, A (1996) The business angel's investment decision: an exploratory analysis, in *Small Firms: Contributions to economic regeneration*, eds R Blackburn and P Jennings, Paul Chapman Publishing, London

Mintzberg, H (1991) The entrepreneurial organization, in *The Strategy Process: Concepts, contexts, cases*, eds H Mintzberg and J B Quinn, Prentice-Hall International, London

Schwenk, C R and Shrader, C B (1993) Effects of formal strategic planning on financial performance in small firms: a Meta-analysis, *Entrepreneurship: Theory and practice*, **17**, pp 53–65

Shirley, S (1989) Corporate strategy and entrepreneurial vision, *Long Range Planning*, December, p 107

Shrader, C B, Mulford, C L and Blackburn, V L (1989) Strategic and operational performance in small firms, *Journal of Small Business Management*, October, pp 45–60

Stevenson, P and Coveny, H (1996) A survey of business angels: fallacies corrected and six distinct types of angel identified, in *Small Firms: Contributions to economic regeneration*, eds R Blackburn and P Jennings, Paul Chapman Publishing, London

Storey, D J (1994) *Understanding the Small Business Sector*, Routledge, London

Storey, D J, Watson, R and Wynarczyk, P (1989) *Fast Growth Small Businesses: Case studies of 40 small firms in northern England*, Department of Employment, Research Paper 67

Wheelen, T L and Hunger, J D (1995) *Strategic Management and Business Policy*, Addison-Wesley, Reading, Mass.

Woo, C Y *et al* (1989) *Determinants of Growth for Small and Large Entrepreneurial Start-ups*, Babson Entrepreneurship Conference

16

The public sector

INTRODUCTION

In 1926 Franz Kafka published *Der Prozess* (*The Trial*) and in the following year *Das Schloss* (*The Castle*). In these books and in his other writings Kafka developed and elaborated a view of the world that has become to be known as Kafkaesque. In essence he wrote not only about the loneliness of human existence but also about the power bureaucracy has over us. In *The Trial* the main character is accused of a crime and summoned to a court to be judged. He never really finds out what he has been charged with or even much about the legal system that is prosecuting him. Chapter after chapter is taken up with his frustration at the literally faceless bureaucrats that inhibit the court buildings. The protagonist has little or no control over his fate. One of the key motifs in *The Trial* is that the protagonist's crime is not to know his crime.

Interestingly Kafka was not for most of his life a professional writer but a civil servant, and so he was presumably drawing upon his experiences to write about the officials that populated his novels. Whatever agenda the protagonists of his novels have these are obstructed easily by the administration he battles with. The castle and the court are there for the officials and not for the protagonists. The internal logic of what the officials do is hidden away from the protagonist leading to more frustration and isolation. These institutions exist for those who work there not for the public they are supposed to be serving. To use a bit of jargon, the people working in the court and the castle were too production-oriented and not sufficiently consumer-oriented.

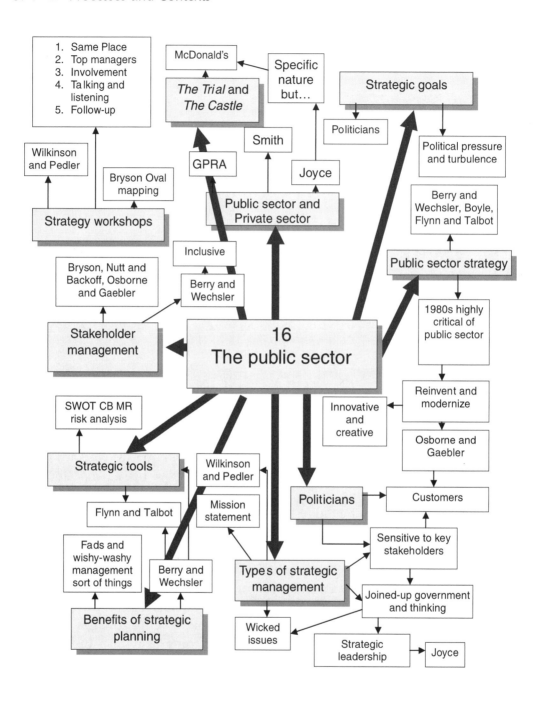

We are now going to risk a joke that has quite a sting in the tail. But it captures some of the frustration of the public with officials. A man walks into McDonald's one day and after being greeted asks, 'I sent a letter three weeks ago about my planning application and I haven't heard anything yet. Could you tell me what is happening?'

The woman at the counter replies, 'Sorry, sir, I think you need the council offices next door. This is McDonald's.'

The man looks a bit startled saying, 'I am sorry.'

As he leaves she smiles, saying, 'Have a nice day.'

Next day the man is back at McDonald's. 'Sorry to bother you but I sent a letter to the council about my planning application and I haven't heard anything yet. You haven't by chance misplaced my letter?'

The woman behind the counter looks puzzled. 'Sorry, sir, weren't you here yesterday about this?'

'Yes.'

'Well I am sorry but this is McDonald's and I think you need the council offices next door.' 'Oh sorry. Thank you.'

'You're welcome. And have a really nice day,' she says with a smile on her face.

Off he goes again in search of his letter.

You've guessed it, next day he is back. 'Hello, I wonder if you can help me?'

'Certainly, sir. What would you like – a Big Mac with fries, perhaps?'

'No, I'm still trying to find out what happened to my planning application.'

'But, sir, I've explained to you that you are in McDonald's not the council offices.'

This time he smiles and replies, 'Yes, I know, but I've figured out that there is as much chance of me finding my letter here as there is in the council offices and at least you deal with me quickly and in such a friendly way!'

For many people, while our treatment in the public sector may not be Kafkaesque, it is often not up to the standard set by the private sector. In this chapter we look at how the public sector is responding to this and other challenges it has in a strategic way.

PRIVATE AND PUBLIC

When we think of strategy it is tempting to focus just on the private sector, but over the last decade or so interest in using strategic planning and management in the public sector has increased (Smith, 1994). This has its roots, in part, in the way governments in the 1980s imposed strict spending limits on public sector organizations. In the 1990s government applied pressure for public services to meet performance targets, to become more responsive to people and business, to be more 'joined up', and to apply information and communication technology to open up new channels for access and increase efficiency. In the United States much of this was done under the banner of 'reinventing government'. Current efforts at reforming the public sector in the UK are referred to as 'modernizing' government. Within all this reform in the UK and elsewhere there has also been explicit support and encouragement by government for more strategic responses by public sector organizations. In the United States the Government Performance and Results Act (GPRA) of 1993 required all federal agencies to produce strategic plans.

What we want to do in this chapter is explore the differences, if any, between public and private sector strategic management. There is a view that the public sector sometimes hides behind alleged differences between the two sectors – some people have said that it is nonsense for public sector managers to concentrate on these differences, and that the public sector should be run more like the private sector.

We believe that there are distinctive features of the public sector located in its relationship to central government and political pressure that do make an important difference, especially in relation to stakeholder management. However, we do not thereby argue for the status quo. Both the modernization of the public sector and the introduction of strategic management can, and should, be done taking account of the specific nature of the public sector environment (Joyce, 1999).

STRATEGIC GOALS IN THE PUBLIC SECTOR

Obviously the public sector contains a range of different types of organizations, consequently generalizations about it are bound to suffer because of its diversity. A key point concerns how public sector organizations fit into political structures. A government department is under the direct control of the minister. The minister, through the cabinet in the UK and the Prime Minister, sets the overall strategy for the department, with senior civil servants advising on strategy and its implementation.

At the other end of the spectrum there are arms-length agencies that work at one step removed in the sense of their management arrangements, but for all that are still dependent on funding from public taxation. Politicians still set the broad agenda in which the agency operates but it has a degree of autonomy in the development and delivery of their service. In many public sector organizations the politician is a distant and remote figure whose words are filtered through many layers of management and bureaucracy before emerging. This sets a peculiar challenge to local managers, as tiers of authority have to be negotiated in the development and implementation of strategy. While we could detail many, quite complex, organizational structures, the main point is that senior managers in the public sector have always to align their organization's goals with the goals of the politicians. This means also that in the last analysis the public sector organization is having to adjust and adapt to political pressures, which in a democratic society mediate between the needs and aspirations of the public and the regulatory and service activities of public sector organizations. It should be stressed that in a democratic society it is the politicians that have legitimacy for decision making, not the public managers appointed to work in public organizations.

The public sector then has at its centre a political agenda to follow. This produces a degree of turbulence as policies change and new problems arise in the political domain. On the other hand, the invisible hand of the market can seem quite a distant threat, unlike for private sector firms. Private sector firms go out of business with alarming frequency. Public sector organizations often have quite a long life compared to the vast bulk of (small) private firms. So while the public sector does suffer from periodical reorganizations, and organizations do get closed down, with employees made redundant, perhaps it does have a degree of stability that the private sector does not. This, though, leads to a degree of inertia, making it harder for senior managers to introduce strategic change into their organizations.

PUBLIC SECTOR STRATEGY

Strategic planning began spreading in the private sector during the 1960s and 1970s, and then began to spread in the public sector in the 1980s and 1990s (Berry and Wechsler, 1995; Boyle, 1995a; Boyle, 1995b; Flynn and Talbot, 1996). So there appears to have been a 10–20 year lag between the two sectors.

During the 1980s considerable public dissatisfaction with levels of taxation and with access to and the quality of public services led to right-wing governments, or at least governments that were prepared to be highly critical of the public services. One of the main reasons put forward for the defects in the delivery of public services was that the managers and other professionals in the sector were not concerned enough about the services the sector provided for the public. Managers and professionals were more concerned with what they saw as good public sector management and service delivery that what the public wanted them to provide. In a real sense public sector officials and professionals thought they knew best. The officials and professionals defined the services – the needs of the public and how they were to be met. The public had little say. The public sector was remote, distant and out of touch.

As the pressure for change increased, strategic management appeared increasingly as part of a package of management innovations designed to 'reinvent' or 'modernize' the public sector (Osborne and Gaebler, 1992). The move from bureaucratic public sector organizations to responsive and innovative public sector organizations was seen as in large part possible by the introduction of strategic planning in government departments, agencies and elsewhere. The concerns that are apparent in the public sector mirror the concerns of the private sector. There is a need to be innovative and creative. To get in touch with and listen to 'customers' and, therefore, to be responsive to a range of influential stakeholders. The introduction of strategy into this context is seen as an essential prerequisite.

We can point to developments in the United States, Britain, Ireland, New Zealand, Australia, and elsewhere in Europe and it is a short step to suggesting a global trend in the use of strategic management in the public sector. Just as we have to be cautious when trying to make generalizations about the private sector, the same applies to the public sector in different national settings. There is yet to be an in-depth and thorough survey of these developments. Attention to local differences and culture are important in understanding the exact form that strategic management takes in the public sector in different national contexts. But there does appear to be in the developed world a trend towards senior managers in the public sector making use of strategic management.

Politicians are pressing for more clarity from managers about how desirable political goals will be pursued and with an emphasis on increased management data capacity. Performance by public sector organizations is being placed within an accountability framework. This accountability is enacted through goals, performance indicators and systems of reporting and auditing performance. The result is that public managers are setting up and embedding fairly classic forms of strategic planning. This means that there is a management capability for identifying performance deficits and planning performance improvement. Consequently, strategic plans in the public sector focus on ensuring that the public sector organization delivers a transparent system of goals and targets.

Can we provide a succinct summing up of the model of strategic management in the public sector? Heymann's (1987) analysis of a number of cases of public sector strategic management in the United States provides a very basic outline of the key elements and processes. The core of strategic management in the public sector is using planning to bring three things into a consistent alignment. These three things are:

- desirable strategic goals linked to the political objectives of elected politicians and public and social needs;
- external support from politicians, the public and other external stakeholders;
- organizational capacity.

It is evident from Heymann's analysis that organized constituencies among the public and business communities are powerful in defining issues that require external

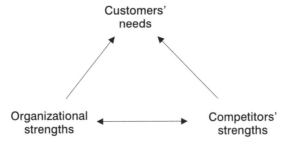

(a) Ohmae'private sector strategic management

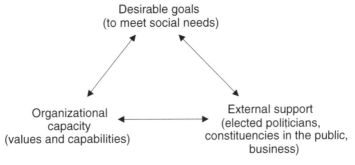

(b) Heymann's public sector strategic management

Figure 16.1 Ohmae's and Heymann's Models

support and thus in defining political objectives and public needs. External support is also important in dealing with the peculiar vulnerabilities of public sector organizations to public attack. The organizational capacity of a public sector organization, it should be noted, is a function of capabilities and values. Finally, we might also mention the importance of public sector leadership to develop interconnecting strategies with other organizations sharing responsibilities.

While we would emphasize the special nature of strategic management in the public sector, especially the involvement of elected politicians, it is also interesting that Heymann's model of strategic management, like that of Ohmae's model of private sector strategic management, is based on a 'triangle'. Indeed, as Figure 16.1 shows, the strategic triangles appear similar in a number of respects.

POLITICIANS

Politicians are sensitive to the views and reactions of key stakeholders. Once upon a time, perhaps, politicians could claim that they spoke for the public simply on the basis that they had been elected by citizens for four or five years. Nowadays politicians are acutely aware of the need to keep in touch with voters and a whole raft of stakeholders.

Arguably politicians must become more involved in strategic planning as it evolves and becomes more concerned with partnerships and involving the public. While organizations are only focused on efficiency and organizational achievement it is possible to see strategic planning as just a mechanism to reinforce goal-oriented behaviour by managers and employees. As the public sector becomes more 'joined up' and more responsive to the public, there arise deeper issues of balancing and negotiating priorities. Managers can do a limited amount of this balancing of priorities – but they lack the legitimacy of the elected politician.

So who does provide strategic leadership – politicians or managers? One answer is that it has to be a partnership of elected politicians and managers (Joyce, 2000). The managers are the junior partners, but there need to be forums in which politicians and managers exchange views, listen to each other, and together arrive at conclusions.

TYPES OF STRATEGIC MANAGEMENT

What types of strategic management currently exist? Some are based on mission and value statements. Another type is an expression of 'joined-up thinking'. In this issues are identified with the help of key stakeholders, partners outside the sector are enlisted, and resources aligned across several departments and even organizations to tackle the issues. A variant on this is to work on the responsiveness of the public organization, as this is one of the key problems the sector is perceived to have. Below we look at each of these types of strategic management in a bit more detail.

Some organizations have built their strategic management processes around a mission statement and set of core values. The content of these values may refer to public service, environmental concerns, valuing employees, equality of opportunity, and so on. The mission statement and core values may be meant to create a unified vision that allows top managers to devolve planning down to service delivery level. This type of strategic management model may stress cultural change and empowerment of managers at operational levels of the organization. The hoped for results may include reduced costs and greater levels of customer care.

Another approach to strategic management puts the emphasis on 'joined-up' government. The organization seeks out other public sector partners and is keen to explore coalignment of activities to address 'wicked issues' that are perceived to have emerged in recent years and be at the forefront of community well-being. In some cases, such as local government, this partnership approach to strategic management is extended to the private and voluntary sectors. The idea is to build networks or consortiums to jointly plan and implement strategy. One consequence of this type of approach is an interest in developing strategic forums in partnership with community representatives and public and private sector leaders. Another approach is to invite representatives of the external constituencies to join internal strategic review processes. The depth of such efforts can vary. In some cases the partners may be very loosely coordinated through the use of forums to develop strategic visions. It is left up to the partners to decide how this will be implemented. In other cases there may be joint planning and explicit agreements about the contribution of financial resources and skills in areas where there are overlapping mandates. This is more likely where the partners are all public sector organizations. The most minimal form of coordination of public sector partners is simple consultation during the process of formulating a strategic plan.

A third style or approach to strategic management is one in which the emphasis is on using the strategic planning process to increase responsiveness to the public. Perhaps the most obvious example of this is the application of whole systems development ideas to the development of a strategic plan (Wilkinson and Pedler, 1996). This involves bringing together all the internal stakeholders with members of the public to develop both the strategic plan and implementation plans. The crux of such a process is carefully orchestrated listening, dialogue, debate and learning in a highly transparent public event.

Of course, there is no reason why public sector organizations should not combine all these different styles either concurrently or in a hybrid form of strategy formulation. In such a case the top managers may be looking for enhanced performance, the benefits of partnership working, community problem solving, responsiveness to public needs, and the fullest possible consensus embracing professionals, other employees, partner organizations and the public. Reading through this it is fairly obvious just how skilled strategists have to be in the public sector. To achieve this a change programme frequently needs to be put in place to bring into line employees with the new strategic direction and thrust of the organization.

BENEFITS OF STRATEGIC PLANNING

The benefits of becoming skilled in the use of strategic tools and thinking strategically often have a bad press from managers and professionals in the public sector. They believe that there are a lot of fads and fashions in management that are pretty meaningless. They feel that things such as business process re-engineering, TQM, etc, achieve little or, worse, have a negative impact on how well they do their jobs.

Training does not easily change these attitudes. Some public managers resist the training. They resent having been sent on a course to learn about strategic planning because senior managers think this is a good idea. They feel that time spent on this training is time wasted as they should have been doing their job.

Also, many managers are professionals trained in fields other than management. Management is seen as a wishy-washy sort of thing where there appears to be no 'one best way' and 'it all depends'. Professionals can have great difficulty with this as their training as a town planner, or engineer, or care worker would not have necessarily encompassed such a degree of uncertainty. They simply have a different mindset. They feel that what they are taught about strategy is either so obvious that it is valueless or so unlikely that it cannot be true. They may also have difficulty with the way knowledge is established and the short shelf-life it appears to have compared to the knowledge they have acquired in their own professional training. All these things can make it hard for public managers to embrace strategy.

In spite of everything we have just said, however, a survey comparing the private sector and local government showed that local government managers did perceive benefits from strategic planning, and they were often the same benefits identified by their private sector counterparts (Flynn and Talbot, 1996).

Benefit	Local Government (n = 241)	Private Sector (n = 132)
	%	%
Achieved goals and objectives	81	81
Specified milestones	70	77
Allowed better use of resources	69	5
Gave staff unified vision	59	64
Provided new opportunities and ideas	54	51
Achieved cost savings	43	68
Put resources into areas of opportunity	41	51
Source: Flynn and Talbot, 1996		

Table 16.1 Benefits of strategic planning (UK study)

The local government managers saw strategic planning as helping to achieve goals and objectives, to specify milestones, to create a unified vision, and to identify new opportunities and ideas. In these respects the local government managers resembled their private sector counterparts. In addition, they also saw strategic planning as helping to make better use of resources. On the face of it, this survey is quite an endorsement for strategic planning by UK local government managers. It seems as though this is a process of considerable value in the public sector as it is in the private sector.

A 1992 survey of directors of US state agencies also found that strategic planning was a positive experience (Berry and Wechsler, 1995). In one question respondents were asked about the important outcomes of the strategic planning process. Seventy-one per cent claimed that service delivery improvements were important outcomes. The most important outcomes, however, were often linked to decision-making requirements. Strategic planning had established the management direction, clarified the priorities of the state agencies, and guided policy and budget decisions. Such benefits, of course, would be most appreciated by top management that has responsibility for such decisions. Berry and Wechlser (1995: 165) commented: 'Based on the positive comments and assessments from senior state executives expressed in this national survey, strategic planning has produced to date very little disillusionment among those who have used it in state agencies.'

Outcomes	Respondents identifying outcomes as 'most important'	Respondents identifying outcomes as 'important'
	%	%
Established management direction	30	90
Clarified agency priorities	17	90
Guide to policy decisions	11	82
Guide to budget decisions	9	73
Gaining support for budget priorities	7	62
Greater commitment to customer satisfaction	6	59
Improved teamwork	4	67
Service delivery improvements	3	71
Source: Berry and Wechsler, 1995		

Table 16.2 Outcomes of strategic planning in state agencies (US study)

This research shows that the scepticism and cynicism that can be shown by some managers towards strategic planning in the public sector may well be unrepresentative. So if you are a manager from the public sector with colleagues who question why you are studying strategy you might like to point these results out to them. This may go some way to persuading them about the benefits.

The benefits of strategic planning may evolve over time. Top managers may early on appreciate the benefits they get from the use of strategic planning to set clear directions and priorities and from having a framework for policy and budgetary decisions. Subsequently, planning may be enhanced to involve more stakeholders and develop more formal plans. Finally, as experience accumulates, perhaps the time horizons for planning lengthen and strategic planning processes are integrated with other management systems (eg budgetary and quality management systems).

STRATEGIC TOOLS

The activities through which strategic plans are formulated and implemented are very varied. However, in the US study by Berry and Wechsler (1995) there was a widespread use of both goal setting and strategic issue management. Other common analytical activities were conducting SWOT analyses, stakeholder analysis and environmental scanning. This is much as might be expected on the basis of textbooks of strategic management.

Flynn and Talbot (1996) also provide some evidence of the types of analytical activities found in local government. They report that the top four techniques were the same for both local government and for private sector managers:

- SWOT analysis;
- cost/benefit analysis;
- market research;
- risk analysis.

Technique	Local Government (n = 392)	Private Sector (n = 183)
	%	%
SWOT	54	57
Cost/benefit	52	42
Market research	47	64
Risk analysis	44	38
Workshops	44	10
Cost analysis	41	14
Executive info systems	40	26
7S framework	29	3
Competitors (Five Forces Analysis)	23	37
Source: Flynn and Talbot, 1996		

Table 16.3 Techniques Used in Strategic Planning (UK study)

However, while the top four activities were the same, the local government managers differed from the private sector managers in the use of workshops for strategy formulation. It is possible that this reflects the greater concern in the public sector to create coalitions for change. Flynn and Talbot (1996: 31) speculate as follows: '... one interpretation is that it clearly seems to be a much more political (in both an organizational and a formal political sense) process which requires more negotiating between key stakeholders, for which workshops are an ideal provisions.' So a greater emphasis on stakeholder analysis and management may be correlated with a greater tendency to employ workshops to formulate strategies. In the public sector it may well be the case that employees are given more say in the development of strategy because they can be more effective in blocking or delaying its implementation. In the private sector senior managers might well worry less about persuading employees to be 'on message' so less use is needed of forums where discussion and persuasion can take place to win over employees to the strategy.

STAKEHOLDER MANAGEMENT

There are powerful arguments in favour of the proposition that the main difference between private and public sector strategic planning relates to the importance of stakeholder management and processes of coalition building in the public sector (Bryson, 1995; Nutt and Backoff, 1992). Osborne and Gaebler (1992: 234) underline this point as follows: 'A government has more stakeholders than a business, and most of them vote. To change anything important, many of those stakeholders must agree. This is the piece most private sector versions of strategic planning miss...'

It is possibly because of the need for consensus that public sector leaders must think in terms of negotiations and issue management as well as in terms of mission-led strategic planning. This can be problematic for senior managers as they may well feel that by the time they have negotiated successfully with various stakeholders the world has moved on and the importance of the original issue has decreased. While stakeholder management, coalition building and issue management may have special importance in the public sector, we may also be witnessing the rise of another difference – the growth of processes for including the public in strategy formulation.

As strategic planning evolves in public sector organizations it appears that the distinctive character of the planning process becomes more adapted to public sector conditions. Hence, Berry and Wechsler (1995) reported that among the changes made to strategic planning by state level agencies was the development of the process to make them more inclusive. This meant that more internal and external stakeholders were included in the process of strategic planning.

Stakeholder analysis can help politicians and managers to formulate mission statements. This involves identifying the relevant stakeholders and the criteria they apply to judging the success or failure of the public sector organization. It is then important to assess the relative ability of the stakeholder groups to have an impact on the organization. The exercise is directly useful in identifying all the potential beneficiaries of the organization's activities. The mission statement can then be framed in a way that looks likely to generate support from powerful or influential stakeholders who might benefit from the organization. This ensures that the strategic goals (defined in terms of benefits) and external support are logically aligned.

Stakeholder analysis can also help when planning the implementation of strategy. As discussed in Chapter 13, this is a matter of anticipating how different stakeholders will be likely to react to a proposed strategy. This may be understood in terms of a continuum from hostility to support. If this then is considered along with the relative importance (power or influence) of the stakeholders, it becomes immediately obvious where the key sources of resistance to change are. Nutt and Backoff (1992) have provided some simple outline guidance on how stakeholders may be managed in the public sector.

STRATEGY WORKSHOPS

Strategy workshops are often organized on the basis of a tightly controlled agenda and timetable of activities that are supervised by process facilitators. The workshops may comprise one or more teams working through a series of analytical steps with presentations, discussions and evaluation. For example, the teams may be asked to do a stakeholder analysis, identify strategic goals, carry out a SWOT analysis and then brainstorm some possible strategic actions. The detail of the activities may be based on the use of techniques to maximize the involvement of participants and to enhance levels of problem solving and creativity. The activities may also be designed to build a consensus among the participants. Consequently, everybody may be invited to use brainstorming to generate ideas and the facilitator will use grouping of ideas and voting to produce agreement. Where the teams consist of management teams from different departments of the same organization, the presentations and evaluation processes used may be employed in a way that increases their public commitments to action plans.

Some workshops may be based on the use of a single technique. For example, Bryson (1995) describes the use of the oval mapping technique. This also emphasizes the use of brainstorming and places a premium on creativity. It is called the oval mapping process because strategic options are placed on oval-shaped pieces of paper and stuck on flip chart paper. These can be moved around and a map of strategic issues, goals and strategic options can be produced. The process can be used with groups of 15 or more managers and tends to be very interactive and enjoyable.

It may be stretching the term a little, but whole systems development events can be seen as a large-scale workshop. These events are ideal for developing very inclusive strategic planning processes. Wilkinson and Pedler (1996) have described one such event at Walsall Council in detail. In this case the Chief Executive and the Head of Policy were anxious to have plans that were owned by as many people as possible. About one-fifth of those who took part – nearly 300 people in all – were service users. The detail of the activities in the Walsall Council event appeared to be designed to get a dialogue going between top management and everybody else. Feedback and presentations were key aspects of the two-day event. Ideas were put on 'post-its' and placed around the hall in which the event was held. People were encouraged to show their support for ideas by ticking them.

Wilkinson and Pedler's report of the event make it clear that public learning by the top management was an important feature of the event. This was critical to the dynamics of the event. Perhaps it is crucial for employees and service users to see their feedback actually influencing the top managers before their very eyes.

The five key principles of whole systems development are as follows. First, getting everybody with a stake in the strategic plan together in the same place. Second, top managers being publicly questioned and getting feedback, and as a consequence changing their direction. Third, involving those who will have to implement the strategy as well as those who are usually seen as the architects of strategy. Fourth, making sure everyone has a chance to have their say and making sure that there is effective listening through the use of small group working. Fifth, the high expectations created by the event must be followed up. If there is poor follow-up then there is a risk that damage will be done to the credibility of the strategic leadership.

Workshops should take a lot of effort. They should be carefully planned. If this trouble is taken and energy is put into them then strategic planning can become much more inclusive.

CONCLUSIONS

Strategic management is rapidly establishing itself within modern public sector organizations. The importance of strategic management in reinventing government – or modernizing the public services – no doubt reflects the range of benefits and functions it is expected to fulfil. It may allow more freedom to managers to manage because it increases accountability to politicians. It provides increased performance and value for the public while providing a framework for innovation. It has the potential to include employees, partners and even the public.

In this chapter we have drawn attention to the distinctive conditions and special features of the practice of strategic management in the public sector. We have underlined the importance of stakeholder management, strategic issue management and coalition building.

Political pressures, and ultimately public demands, have made strategic planning an indispensable tool for public sector managers building modern organizations and responsive and innovative services.

QUESTIONS

1. What is 'joined-up' government and how might it affect strategy development in the public sector?
2. Who is in charge of strategy in the public sector?
3. Why is the public sector moving from a bureaucratic focus to a responsive and innovative one?
4. Who are the customers of the public sector? Are they different from its stakeholders?
5. What role do politicians play in the development and implementation of strategy in the public sector? Should they play such roles?
6. What types of strategic management exist in the public sector?
7. How would you go about convincing a manager in the public sector that they should learn about, embrace and use strategic planning tools?
8. What tools would you recommend a manager in the public sector to learn in order to engage effectively with strategy?
9. Why is stakeholder management so important in the public sector? Is this really any different from the private sector?
10. Write a brief outlining the benefits of holding a strategy workshop in a public sector organization. In the brief sketch out how you would organize a two-day workshop on strategy.

EXECUTIVE EXERCISE

This exercise is designed for executive students currently working in the public services. Performance management within a strategic framework is currently a hot issue in the public services. This simple exercise is designed to encourage you to think creatively about actions to achieve strategic goals and performance targets. In preparation for this exercise you will need to carry out research on your organization in respect of the following:

- The main strategic goals and priorities of the organization.
- Financial plans for the services as a whole and your part of it.
- Performance targets applicable to the whole service and to departments – especially those most closely relating to the main strategic goals and priorities of the whole organization.
- Trends in patterns of usage of the services of your organization – for example, trends in who has used your service over the last seven years, changed user expectations, etc.
- Major social and economic trends over the last seven years – especially those affecting the lifestyles of your service users.

Based on the preparatory research you have done, please identify in Worksheet 1 the top strategic goals of your organization and performance targets based on them for years 1, 2, 3, 4 and 5.

	Annual performance targets (year)				
Strategic goals	1	2	3	4	5
1.					
2.					
3.					
4.					
5.					
6.					
7.					
8.					

Worksheet 16.1

Now identify your organization's main stakeholders. Suggest the criteria used by each of the stakeholders to assess the effectiveness of your organization. Also assess the relative importance of each stakeholder as low, medium or high. Summarize the results of your analysis in Worksheet 16.2.

Stakeholder	Criteria	Importance
1.		
2.		
3.		
4.		
5.		
6.		
7.		
8.		

Worksheet 16.2

Please list in Worksheet 16.3 what you see as the key events, trends and turning points that you think occurred over the past seven years. These may have been inside or outside your organization. Please rate them for importance on a scale of 1 to 10, using 1 for 'only slightly important' and 10 for 'very important'.

Events, Trends and Turning Points	Importance
1.	1.
2.	2.
3.	3.
4.	4.
5.	5.
6.	6.
7.	7.
8.	8.

Worksheet 16.3

Please reflect on the data you have reported in the previous two Worksheets, and list in Worksheet 16.4 the main opportunities and constraints you think will be important now and for the next few years.

Opportunities	Constraints
1.	1.
2.	2.
3.	3.
4.	4.
5.	5.
6.	6.
7.	7.
8.	8.

Worksheet 16.4

Finally, brainstorm some ideas for action based upon taking account of the strategic goals and the opportunities and constraints. List the ideas in Worksheet 16.5.

Ideas for Action	Does Action Address a Strategic Goal and Performance Target?
1.	Yes/No
2.	Yes/No
3.	Yes/No
4.	Yes/No
5.	Yes/No
6.	Yes/No
7.	Yes/No
8.	Yes/No

Worksheet 16.5

REFERENCES

Berry, F S and Wechsler, B (1995) State agencies' experience with strategic planning: findings from a national survey, *Public Administration Review*, March–April, **2**, pp 159–68

Boyle, R (1995a) *Developing Management Skills*, Institute of Public Administration, Dublin

Boyle, R (1995b) *Towards a New Public Service*, Institute of Public Administration, Dublin

Bryson, J (1988, 1995) *Strategic Planning in Public and Nonprofit Organisations*, Jossey-Bass, San Francisco

Flynn, N and Talbot, C (1996) Strategy and strategists in UK local government, *Journal of Management Development*, **15** (2), pp 24–37

Heymann, P (1987) *The Politics of Public Management*, Yale University Press, London

Joyce, P (1999) *Strategic Management for the Public Services*, Open University Press, Buckingham

Joyce, P (2000) *Strategy in the Public Sector*, Wiley, Chichester

Nutt, P and Backoff, R (1992) *Strategic Management of Public and Third Sector Organizations*, Jossey-Bass, San Francisco

Ohmae, K (1982) *The Mind of the Strategist*, McGraw-Hill, London

Osborne, D and Gaebler, T (1992) *Reinventing Government*, Addison-Wesley, Reading, Mass.

Smith R J (1994) *Strategic Management and Planning in the Public Sector*, Longman, Harlow

Wilkinson, D and Pedler, M (1996) Whole systems development in public service, *Journal of Management Development*, **15** (2), pp 38–52

Reading 16.1

Taken from The new manager and learning to manage strategically, in *Managing in the New Local Government* by Paul Corrigan, Mike Hayes and Paul Joyce (1999)

Restructuring, reorganization, change, change and more change

Most, but not all, local government managers take up new managerial positions either as a result of, or in the middle of, some form of restructuring or reorganization of their authority or their department. When most managers take over a new post in local government, they experience in the first few days real problems of confusion and in many cases chaos. Of course some of this is just the experience of 'the new'. But so many of these new experiences are really painful that we believe that something pathological has been, and is, happening in these organizations.

One of the reasons for this experience is the emotion that managers bring to their expectations of the task of management. Too many managers believe that given their title and their job description they should be able to shape their part of the organization in such a way as to make anything happen that should happen. So if their job description is to 'manage effectively the staff under their control', they believe that they should be able to get the staff to do everything that is necessary. Given this new job, and given the fact that it says 'manager' in their title, then it is their responsibility to 'run things'. So they bring an expectation of being able to run things with them to the job.

However, very quickly they experience the world as 'beyond their control'. Immediately things start happening which demonstrate that they are not 'in control'. For many this feeling that they are 'not in control' leaves them feeling that there is nothing they can do.

This can be a common experience for managers, new and old. In fact, all local government managers, whatever they are managing, are a part of a much wider organization. Under those circumstances no one manager is 'in control' of their work. A chief executive and a team leader on a dust cart are both part of a nexus of pressures, most of which come from outside of the whole local authority – from central government, from the public and from the law. There are, of course, also pressures that come from inside the local authority.

In this state managers move between an expectation that they *should* be able to entirely shape the part of the organization that they are 'in charge' of, and the experience that, actually, things constantly occur which undermine that ability to control. It is this contradiction more than anything else that makes people feel confused about how they might manage in their new job. One thing is clear, they cannot 'take control', even if emotionally they feel they need to. One of the things that this chapter will aim to achieve is at least a debate with those emotional expectations.

This means that some managers veer backwards and forwards between the expectation of total control and the experience of not having sufficient power – and in that experience of not having sufficient power they begin to blame themselves. Every chapter in this book addresses that experience, but we want to start by asking the manager to reflect on their experience of entering their new work, the feelings they had when confronting the confusion of their new task and how they dealt with it.

The aim of this chapter is to 'normalize' what would otherwise be an isolating experience. What we mean by 'normalization' is a process which points out to managers that the experience that they might have had, which they may have felt was caused by their personal inadequacies, is in fact a normal one, caused not by their personality but by the interaction between external factors and how they expect management to be.

The process of normalization encourages the individual in a difficult position to understand the structural factors that are making their personal experience so difficult. In commonsense language it makes the point that what you may feel is bad for you as an individual is in fact 'the same for everyone'. How you deal with it may be different, but in truth every single person who takes on a new management task in local government does so with some real trepidation and anxiety about how they will do. That anxiety comes from the very difficult structural situation of change that the whole of local government is taking part in.

How we deal with that anxiety, how we begin to take some small control of this changing world, is the hallmark of what separates a good manager from a bad one. But it is certain that a new manager in modern local government enters the job with some anxiety, and if they do not feel that anxiety then they do not live in the real world.

Task 3.1

If you have just taken up your first management job, or are about to, or are contemplating applying for a promotion, what are your key concerns? If it is now some time since you were appointed to your present management job, can you remember what your concerns were at the outset? Please list the top ones below.

1. _____   4. _____
2. _____   5. _____
3. _____   6. _____

Taking just the most serious concern on the list, what do you think is (was) causing the concern? Is it concern about your own expertise? Is it concern about your ability to lead as well as manage? Is it concern about making sense of the situation and solving problems? Is it concern about how others will act or react? Make a note of what the causes might be, and bear these in mind as we explain how you can handle the adjustment to being a new manager.

Being strategic and not tactical in decision-making

Amongst all of this change it is imperative to try and construct a way of making sense not just of the overall parameters of change but also of the way in which you can influence the situation. It is important, in other words, to make strategic decisions and not just be tactical in decision-making (Drucker, 1955). A great deal of management literature has been written about strategic management. Most of that literature relates to managing whole organizations and the necessity of doing so with an overall strategy (Smith, 1994). But it is important for all managers to be strategic in the sense of analysing their situation and their resources, and not taking the requirements of the situation as given. This means taking the trouble to find the right questions, whereas tactical decisions assume the questions are obvious and just address the need to find the right answers.

The reason for creating a strategy for an organization is to provide some form of possible future map for where that organization is going. Strategic management tries to make the organization pro-active in a difficult world that the organization cannot control. The same is true of strategy within a small part of the organization.

If strategic decisions are well constructed then they are straightforwardly aimed at the problem we outlined at the beginning of the chapter. We explained that some managers felt that they had to be in total control in order to carry out their management tasks and when they found they could not control everything fell into a kind of immobilization where they believed they could achieve nothing. Strategic thinking and decisions provide a kind of plan for the manager by mapping out what they need to address, why they need to achieve certain results, and how they can control or influence actions to bring about the desired results. As a result, the manager is pragmatic in their observance of the limits of what they can control or influence.

There are many different definitions of strategy in books on strategic management. Generally they can be thought of as ideas for actions which are hypothesized to produce outcomes which are important for the organization's performance and long-term success (however that is defined) (Nutt and Backoff, 1992).

So what do we need to create a strategy and how do we do it? We will suggest that we need four things to build a strategy.

1. First it is vital to understand the context in which the part of the organization you are managing is operating.
2. Second it is important to gather as much information as possible.
3. Third it is important to construct a structure of aims, targets and indicators.
4. Fourth it is important to try out these aims and targets within the immediate structure of your work.

This chapter will exemplify the creation of a strategy by looking at those first few weeks of a new job. A time when it is possibly the most difficult to know exactly what you are doing is the best time to try and construct a strategy to give you a view of where you are going. We are not concerned here with the highly technique-oriented approaches found in textbooks, but with the clear and logical decision-making needed by a manager in the thick of operational matters.

The new manager needs to understand the particular context of change

So, imagine the new manager on their first day in their new job in a newly restructured part of the organization. They are sitting in their new chair at their new desk. How can they think and act strategically?

On many occasions, the management job they will have walked into will be completely new as a task to the organization as a whole, let alone new for that particular person. Under these circumstances it is vital as a part of the preparation for starting this new management job to fully understand how their new tasks are a part of that wider restructuring. This process of placing their new work in the wider context of the recent restructuring has two main consequences.

First, and most obviously, it gives the manager a wider understanding of how their work will fit in with the new organization. If the new manager reviews the main changes in local government that we outlined in Chapter 1 they will almost certainly be able to understand their recent reorganization in the context of one or more of those structural changes. If the manager carries out that task they can place their whole reorganization, let alone their particular job, in the wider context. This contextualization will provide important insights into how to do their particular job.

Second, putting their new job in context not only provides them with an intellectual understanding, but will remind them, from the very beginning, that it is not possible for them to manage without that wider context. This strong reminder of context combats the simple way in which the manager's emotions can occasionally lead them to believe that they can 'control' their work.

- Context teaches the manager who may want to control their world that they cannot.
- Context demonstrates that the small part that each manager plays in an organization is dependent on others.
- Context shows that when something changes outside the immediate workplace it can have a dramatic impact on how the manager works.

The manager needs to start their new job by placing it in context and by continuing to look again and again at that context. Throughout this book we will be linking context with the detail of skill development.

 Task 3.2

Look at the last reorganization of your specific work. Look at the main themes in Chapter 1 and locate that reorganization within them. Why did your work change?

Gather intelligence from other staff before the manager starts

One clear way to success for a new manager preparing to enter the difficult experience of a new post when surrounded by possible confusion is to make sure that they talk to all of the main actors who have been, or will be, working there before they start. From the moment the new manager starts the post, they will be expected by most people around them to fill it. Whilst this may be unfair, work in local government rarely paces itself to be a part of a probationary period. When the manager starts, it starts.

First, it may be possible that the post had a previous post-holder who would be prepared to talk with the new manager. Where were the problems? What were the good parts of it and how did they see the job progressing? The new manager should ask advice freely and from an obvious position of ignorance. They can feel free not to know very much, because, well, they don't know much at this point.

It may also be that the previous post-holder has been promoted to become the new manager's future boss. This is obviously a different situation and the intelligence gathered may be less value free. But it is still worth the new manager talking to the person who was last in the chair, sometime before they sit in it.

Second, before the new manager starts, even if the post is at the other end of the country, they should make some appointments to talk through things with their future boss and staff. The first appointment needs to be with their new boss. The new manager needs to talk with them about what their expectations are about the post they are about to fill. The new manager should ask them what the main challenges are in the next year, what they would like to happen, what special problems there are, and what general problems there are for the department and the local authority. They should ask if there are any major changes being planned for the local authority and what the members think they are doing. It is likely that in an hour the new manager will get a very great deal of 'intelligence' about their expectations and about the authority. In this discussion they will not expect much in return, but at some stage the new manager can promise to fill them in with some of the recent experiences that they have had from outside their new authority.

The new manager may also be able to get some of the main bits of paperwork that will govern their job. They should ask their boss for any papers that he or she thinks might be useful. And when the manager has the papers, it is important to read them. They can be very useful for understanding the history and the culture of an authority, as well as for finding out about current service and organizational matters. If there are reports or surveys of what the public think of the services, these too are invaluable.

It will also be wise, if a manager is completely new to an authority, to ask the future boss if any of the staff applied for the job that the new manager will be filling. Given the way in which local government works, it's possible that one of them had been 'acting up' in the post the new manager is about to take up, for about a year. They may even have felt they were 'promised it'. This may not only mean that they are a bit resentful but most of the other staff may feel they are hard done by as well.

Having met the boss for an informal chat, the new manager should do the same with the staff. It's probably over formal to talk to them all before the start, but it's worthwhile having an informal cup of tea with a group of them. Putting names to faces and jobs to desks will make the early days a lot easier. Again, the new manager should ask them if there is anything that he or she should be reading before they come into the job.

All of these meetings and papers provide the new manager with important information about the job and how they can best fill it.

Task 3.3

Think through all of the intelligence that you have about the new job before you start it. Start with the job description and, if there is one, the person specification. Think through the application you made and the interviewing process. Then think through the results of the discussions you have had. From all of this information list the three main problems that you think you will face in your first three months. Think through the main three achievements that you want to make in the first three months. Write these up and keep them.

If you haven't started a new job for some time, think back to what you knew about your current management job before you started it. Think how right or wrong those first impressions were and reflect on how you might have been better prepared.

Set out targets and aims

An appraisal and development system provides one of the main parts of the scaffolding of the structure of a manager's work. Motivating and supporting employees is a core component of most managers' work. Any manager in a new managerial task has to build that scaffolding for their work as quickly as possible. Being appraised is in many ways a lot more difficult than appraising people, since the person being appraised must make demands on their manager for their individual development alongside that of the organization.

A new manager particularly needs to start this process with their new boss. Either within the appraisal and staff development system, or within their first formal interview, the new manager needs to ask their new boss what is expected. The new manager should set some immediate and medium-term joint targets. These should be realistic and capable of being measured. They should not be vague, as in the goal of 'managing my staff successfully'. It is important to ensure that the definition of what counts as success and failure is agreed.

It is important for the manager to gain as much information as possible from this interview about the wider strategies of their department and the council. It is essential that their first draft strategic document fits their part of the management task into an overall council strategy. No organization can move forward unless there are strong relationships between its constituent parts. In management jargon, successful organizations succeed in developing strategic coherence and alignment of functional and service strategies and resources with the overall organizational strategic intent. So, any small strategy must fit in with the large strategy.

Specifically the manager needs to know how this all fits in with what the members of the authority have decided. Every aspect of local authority activity receives its legitimacy for action from some member's decision or another. It is a very good idea for a manager to familiarize themselves with what the members have decided for their area of work. The manager should have copies of the papers that have been passed by the relevant committee, and they may want to meet the relevant chair of the committee at some time.

These are very important aspects of local authority organization since the members provide the legal and democratic legitimacy for actions. Knowing exactly what the members want the council's officers to do is crucial.

It is also important to obtain as much information as possible about what the public think of your area of work. How many recent complaints have there been? Have members' surgeries been inundated with requests about the area of work? Have the local newspapers shown any interest? Have there been any user surveys carried out in your area of work? Increasingly, council officers are wanting to understand the detailed perceptions and needs of the public, and not just whether they are broadly satisfied or not with the services.

As we shall see, managing local authority work must involve a relationship with the public. Therefore finding out as early as possible what evidence there is about what the public think of your work is important. When the manager has obtained the evidence about what the public think about the service, they should make sure that it can be incorporated into any draft strategy that is being drawn up. On many occasions the messages from the public can be very difficult but it is important to incorporate what they think and feel. The public must provide a continual reference point for all public service work in local government.

The main aim of this initial set of discussions between the manager and their boss is to draw up an initial contract with them. It will take some time to work out this contract properly and see it as the cornerstone of any future strategy. It is vital to understand how often the manager will be able to see their boss for supervision and discussion.

Make an early contract with staff

In nearly every single management task in local government the main resource in carrying out that task is the staff. In some parts of local government there may be some important and expensive machines and everywhere there are offices and buildings with IT equipment, but without the staff nothing at all can be achieved. So the development of strategy depends upon a manager's ability to motivate and develop their staff.

Chapter 6 is devoted to the issue of managing people. But in this chapter we are saying that in developing a strategy it is essential to recognize the core importance of staff in that development. One of the main themes in the management literature that covers such issues as creating a vision or developing mission statements or strategies is the importance of stakeholders owning that vision or strategy. What does this phrase mean?

It is the manager's staff who will implement the strategy and they too have to own the direction of their work. Obtaining this ownership is not a mystical process. Staff will want to be involved in discussing it as early as possible. In Chapter 5 we outline how to communicate through meetings and discussion. The manager may need two or three meetings with their staff sorting this through. Starting with an exploratory one and ending with a meeting where the staff 'sign off' with their agreement to the strategy (see the box below for some ideas on the content of these meetings). This may seem a lot of meeting time to spend on one issue, but the strategic document potentially transforms the way in which everyone works, so it is vital that staff members feel a part of it.

A process for carrying out a strategic review with staff

At the very first meeting of a manager and their staff to discuss strategy, the manager is advised to agree the status of the meetings: are the meetings consultative or decision-making ones? Will the manager listen to all the ideas and contributions but make their own decisions? Or, if the manager is willing to make decisions within these meetings, which matters are for decision and which are matters lying outside the scope of these meetings? If these questions are not agreed at the outset the process can get into diffi-culty, with staff feeling that they have been misled.

The meetings themselves can cover eight steps.

1. Identifying the main activities (issues) of the section or unit
The participants should clarify the five or six main activities of the section or unit. These main activities can be further broken down into their constituent activities. An alternative approach is to identify the five or six top issues – especially issues as perceived from the service users' perspective. It can be interesting to ask how well a section or unit's main activities are currently addressing these top issues. We favour this first step being strongly informed by market research and studies of service users' needs and future social trends as we think this is likely to increase the rate of innovation by the section or unit (Thurley and Wirdenius, 1989).

2. Identifying goals
In respect of each main activity, the participants explore why the section or unit carries out this activity. The answer is framed as follows: 'Activity X is done in order to...' This helps the section or unit become clearer about why it does the things it does. The answers can be checked against council goals. It can also be very useful to look at the interconnec-tions between the goals to see if there are any overarching goals. Obviously, the goals of a section or a unit should feature benefits to the public and service users. (A similar dis-cussion can take place in relation to the top issues faced by the section or unit. The par-ticipants can explore why these issues should be addressed.) This second step in the process is not only important for checking whether activities are producing benefits for the public and service users and whether they align with important council goals, it is also an important preparatory stage for defining performance indicators and targets.

3. Identifying ideas for actions
The participants then move on to look at how current activities of the section or unit can be improved. The discussion frames the answers by saying: 'The main activities of the sec-tion/unit can be improved by ...' The participants are encouraged to brainstorm actions which might improve the main activities of the section or unit. These actions need to be thoroughly discussed and evaluated. How feasible are the actions? How acceptable will these actions be to the elected members, senior management, the public, etc? What resources are required to take these actions and are the resources available? (A process focused on issues rather than activities would ask how the issues might be addressed. Proposed actions would be aimed at handling or eliminating the top issues.)

4. Identifying who needs to be involved
For each of the best (ie feasible and most beneficial) ideas for action, the participants in the process ask who needs to be involved. They then plan how this involvement will be obtained and managed.

5. Responsibility charting
On the assumption that service activities are being improved as a result of this process, responsibility charting may be useful to implement changes. According to Beckhard and Harris (1987: 105) responsibility charting 'helps reduce ambiguity, wasted energy and adverse emotional reactions between individuals or groups whose interrelationship is affected by change'. Process participants identify the affected activities, the people involved in these activities, and the behaviour required of each in relation to the activities. Individuals may be identified as: having responsibility for an activity; having the power to approve (veto) activities; being required to support activities with resources; or having the right to be consulted or informed in relation to activities. This can be literally charted with the individuals identified across the top of the chart and the activities listed down the side.

6. Revising roles and procedures
Roles and procedures within the section or unit may need to be revised in the light of the preceding steps in the process. It may be worth bearing in mind, however, that actions which do not require changes in organization and roles may be more economical because they are not disruptive. Bryson (1995) suggests that strategy development includes asking what major actions may be taken within the next year or two with existing staff and within existing job descriptions.

7. Planning training and development of staff
Training and development may be needed to ensure changes are implemented effectively. Whilst managers in local authorities often recognize that, ideally speaking, change can be made more effective by appropriate training and development, they are not always able or willing to deliver this ideal.

8. Setting performance indicators and targets.
Strategy should always be evaluated. But as well as evaluating how well changes are being implemented – which means setting milestones to check on progress – the manager should discuss performance indicators and targets with participants. This is where the work undertaken at the second step – identifying goals – comes in useful. By establishing why activities were important, the manager and his or her staff can now develop performance goals, indicators and targets for the main activities of the section or unit. If the goals identified in the second step included benefits to service users as well as goals stated in terms of efficiency then a balanced set of performance targets should be obtained. It is advisable that the manager and his or her staff should limit the number of performance targets – large numbers of targets are probably counterproductive.

Full ownership will mean that every member of a manager's staff can see their work playing a full part in the overall strategy. A good strategy ensures that everyone on the manager's staff can judge their small part as a part of the larger strategy. They must recognize that if they fail in their work something bigger will stop. And if they succeed, so will something bigger succeed.

17

E-business

INTRODUCTION

This introduction is based on a short story by the Italian novelist Italo Calvino called *The Man Who Shouted Teresa*. One day, not long ago, I was passing through the business district of a large city. I stopped outside an impressive office building that appeared to me to stretch up to the very heavens. I shouted out as loud as I could 'E-business!'

After a few moments of shouting a man stopped and stood next to me. He started to shout with me, 'E-business, e-business, e-business!' at the top of his voice. Unfortunately we were out of time with each other. The man said, 'Come on we can do much better than that if we shout together. After three – one, two three. E-business!'

Still no one appeared at any of the windows in the tall office block. By good fortune a group of my friends appeared from a nearby café and seeing me and my new friend shouting decided to lend a voice (so to speak). After a short rehearsal to make sure we all shouted in time we tried again. 'E-business!' I have to say it was a loud and a clear shout. I doubt, given the time we had to practise, few other groups would have been able to match us in both the noise we made and the clarity of the shout. We were simply brilliant. But still to no effect.

After a few more goes and after swelling our ranks with even more passers-by I detected a change in the atmosphere. The ambience that appeared to me to be so

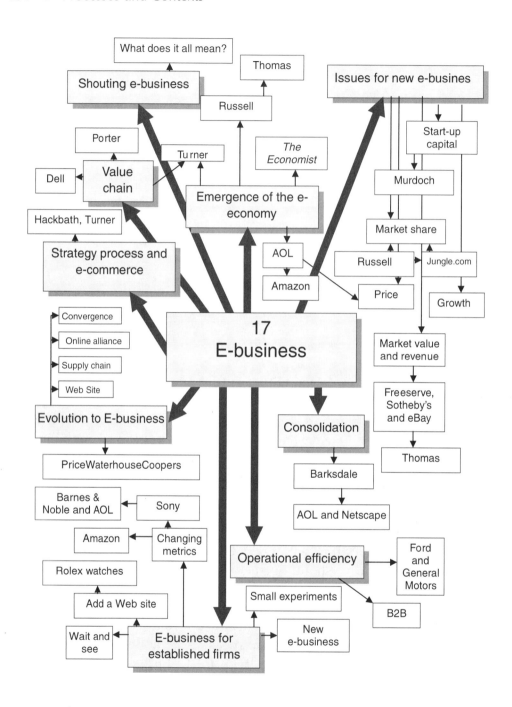

wonderful only a few minutes before had started to change. It is strange how some people pick up things very quickly and then drop them just as quickly. After all we had only been shouting for 30 minutes or so.

One group of shouters (I never did get to know their names) asked me what I took to be a pretty impertinent question, namely, 'Why are you outside here shouting "e-business"? Is there someone in the office block you know, or what?'

Well, I have to say that I felt quite put out by this. What cheek. But being a well-mannered person and not wanting to upset my group (that's how I saw them now) I replied, perhaps a touch coldly but not in an aggressive way, 'Of course not. I've no idea who works in that office block.'

'So why are you shouting "e-business"?'

I still managed, but only just, to keep my cool. 'As far as I am concerned we could all be shouting "business process re-engineering", or "core competencies",' I said.

A rather small man, who I hadn't notice before said, 'Is this some kind of practical joke for the TV? Where's the camera?'

I was very cross about this. So I simply replied 'What?' in the belief that the rest of the large crowd that had now formed around me would have much more common sense than this small man.

For one moment I thought things might turn nasty but someone said, 'One last go and then if nothing happens let's all go home.' So like a well-rehearsed orchestra a mighty shout went up: 'E-business!'

Then the crowd started to drift off. I needed a drink of water – all this shouting had made me a bit hoarse. I must have been about 100 or so yards down the round when I distinctly heard a voice shouting 'E-business, e-business, e-business!' But I can't be sure!

The beauty of Calvino stories lies in your interpretation of them. Our small pastiche of his essay does no justice at all to him but we hope we might have, in a small way, captured something of the original and made you think a bit about e-business. Let's get on with the rest of the chapter.

THE GROWTH OF E-BUSINESS

In the last few years of the 20th century all kinds of companies began to think about doing business through the Internet. This is astonishing given that, according to one view, e-commerce was 'virtually non-existent' in 1995 (Turner, 2000: 41). By 1998 the electronic economy (e-economy) represented 6.5 per cent of US GDP and 1 per cent of Japan's GDP (Source: *The Economist* 26 June 1999). This may not sound very much but the US e-economy was expanding fast – by 65 per cent in 1998. The rate of growth of access to the Internet grew dramatically. Already by 1996 tens of millions of people had access to the Web, but the numbers were doubling each year at that time. At the start of the 21st century some half a dozen countries, including the United States and Germany, had one in five of their population with online access to the Web via their own PCs. Internet service providers proliferated. The United States had over 4,000 of them in 1996. Some, such as America Online (AOL), quickly emerged as strong contenders for leadership of this segment of the e-economy. Then banks, insurance firms, book retailers, travel companies and various other kinds of businesses moved quickly to establish a presence on the Net. Many companies may have done so because they saw opportunities. Many may have joined the Internet bandwagon simply in order to keep up with what their rivals are doing, or might soon do.

'That e-commerce is a growing business is indisputable and that the Internet gives companies a way to achieve rapid growth is fairly commonplace' (Russell, 2000: 18). The emerging e-economy is full of businesses that have grown extraordinarily fast, often returning growth rates that until recently were unimaginable. However, this is not a simple story of new opportunities. Established firms may feel threatened by the development of e-business. According to Thomas (2000), 'Everywhere you look it seems that cyber upstarts are challenging the old order, seemingly teleporting in and threatening established brands in retail, finance and service industries.'

Amazon was one of the first really large businesses on the Internet. Set up in 1994 and located in Seattle, Amazon sold US $0.5 million worth of books online in 1995 and US $16 million worth of books online in 1996. Companies like Amazon used the Net to provide a new kind of service, and a level of service, that broke new ground. Book retailing online could offer consumers a convenient and cheap option and, with a wide range of titles available, also incredible choice.

Some Internet companies enjoyed a growth of turnover that was hard to believe. In the UK the winner of the 1999 Deloitte and Touche National Technology Fast 50 was Data Discovery, a Scottish firm that grew by over 9,000 per cent in one year! It has a Web site at www.datadiscoveries.com/. The second firm was Eurocall Limited that also achieved a growth in excess of 9,000 per cent. It has a Web site at www.eurocall-telecom.com/. Full details of the Technology Fast 50 can be found at www.fast50.co.uk/fast50_99/

ISSUES FOR NEW E-BUSINESSES

E-businesses, like any other kind of business, initially face the issue of raising the necessary capital to start and keep them going until they have sufficient sales revenue from customers. The difficulties of getting start up capital to start an e-business may vary from one country to another. Bookpages was an Internet bookseller based in the UK that was started in 1996. Its founder reported having a difficult time getting the capital he needed. He reports:

> In general, UK venture capitalists saw the Internet market as uncertain and risky and were reluctant to get involved in it. Dealing with a young entrepreneur, the venture capitalists were suspicious of the market opportunities for e-commerce despite my relevant experience in both technology and books. The return on their investment would also take some time to come to fruition and the UK venture capital community seemed to be looking for a faster return on any stake they might invest. (Murdoch, 2000: 213).

Although some capital was eventually provided by a group of US business angels, the founder of Bookpages was approached by Amazon in 1998 with an offer to buy the company, and he went on to become the MD of Amazon's UK arm.

Once the e-business has begun operating, another issue is how to build its share of the Internet market. One approach is to spend money on offline advertising to build an online brand, which can be very expensive. One e-business, called jungle.com, spent £10 million on offline advertising to encourage registrations to its Web site (Russell, 2000).

A different approach to building market share is to compete on price. If this leads to a price war it is possible to have both a massive growth in sales and financial losses. This appears to have been the case of Internet service providers in 1996 when the largest of them were making very substantial losses on top of growing revenue. AOL had made the first move and offered a low flat fee. This produced a surge of customers for AOL's service, and other providers also offered flat fees.

The fortunate e-businesses that have no difficulty in finding or creating a demand for their products or services through the Internet grow fast and have to cope with problems of this growth. Fast Search & Transfer was set up as an Internet company in Norway. It grew from a business employing two people to one employing 60 in 1999, and valued at US $600 million. The company's Chief Executive is reported to have resisted the creation of a salesforce in the United States and have been concerned about the cultural integrity of the company. (Source: *The Economist* 31 July 1999). Rapid growth can also expose problems of capacity. Despite the rapid expansion of the e-retail market in 1999, some Internet retailers hit problems because of delays in meeting customers' orders and because of unreliable suppliers. In other words, they were not effective in managing capacity as the turnover of their businesses expanded.

Yet another issue for the Internet businesses was the disproportion between their market value and their revenue. For example, Freeserve, an Internet service provider started by Dixons, an established UK electrical retailer, had a share price in July 1999 that suggested a market value of just over £2 billion at a time when its revenue was less than £3 million. Thomas (2000) offered a comparison between an old-established firm and a new dotcom firm that makes the same point. He pointed out that Sotheby's had a market worth US $1.7 billion and revenues of US $1.9 billion, where-as eBay, an online auctioneer, was valued at US $17 billion with revenues of only US $125 million. After an initial period of enthusiasm among investors, doubts about the profit potential of e-businesses generally increased. In consequence, share prices dropped for some e-businesses, which also triggered action by some of them to cut jobs and cut costs.

CONSOLIDATION

The development of e-commerce since the mid-1990s has been so rapid that issues of consolidation are already starting to emerge. Jim Barksdale, Chief Executive of Netscape, is reported to have said that all industries consolidate as they mature. (Source: *The Economist* 28 November 1998). This judgement certainly is borne out by the evolution of older industries. The car industry, for example, began in the 20th century with large numbers of small firms using craft-based technology and then proceeded during that century to consolidate in to a small number of large global car businesses with General Motors, Ford and Volkswagen being pre-eminent. So the big question facing the new Internet businesses as the industry evolves is how to be among the survivors that grow and prosper.

In 1998 AOL bought Netscape and did a deal with Sun Microsystems involving licensing of software and sales of equipment. The complementary resources and skills of the three firms were to be combined to offer services to companies wanting to participate in e-commerce.

OPERATIONAL EFFICIENCY

The Internet offers established firms new ways of operating. Firms can increase efficiency by, for example, moving to electronic procurement. They can use the Internet to secure closer integration with business customers. For example, firms may obtain access to their customers' sales information as a way of increasing efficiency and responsiveness. They can use the Internet as a new way to do business with their suppliers. This is not just hypothetical. In late 1999 Ford and General Motors separately announced that they were investing in online purchasing operations. Ford planned to do this through a joint venture with Oracle, and General Motors had selected a supplier of Web-based procurement to assist its development of online purchasing.

E-BUSINESS STRATEGIES FOR ESTABLISHED FIRMS

In addition to looking at operational matters, firms may decide to make a strategic response to the opportunities of the Internet. For example, a firm must decide whether it wants to enter this new competitive space immediately, wait until the nature of the threats and opportunities of the e-economy becomes clearer, or concentrate on becoming more efficient or effective in terms of its current strategic posture.

As with any need to interpret market signals, there is ample scope for internal disagreement within the individual firm. This disagreement can centre on the feasibility and returns of e-business projects. A survey of 171 IT decision makers in organizations with more than 500 employees, which was carried out in 2000, found that a third of those who approve IT spending were 'unclear if e-business projects can justify their return on investment'. (Source: *The Sunday Independent* 3 December 2000: 2). The same survey found that a quarter of IT directors saw internal organizational politics as a barrier to their organization undertaking e-business projects. Over half of the organizations covered were spending less than 10 per cent of their IT budget on e-business.

If established firms decide that a response is needed they have at least two options. As shown by the case of the European insurance industry, they can respond by maintaining their existing business designs but adding a Web site, or by launching a properly designed e-business of their own.

Those firms adopting the first option face problems. Some are relatively minor, such as that of seeking to register the firm's name on the World Wide Web (Source: *The Economist* 8 June 1996) only to find, as Rolex Watches did, that their name had already been registered by someone else. This was an early lesson for established firms. The Internet is a channel of business activity with its own peculiar rules – such as registering names on a first come first served basis. This must add to the sense of uncertainty about the risks and rewards of e-business.

The more serious problem of this option is that adding a Web site does not address the way in which e-businesses are changing 'business metrics'. This can be seen if we look at the success of Amazon in its early years. Online booksellers measure their performance in terms of lower prices, customer convenience and wider customer choice from a large stock of book titles available. In order to meet these business metrics, e-businesses set up processes to take orders, source books not held in their own warehouses, and despatch books to customers quickly. It should be noted that operating such processes Amazon was able to sell books at prices substantially lower than its traditional rivals did. A traditional bookseller in a high street has its investment tied up in its location and book stocks, has high costs of premises because of its location, and the choice it offers customers is physically constrained by its premises. Its business design is simply not optimal for the new metrics.

Established firms in established industries can now see the possibility that e-business will not only create new opportunities for successful pioneers. It also threatens to invalidate established ways of doing business and thus cause the collapse of value chains that have faithfully delivered profits over long periods of time. As we have seen, firms that create a presence on the Net but do not substantially change the way they operate have business processes quite different from their e-business counterparts. Established firms facing the challenge of e-business might have to dismantle parts of their organization and transform the way they operate. They will have to pay as much attention to designing the business processes behind the Web page as to designing the Web page itself.

While established firms wanting to enter the e-economy face challenges in terms of the redesign of their business processes and investment costs, they can also be seen to have a major advantage when they do go on the Net. They have established brands. Firms that are big names generally have an advantage when customers are browsing the Internet. The established firms are noticed, and trusted, because of their names. The evidence for this in the early days of the e-economy's growth was the popularity of the Web sites of firms such as SONY.

One way for firms to respond to the challenges of e-business is to search for new, fast growing Internet-based firms and acquire them. This is a common feature of the new dot economy. Older established firms snap up new, but very innovative, businesses. For example, Britain's BT has acquired small Internet firms in Europe.

Another approach is to work through Internet companies. Barnes & Noble, a bookseller based in the United States, began online retailing through AOL in 1997. Both Yahoo and AOL have partnership deals that provide established businesses access to virtual shopping malls.

EVOLUTION TO E-BUSINESS

The preceding discussion of how established firms respond to the challenge of the e-business might be compared with a model presented by PriceWaterhouseCoopers (1999) (see Turner, 2000: 48–49). According to this model, established businesses might pass through four stages in the transition to e-business:

1. Implement a Web site.
2. Extend the capabilities of the Web site into supply chains.
3. Develop online alliance.
4. Work on industrial convergence.

In the first stage firms use a Web site for buying and selling processes. In the second stage the emphasis is on the closer integration of suppliers. In the third stage alliances develop entailing important shifts in how industry operates. In the fourth stage innovative products result from the convergence of sectors.

STRATEGY PROCESS AND E-COMMERCE

The discussion of how e-commerce (or e-business) strategies relate to corporate strategies is probably inevitably still largely speculative. A firm may decide it needs an e-commerce strategy to ensure that it keeps up with the development of the e-economy. But how does this relate to the strategic plan for the organization?

There is a plausible schema for how the relationship might develop (Kittinger and Hackbarth, 1999; Turner 2000: 49). Initially, e-commerce is a departmental or functional initiative rather than having a corporate focus. Then e-commerce becomes more important and is supportive of the organization's business strategy. Finally, e-commerce becomes very important in terms of the corporate business strategy. An e-commerce strategy, at this stage, supports a 'breakout' of business strategy.

We would build on these ideas to suggest that e-commerce could be transformational in its impact on corporate strategy. By this we mean that there could be corporate strategies which lead to fundamental changes in business design. In our opinion these changes, which are obviously still emerging, might well relate chiefly to more responsiveness by businesses to consumers, the importance of strategic alliances between businesses, and the emphasis by industry leaders on the search for innovations in products and services.

VALUE CHANGE ANALYSIS

Value chain analysis may be useful as a way of thinking about the use of Internet technology to obtain competitive advantages. Value chain analysis has of course become popular as a result of the writings of Porter (1985), but Turner summed it up quite neatly. He suggested that:

> The essential theme of the value chain is one of securing competitive advantage through managing suppliers, assessing the requirements of consumers and adjusting internal processes as appropriate... The value an enterprise creates is measured by the amount buyers are prepared to pay for its product. Thus a business is profitable if the value it creates exceeds the cost of performing these activities. (Turner, 2000: 25)

The main and support activities in the value chain identified by Porter (1985) are:

- inbound logistics;
- operations;
- outbound logistics;
- marketing and sales;
- service;
- firm infrastructure;
- HR management;
- technology development;
- procurement.

The Internet can be used in a number of these activities to reduce costs or improve the value as perceived by the customer. Turner has argued that the integration of Internet technology into supply chains is associated with cost-conscious industries such as PC manufacturing. The potential for the use of the Internet by PC firms can be illustrated using the case of Dell Computer Corporation. According to Turner, suppliers can access Dell's extranet to obtain information about Dell's orders. It offers online sales to its customers. It also allows customers to access the Extranet to obtain information on the processing of their orders. Given the level of cooperation that then becomes possible between a firm and its suppliers and customers because of Internet technology, there is potential for what Turner describes as three-way information partnerships in which there is cooperation to increase the efficiency of the supply chain. Indeed, a key point made by Turner is the way that the Internet enables competitive advantages to be sought through strategic alliances and networking relations.

CONCLUSIONS

The Internet has offered e-business opportunities that have led to high levels of growth for individual businesses. It has resulted in not only new channels for reaching customers, but also radically new business metrics that call for new business designs. E-businesses are much more than businesses with a Web site. The early years of development of e-business have been marked not only by competitive threats to established businesses and brands, but also the use of strategic alliances and new relationships with buyers and suppliers. Also, as Turner (2000) points out, Internet technology may become more integrated into supply chains. This could lead to greater cooperative relations between a firm and its suppliers and customers to improve the functioning of the supply chain.

QUESTIONS

1. What is e-business and e-commerce?
2. When it comes down to it, the problems facing the strategist in a new economy company are just the same as those facing one in an old economy company – same problems, same strategic tools needed to solve them. Is this true?
3. Why is it so hard to value an Internet business and how does this impact on strategy?
4. Just as in the mature motor industry business consolidation has happened, this will occur in the new economy. Can you give examples of this and examine how this might influence strategic thinking in the new and old economy?
5. What are old economy firms doing about the opportunities offered by the Internet? You may like to use the Ford case study to help you answer this.
6. Using the model presented by PriceWaterhouseCoopers, select a company you are familiar with to test how well the model works. Do Kittinger and Hackbarth give a more plausible approach?
7. Using Dell Computer Corporation as an example, how easy is it to apply Porter's value chain?
8. Our small bakery owner is thinking about getting on the Net. How would you draw up a strategy to do this?

REFERENCES

Kittinger, W and Hackbarth, G (1999) Electronic commerce, *The Financial Times*, Information Management Supplement **7**, pp 68–77

Murdoch, S (2000) Venturing into unknown territory – a personal view, in *The Growing Business Handbook: Strategies for planning, funding and managing business growth*, eds R Willsher and A Jolly, Kogan Page, London

Porter, M (1985) *Competitive Advantage*, Free Press, New York

PriceWaterhouseCoopers (1999) *Electronic business outlook*, www.pwc.global.com

Russell, C (2000) Understanding e-commerce, in *The Growing Business Handbook: Strategies for planning, funding and managing business growth*, eds R Willsher and A Jolly, Kogan Page, London

Thomas, I (2000) E-business, a broader view, in *The Growing Business Handbook: Strategies for planning, funding and managing business growth*, eds R Willsher and A Jolly, Kogan Page, London

Turner, C (2000) *The Information E-conomy: Business strategies for competing in the digital age*, Kogan Page, London

Reading 17.1

Taken from Chapter 2 – The information economy and competitive advantage, in *The Information E-conomy* by Colin Turner (2000)

The shift to the information economy highlighted in Chapter 1 is going to have a profound impact on business strategy as enterprises seek to sustain their competitive position in the face of such changes. According to Michael Porter (1985), the ability of the technological change associated with the development of the information economy to translate itself into competitive advantage is determined by the following factors:

1. *Factor conditions.* It is increasingly pivotal (as highlighted in Chapter 1) that the ability of human resources to assimilate information and turn it into value-creating knowledge is key to enterprise success, as is the wide availability and access to capital (notably hardware and software) that facilitates the efficient and effective use of information.
2. *Demand conditions.* The anticipated shift to electronic commerce and corresponding new business models is likely to be driven by the necessity to meet the needs and requirements of consumers. This will be compounded by the desire of users to utilize new technology for the purposes of commercial transactions (see Chapter 3).
3. *Related or supporting industries.* The information economy needs to be supported by an effective and efficient information industry that provides value-adding applications and technologies that constantly innovate to aid competitiveness (see Chapter 4). The products supplied by the information industry need to be accessible to as broad a range of business communities as possible.
4. *Firm strategy, structure and rivalry.* How enterprises use technology within the value chain is key to aiding their competitiveness. The desire to adopt these technologies is a general function of overall strategy and levels of competition faced by enterprises.

This chapter will focus primarily upon the first and last of these factors with the other themes being discussed in the chapters noted. Essentially the purpose and underlying theme behind the diverse range of issues addressed within this chapter is to develop an understanding of how the establishment of the information economy is changing enterprise through stimulating a reassessment of what the business needs to do to sustain its competitive position within such an environment. This should enable the reader to understand fully how and why business models are changing within the information economy and why exactly electronic commerce is becoming such a salient issue (see Chapter 3).

The impact upon enterprise performance and functioning

As this and the following chapter indicate, the application of ICTs is fundamentally alter-ing the manner in which enterprises function. The application of these technologies to business functioning is driven by the compulsion to remain competitive in an era when the intensity of competition is further increasing and when there is correspondingly intensify-ing pressure upon enterprises to maximize their own efficiency (see below). Importantly these pressures create further strategic issues as lower production costs reduce barriers to entry thereby encouraging new entrants, increasing both the intensity of competition and the pressure upon enterprises to deliver these efficiencies on to the consumer. This pres-sure upon the cost functions of enterprises is likely to grow as consumers, through elec-tronic commerce, become able to reach an increasing number of potential suppliers.

The maturing market for information is a testament to its growing strategic importance. Increasingly enterprises do not merely need information strategies but a proper assessment and integration of ICTs (as a symptom of the increasing strategic importance of knowledge and information) throughout their organization. This requires the integration of all the infor-mation aspects of the business (strategy, people, systems, operations and technology) as a means of ensuring that the value added from the application of these technologies is max-imized. Consequently, companies seeking to sustain and enhance their competitive position need to utilize the information they have available at their disposal in a more productive and proactive manner. Information is no longer just stored, analysed and discarded; it is increas-ingly being used as a strategic resource in its own right to generate sustainable competitive advantage.

There are a number of strategic challenges associated with information, which are as fol-lows:

- understanding and recognizing the forms of information valuable to the enterprise;
- assessing the value of the relevant information in business processes;
- identifying the business processes affected by this information;
- assessing how to integrate the relevant information into business processes;
- identifying necessary core-supporting ICTs;
- understanding core legal and statutory legal obligations in the use of the relevant information;
- understanding the need to assess and monitor the quality, relevance and accuracy of information.

These strategic challenges are core concerns that all businesses will need to assess in addressing the commercial impact of the information economy. They highlight how and where the enterprise will need to develop an information profile to sustain its competi-tiveness within the information economy. The information that a company possesses will span most aspects of business operation from essential knowledge about suppliers through to specialist customer and product knowledge. All the factors listed above com-bine to develop a particular identity for the company in terms of how information will shape its corporate position. This highlights how crucial an asset information actually is and how it clearly represents a source of business value. Companies need to develop a clear perspective on what the value of the information available to them actually is and how it can best be used to enhance an enterprise's competitive position. This is leading many enterprises to seek to put a value on information assets within their annual accounts — underlining the key point that information represents business value.

Measuring the value of knowledge in business is important. It helps managers assess the best strategy as well as helping gauge the knowledge assets of competitors. These processes can also assess the cost of knowledge and highlight deficiencies in the information the enterprise possesses in order to achieve its strategic objectives. In this context, three core information resources can be identified:

1. the human element — the information embodied in the work-force that contributes to strategic objectives;
2. the structural element — the information regarding specific markets;
3. the customer element — the information regarding the customer base.

These should enable an enterprise to prioritize information resources and counter the potentially harmful effects of information overload and knowledge deficiency.

From the above, it is evident that there are two critical factors in shaping enterprise operation and functioning in the information economy. The first is how enterprises manage and alter human resources; the second is how the application of ICTs feeds through into enterprise efficiencies (a point more fully explored within the context of value chain analysis in the following sections). Consequently, it is worth while exploring these issues further at this juncture.

Human resources issues

Chattell (1998) underlines that value creation in the information economy depends upon human capital and the ability of organizations to allow the knowledge base of the enterprise to have sufficient freedom to express itself, and to stimulate the necessary invention and innovation to keep the enterprise ahead of its rivals. In truth, because of the complex impact of information upon the value chain (see below), coming to a definitive assessment of the impact of the burgeoning information economy upon human resources and employment is difficult. However, it is already evident that employment will rely less on the distribution of products and more on the transfer of information, with the result that routine, simple tasks will be replaced by increasingly complicated, knowledge-based duties.

Clearly the emphasis for enterprises is upon establishing and accessing a human resource base that has the necessary embedded human capital and flexibility to produce, access, process, assess and apply information in a manner that creates usable and commercially valuable knowledge. Firms (as the emphasis upon knowledge management highlights — see below) need to reconfigure knowledge assets if they are to sustain competitive advantage. This many will do through the medium of ICTs. Human resource functions need to be wired to ensure that available knowledge within staff is maximized and sent to the function where it will be most commercially valuable. In this context, an enterprise's staff is seen as a team of competent people who are more valuable when interacting than when working in isolation. Therefore well-organized team action, where each worker's knowledge is complementary, seems to be central to success, as does the need to manage staff in a cross-functional manner ensuring that the knowledge of each section is shared with all other parts of the organization (see the boxed section, 'Human resources in the information economy: the rise of knowledge management' below).

Firms are likely to be especially keen to protect specific kinds of human capital that are central to strategy and both difficult and costly to replace. Furthermore, firms need to interact with the legal system through intellectual property rights to secure knowledge assets within staff against poaching by other enterprises. These strategies are increasingly underpinned by strategic alliances with other enterprises (notably key suppliers or customers) designed to expand the knowledge resources available to the enterprise. This necessity has to be balanced against the possibility that creating a more knowledge-rich environment leads to a situation of information overload where there is too high a ratio of information to be assimilated to capable staff with the corresponding effect that competitiveness is potentially undermined.

As a result of these and other trends, most developed economies in the late 20th century/early 21st century are experiencing high and rising demand for labour that possesses the necessary information-based skills. This demand is expected to increase as the information economy matures. The onus is therefore upon both policy makers (see Chapter 5) and enterprises to ensure that the pool of available labour resources is able to complement and sustain this growth. It is generally believed that if the wider application of ICTs is to create the desired levels of employment, it needs to be accompanied by moves to stimulate competition within product and service markets as well as by the engendering of higher levels of flexibility into labour markets and work organizations. The latter two imply that there needs to be a concerted effort by economic actors to constantly adjust education and training to reflect the changing requirements of the information economy.

These changes in the labour market are expected to extend right through the enterprise to include the core skills expected of all staff (ie that all staff are IT-literate). These changes could become especially prevalent in an era of electronic commerce, which will require a change in the composition of the work-force as an increased level of sales occur online. Thus levels of retail and sales staff could be trimmed and replaced with the lower levels of specialist employees required to manage an online sales system. This would be especially likely if re-intermediation or disintermediation becomes commonplace (see Chapter 3). Consequently, the emergence of the information economy will lead to a reassessment of the skills businesses require especially if their products and services are now being sold online. In addition, since they no longer need to be near to their market-place they can locate where they can find the right skills at the right price.

This latter point underlines a core concern of many major economies, which fear that the intertwining of the information economy with the process of globalization will stimulate a migration of employment to developing states. There is good reason to believe these fears are overstated especially if the threat stimulates the appropriate policy response. The core challenge for the developed economies is in facilitating the necessary structural adjustment so that the employment costs of the transition from industrial to information economy is minimized. It is already evident that job losses in some sectors are being counterbalanced by the creation of jobs in other areas. The key point is that the information economy — in altering the form and types of job available — should, over the longer term, stimulate higher levels of employment. The universal nature of ICTs, their speed of introduction and the mobility stimulated increases the employment consequences of the information economy through its potential to destroy more jobs than other technological changes. Where there are job losses, it is evident that these will be within the low-skilled sectors of the economy, with growth being within those that require a higher level of both education and skill.

There is an emerging demarcation in terms of the impact of ICTs between organizations where information is an input and those where it is an output. In the former (such as traditional retail outlets), the exploitation of the potential of ICTs has been slow and, where they have been applied, they have been linked to the shedding of labour. Redundancies have been linked to facilitating the necessary investment needed to apply these technologies. In the 'information output' organizations (such as dedicated online enterprises), there has been speedier adoption of these technologies. In these enterprises, the focus has been upon providing the existing work-force with the necessary training, and there has been a general avoidance of major lay-offs.

In increasingly competitive markets, businesses can only really flourish by maximizing the potential of their resources, of which human resources and the knowledge embedded therein are proving increasingly important. Knowledge is the information needed to make key business decisions, and most enterprises have to assess the knowledge capital embedded within the organization's human resources and ensure it is utilized effectively to secure the broad corporate objectives of those enterprises. This core concern has seen knowledge management rise up the strategic agenda of enterprises.

Human resources in the information economy: the rise of knowledge management

Knowledge management is concerned with the collection of processes involved in the acquisition, creation, sharing and use of knowledge within organizations. This encompasses a range of activities from learning processes through to management information systems. Generally knowledge management consists of four central elements:

1. valuing knowledge;
2. exploiting intellectual property;
3. capturing project-based learning;
4. managing knowledge workers.

This means finding and capturing the knowledge staff possess, sharing it and exploiting it for commercial benefit. Thus the knowledge of an enterprise is not merely the explicit knowledge held within databases, intellectual property portfolios or the corporate Internet — it is also the knowledge of staff.

Many see the development of knowledge management as a reaction to business process re-engineering where the application of ICTs was almost solely about cost minimization. The key change represented by knowledge management is that it is about networking people as well as ICTs — though this change may come up against a culture clash because of an inertia to change within organizations. People are central to knowledge management, as they possess the knowledge that will improve enterprise functioning. If people are resistant to sharing knowledge, then that asset as a key business resource is lost. The consequence is that information resources are utilized inadequately with the result that the competitiveness of the enterprise is put in jeopardy.

If a company fails to utilize information through a failure to translate human intellectual capital into organizational intellectual capital (as can happen when a key member of staff leaves), it can damage the enterprise by affecting relationships with a key client or supplier or by the loss of knowledge regarding best practice. A survey conducted for KPMG (1998a) by Harris indicated that companies were failing to exploit the technological infrastructure to improve knowledge management, with only 10 per cent of enterprises surveyed making knowledge of competitors available electronically to all who needed it. This is despite the fact that most companies have in place the necessary technology (intranets, extranets, etc) to support this activity.

A recent survey by KPMG (1998b) highlighted that knowledge management is becoming integrated into enterprise strategy, with many believing that they had commercially lost out through failure to address the core issues it poses. This was especially evident in cases where departing staff or poor information-sharing had damaged relations with a key supplier or client or where staff turnover had led to the loss of expertise in a core operative area. Many enterprises are using the advent of new technology to aid competitiveness through the storing of information about customers, markets, own products and services, competitors and employees' skills. The survey also found that, despite having the technology in place, enterprises are still not enabling easy access to mission-critical information, and that they possess relatively immature strategies for knowledge management. Enterprises also feel that knowledge management strategies can ultimately be frustrated through the lack of time individuals have to seek out the information and garner the necessary knowledge, as well as through the aforementioned problems of corporate culture and organizational inertia.

A notable example of a greater degree of competitiveness being sought through knowledge management is Airbus, Europe's largest aerospace enterprise. Airbus recognized that, despite the recent advances in computer-aided design, advanced technologies are still unable to deal with all the knowledge needed to ensure an aircraft design is successful. This is due in no small part to the large body of both written and unwritten rules upon the practicalities of aircraft design, which cannot be captured in computer-aided design. As aircraft design increases in sophistication and as the development time grows, so there is increased competitive advantage in securing this untapped human knowledge to secure first-mover advantage in terms of the latest aircraft models.

Airbus is seeking to develop a new plane to challenge the long-held dominance of the Boeing 747 over long-haul routes. The sooner it can bring the new aircraft to the market, the sooner its strategy for this market niche can become commercial reality. Its new rival to the Boeing 747, the A340–600, is scheduled for initial delivery in 2002, giving it a small window of opportunity over Boeing. The result is that the enterprise is seeking knowledge management techniques to shorten the design cycle to secure or even enhance this first-mover advantage over its key rival.

To aid this, it is using software that links computer-aided design to the body of knowledge within the enterprise, which includes areas such as product rules, performance data, legislative and safety codes, and best practice in terms of manufacturing. Essentially the business has turned to total business modelling where models are developed that integrate everything of concern to the business. The results so far have been promising. For example, the time taken to make the wings was reduced from one man-year to 10 hours using the advanced software.

Impact upon production costs and productivity

The impact of ICTs upon a firm's internal production and transaction costs falls into three broad categories (OECD, 1998a):

1. the costs of executing a sale — there are savings to be had in selling through the Internet rather than through a physical location, by simplifying the process of order placement and execution, easier customer support and after-sales service, and staffing;
2. the costs associated with the procurement of production inputs (see Chapter 3);
3. the costs associated with making and delivering the product (see the boxed section, 'The supply chain and the information economy' below).

Thus within a system where electronic commerce starts to come to the fore, the cost of doing business can be expected to fall. These cost reductions should enable markets to work more efficiently. This trend is likely to continue as the costs of communication continue to fall. Many of these impacts will be upon the costs involved in selling products through third-party agents or brokers. The moves towards disintermediation are already evident as electronic commerce allows the 'middleman' to be removed from the value chain (see Chapter 3). Alternatively there is re-intermediation as the advent of trade over the Internet creates new dependencies upon online intermediaries (so-called infomediaries) such as those providing Internet search services and directories. This should result in lower barriers to entry and create greater incentives to enter the market-place. The cost pressures upon enterprises could be expected to grow as buyer power becomes more evident and as the competition within respective sectors intensifies.

Enterprises should be able to lower inventory costs through adopting just-in-time production methods and improving the ability to forecast demand more accurately. This can be complemented by the aforementioned efficiencies in sales via enhanced online facilities as well as by using these methods to deliver more efficient after-sales service. As the value chain analysis below indicates, the gains from electronic commerce and other aspects of the information economy are dependent upon enterprise 'openness', as firms need to be willing to open up internal systems to trusted customers and suppliers. On an economy-wide level, the OECD (1998b) estimates that the wider use of electronic commerce would lower physical retail and wholesale trade activity by 25 per cent, leading to a 50 per cent decline in the use of buildings and related services. Other cost savings would also be induced by the lower levels of staffing and capital usage.

These impacts upon enterprise production costs from the application of ICTs have been compounded by rapid declines in the price of the technologies themselves. For example the price of computer processing power has fallen by around 30 per cent per annum in real terms over the last couple of decades, a trend that is expected to continue. Never before has business witnessed such a fall in the costs of a key input — a change that has stimulated a virtuous cycle in terms of the adoption of these technologies. These price changes have not only lowered transaction costs but, with the advent of digital technology, have also meant that information can be moved or transacted both within and between enterprises considerably more effectively and efficiently.

Efficiency gains in terms of the application of ICTs should also be realized through improvements in productivity (the output per unit of input). The application of ICTs should enable enterprises to produce more with a given resource base as better information resources and utilization enable it to work 'smarter'. Despite the intuitive logic of this argument, there is a general absence of any evidence to suggest these effects are occurring: the so-called 'productivity paradox'. Rapid investment in ICTs has had, to date, seemingly little impact upon productivity. Indeed initial evidence seems to suggest that productivity increases have been trailing off, with any increases in productivity being driven by the more 'traditional' factors of labour and capital. Consequently some suggest that ICT investment has been wasted. Others are less dismissive, emphasizing that by their nature these technologies will increase productivity less than other resources, and that economies take time to learn and apply technologies in the most efficient and effective manner. This last point is important, for it suggests that once the market for these products reaches maturity their effects upon productivity will become more evident. A final perspective is simply that changes in productivity from ICTs may simply be difficult to measure — a feature that is a common occurrence across the service sector. Within the service sector, there are generally recognized to be two problems in measuring productivity: in measuring, firstly, changes in output and, second, improvements in quality. Given the broad use of ICTs in the service sector, there is a definite case for believing that productivity gains are there; it is simply that they are not captured through statistics. It also needs to be highlighted that investment in ICT is not always designed to boost productivity. For example, there has been a trend towards using this technology for product differentiation and marketing. These activities clearly do not boost productivity directly.

Overall, the greatest benefits from ICTs seem to be derived when investment in this technology is coupled with other complementary investments — new strategies, new business processes and new organizations. This reflects a basic truism that the impact of ICT will vary on a company-by-company basis (see later). In other areas, it may simply be the case that enterprises have to go online out of necessity as a means of preserving or extending market share and therefore do not end up producing that much extra output for the given resources. The true impact of the increased strategic value of information and associated technologies is best expressed within the context of the value chain.

The information economy and competitive advantage of enterprises: a value chain analysis

The framework of the value chain puts the impact of the information economy upon enterprise functioning and performance noted above in a broader context. It suggests that changes in efficiency and human resource requirements occur because of changes within the industry value chain in which the enterprise operates. The essence of the value chain is that an enterprise takes inputs from suppliers to which it adds 'value' (in the context of the information economy, through the application of knowledge and information resources and associated technologies) to create outputs that are eventually consumed by others. The typical, simplified value chain is identified in Figure 2.1.

Source: Tapscott (1995)

Figure 2.1 *The simplified value chain*

The essential theme of the value chain is one of securing competitive advantage through managing suppliers, assessing the requirements of consumers and adjusting internal processes as appropriate. The latter inevitably needs an assessment of the enterprise's core competencies and internal functioning in relation to the themes highlighted above. The value an enterprise creates is measured by the amount buyers are prepared to pay for its product. Thus a business is profitable if the value it creates exceeds the cost of performing these activities. Consequently to gain competitive advantage an enterprise must either perform these activities at lower costs (through using ICTs to improve efficiency) or perform them in an innovative manner (through the utilization of improved knowledge resources).

Porter (1985) divides the value chain internally into five primary activities and four supporting activities. The five core activities are:

1. inbound logistics — all activities linked to receiving, storing and handling inputs into the production process;
2. operations — all activities involved in the transformation of inputs into outputs, such as machinery, assembly, testing and facilities management;
3. outbound logistics — processes involved in moving the output from operation to end user (including movement, ordering, warehousing, etc);
4. marketing and sales — the process of inducing purchase and enabling those who wish to buy to do so (includes activities such as advertising, distribution channels, etc);
5. service — activities involved in the provision of a service to buyers, offered as part of the purchase agreement (includes spare parts supply, repair facilities, etc).

The four support activities (designed to support the primary functions) are:

1. firm infrastructure — includes accounts, finance and quality management;
2. human resource management — includes all functions involved in the process of staffing the enterprise from training through to rights;
3. technology development — the development of technology to support new product development and stimulate new process improvements;
4. procurement — the process of attaining the enterprise's inputs.

It is already evident that, across these primary and support activities, the application of ICTs is having a tangible effect (in addition to the production and human resources concerns noted above) upon enterprise performance — indeed it is difficult to identify an area where business functioning does not now depend to a greater or lesser extent upon information and the application of ICTs. Many of these effects will be discussed in greater depth in Chapter 3, but it is worth noting by way of illustration that there have been impacts upon advertising (for example, through improved knowledge about customers), the nature of shopping (there are anticipated increases in distance shopping) and logistics (via lower distribution costs). In addition, it is felt that the application of these technologies will (as mentioned) lower entry barriers, generate more efficient markets (through the better allocation of resources) and increase the pressure upon intermediaries and agents. It is also already evident that ICTs are having an impact upon operations through the development of computer-aided design and manufacturing, which is having a tangible effect upon the speed of production cycles, improving the quality of output and lowering the time it takes for new products to reach the market-place (see the boxed section, 'Human resources in the information economy: the rise of knowledge management' above). The impact upon distribution systems is also evident, as the application of ICTs is reducing the time needed to process orders as well as reducing the need for large inventories. In terms of marketing and sales, it is also apparent that a 'digital' shop front is much cheaper to maintain than a physical one, and is able, through Internet technology, to open all hours and reach the global market-place. Finally, the application of these technologies will have an impact upon corporate structure (see below), the nature of human resources (see above) and the location of commercial activities. The support activities (aside from the human resources element mentioned before) are also affected, through the rise of electronic tendering, the need to develop a supporting electronic infrastructure and the application of the correct technology to support the changing information requirements of the enterprise's primary activities.

These reinforce a trend where speed to the market is becoming more important as part of the process of securing competitive advantage, a phenomenon that relies in no small part upon the better use of information. The aim is to lower the unnecessary cost and waste out of the value chain. The savings realized from the improvements in knowledge can be utilized to fund further process enhancement as well as improved products and lower prices. These processes are all core to the enterprise delivering better value added to its customers. These changes, as well as the constant reappraisal of processes and techniques, are necessary in an era of intensifying competition. Strategy therefore constantly has to assess the nature and function of the value chain.

These trends underline the increasingly pivotal role of information in the value chain, which increasingly is not merely about the physical flow of goods and services within and between linked enterprises but is also about the information that flows within and between them. It is evident that branding, customer allegiance and employee loyalty amongst others all depend upon information of various sorts. Supplier relationships are by their very nature based upon channels of communication founded upon the exchange of information. Within these relationships, information can determine the relative bargaining power of the players. Very often one party or the other can gain increased value from the existence of asymmetry of information. In these instances, and where enterprises have better information systems and processes than their rivals, the existence of information can be used as a key determinant of competitive advantage. New advantages will emerge when the value chain, as it is currently developed, deconstructs and is fragmented into multiple businesses, each seeking to define its own competitive advantage. This process is symptomatic of the emergence of a virtual value chain (see the lower segment of Figure 2.2).

The development of a virtual value chain is, as the name suggests, value creation through interactions over the network (via the exchange of information) rather than through direct contact as typified by the traditional value chain. The virtual value chain is essentially the process whereby raw information is transformed into products, delivering value to users through electronic means. It is already evident that information within traditional value chains has had something of a supporting role, acting as a facilitator and often not as a source of value in its own right (for example, in areas such as marketing). Figure 2.2 indicates a number of things. First, it highlights the process of value creation in the production of information-based goods. Clearly the virtual value chain is mirroring the physical value chain as information is collected, processed, packaged and moved to the end user. Second, the growing importance of information means that processes within the virtual value chain can supersede those within the more traditional equivalent. For example, the network can offer alternative means of distribution and can also fundamentally alter aspects of the supply

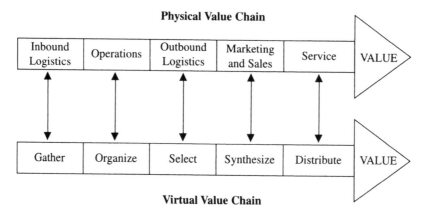

Physical Value Chain

| Inbound Logistics | Operations | Outbound Logistics | Marketing and Sales | Service | VALUE |

| Gather | Organize | Select | Synthesize | Distribute | VALUE |

Virtual Value Chain

Source: Phillips (1994)

Figure 2.2 *The new value chain*

chain (see the boxed section, 'Intranets and extranets' below). This leads to a third (and final) point, that the virtual value chain is more a complement to the existing value chain than its replacement — there are emerging interlinkages between the two value chains. There are evident interlinkages between the virtual and physical value chains in terms of functional areas such as marketing and sales. Over time, as new markets are created and as more and more aspects of the two value chains become interdependent, it is possible to foresee their integration. Overall, the virtual value chain only applies to information businesses, which rely on these technological methods for their business models. For other enterprises, the virtual value chain is an important source of competitive advantage through using information collected as a complement to existing physical processes — a process also highlighted in Figure 2.2.

Information can evidently be captured at all stages of the virtual value chain and used to enhance the performance of the enterprise. This information need not be used merely to aid existing processes but can also be repackaged and analysed to build content-based products or new lines of business. For example, supermarkets are using their customer information in developing banking or other specialized customer products. This not only enables the enterprise to generate loyalty amongst its customers but can also assist it in reaching out to its competitors' customers. The result is to rearrange the value system to create growing interlinkages between various, previously separate, sectors (for example, in the case mentioned above, banking and food retailing) — a variation of the process of convergence most evident in the information industry (see Chapter 4).

The growing use of information and the development of the virtual value chain allow inter-enterprise relationships to expand with added value being generated through alterations to this network to maximize flexibility, speed, innovation and responsiveness (these are evident in terms of the development of virtual enterprises and the impact upon supply chain management noted below). Thus the capabilities of the enterprise to use and share information of common commercial interest create an interdependent network of enterprises whose efficiency can work to the advantage of all parties. The development of such networks (within the context of the wider application of ICTs) as the source of value added is, according to Tapscott (1995), creating new dynamics in terms of:

- improving the accessibility of partners;
- establishing new interdependencies between enterprises;
- creating competitive advantage through co-operation;
- value creation through inter-organizational partnerships;
- speeding up inter-organizational transactions.

These trends highlight that the flow of information along the value chain between the enterprise, its suppliers and its customers can be utilized to ensure that efficiencies and competitiveness are realized. On the supply side, sharing information with suppliers brings obvious benefits to both in terms of efficiency of delivery and avoidance of over-stocking, and is a complement to just-in-time production techniques. Bringing the customer into the enterprise's value chain offers advantages in terms of requiring fewer resources for enterprise functioning, increased speed for the re-engineering of products to meet customer needs, the enabling of mass customization and the avoidance of supply problems, as products can be relayed to the customer quickly and easily. The success of these systems to the competitiveness of enterprises relies upon emphasizing the customer as the key driver of the system. Most businesses have focused upon the supply chain within the logistical system in terms of the use of extranet technologies (see the boxed section, 'Intranets and extranets' below), as this is where they generally exert more influence, but evidently sustaining competitive advantage means integrating consumers.

The above trends indicate that the impact of information upon the value chain (in both its physical and virtual forms) is creating a situation where enterprises are increasingly part of a wider value system. This wider stream of activities, of which the enterprise's value chain is part, consists of the value chains of suppliers through to those of its customers. This system creates interdependence between enterprises and (as noted below) can become a source of competitive advantage in its own right. The external value system is reflected in Figure 2.3.

Supplier Value Chain   *Firm's Value Chain*   *Channel Value Chain*   *Buyer Value Chain*

Source: Porter and Millar (1985)

Figure 2.3 *The external value system*

What this underlines is that the enterprise is part of a network of mutually interdependent value chains, and it highlights how important the virtual value chain can be in allowing information to be utilized effectively to ensure that full competitive advantage is realized from these interdependencies. The virtual value chain should increase the efficiency of these relations through, for example, an enterprise being made aware early of change in the supply of components so that it can then source them elsewhere.

Intranets and extranets

In facilitating the advantages of applying information more completely throughout the value chain, enterprises are utilizing two core Internet-based technologies — intranets and extranets. A brief explanation of each follows, outlining their typical and potential utilization by enterprises.

Intranets

An intranet allows information to be spread around an organization using Internet-compatible standards. Such developments are inevitably interlinked to the emergence of knowledge management as a business issue. By using common Internet protocols in conjunction with their own business applications, enterprises can easily communicate, distribute information and facilitate project collaboration across the business whilst maintaining the necessary security. Use of intranets is growing rapidly. Indeed, it is estimated that internal Web servers are outpacing their external equivalent by a magnitude of five to one. Intranets are fundamentally altering the way companies create and disseminate information, with effects in the following areas:

- internal e-mail;
- collaborative processing;
- accessing enterprise memory;
- order processing;
- personal pages;
- departmental pages;
- group communications;
- enterprise communications;
- product and company information.

Extranets

A complementary, and arguably more important, technology is the extranet — essentially an intranet connected to trusted customers and suppliers. Developing an extranet initiates the concept of the virtual business by allowing all the organizations in an enterprise's value chain to integrate their systems and operations (value chain). The notion of the extranet is by no means new, as electronic data interchange on private networks has performed similar functions for a number of years. Potentially, extranets offer the prospect of removing many of the problems that have prevented firms from sharing their data with customers and suppliers. The more extensive use of extranet technology is intimately linked to greater development of software offering increased security over data.

Generally, companies are using extranets to:

- exchange large volumes of data;
- share product catalogues with wholesalers and other linked parties;
- collaborate with other companies on joint development efforts;
- develop and use training programmes jointly with other companies;
- provide or access services provided by one company to a group of other companies;
- share news of common interest with partner companies.

As highlighted, these intranet and extranet technologies are being used in a number of ways to complement the development of information (and its dissemination) as a key strategic resource to enterprises. Use of these technologies also highlights the trend towards an enterprise being increasingly perceived, within the context of the development of the information economy, as part of a network of mutually supporting businesses. The enterprise's efficient and effective functioning depends on the internal and external communication networks that aid and enhance its competitive positioning.

Organizational implications

The advent of the information economy and its implications for the value chain are having an impact on enterprise structures (as shown in Figure 1.1 and Table 2.1). It is evident from the analysis throughout this chapter that the source of competitive advantage lies within the organization and how it uses ICTs to alter internal and external processes and

Table 2.1 *Changing business models*

	Industrial Economy	**Information Economy**
Companies	inwardly focused	extended/network enterprise
Customers	limited access to manufacturer	direct access to manufacturer
Suppliers	arm's length relationship	electronic relationships
Intermediaries	stand-alone entities/ separate processes	extended enterprise links/shared processes
Employees	hierarchical and functionally managed	empowered and cross-functionally managed

Source: Financial Times (1999a)

structures to secure its strategic objectives. As suggested by the external value system (see Figure 2.3), this is often done within the context of a larger commercial network. The development of electronic links between organizations can alter the concept of the organization, promoting the shift towards virtual organizations. The virtual corporation, in its most basic form, deals with the changes to the internal functioning of the firm in four major areas:

1. decentralization of operational controls as a means of becoming more responsive to commercial pressure;
2. global enterprises moving into more remote locations;
3. the increased use of electronic links between separate business units;
4. redefining the very nature of the workplace.

Such developments are driven by competitive pressure and by a recognition that it is often cheaper to conduct transactions externally than internally.

The shift towards virtual corporations is altering the concept of the organization, as its boundaries become less readily identifiable and it begins to include elements of other organizations as an alternative to the traditional options of horizontal and/or vertical integration. Such arrangements can work towards securing greater efficiency, flexibility and innovation. At the heart of the concept of the virtual organization is knowledge rather than location as the defining factor in the emerging corporate landscape. In effect, the enterprise can minimize the need for many corporate buildings, outsource many peripheral functions and operate as a virtual company. The existence of such companies is rare today but a survey by Andersen Consulting/*Economist* Intelligence Unit indicates that 40 per cent of executives believe their enterprise will be virtual by 2010, up from a 1998 level of only 3 per cent (BT, 1998).

Within this virtual framework, the enterprise is able to call upon more resources through the development of ICT-induced alliances — many of which may be only temporary — as a short-term means of grasping market opportunities. As suggested, the virtual organization is being applied as a means to aid flows of information within and external to the organization so as to achieve greater efficiency and secure more effective supplier and customer relationships. The enterprise will focus on core activities and outsource those functions that may be better done elsewhere. Outsourcing offers benefits in terms of accessing the skills needed to develop effective online solutions, lowering the risk associated with project development and freeing up existing resources.

In terms of external links, the development of the virtual enterprise is very much based upon stimulating value-added partnerships. These partnerships are based upon a set of organizations that co-operate to manage (information about) the flow of products and services in the value chain. The partnerships can be:

● symbiotic — where different organizations offer complementary services;
● vertical — where parties follow one other in the industry value chain;
● horizontal — where the partners are erstwhile competitors.

The point behind each of these agreements is to establish a competitive advantage over those enterprises that are excluded from the network. When examining this within the context of Porter's Five Forces (see below), it is clear that these agreements seek to negate the rivalry between the forces — through co-operation between enterprises, suppliers and sellers — thereby improving the competitive positioning of those that participate in the network. For these effects to be felt, enterprises need effective communication systems.

The existence of electronic communication networks between enterprises can improve co-ordination between firms through either: an electronic brokerage, such that the firm is able to lower the cost of searching for and procuring the relevant goods and services; or an electronic integration effect, where there is a lowering of the costs involved in tightly integrating a supplier into the enterprise's functioning (see below).

The realization of these benefits will depend upon the attributes, the products, the network infrastructure, business environment and network control. These advantages have been employed to great effect by General Electric, which has pioneered the use of devices such as electronic auctions for the purposes of sourcing.

Such enterprises are able to harness the capabilities of many to pursue a strategy of risk sharing. However, it needs to be recognized that virtual firms are likely to face control problems, which may increase with the degree of risk they face. This is important, for the virtual enterprise needs to be a real-time enterprise, responding quickly to changes in business conditions. This relies upon the flexibility and adaptability of staff — underlining that new skills will have to be developed if the enterprise is to succeed with its virtual structure in the information economy. The virtual enterprise will be characterized by flatter hierarchies and a team-based work organization as a means of responding to changes in the business environment and customer demands. The value added is generated through the interworking of these teams.

The supply chain and the information economy

Increasingly the supply chain is being perceived as a key area of competitive advantage for enterprises. Consequently, many enterprises are seeking to achieve efficiency within the supply chain from the innovative use of information and communication technologies. This trend reflects the fact that, for many industries, the use of Internet technology to stimulate supply chain integration is no longer merely a source of competitive advantage but one of competitive imperative. The Internet has aided the integration of supply chains through its reliance on open standards (which allows flexibility in terms of partnerships and avoids lock-in), its relative cheapness (compared to the preceding EDI systems) and its ability to operate securely both inside (intranet) and outside (extranets) the enterprise. Such trends are stimulating a reassessment by many enterprises of their business model, as they realize the application of these technologies can generate extra efficiencies and develop new commercial opportunities (see Chapter 3).

Changes in the supply chain, driven by the application of these technologies, are not merely about cost reduction. They are also a means of revenue creation. The conventional supply chain is built around the assumption that the buyer will come into the traditional 'bricks and mortar' store — with the development of the Internet, this assumption is clearly being challenged. This is in line with the observations regarding disintermediation/re-intermediation within retail markets (see Chapter 3). Internet-based supply chains not only offer businesses a new way to cut costs but also offer forecasting that reflects market conditions more completely. In addition, the sharing of information along the value chain ensures that customers' needs are met more completely, that demands feed through the system and the enterprise's resources meet those demands, and that suppliers are fully aware of market trends and can stock accordingly.

In line with its strategy of offering a greater degree of online sales, Dell (a leading PC manufacturer) is one company that has made progress in terms of using electronic commerce to integrate more completely its supply chain. As its orders are received, information is relayed to its suppliers informing them of its needs in terms of types of components as well as when they are needed and where. This system allows inventories to be kept to a minimum with the newly arrived components emerging as new computers merely hours after they have arrived at the plant. The ability of suppliers to have real-time access to Dell's orders through its corporate extranet allows them to organize their own production and delivery much more efficiently as well as keeping them abreast of changes in demand. This ensures that Dell has just enough parts to keep production running smoothly. The extranet is extended to its customers, allowing them to track their orders. The trend towards the integration of Internet technology into supply chains has been most evident in the most cost-conscious of industries (such as the PC sector) where competition seems to be the most intense. Advances in software have aided this process by enabling enterprises to understand their businesses better and making them more able to identify cost sources. In these sectors, enterprises have been quick to realize, through the more widespread application of Internet-based technologies, that most enterprises paid over-inflated costs for their supplies and operated unnecessarily costly logistical chains. This is reflected in the fact that one of the main sources of efficiencies within the supply chain is the ability to eliminate much of the paper chasing involved in the process.

These trends typify a situation where supply chains are integrated to the extent that they effectively function as a single corporate entity. This integration is driven by the desire to deliver to the end user as efficiently as possible. Thus competition may increasingly occur between supply chains rather than, as traditionally understood, between enterprises. These trends towards integration are already evident in the consumer products sector or where an enterprise has outsourced a great deal of its activity. Highlighting supply chain integration is integral to the virtualization of the enterprise.

These trends indicate how business-to-business electronic commerce is helping to integrate value chains through enabling suppliers and customers to be part of a

three-way information partnership. This partnership is based upon treating all partners within the value chain as collaborators in seeking a common goal of increasing
efficiency across the value chain. It can overcome the increase in consumer power
derived from the Internet by offering a better service and therefore breeding increased
consumer loyalty. The true competitive benefit of such an arrangement relies upon
long-term commitment by the partners to the system and a continuation of the outsourcing process.

The application of electronic commerce to the supply chain directly indicates the
shift towards value chain integration noted above. This process of collaboration
allows for the optimization of all internal and external activities. Enterprises have
developed data warehouses, which can be accessed by their suppliers to enable
them to gauge the sales of their stock. This enables them to predict and plan output.
It also allows savings by allowing new as well as current suppliers to service the
demands of customers. These trends indicate (as mentioned) that the business is no
longer a freestanding entity. The objective is for large enterprises to become electronic business hubs and for smaller enterprises to become spokes vital to the success of the larger enterprise. This implies that the enterprise must let others into its
internal functioning and become familiar with the functions of its business partners.
This underlines the role of the organization as a network bringing in partners and outsourcing a great deal of its activities.

Despite evident benefits, the process of supply chain integration can be retarded
due to the resistance of assorted business partners to open up processes to other
enterprises. This reflects a general lack of willingness to share information. There are
other fears that this new system could lead to a re-intermediation with the emergence
of new — and the removal of existing — intermediaries ('middlemen') (see Chapter
3). These could be natural resisters to change. Finally there are factors that simply
reflect that the technology is not fully available to support these changes.

The competitive paradigm within the information economy

By way of a conclusion to the themes addressed within this chapter, it is evident that the
form and nature of competition is changing within the information economy.
Correspondingly, as businesses respond to the challenges posed by the increased competition associated with the information economy, it is apparent that new sources of competitiveness are emerging. These new sources of competitiveness are reflected throughout
this chapter and are broadly indicated in Table 2.1. This table contrasts the business
model associated with the information economy with the one that characterized the preceding industrial economy. Within the emerging business model, there is, as discussed in
the text, a greater reliance upon using ICTs to develop new commercial arrangements that
exhibit the necessary flexibility and to develop the new relationships that are key features
of the information economy.

The development of this new business model is derived from changes in the industry
structure within which the enterprise is operating, and is needed to secure competitive advan-

tage. According to Porter (1985), industry structure is determined by five competitive forces (the power of buyers, the power of suppliers, the threat of new entrants, the threat of substitutes and rivalry among suppliers). It is evident from the above analysis that all of these competitive forces will be affected by the development of the information economy (as highlighted in Figure 2.4). Many of these changes will be driven by revisions within the value chains of the affected sectors as buyer power and supplier pressures upon the enterprise are intensified. In addition, enterprises are likely to face increasing competitive pressure (both in a potential and actual sense) through the convergence of previously distinct sectors and a lowering of entry barriers.

Such competitive pressures highlight that the development of the information economy extends the enterprise out over ever-widening circles of influence — as witnessed through the external value system (see Figure 2.3). Most immediately affected are its customers and suppliers. To a lesser degree, the suppliers of its suppliers and customers of its customers and so on are also likely to be within the sphere of influence of the enterprise to some extent. Thus as the enterprise extends, there are new requirements to open up the enterprise to customers and suppliers, getting to know customers as individuals, creating mutually successful solutions with suppliers and evaluating alternative sourcing options. These trends will lead to industry transformation. As this happens, so there is a need for the extended enterprise to identify value network roles clearly, develop deep specialization, embrace collaboration and share infrastructure with competitors. Finally, as these industry trends stimulate commercial transformation, so there is pressure upon the enterprise to:

- focus upon customer intentions;
- exploit hybrid markets;
- manage the network of alliances strategically.

Inevitably these changes place pressure upon achieving new forms and sources of competitive advantage in terms of:

- lower costs in a number of areas through the use of the Internet (eg marketing);
- offering greater differentiation through product innovation;
- altering competitive scope through providing increased focus upon customer relations.

These trends highlight that it is especially important that enterprises exploit the full potential of the development of the information economy. In the first case, the cost efficiencies associated with the increased deployment of ICTs become especially important — being a first mover can feasibly deliver market share to the enterprise. The second point stresses the core source of competitive advantage — human resources — and the importance of the enterprise having access to the necessary skills to secure and enhance competitive advantage. The final point stresses, first, the increased importance of information in determining competitive advantage (through, for example, tailored marketing strategies) and,

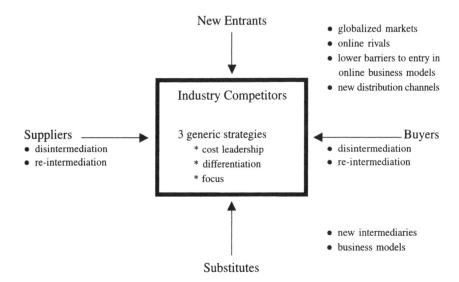

New Entrants

- globalized markets
- online rivals
- lower barriers to entry in online business models
- new distribution channels

Industry Competitors

Suppliers
- disintermediation
- re-intermediation

3 generic strategies
* cost leadership
* differentiation
* focus

Buyers
- disintermediation
- re-intermediation

- new intermediaries
- business models

Substitutes

Source: Adapted from Boch *et al* (1996)

Figure 2.4 *Porter's framework for competitive advantage within the information economy*

second, that many businesses will seek to compete within the information economy through new or evolved business models based around the increased utilization of online business processes. The generic impact of the information economy within the framework provided by Porter is reflected in Figure 2.4.

Figure 2.4 demonstrates how the forces of competitive advantage are all affected by the development of the information economy. Many of these issues are addressed more in Chapter 3 where the impact of electronic commerce is discussed more fully. How competitive advantage is altered depends upon how exposed the industry is to the challenge of online transactions, at least over the short term. As Chapter 3 discusses, those sectors that are especially exposed are developing and implementing new business models to meet head on the challenge and the threat to competitive advantage posed by the information economy. The model is by no means ubiquitous, as the pressure from the development of electronic commerce will be felt asymmetrically across the economy, and is dependent upon the sensitivity of the sector involved.

Clearly strategic goals are influenced and altered by the advent of the information economy. The entire process of competition has the ability to be fundamentally altered by the shift towards the information economy. One of its core features is the creation of new competition by removing barriers between sectors and allowing enterprises from previously distinct sectors to enter one another's — as well as new — markets. This process will be directly affected by the degree of interworking that takes place as a result of the evolution of the information economy. Thus instead of an enterprise carving out a particular niche on a particular value chain, the blurring of demarcations between businesses that results from the information economy will (as mentioned above) lead to integrated value chains across sectors. The result is that organizations will find ways to combine or interwork to establish common strengths. The end point over the medium to longer term is that value chains rather than companies will compete against each other, and the succeeding businesses will be the ones that most successfully integrate their demand and supply chains to enable information of mutual commercial interest to be easily transmitted across companies. Such trends, in terms of the competitive forces model, will integrate the external forces (new entrants, suppliers, buyers and substitutes) much more closely into generic strategy formation. In this context, strategy choice will become an increasingly interdependent (and possibly integrated) phenomenon.

These competitive forces are also shaped by the rules of co-operation and alliance development. The global effects linked to the development of the information economy mean that enterprises will feel pressure to develop value chains that allow them to act in both defensive and offensive ways. The development of these alliances across organizational boundaries will be established through common media such as the Internet. The openness of the system will make both the creation and dissolution of these alliances easier. Competitive forces are clearly changing. The cross-links between virtual and physical value chains and the convergence that is being stimulated are all altering the nature of competition forces within many, and eventually all, sectors.

The development of a new business model (see Table 2.1) and the changing competitive forces that are stimulating it (as formalized within Figure 2.4) are central to understanding the commercial impact of the information economy. They highlight how internal and external processes are responding to the challenges posed by its development. This is especially relevant in terms of the development of electronic commerce explored in Chapter 3. Many of the features of these frameworks — in terms of both the business model and competitive forces — reflect the broad ubiquitous impact of electronic commerce upon the enterprise, both internally and externally. Electronic commerce is the key facilitator behind many of the changes occurring within the value chain (apart, in most cases, from the human resource impact); it is the source of many of the cost efficiencies predicted and allows the organization to 'virtualize' itself. What this suggests is that you cannot really understand deriving competitive advantage from the information economy without comprehending electronic commerce.

Reading 17.2

Taken from Chapter 4 – Does your product or service suit the Internet?, in *Brand Building on the Internet* by Martin Lindstrom and Tim Frank Andersen (2000)

Why are 90 percent of all cinema-goers already in their seats by 7 p.m. when the first advertisement begins and why do they not wait until 7.25 p.m. when the feature film starts? Mainly because they regard the advertisements before the film as a bonus. This statistic illustrates very clearly that correct use of a medium is received positively by the user. This also applies in those cases where it is just a question of traditional advertising and where in principle the user pays, both in the form of time and money.

It is basically a matter of taking advantage of the strong aspects of the medium. Apart from the owner, no-one bothers to watch the slide show with the names of local shops that precedes the advertisements proper in the cinema, for the very reason that the slides do not make full use of the medium's unique characteristics. In the same way the Internet is not used in an optimal way at present. Scanning in a brochure and making it available on the Internet is in principle the same as giving a slide show in a cinema; it will never attract our attention. You can see this from everyday life; if you receive an e-mail of more than 20 lines the first thing you do is to print out the text. This is because you lack an overview of the received letter. All communication that can be printed off from the Internet without losing anything in the form of understanding or involvement is in principle not using the Internet optimally. It is very likely that people will print out an ordinary brochure which has merely been scanned in and put on the net. The user's perception of the company has in theory thereby become worse than if the brochure had been distributed in the traditional way. The picture quality is poorer and the overview more difficult, as the content is spread over several pages, with in some cases random page breaks. Of course the sender will experience a benefit in the short term in being able to distribute the brochure cheaply, but the recipient will not have benefited from the possible additional value that could have been gained had the 'brochure' been interactive. It can thus be very difficult to justify the distribution of such communications via the Internet, where the user's expectations about interactivity correspond to a cinema-goer's expectations concerning the use of the film medium by advertisers.

Television has proved particularly suited to product demonstration and comparison of two situations, e.g. clothes before and after being washed, or between washing powders A and B. This is perhaps why Procter & Gamble – maker of some of the world's most successful washing products – is one of the world's leading television advertisers. Most of their television advertisements are based on comparative advertising.

On the other hand, it would be difficult to make a case that television is suitable to advertise, say, bananas or spices. The additional value of using the medium's visual characteristics is limited. All the same, now and then we see advertisements for both on television. If a parallel is drawn with the Internet, it would not immediately appear appropriate to develop websites for toilet paper, bananas or tampons. And it is here that creativity – as in all other communication – comes into the picture.

Libra (in some countries called Libresse), a feminine protection brand, has established a website that hasn't lost the top position on health websites in countries where Libra is marketed since it was launched. Its case study, in Chapter 8, is a good example of how creativity can make a relatively low-interest product very interesting in a web format. On average a visitor spends 15 minutes on the Libragirl website, returning more than three times a year – a total of 45 minutes annually. Compared with an average television exposure of five minutes, this can be considered very high. Besides the big difference in the number of minutes exposed to the medium, a major difference is also that the consumer voluntarily participates on the Libragirl website. Users of the site searched for the address, waited for the pages to download and surfed through the Libragirl pages. This high involvement is not necessarily the case with regards to Libra television advertising.

In 1998 MTV ran a campaign on their site claiming that unknown people had managed to gain access to the site and had left unauthorised messages. The hacker plot turned out to be a planned MTV action – introducing a new television show. The case is a good example of how creativity can generate the right momentum about a news story.

JoeBoxer is another good example of how creativity can justify why a product should appear on the Internet without any clear consumer benefits. When visiting the JoeBoxer site (www.joeboxer.com) the visitor will be asked to place the body in front of the screen and download a pair of virtual JoeBoxer underwear. The process, which continues in the same tone-of-voice over more than 30 pages, is pure fun but manages to add an extra dimension to the brand. A more detailed description of how to ensure brand-added value on the internet is described in Chapters 7 to 9.

Creativity was also the key word for one of the most acclaimed campaigns ever run on the Internet – in Brazil. The successful campaign, to promote a local Internet company, is best explained via the illustrations they used (and on the net these illustrations were in fact animated).

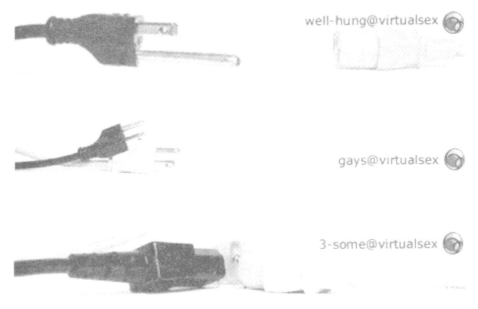

Creativity not only increased the click-through rate but ensured more than 10 international awards for this recent campaign promoting an Internet company in Brazil.

The product's interactive potential is decisive for its relevance on the Internet
Creativity is necessary for the successful integration of the product and the Internet on a branding site in the same way as creativity is the winning factor when it is a question of successful communication on television or in print. The more it is possible to use the medium in an untraditional way, perhaps by combining two familiar elements in a new way, the greater the success.

In principle all products are therefore suitable for exposure on the Internet. Certain lines of business and products are, however, more suitable than others, as they are of a kind which are better suited to the medium's communicative characteristics.

Which products are most suitable for the Internet?

Until three years ago only a few companies could show a positive return from their use of the Internet. However, this has changed drastically. The main reason is that since the end of 1996 many companies have managed to give the customer additional value by the integration of dialogue and interactivity and by the use of the medium's enormous potential for information searching, sales and distribution.

Everyone knows the situation where the number of CDs that people want to listen to in a music shop exceeds the patience of those around them. It is difficult to listen to more than a couple of CDs as a queue forms and both the staff and other customers become irritated. Using the Internet, however, the scenario can provide the customer with extra value. On the Internet the consumers can search for the required type of music, enter the names of musicians as well as seeing the whole of the available range. The consumers can also listen to all the songs they want without being interrupted or feeling guilty. Ordering is carried out online, deliveries are made to the consumer's address and the charge only consists of the delivery costs. That consumers also receive a discount when buying CDs over the Internet is yet another advantage.

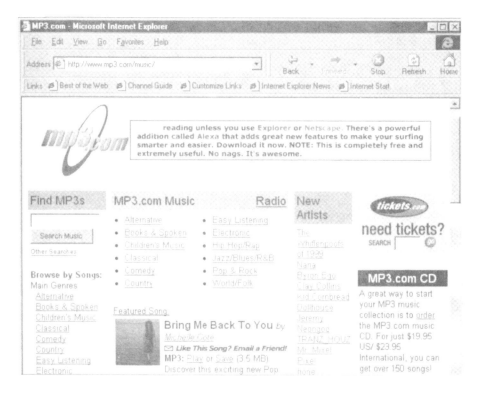

www.mp3.com is the key to more than 18 million songs on the Internet.

The introduction of RIO Diamond (www.diamondmm.com) has pushed the popularity of music on the Internet even further. More than 18 million songs are today available for download via the Internet, several hundred thousand are for free and all are of high sound quality. Downloading a song to RIO Diamond (a portable music device) only takes 10 to 15 minutes (depending on connection type). It is possible to store up to 60 minutes of sound on the RIO Diamond. The Diamond is based on MP3, a file format that stores audio files on a computer in such a way that the file size is relatively small, but the song sounds near perfect.

The technology has not only made life difficult for record companies and provoked the formation of an anti-MP3 organisation called Secure Digital Music Initiative, it has also opened the gates for a whole new world of music amateurs on the Internet. More than 100 amateur hit lists are today available on the Internet with thousands of hits created by 'ordinary' people around the world.

Sony is one of the companies trying to create an alternative to the popular MP3 technology, by introducing the Sony Memory Stick technology. Their hope is to avoid a cannibalisation of the music copyright industry.

The Internet has added value compared with the traditional method of selling recordings and has forced the international music companies to re-invent their whole way of doing business, which clearly has been shown to be out of date in the online business.

The advantage of using the Internet here as a channel of communication, and possibly also sales, is self-evident. This is perhaps one of the reasons why, according to Forrester Research, 19 percent of websites with positive incomes belong to the entertainment industry.

Successful online sales in the year 2002

As previously stated in this chapter, almost every company has a reason for going online. By working with the Internet, however, we have learned that some product categories will gain more value by becoming online than others. In general, all product categories can be classified into three segments – Interactive branding (i-branding), Electronic commerce (e-commerce) and Electronic operations (e-operations) (a more detailed description of this model can be found in Chapter 9). Each segment represents either a way of 'saving' or 'earning' money by being on the Internet.

When deciding why a company should go online it is important to evaluate the site's online objectives. Is it to establish or build a brand, to earn money or to save money by implementing processes that cut existing costs in the organisation?

As is the case for traditional communication, very little research has been conducted to determine the value of online branding. It is a difficult task as a strong brand position does not necessarily mean a sales increase on a short-term basis.

The best way to get a verified indication of which companies today are more suitable on the Internet (within i-branding and e-commerce) than others is by looking at where tomorrow's online sales will be.

The list below covers the projected six most successful revenue categories on the Internet for the year 2002. The research, interestingly enough, shows that only five product

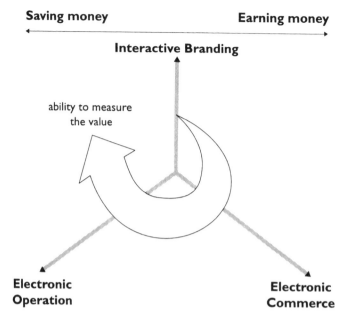

Saving money   **Earning money**

Interactive Branding

ability to measure
the value

Electronic   **Electronic**
Operation   **Commerce**

I-branding sites are today the most difficult sites to measure in a quantitiative way as there is no transaction involved.

categories will cover 90 percent of all e-commerce on the Internet for the year 2002. This clearly indicates why so many websites haven't managed to become successful on the Internet today. The fact is that in far too many cases the 'real' added consumer value when buying online is too low compared with the 'risk' the consumer perceives when making an online purchase.

1.	32%	The computer industry
		Modems, computers, accessories and software
2.	24%	The travel industry
		Travel, hotels and events
3.	19%	The entertainment industry
		Interactive leisure products (edutainment, infortainment and games)
		Music and films (video, DVD and CD)
		Books
4.	10%	Gifts and flowers
		Chocolate, postcards, flowers, gimmicks, merchandising
5.	5%	Food and beverage
		Personal placing of orders and delivery
		Provisions (food, drink, etc.)

6.   10%   Apparel and other product categories
            Insurance and banking
            Search databases/reference works
            Transport, dispatch and communication
            News reporting, research, information

Below is a fuller explanation of each individual category, focusing on utilisation of the medium.

1. Computer-related products

Practically all the users of the Internet have a computer. Providing information about computer-related products and selling hardware and software via the Internet is therefore an obvious step. For example, if you want to upgrade a modem, one of the most appropriate places to look for information about it would be on the Internet. Software is one of the most rapidly growing product categories on the Internet today.

www.macromedia.com is one of the most visited sites in the world, with more than 500,000 visitors per day.

Macromedia, an American company that develops Internet software, stated in its conference in San Francisco in October 1999 that they have more than 500,000 visits to their website each day. Of the 500,000 visitors, 170,000 want to download programs. Macromedia therefore reached the break-even point with their website in the middle of 1997, even though their webmaster team already consists of more than 40 employees.

Purchase of hardware, such as what Dell offers its customers, is not the only type of service that has been shown to be successful on the Internet. Often a discount of 25 percent is offered if software is bought and downloaded directly via the Internet. If you want the coloured version of the instruction manual and the box in which the software was sold the price is 25 percent higher.

But the benefits don't stop here: a frequent and easy update of software has finally become a reality just by accepting 'yes' on the screen. User support can be done online via a new browser setup that enables the user to split the screen in two and receive online support while surfing the net simultaneously.

2. The travel industry

Travel, hotels and events

Due to the Internet's global spread the medium has rapidly proved itself to be particularly well suited to collecting information about other countries and other cultures. The amount of information about all the countries of the world is enormous and of interest to anyone who is planning a journey.

Once the holiday destination has been selected, it is an easy step to book the journey on the Internet. For this reason alone travel agents are justified in being on the Internet. The purchase process could almost be described as a chain reaction. Once the users have become accustomed to obtaining the first half of the information via the medium it seems natural to continue. The winners are the travel agents offering the users the required travel data online and ultimately also providing a booking service for tickets and hotel reservations via the Internet.

Many hotels make it possible to view the rooms and book them online. As far back as 1995 the city of San Francisco drew up a hotel guide which not only made it possible to book hotels but also to see what activities were available in the vicinity of the hotel. www.travelocity.com is another good example of how travel and hotel booking will be one and the same service in the future.

At the same time the Internet has started a war between the airlines, and as a result many US airlines offer standby prices to Internet users. The prices are often 200 to 300 percent lower than the prices obtained by contacting a travel agent in the normal way. By subscribing to a special airline e-mail list, customers are informed about low airfares on a daily basis. This will result in a dramatic change in today's role for travel agents. The traditional travel agency already suffers from substantial costs such as rent, personnel and paper-based infrastructure – costs which in a low-margin business can become life threatening when competing against Internet-based companies that can 'white-out' these burdens.

The next stage in the chain reaction will typically be the selection of local attractions and

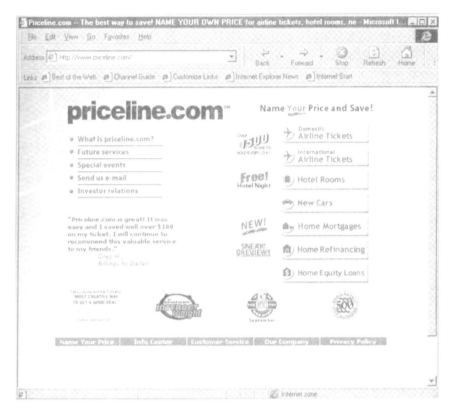

What do you want to pay for a trip from Sydney to Los Angeles? Type in the amount at www.priceline.com and become a part of the airline online auction.

restaurants, booking seats and purchasing tickets. Furthermore, obtaining calendars of local events and not least establishing contact with the local population or other travellers who have recently visited the selected places and have some experience of them is likely to occur.

Comparing Fares

City pair	Internet fare	Full-coach	Advance Purchase		
Washington – Nashville	US Airways, (www.usairways.com), $79	$598	$414,	$210,	$158
Newark – Salt Lake City	Continental, (www.flycontinental.com), 179	1,610	785,	614,	408
Dallas – Cleveland	American, (www.americanair.com), 159	1,296	204,	204,	204
Memphis – Las Vegas	Northwest, (www.nwa.com), 149	1,388	463,	351,	351
Los Angeles – Vancouver	Air Canada, (www.aircanada.com), 197	426	337,	214,	214

Air ticket prices can usefully be studied on the Internet, as price-wise there are great savings to be made. Many airline companies offer Internet users a chance to subscribe to a mailing list that informs them about daily discount tickets.

3. The entertainment industry

Interactive leisure products

One of the most appropriate product categories for exposure on the Internet is products which are based on interactivity. Exposure in the traditional media is difficult as, for example, a game looks neither particularly exciting nor involving in an advertisement or on a poster. The Internet can present extracts from the game (for example, one level) which the user can try out, and can enable the user to download the whole game in return for payment. This means that users do not even need to leave their chairs. Often the price for downloading will be cheaper than the price users would pay for an identical product in a shop because on the Internet there are no costs such as packaging, retail trade distribution and advertising.

The latest methods also take care of automatic updating of new versions of software via the net.

Walt Disney's Disney Blast is an excellent example of how the Internet can be used as an entertainment medium. Disney Blast, the digital Donald Duck comic, is updated daily and 20 to 25 new games and stories are added each week.

Disney (www.disneyblast.com) was one of the first really successful online entertainment concepts on the Internet which managed to charge money for its service.

Already products are marketed which are based on letting the user play the game free of charge. The games are constructed in such a way that the user has to buy equipment in order to make best use of the game. The price is often symbolic, but even if each player only spends a few cents on playing a game, experience shows that this form of payment is a goldmine for the provider. The number of players can be overwhelming due to the easy availability and the low price.

Music and films (books, video, DVD and CD)
The world's largest bookshop – www.amazon.com – is probably one of the most famous success stories on the Internet. The bookshop today has three million books, CDs and video titles on its 'cyber shelves'. The typical delivery time is one week (including carriage by courier). Amazon.com not only specialises in book, CD and video sales but also offers many services linked to the sales process which in themselves can justify its existence on the Internet. Amazon.com's prices are estimated to be up to 40 percent lower than those of an ordinary retailer, primarily because of the lower costs of distribution and marketing.

At amazon.com the readers can write reviews of the books they have read and participate in a weekly competition for the best contribution. Amazon.com's services also include the opportunity to subscribe to a virtual news-list which is modified to suit the interests and profile of the user. You can also match your author or title taste with other amazon.com users' tastes and review suggestions for other titles which may match your taste. Today several hundred thousand users subscribe to this mailing list – an excellent alternative to the traditional book catalogue. Similarly www.amazon.com can recommend to their visitors relevant books on the basis of their existing favourite titles. This is possible because www.amazon.com records the readers' variations in taste each day and links these together with other readers' favourite titles.

4. Gifts and flowers
Chocolate, postcards, flowers, gimmicks, merchandising
www.interflora.com is a good example of excellent use of the Internet. If you order a bouquet of flowers to go from Sydney, Australia to Copenhagen in Denmark via Interflora in the traditional way it costs between $90 and $100 per bouquet including delivery. A bouquet of the same size ordered via Interflora's Internet website costs half as much. The higher price does not give you quicker delivery, more (or prettier) flowers or more lines of text on the greeting card. Another example could be a department store which in the run-up to Christmas might open a Christmas gift catalogue, where users could choose between selected gift ideas in varying prices ranges, have their selection wrapped in their choice of wrapping paper and finally have the present delivered, all via the Internet.

New services have appeared on the Internet. www.123greetings.com and www.e-greetings.com both offer free digital postcards. A newer online promotion is wotch.com, which offers a free download. It might be a reminder of your friend's birthdays or the weekly joke. Basically the more you interact with the application on your desktop the more valuable it becomes. More than 50,000 users download wotch.com per day, making it clear that the future is bright for such promotions.

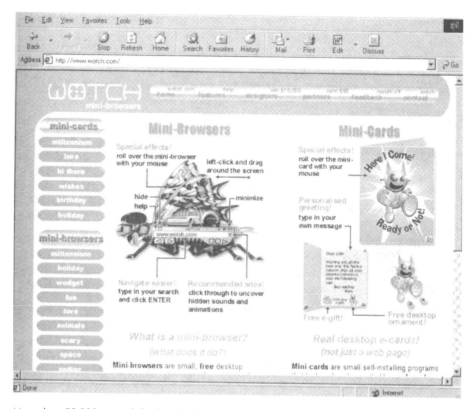

More than 50,000 users daily download a wotch.

5. Food and drink products

This category includes, in principle, all types of ordered purchases, where the actual purchase process can be simplified via the Internet and thus give a particular company added value as a result of its existence on the net. One of the most successful websites in Scandinavia is ISO (www.iso.dk), a Danish supermarket chain, where subscribers order provisions online. The Internet can complement smaller retailers too: HomeDelivery.com (www.homedelivery.com) lets New Yorkers browse local stores, order and get home delivery.

6. Apparel and other product categories

Insurances, brokerage, banking and credit companies

The financial sector should become a winner on the Internet. Already nearly all transactions between financial institutions are electronic. Most US-based banks offer 100 percent online banking for customers – a huge time-saver. Paying bills over the web can save hours of monthly paperwork (and postage). Eventually, billers will close the loop and invoice over the Internet. On the other hand, a PC still can't spit out $20 bills – the web has a way to go before it kills off the ATM. Initially consumers resist changes, but then find

www.foodcom is one of the largest home delivery services on the Internet today.

they can't live without them. When ATM cash dispensers appeared in the 1970s, people distrusted them. Today ATMs are more popular than bank branches.

Insurers face more difficulties than banks. Many consumers rely on local agents to do policy shopping for them. Also, big insurers have aging computer hardware and rely on agents to sell their wares. Similar factors have slowed the progress of retail-oriented broker-age firms like Merrill Lynch onto the Web. If they're not careful traditional insurers, too, could find themselves losing share to Web-based discounters.

The Internet has revolutionised the once-staid investment world. In the 1970s, stock trades were completed on paper: bicycle messengers pedalled down streets with mountains of certificates and payments. Today a quarter of all retail trades are online. Upstarts like E-Trade have a lot of the market but older firms – notably Fidelity Investments and Charles Schwab – have a share, too.

In the long run, the distinction between online and offline financial services will fade away. Banks without websites will be as rare as banks without ATMs. Lenders with no web presence will lose market share. Insurers that don't provide services on the web will shrivel. Eventually, not enabling customers to check balances, originate loans and manage their financial lives over the web will cost institutions business. Financial service providers ignore the web at their peril.

Sixty-six percent of businesses in the West rate e-commerce as important in their overall strategy, according to IBM, while 35 percent of these businesses have an e-business strategy. However, only 31 percent of the US population, according to CDB Research & Consulting Inc., has bought products or services online.

The insurance and banking sectors are particularly suited to the Internet as more and more people manage their finances from their home computer. A total integration with the bank and insurance company is therefore obvious. A survey conducted on 2,929 Internet users in February 1999 found that 83 percent state convenience as the major factor for preferring the Internet.

Most Important Reasons People Shop on the Web		What Information Do You Look For When Buying a Product on the Web?	
Easy to place an order	83%	Detailed information about the product itself	82%
Large selection of products	63%		
Cheaper prices	63%		
Faster service and delivery	52%	Price comparisons	62%
Detailed and clear information about what is being offered	40%		
No sales pressure	39%	Detailed information about the vendor	21%
Easy payment procedures	36%		

Survey conducted by Jacob Neilsen's Alertbox 1999

Not just transactions but also many forms of dialogue between the company and the customer can be carried out more easily via the Internet. In a typical situation where users need to contact their insurance companies, for example to claim on flood damage, they normally have to go through the following procedure: first the insurance company has to be contacted, then the company sends out a (sometimes incorrect) claims form. The claims form then has to be filled in and returned to the company. If the form is not filled in correctly then the whole process has to start again. The claim is processed and the company comes back with a reply. Typical processing time: four weeks.

On the Internet this can be carried out more quickly, easily and cheaply. The claims form can be displayed onscreen and while it is being completed it is possible to obtain supplementary information and ongoing verification of the data. The form is sent online and the reply returns online. The Internet has thus given the company's service an extra dimension – justification for an insurance company or bank to be on the Internet.

Search databases

Search databases filter the chaos of information that is to be found on the Internet at present – for each day brings 250,000 new pages online. The next generation of search

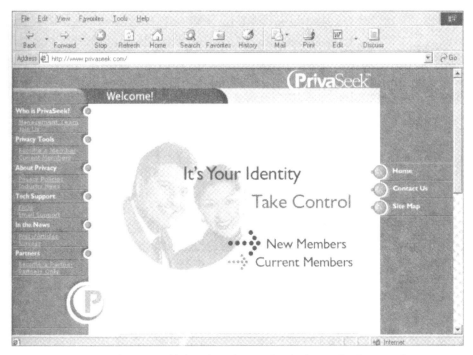

Concepts like privaseek.com are likely toshow the way for the future of online search engines.

databases is very likely to be 'infomediaries'. An infomediary is a third-party search engine that collects data about its user and then acts on the user's behalf, to gain benefits on the Internet. An infomediary can choose relevant links, based on its profile of the user, from the thousands th~t m~v h~ +h~own up by a search, thus creating true one-to-one communication.

The introduction of infomediaries is the first serious trend toward customised negotiation on the Internet. As a negotiator, the infomediary will gain discounts for a user by leveraging its store of your consumer details. Leading search engines, like Yahoo! and excite@home, have acknowledged this recently by taking over some of the world's most respected data-mining companies. It is very likely that search engines and databases will become infomediaries to survive in the future.

Transport, dispatch and communication

FedEX was the first company that offered dispatch tracing of packages and letters. The integration of courier service and the Internet was in many ways something of a small revolution on the Internet as the concept was the first to create concrete added value by incorporating the medium into the company's product portfolio. In 1999 1.3 million people carried out a digital package search via the FedEX website. If this is converted to (telephone) work-hours, it corresponds to a saving of 200 telephone employees per year!

With an unduplicated monthly audience of more than 14.8 million users, the CNN website has the largest reach of any news site on the web.

FedEX's newest technology makes it impossible to receive a package from the company unless the recipient signs for it on a digital signature pad. These signatures are then automatically put into a receipt database which is also available on the Internet. This puts an end to the old excuses from recipients who claim they never received something or other.

FedEX is systematically going about turning its problem areas in customer relations into strategic advantages, all by using the Internet. At the same time the basic processes in the company are being optimised and the customers are serving themselves, and are quite happy to do so. The traditional consumer has become a prosumer, who first produces and assembles the product and then orders it via the Internet. By letting the customer become part of the production apparatus, the company has the opportunity to make considerable savings.

At present, competing courier and transport companies are engaged in a scramble for position. Some have gone even further and by using GPS (Global Positioning System) are able to trace a package to the individual delivery vehicle and determine its exact position.

The future will offer even more advanced interaction. Tests were conducted in 1998 by BMW to enable online tracking of a car's exact position via the Internet. In addition they looked into transferring data about the car's current technical status to an individual website, which could mean that sometime in the future it may be possible for the car to book itself into a workshop and for the mechanic to have ordered the spare parts required before the car even arrives.

The integration between GPS and the Internet has only shown us the tip of the iceberg of what benefits we might gain by having this new technology available. One of the most tangible benefits available today is the ability for consumers to see the current position of the bus they are catching every morning to work. If it is delayed then an estimated arrival time will appear on the site. The system has so far been introduced in only two US cities but has proved to be a major success.

News reporting

The traditional mass media are struggling at the moment to find a balance between traditional news reporting (in newspapers, on radio and television) and news reporting via the Internet. The danger is that the new form of news reporting will cannibalise the original channels of communication. Experience shows that users of the Internet are not yet prepared to pay for this form of interactive service, and many news providers are therefore finding it difficult to justify why they should be on the Internet at all. A number of Internet-based concepts – like news.com – have, however, proved that news reporting on the Internet is justified. At present news.com and CNN.com are free for the end-users, but within a few years the companies will probably demand payment for their services. This will be the acid test of whether users are willing to pay to receive electronic news.

It all takes time ...

As with all new technology, the Internet and the opportunities the medium offers will see major developments in the future. Not only will the medium have new technologies at its disposal which make the visual elements stronger, the interactivity more integrated and the flow of information faster, people will also become more familiar with how to utilise the unique characteristics of the medium.

The examples above all show that they have managed to link together the product, the brand and the Internet in a way which leaves the company more service- and user-oriented than before and which in the long term will help to differentiate them from their competitors.

Part 2

Case Studies

Contents

1.	The Body Shop by Graham Beaver	457
2.	Ford	460
3.	Fujitsu and ICL	469
4.	Glaxo-Wellcome	472
5.	Idealab by Graham Beaver	476
6.	J D Wetherspoon	480
7.	Maison Novelli by Graham Beaver	485
8.	Manchester United	488
9.	Matcon Engineering by Graham Beaver	500
10.	Nissan and Renault	504
11.	Powderject Limited by Graham Beaver	509
12.	Procter & Gamble	514
13.	Raytheon by Graham Beaver	520
14.	Shell	526
15.	Starbucks Coffee	535
16.	Toyota	544
17.	Vodafone	549

1

The Body Shop

by Graham Beaver

© 2001 Graham Beaver

The Body Shop's founder Anita Roddick could not raise a bank loan from her bank manager until she replaced her T-shirt in favour of a suit. The presentation of a business plan can be just as important as the facts and figures contained in it. That was the lesson that Anita Roddick learnt when she approached her bank manager for the start-up capital to open her first Body Shop. She came up with the name after finding her premises between two funeral parlours in Brighton. It was a move that prompted a legal threat from her neighbours, who claimed that the name was a tasteless stunt.

In the week of 24 October 1999, the manufacturer and retailer of bodycare products reported half-year profits up 4 per cent to £9.4 million on sales of £271 million, up from £262 million. In October 1999 the company had a market value of £222 million, operated more than 1,600 outlets in 47 countries and made 400 products. (Source: *The Sunday Times*, 24 October 1999).

The numbers are a far cry from that small shop that Roddick opened in 1976. The story of her rise to fame and her subsequent hiccups has been told many times. Not so well known are the details of how she touted around her first business plan and the prejudice she suffered because of her casual appearance and the fact that she was a woman.

Roddick states:

> The most difficult thing was raising money for the first shop. I knew that I had a good idea and a reasonable business plan, and I thought naïvely that this was all that was important. I went to see my bank manager in my T-shirt, with my two small children in tow.
>
> I thought that my enthusiasm and energy would convince the bank manager to believe in me but he turned me down, which really set me back. My husband, Gordon, told me to have another go but this time dress up like a bloke in pin stripes and leave the kids behind. He came too. After taking his advice, I was able to walk out of the bank with a £4,000 loan.

Roddick had grown up in Littlehampton, Sussex, the daughter of Italian immigrants. 'We never fitted in,' she has said. Her father, who ran his own café, died when she was ten. Roddick had to help her mother who always told her that she would succeed. She did well at school and was 'desperate' to see the world. Before embarking on that, she joined a teacher training course at the University of Bath but fondly remembers being asked to leave one school for writing a swear word on the blackboard to illustrate a linguistic point!

Roddick worked on a kibbutz, travelled, married Gordon and ran a bed-and-breakfast hotel before starting The Body Shop. She had always wanted to start her own business and when, in 1976, Gordon took several months off to make a trip from Argentina to New York, she decided that it was time to realize her ambition.

She herself had travelled extensively. Having run out of shampoo in one remote place, she experimented with rubbing extracts from fruit and vegetables on her hair. 'In its raw state, almost anything that is harvested out of the ground can polish, clean and protect your body.' She has said:

> It wasn't only economic necessity that inspired the birth of The Body Shop. Women, when they want to earn a livelihood, usually earn it through what they are interested in or what they are knowledgeable about. My travels exposed me to the body rituals of women all over the world. Also, the frugality that my mother exercised during the War made me question many retail conventions. Why waste a container, when you can refill it? Why buy more of something than you can use? We refilled, re-used and recycled everything.'

Roddick began with one shop. She paid a friend £25 to design The Body Shop logo and painted the store green to cover the damp mouldy walls. She started by selling 25 hand-mixed products that she produced in various sizes to make the range seem larger at 200 items. She dreamt up some marketing gimmicks that included sprinkling scent on the pavement close to the shop to entice customers.

She took a £4,000 investment from Ian McGlinn, a friend, and within six months had opened a second shop. Another friend wanted to open one in Bognor Regis and a haphazard network of franchises evolved, all taken by women. The Body Shop soon had stores in London and started opening others on the Continent. Gordon came up with the idea of self-financing more new stores, which sparked the growth of a more organized franchised network.

By 1984, The Body Shop was making a profit of £1 million on sales of £5 million. Two years later, it was floated on the stock market and four years after that it made profits of £14 million on sales of £56 million. However, in 1998 profits plunged 91 per cent falling from £38 million to £3.4 million, after the company bought back many of its franchises and embarked on a big restructuring programme.

Roddick says that the business in Britain is hierarchical with 'generals' at the top who stifle creative thinking. She states that: 'There is a real timidity towards energy and passion in this country. You can't make yourself have passion. Curiosity, optimism, a great idea, self-esteem and networking are important in starting a business.'

2

Ford

By the end of 1999 Ford had revenue of US $163 billion and employed 364,550 people. This had been achieved in less than 100 years from a modest start in 1903, with only US $28,000 cash and 10 employees. Right from the beginning the Ford Motor Company was looking for foreign growth. In 1905 it started building its first factory in Canada. Today Ford operates in over 30 nations with representatives in over 200.

PERFORMANCE

In 1999 Ford sold some 7,220,000 cars worldwide made up of 4,787,000 in the United States and the remainder in the rest of the world. This was up 6 per cent on the previous year. Sales and revenue were up 13 per cent to US $162,558,000. This resulted in earnings per share of US $5.86, up 21 per cent. Table A.1 gives more details of this. It is taken from the 1999 annual report found at www.ford.com/finaninvest/stockholder/stock99/operhigh.htm.

TYPICAL PROBLEMS

Being a global company means having manufacturing capacity spread around the world. This has resulted in a feeling that Ford, like GM and other car companies, simply has too many plants in too many countries. Having plants in different companies exposes the company to local labour market laws and practices. Whereas in the UK

Table A.1

	1999		1998		Percentage Change
Financial Results					
Vehicle Unit Sales (in thousands)					
– North America	4,787	✓	4,370		
– Outside North America	2,433		2,453		
Total Worldwide	7,220	✓	6,823		up 6%
Sales and Revenues (in millions)					
– Automotive	$136,973	✓	$119,083		
– Financial Services	25,585		25,333		
Total Company	$162,558	✓	$144,416		up 13%
Automotive Capital Expenditures					
– Amount (in millions)	$7,945		$8,113		down 2%
– As a Percentage of Automotive Sales	5.8%		6.8%		
Automotive Cash at Year-end (in billions)					
– Gross Cash and Marketable Securities	$23.6		$23.8	✓	
– Net Cash and Marketable Securities	11.4		14.0	✓	
Earnings*					
Net Income (in millions)	$7,237	✓	$6,116		up 18%
Earnings per Share	$5.86	✓	$4.86		up 21%
Financial Returns					
After-tax Returns on:					
– North American Automotive Sales	6.2%	✓✓	5.3%		Up 9/10 pt.
– Total Automotive Sales	4.2%	✓✓	4.0%		Up 2/10 pt.
– Common and Class B shareholders' equity	28.1%		25.4%		Up 2.7 pts.
Shareholder Value					
Quarterly Dividends per Share (effective 4th quarter, 1999)	$0.50	✓	$0.46		up 9%
Shareholder Value Added (in billions)*	$2.6	✓	$1.7		up 53%
Total Shareholder Returns	–6%		+89%	✓✓✓	

✓ – All-time Ford record
✓✓ – Best since 1988
✓✓✓ – Top-Quartile performance among S&P 500 companies

*Earnings and Shareholder Value Added are on an operating basis, and for 1998 exclude a non-cash gain of %15,955 million that resulted from Ford's spin-off of Associates First Capital Corporation in 1998.

there is at present a relatively flexible labour market, this is not the case in Germany, for example.

It is pretty clear that car manufacturers will have to do something about emission pollution of cars. Increasingly countries are tightening up on the level of emission allowed. This is forcing the car makers to develop cleaner cars.

The spread of the Internet means that the way cars are sold through dealerships is also under fire, as well as the way spare components are sourced. GM, Ford and Daimler Chrysler are in the process of setting up an Internet-based business-to-business facility to do just this. The e-car is at present a bit of a dream for the makers but it cannot be too far away. By e-car they mean a car that the consumer has been able to specify before the company builds it. This is opposed to the present system where car makers build lots of cars based on market research of what models, colour, etc consumers are going for and then wait for the cars to be purchased.

Sub-contractors are also being targeted by the car makers in order that more value at lower cost can be extracted from them. This is taking the form of better use of the Internet and also trying to reduce delivery costs by relocating sub-contractors and suppliers near, or on site, with the assembly plants.

Car makers are seeking mergers or alliances with other car companies or suppliers. The reasons behind this are several fold; sometimes it is to gain access to markets, to share development costs, to exploit specific competencies or to gain from economies of scale.

There is a drive to develop world cars that can sell around the world. So while production may take place locally, design is centralized. Technically manufacturers want to reduce the number of platforms. Consumers on the other hand appear to want diversity in cars – so-called lifestyle vehicles, sports vehicles, the family car, people carriers etc.

The changes in the former Soviet Union and its satellite nations such as Hungary, the Czech Republic and Poland have presented the car makers with new markets and possible production sites. Other new markets include China and the Asia-Pacific area.

Let us look at three specific strategic issues that are facing Ford at present –manufacturing location, business-to-business (B2B), and the environment and corporate citizenship.

MANUFACTURING LOCATION

One of the hardest things a global company like Ford has to do is to decide on the 'best' places to manufacture its products. The building and bringing into production of a new plant is an extremely expensive business, as is taking out of production old plant. Mistakes can be very, very expensive. Ford's decision to close car production at Dagenham is instructive of this.

Sometime in 1999 senior executives at Ford started to think about whether the closure of one of its plants making the Fiesta in Europe should take place. While its overall global position was healthy, the last quarter of 1999 had seen continuing poor results from Europe. In fact there had been some slight improvement in Europe with losses down from US $75 million in the previous quarter to US $55 million – but this was still felt to be unacceptable. As the 1999 Ford annual report stated, 'Europe continues to be a fiercely competitive market, and our recent results there are unacceptable.' Eventually the Fiesta facility at Ford's plant in London, based in Dagenham, was selected for closure with the loss of nearly 200 jobs and productive capacity increased in its plant in Cologne, Germany. Why?

Several possible reasons might have been behind this. Firstly, the high value of the pound against the euro makes it hard for manufacturers based in the UK to compete with firms in the euro area. For several months the high value of the pound had led leading industrialists to lobby for either the UK to join the euro or for the pound to be devalued by lowering UK interest rates. Taking the strategic view on this is difficult. The UK Government's policy on the pound has been to let the Bank of England set interest rates in line with its overall aim of keeping inflation low. On the one hand this has worked, as inflation in the UK is low even though the economy is growing at a historically high rate. In the past this level of economic growth would have led to inflationary pressure and eventually to a slowdown in the economy. This, at present, has not happened. By manipulating interest rates the bank of England has kept the lid on inflation. On the other hand increases in interest rates, while keeping inflation in check, has kept the pound high against the euro. It would, of course, be wrong to maintain that the poor performance of the euro is all down to the high value of the pound. The euro countries have their own problems but high interest rates in the UK make it hard for the pound to reduce in value against a poorly performing euro.

In the short to medium term it looks unlikely that the euro will improve even given strong support from other central banks such as the US. In the long run the strategic position is even more complex as after the next general election in the UK, sometime between May 2001 and May 2002, if re-elected the Labour Party is committed, if the economic conditions are right, to hold a referendum on the pound joining the euro. If this were to happen it is unclear whether or not the UK would join as public opinion is divided on this. If the Conservative Party won the next election they have ruled out joining for the time being. Whatever happens, Ford is placed in a difficult position because of the uncertainty over whether or not the UK will join. What is certain, at present, is that the pound is high against the euro making it relatively more expensive to manufacture in the UK than elsewhere in Europe.

Secondly, was productivity lower at Dagenham compared to Cologne? How productive a plant is not only depends on the labour force and management but on the quantity and quality of capital employed. Older plants are almost certainly bound to be less productive than newer ones, as the newer ones use more up-to-date technologies. In this case the quantity and quality of the capital used in the two plants needs to be compared before decisions on the reasons for any productivity differences can be established. In this instance both plants were built about the same time: Cologne in 1930 and Ford in 1931. Both produce about 200,000 cars a year. So on the surface the two locations look remarkably similar. How much the image of the British car worker as being 'militant' compared to their German counterpart played a part is hard to say. Certainly the British car worker had this image in the 1960s and 1970s but industrial relations in the car industry of the 1990s in the UK are a far cry from that of the past. Fred Kite of 'I'm all right Jack' fame has long gone – but perhaps even in the hard-headed business world of today past echoes still sound.

Thirdly, there had been cases of alleged racial discrimination at Dagenham previously, which for a global company was simply unacceptable. This had absorbed senior executives' time and energy, as well as generating negative stories about the company. Again just as with the 'image' of the Dagenham car worker the impact of these cases on the decision to move production might have proved to be crucial.

Lastly, the introduction in the 1980s of what is called 'labour market flexibility' in the UK played a part. Labour market flexibility lowered the cost of employing and making redundant workers in the UK, and made the UK an attractive site for global businesses to set up in. Because of the flexibility of UK labour markets the price for closing Fiesta production at Dagenham was significantly cheaper than it would have been to close it in Germany – the company would have been committed to relatively generous settlements in Germany. Therefore labour market flexibility made it easier and cheaper for Ford to close car production at Dagenham as opposed to Cologne.

Looking just at the Dagenham v Cologne case the strength and uncertainty of the pound against the euro seems to be important, as is the cost of closing one production site. The differences between the two sites in terms of productivity and the culture of each workforce are harder to define.

What this illustrates is some of the complexities of fixing on the 'right' worldwide distribution of productive capacity. Strategically would Ford be better off by focusing productive capacity at fewer sites around the world, producing more or less standard engines and bodies, or spreading out production to minimize the difficulties it might encounter if any of its manufacturing centres become unviable for any reason? In terms of both Dagenham and Cologne, political stability and economic stability are high, as are local workforce skills. Also access to other European markets is easy. In other parts of the world instability might be higher, skills lower but wages costs lower and access to rich markets more difficult. As we said above, decisions about distribution of productive capacity are long-term decisions that, once made, commit the company to large investments over several years before profits can be made.

BUSINESS-TO-BUSINESS (B2B)

Business-to-business, or B2B, is a way that large companies can cut prices charged by their suppliers by combining their purchasing power. Also, by using the Internet, it should prove possible to reduce the number of intermediaries involved in purchasing and provide better information on what is available at what sort of price. Regulatory authorities on both sides of the Atlantic are concerned over possible price-fixing in B2B exchanges especially when very large companies such as car makers are concerned.

GM, Ford and Daimler Chrysler have named their proposed B2B Internet exchange Covisint. At present they are facing problems over its launch from two sources: firstly, due to the sheer complexity of the system envisaged, and secondly, in the United States and EU from anti-trust authorities. There are also fears from suppliers that the system will be used to further lower margins for them or exclude some of them completely. The exact configuration of Covisint is somewhat unclear at present. For instance, Ford has recently purchased a minority shareholding in eSteel and expects to source from it about one half of its steel requirements. The remainder will be sourced through Covisint. But another rival steel exchange to eSteel, MetalSite, is a major supplier to GM. While all this is happening, other major suppliers such as Delphi Automotive Systems and Federal-Mogul are deciding on how to respond to the Covisint proposal. GM, Ford and Daimler Chrysler are wooing Toyota to join Covisint but for the time being Toyota does not see sufficient commercial gain to participate in it. Renault/Nissan have now joined Covisint.

Certainly B2B is going to change the way business is done. What is hard to work out is exactly how this is going to happen. It is one of those things that businesses such as Ford cannot afford to ignore but making the 'best' or even a 'good' choice is not going to be easy. Businesses as big and powerful as Ford have to be in there shaping B2B, whilst at the same time learning how to get the best out of it.

THE ENVIRONMENT AND CORPORATE CITIZENSHIP

Like all big businesses Ford is acutely aware of its environmental responsibilities. Ford's environmental pledge is as follows:

> Ford Motor Company is dedicated to providing ingenious environmental solutions that will position us as a leader in the automotive industry of the 21ˢᵗ century. Our actions will demonstrate that we care about preserving the environment for future generations.

Ford's 1999 environmental report stated:

> At Ford Motor Company, dedication to personal mobility and the environment is a way of business. It is a mind set found throughout the Ford team from employees on the factory floor to senior corporate executives to the Board of Directors. Indeed, Ford's commitment to the environment is alive more than half a century after the passing of founder Henry Ford.

Ford goes on to show the seriousness of its intent by publishing its targets for manufacturing over the next few years:

> Our 1998 Manufacturing Business Plan Targets exemplify this new way of doing business:
>
> - Certify all of our manufacturing plants worldwide to the ISO 14001 standard by year-end 1998. This objective has been achieved.
> - Achieve 90 per cent returnable container usage in our facilities by 2001. We achieved this goal in 1998, ahead of schedule.
> - Reduce paint shop emissions to 60g/m2 by 2005.
> - Phase out all PCB transformers by 2010.
> - Reduce energy usage by 1 per cent per year.

Ford, in both its European and home markets, is facing, along with all car makers, pressure to 'clean up its act'. The car is seen as a major contributor to pollution and to greenhouse gases. The pressure is on for Ford to develop both cleaner petrol cars and alternative forms of engines. The purchase of a 51 per cent stake in Th!nk, a Norwegian company that produces electric cars, is a sign of how Ford is responding to tougher CO_2 emission. Not only is Ford interested in the development of the electric car but also in the way the car is assembled. Unlike standard cars, production of the electric car requires very little in the way of modern paint shops or sophisticated welding equipment. Ford believes it will learn a lot from being associated with this project that might have implications for other projects. Apart from this Ford has several initiatives it has been pursuing for many years to develop non-petrol cars, combined electric and petrol cars and more efficient petrol cars.

Ford in its first corporate citizenship report *Connecting with Society* looked at the effects its sports utility vehicles (SUVs) had on the environment. SUVs are known for having poor fuel efficiency and being major polluters. Ford has to face up to the environmental threat SUVs pose but also the effect not making them will have on profitability. Its strategy for SUVs is as follows:

Ford has taken significant steps to address SUV issues, including those raised by environmentalists, safety advocates and other stakeholders. More than 80 percent of an Explorer is recyclable today and a number of parts are made from recycled plastic and rubber. In addition, all Ford SUVs (and F-series pickup trucks and minivans) sold in the US and Canada are certified as Low Emission Vehicles (LEV), years ahead of any regulatory requirement to do so – a commitment still not matched by the competition. The LEV pledge cut smog-producing emissions by approximately 50 percent, and we recognize the need to go further.

For environmental and customer satisfaction reasons, Ford will continue to improve the fuel economy of its products. The challenge is to achieve substantial gains in fuel economy without increasing costs or compromising the functions desired by customers. A smaller SUV, the Ford Escape, will be introduced later this year to meet the needs of SUV buyers who do not require as much space, and a hybrid electric Escape will be offered in 2003, designed to achieve 40 mpg in stop-and-go traffic. Our research and product development community is aggressively pursuing advanced technologies and lightweight materials to improve fuel economy.

We also have acknowledged vehicle compatibility issues – some of which will always exist because of the basic laws of physics. We are, however, exploring ways to address the concerns while continuing to produce different styles and weights of vehicles. For example, we introduced the BlockerBeam™ on the Ford Excursion, which is designed to reduce the risk of lower-riding cars sliding beneath the Excursion in collisions.

Long Term

Longer term, there may be new and different issues raised about SUVs. Market dynamics may change customer needs and wants. Technology breakthroughs may allow significant emissions reductions and fuel economy improvements without loss of function. In addition, SUVs will be required to meet the same emissions standards as passenger cars.

We believe that the steps Ford has taken to date are only a beginning in addressing the issues raised by these products. Our task is to develop additional technological solutions and identify and implement alternative ways to satisfy customers that build a sustainable competitive advantage while meeting our environmental, social and economic objectives.

Responding to both its environmental and citizenship responsibilities Ford set out, in its *Connecting with Society* report, the following table to illustrate its strategic response. (See Table A.2.)

Web resources

www.ford.com/ – to read more about the history of Ford see its Web site at www.ford.com/default.asp?pageid=95&storyid=916

Table A.2

Corporate Citizenship Strategy Elements

	2000	2001	2002–2005
Values and Business Principles	Conduct values alignment process. Develop draft of Business Principles	Test, refine and adopt Business Principles	Integrate Business Principles into strategic decision-making processes
Stakeholder Engagement	Internal engagement on Business Principles Internal and external engagement on what corporate citizenship and sustainability mean to Ford; development of transformational goals	Internal engagement on business principles and transformational goals Internal and external engagement on key corporate citizenship/ sustainability issues	Engagement on implementation issues Development of partnerships for implementation
Transformation/Action	Develop baseline environmental/social footprint Develop transformational goals Establish short-term goals Continue learning and discussion of key performance indicators	Make progress on short-term and transformational goals Develop key performance indicators	Continue integration of corporate citizenship/ sustainability thinking into core business Measure and report performance using key performance indicators
Transparency	Issue Corporate Citizenship report Explore verification issues	Issue Corporate Citizenship report and explore additional venues for communication and dialogue with stakeholders Adopt verification process	Continue reporting and verification practices

Source: Corporate Citizenship Strategy
http://www.ford.com/default.asp?pageid=399&storyid=830

3

Fujitsu and ICL

Fujitsu consists of some 500 companies and associates operating around the world. Fujitsu's revenue is nearly US $50 billion, and the group employs nearly 200,000 staff. Companies in the group include Amdahl, DMR Consulting and ICL, the company featured in this case study.

This case study revolves around the abandoning of the ICL flotation in the summer of 2000. It had been the intended goal of ICL and Fujitsu sometime in 1999 or 2000. What went wrong? First, let's look at a bit of ICL's history.

ICL – COMPANY HISTORY

ICL emerged as a company by the merger of English Electric Computers and International Computers and Tabulators (ICT) in 1968. One of the reasons for this was for the new company to compete effectively against the industry giant, IBM. ICL produced computers, including the 1900 series and its operating systems – the George series. In the days before desktop machines and the dominance of Microsoft, computers were big and only large companies could afford them. Competition in the computer market intensified throughout the 1970s. In 1981 ICL and Fujitsu signed a collaboration agreement to allow ICL to move into network computing. In 1984 Standard Telephone and Cables (STC) acquired ICL. Again size was one of the driving forces behind this as to compete successfully required large-scale operations. In 1990 Fujitsu bought an 80 per cent holding of ICL and Nortel later bought STC. In

1998 Fujitsu purchased from Nortel the remaining 20 per cent of ICL that Nortel had from its purchase of STC.

In 1995 Keith Todd become Chief Executive and started the move away from manufacturing of computers towards systems and services. Soon ICL had no involvement in the manufacturing of computers. Keith Todd not only wanted ICL to concentrate on systems and services but he also wanted to float them on the London Stock Exchange, preferably before 2000. In 1995 when he took over, ICL made losses of £188 million but this included an exception item of £151 million for restructuring derived from the decision to get out of manufacturing. In 1997 the company saw a loss of only £2.5 million. The progress made by Todd can be seen in the pre-tax profit for the year ending March 2000 – £96.1 million. There was an operating loss of £70 million but income was boosted by £187 million by selling some of ICL's businesses. The previous year had seen a loss of nearly £120 million. ICL under Todd got involved in a scheme to automate nearly 20,000 post offices in the UK. Todd also bought a 10 per cent stake in the lottery company Camelot.

Let's move the story on to 2000. ICL had by now transformed itself from a poorly performing, loss making computer company into (it hoped) a leading e-business service group. As part of the run-up to its float, ICL was going to float Invia, a subsidiary, on the Helsinki Stock exchange in May 2000. In what can now be seen as an ominous sign, ICL pulled out of this plan. While all this was going on the allure of so-called dotcom companies was wearing thin for investors. For instance, in March shares in lastminute.com fall sharply. In May boo.com, a fashion retailer, went out of business. In June amazon.com lost in one day 20 per cent of its value and in July click-mango closed down.

On 2 August 2000 Fujitsu and ICL jointly announced that the float was being put off for the indefinite future. And in a flash Keith Todd vanished from ICL as the company's press statement said, 'Keith has been instrumental in redefining ICL's business model and has managed the successful transformation of ICL from a computer manufacturer to one of Europe's leading e-business service companies. He goes with our thanks and good wishes.' The reason given for postponing the float by the company was its continued poor financial performance and not the depressed state of e-business shares on the world's stock exchanges. The Acting Chief Executive, Richard Christou, said simply 'our operating performance does not justify a flotation'.

Now we move on to a statement made in autumn 2000:

> With the disappointments of the summer over and a new senior management team in place ICL is now concentrating on developing further its IT solutions. ICL's mission is to unlock the full potential of the knowledge society for our customers. To achieve this ICL has reoriented its business model to embrace this opportunity, ensuring clarity and operational focus which defines the shape of the group's business for the long term. We are

playing to our strengths in the industry markets we know best – retail, financial services, government, telecommunications, utilities and travel – and focusing our capabilities into three key sets of offerings: e-Innovation, e-Applications and e-Infrastructure. (Source: www.icl.com/about/index.htm).

On e-Innovation ICL implements solutions that go far beyond technology and engage all aspects of your business. We help you develop new ways to relate to your partners and staff. For e-Applications ICL has a rich knowledge of the markets in which we operate. We can provide you with solutions that are based on this knowledge, with integration skills that can link them to the e-World. And for E-business it says, success in e-Business requires a fundamental change to traditional inward looking IT infrastructures – and the people who manage them. A customer-centric rather than technology-centric view is now essential when planning IT strategies. (Source: www.icl.com/services.htm.)

Web resources

www.fujitsugeneral.co.jp/
www.icl.com/

4

Glaxo-Wellcome

Glaxo-Wellcome was formed on the 16th March 1995, when Glaxo acquired Wellcome plc. The company employs over 67,000 people. Glaxo-Wellcome has an impressive range of drugs including Flixotide, Ventolin and Serevent for asthma; Combivir, taken by 50 per cent of Americans being treated for HIV; Epivir for HIV/AIDS; and Fionase, a nasal spray for allergies. Patents on Zantac, a heartburn treatment, and Zovirax, for herpes, have though now expired. The company produces in 33 countries and sells in over 150 with about 40 per cent of its sales in the United States. In 1998 it acquired Biddle Sawyer and a majority holding in Polfa Pozan but sold its stake in Warner-Lambert.

Glaxo-Wellcome has recently merged with SmithKline Beecham. SmithKline brings with it (among other things) existing successful drugs such as Seroxat, an anti-depressant, and Augmentin, an antibiotic.

Both companies secured shareholder approval for this merger on 31 July 2000. The merger had a somewhat chequered history. After several months of negotiation the first attempt at merging fell through in February 1998 but by the autumn of 1999 speculation had increased about the possibility of the two companies merging. By early 2000 both boards had agreed to the merger subject to both shareholder and regulatory agreement. One of the key figures in this was Jan Leschly, SmithKline's Chief Executive, who in 1998 had appeared to be against the merger. With the announcement of the merger in 2000 Leschly decided to stand aside in April with six months of his contract still to run.

WHY MERGE?

According to the Glaxo-Wellcome annual review 1999, a merger was seen as beneficial because:

> The new company, with a range of experience in emerging technologies, will possess significantly enhanced scale and scope to discover, develop and deliver new and better medicines in a faster and more efficient way.

Emerging technologies
Glaxo SmithKline will be well positioned with a range of experience in emerging technologies. Glaxo Wellcome is an industry leader in combinatorial chemistry and human genetics; SmithKline Beecham is at the forefront of using genomics to discover a wide variety of unique targets for discovery. Both companies are also leaders in the area of bioinformatics.

Sales and marketing
Glaxo SmithKline will have an industry-leading global sales and marketing force. In the all-important managed care segment of the US market, Glaxo SmithKline will provide many key accounts, which normally contract with several pharmaceutical companies to obtain the medicines they need, with the convenience of one-stop shopping as a result of the breadth of its product line.

Cost savings
It is estimated that annual pre-tax cost savings of £1 billion (US $1.6 billion) are achievable from the third anniversary of the completion of the merger, of which £250 million (over US $405 million) is expected to be reinvested in R&D. These savings are in addition to the £570 million (US $923 million) of savings already targeted by both companies from restructuring manufacturing activity. The total cost of achieving the savings from the merger is expected to be approximately £1.1 billion (US $1.8 billion).

There were, then, three reasons for wanting to merge. First, the new company has a valuable range of experience in emerging technologies. If it is to compete in the world market for new genetic-based treatments enormous amounts of money are required. The company believed that following the merger it would be able to compete in this market. Second, the merger will give the new company immense marketing capabilities. Third, of course, a merger of this scale gives a great opportunity to reduce costs and employment making the new company more efficient. As we see above, Glaxo-Wellcome estimated possible cost savings of around £1.1 billion as a result of the merger. While the companies will not give estimates of job losses, unions involved have said that up to 15,000 job losses are probable.

REGULATORY AGREEMENT

The two companies had hoped to complete the merger by the end of September 2000 but this was put back because of regulatory concerns from the United States Federal Trade Commission relating to a range of issues including smoking cessation treatments. Both companies have products in this area – Zyban from Glaxo-Wellcome and Nicorette from SmithKline Beecham. In the summer of 2000 SmithKline Beecham agreed subject to the completion of the merger to sell Kytril, a drug used in chemotherapy and radiotherapy, to Roche and the drugs Famvir and Vectavir/Denavir, used in the treatment of herpes, to Novartis in order to comply with regulatory demands.

ISSUES

The merger raises the following issues:

- **Is big beautiful and if it is how should it be achieved?** Consolidation is happening in the industry with not only the merger of Glaxo Wellcome and SmithKline but also other important players such as Pfizer and Pharmacia & Upjohn actively looking for acquisitions. Others, such as Merck, while wanting to grow, see organic growth as their preferred strategy with acquisitions being of secondary importance. An acquisitions strategy entails quite difficult problems, such as creating the new company culture and ways of doing things, eliminating duplication etc.

  Also while big might just be beautiful in terms of R&D it may not work so well on the sales front. Increasing the number of salespeople might quickly become counter productive. There are doubts that Glaxo SmithKline's huge salesforce is good value for money, especially in the United States, where it consists of around 40,000 sales staff.

  The simple sheer size of the new company, created more or less overnight, will require quite a bit of senior management resource to handle it effectively in the first few years of its existence.

- **How will developments in genetics affect the development of new treatments?** The success of the human genome project and other developments in genetics has opened up huge new areas of R&D for the drug companies. But to succeed in this you need lots of money. The merger, it is believed, will provide the scale of resources needed to develop the new drugs of the 21st century. On the other hand there are lots of relatively small companies out there working on genetic-based developments that could easily find the new peni-cillin or HIV wonder drug. Large companies have access to vast amounts of research money but their very scale may mean that they become somewhat distant and impersonal for the scientists, with layers of bureaucracy stifling innovation and creativity. Small companies may lack the resources but may compensate for that by having a company culture of innovation, creative and swift decision making, with little formal bureaucracy. Whatever size is 'best', what is true is that it is 'now or never' for the development of the important patents that are going to be the profit makers of the next two decades.

- **Where are the new markets?** Drugs are expensive and while Western coun-tries can afford treatments for conditions such as HIV this is not so in other parts of the world. Glaxo SmithKline will need to expand its markets in the poorer and emerging economies such as China but most local or state health services cannot afford its prices. The rich West will provide the bedrock of its business while it continues to move into other markets where its products are needed but remain mostly far too expensive to obtain. This will expose the company to social and moral pressure to lower prices. In those countries that can afford the treatments there is often an ageing, but relatively well-off pop-ulation who can afford to buy Glaxo SmithKline products. This will also be an important market to exploit.

- **What will be the effect of the Internet on traditional distribution channels?** Like all firms, Glaxo SmithKline will have to develop its strategy for the Internet. We know already that patients often consult the Internet before vis-iting their doctors armed with the latest advice and information about the drugs for what they believe they have wrong with them. To what extent this will change the key decision-maker from the doctor to the patient in the use of a particular drug is hard to estimate but it is something the drug compa-nies are watching. Selling non-prescription drugs direct to the public bypass-ing pharmacists is a possibility but for the foreseeable future prescription drugs will have to be prescribed by a doctor and purchased from a pharma-cist in most Western countries.

B2B does offer some advantages to Glaxo SmithKline in cost savings but it might make it much harder for the company to charge different prices in different markets and to keep such a firm control of prices.

Web resources

www.glaxowellcome.com/

5

Idealab

by Graham Beaver

© 2001 Graham Beaver

Much has been written about the impact of information technology on the fortunes and operating practices of business and organizations in their seemingly relentless quest for competitive advantage. Information about customer trends, buying behaviour and payment methods together with the response of enlightened management to cater for such changes in a proactive, strategic manner, has taken Tesco to a 22 per cent market share and record profitability. And this is in an industry that, as one commentator put it, 'does not take any prisoners'.

There appear to be many examples where corporate management has embraced information technology systems to its strategic advantage and as a consequence has improved its operating context through, for example, raising entry barriers or improving the value chain to enhance a differentiation strategy (Porter, 1979; Porter, 1985).

IDEALAB'S FORMATION AND DEVELOPMENT

Who would have thought, though, that the development of the Internet (or World Wide Web) would radically transform business practices in many industries and create whole new opportunities for intellectual property development and entrepreneurial creation? This case history examines the formation and development of Idealab, by Bill Gross, described in the popular press as a 'high tech entrepreneur'. It seems fitting to begin this account with an introduction from the December–January issue of *Fast Company Magazine* (1997) that states:

> Bill Gross, Chief Executive Office of Idealab, has started 18 companies in 9 months. On the Net, he says, 'Time is more important than money.' Gross has been starting companies since he was sixteen but it was not until he met Steven Spielberg that he came up with his ultimate entrepreneurial idea... a company dedicated to ideas themselves.

Thus was born Idealab, a Pasadena-based think tank that conceives and funds new ventures on the Internet. Unlike many of the new Web enterprises, Idealab is more than an indulgence for its 39-year-old founder. It represents a radical new model for starting and developing new companies that reflects both the volume and potential of ideas on the Internet and the challenges of doing business there. Gross launched the new company in March 1996, with the stated objective to develop ten new businesses with a market capitalization of some US $100 million each, that was capable of going public or being sold by the end of the decade. At the time of writing, Idealab has started 18 different ventures, 6 of which are now fully operational. One of these companies, CitySearch, already appears to be enjoying considerable success, having achieved a strong market position against the formidable competition from Microsoft and America Online in the creation of online information services for urban communities.

The creation of new companies would appear to be a process that comes naturally to Gross. He paid for his US college education (at the California Institute of Technology) by selling patented stereo speakers that he designed himself. Probably his best known start-up is Knowledge Adventure, which is now placed as the fourth largest educational software company in the United States. Impressive though his business development track record may be, Gross is on record as stating that it does not really count for much when it comes to starting companies on the Internet, which is an entrepreneurial medium like no other. When asked what is the fundamental key to success on the Internet, Gross was in no doubt: 'Speed is of the essence here. Time is more important than money. If a company can not go from concept to launch in nine months, it's not going to make it. This is the toughest business in the world.'

ACHIEVING COMPETITIVE ADVANTAGE

For readers keen to know of new ways and methods of achieving competitive advantage, the formula embraced by Idealab is constructed on four principles.

The first principle is to evaluate new ideas quickly... and thoroughly. Time is not wasted if a promising new idea is found to have no real commercial viability. The timetable set by Gross for Idealab is, to say the least, ambitious. Over the next five years he aims to identify one new and potentially profitable idea per month and to launch one new company every quarter. The evaluation process is both professional and comprehensive with very little left to chance. Idealab has assembled a panel of ten Internet luminaries as its commercial evaluation advisors. They include MIT Professor Sherry Turkle, an expert on the sociology of the Internet; Richard Wurman, creator of the very influential TED conferences; and Bob Kavner, the successful AT&T executive who now runs the On Command Corporation. To again quote Gross:

> These advisors don't just provide commercial insight, they also provide credibility... We have some amazing people working with and funding us; once we persuaded Bob Kavner to become Chairman of our Board of Directors, we got Goldman Sachs and AT&T as investors. Once you get those first few breaks, the rest is like a chain reaction.

The second principle is based around people, or rather the acquisition of a balanced managerial team that is capable of turning the new ideas into commercial and viable enterprises. Idealab companies, according to Gross, are fanatical about recruiting:

> The biggest difference between success and failure on the Internet is the selection and recruitment of the right people. We have eighteen companies in various stages of development and the only thing that is holding us back from having all eighteen companies fully operational is people. Our biggest challenge every day is where are we going to find really talented people to execute the ideas.

The third principle to promote speed in the selection and execution of new ideas is to provide the necessary support infrastructure that is so often missing in the new entrepreneurial venture and may well delay or frustrate commercial viability. Idealab has a central support staff that undertakes all the vital activities such as negotiating for office space, creating the required corporate identity and protecting intellectual property. For example, graphic designer Tom Hughes, who created the Macintosh logo for Steve Jobs, is responsible for creating the individual corporate identity and supporting marketing collateral for all of the companies in the Idealab portfolio. Gross states: 'With the provision of these excellent and dedicated and shared resources, I can reckon being at least three times faster than someone starting a company in the normal way.'

The fourth principle is to have an enlightened approach to ownership and control of corporate assets. Idealab does not take a controlling interest in its portfolio of companies. In return for the start-up capital that it negotiates, Idealab receives a 49 per cent equity holding, the remainder being reserved for managerial investment and subsequent investors that may be needed to fund future business expansion. Gross puts this very succinctly: 'The way to create wealth quickly on the Internet is to spread it around.'

There is no doubt that the Internet will continue to provide the medium for future new venture creation but the rate of commercial success is likely to be far outstripped by the rate of failure. Speed, as an essential ingredient for both idea generation and exploitation must be matched with strategic thinking, which, as Rosabeth Moss Kanter (1989; 1995) reminds us, is a scarce resource. Of the many ingredients that constitute Idealab's success to date, and let us hope in the future also, strategic thinking is embracing the concept of value chain management (Porter, 1979; Porter, 1985; and Porter, 1996). Gross, not surprisingly, does not use the strategic management vocabulary that readers of this case study are familiar with, but this last comment on corporate success is left to him, and it does seem to have a familiar ring to it!

> The way to get speed... and a successful business, is to create shared knowledge about this medium as quickly as possible...Your competitors won't share what they know, so you have to find long-term allies and form lasting reciprocal relationships that improve the quality of business for everyone. I am trying to create a family of companies that are allied with one another in a commitment to increase the speed at which we do and enjoy doing business.

Web resources

www.idealab.com

REFERENCES

Kanter, R M (1989) *When Giants Learn To Dance*, Unwin Hyman, London

Kanter, R M (1995) Entrepreneurial Organisations, BBC *In-Business*, screened November 1995, London

Porter, M (1979) *Competitive Strategy*, Free Press, New York

Porter, M (1985) *Competitive Advantage*, Free Press, New York

Porter, M (1996) What is strategy? *Harvard Business Review*, November–December, pp 61–78

6

J D Wetherspoon

Tim Martin acquired his first pub, called Wetherspoons, in 1979 in North London concentrating on providing a range of cask-conditioned beers drank in a music-free environment. Twenty-one years on, J D Wetherspoon, as the company is now called, has more than 370 pubs. The strategy behind this success story is deceptively simple – provide a range of beers, spirits and soft drinks at competitive prices and serve food all day in a music- and television- free environment in, typically, a refurbished bank. J D Wetherspoon was also one of the first pub chains to introduce non-smoking areas.

Why J D Wetherspoon as a name and why so many moons? Well, evidently the J D comes from the character J D Hogg in the television series *The Dukes of Hazzard* and Wetherspoon was the name of one of Tim Martin's teachers. Early pubs in the chain often had the word moon in their name. This was derived from a pub that George Orwell (author of *Animal Farm* and *1984*) wrote about in the *Evening Standard* called The Moon under Water.

J D Wetherspoon was successfully floated on the stock exchange in 1992 providing funds for even more expansion with its first Midland's pub, The Square Peg in Birmingham, which opened in 1994. Pubs in other cities soon followed. Recently the company has turned its attention to Northern Ireland by opening two outlets. J D Wetherspoon's pub-opening programme is impressive. The firm opens between 60 and 90 pubs a year and has ambitious plans for more. It has aimed at opening a further 500 by 2004. In recent months it has opened the Last Post in Beeston (August 2000) and the Robert the Bruce in Dumfries.

Financial data for the company is shown in Table A.3.

Table A.3

	2000 (£000s)	Before Exceptional Items 1999 (£000s)	After Exceptional Items 1999 (£000s)
Turnover	369,628	269,699	269,699
Operating Profits	46,278	36,226	35,389
Net Interest Payable	(10,226)	(10,012)	(10,012)
Profit on Disposal of Tangible Fixed Assets			22,625
Profit on Ordinary Activities Before Tax	36,052	26,214	48,002
Tax on Profit on Ordinary Activities	(1,785)	(751)	(751)
Profit on Ordinary Activities After Tax	34,267	25,463	47,251
Dividends	(5,599)	(4,809)	(4,809)
Retained Profit for the Year	28,668	20,654	42,442
Earnings per Ordinary Share	16.8p	12.9p	24.0p
Fully Diluted Earnings per Ordinary Share	16.4p	12.8p	23.8p

In the jargon of the pub trade, J D Wetherspoon concentrates on the 'destination' pub as opposed to the 'community' pub (also know as the 'local'). Destination pubs are targeted at the more affluent and younger drinker, are 'women-friendly', and are invariably situated in city-centre locations in refurbished banks, cinemas or other good quality real estate. In general community pubs are losing market share to destination ones. With the steady decline in community pubs major brewers have been looking to divest these to companies such as Enterprise Inns or to refurbish them into destination pubs. Enterprise Inns has as its growth strategy the purchase of unwanted community pubs from brewers. For example it bought 217 community pubs from Bass. This contrasts with J D Wetherspoon's strategy of buying good sites and refurbishing them into destination pubs. This strategy is possible in part because of the number of sites that are becoming available in town centres as a result of the move in banking away from local branches.

PRICING POLICY

A key element in the success of J D Wetherspoon is its pricing policy. In September 1999 the company revealed that it would sell popular drinks at anything up to one third cheaper than other competitors. Outside Central London it was aiming to sell Boddingtons at £1.29 a pint and Carling for £1.49. It was also offering savings on other brands including spirits and soft drinks. As a response to the Yates's Wine Lodge, a competitor, it lowered some of its prices within Central London as well as outside, but admittedly only for certain times in the day.

SEGMENTED MARKETS

Starting in September 2000, J D Wetherspoon designated Wednesday nights as students' nights in their pubs excluding pubs at airports and in Central London. These nights are advertised as 'Wicked Wednesday' nights. Special prices for such drinks as Budweiser and Diamond Red were designed to bring in the student market. However, the company went to some lengths to say that not only students but also other customers could benefit from the low prices. The student market is seen to be an important one with the growth of students in the UK set to increase both at universities and at colleges of further education under existing government policy.

COMPETITORS

Yates's Wine Lodge

A major competitor to J D Wetherspoon is Yates's Wine Lodge. In the financial year 1999–2000 Yates's opened 31 new branches of which 25 were Wine Lodges. The other six were Ha! Ha! branches and Canteens. The company also consolidated its expansion into the South East of England increasing the percentage of its pubs there from 33 per cent to 42 per cent. At present Yates's have some 143 branches. Part of Yates's strategy is to market the chain as a place to go for celebrations – birthday parties, Christmas, the New Year etc. The success of its policy on millennium eve opening demonstrated just this. The company decided on a policy of free entry, free soft drinks and a 2.00 am close. It resulted in packed branches throughout England. Yates's is looking at expansion into franchised outlets as a way of increasing its profits and hopes to open a branch at Gatwick airport shortly to test the feasibility of such a move. Yates's has also invested heavily in Ha! Ha! and while some branches of Ha! Ha! have initially struggled, the concept does appear to be catching on especially with young people and students.

Bass plc

Compared with J D Wetherspoon and Yates's, Bass is big and only part of its business is in pubs and bars. It owns and manages over 3,000 pubs, bars, restaurants and leisure sites in the UK. Its brands include All Bar One, Harvesters, It's a Scream and Vintage Inns. Through its branded outlets it can focus on different market segments. For instance, its Vintage Inns is a traditional English pub, while All Bar One attracts younger, single businesswomen. It's a Scream is aimed at students.

Table A.4 compares the last few years' turnover and pre-tax profits for the three companies.

Table A.4

Yates's Wine Lodge						
Year Ended 31 Mar		1996	1997	1998	1999	2000
Turnover	£m	61.2	75.7	97.8	120	144
Pre-tax Profit	£m	7.48	10.5	13.6	14.1	14.9
J D Wetherspoon						
Year Ended 31 Jul		1996	1997	1998	1999	2000
Turnover	£m	100	139	189	270	370
Pre-tax Profit	£m	13.1	17.6	35.1	48.0	36.1
Bass						
Year Ended 30 Sep		1995	1996	1997	1998	1999
Turnover	£m	4541	5109	5254	4609	4686
Pre-tax Profit	£m	599	671	477	834	572

WHAT SHOULD J D WETHERSPOON DO NOW?

The two key ingredients of J D Wetherspoon's success are to be found in its ability to source drinks cheaply and create an ambience that is attractive to consumers who are looking for destination venues. The competition is hotting up though. The student and young adult market is becoming crowded with copycat venues and alternative themed venues. Competition on prices is also becoming keener. And perhaps a major problem for the future will be the availability of new sites for refurbishment. J D Wetherspoon was fortunate when it started to expand, as there was a good supply of high quality city-centre sites available mainly because of restructuring in other industries such as banking. This supply may well be coming to an end and other high street retailers on the look-out for similar sites will push prices up. The move away from its traditional English base into Northern Ireland and perhaps later, Europe, will start to stretch managerial resources as well as capital. The ambitious growth targets it has set itself may not be possible in the future. Lastly there is now the possibility of a takeover as the business is of such as size to attract others.

Web resources

www.jdwetherspoon.co.uk/

7

Maison Novelli

by Graham Beaver

© 2001 Graham Beaver

As a consequence of the many contacts and networks from research undertaken in the hospitality industry, the author was invited to interview Jean-Christophe Novelli, a prominent chef and restaurateur, to discuss his plans and hopes for business expansion. The time set for the interview came and went and an hour passed with the PR assistant / receptionist looking increasingly flustered and offering apologies on a regular basis. As the time dragged on tempers began to fray and thoughts of departure were seriously entertained.

Finally the subject of the interview arrived, and entered the room smiling and totally apologetic. His voluble charm and pleasant demeanour swept all thoughts of resentment and surliness aside. 'I am so very sorry for the delay and I do hope that my lateness has not inconvenienced you too much. I have had so many invitations from different people to talk about my plans for the business that I lost track of the time. Forgive me!'

When the interview took place, Jean-Christophe Novelli, one of the bright new hopes of the restaurant business, was at the pinnacle of his career and promised to deliver much for the industry that was new and innovative. At 37 years old he had worked in some of the finest hotels in the UK and was in the process of opening his sixth restaurant in the heart of London's fashionable Mayfair district. With a staff of around 120, a reputation for exciting and creative cooking and the recent award of a Michelin star, he was popularly regarded as the new role model of restaurant success and achievement.

Novelli's enthusiasm and passion for good cooking was contagious and his energy and determination to succeed was admirable. He rarely slept more than five hours a night and most times would lull himself to sleep conceiving and composing new recipes for his restaurants. He received loyalty bordering on adulation from his staff and taught talented chefs to become great ones – paying them a pittance of £50–£75 a week in the first three restaurants, because that was all he could afford – and giving them small shareholdings in the business in lieu of bonuses. All the profits generated by the restaurants in the three years of business to that point had been reinvested into the company.

At the time of the meeting, the plan was for some 40 per cent of the company to be floated on the Alternative Investment Market (AIM) which would have valued the business somewhere in the region of £5.75 million. For a business just over three years old that was some accomplishment. However, whilst Novelli was a gifted chef and motivator, his business acumen was at best questionable. By his own admission he had little thought for material things despite a poor childhood and Spartan upbringing. He said: 'If I need a cab fare, I'll take a fiver out of the till.'

The business began to experience difficulties when Novelli returned from a booksigning visit to the United States in June 1999. The bank had told him that the company was some £75,000 overdrawn – with no previously agreed overdraft facility – suppliers were owed about £50,000 and there was an outstanding staff wages account of £100,000. Novelli was given three days to find the money which, by the rapid sale of some of the restaurants and substantial offers of help from friends, he managed to do, but that was the beginning of the end. The outgoings from the company continued in excess of the revenues and four of the restaurants were closed during 1999 and the fifth in March 2000. At one point, Novelli was forced to approach his suppliers to pay his wages bill. The two remaining restaurants, the original Maison Novelli and the sister bistro EC1, went into voluntary liquidation at the end of June 2000, the restaurants having been sold a few weeks earlier to JJ Restaurants. Novelli is currently cooking in both of them.

The liquidator, Morison Stoneham, confirmed that according to the financial statement presented by the business to Companies House, Maison Novelli owed a total of some £205,487 and had assets of £13,000. The Customs and Excise and the Inland Revenue were owed respectively £14,000 and £24,743. The largest creditor claim was from J.C. Novelli for £53,000. Some 63 other trade creditors were owed around £113,000.

Novelli's explanation of his business difficulties was refreshingly direct and straightforward: 'I blame it on poor planning and bad financial management which was all my fault. I should have stuck to the cooking and menu creation part of the business and got somebody else to take care of all the other parts.'

An explanation hard not to agree with – but good management is easier said than done!

8

Manchester United

Why have a case study about a football club? Well, nowadays football is big business and the leisure industry is fast becoming an important sector worldwide. Football clubs are invariably thought of as occupying a special place in society, more so than most businesses. Football touches some people's lives in extraordinary ways that other business does not. Football clubs have a role in most Western societies far beyond their size (except in the United States, a country with its own sports, notably US football, baseball and basketball, to which these arguments could equally apply). Football matches are watched avidly in stadiums and on television, and news about matches features prominently in the media, many feel disproportionately so. To some, football is not about life or death, it is more important than that! The supporters are only one stakeholder group; there are other stakeholders such as the shareholders and the wider community.

THE CLUB AND ITS FINANCES

Manchester United plc wholly owns the following:

- The Manchester United Football Club plc;
- Manchester United Merchandising Limited;
- Manchester United Catering Limited;
- Manchester United International Limited.

Table A.5 Summary of Manchester United's recent finances (£m)

	2000	1999	1998	1997	1996	1995
Gate Receipts	36.6	41.9	29.8	30.1		
Merchandising		21.8	24.1	28.7		
Television	30.5	22.5	16.2	12.6		
Sponsorship		17.5	11.8	11.1		
Conference and Catering		7.0	6.0	5.4		
Turnover	116.0	110.7	87.9	87.9	53.3	60.6
Net transfers			15.5	–0.3		
Wages and Salaries	44.7	36.9	26.7	21.8		
Pre-tax Profit	16.8	22.4	27.8	27.6	15.4	20.0

Major shareholders are BSkyB with a 9.1 per cent stake in the club and the Royal & Sun Alliance Group plc that has a 3.1 per cent stake. Other major shareholders include Martin Edwards and E M Watkins. Table A.5 shows a summary of Manchester United's recent finances.

Manchester United is growing fast. In 1997 its turnover was £87.9 million. By 1999 it had risen to £110.7 million – an increase of one quarter. By 2000 turnover was £116 million. Pre-tax profits in 1997 were £27.6 million, in 1999 £22.4 million and in 2000 £16.4 million. Income from television rose sharply from under £13 million in 1997 to over £30 million in 2000. However, wages and salaries increased from £21.8 million in 1997 to nearly £45 million in 2000.

Manchester United is the most successful club in the English Premier League. In 1999 it won the Premier League, the FA Cup and the Champions Cup. The following year it again won the Premier League and in all likelihood would have won the FA Cup but instead withdrew from it to play in South America in a FIFA-sponsored tournament. Its ground capacity is 67,000 and apart from receiving money from gate receipts it has extensive merchandising and other commercial activities such as cafés, a share in a hotel and a share in a cable channel, MUTV.

As a comparison, Chelsea Village plc, the umbrella company for Chelsea Football Club and associated businesses, grew from £23.7 million turnover in 1997 to £91.5 million in 1999 (an even more staggering increase than in Manchester United's case) but Chelsea made a pre-tax loss of £0.5 million. The increase in turnover was possible because of the investment Chelsea had made in hotel and restaurant facilities at its West London Stadium. In the 1999–2000 season Chelsea won the FA Cup, which is an important trophy but winning it is not as significant as winning the Premier League. Manchester United, though much more successful on the football pitch, needs to keep a close eye on Chelsea's strategy of growing its football-related businesses by exploiting its brand image. Newcastle United, another top Premier League team, had a turnover of £41 million in 1997, rising slightly to £45 million in 1999. And lastly Tottenham Hotspur had a turnover of £43 million in 1999 up from £28 million in 1997.

Manchester United is therefore much bigger in financial terms than other clubs in the Premier League except Chelsea. This gives Manchester United a significant advantage in buying the very best players, who often cost more than £5 million, and paying the salaries required, which are often in excess of £30,000 per week.

BRAND IMAGE

Nowadays football is not just about winning on the field – for the big clubs it is a potential lucrative business and to get the best return on its assets a company has to be able to exploit its brand identity. As the figures above show, merchandising contributed significantly to Manchester United's revenue. Merchandising contributed even more significantly to profitability – Manchester United's products such as replica strips cost relatively little but can be sold with a large mark-up because of the club's brand image. Just as Coca-Cola and Microsoft have strong brand images so does Manchester United.

The contribution that merchandising makes to turnover and profitability illustrates the strength of Manchester United's brand image, but how was this brand image acquired? Manchester United has for many years been more than just a Manchester club. It is known throughout the world. It is quite hard to pin down why this is. But the usual reasons put forward include (sadly) the Munich tragedy of 1958 which killed eight of the so-called 'Busby Babes' named after the manager Matt Busby and the number of young players then in his team. At the time the Football Association had with some reluctance allowed English clubs to compete in Europe after years of refusing permission to do so. This permission was granted on the condition that it did not interfere with league games. Travelling to some of the European ties was not as easy and straightforward as it is today and Manchester United were under pressure to return from Munich quickly to play a league game. In appalling conditions the plane they were on attempted to take off but it could not gain sufficient height and power because ice had built up on its wings. The plane crashed with the loss of eight lives. Busby was also seriously injured and for a while his life hung in the balance. Public interest in the tragedy drew in people who only had a marginal or little interest in football or the club, not only in Britain but also around the world. This helped considerably to establish the name of the club.

The club made a remarkable recovery after the Munich tragedy. Eventually, in 1968, Manchester United became the first English club to win the European Cup. Matt Busby, a driven man by all accounts, had even before the Munich air crash wanted Manchester United to become the dominant European team. After the crash his determination had strengthened further. It had become a crusade for him. He managed to transmit this not only to his players but also to supporters who were increasingly not locally based. The winning of the European Cup was the culmination of his managerial career. Although Celtic, a Scottish football club, had become the first British team to win the European Cup, Manchester United was the first team from the English Football League to do so. This encouraged people who lived many miles from the ground to adopt them as their team.

In the team at that time was one of the most exciting footballers of all time. He was seen as the first 'pop star/superstar footballer'. George Best, often called the 'fifth Beatle', drew in a whole new supporter base. Best, with his long hair, lavish lifestyle and sublime footballing skills became an international celebrity.

Apart from Best, the team also had a reputation for playing exciting, attacking football with Charlton and Law adding to the brilliance of the team. These four factors somehow combined to raise Manchester United from a provincial football team, albeit a large one, to an international team. What happened next is instructive as to the strength of the brand created but also to the fact that very few people realized just how strong the brand was and how it could be exploited.

Matt Busby's tenure as manager lasted from 1945 to 1971. He was always going to be a hard act to follow. In retrospect perhaps he stayed on too long after the triumph in 1968 and was remarkably loyal to his players, some who were past their best. In the past Busby and the club had, like most top clubs, a ruthless streak when it came to changing the team. As soon as a player had reached his peak and started to decline he would be sold and a new player bought in. Busby kept a few players longer than he might have done in his younger days and probably did not control Best sufficiently when Best's lifestyle started to affect his football.

After Busby a series of managers were hired and dismissed and until the 1990s, under Ferguson's management, the club never quite found either the players or the managers to compete at the very top level. Nor did it realize for a long time just how valuable its assets were. The club was nearly sold for £20 million in 1989 to Michael Knighton, showing what a low value was placed upon a business that 11 years later was valued at £1 billion. But in the period 1971–1990, between Busby's retirement and the start of Ferguson's success, support for the club and attendance held up despite relative poor performances and even relegation.

The traditional wisdom in football is that attendance is strongly associated with on-pitch performance. For Manchester United this does not appear to hold. It is easy to see why people support Manchester United now – the team does win lots of trophies – but the fans seem to be incredibly loyal even in periods when the team is doing badly. Ferguson was an inspired choice as manager and under him the team again started to reach the heights attained under Busby. Ferguson came from much the some background as Busby, both being Scottish and both driven to achieve success on the football pitch. Ferguson's drive and self-belief were transmitted to the team making it over the years the great team it is today.

In the period between Busby's retirement and when Ferguson's team started to win trophies, Liverpool was the dominant football club both in England and in Europe. Unfortunately for them, this was before really large amounts of money started to flow into football from television and sponsorship. It was also when football's image was harmed by problems of violence between fans at and around football grounds. Liverpool had the misfortune of being easily the best team around at the wrong time. Manchester United's revival coincided with more money coming into the game and it was able to exploit this. We can speculate that if there had been the amount of money available for the top team when Liverpool were in the ascendancy they would have gained the competitive advantage Manchester United enjoys today.

So a tragic accident, two driven managers, exciting football played by exciting, distinctive players, supporters who keep the faith through bad times and the luck to be one of the best teams at the right time have got the club to where it is today.

MANAGEMENT AND STRATEGY

There are tensions between what some refer to as the 'real' fans and the club. To understand this we need to look in more depth at how the club makes its money and who its customers are.

Merchandising

You will often see supporters wearing a Manchester United top, with either the name of their favourite player on the back or their own name, many miles from Manchester. Supporters of the club, both young and old, whether or not they ever go to see the club live at its home ground at Old Trafford, want to buy the latest replica kits and so the club can make money out of changing the kit the players wear. This works not only for the first team home strip, but the away strip as well. By changing these frequently the club can sell more. The difficulty with this is that some supporters get fed up with having to buy a new strip each season, as they are not cheap. As young children are particularly prone to wanting to wear a replica strip this puts pressure on parents to buy it even though it may only be a few months since the parents bought the last, now superseded, one. The club of course sees this as making more profit for its shareholders.

According to the club's 1998 annual report, merchandising income fell by 16 per cent and one reason given for this was that the home sales kit was now in the second year of its two-year cycle. Most supporters who wanted to own the home kit had already bought it but many supporters decide they have to have the new one, irrespective of the fact that they have a perfectly good one already. The club has been criticized for changing replica strips so frequently. It has been suggested that a code of practice is introduced on replica strips to limit the number of changes allowed over a two- or three-year-period. Shareholders, on the other hand, want to see the returns from replica strips and other merchandising maximized.

Why would you not change your products frequently if people were prepared to pay for the new ones? One reason for not doing so is the place football has in the wider society. The argument is that you should not exploit your supporters in this way, because supporters are not customers. Being a major football club is not like being a profit-maximizing company. It is different. The clubs have a bond between themselves and their supporters, which is more than what exists between other companies and their customers. So even if a club can exploit its brand by changing its strip frequently and increasing merchandising it should not. Its supporters wear the shirts to show they are true to the club. They have to buy the latest shirt because of the unique role the club plays in their lives. Very few products have this type of psychological hold over their customers and some believe it is wrong to exploit this.

We have to say this happens with all football clubs, even clubs in the lower division such as Brentford and Brighton, as well as clubs outside of the football league which have dedicated supporters who buy the latest kit. What is special about Manchester United is the sheer number of people who want to buy their replicas, not only in the UK but abroad. And the vast majority of these never or rarely go to Old Trafford to see them play! Manchester United, clearly, is for many people a strong brand.

Gate receipts

Just as the strong brand helps merchandising, it helps attendance. With the club's recent successes the number of people wanting to see Manchester United play means that home games are sold out. The club has undertaken a building programme to increase attendance up to 67,000. Gate receipts contribute between 30 and 35 per cent to annual turnover. The figure varies because of the number of home games the club plays in the year. While the number of Premier League games is guaranteed, cup games and European games depend on how well the team does in them. A successful European campaign and a good cup run can increase gate receipts markedly.

Normally if you had a product that was in limited supply and the demand for it exceeded the supply you would raise the price. If the club did this revenue would rise as the demand for tickets far exceeds the supply. Why does it not do so? To answer this we again need to take account of the traditional roots of English football.

Manchester United's home ground, like many British football clubs, is in a working class area of Manchester, as this is where clubs had their traditional supporter base. But going to home games now is not cheap and richer supporters living, in some cases, many miles from the ground, have for many years displaced local supporters. A football chant supporters of other clubs sing when Manchester United play away is 'You are all doctors from Surrey!' Increasingly there are complaints that the 'real' supporter cannot afford to see the team play live anymore. Manchester United, again, like all the top teams, has when redeveloping its grounds replaced cheap terrace places where supporters traditionally stood with expensive seats, because of legal requirements introduced following the Hillsborough Disaster at which Liverpool fans were killed following severe overcrowding in a cup semi-final. Manchester United has also taken out capacity by building expensive corporate hospitality accommodation. Revenue has increased enormously because of this but at the expense, it is argued, of the 'real' fan.

The days of turning up without a ticket to the match have long gone for the club. One way to secure a seat is to buy a season ticket, something that traditional working class supporters might find difficult to afford. Alternatively, the options are to get invited to one of the corporate boxes or buy a ticket on the black market. If richer fans who travel a long way to see home games are displacing 'real' fans, why not put prices up even more? There must be quite a debate at board level over this, as given that the ground is usually sold out, an increase in prices would raise revenue considerably. Is the reason why this does not happen to do with the relationship the club feels it still has with its supporters? So while seeing a home game is expensive it is not as expensive as it could be if market forces were allowed free-rein.

Manchester United, like all big clubs, does offer corporate hospitality deals through which companies can buy seats in corporate boxes. This is a way of increasing the sales price of a seat at a game. The club charges anything up to £400 per seat for something it charges elsewhere in the ground between £14 and £20. The corporate client is given a tour of the ground, pre- and post-match buffet and drinks with some past players, plus the luxury of watching the game in warm and comfortable surroundings. 'Real' fans don't watch the game behind glass, sipping drinks.

For the club there is a need to balance the needs of the 'real' fan and the richer fans and the corporate sector. This is a balance between meeting the needs of someone who will not disappear once performances on the pitch deteriorates, and making money from the richer supporters and corporate sector. This balance is not easy. Some clubs, when the team starts doing badly, find that not only has the corporate market dried up but also its core of supporters has shrunk because they have been excluded in the past.

Television receipts

Over the last 20 years revenue derived from television has gone up for clubs such as Manchester United. To understand why a little background is required.

The 1937 FA Cup Final was the first match to be shown live on British television. For the record, Preston North End lost to Sunderland 3–1. It took nearly 50 years before live league games, that is not the Cup Final and some Internationals, were regularly broadcast live. The cost of the contract for this was £2.3 million for the 1983 season with the 92 football league clubs getting £28,261 each. The cost of the contract went up to £3.1 million per season in 1986. In 1988 the cost was £11 million per season. Then, in 1989, Sky started its UK satellite broadcast. Sky's strategy to sell more satellite dishes than its rival satellite company BSB was in part based on getting the rights to broadcast football live. It won these rights with a bid of £49 million a season starting in the 1992–93 season. The BBC paid £4 million for the highlights. The next round of bidding was for the rights to the period 1997–98 to 2000–01. BSkyB (formed from the merger of Sky and BSB) successfully won this round with a bid of £670 million while the BBC paid £73 million for the highlights. The last period bid for was 2001–02 to 2003–04. Rights for live matches reached a staggering £1.1 billion for this three-year period.

How much were Premier League clubs expected to get from all this? For the very first deal Manchester United received £28,261 (1983–84 season), as did every league club. According to Manchester United's 1998 annual report the club received £16.2 million from television. For 2000 it got a massive £30.5 million. This is probably easily more than the turnover of most of the clubs in the football league, as well as many clubs in the Premier League. For the period 2001–04 it can expect to receive even more than this. It is probable that income from television will become the single most important source of revenue for the club over this period. It will also help it maintain its brand image because of the exposure it will receive not only in the UK but also in programmes being relayed around the world. The money it receives from television should allow it to compete in the market for players thus reinforcing its position over other English and, increasingly important for the club, European teams.

Live television rights, although generating massive incomes for the club, have been granted again to BSkyB which has a subscription-based service for viewers. This means that supporters wanting to see Manchester United play live on television have either to buy a subscription from BSkyB and the necessary satellite dish and technology or watch it in a local pub. Again the 'real' supporter, some argue, is being excluded from watching the club. BSkyB anyway may well increase how much it charges customers for watching football; or begin moving more of the games from its analogue to its digital system – again involving more expenditure for those who want to watch the match live. On the other hand BSkyB has significantly increased the number of people who can watch the game live. Old Trafford only holds about 67,000 spectators but over 2 million people might watch on television an important match against another top club. The club can sell club-related merchandise to these viewers and thus gain more income.

The share Manchester United takes from television income is a dilemma. If it takes too big a slice other clubs, not only in the lower leagues but also in the Premier League, will find it increasingly difficult to compete with them. The club can afford the best players. This at first sight might appear to be a good thing, as the club will win more trophies. However, if competitors do not have access to the money required to compete effectively, people might soon tire of seeing Manchester United easily win everything. The success of a small, unfashionable club, such as Bradford City, keeps the game 'alive'. If the big clubs such as Manchester United rarely lost any trophy, the interest in the game would soon evaporate. The brand image of the club is interwoven with the brand of the game. If the game's brand starts to falter so will the club's. It is important that money from television filters down through the leagues to allow the possibility of clubs from the lower divisions creating new interest in the game by challenging the existing status quo. At first sight this may appear not to be in the interest of the club, as it would allow other teams to challenge them effectively but without this the Premier League could easily become sterile.

On the other hand to compete at the very top level in the Premier League and in the European Champions Competition the club needs to buy the very best players. Other top English clubs such as Arsenal and Liverpool, as well as top European clubs, are also very wealthy and can afford the high transfer fees and wages required to secure the very best players. Manchester United has to be able to compete with these clubs for the services of players. If Manchester United is to mount a challenge for domestic and European trophies it needs to secure the maximum it can from the Premier League television rights in order to buy and pay the top players

If the club takes too large a share of television income, domestic competition could be undermined, with the brand image of the game as a whole undermined. It it takes too small a share, domestic and European competition becomes problematic, with support being affected.

There is a further dimension to television revenues as BSkyB, the provider of television coverage, is an important stakeholder in the club. In 1999 BSkyB attempted to buy Manchester United with a bid of £623m. The Department of Trade and Industry blocked this. The company changed its strategy on football club acquisitions after this rebuff. Instead of buying up clubs it switched to buying stakes in leading premier clubs. At present BSkyB owns a 9.9 per cent stake in Chelsea, a 9.9 per cent stake in Manchester United, a 9.08 per cent share of Leeds United and a 9.9 per cent share of Manchester City. Other media companies have shares in Newcastle United, Aston Villa and Liverpool. For example, Granada has a 10 per cent stake in Liverpool and a 5 per cent stake in Arsenal. As a major shareholder in Manchester United, BSkyB needs to make sure that the brand images of the club and of the Premier League are maintained. BSkyB has to make sure that its customers are subscribing to its football services. At present it has not introduced pay-for-view for football; instead customers buy a subscription to watch a number of games. It has, though, experimented with pay-for-view for boxing matches. The company must be tempted to introduce pay-for-view for top football games, as the potential income is enormous. However, the UK tradition is to show edited highlights on terrestrial television with a subscription service via satellite for live games.

BSkyB's purchase of shares in Premier League teams is seen as an attempt to consolidate its monopoly to show live games. It does have some influence in the boardroom of these clubs when negotiations for a new contract begin. Other media companies, such as Granada and NTL, are now positioning themselves for this eventuality by buying stakes in other clubs. At present the maximum stake allowed is 10 per cent but this could change under pressure from the clubs. Whoever owns the rights to show football also has to make sure that football stays exciting and this means that a league dominated by Manchester United will not, in the long run, sell. In other industries the elimination of competition is seen as a good thing but in competitive sport competition has to be kept reasonably sharp to maintain consumer interest. The beauty of games such as football lies in their ability to surprise us from time to time. Or at least give us hope that there might just be a surprise.

Sponsorship

Manchester United makes money out of being sponsored by companies such as Vodafone and is presently negotiating a deal with Nike for a reputed £20m a year for 15 years. With this additional enormous income Manchester United will be able to spend even more on acquiring the very best players available, but the same point comes up again – the club might simply become too good for the Premier League, winning the league with comparative ease because of its superior resource base. Whether this sort of money, coupled with the increased income it is going to earn

from television, is enough to mount a challenge for the European Cup is more difficult to say as some European clubs have access to even more money than Manchester
United does.

STRATEGIC PROBLEMS

Looking at the sources of Manchester United's revenue, two potential difficulties
emerge. Firstly, the possible exclusion of the 'real' fan and the breaking down of the
bond between the club and its traditional supporters. Recognition of this bond means
that the club is more conscious of changing its kit and charging high prices for seats
than perhaps a traditional business would be. Second, demanding too much from
television and sponsorship might undermine the market for football as a commodity
as competition might be seriously weakened making games sterile. Alternatively, by
not getting the best deal possible the club may find it does not have the resources to
compete at the very highest level in Europe. These are strategic problems the club has
to grapple with. The club also has other long-term concerns about the English game
that it needs to analyse carefully.

Who plays for Manchester United?

With the EU's freedom of movement of labour and the growth in income that top
clubs such as Manchester United have achieved, there has been a large increase in the
number of non-British players in the Premier League. For many years there was,
more or less, a complete ban on non-British or non-Irish players in the Football
League. This was slowly relaxed, first allowing only two such players, and now there
are almost no restrictions on foreign players. (There is a restriction relating to non-EU
players but in practice even this hardly applies.) Clubs such as Manchester United
can now, more or less, compete against top clubs in Italy and Spain for the very best
players.

   The growth in foreign players in UK clubs has had an effect on domestic players, as
they are not getting the chance to play at the highest level. Recently Chelsea fielded a
team entirely made up of foreign players. Their player-acquisition strategy is to buy
well-established foreign players. Manchester United, on the other hand, has an excellent record of bringing on young, home grown talent starting with the famous Busby
Babes of the 1950s. Today's team has several players nurtured through its youth
scheme such as Beckham, Scholes, Giggs and Butt. But the temptation is there to buy
established players, often from abroad. The effect of this in the long run will be to
undermine the ability of the national team to compete in the European and World Cup
successfully, as the players available for selection will not have had sufficient

experience of playing at the highest level in the domestic league. The pressure on the club is to win now and if this means buying foreign players so be it; but in the long term this could dilute the game's brand as the national team will not be able to win anything and support will drift away to sports where the national team does do well.

So it can be argued that Manchester United not only has a problem if it becomes too dominant in the Premier League (as this will undermine the excitement value of the game and consequently the club's own support), it also has to be aware that if the national team does not do well the national game will decline and, again, support for the club will wane.

Web resources

www.manutd.com/

9

Matcon Engineering

by Graham Beaver

© 2001 Graham Beaver

Having a good product is not always enough to turn a small firm into an international success. Once a company starts operating in a wider market it needs experienced management to take it forward.

MATCON ENGINEERING'S CORE PRODUCT

For almost 17 years, Ivan Semenenko was Matcon Engineering. An inspired and brilliant engineer, he invented the company's core product – a steel cone that revolutionized the way that grain is discharged from storage silos. Semenenko called it the cone-valve system, took out worldwide patents, and set up Matcon Engineering in 1981 with business angel finance from Sir John Aird, an old Etononian baronet with an interest in engineering.

When Semenenko started he was producing his cone valves for farmers who fitted them on their silos. The cone replaced the age-old method of discharging grain – running up a ladder and thumping the sides of a silo with a sledgehammer! Installing a steel cone that pumped up and down in the base of the silo broke up the grain and allowed it to flow through a gap evenly. The average size of a contract was £4,000.

BRANCHING OUT

Over the years, Semenenko, the son of a World War II refugee, used his base technology to branch out into more complex systems designed to help the food and drugs industries handle powders safely and efficiently. Matcon has developed a range of technologies that contribute to the safe storage, measurement, mixing and discharge of powders such as paracetamol and detergent. Safety is paramount when handling these products in concentrated pre-processed form. Inhaling even a tiny amount of paracetamol dust could kill a worker. People who work with the enzymes used in some detergents, which can be as damaging as radiation, could suffer serious health problems if particles escape into the air; and companies involved with explosives have to transfer and store them without the risk of contamination.

PROBLEMS AND SOLUTIONS

Although Matcon has gained an enviable reputation for innovation, by the-mid 1990s the delivery of its products and services was uncertain and there was a staff turnover problem. 'Our attention span was too short,' says Charles Lee, CEO of Matcon. 'We were developing innovative products but as an organization we had a habit of generating expectation in excess of our capacity to deliver. That created a lot of internal stress. There was high staff churn and we were not seen as a good place to work.'

There have been changes in the company's ownership and management. Aird and Semenenko sold 10 per cent of their shares to the staff and an experienced non-executive director was appointed to provide 'a calm voice of reason in board meetings'. In 1997, Semenenko sold his remaining stake to existing shareholders and a venture capital company.

In 1999 Matcon was on target to make profits of £1m on sales of £15.6m. There was however a problem about growing the business. The company had reached a point where it had a huge market opportunity yet it continued to remain a small engineering business. Aird said in 1999:

> Today, we calculate the size of the potential market to be about £400 million. Our technology is applicable to an enormous variety of sectors, from pharmaceuticals, chemicals and paints to foods and fertilizers. We're not even scratching the surface of it… The qualities that made a successful founder-entrepreneur, such as energy, determination and unstoppability, do not necessarily enable a company to make a successful transition to a larger, professionally managed organization.

Matcon has worked hard to counter its problems. To stem the level of staff turnover that had built up, it developed a more democratic structure, giving senior managers a say in key decisions as well as equity. The company has tried to establish clear lines of accountability as well as administrative and communication systems that, according to Lee, 'May add nothing to a project in technical terms but are crucial in keeping everybody on board.' Matcon is also recruiting more senior staff to provide greater management depth.

THE FUTURE

Matcon has now reached a level of organizational maturity and its board reckons that it is now in a better position to seize opportunities. However, its future is still unclear and the company has still to make important decisions to decide on its path of development.

The company's customers are global organizations such as Roche, Unilever, Procter & Gamble and Pfizer, so it has to change its supply methods. It cannot simply ship bits of machinery from its Moreton-in-the-Marsh, Gloucestershire headquarters. Its systems are large and complex and need to be embedded at the heart of a customer's factory.

Customers want on-site consultation about which system to install, project management of its installation, including dealing with local contractors such as fitters and service engineers, training of workers in their own languages and back-up support and maintenance. This is a big task for a company with only 140 staff. 'It is a real problem for a small company to meet these selling and service requirements,' says Aird. 'We are in an ongoing debate about the best way of managing them.'

Matcon has tried to achieve global reach through setting up overseas subsidiaries, signing joint ventures and recruiting licensees. It has operations in the United States, Australia, France, Japan, Holland and Scandinavia and is studying them to decide which is the best model for development.

'Joint ventures tend to be an enormous administrative burden on the home base,' says Aird. 'With licensees you run the risk of transferring knowledge to a competitor since it is hard to manage and protect territories in a global environment. And subsidiaries require capital input, which is only justified by high-volume sales.'

The company's preferred strategy is to deploy specialist engineers who work with customers in the field, send back specifications to Matcon's headquarters and manage the installations of the systems when they are sent out to the client. The attraction is that costs are kept low because there is no need to duplicate the expensive technical design and engineering base abroad and no knowledge is passed to potential competitors.

This strategy does depend though on being able to recruit the right calibre people. High-performing sales engineers must have excellent technical and commercial skills and be able to speak to an executive of a multinational – and for example, Portuguese to a Brazilian operator or service engineer. 'The only real constraint on our growth now is the capacity to find and train high-quality committed sales engineers,' says Aird.

Since powder handling is a young industry and there is a shortage of engineers with the relevant skills, Matcon has had to recruit likely candidates and train them. The training, which lasts at least a year, builds technical and commercial skills as well as a strong relationship with base camp. 'We aim to make them part of the Matcon family before they move out to work in remote territories,' says Lee. 'The worst thing that you can do is to download a whole lot of information on people for several months and then see them go off and join a competitor.'

Matcon will not get the best from its field engineers unless it keeps them informed about what their colleagues are doing. The proliferation of sales operations has meant that people are selling into the same organization at different points. Recently, a Matcon representative in Texas was advising a Japanese drug company about a system for transporting products from Japan to a plant in Texas. At the same time Matcon's Japanese licensees were advising the company's Tokyo head office on the same operation. It did not take the Japanese company long to start playing one end off against the other, asking for modified quotes based on inside information. 'We only found out by accident,' says Lee. 'Hopefully in time to make price information at both ends compatible. But the experience made it clear to us that we have to build a coordinated strategy so that our people are not competing against each other.'

Finally, Matcon has to decide whether its enormous potential market is best served by going it alone or forming an alliance. Central and Eastern Europe are today's new markets while Latin America and China are expected to be tomorrow's. With the capacity to train only three new sales engineers each year, Matcon is in no position to exploit the potential market for its products alone. Thus there is a lengthy internal debate about whether it should seek an alliance or merger with a bigger organization selling to the same type of customers. 'We would then be able to deliver our products and services through their distribution channels,' says Lee.

Aird says of Matcon's technology: 'A man with a shovel and a large hammer can do everything we can do but not as efficiently and safely. As manufacturing standards become more rigorous worldwide there will be a huge increase in demand for our products.'

What are the principal issues and challenges facing the company in its quest for growth, organizational development, control and profitability?

10

Nissan and Renault

On 26 December 1933 Jidosha-Seizo Kabushiki-Kashia (Auto Manufacturing Company Limited) began manufacturing Datsuns under the direction of Yoshisuke Aikawa. By June 1934 the company had changed its name to Nissan. In 1935 it started exporting Datsuns to Australia. After World War II the Americans occupied half of the company's plant at Yokohama and a large part of its dealer network was taken over by Toyota. This impeded Nissan's progress considerably. Even when production started to grow again labour disputes were not uncommon with the company suffering a 100-day strike in 1953. The seeds for the company's collaborative approach to labour relations were sown around this time. In the early 1950s it started to explore foreign alliances. It made an agreement with Austin (a UK car company) to build Austin cars in Japan. The first one was produced in 1953.

Nissan also began to explore ways of excelling at the technical side of manufacturing. By 1960 it won the prestigious Deming Prize for engineering excellence, the first Japanese company to do so. In the 1960s Nissan benefited from the freeing up of investment funds in Japan by embarking on a growth path that included acquisitions and new plant capacity. In the 1970s the company profited from the oil crisis that increased the demand both in Japan and outside for smaller, more efficient cars. In 1973 its Sunny won a fuel economy test in the United States demonstrating its success in manufacturing fuel-efficient cars.

In the 1980s Nissan embarked on major overseas expansion with the establishment in 1980 of the Nissan Motor Manufacturing Corporation USA and in 1984 the Motor Manufacturing (UK) Limited.

PROBLEMS

The early 1990s saw company results starting to decline and, as the decade wore on, the problems it faced started to appear so great that it needed outside help. So on 27 March 1999 Nissan entered into a strategic alliance with Renault when Renault bought 37 per cent of Nissan. Why did Nissan do this? It felt it had to improve or go out of business! It urgently needed to start making profits again after several years of very poor results. It had experienced declining market shares around the world including in Japan, where its share of the market had dropped from nearly 24 per cent in 1988 to under 20 per cent in 1998. Its global market share had reached 6.6 per cent in 1991 but had fallen back to just under 5 per cent in 1998. Renault on the other hand wanted to sell more cars in Japan and Asia. If Renault could turn around Nissan its 37 per cent stake would be very good business for it.

According to Nissan there were five reasons for its poor performance:

- The company had lost its profit orientation.
- It had ceased to be customer focused.
- It had difficulty in integrating across functions and markets and also had become too hierarchical.
- Increased bureaucracy meant that it lacked a sense of speed in getting things done.
- Perhaps most damning of all, the company felt it had lost a sense of common vision leading to disputes over the direction it should be going and frustration between the different business units both in Japan and overseas.

Nissan had been trying for several years to sort itself out but, as its results had shown, this was simply not working. In 1996 it believed it was on its way to improved performance – its annual report was called 'We've turned the corner.' Some of the key components of its plan at that time were cost reductions and management restructuring and these measures appeared to be having the desired effects. In 1994 net income was negative at over –86 billion yen (–86,915,000,000 yen), in 1995 net income worsened to just over –166 billion yen (–166,054,000,000 yen) but this was reduced to over –88 billion yen (–88,418,000,000 yen) in 1996. 1997 did indeed see positive net income of more than 77 billion yen (77,743,000,000 yen) but through to 1999 net income was again negative reaching more than –684 billion yen (–684,363,000,000 yen) in 1999. Nissan's 1997 annual report was entitled 'Back on track and shifting to a higher gear' but the next year's was entitled 'Strategic reform is the message at Nissan' as net income had slumped to just over –14 billion yen (–14,007,000,000 yen). The company's 1999 report was called 'A new alliance for the millennium.'

THE ALLIANCE IN EUROPE

In Europe the Renault Nissan alliance aim is to achieve a market share of 17 per cent by 2005 to become the number one in Europe ahead of Ford and Volkswagen. At present the alliance has a market share of about 14 per cent. The plan to achieve 17 per cent has two basic parts. First, the alliance will restructure dealer and support networks and second, in the short term, some narrow cross-badging will take place. The introduction of shared engines and bodies will take some time – for example the Nissan Micra and Renault Clio will share the same basic platform by 2003–04.

The restructure of the dealer and support network in Europe will involve reducing the current joint number of dealers to create fewer but larger hubs or super dealers. These will look after back office functions such as accounting and legal services, along with parts and accessories, for both companies while still presenting the two companies to customers separately. This will be a tricky task as both companies have built up their own dealer networks, back-office facilities and management structures that will have to be gradually realigned into the new structures. By 2002 up to 70 per cent of the hubs will be providing services for Renault and Nissan and presenting the two companies to customers. By 2005 there will be 450 hubs, 90 per cent of which will be serving the two companies. The aim of this is to increase sales through better marketing and reduce cost through savings. The current thinking of the alliance is for Renault to direct all sales and marketing including Nissan in Germany, the Netherlands and Switzerland but with Nissan to be in charge of the Nissan front office. In France, Italy, Spain and the UK both will retain marketing but Renault will be responsible for the back office. If the plan works this will result eventually in a reduction of over 500 staff in sales and marketing. Nissan's workforce in these areas will be reduced by over half but Renault's will increase by about 8 per cent due to work in the new hubs. One effect of this restructuring could be a reduction of the number of small dealers as they merge to provide the scale the alliance thinks necessary to compete effectively in Europe.

THE ALLIANCE ELSEWHERE

Worldwide Nissan is looking for a reduction in dealerships and a concentration of back-office functions. For instance in Japan it aims to close 20 per cent of its dealer affiliates and 10 per cent of its retail outlets, while at the same time concentrating back-office functions.

In Japan Renault believes that it can significantly increase sales with the help of Nissan. It has set up Renault Japan to be the sole importer of Renaults into Japan. In

1999 Renault sold around 3,000 vehicles in Japan. By 2004 it aims to be selling 15,000 a year there. As a comparison, in 1999 in Europe Renault sold 1.9 million vehicles. Nissan's know-how in the Japanese market, its existing dealer network and back-office capabilities will be an important factor in achieving the desired sales growth. At present the brand identities will remain separate.

In the Mercosur market (Argentine, Brazil, Paraguay and Uruguay) the alliance aims to increase joint sales to 150,000 vehicles by 2010, that is, about 15 per cent of the market. Again it believes this can be achieved by enhancing the efficiency of its back-room operations and by eventually having joint production facilities and shared models.

MORE ON COST SAVINGS

The alliance has three areas where savings can be made: manufacturing, global stocks and labour productivity.

In Japan in 1999 the alliance was manufacturing 24 makes in nine plants. By 2002 it wants to reduce this to 15 makes and four plants and within two years to have reduced the makes to 12. (In this period one plant at Kyoto will produce a small number of Civilians only.) Similar savings are envisaged in the alliance's overseas plants by concentrating production and reducing the number of models. In time Renault design expertise will be introduced to revamp the image of Nissan and shared models will be launched.

To achieve other savings and improvement of practice, high-level executive exchanges and numerous low-level ones are planned as best practice is transferred between the two partners. A small example of this is Nissan is now going to adopt the Renault manufacturing guideline that any component that has to be lifted by the workforce on the plant floor can be done safely using one hand. Also Nissan is moving to the implementation of 14-day car delivery instead of 21-day delivery, and a significant reduction in the amount of stock carried.

Nissan further wants to reduce the number of suppliers it relies on. In 1999 it had nearly 1200 suppliers and aims to reduce this to 600 by 2002 with the aim of saving in logistics and paperwork and possible gains from larger batch orders at lower unit cost.

MANAGEMENT

How is Nissan going to tackle what it believes has been a failure in its senior management structure that it felt had become fragmented across functions and countries? It aims to solve this by radically restructuring itself from a multi-regional organization to a global one. Global headquarters will be involved in deciding upon and implementing strategy. Other functions will be directed globally including R&D, finance, HR, purchasing and manufacturing systems. Brand management will also be directed from here.

The workforce needs to become more productive for Nissan to move back into profits. It aims to reduce its workforce by some 21,000 employees through natural wastage, spin-offs, early retirement and more flexible working hours. About 4,000 jobs will go in manufacturing and 6,500 in the dealerships. Other reductions will be in the back offices and into spin-offs. Nissan intends to introduce stock options schemes and bonuses for managers to encourage increases in productivity.

Will Renault's magic work?

Web resources

www.nissan.co.uk/
– for details of Nissan's revival plan see its PowerPoint presentation at www.nissan.co.jp/NRP/SUPPORT/index-e.files/frame.htm

11

Powderject Ltd

by Graham Beaver

© 2001 Graham Beaver

Pharmaceutical companies pump millions of pounds into research and development before seeing a profit. Powderject, which is pioneering needle-free injections, wants to keep costs down and make sure its products are successful with the public.

BACKGROUND

Biotechnology has proved fertile ground for smaller-company growth, but as Paul Drayson, CEO of Powderject knows all too well, growth is achieved only after big cash outflows on R&D. Drayson has to get the balance right between investment and cash management. 'My challenge is control the cash burn,' he says. 'I have to get the products to market within the timetables established. We are running a commercial operation, not a research institution.'

So far, Drayson has kept the show on the road. Despite losses of £4.5 million during 1999, Powderject's market value has risen to £289 million since it was founded in 1993 to commercialize the research findings of Brian Bellhouse, Director of Oxford University's Medical-Engineering Unit.

Bellhouse had invented a way of giving injections without needles in the manner of Dr McCoy in *Star Trek*. A helium gas trigger delivers a powdered drug with sufficient speed to penetrate the skin. Not only is the injection pain-free – it feels like a puff of air – it may also be more effective than an injection via a needle since the drug can be targeted more accurately. The company owns worldwide patents to this method, an attractive asset with the drug-delivery sector growing at twice the rate of the pharmaceuticals industry as a whole.

Drayson's success may be due partly to his background, which is in industrial management rather than the research laboratory. In fact, he learnt 'the commercial ropes' in biscuits. By the time he was 30 he had set up a subsidiary for Trebor, the sweets company now owned by Cadbury Schweppes, developing a high-quality snack product. He sold the business at a big profit, learnt of Bellhouse's invention and invested his own money to start up Powderject. 'I had the experience of taking a product from concept to the supermarket shelf,' he says. 'It is an exhilarating feeling to see people buying something that you created – and when you are running a biotech company, with such long lead times in bringing a product to market, it is important to remember what the goal is.'

FINANCIAL SITUATION

Powderject, which has been growing at 50 per cent a year, went public in 1997 and has raised £35 million to fund development. Drayson then told investors how he planned to spend the money over two years. He recognized that his war chest had to be managed carefully. 'The impulse, when you have raised a lot of money is to go out and spend it,' he said. 'But every pound we spend we have to earn back. My job is to make sure all those involved in the Powderject process get a good return for their investment.'

Budgets are reviewed monthly and managers who do not meet them are carpeted. Drayson encourages a lean and hungry atmosphere: there are no company cars and pension contributions and rewards are made up of basic salary and share options. 'I started my biscuit company in the recession. I had to go back to bank managers and beg for an extension of my overdraft facility. I remember kicking myself for spending £2,000 on office furniture I could have done perfectly well without,' he remembers.

Drayson has had some difficulty in applying the performance measures he used for biscuits to biotechnology. 'I learnt biscuits through ratios,' he says. 'Sales to cost of sales, cost of sales to overheads to net profits and so on. These disciplines are harder to apply in the more nebulous world of biotechnology.' As a result, he is working with accountants to build performance measures that can be applied to high-technology businesses where a lot of money is spent before big sales are seen. The model includes measuring such items as overheads per worker, current and potential sales per worker and product milestones achieved per worker.

Drayson tries to maintain commercial focus by outsourcing early stage research to Oxford University. 'I believe the early-stage innovation engine should continue to be in the University,' he says. He pays scientists on the understanding that Powderject is allowed to commercialize any relevant findings. This reduces laboratory overheads and allows the company to use its own laboratory specifically for development.

The business earns money from partnerships with big companies that pay Powderject to develop their drugs for powder delivery. Payment starts with a fee when a deal is signed, continues with milestone payments as a drug passes through the various development stages and ends with royalties of 6 per cent to 12 per cent when it reaches market.

Drayson's biggest achievement to date is a deal with Glaxo Wellcome to develop their genetic vaccines for hepatitis B, AIDS and cancer for powder delivery. At £180 million before commercialization, this is said to be Europe's biggest R&D collaboration. It is also a big endorsement of Powderject since these drugs will be developed for powder delivery only.

MANAGING CHANGE

While the partnership method has offered Powderject fast growth, it brings its own pressures. The company grew from 5 staff to 126 in 5 years and now has offices in Oxford, Wisconsin, and Palo Alto, California. 'We were a company of only 10 people when we set up the Palo Alto office,' says Drayson. 'It was a risk but it was one of the best things that we have done. The US West Coast is way ahead of us in the area of drugs delivery – it was a huge wake-up call for me about the strength of the competition. And I spend quite a lot of my time there to get a shot in the arm of entrepreneurial energy.'

Half of Powderject's staff is now in the United States, the world's largest drugs market. Modern technology helps them to keep in touch – Powderject uses an Intranet, videoconferencing and e-mail – but Drayson knows that the growth rate creates problems. 'It puts a lot of strain on people to be adaptable,' he says. 'But if you start off with the right culture, the expectation of continual change – it can be managed.'

Continual change is not everyone's cup of tea. Even in terms of desk space, the company is growing at a rate that does not allow people to get stuck to their chairs. As drugs proceed through clinical trials towards manufacture and distribution,

Drayson has to hire new people over the heads of existing staff to direct these new and complex processes. He tries to manage this by involving existing staff in the interviewing process but knows that the rate of change does not suit everyone. 'When you are redefining jobs and organizational structures rapidly, you will always lose some people,' he says. 'Sometimes a person who has done a brilliant job to a certain point is just not suitable for the next stage. Then I look on it as my responsibility to help them as easily as possible into their next situation.'

Drayson has learnt something about how to accommodate growth from Auragen, its recent US purchase from WR Grace. As a subsidiary of a big company, Auragen had established procedures on many aspects of operations. Drayson says: 'If you wanted to paint your office wall, there were rules to tell you what colour it should be. It is surprising just how much time these kinds of operational issues can take up when there is no settled procedure.' Drayson says that he has swallowed whole what he found useful in the Auragen rulebooks.

ESTABLISHING THE BRAND

Drayson's big challenge is to build a brand solid enough to survive beyond the expiry of the Powderject patents. If he has built a brand that commands strong customer loyalty, it will be a potential barrier to entry in his field. He points to the Intel chip, used inside PCs and also the breathable fabric Goretex, used inside well-known sportswear brands. 'If you buy a Ralph Lauren ski suit you are not just buying the brand and the design, but also the Goretex label inside,' he says. 'It comes as a package.'

His ambition is to establish Powderject as the customers' favoured form of taking powdered injections. To do this, he must make sure that the needleless injection is branded whenever it is delivered, so that the patient knowingly takes an anaesthetic for dental surgery or a Glaxo vaccine for cancer with a Powderject device. He is confident of achieving this ambition. There is a growing trend towards patient choice in healthcare on both sides of the Atlantic.

The Powderject technology itself assists in the process since it removes the necessity for an injection to be taken under medical supervision. With self-administration of injections, patient choice looks likely to play an important part in the creation of healthcare brands. 'As a lifetime asthmatic, I have a strong relationship with my inhaler,' says Drayson. 'As a child I noticed that there were differences between inhalers – some were more effective than others – and if pharmaceutical companies had branded them more powerfully, I would have insisted on being given a particular type.'

ISSUES FOR DISCUSSION

Consider the following issues:

1. The control and management of spending when a lot of money has to be spent on R&D before seeing significant revenues.
2. The need to develop organizational structures to manage the rapid growth which, it is hoped, will materialize.
3. The requirement to establish Powderject as a major brand that will both survive and prosper beyond the expiry of its patents.

12

Procter & Gamble

This case study starts in Cincinnati in 1837 and ends there on 1 July 2000.

HISTORY

William Procter and James Gamble came to the United States from England and Ireland respectively. They married the two Norris sisters, Olivia and Elizabeth. William's previous wife, Martha, had only recently died and it is interesting to consider that if she had lived Procter & Gamble might never have existed as a business. It was the two men's father-in-law who suggested that they go into business together. William was a candle maker and James was a soap maker. So in 1837 in Cincinnati the business was formed. Despite fears of an economic collapse and competition from existing candle and soap makers in Cincinnati the business flourished. By 1859 Procter & Gamble employed 80 people and had sales of US $1 million. During the American Civil War the company supplied soap and candles to the Union Army and when the war was over soldiers returning home started to buy its products in their hometowns. A cheap white soap developed by James Norris Gamble, named Ivory in 1879, was the first of their products to be advertised across the United States in 1882 and became a great success. In 1887 the company introduced a profit sharing scheme for its employees instigated by William Cooper Procter, grandson of the founder.

The company started to expand rapidly, investing heavily in new products. Products such as Dreft (a detergent), Ivory Flakes (for washing clothes) and Crisco (cooking oil) appeared. Central to the success of the company was the combination of in-house R&D on new products coupled with market research of consumers. The company was also at the forefront of advertising. In 1933 it launched *Ma Perkins* on the wireless, sponsored by P&G's Oxydol soap powder – yes, you've guessed it, the programme was a soap opera. So when you are watching *EastEnders* or *Home and Away* think of P&G's Oxydol. Today the company is still involved with soap operas through its sponsorship of *Guiding Light* and *As the World Turns*.

By 1937, 100 years after James and William started the business, P&G was worth £230 million. Underpinning its commitment to R&D and marketing was the company's commitment to its workforce. In 1919 Procter & Gamble changed its Articles of Incorporation to include the following statement: 'Interests of the Company and its employees are inseparable.'

After World War II the company continued to introduce new products including Tide (washing powder) and Crest (fluoride toothpaste) and then in 1961 the first disposable nappy, Pampers, something those of us with children are eternally grateful for. Apart from these new products the company started to look at buying other companies both in the United States and abroad to strengthen its market position. In 1980, Procter & Gamble had sales of US $11 billion derived from operating in 23 countries.

GOING GLOBAL

The next step in Procter & Gamble's development was to become a global company. To achieve this it invested heavily in two new areas, pharmaceuticals, with the purchase of Norwich Eaton in 1982 and Richardson-Vicks in 1985, and cosmetics, with the purchase of Max Factor, Novell (with its brand Cover Girl) and Ellen Betrix in the same period. In 1990 it acquired Shulton's Old Spice brand. It had a strong presence in Western and the Japanese markets. With the collapse of the Soviet Union it started to look for markets and acquisitions in Eastern Europe. In 1991 it purchased Rakona, a Czech company. By 1993 sales were over US $30 billion with the majority from outside the United States for the first time. In little over 150 years the small Cincinnati soap and candle makers had become a global business. Today about 5 billion of us buy their products. They operate in 70 countries and sell in 140, employing over 100,000 people. New products include a line of snacks cooked in Olean, based on Olestra, a fat-free and calorie-free cooking oil.

PERFORMANCE

Procter & Gamble set itself the aim of doubling business every decade. By 1996 revenue and profit were at record levels. Everything looked fine for Procter & Gamble but behind these excellent figures were some worrying signs. The company was living off past success. Its leading products – Tide, Pampers and Ivory – were old. Some of them were slowly modified over the years by the vast army of research scientists the company employed. Procter & Gamble had built its business by careful product and market research but in the fast-moving modern world the products were taking too long to reach the market. Other firms were beginning to beat Procter & Gamble to market, but still in 1996 Procter & Gamble held over 40 per cent of the disposable nappies market and nearly a third of the laundry detergent market.

The company's profits had been boosted by the cost-cutting campaign instigated in 1992 by CEO John Pepper that had by 1996 reduced costs by some US $3 billion. While this had helped the bottom line it disguised, to a degree, the need for the company to come up with the new Tide or Pampers for the future.

The company's culture, which had served it well in the past, was one of conservatism and caution. Most of the senior managers had worked for the company for years and had internalized this culture. Undertaking new risky innovations was difficult. Decision making often took months and sometimes resulted in more information being asked for, more research being undertaken. The company had developed over the years rules for most things. Memos, for instance, had only to be so long, a new business proposal followed a certain template, recruitment looked at certain key features etc. Even so, in 1996 the company seemed to be on course to fulfil the aim of doubling its business within the decade.

In 1997 sales growth was only up just over 1 per cent on the previous year but the company had managed to find another US $1 billion of savings. It was also moving towards building global brands but the leap forward it needed in innovation and market share was still not happening. By 1998 it become clear to the company that its existing strategy was not going to achieve the goal of doubling sales. Something else had to be done.

CHANGE AT THE TOP

Jager replaced John Pepper, the CEO, in January 1999. A new strategy, called Organisation 2005, was started. This strategy will ensure that Procter & Gamble almost double turnover from US $38 billion to US $70 billion by 2005. To do this Jager identified major cultural changes that needed to take place within the company, coining the phrase 'speed, innovation and stretch' to encapsulate the strategy.

Jager wasted little time in implementing the changes he believed necessary to turn the company around. In June 1999 he announced that by 2005 the workforce would be cut by 13 per cent involving some 15,000 job losses and ten factory closures. The company would be reorganized into seven global Business Units and corporate services would be centralized. Importantly, he committed the company to tripling its introduction of new products while reducing the time to get them to market by 50 per cent.

In the summer of 2000, there had been three profit warnings in six months and the writing was on the wall for Jager. He stepped down. In March Procter & Gamble's stock had dropped 29 per cent following a profits warning. In response to this Jager commented that the company restructuring necessary for Organisation 2005 might have sucked in too much of the day-to-day managerial resources. Attempts to buy two drug companies had failed, further lowering Jager's standing internally and externally. Lafley took over as CEO and Pepper (who Jager had replaced only 18 months previously) reappeared as Chairman. Lafley, commenting on the results for the fiscal year 1999–2000, says:

> Fiscal 2000 was a tough year. Earnings came in below the goals we had originally established and felt we could achieve. In our drive to meet changes in the marketplace – globalization, the Internet, consolidation among retailers – we tried to do too much too fast. As a result, we lost critical balance in several key areas:

- We grew top-line sales more than we had over the past few years, but bottom-line earnings growth came in below historical rates.
- We introduced more new brands than during any other period in our history, but our biggest, most profitable brands didn't grow at acceptable rates.
- We invested for the future – in new businesses and developing markets – but some costs grew faster than revenues.
- We made important leadership changes, placing people into new jobs as part of our organizational restructuring, but we lost continuity in some parts of the business.

And finally Lafley says of the company:

> While these results demonstrate progress, P&G is capable of delivering better results. We are confident we can re-establish the balance needed to deliver top-line revenue growth and bottom-line earnings growth. We have the core competencies and strengths to win; (and) our new organizational design remains fundamentally right...

FINANCIAL DATA

In 1996 net sales were some US $35.3 billion. In 1997 net sales nudged up to US $35.8 billion – an increase of less than 1.5 per cent. The following year saw net sales rise by nearly 4 per cent to US $37.2 billion. The next year sales rose by US $1.1 billion to US $38.3 billion, an increase of just under 3 per cent. Table A.6 shows details of the company's three-month earnings from June 1999.

Table A.6

	3 Months to End June 00	3 Months to End Mar 00	3 Months to End Dec 99	3 Months to End Sep 99
Net Sales	9,661	9,783	10,588	9,919
Cost of Sales	5,418	5,327	5,563	5,206
Gross Profit	4,243	4,456	5,025	4,713
Total Operating Expenses	8,716	8,463	8,746	8,072
Earnings Before Tax	885	1,191	1,715	1,745
Earnings After Tax	516	753	1,126	1,147

Table A.7 shows Procter & Gamble's consolidated earnings information for the three months ended 30 June 2000. All amounts are in millions of dollars.

Table A.7

	Net Sales	% Change on Year	Earnings Before Tax	% Change on Year	Net Earnings	% Change on Year
Fabric and Home Care	2,890	1	433	−14	277	−6
Paper	2,920	−1	361	−23	214	−25
Beauty Care	1,768	−2	256	−20	165	−19
Health Care	959	41	27	−45	19	−44
Food and Beverage	1,128	−1	100	1	71	9
Corporate (excluding Organisation 2005)	(4)	N/A	(5)	N/A	31	N/A
Total Company Core	9,661	2	1,172	−8	777	−3
Organisation 2005	N/A	N/A	(287)	N/A	(261)	N/A
Total Company	9,661	2	885	12	516	25

Table A.8

	Net Sales	% Change on Year	Earnings Before Tax	% Change on Year	Net Earnings	% Change on Year
Fabric and Home Care	12,157	7	2,318	–4	1,450	–3
Paper	12,044	–1	1,817	–17	1,069	–16
Beauty care	7,389	0	1,393	–4	984	–3
Health care	3,909	36	540	45	335	38
Food and Beverage	4,634	0	566	7	364	11
Corporate (excluding Organisation 2005)	(182)	N/A	(284)	N/A	118	N/A
Total Company Core	39,951	5	6,350	0	4,230	2
Organisation 2005	N/A	N/A	(814)	N/A	(688)	N/A
Total Company	39,951	5	5,536	–5	3,542	–6

Table A.8 gives Procter & Gamble's consolidated earnings information for the 12 months ended 30 June 2000. All amounts are in millions of dollars. (Source for tables: P&G corporate news release 1 August 2000.)

Commenting on the financial results Lafley said:

> P&G is capable of delivering better profit results and will. Our plan is to focus on big, leadership brands, big markets and big customers; smarter, more effective and efficient commercialization of innovation; and better cost control and cash management. We're committed to delivering a better balance of top-line sales growth and bottom line-earnings progress.

Looking at the 3 months' and 12 months' returns it is plain that the Organisation 2005 programme is eating up resources. On earnings before tax of US $6,350 million Organisation 2005 cost US $814 million, or about 13 per cent. For the 3-month period it cost US $287 million or very nearly 25 per cent of earnings before tax. This is proving to be a very expensive reorganization. For the year, on sales of US $12,157 million Fabric and Home care returned earnings before tax of US $2,318, or about 19 per cent; and for the 3-month period 15 per cent. For the 12 months Health care returned earnings before tax of about 14 per cent and for the three months only 3 per cent. There is still a long way to go before P&G is turned around.

Web resources

www.pg.com/main.jhtml

13

Raytheon

by Graham Beaver

© 2001 Graham Beaver

Readers of this case will almost certainly be very familiar with the current 'tensions' in the debate over the role, contribution and relevance of strategic management. There are many writers questioning the value of traditional techniques and concepts that seemed to owe both their currency and existence to companies and operating contexts that have long gone out of both fashion and profitability. Let us consider two recent examples of this 'search for the new role for strategy' that are not only thought provoking and exciting, but also quite disturbing in their challenge to established orthodoxy. The first comes from Coyne and Subramaniam (1996). Their article begins:

> Strategy today is an extraordinarily demanding, complex, and subtle discipline. But you would never know that from reading the management journals and business best sellers of the past five years. Each season brings a new crop of experts proclaiming that their framework – core competencies, customer retention, management ecosystems, strategic intent, time-based competition, TQM, white-spaces, managing chaos, value migration – is the definitive way to think about strategy.

Their very readable and thought provoking paper proceeds to examine the short-comings of the traditional approach to strategy discussing the relevance of industry structure, sources of advantage and levels of uncertainty. This leads to a new definition of strategy in which they discuss the role of 'strategic posture' and 'tailored value delivery systems'. They conclude:

> Traditionally, strategic management has meant little more than staying the course. Today, however, it means actively managing the way in which strategy unfolds, month after month, year after year... We have examined over 25 separate strategy concepts proposed over the past few years. Close examination of any of these reveals how their underlying assumptions limit the circumstances in which they can be used. Consequently, strategists should be familiar with all of these concepts, but not biased towards any of them... In today's diverse business world, they must take into account a wider range of industry structures and bases of competitive advantage, and a higher degree of uncertainty.

The second example of the challenge to strategic orthodoxy comes from perhaps one of the most influential and articulate contributors to contemporary strategic thinking, Gary Hamel. Currently Visiting Professor to the London Business School, his rise to fame came about partly from the best selling volume that he co-authored with fellow academic C K Prahalad *Competing For The Future* (1994). This book propelled them both to 'superguru' status (in the words of *The Economist*), the leaders in the new wave of thinking about strategy. Hamel (1999) has recently argued, 'We live in a discontinuous world. Digitalisation, deregulation and globalisation are profoundly reshaping the industrial landscape.' Furthermore, he claims that there is a need for innovation and invention:

> What it takes, is a deep capacity for strategy innovation – an ability to reinvent the basis of competition within existing industries and to entirely invent new industries... For many companies, it will not be enough to reengineer processes; to survive they will also need to reinvent core business models. The challenge is to become the author of industry revolution.

Is this revolutionary thinking, or just plain common sense? After all, even Microsoft, one of the great success stories of recent times, was taken off-guard by the extraordinary rise of the Internet and has had to rethink its strategy or risk being replaced as the industry leader by the likes of Netscape. Hamel is fond of quoting Bill Gates's comment that 'Microsoft is always just two years away from failure' as a reminder to the complacent.

This is a case study that begins with the premise that strategic management is a dynamic activity, actively managing the way in which strategy unfolds. It also stresses the innovative role of corporate strategy and the need to reinvent industries. The comparatively recent (August 1998) US $1.4 billion deal with the US defence company Raytheon, to provide a system to monitor the exploitation of the rainforest for the Brazilian Government, is used as an example of the two aspects of strategic management.

ECOLOGICAL SECURITY AND BRAZIL'S RAINFOREST

In 1994, the Brazilian Government, following sustained pressure from environmental pressure groups all over the world, to do substantially more to protect its rainforest heritage, underwent a radical change in political intent. 'Ecological security' became a major priority for the Government, but how do you police an area of 5.2 million square kilometres of tropical rainforest that comprises some 60 per cent of Brazil's territory? The Raytheon Company of America, an organization best known as a defence contractor, successfully bid for the contract offered by the Brazilian Government to 'bug, tape, monitor via satellite, and otherwise track every move being made' to afford the Government professional monitoring of its rainforest environment. A company spokesman for Raytheon commenting on the successful outcome of the deal said: 'It's one of those arrangements that looks good from both viewpoints; Raytheon gets US $1.4 billion and the opportunity to enter a major new business area and Brazil gains control of its rainforest. In the still emerging US $25 billion industry of environmental monitoring, this deal is a bonanza, and the Amazon is the Wild West!'

Clovis Bragagao, a professor at the Candido Mendes University in Rio de Janeiro is the author of a best selling book that predicts that the importance of 'ecological security' will soon rival that of national security in regions such as the Amazon. He has stated, 'Environmental monitoring is an exceptional technological advancement and really the only way to watch the environmental impact of development.'

This is an ambitious, some would say intimidating, contract for Raytheon and the stakes are high, with other Governments and high-technology competition watching to see whether Raytheon is capable of coordinating all the disparate elements into a cohesive, professionally managed project.

Raytheon would probably get Hamel's endorsement as a company that is not short of strategic vision or afraid of adopting 'new perspectives'. It also scores highly on the corporate innovation index, having pioneered the world's first microwave oven and developed the Patriot anti-missile system that contributed to the downfall of Iraq in the Gulf War.

Raytheon, with sales of US $12.5 billion in 1996, has a 75-year history of innovative projects. Although best known as a defence contractor, the company also makes considerable annual revenue from selling electronics, aircraft and major appliances. It appears appropriate, then, that the package sold by Raytheon to the Brazilian government is a virtual patchwork of electronic and high technology wizardry. It is based on a system best known by its Portuguese acronym SIVAM (roughly translated as the system for the vigilance of the Amazon). The integrated network of precision-engineered products and support equipment includes air traffic control radar, airborne and ground-based surveillance, infrared, optical and satellite-based sensors, weather radar systems and a seemingly endless list of telecommunications capabilities.

Raytheon is purchasing first-class components from selected sub-contractors, such as IBM-Brazil and the Embraer Aircraft Corporation of Brazil. However, the performance of Raytheon's employees at the company's headquarters in Lexington, Mass, is critical. In 1998 Barry French, the International PR Director for the company stated:

> The significance of this project is not lost on us. This is the largest contract ever awarded by Brazil to a foreign company. By the year 2000, Brazil's regulators and forest officials will be able to monitor borders that were formally inaccessible, locate oil and mineral deposits that were undetected, and track weather patterns that were formerly a mystery. Furthermore, the government's enforcers will be able to detect unauthorised mining, forest burning, and hunting, spot planes used for smuggling and intercept contraband, and police border activity. Brazil is getting the best technology in the world in one of the most comprehensive networks ever designed, in one of the most untouched places on the earth. Besides that it's just plain cool!

The juxtaposition of the primitive nature of many of the jungle peoples and the state-of-the-art technology is almost surreal. Million-dollar satellites will send and receive digital data over the heads of native peoples living in thatch huts with no formal monetary system. To use French's vocabulary, what indeed could be cooler? Raytheon will be using the most sophisticated wide-area surveillance technology in the world derived from the best spy equipment designed for the best armies to catch criminals in a rainforest that is regarded by some as heaven on earth. A daunting task, especially when you consider that this tropical environment is more than half the size of the United States, contains one third of the world's rainforests, 25 per cent of the world's fresh water, and more than half of the known species of animals and plants.

SOCIAL RESPONSIBILITY ISSUES

Although this is an impressive undertaking, in the eyes of some observers corporations such as Raytheon should not be making revenues from environmental management. Mary Helsaple, who produces wildlife films for the Discovery channel, PBS and ABC networks and has worked for the last 10 years on rainforest projects, puts the alternative perspective:

> The resources are there, and ultimately they will be exploited, so protecting them is a worthy goal. The problem is that the very act of installing these systems will entail some intrusion and destruction. No matter how altruistic your purpose, when you contact people who were previously uncontacted, when you introduce computers to people who

would rather have a good cooking pot, you upset the balance of their world and you take something away from them. Offer them some fishing hooks or a laptop, and you will be left holding the laptop.

There are criticisms from environmentalists that SIVAM could result in further exploitation of the rainforest by helping industries more accurately locate natural resources such as minerals, oil and specialist timbers. However, if those resources are going to be developed, then at least it will be done legally and with the ability of the government to manage the development responsibly.

Mary Helsaple agrees with this point stating, 'The resources of the rainforest will ultimately be tapped, the population of the world demands it. What the government really has to manage is the greed factor. I am sure that other countries with large rainforest areas will soon be installing similar capabilities.'

THE FUTURE

There is no doubt that the emerging market of environmental surveillance could prove to be a rich and profitable one, especially when at a time of relative worldwide peace, transferring technology primarily developed for defence is an appropriate strategic move. The list of potential international customers, according to Raytheon officials, includes the governments of Malaysia, Indonesia, Venezuela, Mexico and Peru. This may, paradoxically, partially explain Raytheon's recent actions to become even more focused in defence technology. The recent acquisition of Texas Instruments' defence and electronics business for US $2.95 billion and the US $9.5 billion merger with Hughes Electronics has given Raytheon added capability to conduct business in a market that promises to deliver large revenues.

The future of corporate strategy is, Gary Hamel contends, one of organizations redefining their 'core-competences' – a phrase which Hamel helped to coin and which has now, as he says, become 'part of the vernacular'. If this is right, then Raytheon is an organization that appears to be doing just that.

Companies are often less than rigorous when trying to define their own core competencies. Hamel claims that: 'They lose sight of three clear criteria: that they make a substantial contribution to customer value or cost reduction; that they are skills hard to duplicate; and that you can imagine a way of leveraging them into new opportunities.' Raytheon may, therefore, also need to ensure consistency, commitment and clarity of direction if it is to enjoy the benefits of continued business development and superior profitability.

REFERENCES

Coyne, K and Subramaniam, S (1996) Bringing discipline to strategy, *The McKinsey Quarterly*, 1996, 4

Hamel, G (1999) *The Search For Strategy*, The Strategos Manifesto, info@strategosnet.com

FURTHER READING

Hamel, G and Prahalad, C K (1994) *Competing For The Future*, Harvard Business School Press, Boston

14

Shell

In the 1830s Marcus Samuel sold seashells in London. His business flourished, helped by the growing interest in natural history and soon he was importing and exporting a large volume of shells to satisfy the growing demand. This took him, and later his son, Marcus Junior, around the world in search of new sources of supply. On one such visit Marcus Junior visited Baku on the Caspian Sea. Here he saw oil being exported and realized that if he could find a cheap way of transporting it to the Far East he might be able to compete with Standard Oil. The opening of the Suez Canal in 1869 provided a cheap sea route and the building of an oil tanker, ready by 1892, provided the means. But what about the Dutch connection?

In the early 1890s a Dutch Company, called simply NV Koninklijke Nederlandsche Maatschappij tot Explotatie van Petroleum-bronnen in Nederlandsch-Indië, was exploring for oil in Sumatra. When oil was discovered, the company started to ship it, in competition with Shell. By 1903 the two companies had set up the Asiatic Petroleum Company. By 1907 this new company had expanded its operations and renamed itself the Royal Dutch/Shell Group of Companies. Today the group consists of about 1,700 companies, owned 60 per cent by Royal Dutch Petroleum and 40 per cent by the Shell Transport and Trading Company. Both companies (that is Royal Dutch and The Shell Transport and Trading Company) kept their separate identities.

BUSINESS PRINCIPLES

The group has nine principles by which they operate. These are:

- **Principle 1. Objectives.** The objectives of Shell companies are to engage efficiently, responsibly and profitably in the oil, gas, chemicals and other selected businesses and to participate in the search for and development of other sources of energy. Shell companies seek a high standard of performance and aim to maintain a long-term position in their respective competitive environments.
- **Principle 2. Responsibilities.** Shell companies recognize five areas of responsibility:
  - To shareholders: to protect shareholders' investment, and provide an acceptable return.
  - To customers: to win and maintain customers by developing and providing products and services which offer value in terms of price, quality, safety and environmental impact, and which are supported by the requisite technological, environmental and commercial expertise.
  - To employees: to respect the human rights of their employees, to provide their employees with good and safe conditions of work, and good and competitive terms and conditions of service, to promote the development and best use of human talent and equal opportunity employment, and to encourage the involvement of employees in the planning and direction of their work, and in the application of these principles within their company. It is recognized that commercial success depends on the full commitment of all employees.
  - To those with whom they do business: to seek mutually beneficial relationships with contractors, suppliers and in joint ventures and to promote the application of these principles in so doing. The ability to promote these principles effectively will be an important factor in the decision to enter into or remain in such relationships.
  - To society: to conduct business as responsible, corporate members of society, to observe the laws of the countries in which they operate, to express support for fundamental human rights in line with the legitimate role of business and to give proper regard to health, safety and the environment consistent with their commitment to contribute to sustainable development.

These five areas of responsibility are seen as inseparable. Therefore, it is the duty of management continuously to assess the priorities and discharge its responsibilities as best it can on the basis of that assessment.

- **Principle 3. Economic principles.** Profitability is essential to discharging these responsibilities and staying in business. It is a measure both of efficiency and of the value that customers place on Shell products and services. It is essential to the allocation of the necessary corporate resources and to support the continuing investment required to develop and produce future energy supplies to meet consumer needs. Without profits and a strong financial foundation, it would not be possible to fulfil the responsibilities outlined in this section.

  Shell companies work in a wide variety of changing social, political and economic environments, but, in general, they believe that the interests of the community can be served most efficiently by a market economy.

  Criteria for investment decisions are not exclusively economic in nature but also take into account social and environmental considerations and an appraisal of the security of the investment.

- **Principle 4. Business integrity**. Shell companies insist on honesty, integrity and fairness in all aspects of their business and expect the same in their relationships with all those with whom they do business. The direct or indirect offer, payment, soliciting and acceptance of bribes in any form are unacceptable practices. Employees must avoid conflicts of interest between their private financial activities and their part in the conduct of company business. All business transactions on behalf of a Shell company must be reflected accurately and fairly in the accounts of the company in accordance with established procedures and be subject to audit.

- **Principle 5. Political activities.**
  - Of companies. Shell companies act in a socially responsible manner within the laws of the countries in which they operate in pursuit of their legitimate commercial objectives. Shell companies do not make payments to political parties, organizations or their representatives or take any part in party politics. However, when dealing with governments, Shell companies have the right and the responsibility to make their position known on any matter which affects themselves, their employees, their customers, or their shareholders. They also have the right to make their position known on matters affecting the community, where they have a contribution to make.
  - Of employees. Where individuals wish to engage in activities in the community, including standing for election to public office, they will be given the opportunity to do so where this is appropriate in the light of local circumstances. Some of the issues in this Principle are hard to measure, and

little quantified evidence is available. Shell companies are trying to develop suitable measures so that they can track and publish their future performance. If you have any suggestions on the sort of evidence you would like to see, please send them an e-mail or participate in the relevant forum.

- **Principle 6. Health, safety and the environment.** Consistent with their commitment to contribute to sustainable development, Shell companies have a systematic approach to health, safety and environmental management in order to achieve continuous performance improvement. To this end, Shell companies manage these matters as any other critical business activity, set targets for improvement, and measure, appraise and report on performance.
- **Principle 7. The community**. The most important contribution that companies can make to the social and material progress of the countries in which they operate is in performing their basic activities as effectively as possible. In addition, Shell companies take a constructive interest in societal matters which may not be directly related to the business. Opportunities for involvement – for example, through community, educational or donations programmes – will vary depending upon the size of the company concerned, the nature of the local society, and the scope for useful private initiatives.
- **Principle 8. Competition.** Shell companies support free enterprise. They seek to compete fairly and ethically and within the framework of applicable competition laws; they will not prevent others from competing freely with them.
- **Principle 9: Communication.** Shell companies recognize that, in view of the importance of the activities in which they are engaged and their impact on national economies and individuals, open communication is essential. To this end, Shell companies have comprehensive corporate information programmes and provide full relevant information about their activities to legitimately interested parties, subject to any overriding considerations of business confidentiality and cost.

CURRENT AND FUTURE ACTIVITIES

Today there are three main players in the oil business – Royal Dutch Shell, BP Amoco and Exxon Mobil. At the centre of all their businesses is the production of energy. As fossil fuels such as gas and oil start to run out companies have increasingly focused on finding newer deposits of fossil fuel. These deposits are, typically, in quite difficult operating environments such as the North Sea, or in countries that are politically unstable, hostile to the West or have a poor record on human rights. At the same time the companies have been looking at renewable forms of energy.

Conditions in the oil business in the 21st century will differ from those of much of the 20th century. One of the key differences is going to be a concern for the environment. Both Royal Dutch/Shell and BP Amoco are pushing ahead with strategies that attempt to turn the traditionally viewed environmentally unfriendly business into a friendly one. BP Amoco has signalled this with its *Beyond Petroleum* campaign started in the summer of 2000. Royal Dutch/Shell has for its part identified several areas that will need to be tackled that relate to environmental and social issues. These areas are:

- **Climate change.** It is pretty clear that the burning of fossil fuels has contributed significantly to the so called 'greenhouse effect' whereby the world is getting warmer. In the summer of 2000 the North Pole instead of being frozen had in places melted giving another indication of the potential seriousness of continued global warming. The Kyoto Agreement is an attempt to reduce greenhouse gas emission by around 5.2 per cent by 2012. In the foreseeable future there will be increased pressure to reduce further the impact fossil fuels have on the global climate. This is a serious problem for Shell. The company has committed itself to reduce its 1990 emissions by 10 per cent by 2002 and aims always to better the targets set by the Kyoto Agreement. In pursuit of this it has set up STEPS (Shell Tradable Emission Permit System) to monitor its own emissions and trade across the group emissions to reduce the group's total emissions. Shell is working with customers to reduce their emissions, by developing low carbon fuels such as liquid petroleum gas and by investing in renewable alternatives. Shell is also exploring ways of absorbing more of the dangerous emissions by, for instance, embarking on a large tree-planting programme. Clearly, being involved in energy means that Shell has contributed to climate warming in the past and will do in the future. The extent to which Shell will be forced to reduce emissions further will be a political decision as much as a business choice by the company.
- **Sustainable development.** Defined by the Brundtland Commission in 1987 as 'meeting the needs of the present without compromising the ability of future generations to meet their own needs'. This definition, while it has its supporters, has been challenged as it does not stress sufficiently the ecological costs and benefits of development. This said, Shell is committed to embedding the Brundtland Definition into the way it does business. It does this, in part, through its sustainable development management framework (SDMF).
- **Concern for others.** This is a key feature of sustainable development. Shell operates in many locations that have a poor record on human rights. How does the company square this with its concern for people it comes into contact with? Shell has been involved in several initiatives, such as The Global Sullivan principles and the OECD's Guidelines for Multi-nationals, as well as

taking part in the Global Compact between the UN and multi-national companies. A particular concern is the use of child labour in the developing world. Shell has, in Brazil, introduced a clause in its contract to sugar refiners that bans the use of child labour. But the problem of child labour and to a lesser extent low pay in the developing world is one that is going to be hard to solve. While in the West it appears clear that the exploitation of local labour is morally wrong, this does not take into account local cultures, something that multinationals have to be aware of. What appears a very dubious practice at home may, in fact, be quite normal elsewhere. Shell is addressing this difficulty. Further, by operating in countries whose record on human rights is poor, Shell is confronted with hard choices. Should it refuse to do business there until basic human rights are restored; should it try to work for change internally; or should it adopt a neutral stance? Shell's business in Iran is an example of such a dilemma.

- **Clearing up.** In the past the way energy was produced and consumed has meant that today we are faced with clearing up the pollution caused. The disposal of one of Shell's North Sea oil platforms – Brent Spar – demonstrated the complexity of the issues involved. In different operating environments different standards of clearing up are required: in the EU and the United States the law requires quite high standards, but this is not necessarily the case elsewhere.

THE BRENT SPAR PLATFORM

The difficulty Shell had with the disposal of its Brent Spar platform is illustrative of the strategic choices the company faced. Starting in the 1960s, Shell had been exploring and then extracting oil and gas from the North Sea. Technical advances in extraction had made it possible to locate and extract oil and gas in harsh environments such as the North Sea. By the start of the 1990s some of the original equipment used in extraction and storage of the oil and gas had reached the end of its useful life. Not only was some of the existing equipment becoming uneconomic to maintain, but also Shell was in the process of switching the balance of extraction away from oil towards gas in its Brent fields; consequently some of the storage platforms used for oil were redundant. The Brent Spar platform was in this category and in 1991 the decision was made to shut it down.

Shell commissioned many studies to look at the best way of disposing of the platform, the first one in the North Sea requiring disposal. Options considered included moving the platform to dry land and cutting it up, blowing the platform up with high explosives, moving the platform to another location in the North Sea fields and using it there, sinking the platform, or modifying it to be used in situ. After many months of deliberation Shell decided that the platform should be sunk in a suitably deep location in the North Sea. The North Feni Ridge was selected as providing the depth required to minimize the environmental impact of the platform. In fact a study carried out at the time by geologists and reported in the authoritative scientific journal *Nature* in June 1995 went so far as to suggest that the environmental impact of sinking the platform here would be zero.

Shell obtained permission to sink the platform in 1995 from the British Government on the basis that not only would this provide a minimum impact on the environment but also that other disposal methods, such as cutting up the platform on dry land, would carry a significant risk of accidents. So far so good. Shell had acted responsibly by looking at various options generated by independent experts and had persuaded the relevant authority, the British Government, that deep sea disposal was the best solution based on exemplary scientific option. But Greenpeace was not convinced.

Greenpeace was founded in 1971 with the aim of raising public awareness to environmental issues. A tactic it had used successfully in other environmental campaigns – such as protest against French nuclear tests in the Pacific – was to grab media attention. On 30 April 1995 four Greenpeace activists managed, in a commando-style raid, to gain access to the platform. The media spotlight was theirs. Under massive pressure Shell was forced to reconsider the disposal as boycotts of Shell products escalated across Europe. On 20 June 1995 Shell decided to climb down – Greenpeace had won. The platform was moved to Erflord in Norway for disposal. Even after this the scientific debate about the best way of disposing of the platform continued. Within a few weeks Greenpeace admitted that the estimate it had used about possible oil leakage was in fact wrong. Whether this would have undermined its campaign fatally if it had become public at the time is hard to assess. Greenpeace not only focused on the facts of the disposal but also managed to tap into many people's consciousness about the polluting effects of big business, especially oil companies in general, irrespective of the rights and wrongs of this particular case. In a study commissioned by the British government, eminent scientists concluded that in itself the deep-sea disposal of Brent spar would have had only a small impact but if more platforms were disposed in this way in the same area a cumulative, environmental threat could emerge.

SOCIAL RESPONSIBILITY

Royal Dutch Shell now operates in a world markedly different from that of a generation ago. A key feature of the new landscape is the tension between keeping its shareholders happy and meeting its wider social obligations. Royal Dutch Shell is committed to pursuing a strategy that centres on sustainable development and is busy implementing social accountability throughout its business. It believes that by the middle of the century renewable energy will be its major source of energy as fossil-based fuels decline both from exhaustion and from environmental pressure to stop using them because of pollution. Shell says:

> The multi-faceted commercial strengths of Shell companies are underpinned by deeper common values – of honesty, integrity and respect for people. These are clearly spelled out for anyone to read in the Group's Statement of General Business Principles. Subsumed under those principles is a Group-wide commitment to contribute to sustainable development: to integrate the economic, social and environmental aspects of everything Shell companies do while balancing short-term wants with long-term needs.

While the pressure is being intensified on the social and environmental front, restructuring of the industry, reducing the number of players down to three – Exxon Mobil, Royal Dutch Shell and BP Amoco – has meant that competition is keen. Being a successful energy company requires a consistent search for new sources of energy and these new sources are typically being discovered in challenging environments. Not only do these new environments pose significant new technical problems – deeper drilling, making discoveries far from markets, operating in harsher climates – but also they are often in countries that are politically unstable or hostile to the West. Considerable senior managerial skill, time and resources are required to operate in these environments.

PRICES

A further problem for Shell (and other oil companies) is that the price of its core product can vary considerably as OPEC manipulates the basic price by controlling the supply of oil from its members. After several years of low prices oil recently reached more than US $30 per barrel mainly because of the ability of OPEC to control the supply. High oil prices mean that fields that were considered to be uneconomic become economic but, and it's a big but, Shell has to take the long view as exploiting new fields may take many years. It is possible that OPEC can only temporarily influence the price of oil and, if the past is any guide, it will increase production again under pressure from the West, especially the United States. Then oil prices will fall, perhaps to as low as US $15 a barrel. Also, while high oil prices suggest higher profits for Shell this may not happen: if world economic activity slows down because of the high price of oil, the demand for oil will slow or even fall, leading to lower sales for Shell and perhaps lower profitability.

QUESTIONS FOR DISCUSSION

What sort of strategic choices does Shell face in the future? Consider the following questions:

1. Should Shell pay even more attention to the environment?
2. Should it contemplate moving away faster from fossil fuels and into renewable forms of energy say by 2035?
3. Should it concentrate even more on social accountability?
4. Should it pay even more attention to human rights issues in the Third World?

Web resources

Extensive material is available at the Shell site
www.shell.com/royal-en/directory/0,5029,25414,00.html)

15

Starbucks Coffee

Go into a Starbucks coffee shop and you will be served high-quality coffee with, to those with a taste for coffee, a slightly charred taste, by a well-trained and friendly member of staff called baristas. Starbucks also sells coffee-related products and equipment, along with fresh coffee beans for home use. Starbucks' apparently simple formula has been incredibly successful and the company just keeps growing.

At the centre of this is Starbucks' brand name, which it is now increasingly using for complementary products to coffee, such as Tazo tea, Tizza and Frappuccino and, in some cases, completely unrelated products, such as music CDs. At present, according to Interbrand, a company that specializes in ranking leading brand names in the world, Starbucks is number 72. Establishing Starbucks as a key brand globally is the company's ultimate aim: Starbuck's Web site states:

> The Company's objective is to establish Starbucks as the most recognized and respected brand in the world.
> To achieve this, the Company plans to continue to rapidly expand its retail operations, grow its specialty sales and other operations, and selectively pursue opportunities to leverage the Starbucks brand through the introduction of new products and the development of new distribution channels.

ORIGINS

Starbucks started in 1971 with one shop at Pike Place Market, Seattle. In 1983 Howard Schultz, its Retail Director, travelled to Milan and, realizing the potential of Italian-style coffee shops in the United States, started Il Giornale in Seattle. Il Giornale sold Italian-style coffee made from Starbucks' beans. This proved to be so successful that by 1987 Il Giornale was able to acquire Starbucks' assets and name. Il Giornale became the Starbucks Corporation.

EXPANSION

By the end of 1987 there were 17 Starbucks stores. By 1990 Starbucks had expanded outside Seattle, and had over 80 stores. By 1993 there were stores in most US cities and 272 stores in total. In 1995 the company started looking for overseas growth especially in Japan and the UK. By now it had over 650 outlets. In 1996 overseas stores opened in Japan and Singapore. In the same year the 1000th store opened. In 1998 Starbucks acquired Seattle Coffee to give it market share in the UK. By the end of 1999 it had over 1800 stores around the world. Late in 1999 Starbucks opened its 100th store in the UK situated in Oxford Street, London and in early 2000 it opened its 100th store in Japan in The Sanno Park Tower, Tokyo. Starbucks also has a presence in China, where it opened its first store in Beijing in January 1999. There are now more than 10 stores in Beijing.

In the year to August 2000 the company opened over 900 new stores bringing its total worldwide to 3,382 of which nearly 2,900 are in the United States. It has 485 overseas stores, about 14 per cent of the total, of which 212 were opened between August 1999 and August 2000. This represents a growth rate of about 33 per cent per year. The company aims to have 500 stores in Europe and another 500 in Asia and the Pacific Rim by the end of 2003. Figure A.1 shows just how quickly Starbucks has grown since 1987. It has regularly exceeded a growth rate of 50 per cent. The company believes that 20,000 (yes, twenty thousand) outlets are possible.

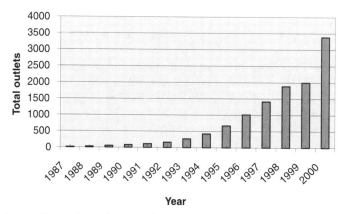

Starbucks

Figure A.1 Note: total number of stores for 2000 is up to August only.

HOW WAS IT ACHIEVED?

First and foremost, Starbucks celebrated excellent coffee. Consumers were used to quite low-quality coffee and when people first tasted Starbucks they often remarked: 'This is the best coffee I have ever tasted outside of Italy.' Achieving consistency in coffee taste in so many outlets is one of the keys to Starbucks' success. It's one thing saying you serve great coffee. It's another being able to deliver it day in and day out, across the world.

Starbucks serves high-quality coffee, invariably brewed from superior Arabica beans, that attracts a higher price than the basic blends based on the inferior Robusta bean, but to be able to do this requires a lot of effort. Getting the coffee in the cup starts from buying the very best Arabica beans available. Starbucks routinely checks samples of the beans it is thinking of buying and if it feels the beans are not up to its standard it rejects the whole shipment.

Once the beans have been purchased, the next stage is roasting. Starbucks pays great attention to this, having a database of roasting settings to ensure just the right taste at the end. As Starbucks say about their particular roasting techniques, 'At Starbucks, we're passionate about the way we roast our coffee. We call our roast the Starbucks Roast®. It's more than a color: it is the cumulative, positive and dramatic result of roasting each coffee in a unique way, helping each one reach its maximum flavor. The color can be duplicated – but the taste cannot.'

Those who know about these things tell us that the key feature of Starbucks coffee is a slight charred taste. It has proved to be a taste many people like.

The next stage is the blending of different roasts to produce just the taste needed. To do this well requires years of experience. It can take months of trial and error and sheer inspiration. As Starbucks say of their blenders:

> Cup after cup they evaluate the flavor performance of many samples of an individual coffee. In general, they are seeking blend components that show an extraordinary strength in one flavor dimension – like brightness, earthiness or spiciness. Rare or unusual coffees often make wonderful blend components because of the unmistakable flavor they impart. Yemen Mocha plays this role in Arabian Mocha Java.

After this the Starbucks coffees emerge. For instance Arabian Mocha Sanani is described as: 'Sanani is truly an exotic coffee, displaying a dazzling array of spice, cocoa, port, rum and berry flavors. It is both tantalizing and challenging at any time of day, at any temperature.' And of French roast they say, 'Our darkest roast, French Roast is a light-bodied blend of Latin American coffees that is very low in acidity and intensely smoky. These beans can 'take the heat" – standing up to a roast that would cause many other coffees to go up in flames.'

Even after blending, getting the coffee to the shop is difficult: the quality will deteriorate considerably if oxygen enters the package but the coffee itself produces gases that have to be vented from time to time. To overcome this a one-way valve system is incorporated into the package to allow the gases to escape but to exclude oxygen contamination. As a norm Starbucks has a three-month shelf life for its unopened packaged coffee and a one-week one for opened packages. Given the number of stores it has, a long shelf life for its unopened packages is essential as it eases the logistical problems of supplying the stores. Other smaller, regional coffee shops, which also serve high-quality coffee, have stayed regional because the deterioration in coffee that has been in the packet too long was seen as a major obstacle to building a wider network of outlets.

So the coffee is now in the shop ready to be turned into a drink or sold for home use. All the careful preparation that has gone before could easily be wasted if the coffee is not brewed correctly. As you probably suspect, Starbucks continues its high attention to detail in turning the coffee into a drink. Take the making of a cup of coffee latte:

> A soothing beverage composed of three layers: a freshly drawn shot of espresso, milk steamed and poured to fill the cup and finally, a quarter-inch dollop of foamed milk to create a delicate first impression. A Latte Macchiato is made in a similar fashion to a Caffè Latte except the espresso is poured over the steamed milk, thus 'marking' the milk.

To summarize: buy the very best Arabica beans you can. Check frequently that the beans are of the high standard you want. Roast them to perfection. Pack them in such a way that they maintain their flavour. Starbucks does not stop there in its desire to serve the very best coffee – it employs the best baristas to serve it.

Starbucks treats its staff as partners in the business not just employees. The company's Bean Stock programme offers stock options to its partners (employees) as one way that the company shows that it values its employees. As Starbucks says of its partners:

> Our ability to accomplish what we set out to do is based primarily on the people we hire – we call each other partners. We are devoted to investing in, supporting and engaging our partners in the constant reinvention of Starbucks. In fact, the first guiding principle in our Mission Statement is to 'provide a great work environment and treat each other with respect and dignity'.

The training the baristas get in coffee is legendary. As already emphasized, Starbucks goes through a lot of trouble to brew the best possible coffee. It has to make sure that its partners can make the coffee perfectly each time and answer customers' questions knowledgeably. To do this requires extensive investment in training. Starbucks makes this investment. In an industry where labour turnover is high, Starbucks has a well-earned reputation for keeping its staff significantly longer than others.

Second, it has become fashionable to go to a coffee shop and just chat and watch other people. Schulz saw people doing this when he went to Milan in 1983 and it convinced him there was a huge potential market for this in the United States. He was right. Now how much Starbucks and other coffee shops have created this and how much it was waiting to happen is hard to say, but Schulz was right in believing that it would be possible to have many, many more coffee outlets in US towns than there were at the time. Locating the coffee shops near the shopping and entertainment districts of large towns is vital. The ambience created by the Starbucks brand and style also draws in customers who may be visitors or tourists to the area as they recognize the brand so feel 'at home' with the outlet.

Third, the company has been helped by changes in consumer behaviour that has increased the market for coffee and related products purchased on the way to work, at lunchtime and on the way home from work. To what extent the change from in-house catering towards self-vending or no service at all has helped the company is hard to estimate. Certainly the quality of coffee served at Starbucks is much better than self-vending coffee or what is normally available at work. Many office workers buy their coffee 'to go' at Starbucks. Choice of location is important in this with prime sites commanding a premium. Starbucks is not afraid of clustering its outlets if the location supports several, so in busy business districts it is not uncommon to see several outlets within easy walking distance of each other.

Fourth, not only was Starbucks' coffee excellent but the surroundings and staff were also much better than what was usually on offer.

Fifth, the company innovated. For instance, it started a mail order facility as early as 1988. It has always been on the lookout for new products, for example it launched Frappuccino in 1995 and in 1996 it introduced Starbucks Ice Cream. In 1998 Tea Latte and Tiazzi Blended Juiced Tea first sold. Coffee-related products such as espresso machines and mugs have also been introduced.

Sixth, Starbucks worked with strategic partners to expand its market reach. For instance, in 1991 in partnership with Host Marriott Services, Starbucks opened its first licensed airport outlet and in 1995 joined with the Canadian company, Chapters, to provide in-store coffee. It sought out international partners to reach overseas markets. For instance, in 1996 it agreed with SAZABY Inc, a Japanese retailer and restaurateur, to develop the business in Japan and in 1998 acquired the Seattle Coffee Company in the UK.

Driving this has been an unshakeable belief in the Starbucks brand and what it stands for. The company's mission is: 'To establish Starbucks as the premier purveyor of the finest coffee in the world while maintaining our uncompromising principles as we grow.'

STARBUCKS' PRINCIPLES

The company's six principles are:

1. Provide a great work environment and treat each other with respect and dignity.
2. Embrace diversity as an essential component in the way we do business.
3. Apply the highest standards of excellence to the purchasing, roasting and fresh delivery of our coffee.
4. Develop enthusiastically satisfied customers all of the time.
5. Contribute positively to our communities and our environment.
6. Recognize that profitability is essential to our future success.

FUTURE PLANS

The 1999 company report states:

> The Company's retail goal is to become the leading retailer and brand of coffee in each of its target markets by selling the finest quality coffee and related products and by providing superior customer service, thereby building a high degree of customer loyalty. Starbucks strategy for expanding its retail business is to increase its market share in existing markets and to open stores in new markets where the opportunity exists to become the leading specialty coffee retailer.

And as we said above, ultimately the company wants to have over 20,000 outlets worldwide.

It has to find new customers for its existing products. This means in the United States opening outlets in under-served districts in large metropolitan areas such as Harlem and South Central in Los Angeles. It is doing this under the auspices of Earvin 'Magic' Johnson's Johnson Development Corporation. Overseas it is looking to expand its existing customer base in the UK and Japan, as well as looking at new areas. Recently it has opened outlets in the Lebanon and Kuwait and has just signed an agreement with the Bon appétit group to open outlets in Switzerland.

It is trying to become more than just a coffee shop by introducing a wider range of food apart from the usual Danish pastries to encourage customers to have or buy lunch at the shop. This will require the development of new skills and products.

It is attempting sell more of its products through other distribution channels. Frappuccino and its ice cream are now sold through normal retail channels, such as supermarkets.

It is increasing the number of its outlets in different locations such as supermarkets, universities and colleges.

It is looking at the Internet to reach new customers or sell more to existing customers. This has not been wholly successful as Starbucks lost its investment of over £14 million in Living.com when the company failed. Still Starbucks believes there is potential for further investment in the Internet. The key to future Internet development centres on to what extent Starbucks can use its excellent brand image to lever in sales in unrelated products through this new distribution channel.

By exploiting its brand and business skills ultimately Starbucks would like to be seen as 'a lifestyle portal'. This is somewhat problematic revolving around whether its core business is coffee or something to do with creating lifestyle. When you purchase your Latte to go you think you are buying coffee but what you are really buying is a lifestyle with coffee as one of the components. The failure of Living.com can be attributed to two main difficulties: the difficulties a lot of dotcom start-ups are having in establishing themselves; and Starbucks getting involved in something – selling furniture – in which it had no core competencies.

It will have to continue to innovate in its products to maintain and increase its customer base.

COPYCATS

The market for coffee outlets like Starbucks is more crowded now than it was when the company started. In prime metropolitan locations other chains have emerged to challenge Starbucks and existing small retailers have responded by 'sharpening up' their own image, often copying the look and feel of Starbucks. The company is starting to face competition the way Kentucky Fried Chicken does now that it has hosts of small local imitators, such as Keenly Fried Chicken and others, all with shop colours and design similar to the original. The very success of Starbucks in building up the market means that others are now copying the formula. Not only on the high street are others getting in on the act, but in-store locations in supermarkets are also being viewed by other specialized retailers or by the supermarkets themselves to provide their customers with quality coffee. Moreover Starbucks's Frappuccino is not the only iced coffee available as Havana Cappucciono has its own iced cappucciono brand. Other competing products now include Blue Luna, Planet Java and Coca-Cola is testing Cafielle in the United States. On the other hand Nescafé have dropped their own iced coffee and the future of Procter & Gamble's Jakada is uncertain. What is certain is that Starbucks will not have the market to itself.

This said Starbucks has competencies and skills that will be very hard for others to imitate easily. The care and attention to detail it puts into getting its coffee just right is not easy. Competitors will struggle to emulate this, as well as the training and consequent quality of Starbucks' employees.

THE ENVIRONMENTAL AGENDA

As Starbucks has grown it has become the target of environmental groups who complain about the exploitation of Third World labour in the growing and harvesting of coffee. As Starbucks is so big it has become a high profile target for activists. Responding to this agenda will divert resources and company energy away from its core activities. It is at present involved in a large literacy project through Starbucks Foundation and contributes to CARE, an organization that helps families in coffee producing countries. These are examples of how it is at present responding to the 'social' and environmental obligations of being a big, successful company.

CULTURE

Another problem with its size is maintaining the culture of the company grown through several years that consciously values and rewards its partners (employees). One of the key features of going into a Starbucks is just how well-trained and pleasant the people serving you are. Will it be able to maintain this as the company grows even more?

MAINTAINING HIGH GROWTH

Starbucks has set itself very ambitious growth targets. There will come a time when these become increasingly difficult to meet. It seems unlikely that it can keep growing at its past rate. If it does without at some time running into the buffers, it will be a great achievement. Further, the move into other areas could be problematic as its Internet venture showed.

THREAT OF TAKE-OVER

The company is now of a size that could easily attract a hostile take-over bid. Its brand is excellent. It operates out of some great locations and has a range of valuable products. It may well face a bid sometime in the future, especially if it starts to miss its ambitious targets.

THE STARBUCKS' BRAND

To become a leading 'lifestyle portal' by exploiting the strength of its brand Starbucks will need to think carefully about why its brand is so strong and what it needs to do to maintain this. Starbucks is certainly great at supplying coffee and it has a company culture that strives to get the very best out of its employees but will it be able to take the competencies it has acquired in achieving this into other areas? That, as they say, is the US $64,000 question, except in this case success or failure will be measured in millions if not billions of dollars.

Web resources
www.starbucks.com/
www.starbucks.com/company/

16

Toyota

Toyota is number four in the world of car makers behind GM, Ford and Daimler Chrysler. It is number one in Japan. It manufactures a range of cars including the Camry (a sports utility vehicle) the Lexus (a luxury car) and the Prius (a petrol and electric car). It employs about 184,000 people. It started in 1937 with the AA and AB Phaeton cars, the GA truck and the DA bus. In 1951 it introduced the all-terrain vehicle the Land Cruiser and in 1955 the Crown shortly followed by the Corona. Exports slowly grew throughout the 1950s and the 1960s with the company successfully selling cars around the world including in Europe and the United States. Some time in 1988 the 50 millionth Toyota was built. In the 1990s Toyota started to manufacture the Lexus in order to break into the high end of the car market. Later in the 1990s it developed and launched the world's first hybrid car combining petrol and battery power – the Prius. By 2000 more than 35,000 of these had been sold in Japan. Interestingly Sakichi Toyoda, the founder of Toyota, offered a large prize in the 1920s for any inventor who could power an aircraft by batteries. Needless to say no one won the prize but now his company has made a mass-market car powered in part by batteries.

ENVIRONMENTALISM

Toyota has in recent years placed considerable emphasis on being an environmentally friendly company. It was the first car maker to win the Global 500 Award for environmental initiative sponsored by The United Nations Environment Programme (UNEP). When Toyota won the award attention was drawn to three specific areas of its business: the Prius is the world's first mass-produced hybrid passenger car; Toyota is committed to ISO 14001 – an internationally recognized environmental management standard; and the company's Eco-Project was mentioned. As its citation for the Global 500 award says:

> The Toyota Motor Corporation of Japan is increasingly trying to meet the challenges facing our planet by developing vehicles that are environment-friendly. Every aspect of their industry, from research, production, distribution, sales and service focus on sustainable development and the improvement of overall corporate excellence.

Each year Toyota produces an environmental report that sets out the company's commitment to the environment. In its 1999 environmental report it says of its activities:

> It is imperative that we develop automobiles, such as hybrid vehicles, that are fuel-efficient and have clean exhaust emissions. Furthermore, we must enhance the recoverability of these vehicles and produce them using methods with the least possible environmental impact, and provide them to consumers at a reasonable price. We need to strive for 'zero emissions' at all stages of the automobile life cycle from production through use and disposal, and to pursue every possible approach offered by environmental technology.

COSTS

How much does all this cost? In the financial year 1998 total environmental costs were equal to about 1 per cent of net sales. In this year maintenance costs were reduced by just over 20 per cent but R&D on environmentally conscious products increased by about 13 per cent. Overall environmental costs increased by 8 per cent.

Toyota set itself ambitious challenges in terms of its commitment to the environment. This quote is taken from the 1998 company report:

> One of our teams was tackling long-range issues in body engineering. It was working on a vehicle 'package' that would support dramatic gains in fuel economy and, thus, a big reduction in output of carbon dioxide. The team members thought initially of powering their package with a gasoline engine, perhaps equipped with direct injection. They were eyeing the ambitious goal of improving fuel economy 50 per cent. They knew that would be tough with gasoline power alone. But they thought it might be possible with some tweaking. Then, a senior executive turned their world upside down. 'A 50 per cent improvement is too small for anyone to get excited about,' scoffed the boss. 'And competitors would catch up quickly. Don't settle for anything less than a 100 per cent improvement.' One hundred per cent. In other words, double fuel economy. That settled the issue of power trains. Toyota's first step into the 21st century would be a hybrid-powered stride. Hybrid power was the only technology near commercial viability that would allow for doubling fuel economy.

Why does Toyota place such an emphasis on being 'green'? The simple reason is that if car makers are going to continue into the future cars will have to be designed to be less polluting. They are one of the major causes, if not the major cause, of so-called greenhouse gases that lead to global warming and the depletion of the ozone layer around the earth. Environmental pressure groups, such as Greenpeace, have for many years highlighted the environmental consequences of continuing to pollute the environment. This has become a big political issue, with governments introducing tougher and tougher laws on, for instance, CO_2 emission, with the support of the general public. In California by 2003 up to 10 per cent of all cars sold by major manufacturers, including Toyota, must have zero emission or near zero emission. Of this 10 per cent, 4 per cent must be zero emission (this presently means electric as only electric cars have zero emission) and the other 6 per cent near zero emission. This means effectively moving from selling about 2,300 zero emission and near zero emission vehicles at present to 22,000 by 2003 spread over the leading six manufacturers.

Consumers are also becoming more receptive to the 'green' message, consequently demanding less polluting and more environmentally friendly products. Toyota sold more than 3,000 of the Prius, its hybrid car, in the first month it went on sale in the United States. Late in 2000 Toyota will start to sell the Prius in Europe with the aim of selling about 5,000 a year with sales increasing quickly as consumers start to switch from petrol cars to hybrids. Not only will consumers switch because of its environmental features and its performance but because petrol prices are set to remain high and increase in Europe in the future.

Perhaps this is a bit cynical as it suggests that the only reason Toyota is doing this is for good solid business ones – 'green' products sell and the political pressure is on to produce 'green' cars. You will have to decide for yourself on this but a strong case can be made out that Toyota is doing this for a mixture of business reasons and sincerely held environmental ones. The winning of a Global 500 award demonstrates the progress Toyota has made in becoming environmentally friendly.

ELECTRIC CARS AND REDUCING EMISSIONS

Toyota has been engaged for several years in the electric vehicle (EV) project. There are, though, great technical difficulties in producing an EV that can compete effectively with petrol cars. The range of the EV before the batteries need recharging is a problem compared to the range of petrol cars, as is its performance. Market research shows that very, very few consumers are prepared to pay the sort of price Toyota would have to charge for the car to make it commercially viable. According to company figures there are about 1,000 of its RAV 4 EV used worldwide. One possible way

EVs could catch on is for them to be used in specific settings, such as large conference sites, amusement parks and university campuses. Other uses might be as part of a localized urban campaign to reduce emissions; in fact, in California there is a debate taking place on the so-called zero emission vehicle (ZEV) and cars such as the RAV 4 EV would be able to play an important role in this. Toyota is also developing the E-Com, another electric car, which it hopes will become a popular electric commuting vehicle.

Toyota is not only looking at the development of EVs but at other ways of reducing emissions as follows:

- The company is looking at alternative energy such as natural gas to replace petrol.
- It has spent a lot of money improving existing petrol engines by using lean burn and direct injection technology.
- It is looking to reduce pollution significantly by using a variety of power sources, petrol and electric, in a hybrid car.
- It is looking at returning energy used in braking back to propulsion.
- It is developing commercially viable vehicles based on emerging fuel cell technology. Fuel cells combine hydrogen and oxygen to generate water and electricity. The electricity can then be used to drive the vehicle. Levels of emission are markedly less than those of the most efficient petrol engines.

MANUFACTURING

Manufacturing cars creates pollution. Apart from exploring ways of making cars less polluting, Toyota has also looked at ways of reducing the impact on the environment caused by car manufacture.

As early as 1963 a Plant Environment Committee was set up in one of Toyota's Japanese factories to monitor and innovate new, less polluting ways of manufacturing. This now has become a common feature of the company. Apart from developing a cleaner car the Plant Environment Committee looks at ways of reducing polluting CFCs in the company's manufacturing processes, as well as reducing the use of lead, mercury and other dangerous substances. Further, the use of recycled material is monitored and improved. Toyota was awarded ISO 14001 as recognition of its success in this. ISO 14001 is an internationally recognized environmental management standard similar to the ISO standard for quality, ISO 9000. ISO 14001 is increasingly being recognized as the environmental benchmark businesses need to aspire to, just as ISO 9000 is the quality benchmark. In 1998 11 Japanese plants and 11 overseas ones had achieved ISO 14001 certification. Toyota not only spends resources in the development of new 'greener' products but it also looks at management and reporting systems that can monitor and evaluate how well it is doing against target. It encourages all employees to becoming active in this and works with its suppliers to raise their standard of environmental awareness and commitment.

As an example of its commitment to use alternative sources of energy in its plants, in the summer of 2000 Toyota contracted with Green Mountain, an electrical supply company in California, for it to supply electricity to its US headquarters in Torrance, California. Green Mountain is a 'green' supplier of electricity using both wind and solar sources of energy.

Web resources

www.toyota.co.jp/
www.toyota.com/

17

Vodafone

HISTORY

Vodafone's history is summarized in Table A.9.

TELECOMMUNICATIONS

To appreciate Vodafone's strategy it is necessary to first have a look at the way telecommunications has changed. It has moved away from the delivery of phone services by fixed line, run usually either by a state monopoly or two or three large private firms, to a situation where there are many providers of service and wireless (that is, mobile) phones.

In the past, would-be providers of fixed line (wire) services would have to invest heavily in capacity before they could start attracting customers. This cost was associated with running a wire to each subscriber etc. Alternatively they could buy capacity from existing suppliers and use the existing lines to service their customer base. When there was a state monopoly potential entrances were barred from doing either of these. With the liberalization of the market, wire-based companies were allowed to buy capacity from existing suppliers such as British Telecom in the UK and invest in new capacity themselves, such as cable and fibre networks, to find new customers. Changes in technology made it possible to use different suppliers at different times on

Table A.9 Summary of Vodafone history and activities

Year	Number of UK customers	% change	Major events
1985	19,000		1 January first cellular mobile call made from Trafalgar Square in London to Newbury where Vodafone had its headquarters
1986	63,000	232%	
1987	136,000	116%	Services include *The Financial Times* CityLine and AA Roadwatch
1988	264,000	94%	20% of Racal-Vodafone floated
1989	482,000	82%	Introduction of back-up network to increase reliability of service
1990	665,000	38%	Paknet launched for business users – joint venture between Racal Telecom and Wireless/Mercury Communications
1991	697,000	5%	Racal and Vodafone split. With Telecom Finland first international roaming call made. Vodafone start first UK digital service
1992	795,000	14%	'LowCall' tariff introduced
1993	1,051,000	32%	First Vodafone high-street store opened and agreement with Comet signed. International partners in Germany, Australia, and South Africa
1994	1,638,000	55%	Data, fax and short-message services start. Agreement with Globalstar to develop Low Earth Orbiting Satellite
1995	2,330,000	42%	Growth of retail outlets including deals with John Lewis, AA Stores and The Link
1996	2,800,000	20%	Pre-pay pricing introduced
1997	3,259,000	16%	Internal reorganization from six into three units: Vodafone Corporate, Vodafone Retail and Vodafone Connect. 100th roaming agreement signed. Pay-as-you-talk package started
1998	4,874,000	50%	Sir Gerald Whent retires. Continued search for overseas agreements and partnerships, including Egypt and New Zealand
1999	6,860,000	41%	Merger of Vodafone and AirTouch Communication Inc, an American company. Vodafone renamed Vodafone AirTouch Plc
2000			Acquire Mannesmann AG and with this Mannesmann's stake in Orange. Customers in Europe nearly 33 million. Estimated world customers 59 million. Now one of the top ten companies in the world as measured by market capitalization. Bids successfully for UK and German third-generation mobile licences. Sells Orange to France Telecom. 31 July changes name to Vodafone Group Plc

lines owned by other companies. The growth of companies that sell cheap calls to overseas destinations is an example of this. Wireless services require the building up of receiving and transmitting stations and access to local wire-based services. When you use a mobile phone a signal is sent to a local station, then it is sent by wire over existing lines to either the nearest station to the mobile you are trying to contact or straight to a fixed phone. In 1991 the UK liberalized its market for telecommunications allowing about 50 telecommunication operators and 60 cable operators to compete in the market.

To succeed in this market you have to have subscribers and the more the better. As your customer base increases you can build more fixed stations to provide a better service for your customers. If your customer base is small you cannot generate sufficient investment funds to build more capacity, consequently existing subscribers find they often cannot get through as your network has temporarily reached full capacity. Building market share becomes your key strategic goal. If you look at the phenomenal growth of subscribers to Vodafone you can see how each year the company increases its customer base, allowing it to invest more in capacity. To attract customers mobile phone companies were, and still are, prepared to sell mobile phones at prices way below what they have cost to make. In some cases these companies literally give mobile phones away. What they want is for you to subscribe to their network, as this is where they make money. Vodafone's entry into high street retailing in 1993 is an example of just this.

Vodafone also had to make sure that it had access to overseas markets. So part of its strategy has been to buy into foreign companies such as the US company AirTouch Communications, and the German company Mannersmann AG, to build foreign markets. Vodafone has entered into numerous agreements with other overseas providers in Australia, New Zealand and Finland, for example, to further build overseas markets.

As technology changes, existing mobile operators have to have access to the new capacities. At first mobiles used first generation analogue technology. This delivered a reasonable quality of service but with the next generation using digital technology quality improved considerably. Nowadays the quality is so good it is impossible to detect whether the person on the other end is on a fixed line or mobile. The latest technology, third generation (3G), allows high-speed Internet access and videophones. Governments have the rights to the new airwaves that 3G uses and are in the process of selling these rights to individual companies such as Vodafone.

GAINING ACCESS TO 3G TECHNOLOGY

If you are a player in this business, each stage of the development of mobile phones has been about making sure that you have access to the network. No access means no growth in customers and being left with out-of-date technology. The existing big players are worried that if they are excluded from 3G technology, eventually, their customers will desert them for companies using the newer technology. They cannot afford to be left out. This means they are prepared to pay extraordinary amounts of money for the privilege of using the new airwaves. Unlike the sale of previous licences for accessing the first and second generation capacity, where access to the airwaves was comparatively cheap, the sale of 3G licences was organized by governments who 'owned' the rights to yield considerably more money. How was this achieved?

There are several ways a country can allocate 3G licences and in fact any scarce resource it wishes either to sell or license. Firstly it could run a 'beauty contest'. In this interested parties are asked to provide detailed information to the government about the service they are going to provide and the price they are prepared to pay for the use of the allocated airways. All bids are then analysed and the airways are allocated. The highest bidder(s) do not necessarily win in this system, as the price offered is only one consideration. For instance, the quality of the service, the price charged, and often political factors such as jobs created and their location will influence the decision. The first allocation of mobile phone airways in the UK was on this system with the lucky winners, in retrospect, paying very little for the rights.

Alternatively, a one round sealed-bid system could be used. Here interested parties are simply asked to bid once for the rights. There are several variations on this. For example, the bidders say how much they are prepared to pay for what proportion of the rights or perhaps for all the rights, with the highest bid(s) winning.

Another more favoured method is a series of increasing bids with companies pulling out at various stages, as they calculate that the rights are not going to be profitable for them, until only three or four remain and the rights are allocated to them. This method has the advantage to the rights-holder as it tends to generate higher bids then other methods and it has the advantage to the bidders as at each round their competitors signal through their bids their calculations on how much the rights are worth to them. In this situation companies run many simulations of rivals' possible bids, reaction to this and their rivals' subsequent reaction, etc. Occasionally this does break down as in a recent New Zealand auction when some airwaves rights were secured for just 6 New Zealand dollars.

Recent bidding for 3G licences

In the UK in 2000 there were 13 bidders for five licences for various bands of the spectrum being licensed. The bidders were as follows: British Telecom; Crescent Wireless; One2One; Orange; TIW; One.Tel; Eircom (3G); Nomura; Telesystem International Wireless; Telefonica; SpectrumCo; NTL/France Telecom; and Vodafone.

The bidding continued until only five companies were left. The process went through 150 rounds of bidding with the big four; Vodafone, BT, One2One and Orange being joined by Telesystem International Wireless.

The combined bids totalled £22.48 billion against government and independent experts' estimates of about £3 billion. To put the money into some sort of perspective it is equivalent of giving each household in the UK about £1,000. Vodafone secured licence B with a bid of £5.96 billion. This compares with BT's bid of £4.03 billion for licence C and One2One's bid of £4 billion for licence D. This demonstrates just how far Vodafone and the other providers were prepared to go to maintain their market position in the UK.

In Germany, six companies, including Vodafone through its subsidiary Mannesmann, paid £31.62 billion for the licences. Vodafone paid £5.14 billion for its German allocation compared with the £5.96 billion it paid in the UK.

The immediate impact of paying this kind of money for the licences was on the company's long-term credit worthiness. Standard and Poor lowered its long-term rating of Vodafone from A to A- but when Vodafone announced that it was to sell its stake in Orange (acquired through Mannesmann) to France Telecom it was upgraded to A. The reason for the downgrade was market speculation that Vodafone, like the other mobile phone companies, had paid too much for the 3G licences. This might make it unlikely that they would ever make money out of them.

STRATEGIC ISSUES

Vodafone has spent several years building up its worldwide customer base. In the past access to the airwaves required for mobile phones was relatively cheap but as the auctions for the 3G licences have shown this is no longer the case. For Vodafone to make a decent return on the money it has spent acquiring licences is not going to be easy. It may be possible for the company to gain from the economies of scale it can now exploit because of the number of subscribers it has. It may be able to find the new, innovative services that will bring it customers from other mobile phone companies. Vodafone's development of WAP services might well, if it can keep ahead of its rivals, maintain its profitability even in the face of the debt incurred in the 3G auctions. However, new markets are going to be harder not easier to find, and while the future may well not be Orange anymore, it is not necessarily going to be Vodafone.

Web resources

www.vodafone-airtouch-plc.com

Notes and references for the readings

READING 3.1

Thompson, P (1999) *Persuading Aristotle*, Kogan Page, London

READING 3.2

Corrigan, P (1999) *Shakespeare on Management*, Kogan Page, London
Peters, T (1994) *The Pursuit of Wow*, Macmillan, New York
Peters, T and Waterman, R (1982) *In Search of Excellence*, HarperCollins, London

READING 4.1

Bennis, W (2000) *Old Dogs, New Tricks*, Kogan Page, London

READING 5.1

Anthony, R N (1965), in *Planning and Control Systems: A framework for analysis*, Graduate School of Business Administration, Harvard University
Argenti, J C (1989) *Practical Corporate Planning*, Unwin

Binnersley, M (1996) Do you measure up?, *Management Accounting*, November

Booth, R (1997) Performance management: making it happen, *Management Accounting*, November

Booth, R (1998) Measures for programmes of action, *Management Accounting*, July / August

Brander Brown, J and McDonnell, B (1995) The balanced scorecard: short-term guest or long-term resident?, *International Journal of Contemporary Hospitality Management*, **7**(2/3)

Broadbent, M (1999) *Measuring Business Performance*, CIMA/Kogan Page, London

Coates, J B *et al* (1993) *Corporate Performance Evaluation in Multinational Companies*, CIMA

Drucker, P F (1989) *Practice of Management*, Heinemann

Evans, H *et al* (1996) Who needs performance management?, *Management Accounting*, December

Freund, Y P (1988) Critical success factors, *Planning Review*, **16**(4)

Innes, J (1995) Activity performance measures and the Tableaux de Bord, in *Accounting and Performance Measurement*, ed I Lapsley and F Mitchell, Paul Chapman

Johnson, G and Scholes, K (1997) *Exploring Corporate Strategy, Text and Cases*, 4th edn, Prentice-Hall

Kaplan, R S and Norton, D P (1992) The balanced scorecard – measures that drive performance, *Harvard Business Review*, **70**(1).

Lebas, M (1993) 'Tableaux de Board and performance management', conference paper, Management Accounting Research Group, London School of Economics, April

Lowe, E A and Soo, W F (1980) Organisational effectiveness – a critique and proposal, *Managerial Finance*, **6**(1)

Mintzberg, H (1983) *Power In and Around Organisations*, Prentice-Hall

Otley, D T (1997) Better performance measurement, *Management Accounting*, January

Pearce, J A and Robinson, R B (1985) *Strategic Management, Strategy Formulation and Implementation*, Irwin

Porter, M E (1985), *Competitive Advantage*, Free Press

Society of Management Accountants of Canada (1994), Developing comprehensive performance indicators, *Management Accounting Guideline* No 31

Wilson, R M S (1994) 'Criteria for measuring marketing performance', paper presented at the Performance Measurement and Control Seminar, CIMA Research Foundation

Wilson, R M S and Chua, W F (1993) *Managerial Accounting: Method and meaning*, 2nd edn, Chapman & Hall

READING 5.2

Drennan, D and Pennington, S (1999) *12 Ladders to World Class Performance*, Kogan Page, London

READING 6.1

Cook, M and Cook, C (2000) *Competitive Intelligence: Create an intelligent organization and compete to win*, Kogan Page, London

Fuld, L M (1995) *The New Competitor Intelligence: The complete resource for finding, analyzing, and using information about your competitors*, Wiley, New York

Kahaner, L (1996) *Competitive Intelligence: From black ops to boardrooms*, Simon & Schuster, New York

READING 6.2

Willsher, R and Jolly, A (eds) (2000) *The Growing Business Handbook*, Kogan Page, London

READING 7.1

Argyris, C (1964) *Integrating the Individual and the Organization*, Wiley, New York

Bennis, W (1972) A funny thing happened on the way to the future, in *The Management of Change and Conflict*, ed J Thomas and W Bennis, Penguin Books, Harmondsworth

Burke, T, Maddock, S and Rose, A (1963) How ethical is British business? Research Working Paper, Series 2, No 1, University of Westminster

Burns, T and Stalker, G (1963) *The Management of Innovation*, Tavistock, London

DiMaggio, P J and Powell, W (1983) The iron cage revisited: institutional isomorphism and collective rationale in organizational fields, *American Sociological Review*, **48**, 147–60

Donaldson, J (1989) *Key Issues in Business Ethics*, Academic Press, San Francisco

Donaldson, J and Waller, M (1980) Ethics and organization, *Journal of Management Studies*, **17**(1)

ENDS (1993) Jury still out on responsible care, Industry Report No 55, ENDS 222, July

Friedman, M (1963) *Capitalism and Freedom*, Phoenix Books, University of Chicago Press, Chicago

Hartley, R F (1993) *Business Ethics: Violations of the public trust*, Wiley, New York

Holloway, R J and Hancock, R S (1968) *Marketing in a Changing Environment*, Wiley, New York

Luthans, F (1985) *Organizational Behaviour*, 4th edn, McGraw-Hill, New York

Mintzberg, H (1979) *The Structuring of Organizations*, Prentice-Hall, New York

Welford, R J (1989) Growth and the performance-participation nexus: the case of UK producer cooperatives, *Economic Analysis and Workers Management*, **23** (1)

Welford, R J (1992) Linking quality and the environment: a strategy for the implementation of environmental management systems, *Business Strategy and the Environment*, **1**(1)

Welford, R J (1993) Local economic development and environmental management: an integrated approach, *Local Economy*, **8**(2)

Welford, R (2000) *Corporate Environmental Management 3*, Earthscan, London

Westing, J H (1968) Some thoughts on the nature of ethics in marketing, in *Marketing Systems*, ed R Mayer, 1967 Winter Conference Proceedings, Marketing Association, Chicago

READING 8.1

Romm, J J (1999) *Cool Companies: How the best businesses boost profits and productivity by cutting greenhouse gas emissions*, Earthscan, London

1. John S. Jennings, "Sustainable Development," Shell International, London, April 17, 1997. If the merger between Exxon and Mobil is approved, Shell will no longer be the world's largest, publicly traded oil company.

2. Shell's projected greenhouse gas emissions reductions are derived from *Health, Safety, and Environment Report '98,* Shell International, London, 1998; *People and the Environment,* the 1997 Shell International Exploration and Production Health, Safety, and Environment Report, Shell International Exploration and Production, The Hague, Netherlands, 1998; and information available on their website (www.shell.com).

3. *Economist*, September 28, 1991. See also Peter Senge, *The Fifth Discipline* (New York: Doubleday, 1990), p. 181.

4. Pierre Wack's quotes come from two articles, "Scenarios: Uncharted Waters Ahead," *Harvard Business Review*, September/October 1985, pp. 73–89, and "Scenarios: Shooting the Rapids," *Harvard Business Review*, November/December 1985, pp. 139–150.

5. Both Wohlstetter and Fuchida are quoted in Wach, "Scenarios: Shooting the Rapids," pp. 148–149.

6. The discussion of Shell and its two scenarios is based on meetings with Shell staff, including Ged Davis, Kurt Hoffman, Peter Langcake, Douglas McKay, Gerry Matthews, and Jan Smeele during an October 1998 visit to Shell's London headquarters; Ged David, "Global Warming: The Role of Energy Efficient Technologies," Shell International (SI), London, October 1989; Peter Kassler, "Energy for Development," SI, London, November 1994; E. J. Grunwald, "Energy in the Long Term," SI, London, 1994; Chris Fay, "Fossil Fuels and Beyond—Meeting the Energy Needs of the 21st Century," SI, London, 1995; "The Evolution of the World's Energy Systems," SI, London, 1996; John Jennings, "Sustainable Development"; "Shell Invests US$0.5 Billion in Renewables," press release, SI, London, October 16, 1997; Mark Moody-Stuart, "A Force for Progress—The Royal Dutch/Shell Group in the 21st Century," SI, London, February 10, 1998; "Connecting You to the Sun," SI, London, 1997; *Profits and Principles—Does There Have to be a Choice?* SI, London, July 1998; Jeroen van der Veer, "The Greenhouse Challenge," SI, London, August 31, 1998; information available on various websites (www.shell.com, www.shellpro.brentstar.com, and www.foe.org/orgs/ga/niger/html); *Financial Times*, October 17, 1997; and *The Washington Post*, August 2, 1998, pp. H1, H5.

7. Shell's scenario does not anticipate significant increases in nuclear energy. "Future societal attitudes towards nuclear power, which are currently largely negative, are hard to foresee, but it is possible to say that, for many years into the future, the world's energy demand could be met without significant additional nuclear capacity." E. J. Grunwald, "Energy in the Long Terms," p. 6.

8. *New York Times*, February 13, 1996, p. A1.

9. *Oil & Gas Journal*, November 24, 1997, pp. 29–36.

10. *Washington Post*, p. C13, April 22, 1998.

READING 8.2

Hawken, P, Lovins, A B and Hunter Lovins, L (1999), *Natural Capitalism: The next industrial revolution*, Earthscan, London

1. Marine Conservation Biology Institute 1998: "Troubled Waters: A Call for Action," MCBI, Redmond, WA, Jan., www.mcbi.org, and U.S. National Academy of Sciences and British Royal Society, 1992.
2. Daily, G. C., ed., 1997: *Nature's Services: Societal Dependence on Natural Ecosystems*, Island press, Washington, DC.
3. Coral Reef Alliance 1998: "Reefs in Danger: Threats to Coral Reefs Around the World," Oct. 22.
4. Worldwide Fund for Nature Europe 1998: "A third of the world's natural resources consumed since 1970: Report," Agence France-Presse, October.
5. Costanza, R., d'Arge, R., de Groot, R., Farber, S., Grasso, M., Hannon, B., Limburg, K., Naeem, S., O'Neill, R. V., and Paruelo, J., 1977: "The Value of the World's Ecosystem Services and Natural Capital," *Nature* 387:253–260, May 15, using 1994 dollars in which the value was at least $33 trillion.
6. Details are in World Bank 1995: *Monitoring Environmental Progress: A Report on Work in Progress*, Environmentally Sustainable Development, World Bank, Washington, DC, at 57–66, and World Bank 1997: *Expanding the Measure of Wealth: Indicators of Environmentally Sustainable Development*, Environmentally Sustainable Development Studies and Monographs Series No. 17, World Bank, Washington, DC.
7. Deane, P. and Cole, W. A., 1969: *British Economic Growth, 1688–1959*, 2nd edn, Cambridge U. Press, Cambridge, England.
8. Vitousek, P., et al., 1986: "Human Appropriation of the Products of Photosynthesis," *BioScience* 34:368–73, May, and Vitousek, P. M., Mooney, H. A., Lubchenco, J., and Melillo, J. M., 1997: "Human Domination of Earth's Ecosystems," *Science* 277:494–99, July.
9. International Labor Organization 1994: *The World Employment Situation, Trends and Prospects*, press release, ILO, Washington, DC, and Geneva, Switzerland, Mar. 6.
10. Daly, H. E. 1997: "Uneconomic Growth: From Empty-World to Full-World Economics," Rice University, DeLange-Woodlands Conference *Sustainable Development: Managing the Transition*, Houston, TX, Mar. 3, in press in Columbia U. Press conference volume.
11. Schmidt-Bleek, F. et al., 1997: "Statement to Government and Business Leaders," Wuppertal Institute, Wuppertal, Germany.
12. Present at the Club in September 1996 were: Jacqueline Aloise de Larderel, Director, UNEP-IE, Paris; Willy Bierter, Director, Institut für Produktdauer-Forschung, Giebenach, Switzerland; Wouter van Dieren, President, Institute for Environment and Systems Analysis, Amsterdam; Hugh Faulkner, formerly Executive Director, Business Council for Sustainable Development; Claude Fussler, Vice President/Environment, Dow Europe; Mike Goto, Director, Institute of Ecotoxicology, Gakushuin University, Tokyo; Leo Jansen, Director, Dutch Sustainable Technology Programme; Ashok Khosla, President, Development Alternatives, New Delhi; Franz Lehner, President, Institute for Labor and Technology, Gelsenkirchen, Germany; Jim MacNeill, MacNeill & Associates,

formerly Secretary General, Brundtland Commission, Ottawa, Canada; Wolfgang Sachs, Chairperson, Greenpeace Germany; Ken Saskai, Osaka University; Friedrich Schmidt-Bleek, Vice-President, Wuppertal Institute; Walter Stahel, Director, Institute de la Durabilité, Geneva; Paul Weaver, Director, Centre for EcoEfficiency and Enterprise, University of Portsmouth; Ernst Ulrich von Weizsäcker, President, Wuppertal Institute; Jan-Olaf Willums, Director, World Business Council for Sustainable Development, Geneva; Heinz Wohlmeyer, President, Austrian Association for Agroscientific Research; Ryoichi Yamamoto, President of MRS-Japan, Institute of Industry Science, University of Tokyo.

13. Gardner, G., and Sampat, P., 1998: "Mind Over Matter: Recasting the Role of Materials in Our Lives," Worldwatch Paper 144, Worldwatch Institute, Washington, DC, Dec., at 26 provides a useful summary of many such initiatives.

14. Romm, J. J., and Browning, W. C., 1994: "Greening the Building and the Bottom Line: Increasing Productivity Through Energy-Efficient Design," Rocky Mountain Institute Publication #D94-27.

15. Ayres, R. U., 1989: *Technology and Environment*, National Academy of Sciences, Washington, DC.

16. American Institute of Physics 1975: *Efficient Use of Energy*, American Physical Society Studies on the Technical Aspects of the More Efficient Use of Energy, Conf. Procs. No. 25, AIP, New York, NY, adjusted for progress and new insights since then.

17. Stahel, W. R., and Reday-Mulvey, G., 1981: *Jobs for Tomorrow; the Potential for Substituting Manpower for Energy*, Vantage Press, New York, NY.

18. Friend, G., 1996: "Ecomimesis: Copying ecosystems for fun and profit," *The New Bottom Line*, Feb. 4, gfriend@igc.apc.org.

19. Stahel also coined the term "extended product responsibility" (EPR), which is cradle-to-cradle from the manufacturer's point of view. EPR is now becoming a mandated or voluntary standard in many European industries.

20. Stahel, W. R., and Børlin, M., 1987: Strategie économique de la durabilité, Société de Banque Suisse, Geneva, Switzerland.

21. Emerson, R. W., 1994: *Nature and other writings*, Shambhala, Boston, MA, at 9–10.

22. As far as we know, the term "technical nutrient" was first used by Michael Braungart in a conversation with William A. McDonough.

23. Stahel 1981.

24. Womack, J. P., and Jones, D. T., 1996: *Lean Thinking: Banish Waste and Create Wealth in Your Corporation*, Simon and Schuster, New York, summarized in "Beyond Toyota: How to Root Out Waste and Pursue Perfection," *Harv. Bus. Rev.* 140–158, Sept./Oct., Reprint 96511; Womack, personal communication, 28 February 1999.

25. *San Francisco Chronicle* 1998: "Natural Disasters Around World Cost Record $89 Billion in 1998," Nov. 28.

26. Kaplan, R., 1994: "The Coming Anarchy," *Atlantic Monthly*, Feb., and Kaplan, R., 1997: "The Future of Democracy", *Atlantic Monthly*, Dec.

27. Yergin, D., 1991: *The Prize: The Epic Quest for Oil, Money, and Power*, Simon and Schuster, London.

28. Gleick, P. H., 1998: *The World's Water 1998–1999: The Biennial Report on Freshwater Resources*, Island Press, Washington, DC; updated at www.worldwater.org.

READING 12.1

Wooton, S and Horne, T (2000) *Strategic Thinking: A step-by-step approach to strategy*, 2nd edn, Kogan Page, London

READING 13.1

Haines, S G (1998) *Successful Strategy Planning: How to build a high-performance team or business*, Kogan Page, London

READING 13.2

Hussey, D (1998) *How to be Better at Managing Change*, Kogan Page, London

READING 14.1

Vasconcellos e Sá, J (1999) *The Warlords*, Kogan Page, London

1. The term 'strategy' comes from the Greek *strategos,* a civil and military governor of a province.
2. von Clausewitz, Karl (1978) *Von Kriege*, Penguin Classics.
3. The first book on military strategy dates from the 4th century AD – *The Art of War* by Sun Tzu.
4. To ask which business administration area is more important makes as much sense as to ask which wing of an airplane is most important, or which tyre of a car we not longer need. Left? Right? Rear? Front? That is why there is an old military saying that *there are no victories in strategy*, meaning strategy is never a *sufficient* condition for success but solely a *necessary* one, a prerequisite. Without good tactics, excellence in strategy usually falls short of delivering. On the other hand, if you excel in tactics but do not complement that with a sound strategy, you may win battles but you will lose the war. That is, you will never achieve long-term results and excellence.
5. Today many books on operational areas use the word 'strategy' for marketing purposes. A book which previously would have been called simply 'financial management' nowadays has the title 'strategic financial management'; and production management now appears on the market as strategic production management, and so on. This is a simple technique to sell more (books) which is associated with the popularity of the term 'strategy' (a concept whose use has developed during the last two decades). All subjects have their myths, but the more seriously we take them, the less we should become involved.

6. Until then the subject was called Business Policy or Management Policy and was based on case studies which attempted to analyse problems of coordination between the operational areas of management (marketing, finance, etc). The field of strategy had very few concepts, theories and autonomous techniques.

7. It is significant that in 1943, when Peter Drucker, then Professor of Philosophy in New York University, was invited by Alfred Sloan, President of General Motors, to do some consulting work, the former went to the New York Municipal Library and in the index tried to find which books were available on the subject of management. There were few and all were on the operational areas of accounting, financial management, taxation and engineering; that is, production management. There was nothing about personnel, marketing and information systems of management and certainly nothing about strategy. All this has been developed since the 1940s.

8. In the remainder of this book the word 'market' will be used as a synonym for industry or geographical area.

9. Banks have always been special institutions. They have four types of potential clients: active companies, passive companies, active individuals, passive individuals. Most other institutions only have active clients. Bank clients can be persons or companies, while other institutions either sell industrial goods (the clients are usually companies) or consumable goods (the clients are persons). The strategic decisions of the banks must be based on two segmentation matrices: one for the retail bank and another for the corporate bank. The most usual segmentation matrix for the retail bank is presented in Figure 2.7, in which the two dimensions are the social class and the life-cycle phase.

10. Special situations are excluded in which for cultural, social and/or ethical reasons the entrepreneur opts for a certain industry/geographical area. The situation should then be seen in terms of the company trying to maximize profit subject to this type of restriction.

11. On this subject see Vasconcellos e Sá, J and Amaral, MC (1996) *The Modern Alchemists*, Instituto do Emprego e Formação Profissional, Lisbon, which has a chapter on the establishment of objectives for a company's business units.

12. It also aimed to be the beer to drink at the weekends (as the slogan says, 'It is good to drink something better at the weekends, isn't it?').

13. Like Marlboro for cigarettes.

14. Justifying the motto to be adopted in its sponsorship: 'Tell me who you live with, and I will tell you who you are.'

15. An interesting question is *whether tactics also influence strategy.* For instance, if Hannibal's army had been composed mainly of sailors it would have had to follow another strategy: to attack the Roman fleet in the Mediterranean. In business, if a firm lacks a certain raw material or cannot find a specifically skilled labour force, certain market segments (strategies) are precluded. In such instances, tactics also seem to influence strategy. Two aspects, however, are noteworthy. First, in these situations tactics exert *a veto rule* over strategy; that is, they veto some strategies but they do not indicate *which* strategy to follow. That is considerably different from the influence of strategy upon tactics since (as previous examples illustrate) strategy does not indeed determine in a narrow sense the tactics to follow; what sales promotion should be, what advertising should be, what type of service should be offered, etc. Second, the cases where one

starts by drawing a strategy and then after defining the tactics one concludes that the former must be reviewed are very rare – since they mean that very important and totally unpredictable events occurred after defining the strategy and before implementing it. Another explanation is that the strategy was badly formulated in the first place. The reason is simple. One of the criteria when evaluating alternative strategies is an organization's (or army's) strengths or special qualities. Therefore, only if these were not considered at all, or were wrongly evaluated is it necessary to conclude that a given strategy cannot be implemented.

16. See the very interesting article on this subject by David L Hoyer (1990) 'Corestates New Jersey National Bank Markets to the Affluent by Shunning Mass Marketing', *Bank Marketing*, November.

17. As is demonstrated by Lone Star, which was adapted to the taste of Texas.

18. Segmentation raises very interesting questions, such as how to segment an industry and how far it should be taken (how many segments create an industry). For these procedural aspects, see Vasconcellos e Sá, J and Amaral, MC (1996) *The Modern Alchemists*, Instituto do Emprego e Formação Profissional, Lisbon. For space reasons only aspects of contents (and not process) are focused upon here.

19. It is easy to understand why. At one extreme, if there are as many companies as strategic groups, there will be a ratio of one to one, which would mean that each company would follow a specific behaviour (strategy) within the industry. There should be no reasons concerning the interrelation among the segments which would make one enterprise that is in segment X to go into segment Y. Entry into other segments would be dictated by attractiveness and strong points of the company, and not the synergetic relationship between the segments.

20. This analysis is, *ceteris paribus*, in terms of attractiveness; that is, with the exception of the case when the enterprise is already present these segments would be less attractive than segments empty at the moment. In any case the segments where enterprise C is alone are probably among the most synergetic together with those where the enterprises C and D are together.

21. Banks have enlarged their services to the area of insurance, in addition to offering a panoply of financial products; auditing companies have enlarged their activity to services of taxation, bookkeeping, recruitment of personnel, etc, all within consultancy and so on (see Figure 2.16).

22. A third type of strategy is that which the managers sometimes think they have and which has nothing to do with reality or present strategy. As W Rogers says, 'The problem with some people is not that they do not know, but that what they think they know in fact does not correspond to the truth. It is the difference between conscious ignorance and unconscious ignorance.'

READING 14.2

Matthews, C (1999) *Managing International Joint Ventures: The route to globalizing your business*, Kogan Page, London

READING 16.1

Beckhard, R and Harris, R T (1987) *Organizational Transitions*, Addison-Welsey, Reading, MA

Bryson, J M (1995) *Strategic Planning for Public and Nonprofit Organizations*, Jossey-Bass, San Francisco

Corrigan, P, Hayes, M and Joyce, P (1999) *Managing in the New Local Government*, Kogan Page, London

Drucker, P (1955) *The Practice of Management*, Pan, London

Nutt, P C and Backoff, R W (1992) *Strategic Management of Public and Third Sector Organizations*, Jossey-Bass, San Francisco

Smith, R J (1994) *Strategic Management and Planning in the Public Sector*, Longman, Harlow

Thurley, K and Wirdenius, H (1989) *Toward European Management*, Pitman, London

READING 17.1

BT (1998) *World Communication Report 1998*, London

Chattell, A (1998) *Creating Value in the Digital Era*, Macmillan, London

Financial Times (1999a) *Guide to Digital Business*, Supplement, Autumn

KPMG (1998a) Managing transformation in the new economy, http://www.kpmg.ca

KPMG (1998b) *Knowledge Management: Research report 1998*, London

OECD (1998a) *Industrial Performance and Competitiveness in an Era of Globalisation and Technological Change*, DSTI/IND(97)23/Final

OECD (1998b) *The Economic and Social Impact of Electronic Commerce*, October, DSTI/ICCP(98)15/REV, Paris

Porter, M (1985) *Competitive Advantage*, Free Press, New York

Tapscott, D (1995) *The Digital Economy*, McGraw-Hill, New York

Turner, Colin (2000) *The Information E-conomy*, Kogan Page, London

READING 17.2

Lindström, M and Andersen, T F (2000) *Brand Building on the Internet*, Kogan Page, London

INDEX

NB: numbers in italics indicate drawings, figures, graphs and tables

3G technology   241, 551–53
12 Ladders to World Class Performance (reading
    5.2) 106–14 *see also* performance, evaluat-
    ing
  attaining world class status   106–07
  learning from others   113
  priorities for company   110–11
  results, achieving   112
  setting standards   112–13
  the 12 ladders   113–14
  world class, definition and examples of   107,
    108, 108
  world class status as seen by customers
    109–10

Airbus   285–86
Alexander, L D   280, 281, 285, 290
Amazon   406, 407, 409–10, 470
America Online (AOL)   318, 406, 407, 408

analysis: turning information into intelligence
    (reading 6.1)   128–49 *see also* markets and
    customers, analysing
  company analysis   138–49
    company profiling/worksheets   141, 142–44
    current ratio   144
    event analysis   146–47
    inventory turnover ratio   145
    merger analysis   148–49
    patent analysis   147
    personality profiling   147–48
    profitability ratios   146
    quick ratio   144–45
    ratio analysis   144
    SWOT analysis   139
    total debts to assets ratio and debt servicing
      ratio   145–46
  effective decision-making, analysis as key to
    128–29

industry analysis   134–38
   competition within the industry   135
   competitor profiling   137, *137*, 138
   influence of buyers   136
   influence of suppliers   136
   Porter's five forces model   134–35, 136
   threat of alternatives or substitutes   136
   threat of new competition   135–36
market analysis   129–34
   economic analysis   131–32
   industry analysis   133
   intelligence mapping   133–34
   market factors analysis   130
   political analysis   130–31
   social analysis   132
   technology analysis   133
Andersen, T F   347–53
Ansoff, H I   5, 7, 9, 15, 20, 25, 28, 33, *36*, 39, 155, 156, 158, 163, 235, 236, 242, 250, 251, 252, 255, 261, 265, 268
Apple Computers   283–84
Argenti, J   30, *36*, 39, 156
Argyris, C   178, 190, 194
Aronoff, C E   365, 371
auctions on-line   408

Backoff, R W   34, *36*, 41, 160, 163, 265, 266, 267, 268, 283, 284, 285, 290, 385, 386, 392, 395
balanced scorecard   32, 89–90, 91, 102, *105 see also* Web site(s)
Barrett, H   247, 255
Bart, C K   69, 70, 71, 77
BBC   88, 91, 495 *see also* performance, evaluating
benchmarking   90, 91, 125, 248 *see also* Web site(s)
Berry, F S   377, 383, *383*, 384, 385, 392
Blackburn, V L   365, 372
BMW   325, 340, 452
Body Shop   161, 363, 457–59
Boeing   233, 285, 421
booksellers on-line   406, 407, 409–10
Boston Consulting Group (BCG)   316–18 *see also* Web site(s)
  matrix   31, 316, *317*, 317–318, 327
Boyatzis, R E   39

Boyle, R   377, 392
Bracker, J S   364, 371
Brand Building on the Internet   437
Branson, R   316, 323, 327, 363, 369
British Airways   66–67, 70, 107, *108*
   see also mission statements
British Telecom (BT)   325, 410, 549, 552, 553
Bryson, J M   248, 255, 285, 290, 385, 386, 392, 401
Burns, T   178, 283, 290
Burrows, R   365, 371
business opportunities, suggesting new   221–30
  characteristics, combining   225–26, 229
   combination method *226*
   Dell example   226 *see also* Web site(s)
  conclusions   229
  differentiation   226–28
   restaurants example   227
   social pattern, changes in   227–28
   value chain   227
  empathy method   225, 229
   focus groups   225
   shop floor schemes   225, 264
  executive exercise   230
  latent needs   228–29
   importance of identifying   228
   restaurant/dancing example   228–29
   strategic management, development of   228
  mind map *222*
  new ideas and creativity   223–24
   brain, left and right hemispheres of   223–24
   creativity and imagination, freeing   224
   drawing techniques   224 *see also* Web site(s), creativity/drawing
   mind-mapping   224 *see also* Web site(s), creativity/drawing
   serendipity   224
   thinking techniques   224 *see also* Web site(s), creativity/drawing
  questions   229
  references   230
  television story   221, 223

case studies   455–553 *see also individual entries*
Castle, The   373
Cauley de la Sierra, M   325, 328

Chandler, J   31, 39
Collins, J C   74, 77
Compaq Computer Corporation   117–18, 234,
    280
Competing for the Future   521
Competitive Intelligence   128–49
*Competitive Intelligence from Black Ops to
    Boardrooms*   140
Cool Companies   195–204
core competencies   8, 34, *244, 249,* 249–52, 286,
    319
Corporate Environmental Management   3, 164–80
Coveny, H   364, 372
Coyne, K   520, 525
creating more options (reading 12.1)   269–76
    see also strategic options, identifying creative
    change nothing   272
    creativity, techniques to aid   273–76
        attribute listing   274
        brainstorming   274–75, *275*
        forced relationships   275–76
    divestment, strategies for   273
    external growth, strategies for   272–73
    identifying strategic option*s   270*
    internal growth, strategies for   272
    prompt sheets   *271, 276, 276*
Curran, J   365, 371
customers, latent needs of   118–19, 124, 228–29

Daimler Chrysler   149, 202, 233, 462, 465, 544
David, F R   85, 92
De Kluyver, C A   90, 92
de Vries, M F R   37, 39
De Wit, B   286, 290
Dell Computer Corporation   118, 224, 226, 318,
    412, 413, 432, 444 *see also* Web site(s)
Demb, A   321, 328
Digital Equipment Corporation   184, 234, 280
does your product or service suit the Internet?
    (reading 17.2)   437–53 *see also* e-business
    news reporting   453
    product's interactive potential   439
    products most suitable for Internet   440, *440,*
        441
    search databases   450, *451,* 451

successful online sales/sales categories   441,
    442, 442–43, *443,* 444, *445,* 445, 446, *446,*
    447–50
transport, dispatch and communication
    451–53
Drucker, P   106, 261, 268, 395
Dupuis, M   247, 255
Durand, T   286, 290

e-business   156, 189–90, 403–53
    Calvino story, *The Man Who Shouted Teresa*
        403, 405
    conclusions   412–13
    consolidation   408
    does your product or service suit the Internet?
        (reading 17.2)   437–53 *see also main entry*
    evolution to   410–11
    growth of   405–06 *see also* Internet compa-
        nies/servers
    information economy and competitive
        advantage, the (reading 17.1)   415–36
        see also main entry
    issues for new   406–08
    mind map *404*
    operational efficiency   408–09
    questions   413
    references   413–14
    strategies for established firms   409–410
    strategy process and e-commerce   411
    value change analysis   411–12 *see also* value
        chain analysis
e-commerce   156 *see also* e-business
Eastlack, J   20, 25
Economist, The   196, 249, 280, 282, 287, 324, 325,
    405, 407, 408, 409, 430
environmental concerns/issues   156–57, 189,
    384, 462, 465–67, 529, 530–33, 544–47
    see also Shell *and* Toyota
environmental planning   384 *see also* public
    sector, the
euro, issues surrounding the   463 *see also* Ford
evaluating performance *see* performance, evalu-
    ating
evaluating strategic options *see* strategic options,
    evaluating

Falmer, R   20, 25
Fast Company Magazine   477
Ferlie, E   262, 268
Fiat   249–250, 286
Financial Times   429
Five Forces Analysis/Model   6, 126, 134–35, 431
   see also Porter, M
Fletcher, M   364, 372
Flynn, N   20, 25, 377, 382, *382*, 384, *384*, 385, 392
football leagues/clubs   489–90, 496, 497
   see also Manchester United plc
football managers   88
   see also Manchester United plc
football on television   495–97
   see also Manchester United plc
football players *see* Manchester United plc
Ford   202, 267, 328, 408, 409, 460–67, *468*, 506,
   544 *see also* Web site(s)
   business-to-business (B2B)   462, 465
   Connecting with Society   466, 467
   environment and corporate citizenship   462,
      465–67, *468*
      environmental pledge   465–66
      manufacturing targets   466
      SUV issues   466–67
   history Web site *see* Web site(s)
   manufacturing location   462–65
   performance   460, *461*
   problems and strategic issues   460, 462
Ford, Henry   224, 267
formulating missions and goals *see* missions and
   goals, formulating
Frankenstein, or, the Modern Prometheus   231
Frost-Kumpf, L   262, 268
Fujitsu   469–71 *see also* ICL *and* Web site(s)
Fuld, L M   133–34

Gaebler, T   377, 385, 392
Galagan, P A   7, 14
General Motors   188, 195, 282–83, 408, 409, 462,
   465, 544
Ghent, N   150
Gillies, C   7, 9, 20, 22
Glaxo-Wellcome   241, 472–75 *see also* Web site(s)
   drugs, range of   472, 474
   history   472

merger with SmithKline Beecham   472, 473,
   474–75
   regulatory agreement   474
global organizations/globalization   189, 278,
   323–24, 515, 521
Globe Theatre, London   88–89, 91 *see also* performance, evaluating
Grant, R M   29, 39, 184, 194
Greenley, G E   20, 25
Greenpeace   126, 532, 546
Growing Business Handbook, The   150

Hackbarth, G   411, 413
Haines, S G   291
Hall, G   364, 372
Hambrick, D C   22, 25
Hamel, G   7, 8, 14, 23, 25, 34, 35, 36, *36*, 39, 70,
   124, 127, 185, 225, 228, 230, 248, 249, 250,
   251, 252, 255, 264, 268, 287, 289, 290, 318,
   324, 328, 521, 524
Handy, C   3, 14, 15
Harrison watches   82, 84, 88, 361
Harvey Jones, J   28, 40
Heath, R L   156, 161, 163
Herold, D M   19, 25
Heymann, P B   5, 15, 378, 379, *379*, 392
Hiscocks, P G   251, *251*, 255
Horne, T,   237, 241, 242, 269–76
House, R J   20, 25
How To Be Better at Managing Change   302–13
Howe, F   160, 163
Hunger, J D   320, 328, 365, 372
Hussey, D   90, 92, 121, 127, 234, 242, 247, 255,
   281, 290, 301–13

IBM   188, 321, 469 *see also* Raytheon
ICL   126, 289, 327, 469–71 *see also* Web site(s)
   company history   469
   e-business   470–71
Idealab   476–79 *see also* Web site(s)
   competitive advantage, achieving   477–79
   formation and development   476–77
   references   479
identifying creative strategic options *see* strategic
   options, identifying creative
implementation, planning   277–313

car and the ravine story   277, 279
change, an age of   280
conclusions   288
executive exercises   289
mind map   *278*
organization   286–88
   chaordic structure   286
   corporate approach   287
   corporate centres, size of   287, 288
   structural design   287–88
politics   282–85
   company examples   282–84
   conflict element   283, 284
   stakeholder management/stakeholder
      reactions   284–85
questions   288–89
references   290
resources   285–86
   analytical steps in planning   285
   company examples   285–86
   core competencies/new skills, acquiring
      286
strategy implementation   280–82
   changes implemented by new chief execu-
      tives   281–82
   components for managing   281
   five measures to improve   281
   vision statement, need for   281–82
working through the change process (reading
    13.2)   302–13 *see also main entry*
information and communication technology
    (ICT)   319, 416–24, 427–34, 511 *see also*
    e-business
Information E-conomy, The   415
information economy and competitive advantage,
    the (reading 17.1)   415–36 *see also*
    e-business
   competitive paradigm within the information
      economy   433–34, *435*, 435–36
   enterprise performance and functioning,
      impact upon   416–17
   human resources in the information economy
      419–21
   human resources issues   417–419
   impact upon production costs and
      productivity   421–23

   intranets and extranets   428–29
   organizational implications   429, *429*, 430–31
   supply chain and the information economy
      431–33
   value chain analysis   423, *423*, 424–25, *426*,
      426–27, *427*, 428
Internet   13, 76, 89, 156, 234, 433, 465, 476–79,
    521, 541, 551 *see also* e-business
Internet companies/servers   363, 406, 407, 408,
    410, 465, 470, 521
issues, identifying and addressing   153–80
   conclusions   161
   executive exercise   162
   managing strategic issues   159, *159*, 160–61
      senior management responsibilities   160
      stakeholder reactions/management   160
      SWOT analysis   160
   mind map *154*
   other approaches   158–59
      SWOT analysis   158
   profitability issues, identifying   157–58
   questions   161
   references   163
   social and ethical issues for sustainable
      development (reading 7.1)   164–80
      see also main entry
   strategic issue, definitions of a   155–56
   strategic issues, source of   156–57
      environmental management/sustainable
         development   156–57
      technological change   156
   vacuum cleaner story   153, 155

J D Wetherspoon   161, 253, 254, 480–84 *see also*
    Web site(s)
   competitors   482–83, *483*
   financial data   *481*
   future, the   483–84
   history and name   480
   pricing policy   482
   segmented markets   482
Jager, D   261–62
Jantsch, E   34, 40
Jenster, P   90, 92, 121, 127, 247, 255
Johnson & Johnson   79, 322, 327 *see also* Web
    site(s)

Joyce, P   33, 40, 68, 77, 186, 194, 364, 366, 372, 376, 380, 392
Judge, W Q   37, 40, 321, 328

Kahaner, L   140, 141
Kanter, R M   106, 479
Kaplan, R S   32, 40, 89, 92, 102
Karger, D W   20, 25
Keats, B W   364, 371
Kennedy, President and space programme   70, 72, 75, 104, 187 *see also* mission statements
key factors for success (KFS)/core competencies   243–55
  conclusions   252–53
  core competencies   249–52
    activities of the business, mapping and rating   252
    capability profile, an approach to   250–51
    identifying   250–52
    organizational politics   252
    skill mapping   251, *251*
    skills and technologies as basic elements of   250
    tests for   250
  Enigma machine story   243, 245
  executive exercise   254–55
  key factors for success (KFS)   245–49 *see also main entry*
    exemplars   246–47
    identifying KFS   248
    importance of KFS, decline in?   248–49
    research on importance of KFS   247
    shift from KFS to core competencies   *249*
    specific function, strength in a   246
  mind map   *244*
  questions   253–54
  references   255
Khandwalla, P   37, 40
Kilman, R H   37, 40
Kind, J   237, 242
Kinsella, R P   364, 372
Kittinger, W   411, 413
Klein, H E   184, 194
Klein, J A   251, *251*, 255
Knowledge management (reading 6.2)   150–52
    see also markets and customers, analysing

case studies   151–52
new guidelines   151
vertical leap, the   150–51
KPMG   248, 420 *see also* Web site(s)
Kuhn, T S   258–59, 268

Laforge, R L   20, 25
Larsen, G   247, 255
lead from voice and vision (reading 4.1)   78–81
    see also missions and goals, formulating
  dream, manage the   79–80
  vision, clarify the   78–79
  wisdom, leading with   80–81
learning to manage strategically (reading 16.1)   393–402 *see also* public sector, the
  decision-making, being strategic   395
  new manager, talking to staff   396–98
  new manager and context of change   396
  restructuring, reorganization, change   393
  staff, making an early contract with   399
  strategic review, process for   400–02
  targets and aims, setting out   398–99
Levitt, T   323, 324, 328
Linneman, R E   184, 194

McDonald, P   20, 25
McDonald's   112, 323, 328, 375
McDonnell, E   9, 102, 105, 155, 156, 158, 163, 261, 265, 268
McGrath, R G   286, 290
McKee, L   262, 268
McNulty, T   37, 41, 321, 328
Maison Novelli   485–87
  business difficulties   486–87
  interview with Jean-Christophe Novelli   485–86
Malik, Z A   20, 25
Managing International Joint Ventures   347–58
Manchester United plc   126, 161, 488–99 *see also* Web site(s)
  brand image   490–92
  finances and shareholders   488, *489*, 489–90
  management and strategy   492–98
    gate receipts   493–95
    merchandising   492–93
    sponsorship   497–98

television receipts   495–97
strategic problems   498–99
markets and customers, analysing   115, *116*,
        117–52
    analysis: turning information into intelligence
        (reading 6.1)   128–49 *see also main entry*
    competitor analysis   122–23
    conclusions   125
    customers   117–19
        concentrating on as key activity   117
        definition and needs of customers   118–19
        see also studying customers
    Five Forces Model   120, *121*, 121–22 *see also*
        Porter, M
        pragmatic strategy   121–22
        value chain   121
    further reading   127
    Knowledge management (reading 6.2)   150–52
        see also main entry
    mind map   *116*
    questions   126
    references   127
    Romanov family / Russian Revolution story
        115, 117
    studying customers   123, *123*, 124–25 *see also*
        Starbucks Coffee
        benchmarking   125
        customer types and groups   124
        latent needs of customers   124
        product-market matrix   123, *123*, 124, 125
    value, the subjective side of   119
Marks & Spencer   107, 108, 234, 241, 253
Martin, B   247, 255
Mason, C   364, 372
Matcon Engineering   500–03
    branching out   501
    core product   500
    future, the   502–03
    problems and solutions   501–02
Matthews, C   347–58
Meadows, M   191, 194
mergers
    Boeing / McDonnell Douglas   233
    Daimler-Benz / Chrysler   233
    Warner Communications / Time Inc   233
Meyer, R   286, 290

Microsoft   107, 318, 324, 469, 477, 490, 521
Miller, D   37, 40
mind maps   12, 224
    analysing markets and customers   *116*
    does strategy work?   *17*
    e-business   *404*
    evaluating performance   *83*
    evaluating strategic options   *232*
    formulating missions and goals   *65*
    formulating scenarios   *182*
    identifying and addressing issues   *154*
    identifying creative strategic options   *257*
    identifying key factors for success (KFS) and
        core competencies   *244*
    multi-businesses   *315*
    small businesses   *360*
    suggesting new business opportunities   *22*
    the strategic manager   *27*
    what is strategic management?   *4*
Minder   359, 361
Mintzberg, H   7, 14, 33–34, 35, *36*, 38, 40, 95, 174,
        283, 290, 362, 366, 369, 372
missions and goals, formulating   64–81
    conclusions   75
    executive exercise   76
    lead from voice and vision (reading
        4.1)   78–81 *see also main entry*
    mind map   *65*
    mission statements   64, 66, *66*, 67–68, *69*,
        69–75 *see also main entry*
    questions   75–76
    references   77
    Star Trek story   64, 66
mission statements   64, 66, *66*, 67–68, *69*, 69–75,
        87 *see also* missions and goals, formulating
    British Airways   66–67, 70, 71, 74
    Brunel University   68
    Central Intelligence Agency (CIA), USA
        67–68, 70
    Foreign and Commonwealth Office (UK)   68
    Kennedy, President and US space programme
        70, 72, 75
    Internet spoofs   68, 74 *see also* Web site(s),
        Dilbert
    mission statements / measurement of strategic
        effectiveness   *66*

missions, goals and strategy   75
missions and performance measurement
   73–75
producing mission statements that matter
   71–73
reasons for   69–71
Royal College of Surgeons of England, The
   68
Salvation Army   68
vision, meanings of   70–71
Mitroff, I I   37, 40
Moore, M   5, 15
Mulford, C L   365, 372
multi-businesses   314–58
   BCG matrix   316, *317*, 317–18
      benefits of   317–18
      problems with   318
      stars, dogs, cash cows and question marks
         317
   board, the   320–21
      rubber stamp boards   321
      shareholders' interests, protecting   321
      strategic management/financial perfor-
         mance/away days   321
   business units, integration of   322–23
      company examples   322, 323
      linkages   322–23
      synergy/shared activities   322, 323
   competing   316–19
      core competencies   319
      ICT   319
      innovation, emphasis on   319
   conclusions   327
   corporate centre, the   320
      intrapreneurship, encouraging   320
   global business, the   323–24
      company examples   323, 324
      culture, homogenization of   323–24
   mind map *315*
   partners, selecting   325–26
   questions   327–28
   references   328
   strategic alliances   324–25, 326
      acquisitions/alliances   324, 325
         making them work   326
         management of   325
         trust and reciprocity   326
   strategy and tactics (reading 14.1)   329–46
      see also main entry
   trends (reading 14.2)   347–58 *see also main*
      entry
   zoological gardens story   314, 316
Murdoch, S   407, 413

Natural Capitalism   205–20
Nature   532
Neubauer, F F   321, 328
New Competitor Intelligence, The   133
New Shorter Oxford English Dictionary, The   10,
   363
next industrial revolution, the (reading 8.2)
      205–220 *see also* scenarios, formulating
   biomimicry   215–16
   conventional capitalism   208–11
   natural capital/capitalism   206–08, 211–12
   natural capital, investing in   218–20
   resource productivity   212–15
   service and flow   216–18
Nissan   161, 253, 289, 328, 504–08 *see also* Nissan
   and Renault
Nissan and Renault   465, 504–08 *see also* Web
   site(s)
   alliance in Europe   506
   alliance worldwide   506–07
   cost savings   507
   history   504
   management   507–08
   problems/poor performance   505
Nokia   34, 235, 318
nominal group technique   265, 266
non-financial indicator (NFI)   89, 91
Norton, D P   32, 40, 89, 92, 102
Nucor   246–47, 253, 322 *see also* key factors for
   success/core competencies
Nutt, P   34, *36*, 41, 160, 163, 265, 266, 267, 268,
   283, 284, 285, 290, 385, 386, 392, 395

O'Brien, F A   191, 194

Ohmae, K   5, 8–9, *9*, 15, 35–36, *36*, 41, 123, *123*,
        124, 127, 157, 158, 163, 190, 192, 193, 194,
        225, 230, 236, 238, 242, 245–46, 247, 250,
        251, 253, 255, 260, 264, 265, 268, 287, 289,
        290, 379, *379*
Old Dogs, New Tricks   78–81
OPEC (Organization of Petroleum Exporting
        Countries)   184, 205, 533
Osborne, D   377, 385, 392

Pearson, J N   364, 371
Pedler, M   381, 387, 392
Pennington, S   106–14
performance, evaluating   82–114
    12 Ladders to World Class Performance (reading
        5.2)   106–14 *see also main entry*
    balanced scorecard, the   89–90 *see also* Web
        site(s)
    benchmarking   90
    conclusions   91
    executive exercise   92
    financial indicators   86–87
    financial performance and data   84, 86–87
    Harrison and longitude story   82, 84
    mind map   *83*
    non-financial measures   87–89
        creative industries   88–89 *see also* Globe
            Theatre, London
        league tables   87–88
    questions   91
    references   92
    strategic planning and performance   84–85, *85*
    what you measure is what you get (reading
        5.1) 93–105 *see also main entry*
performance evaluation   88
performance indicators, categories of   89
persuasion, what Aristotle taught (reading 3.1)
        42–48 *see also* strategic manager, the
    Aristotle, what he taught   44, *45*
    artistic persuasion   45–46
    background   42–44
    Bell, John   47–48
    ethos or character   46
    five principles, the   44–45
    logos or reasoning   46

pathos or passion   46–47
Peters, T   28, 36, 41, 49–52, 63, 106, 186, 194, 223,
        230, 286, 287, 290, 320, 328, 366
Pettigrew, A   8, 37, 41, 262, 268, 281, 283, 290,
        321, 328
Pinchot, G   262, 268
plan to implement (reading 13.1)   291–301
        see also implementation, planning
    annual review and update   299, *299*
    annual strategy review (and update)   298–99
    implementing change successfully   291, *291*,
        292
    leadership steering committee: the key to
        success   294–98
    questions to address   292–293, *293*, 294, *294*
    strategy implementation and change   298
    summary / goals   300–01
planning implementation *see* implementation,
        planning
Porras, J I   74, 77
Porter, M   6, *6*, 15, 31, 34, *36*, 106, 120–21, 122,
        123, 126, 127, 226, 227, 230, 249, 253, 316,
        322, 323, 328, 369, 411, 412, 413, 415, 423,
        431, 434, 476, 479
    Five Forces Analysis / Model   6, 98, 120, *121*,
        121–22, 126
    value chain   6, 126, 227, 411–12, *413*, 479
Powderject Ltd   509–13
    background   509–10
    brand, establishing the   512
    financial situation   510–511
    Glaxo Wellcome, collaboration with   511
    issues for discussion   513
    managing change   511–12
        Auragen operational procedures   512
pragmatism   10–11, 13, 121
Prahalad, C K   7, 8, 14, 23, 25, 34, 35, 36, *36*, 39,
        70, 124, 127, 185, 225, 228, 230, 248, 249,
        250, 251, 252, 255, 264, 268, 287, 289, 290,
        318, 324, 328, 521
Prime, N   247, 255
Procter & Gamble   193, 261–62, 267, 323, 327,
        437, 514–18, *518–19*, 519, 541 *see also* Web
        site(s)
    change at the top   516–18

financial data *518–19*, 519
going global/acquisitions 515
history 514–15
performance 516
product-market matrix 123, *123*, 124, 125
Prometheus Unbound 231, 233
public sector, the 373–402
   conclusions 387–88
   executive exercise/worksheets 388–92
   Kafka and McDonald's 373, 375
   learning to manage strategically (reading 16.1)
      393–402 *see also main entry*
   mind map *374*
   politicians 379–80
   private and public 375–76
   questions 388
   references 392
   stakeholder management 385–86
   strategic goals 376–77
   strategic management, types of 380–81
   strategic planning, benefits of 381–82, *382*,
      383, *383*, 384
   strategic tools 384, *384*, 385
   strategy, public sector 377–78, *379*, 379
      global trends 378
      strategic management models 378–79
   strategy workshops 386–87
      oval mapping technique 386–87
      principles of whole systems development
      387

Quinn, J B 5, 7, 15

R & D *see* research and development
rainforest exploitation *see* Raytheon
Raytheon 520–25
   background 520–21
   ecological security and Brazil's rainforest
      522–23
   further reading 525
   future, the 524
   references 525
   social responsibility issues 523–24
readings
   12 Ladders to World Class Performance 106–14

analysis: turning information into intelligence
   128–49
creating more options 269–76
does your product or service suit the Internet?
   437–53
information economy and competitive
   advantage, the 415–36
Knowledge management 150–52
lead from voice and vision 78–81
learning to manage strategically 393–402
next industrial revolution, the 205–220
persuasion, what Aristotle taught 42–48
plan to implement 291–301
Shakespeare to Tom Peters 49–63
social and ethical issues for sustainable
   development 164–80
strategic planning in the greenhouse 195–204
strategy and tactics 329–46
trends 347–58
what you measure is what you get 93–105
working through the change process 302–13
references 15, 25, 39–41, 77
Rejewski, M 243, 245, 246 *see also* key factors for
   success/core competencies
Renault *see* Nissan and Renault
research and development 36, 119, 252, 261, 322,
   324, 325, 474, 508, 509, 511, 513, 515, 545
*Retail and Distribution Management, International
   Journal of* 253
return on capital employed (ROCE) 86, 356
Rigby, D 7, 9, 20, 22, 25
Ringland, G 188, 194
Roddick, Anita *see* Body Shop
Rogers, A 364, 372
Ross, C 365, 371
Royal Dutch/Shell *see* Shell
Royal Opera House, London 88, 91
      see also performance, evaluating
Rue, L 20, 25
Russell, C 406, 407, 413
Ryanair 246–47, 253 *see also* key factors for
   success/core competencies

Samuel, Marcus *see* Shell
SBU *see* single strategic business unit

scenarios, formulating   181–220
   commedia dell'arte story   181, 183, 188
   conclusions   192
   executive exercise   193–94
   forecasting   183–85, *185*, 187
   foresight   185–86
   mind map   *182*
   next industrial revolution, the (reading 8.2)
      205–220 *see also main entry*
   post-modernism   186–87
   questions   192–93
   references   194
   scenario planning   188–90
      Delphi technique   190
      double-loop and single-loop learning   190
      four scenarios   189–90
      scenario preparation   190, *191*, 191–92
Schwenk, C R   364, 372
Seaman, C   364, 372
Selling of the President, The   117
Shakespeare   256, 258, 263
Shakespeare on Management   49–63
Shakespeare to Tom Peters (reading 3.2)   49–52
      see also strategic manager, the
   listening to fools and knaves (reading 3.2)
      52–63
      Falstaff   52–54, 55, 56–61, 62, 63
      Hotspur   55, 56, 58, 59
      Prince Hal   53–62, 63
   Shakespeare, leadership and the modern
      manager   49–50
   speeches   50, 54, 55, 56, 57, 58, 59
Shell   161, 188, 195–204, 526–34 *see also* Web
      site(s)
   background / history   526
   Brent Spar platform   531–32
   business principles   527–29
   current and future activities   529–31
   environmental and social issues   530–31
   prices   533
   questions for discussion   534
   social responsibility   532–33
Shirley, S   365, 372
Shrader, C B   364, 365, 372
skunk works   262, 286

small businesses   359–72
   conclusions   369
   entrepreneurs / serial entrepreneurs   362–63
      definition of   363
   executive exercise   370–71
      cognitive mapping   *371*
   mind map   *360*
   planning and strategic management   364–66
   effects on performance   364
   reasons for lack of planning   365–66
   questions   369
   references   371–72
   stereotypes   361–62
strategic management, nature of   367, *367*, 368,
      368
   television comedy story   359, 361 *see also* Web
      site(s)
   vulnerability of   363–64
Smith, R J   375, 392
social and ethical issues for sustainable
      development (reading 7.1)   164–80
      see also issues, identifying and addressing
   codes of conduct and standards   168–71
      Responsible Care Programme   170–71
   competition over cooperation, dominance of
      173
   conclusions   179–80
   environmental management, the dominant
      ideology towards   174–75
   ethics of business, defining   165–68
   expediency and indifference   174
   international trade   177
   operational barriers to ethical business and
      environmental management   176
   product responsibility   177
   promotional activities   177
   senior management ethics, pervasiveness of
      175
   short-term performance, overemphasis on
      172–73
   structural barriers to ethical business and
      environmental management   175
   sustainable development strategies,
      contribution of ethics to   171–72
   sustainable development through industrial
      democracy, moving towards   178–79

Sony   23, 136, 184, 325, 410
  Walkman   118, 136, 184
Sparkes, J R   29, 30, 41
Stagner, R   20, 25
Starbucks Coffee   124, 126, 253, 535–43 *see also*
        Web site(s)
  brand, the   543
  coffee education events   124
  copycats   541
  culture   542
  environmental agenda   542
  expansion   536, *536*
  future plans   540–41
  high growth, maintaining   542
  how was it achieved?   537–39
      coffee, excellence of the   537
      company's mission   539
      training of baristas   538–39
  origins   535–36
  principles, company's six   540
  take-over threat   542
Stevenson, P   364, 372
Storey, D J   364, 365, 372
stories
  car and the ravine   277, 279
  commedia dell'arte   181, 183 *see also* Web site(s)
  Enigma machine   243, 255
  Harrison and longitude   82, 84
  Italo Calvino, *The Man Who Shouted Teresa*
        403, 405
  Prometheus   231, 233
  Romanov family/Russian Revolution   115,
        117
  Shakespeare; Gilbert and Sullivan, and
        scientific paradigms   256, 258–59
  Star Trek   64, 66
  television   221, 223
  television comedy   359, 361
  vacuum cleaners   153, 155 *see also main entry
        and* Web site(s)
  Zen   26, 28
strategic management, does it work?   16, *17,*
        18–25
  arguments/counter-arguments   19
  conclusions   23–24

functional view, a   21, *21,* 22
innovation, benefits of strategic   22, *22,* 23
mind map   *17*
mission statements/written strategic plans   19
planning, benefits of strategic   19–20
practitioners   20
questions   24
references   25
strength and performance   22
vocabulary of strategic management   18–19
strategic management, what is it?   3, *4,* 5–15
  CD ROM, Internet and Web site   13
  contents of the book   12–13
  customer benefits/organizational capacity,
        linking   7–8
  Greek myths and gods story   3, 5
  implementation   7
  intentions, author's   10–12
      experimentation   11
      knowledge, value of   11
      pragmatic approach   10–11
      strategic thinking, encouraging   11
  mind map   *4*
  planning   5–6, *6,* 7
      analytical strategic thinking   *6, 6*
      Five Forces Analysis   6
      value chain   6
  questions   14
  references   15
  strategic management and capability profile
        9–10
  working definition of strategic management
        8–9
strategic manager, the   26, *27,* 27–63
  conclusions   38
  describing strategy   28, *29,* 29–31, *32,* 32–36,
        36 see also strategy, describing
      strategy as calculating   29–31, *32,* 32
      strategy as discovering   33–34
      strategy as making   34–36, *36*
  executive exercise   39
  mind map   *27*
  persuasion, what Aristotle taught (reading
        3.1) 42–48 *see also main entry*
  questions   38–39

references   39–41
Shakespeare to Tom Peters (reading 3.2)
    49–63 *see also main entry*
studies of strategic managers   37–38
Zen story   26, 28
strategic options, evaluating   231, *232*, 233–42
conclusions   240
cost–benefit impact of a strategic move
    236–37
executive exercise   241
mind map *232*
Prometheus story   231, 233
questions   241
rational approach, a   235–36
    analysis of risks/decision theory   235–36
    costs and returns of strategic moves   236
references   242
scoring systems   237–38
strategic choice   233–34
    company examples   234
    fashion, influence of   234
    mergers   233–34 *see also main entry*
Too Hot To Handle (Salsa restaurant)   238,
    239–40, 241, *240*
Word 97 template   238, *240*
strategic options, identifying creative   256–76
assumptions, challenging   264–65
    key factors for success   264
    management mindsets   264–65
conclusions   267
constraints, challenging   265
creating more options (reading 12.1)   269–76
    see also main entry
creativity techniques for managers   265–67
    cued brainwriting   265, 266
    nominal group technique   265, 266
    synectics   265, 266–67
mind map *257*
orthodoxy, challenging the   262–64
    creating intrapreneurship   262
    dress down days/casual dressing   263
    employee away days   263–64
    shop floor schemes   264
    skunk works   262
paradigms/scientific paradigms   258, 259–260

questions   267
references   268
Shakespeare; Gilbert and Sullivan, and
    scientific paradigms   256, 258–59
success models   261–62
    creativity and innovation   261
    visionary leadership   262
    thinking 'out of the box'   260
strategic planning in the greenhouse (reading 8.1)
    195–204 *see also* scenarios, formulating *and*
    Shell
planners of Royal Dutch/Shell   196–98
scenario one: sustained growth (with cool
    power)   198–99
scenario two: dematerialization (with energy
    efficiency)   199–200
strategic change at Shell, driving   200–04
Strategic Thinking   269–76
strategy, describing   28, *29*, 29–31, *32*, 32–36, *36*
    see also strategic manager, the
strategy as calculating   29–31, *32*, 32
    balanced scorecard   32
    forecasting techniques   29–30
    gap analysis   30
    investment appraisals   30
    key performance indicators, financial   30–31
    portfolio management (BCG matrix)   31
    single strategic business unit (SBU)   31, 32
    stars, cash cows and dogs   31
strategy as discovering   33–34
    interconnected boxes diagrams   33
    thinking and doing, splitting   33–34
strategy as making   34–36, *36*
    company examples   34
    creativity   35
    normative technological forecasting   34–35
    resources, deployment of   36
strategy and tactics (reading 14.1)   329–46 *see*
    also multi-businesses
applying the concept of strategy to business
    333–34, *334*, 335, *335*, 336, *336–37*, 337
concepts of   330, *330*
superiority of concept   331, *331*, 332, *332*, *333*,
    333
ten important aspects of strategy   337, *338*,

338, *339*, 339, *340*, 340, *341*, 341, *342*, *343*, 343, *344*, 344, *345*, 346
Subramaniam, S   520, 525
Success Strategy Planning   291
suggesting new business opportunities *see* business opportunities, suggesting new
Sunday Independent, The   409
Sunday Times, The   457
SWATCH (ETA) watches   23, 34
SWOT analysis   139, 158, 160, 161, 368, 384
synectics   13, 265, 266–67

Tabone, J C   69, 70, 71, 77
Talbot, C   20, 25, 377, 382, *382*, 384, *384*, 385, 392
Taylor, B   29, 41
television   221, 223
Thomas, I   406, 408, 414
Thompson, J L   271
Thune, S S   20, 25
Thurley, K   5, 15, 400
Toulouse, J   37, 40
Toyota   192, 195, 246, 328, 465, 504, 544–48
    see also Web site(s)
    background/history   544
    costs   545–46
    electric cars and reducing emissions   546–47
    environmentalism   544–45, 546, 547, 548
    Global 500 Award   544, 545
    ISO 14001 standard   545, 547–48
    manufacturing   547–48
trends (reading 14.2)   347–58
    see also multi-businesses
    economic cycles   347, *348*, 348, *349*, 349
    economies of scale   354
    emerging markets   351, *351*, 352
    financial   355–58
        funding options   357–58
        investment criteria   356–57
        is the profit motive cyclic?   355–56
        trends in financial management *357*
    key points   358
    management style   354, *354*, 355
    political stability   350–51
        quality, the drive for   352
        summary   358
    technology and manufacturing   352–53

wealth, growth of   350
Trial, The   373
Turner, C   405, 410, 411, 412, 413, 414, 415–36

vacuum cleaners   153–54, 156 *see also* stories *and* Web site(s)
value chain   6, 126, 227, 411–12, 413, 423, *423*, 424–25, *426*, 426–27, *427*, 428
Vasconcellos, J A   22, 25
Vasconcellos e Sa, J   329–46
Virgin Group companies   316, 323, 327 *see also* Web site(s)
Vodafone   241, 497, 549–53 *see also* Web site(s)
    3G technology, gaining access to   551–53
    history *550*
    strategic issues   553
    telecommunications, changes in   549, 551
    WAP services   553
Volkswagen   280, 408, 506

Walkman *see* Sony
Wall Street Journal   185
WAP *see* wireless application protocol
War Lords, The   329–46
Ward, J L   365, 371
Waterman, R   36, 41, 186, 223, 230, 286, 287, 290, 320, 328, 366
Waters, J A   33, 40
Watson, R   365, 372
Web site(s)   13
    balanced scorecards
        home.sol.no/mst/balance.htm   89
        w3.corvu.com/   89
        www.balancedscorecard.com/   89
        www.gentia.com/   89
        www.intrafocus.com/balancedscorecard.htm   89
    benchmarking:
        www.benchmarking.co.uk   248
        www.cateringnet.co.uk/monthly/month029 8/experia1.htm   248
        www.fsbba.org   248
        www.hefce.ac.uk   248
        www.kpmg.co.uk/   248
    commedia dell'arte: www.commedia-dell-arte.com/links.htm   183

creativity/drawing:
  Buzan, Tony: www.buzancentre.com/ 224
  de Bono, Edward: www.edwdebono.com/
    debono/ 224
  Edwards, Betty: www.drawright.com/ 224
Data Discovery: www.datadiscoveries.com/
  406
Dell Corporation: www.euro.dell.com/coun-
  tries/uk/enu/gen/default.htm 226
Dilbert: *www.unitedmedia.com/comics/dilbert/*
  career/bin/ns2.cgi 68, 74
Dyson: www.dyson.com/ 153
Eurocall Limited: www.eurocall-
  telecome.com/ 406
Ford: www.ford.com/default.asp?pageid
  =95&storyid=916 467
  www.ford.com/finaninvest/stockholder/sto
  ck99/operhigh.htm 460
Fujitsu: www.fujitsugeneral.co.jp/ 471
GlaxoWellcome: www.glaxowellcome.com/
  475
ICL: www.icl.com/ 471
Idealab: www.idealab.com 479
J D Wetherspoon: www.jdwetherspoon.co.uk/
  484
Johnson & Johnson: www.johnsonandjohn-
  son.com/home.html 322
Lockheed Skunk Works: www.skunkworks.net
  262
  shop: www.lumsw.external.lmco.com/lerc
  /index.html 262
Manchester United plc: www.manutd.com/
  499
National Technology Fast 50:
  www.fast50.co.uk/fast5099/ 406
Nissan: www.nissan.co.uk 508
Nissan, Powerpoint presentation: www.nis-
  san.co.jp/NRP/SUPPORT/index-
  e.files/frame.htm 508
Procter & Gamble: www.pg.com/main.jhtml
  519
Shell: www.shell.com/royal-en/directo-
  ry/0,5029,25414,00.html 534
Starbucks: www.starbucks.com 124, 535, 543
  www.starbucks.com/company/ 543
television comedy (British): www.phill.co.uk/
  comedy/index.html 359

Toyota: www.toyota.co.jp/ 548
  www.toyota.com/ 548
vacuum cleaners, history of early:
  www.designmaker.com/vacuums/vachist
  2.htm 153
Vodafone: www.vodafone-airtouch-plc.com 553
Wechsler, B 377, 383, *383*, 384, 385, 392
Weinstein, A 247, 255
Welford, R 157, 163, 164–80
Westphal, J D 37, 38, 41
what is strategic management? *see* strategic management, what is it?
what you measure is what you get (reading 5.1)
  93, *93*, 94–104, *105 see also* performance,
  evaluating
  critical success factors 97,–98, *98*, 99
  efficiency and effectiveness 102, *103*, 104, *105*
  framework for consideration 94, *94*, 95, *96*,
    96, 97, *97*
  key performance indicators 99–102
Wheelan, T L 320, 328, 365, 372
Whipp, R 8, 281, 283, 290
Wilkinson, D 381, 387, 392
Wills, G 35, *36*, 41
Wirdenius, H 5, 15, 400
wireless application protocol 235, 553
Woo, C Y 364, 372
Wood, D R 20, 25
Woods, A 33, 40, 186, 194, 364, 366, 372
Wootton, S 237, 241, 242, 269–76
working through the change process (reading
  13.2) 302–13 *see also* implementation,
  planning
  EASIER approach *302*, 303
    activating 304–06
    ensuring 310–11
    envisioning 303–04
    installing 307–10
    knowing when to call a halt 312–13
    recognizing 311–12
    supporting 306
World Wide Web 406, 409
Wynarczyk, P 365, 372

Zeithaml, C P 37, 40, 321, 328
Zen story 26, 28